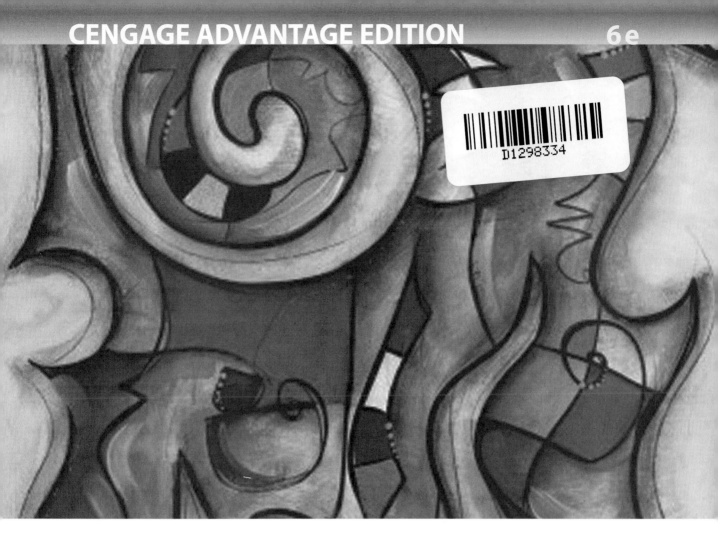

COMMUNICATION
in Our Lives

LINEBERGER DISTINGUISHED PROFESSOR OF HUMANITIES

CAROLINE H. AND THOMAS S. ROYSTER DISTINGUISHED PROFESSOR OF GRADUATE EDUCATION

THE UNIVERSITY OF NORTH CAROLINA AT CHAPEL HILL

WADSWORTH
CENGAGE Learning™

Australia • Brazil • Japan • Korea • Mexico • Singapore • Spain • United Kingdom • United States

**Communication in Our Lives, Sixth Edition
Cengage Advantage Edition**
Julia T. Wood

Senior Publisher: Lyn Uhl

Publisher: Monica Eckman

Senior Assistant Editor: Rebekah Matthews

Editorial Assistant: Colin Solan

Media Editor: Jessica Badiner

Marketing Manager: Amy Whitaker

Marketing Coordinator: Brittany Blais

Marketing Communications Manager:
Courtney Morris

Content Project Management: PreMediaGlobal

Senior Art Director: Jill Ort

Manufacturing Planner: Doug Bertke

Acquisition Specialist, Text: Mandy Groszko

Text Designer: Brenda Grannan, Grannan
Graphic Design

Cover Designer: Grannan Graphic Design

Cover Image: Swirls II © Eric Waugh

Compositor: PreMediaGlobal

For product information and technology assistance, contact us at
Cengage Learning Customer & Sales Support, 1-800-354-9706

For permission to use material from this text or product, submit all requests online at **www.cengage.com/permissions.**
Further permissions questions can be emailed to
permissionrequest@cengage.com.

Library of Congress Control Number: 2011930813

ISBN-13: 978-1-111-35362-9

ISBN-10: 1-111-35362-X

Wadsworth
20 Channel Center Street
Boston, MA 02210
USA

Cengage Learning is a leading provider of customized learning solutions with office locations around the globe, including Singapore, the United Kingdom, Australia, Mexico, Brazil, and Japan. Locate your local office at: **international. cengage.com/region**

Cengage Learning products are represented in Canada by Nelson Education, Ltd.

For your course and learning solutions, visit **www.cengage.com.**

Purchase any of our products at your local college store or at our preferred online store **www.cengagebrain.com.**

Instructors: Please visit **login.cengage.com** and log in to access instructor-specific resources.

Printed in Canada
1 2 3 4 5 6 7 15 14 13 12 11

Brief Contents

Contents

List of Boxes

RESEARCH IN **ACTION**

Preface

When I was an undergraduate student, I fell in love with the field of communication. In my first communication course I discovered that communication was more central to my life than anything else I could study. That feeling grew stronger with each communication course I took during my undergraduate and graduate studies.

I wrote *Communication in Our Lives* to share with students my love of communication and my belief that it is critically important in our everyday lives. Because I want this book to engage students, I've tried to make it as interesting and substantive as communication itself. I use a conversational style of writing and weave into all chapters examples, reflections from students, and applications that invite students to engage material personally. Because I want this book to help students develop their competence as communicators, I emphasize concrete skills and hands-on applications.

DISTINGUISHING FEATURES OF COMMUNICATION IN OUR LIVES

Communication in Our Lives has three distinct conceptual emphases. In addition, it includes a number of pedagogical features designed to highlight the relevance of communication to students' everyday lives and experiences. Some of these features have been retained from the fifth edition, and some, as well as additional content, are new to this sixth edition.

Conceptual Emphases

Three conceptual goals guided my writing of this book: (a) to emphasize theories and research developed by scholars of communication, (b) to integrate coverage of social diversity as it relates to communication, and (c) to respond to student and faculty feedback about previous editions.

Emphasis on Communication Theory, Research, and Skills *Communication in Our Lives* highlights theories, research, and skills developed by scholars of communication. For example, Chapter 9 provides coverage of relational dialectics, a theory primarily developed by Leslie Baxter, a professor of communication at the University of Iowa. Chapter 13 relies on recent research by scholars of social media to sharpen understanding of how various digital technologies are making our lives ever more connected. Chapters 14 through 18 draw on communication scholars' research principles of effective public communication. For instance, Clella Jaffe (2007) has identified the wave pattern as a way of organizing speeches that is more common in ethnic groups with strong oral traditions, and James McCroskey and Jason Teven (1999) have shown that speakers who demonstrate good will toward listeners tend to have higher credibility than those who don't. I emphasize the work of communication scholars both because their research is valuable and because I want students to appreciate the intellectual richness of the communication field. Although I emphasize the work of communication scholars, I don't ignore relevant research conducted by scholars in fields such as sociology, psychology, and anthropology. Thus, this book draws on research and theories in these and other related disciplines.

Integrated Attention to Social Diversity   I have woven discussion of social diversity into the basic framework of this book. I do not do this to be "politically correct" or to advance a liberal social agenda. Instead, I aim to provide integrated attention to social diversity because it is one of the most significant features of contemporary life in the United States. Our culture includes people of different ethnicities, ages, genders, physical and mental abilities, sexual orientations, economic classes, and religious and spiritual commitments.

Communication in Our Lives encourages students to appreciate social diversity as a fact of cultural life that has profound implications for our communication with others. Because social diversity affects our communication in all contexts, I weave discussion of diverse cultures and communication practices into all chapters of this book. For example, in Chapter 10 I note how cultural values affect communication in groups and teams. In discussing personal identity in Chapter 3, I point out how social views of race, economic class, gender, and sexual orientation affect self-concept.

In addition to weaving social diversity into all chapters, Chapter 7 is devoted exclusively to communication and culture. This chapter provides a sustained and focused exploration of the reciprocal relationship between culture and communication.

Evolution in Response to Student and Faculty Feedback   Like communication, books are dynamic—they evolve and change over time. This edition of *Communication in Our Lives* attempts to retain the strengths of previous editions while also incorporating feedback from students and faculty. Before beginning work on this edition, I read feedback from hundreds of faculty members and students who used previous editions. Their suggestions and comments led me to make a number of changes in this new edition.

The most significant change in this edition is increased emphasis on active learning. I've taught college students for many years, and I've become convinced that real learning occurs only if students actively engage and work with course content. Active learning happens when students do something with ideas in a book— they apply theories to their communication experiences; they use new concepts to analyze relationships in their families and work places; they think about how a discussion in a textbook illuminates their own lives. Inserted into the margins of each chapter are questions that prompt students to connect material to their lives. I invite students to analyze, reflect, apply or otherwise actively engage the ideas they've read.

In preparing this edition of *Communication in Our Lives*, I kept in mind the frequent complaint from instructors that each new edition of a textbook gets longer because authors add new material without taking out other material.

I resisted this tendency. I have *streamlined all chapters* by deleting dated material and references and tightening prose. I also reduced the number of features in chapters so that pages are less "busy" than in the previous edition.

Because many faculty assign speeches in the first weeks of a term, and to lay a foundation for the public communication chapters that constitute Part 3, I weave *speech activities into early chapters* of the book. For instance, Chapter 1 includes a Sharpen Your Skill activity that invites students to prepare and present a short speech of introduction. By completing public speaking activities in early chapters, students gain valuable speaking experience and they appreciate connections between public speaking and other forms of communication. I have also further integrated Speech Builder Express™ 3.0 and Speech Studio™ into Chapters 14–18, which focus on public speaking. Wherever appropriate within these chapters, I mention the program's speech outlining and development resources. Additionally, at the end of these chapters, I suggest specific activities designed to help students make use of this online tool. Speech Builder Express and Speech Studio are described further in the section on student resources.

In recent years, ethical—and unethical—actions have gained renewed prominence in cultural life, and this edition of the book reflects that. Communication instructors know that they need to teach students to recognize *ethical issues* in communication that occurs in personal relationships, the work place, or public speaking. To underline the ethical dimension of communication, this edition calls attention to ethical issues and choices in communication. In addition to identifying ethical aspects of communication in each chapter, I include one question at the end of each chapter, flagged with an icon, that focuses on ethics.

This edition of *Communication in Our Lives* also reflects changes in scholarship and modes of interaction. Those familiar with the fifth edition of this book will notice that the current edition includes *more than 150 new references.* Finally, this edition includes *amplified attention to social media*—cells, iPods, BlackBerrys, and so forth—that are increasingly part of our everyday lives.

Pedagogical Features

In addition to the conceptually distinctive aspects of this book and its thorough integration of and emphasis on social diversity, several other features are designed to make it interesting and valuable to students.

First, I adopt a *conversational style of writing* rather than the more distant and formal style often used by textbook authors. I share with students some of my experiences in communicating with others, and I invite them to think with me about important issues and difficult challenges surrounding communication in our everyday lives. The accessible, informal writing style encourages students to personally engage the ideas I present.

A second feature of this book is *student commentaries.* Every chapter is enriched by reflections written by students in my classes and other classes around the country that adopted previous editions of this book. The questions, thoughts, and concerns expressed by diverse students invite readers to reflect on their own experiences as communicators. I welcome ideas from students around the country, so students in your class may wish to send their insights to me for inclusion in future editions of this book.

Communication in Our Lives also includes pedagogical features that promote learning and skill development. At the end of each chapter I provide two *Sharpen Your Skill* exercises to encourage students to apply concepts and develop skills discussed in the text. Many of these exercises end with a prompt to the book's online resources, which offer additional opportunities for skill application. Each chapter also includes *Communication Highlights*, which call attention to interesting communication research and examples of communication issues in everyday life.

New to this edition of the book are two features. The first, *Beyond the Classroom*, appears at the end of chapters in Parts I and II. This feature offers suggestions for taking the material in the chapter beyond the classroom in three ways: considering the chapter's relevance in the workplace, probing ethical issues raised in the chapter, and connecting chapter material to civic and social engagement with the broader world. The second new feature, *Research in Our Lives*, appears in selected chapters. Each Research in Our Lives feature highlights communication research that is particularly relevant to issues and contexts of students' lives. The purpose of this feature is to show students that communication research really does make a difference in the "real world."

Case studies are another feature that encourages students to engage ideas actively. These brief scenarios and speeches appear at the end of each chapter to bring to life the ideas and principles presented. Rather than using generic case studies, I wrote the ones used in this book so that they would directly reflect chapter content and provide students with representative examples of communication theories and skills—this edition features a new case study on groups and teams for Chapter 10. In addition to their presentation in the book, the case studies are featured on the CourseMate for *Communication in Our Lives* as short interactive video activities that include questions for discussion and analysis. (See the section on student resources for details about CourseMate.) With the multimedia enactments of the scenarios, instructors and students can analyze not only verbal messages but also nonverbal communication. Appendix A provides a collection of *annotated speeches* for student analysis.

Each chapter concludes with the **Communication in Our Lives Online** section, which provides both an introduction to the text's many online resources and the print version of the text's learning aids—a list of **key concepts** with corresponding page numbers, the Sharpen Your Skills exercises, and then a series of For Further Reflection and Discussion questions that encourage students to reflect on and discuss the chapter's material. Each set of these questions includes at least one question that focused on **ethics**. Finally, as I discussed earlier, at the very end of each chapter in Part 3, Public Communication, I suggest a related **Speech Builder Express** or Speech Studio activity.

RESOURCES FOR INSTRUCTORS

Katrina Bodey, the University of North Carolina at Chapel Hill, and I have written an *Instructor's Resource Manual* that describes approaches to teaching the basic course, provides a wealth of class-tested exercises including new teaching resources for the public speaking segment of your course, and provides suggested journal topics and sample test items.

The PowerLecture CD-ROM contains an electronic version of the Instructor's Resource Manual, ExamView® Computerized Testing, predesigned Microsoft® PowerPoint® presentations, and JoinIn® classroom quizzing. The PowerPoint presentations contain text, images, and videos of the case studies and can be used as is or customized to suit your course needs.

The Teaching Assistant's Guide to the Basic Course by Katherine G. Hendrix is also available to adopters of this text. Designed specifically for the new communication teacher and based on leading teacher-training programs in communication, this guide includes general teaching and course management topics and specific strategies, such as giving performance feedback, managing sensitive class discussions, and conducting mock interviews.

Wadsworth Cengage Learning's extensive video library includes the *Student Speeches for Critique and Analysis* and *Communication Scenarios for Critique and Analysis,* which include sample student speeches and the interpersonal and group communication scenarios featured as case studies in this text. These videos provide realistic examples of communication that allow students and teachers to identify specific communication principles, skills, and practices, and to analyze how they work in actual interaction.

With the **TeamUP Technology Training and Support**, you can get trained, get connected, and get the support you need for seamless integration of technology resources into your course. This unparalleled technology service and training program provides robust online resources, peer-to-peer instruction, personalized training, and a customizable program you can count on. Visit **http://www.cengage.com/teamup/training/** to sign up for online seminars, first days of class services, technical support, or personalized, face-to-face training. Our online or onsite trainings are frequently led by one of our Lead Teachers, faculty members who are experts in using Wadsworth Cengage Learning technology and can provide best practices and teaching tips.

With Cengage's **Flex-Text Customization Program**, you can create a text as unique as your course: quickly, simply, and affordably. As part of our flex-text program you can add your personal touch to *Communication in Our Lives* with a course-specific cover and up to 32 pages of your own content, at no additional cost.

I encourage you to contact your local Cengage Learning representative or http://www.cengage.com/highered/ for more information, user names and passwords, examination copies, or a demonstration of these ancillary products. Available to qualified adopters.

RESOURCES FOR STUDENTS

If you want your students to have access to the online resources for *Communication in Our Lives,* please be sure to order them for your course. These resources can be bundled with every new copy of the text or ordered separately. If you do not order them, your students will not have access to these online resources. *Contact your local Wadsworth Cengage Learning sales representative for more details.*

The **student companion workbook,** co-authored by Miri Pardo, St. John Fisher College, and me, is available online through CourseMate for

Communication in Our Lives and provides practical exercises and inventories that guide students in applying concepts and developing skills discussed in the book. It includes chapter outlines, class-tested activities, and self-tests.

The **Speech Communication CourseMate** brings course concepts to life with online interactive learning, study, and exam preparation tools like the interactive eBook, Audio Study Tools, flashcards, chapter notepads, Communication Highlight Activities and Sharpen Your Skills Activities that support the printed textbook. Watch comprehension soar as your class works with the printed textbook and the textbook-specific website. The Speech Communication CourseMate for *Communication In Our Lives* goes beyond the book to deliver what you need!

The *Communication in Our Lives* **book companion website** features study aids such as chapter outlines, flash cards and other resources for mastering glossary terms, and chapter quizzes that help students check their understanding of key concepts. Also included are student resources such as an interactive version of the Personal Report of Communication Apprehension (PRCA) and speech preparation worksheets.

The *Communication in Our Lives* interactive video activities feature videos of the sample speeches and interpersonal and group communication scenarios featured in the book's case studies. This multimedia tool allows students to evaluate the speeches and scenarios, compare their evaluation with mine, and, if requested, submit their response electronically to their instructor.

The end-of-chapter activities in Part 3, Public Communication, can be completed with Speech Builder Express 3.0 organization and outlining program. This interactive web-based tool coaches students through the speech organization and outlining process. By completing interactive sessions, students can prepare and save their outlines—including a plan for visual aids and a works cited section—formatted according to the principles presented in the text. Text models reinforce students' interactive practice.

Practice and present with Speech Studio™. With Speech Studio, you can upload video files of practice speeches or final performances, comment on your peer's speeches, and review your grades and instructor feedback. Speech Studio's flexibility lends itself to use in traditional, hybrid, and online courses. It allows instructors to: save valuable in-class time by conducting practice sessions and peer review work virtually; combine the ease of a course management tool with a convenient way to capture, grade, and review videos of live, in-class performances; simulate an in-class experience for online courses.

If you order the online resources packaged with the text, your students will have access to InfoTrac College Edition with InfoMarks. This virtual library's more than 18 million reliable, full-length articles from 5,000 academic and popular periodicals and retrieve results almost instantly. They also have access to InfoMarks—stable URLs that can be linked to articles, journals, and searches to save valuable time when doing research—and to the InfoWrite online resource center, where students can access grammar help, critical-thinking guidelines, guides to writing research papers, and much more.

The Audio Study Tools for *Communication in Our Lives* provides a fun and easy way for students to review chapter content whenever and wherever. For each chapter of the text, students will have access to the audio of the case study for that chapter, learning objectives, and a chapter summary. Students can purchase the eAudio for *Communication in Our Lives* through CengageBrain and download files to their computers, iPods, or other MP3 players.

Many Cengage Learning texts are available through **CengageBrain**, our textbook rental program or also available as an eBook where you can buy by the chapter. Keep CengageBrain in mind for your next Cengage Learning purchase. Visit http://cengagebrain.com for details.

A Guide to the Basic Course for ESL Students by Esther Yook of Mary Washington College is an aid for non-native speakers. This guide includes strategies for accent management and overcoming speech apprehension, in addition to helpful web addresses and answers to frequently asked questions.

Finally, *The Art and Strategy of Service Learning Presentations* by Rick Isaacson and Jeff Saperstein is an invaluable resource for students in the basic course that integrates or will soon integrate a service learning component. This handbook provides guidelines for connecting service learning work with classroom concepts and advice for working effectively with agencies and organizations. It also provides model forms and reports and a directory of online resources.

ACKNOWLEDGMENTS

All books reflect the efforts of many people, and *Communication in Our Lives* is no exception. A number of people have helped this book evolve from an early vision to the final form you hold in your hands. My greatest debt is to my editor, Monica Eckman, and my development editor, Rebekah Matthews. From start to finish, they have been active partners in the project. This book reflects their many insights and their generous collaboration.

Other people at Wadsworth Cengage Learning have been remarkable in their creativity, attention to detail, and unflagging insistence on quality. I am in debt to Elm Street Publishing Services, for thoughtful copyediting. Thanks also to Michael Lepera, senior content project manager; Eric Arima, service and production manager; Brenda Grannan, text designer; Jaime Jankowski, photo researcher; Linda Helcher, art director; Mandy Groszko, image rights acquisition specialist; Katie Huha, senior text rights acquisition specialist; Sarah D'Stair, text permissions researcher; Justin Palmeiro, senior print buyer; Jessica Badiner, media editor; Colin Solan, editorial assistant; and Tami Strang, senior marketing manager.

I am also grateful to the people who reviewed previous editions of this book, who have been most generous in offering suggestions for improving the book.

Reviewers who worked with me in developing this edition, and to whom I am especially grateful, are Theresa Albury, Miami Dade College; Martha Antolik, Wright State University; Emily Bermes, Indiana University-Purdue University Fort Wayne; Christine Hirsch, State University of New York at Oswego; Scott McLean, Arizona Western College; Randall Mueller, Gateway Technical College; Kim Parker, Collin County Community College; John Parrish, Tarrant County College; Trudi Peterson, Monmouth College; Janice Stuckey, Jefferson State Community College; and Esin C. Turk, Mississippi Valley State University.

I could not have written this book without the undergraduate students in my classes. They allow me to experiment with new approaches to teaching communication and help me refine ideas and activities that appear in this book. Invariably, my students teach me at least as much as I teach them, and for that I am deeply grateful.

I also thank my friends who are sources of personal support, insight, challenges, and experience—all of which find their way into what I write. Finally, and always, I acknowledge the support and love of my partner Robbie (Robert) Cox. Like everything else I do, this book has benefited from his presence in my life. Being married to him for 36 years has enriched my appreciation of the possibilities for love, growth, kindness, understanding, and magic between people. In addition to being the great love of my life, Robbie is my most demanding critic and my greatest fan. Both his criticism and support have shaped the final form of this book.

Julia T. Wood
Chapel Hill, NC

Robbie Cox

Julia T. Wood is the Lineberger Distinguished Professor of Humanities, the Caroline H. and Thomas S. Royster Distinguished Professor of Graduate Education, and a professor of Communication Studies at the University of North Carolina at Chapel Hill. Since completing her Ph.D. (Pennsylvania State University) at age 24, she has taught classes, conducted research, and written extensively about communication in personal relationships and about gender, communication, and culture. In addition to publishing more than 70 articles and chapters, she has authored or co-authored 17 books and edited or co-edited 9 others. The recipient of 12 awards for outstanding teaching and 14 awards for distinguished scholarship, Professor Wood divides her professional energies among research, writing, and teaching.

Professor Wood lives with her partner, Robert (Robbie) Cox, who is also a professor of Communication Studies at the University of North Carolina and who is on the Board of Directors of the national Sierra Club. Completing their family is their dog, Cassidy. When not writing and teaching, Professor Wood enjoys traveling, legal consulting, and spending time talking with students, friends, and family.

For Carolyn

For so many reasons

PhotoLibrary

Introduction

FOCUS QUESTIONS

- A friend comes to you with a problem, and you want to show that you support him.
- A group you belong to is working on recycling programs for the campus, and you're frustrated by the group's inefficiency. You want to make meetings more productive.
- At the end of the term, the person you've been seeing will graduate and take a job in a city 1,000 miles away, and you wonder how to stay connected across the distance.
- You met an interesting person on FaceBook. At first, you enjoyed interacting with him, but lately he's been sending you IMs incessantly, and you feel he's intrusive.
- The major project in one of your courses is an oral research report, so your grade depends on your public speaking ability.

Situations like these illustrate the importance of communication in our lives. Unlike some of the subjects you study, communication is relevant to every aspect of your life. We communicate with ourselves when we work through ideas, psych ourselves up to meet challenges, and rehearse ways to approach someone about a difficult issue. We communicate with others to build and sustain personal relationships, to perform our jobs and advance our careers, to connect with friends and meet new people online, and to participate in social and civic activities. Every facet of life involves communication.

Although we communicate all the time, we don't always communicate effectively. People who have inadequate communication knowledge and skills are hampered in their efforts to achieve personal, professional, and social goals. On the other hand, people who communicate well have a keen advantage in accomplishing their objectives. This suggests that learning about communication and learning how to communicate are keys to effective living.

Communication in Our Lives is designed to help you understand how communication works in your personal, professional, and social life. To open the book, I'll introduce myself and describe the basic approach and special features of *Communication in Our Lives.*

INTRODUCTION TO THE AUTHOR

As an undergraduate, I enrolled in a course much like the one you're taking now. In that course, I began a love affair with the field of communication that has endured for more than 40 years. Today I am still in love with the field—more than ever, in fact. I see communication as the basis of cultural life and as a primary tool for personal, social, and professional satisfaction and growth. This makes communication one of the most dynamic and important areas of study in higher education. It is a field that is both theoretically rich and pragmatically useful. I know of no discipline that offers more valuable insights, skills, and knowledge than communication.

Because communication is central to our lives, I feel fortunate to teach communication courses and conduct research on human interaction. Working with students allows me to help them improve their communication skills and thus their effectiveness in many arenas. Research and writing continually enlarge my understanding of communication and let me share what I learn with others like you.

Because you will be reading this book, you should know something about the person who wrote it. I am a middle-aged, middle-class, Caucasian heterosexual woman. For 36 years, I have been married to Robert (Robbie) Cox, who is also a communication scholar. As is true for all of us, who I am affects what I know and how I think, act, interact, and write. My race, gender, social-economic class, and sexual orientation have given me certain kinds of insight and obscured others. As a woman, I understand discrimination based on sex because I've experienced it personally. I do not have personal knowledge of racial discrimination because Western culture confers privilege on European Americans. Being middle class has shielded me from personal experience with hunger, poverty, and class bias; and my heterosexuality has spared me from being an object of homophobic prejudice. Who you are also influences your experiences and knowledge and your ways of communicating.

COMMUNICATION
in Your Life

How does
your identity
enable and
limit what you
know?

Although identity limits our personal knowledge and experiences, it doesn't completely prevent insight into people and situations different from our own. From conversations with others and from reading, we can gain some understanding of people and circumstances different from our own. What we learn by studying and interacting with people of diverse cultural heritages expands our appreciation of the richness and complexity of humanity. In addition, learning about and forming relationships with people different from ourselves enlarges our personal repertoire of communication skills and our appreciation of the range of ways to communicate.

INTRODUCTION TO THE BOOK

To provide a context for your reading, let me share my vision of this book. The aim of *Communication in Our Lives* is to introduce you to many forms and functions of communication in modern life. The title reflects my belief that communication is an important part of our everyday lives. Each chapter focuses on a specific kind of communication or context of interaction.

Coverage

Because communication is a continuous part of life, we need to understand how it works—or doesn't—in a range of situations. Therefore, this book covers a broad spectrum of communication encounters, including communication with yourself, interaction with friends and romantic partners, work in groups and teams, interaction in organizations, mass and social media, interaction between people with diverse cultural backgrounds, and public speaking. The breadth of communication issues and skills presented in this book can be adapted to the interests and preferences of individual classes and instructors.

Students

Communication in Our Lives is written for anyone interested in human communication. If you are a communication major, this book and the course it accompanies will provide you with a firm foundation for more advanced study. If you are majoring in another discipline, this book and the course you are taking will give you a sound basic understanding of communication and opportunities to strengthen your skills as a communicator.

Learning should be a joy, not a chore. I've written this book in an informal, personal style; for instance, I refer to myself as *I* rather than *the author*, and I use contractions (*can't* and *you're* instead of the more formal *cannot* and *you are*), as we do in normal conversation. To heighten interest, I punctuate chapters with concrete examples and insights from students at my university and other campuses around the country.

Theory and Practice

Years ago, renowned scholar Kurt Lewin said, "There is nothing so practical as a good theory." His words remain true today. In this book, I've blended theory and practice so that each draws on and enriches the other. Effective practice is theoretically informed: It is based on knowledge of how and why the communication process works and what is likely to result from different kinds of communication. At the same time, effective theories have pragmatic value: They help us understand experiences and events in our everyday lives. Each chapter in this book is informed by the theories and research generated by scholars of communication. Thus, the perspectives and skills recommended reflect current knowledge of effective communication practices.

FEATURES

Ten key features accent this book:

Integrated Attention to Cultural Diversity

Diversity is woven into the fabric of this book. The world and the United States have always been culturally diverse. Awareness of diversity is integral to how we communicate and think about communication; it is not an afterthought. I integrate cultural diversity into the text in several ways.

First, each chapter includes research on diverse people and highlights our commonalities and differences. For example, Chapter 9, on personal relationships, identifies general differences in women's and men's communication and provides clues about how the sexes can translate each other's language. Other chapters trace the impact of ethnicity, sexual orientation, gender, and other facets of identity on self-concept and communication practices.

You'll also notice that the photos I chose for this book include people of different races, ages, religions, and so forth. Likewise, each chapter includes examples drawn from a range of people, walks of life, and orientations, and the case studies feature diverse people.

In addition to incorporating diversity into the book as a whole, in Chapter 7 I focus exclusively on communication and culture. There you will learn about cultures and social communities (distinct groups within a single society) and the ways cultural values and norms shape how we view and practice communication. Just as important, Chapter 7 will heighten your awareness of the power of communication to shape and change cultures. In addition, it will enhance your ability to participate effectively in a culturally diverse world.

To talk about social groups is to risk stereotyping. For instance, a substantial amount of research shows that women, in general, are more emotionally expressive than men, in general. A good deal of research also reports that blacks, in general, speak with greater animation and force than whites, in general. Yet, not all women are emotionally expressive, not all men are emotionally inexpressive, not all blacks communicate forcefully, and not all whites communicate blandly. Throughout this book, I try to provide you with reliable information on social groups while avoiding stereotyping. I rely on qualifying terms, such as *most* and *in general*, to remind us that there are exceptions to generalizations.

Student Commentaries

Communication in Our Lives also features commentaries from students. In my classes, students teach me and each other by sharing their insights, experiences, and questions. Because I learn so much from students, I've included reflections written by students at my university and other campuses. As you read the student commentaries, you'll probably identify with some, disagree with others, and be puzzled by still others. Whether you agree, disagree, or are perplexed, I think you'll find that the student commentaries valuably expand the text by adding to the voices and views it represents. In the students' words, you will find much insight and much to spark thought and discussion in your classes and elsewhere. You may have insights about material covered in this book. If so, I invite you to send me your commentaries so that I might include them in the next edition of this book.

Communication in Your Life

Each chapter includes "Communication in Your Life" features, which invite you to connect what you are reading about to your own experiences as a communicator. When you encounter these features, pause in your reading to apply ideas in the text to your own life. The first "Communication in Your Life" feature appeared on page xxxii of this introduction.

Communication Highlights

"Communication Highlights" call your attention to especially interesting findings from communication research and news reports involving communication in everyday life. The "Communication Highlights" offer springboards for class discussions.

Experiencing Communication in Our Lives

Following each chapter is a case study, "Experiencing Communication in Our Lives." With each one, I invite you to think about how principles and skills we discuss in that chapter show up in everyday life. I ask a few questions about the case study that allow you to apply what you have learned in a chapter to analyzing real-life communication and developing strategies for improving interaction. You can access videos that depict each case study via the Online Resources for *Communication in Our Lives*.

Beyond the Classroom

Following chapters in Parts I and II is a "Beyond the Classroom" feature. It asks you to take the material in the chapter and extend it in three ways: asking how it applies to the workplace, how it involves ethical issues and choices, and how it applies to civic and social life. By thinking through these three issues for each chapter, you will actively engage the material and understand it more deeply.

Sharpen Your Skill

At the end of each chapter you will find two "Sharpen Your Skill" exercises. These bring to life the concepts we discuss by showing you how material in the text pertains to your daily life. They invite you to apply communication principles and skills as you interact with others. Some of the "Sharpen Your Skill" features suggest ways to practice particular communication skills. Others encourage you to notice how a specific communication principle or theory shows up in your interactions. If you do the "Sharpen Your Skill" exercises, you will increase your insight into communication in general and your own communication in particular.

Critical Thinking

Communication in Our Lives strongly emphasizes critical thinking. Competent communication demands critical thinking: distinguishing logical arguments from illogical ones, drawing sound conclusions from evidence, and applying concepts from one context to a different context. Each chapter calls attention to critical thinking by pointing out specific topics and issues that require critical thought.

Ethics

Because ethical issues are entwined with all forms of communication, I've integrated ethics into all chapters. As you read the chapter, you'll notice that I point out particular ethical questions and considerations. Also, I've included one question focused on ethics at the end of each chapter and an ethical extension is part of each Beyond the Classroom feature.

Research in Our Lives

A final feature, "Research in Action," appears in selected chapters. This feature is an attempt to answer a question that students often raise: How does research affect the "real world?" To show you that research conducted by communication scholars has important impact on real life I offer in-depth descriptions of particular research studies that are relevant to issues in today's world and your own life.

I hope you enjoy reading this book as much as I've enjoyed writing it. I also hope that this book and the class it accompanies will help you develop the skills needed for communication in your life. If so, then both of us will have spent our time well.

Jon Feingersh/Blend Images/Jupiter Images

The way we communicate with others and with ourselves ultimately determines the quality of our lives.

Anthony Robbins

The World of Communication

Mike closes his cell and shakes his head; talking with Chris is awkward now that they live 800 miles apart. They were buddies in high school but drifted apart after they enrolled in different universities. They talk by cell and IM frequently and post on each other's My Space pages, but it's not the same as hanging out together. Shrugging, he turns on the TV while he finishes dressing for dinner with Coreen. The top news story is about another school shooting. He grimaces, thinking that the world has become a pretty mean place. Turning his thoughts back to Coreen, Mike hopes she won't want to talk about their relationship again tonight. He can't see the point of analyzing and discussing their relationship unless something is wrong, but she likes to talk about it when everything is fine.

As he dresses, Mike thinks about his oral presentation for Thursday's

SHARPEN YOUR SKILL

At the end of this chapter, refer to the Sharpen Your Skill features, Giving a Speech of Self-Introduction and Your Mediated World, to apply concepts from Chapter 1.

sociology class. He has some good ideas, but he doesn't know how to turn them into an effective speech. He vaguely remembers that the professor talked about how to organize a speech, but he wasn't listening. Mike also wishes he knew how to deal with a group that can't get on track. He and six other students have worked for three months to organize a student book co-op, but the group can't get its act together. By now everyone is really frustrated, and nobody listens to anyone else. He checks his voicemail and finds angry messages from three of the group members. He shrugs again, turns off the TV, and leaves to meet Coreen.

Like Mike, most of us communicate continually in our daily lives. Effective communication is vital to long-distance friendships, romantic relationships, public speaking, interviewing, classroom learning, and productive group discussion. Communication opportunities and demands fill our everyday lives.

Mike—and the rest of us—rely on communication long after our college years. Even if you don't pursue a career that relies centrally on public speaking skills, such as teaching or law, communication will be essential in your work. You may need to talk with clients or patients, make progress reports, engage in public dialogues, and present proposals. You may want to persuade your boss you deserve a raise, represent your company at a press conference, or work with colleagues to develop company policies. You will have conflicts with co-workers, supervisors, and subordinates. You may need to deal with superiors who email inappropriate content or with whom you simply disagree. Beyond your career, you'll communicate with family members, friends, and social acquaintances in a range of settings, each of which will call for communication skills.

WHY STUDY COMMUNICATION?

Because you've been communicating all of your life, you might wonder why you need to study communication. One answer is that formal study can improve skill. Some people have a natural aptitude for playing basketball. They become even more effective, however, if they study theories of offensive and defensive play and if they practice skills. Likewise, even if you communicate well now, learning about communication and practicing communication skills can make you more effective (Hargie, 2006).

Another reason to study communication is that theories and principles help us make sense of what happens in our lives, and they help us have personal impact. For instance, if Mike learned about different gender communities, he might understand why Coreen, like many women, enjoys talking about relationships even when there is no problem. If Mike had better insight into the communication that sustains long-distance relationships, he might be able to enrich his friendship with Chris despite the miles between them. If he knew how to develop an agenda, he might be able to get his group on track. Studying public speaking could help Mike design a good presentation for his class report. Learning to listen better would help Mike retain information like his professor's tips on organizing oral reports. Communication theory and skills would help Mike maximize his effectiveness in all spheres of his life.

Communication in Our Lives will help you become a more confident and competent communicator. Part One clarifies how communication works

(or doesn't work) and explains how perception, personal identity, language, nonverbal communication, listening, and cultural factors affect the overall communication process. In Part Two, we'll look at communication in five contexts: personal relationships, small groups, organizations, interviews, and mass communication. Part Three focuses on public speaking.

This chapter lays a foundation for your study of communication. We'll first define communication. Next we'll discuss the values of communication in many spheres of your life. Then we'll examine some models of communication to clarify how the process works. In the third section of the chapter, we'll describe the breadth of the communication field and careers for communication specialists.

DEFINING COMMUNICATION

Communication* is a systemic process in which people interact with and through symbols to create and interpret meanings. Let's elaborate the key parts of this definition.

The first important feature of this definition is **process**. Communication is a process, which means it is ongoing and always in motion, moving ever forward and changing continually. It's hard to tell when communication starts and stops because what happened long before we talk with someone may influence interaction, and what occurs in a particular encounter may have repercussions in the future. We cannot freeze communication at any one moment.

Communication is also **systemic**, which means that it occurs within a system of interrelated parts that affect one another. In family communication, for instance, each member of the family is part of the system (Galvin, Dickson, & Marrow, 2006). In addition, the physical environment and the time of day are elements of the system that affect interaction. People interact differently in a formal living room and on a beach, and we may be more alert at certain times of day than at others. If a family has a history of listening sensitively and working out problems constructively, and then when one family member says, "There's something we need to talk about," it's unlikely to cause defensiveness. On the other hand, if the family has a record of nasty conflicts, then the same comment might arouse strong defensiveness. A lingering kiss might be an appropriate way

· · · · · · · · · · · · · · · ·
*Boldfaced terms are defined in the glossary at the end of the book.

to show affection in a private setting, but the same action would raise eyebrows in an office. To interpret communication, we have to consider the system in which it takes place.

Our definition of communication also emphasizes **symbols**, which include all language and many nonverbal behaviors, as well as art and music. Anything that abstractly signifies something else can be a symbol. We might symbolize love by giving a ring, by saying "I love you," or by embracing. Later in this chapter, we'll have more to say about symbols. For now, just remember that human communication involves interaction with and through symbols.

Finally, our definition focuses on meanings, which are the heart of communication. Meanings are the significance we bestow on phenomena—what they signify to us. Meanings are not in phenomena. Instead, meaning grows out of our interaction with symbols; that is how we interpret words and nonverbal communication.

There are two levels of meaning in communication. The **content level of meaning** is the literal message. For example, if someone says to you, "Get lost!" the content level of meaning is that you should get lost. The **relationship level of meaning** expresses the relationship between communicators. In our example, if the person who says, "Get lost!" is a friend and is smiling, then you would probably interpret the relationship level of meaning as indicating that the person likes you and is kidding around. On the other hand, if the person who says, "Get lost!" is your supervisor, and she is responding to your request for a raise, then you might interpret the relationship level of meaning as indicating that your supervisor regards you as inferior and dislikes your work.

VALUES OF COMMUNICATION

Now that we have a working definition of communication, let's consider its value in our lives. We spend a great deal of time communicating. We talk, listen, have dialogues with ourselves, participate in group discussions, present oral reports, watch and listen to mass communication, and so forth. From birth to death, communication shapes our personal, professional, and social lives as well as the culture in which we live.

Personal Values

George Herbert Mead (1934)[†] said that humans are "talked into" humanity. He meant that we gain personal identity as we communicate with others. In the earliest years of our lives, family members tell us who we are: "You're smart." "You're strong." "You're a clown." Later, we interact with teachers, friends, romantic partners, and co-workers who communicate their views of us. Thus, how we see ourselves reflects the views of us that others communicate.

The profound connection between identity and communication is dramatically evident in children who have been deprived of human contact. Case studies of children who were isolated from others for long periods of time reveal that

> **COMMUNICATION in Your Life**
>
> **Identify the relationship level of meaning in a recent interaction with a friend.**

[†] I am using the American Psychological Association's (APA) method of citation. If you see "Mead (1934)," I am referring to a work by Mead that was written in 1934. If you see "Mead (1934, p. 10)" or "(Mead, 1934, p. 10)," I am specifically citing page 10 of Mead's 1934 work. The full bibliographic citations for all works may be found in the References section at the end of the book.

they lack a firm self-concept, and their mental and psychological development is severely hindered by lack of language (Shattuck, 1980).

The headline of a recent *New York Times* article is "Strangers May Cheer You Up, Study Says" (Belluck, 2008). The article summarized research showing that positive, cheerful messages from friends, neighbors, or even strangers affect our happiness. This is consistent with a large body of research that shows that communicating with others promotes health, whereas social isolation is linked to stress, disease, and early death (Fackelmann, 2006; Kupfer, First, & Regier, 2002). People who lack close friends have greater levels of anxiety and depression than people who are close to others (Lane, 2000; Ornish, 1999; Segrin, 1998). One group of researchers reviewed scores of studies that traced the relationship between health and interaction with others. They reached the conclusion that social isolation is as dangerous statistically as high blood pressure, smoking, obesity, or high cholesterol (Crowley, 1995). Many doctors and researchers believe that loneliness impairs the immune system, making us more vulnerable to a range of minor and major illness (Sheehan, 1996).

Life-threatening medical problems are also affected by healthy interaction with others. Heart disease is more common among people who lack strong interpersonal relationships (Ornish, 1998; Ruberman, 1992). Heart patients who feel the least loved have 50 percent more arterial damage than those who feel the most loved, and those who live alone are twice as likely to die within a year of having a heart attack (Crowley, 1998). Women with metastatic breast cancer double their average survival time when they belong to support groups in which they talk with others (Crowley, 1995). Clearly, healthy interaction with others is important to our physical and mental health.

Relationship Values

Daniel Goleman, author of *Social Intelligence* (2007) says humans are "wired to connect" (p. 4). And communication—verbal and nonverbal—is the primary way that we connect with others. Marriage counselors have long emphasized the importance of communication for healthy, enduring relationships (Beck, 1988; Gottman, 1994a, 1994b; Gottman & Carrère, 1994). They point out that the failure of some marriages is not caused primarily by troubles and problems or even by conflict because all marriages encounter challenges and conflict. A major distinction between relationships that endure and those that collapse is effective communication. In fact, results of a national poll taken in 1999 showed that a majority of Americans perceive communication problems as the number one reason marriages fail—far surpassing other reasons such as sexual difficulties, money problems, and interference from family members (http://www.natcom.org/research/Poll/how_americans_ communicate.htm).

Communication is important for more than solving problems or making disclosures. For most of us, everyday talk and nonverbal interaction are the very essence of relationships (Wood & Duck, 2006). Unremarkable, everyday interaction sustains intimacy more than the big moments, such as declarations of love. By sharing news about mutual acquaintances and discussing ordinary topics, partners keep up the steady pulse of their relationship (Duck, 2006; Schmidt & Uecker, 2007; Wood, 2006a, 2006b). For this reason, one of the biggest challenges of long-distance relationships is not being able to share small talk.

COMMUNICATION HIGHLIGHT

Communication and Health

Effective communication is closely linked to physical and psychological health. Humans have a basic need to interact with others and feel that they belong in communities (Lane, 2000). After years of studying healthy and sick people, Dr. Dean Ornish (1998) concluded that one consistent difference between them is satisfying interactions and relationships.

CourseMate

In an interview with *Newsweek* reporters, Dr. Ornish stated, "Love and intimacy are at the root of what makes us sick and what makes us well. I am not aware of any other factor in medicine—not diet, not smoking, not exercise—that has a greater impact" (Hager & Springen, 1998, p. 54).

SANDY   *When my boyfriend moved away, the hardest part wasn't missing big things in each other's life. What really bothered us was not being able to talk about little stuff or just be together. It was like we weren't part of each other's normal life when we couldn't talk about all the little things that happened or about our feelings.*

Professional Values

Communication is the seventh most popular field of undergraduate study (McKinney, 2006). One reason for this is that communication skills are closely linked to professional success. The importance of communication is obvious in professions such as teaching, business, law, sales, and counseling, in which talking and listening are primary. Many attorneys, counselors, businesspeople, and teachers major or minor in communication before pursuing specialized training.

In other fields, the importance of communication is less obvious but nonetheless present. When companies are surveyed to find out what applicant qualities they consider most important, communication tops the list (Schneider, 1999; Windsor, Curtis, & Stephens, 1997). Health-care professionals must communicate effectively to explain medical problems to patients, describe courses of treatment, and gain information and cooperation from patients and their families (Beckman, 2003; Levine, 2004; Mangan, 2002). Doctors who do not listen well are less effective in treating patients, and they're more likely to be sued than doctors who do listen well (Levine, 2004; Milia, 2003). Human resources professionals say that good communication skills are critical to their on-the-job effectiveness (Morreale, 2001). Even such highly technical jobs as computer programming, engineering, and systems design require communication skills (Darling & Dannels, 2003). Specialists must be able to listen carefully, work in groups and teams, and explain technical ideas to people who lack their expert knowledge.

In professional life, the costs of poor communication are great. Executives in large companies report that 14 percent of each work week is wasted because of poor communication (Thomas, 1999). In the workplace, poor communication means that errors and misunderstandings occur, messages must be repeated, productivity suffers, and—sometimes—people lose jobs. No matter what your career goals are, developing strong communication skills will enhance your professional success.

Cultural Values

Communication skills are important to the health of our society. To be effective, citizens in a democracy must be able to express ideas and evaluate the ideas of others. One event typical of presidential election years is a debate between or among candidates. To make informed judgments, viewers need to listen critically to candidates' arguments and their responses to criticism and questions. We also need listening skills to grasp and evaluate opposing points of view on issues such as abortion, environmental policies, and health-care reform. To be a good community member, you need skills in expressing your point of view and responding to those of others. In pluralistic cultures such as ours, we interact with people who differ from us, and we need to know how to understand and work with them. Both civic life and social life depends on our ability to listen thoughtfully to a range of perspectives and to communicate in a variety of ways.

JANET   *There are so many people from different cultures on this campus that you can't get by without knowing how to communicate in a whole lot of ways. In my classes and my dorm, there are lots of Asian students and some Hispanic ones, and they communicate differently than people raised in the United States. If I don't learn about their communication styles, I can't get to know them or learn about what they think.*

Janet is right. When she was a student in one of my courses, she and I talked several times about the concern she expresses in her commentary. Janet realized she needed to learn to interact with people who differ from her if she is to participate fully in today's world. She has learned a lot about communicating with diverse people, and no doubt she will learn more in the years ahead. Like Janet, you can improve your ability to communicate effectively with the variety of people who make up our society.

Communication, then, is important for personal, relationship, professional, and cultural reasons. Because communication is a cornerstone of human life, your choice to study it will serve you well. To understand what's involved in communication, let's now define the process.

Celia Mannings/Alamy

Verbal and nonverbal communication reflect cultural backgrounds and understandings.

COMMUNICATION HIGHLIGHT

U.S. Demographics in the Twenty-First Century

The United States is home to a wide range of people with diverse ethnic, racial, cultural, and geographic backgrounds. And the proportions of different groups are changing. Currently, one in three U.S. residents is a minority. By 2050 more than one in two U.S. residents will be a minority, and by 2050 non-Hispanic whites will be a minority. The following shifts in the ethnic makeup of the United States are predicted to take place between 2005 and 2050 ("Demographics," 2009; Roberts, 2008):

	2008	2050
African Americans	13%	13%
Asians	4%	8%
Caucasians	66%	46%
Hispanics (of any race)	15%	30%
Other	3%	5%

More and more people are convinced that a key function of higher education is to prepare people to function effectively and comfortably in a diverse society. Two-thirds of Americans polled by the Ford Foundation (1998) say it is very important for colleges and universities to prepare students to live and work in a society marked by diversity. Fully 94 percent of Americans polled said it is more important now than ever before for all of us to understand people who are different from us. Interestingly, strong support for weaving diversity into education was not tied to political stands. Fifty-one percent of respondents said they were either conservative or very conservative politically. Still, the majority of those polled believed that every college student should be required to study different cultures and social groups to graduate.

Learn more about diverse groups and their impact on the United States by visiting **WebLink 1.1** via your Online Resources for *Communication in Our Lives*. (To learn how to get started with your Online Resources, see the inside front and back covers of this book.)

MODELS OF COMMUNICATION

Over the years, scholars in communication have developed a number of models, which reflect increasingly sophisticated understandings of the communication process.

Linear Models

One of the first models (Laswell, 1948) described communication as a linear, or one-way, process in which one person acted on another person. This model consisted of five questions that described early views of how communication worked:

> Who?
> Says what?
> In what channel?
> To whom?
> With what effect?

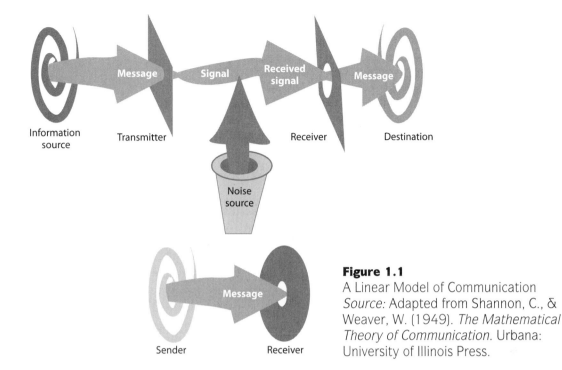

Figure 1.1
A Linear Model of Communication
Source: Adapted from Shannon, C., & Weaver, W. (1949). *The Mathematical Theory of Communication*. Urbana: University of Illinois Press.

A year later, Claude Shannon and Warren Weaver (1949) advanced a model that included noise, or interferences, which distort understanding between communicators. Figure 1.1 shows Shannon and Weaver's model. Although these early models were useful starting points, they were too simplistic to capture the complexity of most kinds of human communication.

Interactive Models

The major shortcoming of linear models was that they portrayed communication as flowing in only one direction, from a sender to a receiver. This suggests that speakers only speak and never listen and that listeners only listen and never send messages.

Realizing that receivers respond to senders and senders listen to receivers led communication theorists (Schramm, 1955) to adapt models to include **feedback**. Feedback may be verbal, nonverbal, or both, and it may be intentional or unintentional. Research has confirmed Schramm's insight that feedback is important. Supervisors report that communication accuracy and on-the-job productivity rise when they encourage their subordinates to give feedback: ask questions, comment on supervisors' messages, and respond to supervisory communication (Deal & Kennedy, 1999).

The interactive model also shows that communicators create and interpret messages within personal fields of experience. Adding fields of experience and feedback allowed Schramm and other communication scholars to develop models of communication as an interactive process in which both senders and receivers participate actively (Figure 1.2).

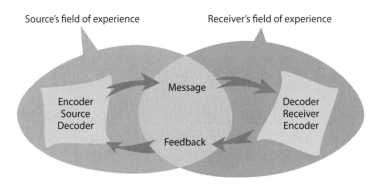

Figure 1.2
An Interactive Model of Communication *Source:* Adapted from Schramm, W. (1955). *The Process and Effects of Mass Communication.* Urbana: University of Illinois Press.

NISHA   *I lived in India until I was 14, and my family is still very Indian culturally. I am always surprised by how much U.S. college students disregard their parents' wishes. My parents insist that I marry an Indian so they do not want me to date Americans or other non-Indians. My friends say it is not my parents business who I date. They don't care if their parents don't approve of their boyfriends and girlfriends.*

COMMUNICATION in Your Life

How has your communication with one friend changed over time?

Transactional Models

A serious limitation of interactive models is that they don't acknowledge that everyone involved in communication both sends and receives messages, often simultaneously. While giving a press release, a speaker watches reporters to see whether they seem interested; both the speaker and the reporters are "listening," and both are "speaking."

Interactive models also fail to capture the dynamism of communication. To do this, a model would need to show that communication changes over time as a result of what happens between people. For example, Mike and Coreen communicated in more reserved and formal ways on their first date than after months of seeing each other. What they talk about and how they talk have changed as a result of interacting. An accurate model would include the feature of time and would depict features of communication as dynamically varying rather than constant. Figure 1.3 is a transactional model of communication that highlights these features and others we have discussed.

Our model also includes **noise**, which is anything that interferes with the intended communication. This includes sounds like a lawn mower or others' conversations, as well as "noise" within communicators, such as fatigue and preoccupation. In addition, our model shows that communication is a continuous, constantly changing process.

The outer lines on our model emphasize that communication occurs within systems that themselves affect communication and meanings. Those systems include contexts that both communicators share (e.g., a common campus, town, and culture) as well as each person's personal systems (e.g., family, religious associations, and friends). Also notice that our model, unlike previous ones, portrays

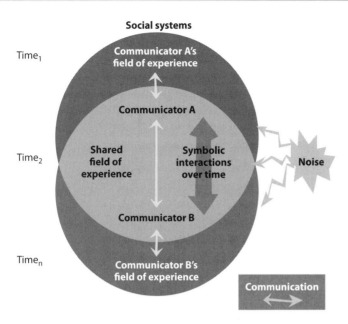

Figure 1.3
A Transactional Model of Communication
Source: Adapted from Wood, J. T. (2010). *Interpersonal Communication: Everyday Encounters* (6th ed.). Belmont, CA: Wadsworth.

each person's field of experience and the shared field of experience between communicators as changing over time. As we encounter new people and grow personally, our field of experience expands.

Finally, our model doesn't label one person a "sender" and the other a "receiver." Instead, both people are defined as communicators who participate actively in the communication process. This means that, at a given moment in communication, you may be sending a message (speaking), receiving a message (listening), or doing both at the same time (interpreting what someone says while nodding to show you are interested).

THE BREADTH OF THE COMMUNICATION FIELD

The discipline of communication dates back more than 2,000 years. Originally, the field focused almost exclusively on public communication. Aristotle, a famous Greek philosopher, believed that effective public speaking was essential to citizens' participation in civic affairs (Borchers, 2006). He taught his students how to develop and present persuasive speeches to influence public affairs.

Although public speaking remains a vital skill, it is no longer the only focus of the communication field. The modern discipline includes seven major areas of research and teaching: intrapersonal communication, interpersonal communication, group communication, organizational communication, public communication, mass communication and new technologies, and intercultural communication.

Intrapersonal Communication

Intrapersonal communication is communication with ourselves, or self-talk. We engage in self-talk to plan our lives, to rehearse different ways of acting, and to prompt ourselves to do or not to do particular things. You might be wondering whether the term *intrapersonal communication* is just jargon for the term *thinking*. In one sense, it is. Intrapersonal communication is a cognitive process that goes on inside us. Yet, because thinking relies on language to name and reflect on phenomena, it is also a kind of communication. Donna Vocate's (1994) book *Intrapersonal Communication*, which is devoted entirely to intrapersonal communication, reflects the importance of this area of study and teaching.

Many counselors focus on enhancing self-esteem by changing how we talk to ourselves (Rusk & Rusk, 1988; Seligman, 1990, 2002). For instance, you might say to yourself, "I blew that test, so I'm really stupid. I'll never graduate; even if I do, nobody will hire me." Because what we say to ourselves affects our feelings, we should challenge negative self-talk by saying, "Hey, wait a minute. One test is hardly a measure of my intelligence. I have a decent overall college record." What we say to ourselves can enhance or diminish self-esteem and thus our effectiveness in contexts ranging from interviews to public speaking to social conversation.

Intrapersonal communication allows us to rehearse alternative scenarios so that we can evaluate how each might turn out. To control a disruptive group member, Mike might consider (1) telling the person to shut up, (2) suggesting that the group adopt a rule that everyone should participate equally, and (3) taking the person out for coffee and privately asking him to be less domineering. Mike can think through the various ways of approaching the group member, weigh the likely consequences of each, and then choose one to put into practice. We engage in internal dialogues continually as we reflect on experiences, sort through ideas and options for communicating, and test alternative ways of acting.

Interpersonal Communication

A second major emphasis in the field of communication is **interpersonal communication**, which deals with communication between people. In one sense, everything except intrapersonal communication is interpersonal. But such a broad definition doesn't create useful boundaries for the area of study.

Interpersonal communication exists on a continuum from impersonal to highly personal. The most impersonal kind of communication occurs when we ignore another person or treat another as an object. In the middle of the continuum is interaction with others within social roles. The most personal communication occurs in what philosopher Martin Buber (1970) called "I–Thou" relationships, in which each person treats the other as a unique and sacred person. Figure 1.4 illustrates the communication continuum. The more we know and interact with another person as a distinct individual, the more personal the

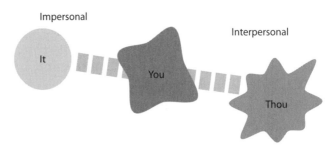

Figure 1.4
The Communication
Continuum

communication is. Using this criterion, we would say that a deep conversation with a friend is more personal than a casual exchange with a salesclerk.

Interpersonal communication scholars study how communication creates and sustains relationships and how partners communicate to deal with the normal and extraordinary challenges of maintaining intimacy over time (Duck & Wood, 1995; Wood & Duck, 1995a, 1995b, 2006).

Research indicates that communication is the lifeblood of close friendships and romantic relationships. Communication is the primary way people develop intimacy and continuously refashion relationships to meet their changing needs and identities. Intimates who learn how to listen sensitively and talk with each other have the greatest chance of enduring over time.

Group Communication

A third important branch of communication study is small-group communication, including therapeutic groups, social groups, decision-making committees, and work teams. Small-group communication scholars study leadership, member participation, agendas for decision making, and disruptive and constructive conflict. Chapters 10 and 11 will help us understand how communication affects each of these aspects of group life and how we can participate effectively in groups.

Group communication scholars also study teams, which are special types of groups that pull together people with diverse skills and experiences and which develop especially strong cohesion. Teamwork is increasingly part of the workplace, with the average executive spending 700 hours a year in team meetings (Tubbs, 1998). Learning to communicate effectively in teams has become a criterion for success and advancement in careers.

Organizational Communication

Communication in organizations is another growing area of interest. Communication scholars have identified communication skills that enhance professional success, and they have traced the impact of various kinds of communication on morale, productivity, and commitment in organizations. Scholars of organizational communication have studied aspects of work life such as interviewing, listening, organizational structure, presentations, leadership, and decision making.

In addition to continuing to study these topics, organizational scholars have begun to focus on organizational culture. The term **organizational culture** refers to understandings about identity and codes of thought and action shared by members of an organization (Nicotera, Clinkscales, & Walker, 2002). From this understanding emerge rules for interaction and perspectives on work. The impact of organizational culture was vividly highlighted in July 1994 when a Colorado wildfire became a raging inferno in which 14 firefighters lost their lives. A detailed investigation revealed that a primary contributor to the loss of lives was a "can-do" culture among firefighters. Trained to believe that they could do what others could not and that they could perform heroic feats, the firefighters didn't observe critical safety regulations. Ironically, the can-do

COMMUNICATION in Your Life

Identify one I-It, one I-You, and one I-Thou relationship in your life.

culture essential to such a dangerous job also led to disregard for important precautions and the subsequent loss of 14 lives.

Organizational communication scholars have also revealed that organizations are fundamentally gendered. Their research has shown that communication practices in organizations institutionalize and sometimes challenge gender-based, hierarchical power relations (Allen, 2006; Ashcraft, 2006; Ashcraft & Mumby, 2004; Buzzanell & Lucas, 2006; Mumby, 2006a, 2006b). We have also learned that in a number of ways, women and men communicate differently, and they often misunderstand one another (Murphy & Zorn, 1996; Wood, 1993b, 1995a, 1996b, 1998, 2011). Women tend to make more "listening noises," such as "um," "uh-huh," and "go on," than most men do. If men don't make these noises when communicating with women colleagues, the women may think the men aren't listening. Conversely, men are likely to misinterpret the listening noises women make as signaling agreement rather than just interest. Such misunderstandings can hinder communication on the job (Murphy & Zorn, 1996).

Another area of increasing interest among organizational scholars is personal relationships between co-workers. As we increase the number of hours we spend on the job, it is natural for personal relationships between co-workers to increase. This adds both interest and complications to organizational life. In one study of personal relationships between co-workers, communication scholar Ted Zorn (1995) studied "bosses and buddies," relationships in which one friend is the boss of the other. Zorn discovered a number of ways people cope with the often contradictory rules for communication between friends and between superiors and subordinates.

> **COMMUNICATION in Your Life**
>
> Have you ever had a close personal relationship with a co-worker? If so, how did it add to and complicate your working relationship?

MELBOURNE *It was a real hassle when my supervisor and I started going out. Before, he gave me orders like he did all the other waitstaff, and none of us thought anything about it. But after we started dating, he would sort of ask me, instead of tell me, what to do, like saying, "Mel, would you help out in Section 7?" Another problem was that if he gave me a good station where tips run high, the other waits would give me trouble because they thought he was favoring me because we go out. And when he gave me a bad station, I'd feel he was being nasty. It was a mess being his employee and his girlfriend at the same time.*

Mass and Social Media

For some time, communication scholars have studied mass communication media such as film, radio, newspapers, magazines, and television. Their research has given us insight into how mass media work and how they represent and influence cultural values. For instance, the cultural feminine ideal, which centers on youth and beauty, is perpetuated by the use of young, beautiful women as models in ads and as news reporters and anchors.

A more recent focus of media scholars is social media. How do iPods, PDAs, cell phones, and other social media influence our thinking, working, and relating? Do they increase social contact and productivity (Wood & Smith, 2001)? Does the vast amount of information now available to us create confusion and information overload, as some scholars suggest (Nie, 2004; Young, 2005)?

New technologies allow us to interact with people we've never met in person.

Clearly, the verdict on the effects of new technologies will not be in for some time. Meanwhile, all of us struggle to keep up with our increasingly technological world. Technologies of communication pervade many aspects of our lives. Videoconferencing now makes it possible for people who are separated by many miles to talk with and see each other. Many public presentations now include PowerPoint images and other forms of technological assistance. Friends, family members, and romantic couples rely on email to stay in touch. Woven into later chapters of this book are discussions of the ways in which new technologies affect how, when, and with whom we communicate.

Public Communication

Even though most of us may not seek careers that call for extensive formal speaking, most of us will have opportunities to speak publically. When we join new groups, we may be asked to "say a few words about yourself," and others' first impressions of us will be based on our self-introductions.

In addition, we all will be in situations where speaking up is a responsibility. My editor speaks to her sales representatives to explain what her books are about and how to point out important features to faculty. I recently coached my doctor in public speaking so she could address her colleagues on a development in the treatment of kidney disease. My plumber presents workshops to his staff to update them on new plumbing products and to teach them how to communicate effectively with customers. My brother-in-law relies on public speaking skills when he's trying cases in court or mediating disputes. My editor, doctor, plumber, and brother-in-law don't consider themselves public speakers, but public speaking is a part of their lives, and doing it effectively is important to their success.

Ghislain & Marie David de Lossy/Cultura/Alamy

Public speaking is part of most people's lives, and when done well, it's a powerful way to communicate information, beliefs, and ideas to foster understanding, build commitment, and motivate action.

Scholars of public communication focus on critical evaluation of speeches and on principles for speaking effectively. Rhetorical critics study important communication events, such as Martin Luther King Jr.'s "I Have a Dream" speech and presidential speeches announcing wars. Critics often take a role in civic life by evaluating political debates and speeches to help voters understand how well candidates support their positions and respond to challenges from opponents.

Scholars of public communication also study principles of effective public speaking. As we will see in Chapters 14 through 18, we know a lot about what makes speakers seem credible to listeners and how credibility affects persuasion. Research has also enlightened us about the kinds of argument, methods of organizing ideas, and forms of proof that listeners find effective. If Mike studied this research, he could glean useful guidelines for his oral report in class.

Intercultural Communication

Intercultural communication is an increasingly important focus of research, teaching, and training. Although intercultural communication is not a new area of study, its importance has grown in recent years. The United States has always been made up of many peoples and cultures. Demographic shifts in the last decade have increased this, making our country richly pluralistic. Growing numbers of Asians, Indians, Eastern Europeans, Latinas and Latinos, Hispanics, and people of other nations are making the United States their home. Immigrants bring with them cultural values and styles of communicating that differ from those of people whose ancestors were born in the United States.

Scholars of intercultural communication increase awareness of different cultures' communication practices. For example, a Taiwanese woman in one of my classes seldom spoke up and wouldn't enter the heated debates that characterize graduate classes. One day after class, I encouraged Mei-Ling to argue for her ideas when others challenged them. She replied that that would be impolite. Her culture considers it disrespectful to argue or assert oneself and even more disrespectful to contradict others. Understood in terms of the communication values of her culture, Mei-Ling's deference did not mean she lacked confidence.

MEIKKO   *What I find most odd about Americans is their focus on themselves. Here, everyone wants to be an individual who is so strong and stands out from everyone else. In Japan, it is not like that. We see ourselves as parts of families and communities, not as individuals. Here* I *and* my *are the most common words, but they are not often said in Japan.*

A particularly important recent trend in the study of intercultural communication is research on different social communities within a single society. Cultural differences are obvious in communication between a Nepali and a Canadian. Less obvious are cultural differences in communication between people who speak the "same" language. Within the United States, there are distinct social communities based on race, gender, sexual orientation, and other factors. Intercultural communication scholars (Samovar, Porter, & McDaniels, 2009) have identified distinctive styles of communication used by women, men, blacks, whites, certain American Indian tribes, homosexuals, people with disabilities, and other groups. For example, women, more than men, tend to disclose personal information and to engage in emotionally expressive talk in their friendships (Wood, 1993b, 1994a, 1994d, 2011). Many blacks are socialized in a culture that encourages dynamic talk, verbal duels, and other communication routines that have no equivalents in white speech communities (Houston & Wood, 1996). Participating effectively in a pluralistic society requires us to recognize and respect the communication practices of distinct social communities.

UNIFYING THEMES IN THE FIELD

After reading about the major branches of the modern field of communication, you might think that the field is a collection of separate, unrelated areas of interest. Actually, this isn't the case. The field of communication is unified by a pervasive interest in symbols, meaning, critical thinking, and ethics.

Symbolic Activities

Symbols are the basis of language, thinking, and much nonverbal behavior. A wedding band is a symbol of marriage in Western culture; your name is a symbol for you; and a smile is a symbol of friendliness. Because symbols are abstract, they allow us to lift experiences and ourselves out of the concrete world of the here and now and reflect on our experiences and ourselves. Because symbols let us represent ideas and feelings, we can share experiences with others, even if they have not had those experiences themselves.

Whether we are interested in intrapersonal, interpersonal, mass, group, public, or intercultural communication, symbols are central to what happens. Thus, symbols and the mental activities they enable are a unifying focus of study and teaching about all forms of communication. We will discuss symbols in greater depth in Chapter 5, which deals with verbal communication, and in Chapter 6, which focuses on nonverbal communication.

Meaning

Closely related to interest in symbols is the communication field's pervasive concern with meaning. The human world is one of meaning. We don't simply exist, eat, drink, sleep, and go through motions. Instead, we imbue every aspect of our lives with significance or meaning. When I feed my dog, Cassie, she eats her food and then returns to her canine adventures. For her, eating is a necessary and enjoyable activity. We humans layer food and eating with significance. Food often symbolizes special events or commitments. For example, kosher products reflect commitment to Jewish heritage, turkey is commonly associated with commemorating the first Thanksgiving in the United States (although vegetarians symbolize their commitment by *not* eating turkey), eggnog is a Christmas tradition, mandel brot is a Hanukkah staple, and birthday cakes celebrate an individual.

Some families consider meals an occasion to come together and share their lives, but in other families meals are battlefields where family tensions are played out. A meal can symbolize romance (i.e., candles, wine), a personal struggle to stick to a diet, or an excuse to spend two hours talking with a friend. Our experiences gain significance as a result of the meaning we attach to experience.

To study communication, then, is to study how we use symbols to create meaning in our lives. Communication scholars see romantic bonds, friendships, families, groups and teams, and organizations as relationships that individuals collaboratively create in the process of interaction (Andersen, 1993; Wood, 1992, 1995b). Leslie Baxter (1987, p. 262) says that "relationships can be regarded as webs of significance" spun as partners communicate. By extension, all human activities are webs of significance spun with symbols and meaning.

BENITA *It's funny how important a word can be. Nick and I had been going out for a long time, and we really liked each other, but I didn't know if this was going to be long term. Then we said we loved each other, and that changed how we saw each other and the relationship. Just using the word love transformed who we are.*

Critical Thinking

A third enduring concern in the communication field is **critical thinking**. To be competent communicators, we must be able to think critically. This means that we must examine ideas carefully to decide what to believe, think, and do in particular situations (McCarthy, 1991; Wade & Tavris, 1990). Someone who thinks critically weighs ideas thoughtfully, considers evidence carefully, asks about alternative conclusions and courses of action, and connects principles and concepts across multiple contexts. Table 1.1 identifies key skills of critical thinking that affect communication competence.

The skills of critical thinking highlighted in Table 1.1 apply to all types and contexts of communication. Carol Wade and Carol Tavris (1990) wrote an entire book about the importance of critical thinking to personal relationships. They show that the skills of critical thinking can enhance communication in friendships, romantic relationships, and family relationships.

Critical thinking is important in your life as a student. For instance, during a class lecture, your teacher states that Americans are highly individualistic and assertive. You know that you are not assertive and that you are more communal than individualistic. Should you dismiss what the teacher says as untrue? If you have critical thinking skills, you will realize that although the statement doesn't describe you accurately, it may well be true of most Americans.

Critical thinkers also work to apply concepts, skills, and principles they learn in one context to other contexts. For instance, in Chapter 8 we discuss ways to build supportive communication climates in the context of personal

Table 1.1	Critical Thinking Skills for Effective Communication

- Identify assumptions behind statements, claims, and arguments.
- Distinguish between logical and illogical reasoning.
- Separate facts from inferences.
- Evaluate evidence to determine its reliability, relevance, and value.
- Connect new information and ideas to familiar knowledge; apply concepts learned in one context to other contexts; recognize when and where specific principles are and are not appropriate.
- Distinguish between personal experiences, attitudes, behaviors, and generalizations about human beings.
- Identify and consider alternative views on issues, solutions to problems, and courses of action.
- Define problems and questions clearly and precisely.
- Draw reasonable conclusions about the implications of information and argument for thought and action.
- Determine how to find answers to important questions by considering what needs to be known and what sources might provide relevant knowledge.

Learn more by accessing **WebLink 1.2** via your Online Resources for *Communication in Our Lives* to visit the website of the Foundation for Critical Thinking. (To learn how to get started with your Online Resources, see the inside front and back covers of this book.)

relationships. The same skills discussed there are relevant to developing supportive climates in small group deliberations, public presentations, and organizational contexts. The ability to generate and evaluate solutions to a problem, which we consider in the context of group discussion (Chapter 11), is also relevant to addressing problems in personal relationships. Throughout this book, you will encounter opportunities to develop and test your critical thinking skills.

Ethics and Communication

A final theme that unifies research and teaching is ethical communication and interpretation of others' communication. Because all forms of communication involve ethical issues, this theme infuses all areas of the discipline. For instance, ethical dimensions of intrapersonal communication include the influence of stereotypes on our judgments and beliefs. In the realm of interpersonal communication, scholars who focus on ethics are concerned with issues such as honesty, compassion, and fairness in relationships. Pressures to conform that sometimes operate in groups are an ethical concern of scholars who specialize in group communication. Ethical issues also surface in public communication. For example, Linda Alcoff (1991) is concerned that people who speak for others who are oppressed may misrepresent others' experiences or even reinforce oppression by keeping others silent.

Another ethical issue relevant to a range of communication contexts concerns attitudes and actions that encourage or hinder freedom of speech: Are all members of organizations equally empowered to speak? What does it mean when audiences shout down a speaker with unpopular views? How does the

COMMUNICATION HIGHLIGHT

Thinking Critically about Language and Social Groups

It's especially important to think critically when using, listening to, or reading generalizations about social groups. The value of generalizations is that they allow us to recognize general patterns that can be useful starting points in understanding others. We can't learn about Koreans, blacks, whites, or Buddhists if we cannot use group labels such as *Korean* and *Black*. At the same time, generalizations do not necessarily apply to particular individuals. For instance, it is true that Koreans in general are more communal than native-born Americans, particularly whites, in general, but a particular Korean may be very individualistic, and a particular native-born American may be very communal.

In this book, you will read many generalizations about various social groups. These generalizations are based on research, usually including research conducted by members of the social group being discussed. That doesn't mean that a generalization about men or whites is true about all men or all whites. You may well be a living exception to some of the generalizations about groups to which you belong.

To prevent ourselves from mistaking generalizations for absolute truths, it's important to use qualifying words such as *usually, in general, typically,* and *in most cases.* These remind us that there are exceptions to generalizations. As you read this book, notice how I qualify generalizations so we don't mistake them for universal truths. Notice also whether generalizations are appropriately qualified on television, in newspaper stories, in magazine articles, and in everyday conversations.

To explore your own experience with a generalization you applied to someone that turned out to be inaccurate or misleading, complete the Communication Highlight Activity for Chapter 1 via your Online Resources for *Communication in Our Lives.* (To learn how to get started with your Online Resources, see the inside front and back covers of this book.)

balance of power between relationship partners affect each person's freedom to express himself or herself? Because ethical issues infuse all forms of communication, we will discuss ethical themes in each chapter of this book.

In the questions at the end of each chapter, the ethics icon will call your attention to a question focused on ethics of communication.

CAREERS IN COMMUNICATION

Studying communication prepares you for a wide array of careers. As we've seen, communication skills are essential to success in most fields. In addition, people who major in communication are particularly sought after in a number of occupations.

Research

Communication research is a vital and growing field of work. A great deal of study is conducted by academics who combine teaching and research in faculty careers. In this book, you'll encounter much academic research, and you'll be able to evaluate what we learn from doing it.

In addition to academic research, communication specialists do media research on everything from message production to marketing (Morreale & Vogl, 1998). Companies want to know how people respond to different kinds of advertisements, logos, and labels for products. Before a new cereal or beer is named, various names are test marketed to test how customers will respond to different names. In addition, businesses research the audiences reached by different media, such as newspapers, magazines, radio, and television.

Education

Teachers are needed for communication classes and often whole curricula in secondary schools, junior colleges, colleges, universities, technical schools, and community colleges.

The level at which a person is qualified to teach depends on how extensively he or she has pursued the study of communication. Generally, a bachelor's degree in communication education and certification by the board of education are required of teachers in elementary and secondary schools. A master's degree in communication qualifies a person to teach at community colleges, technical schools, and some junior colleges and colleges. The doctoral degree (Ph.D.) in communication generally is required for a career in university education, although some universities offer short-term positions to people with master's degrees (National Communication Association [NCA], 2000).

Although generalists are preferred for many teaching jobs, at the college level, instructors can focus on areas of communication that particularly interest them. For instance, my research and teaching focus on interpersonal communication and gender and communication. A colleague in my department specializes in environmental advocacy and social movements. Other college faculty concentrate on areas such as oral traditions, intercultural communication, family communication, organizational dynamics, and the influence of mass media on cultural values.

Communication educators are not limited to communication departments. People with advanced degrees in communication hold positions in medical and business schools or as communication managers in corporations. Good doctors not only have specialized medical knowledge but also know how to listen sensitively to patients, how to explain complex problems and procedures, and how to provide comfort, reassurance, and motivation. Similarly, good businesspeople know not only their businesses but also how to explain them to others, how to present themselves and their companies or products favorably, and so on. Because communication is essential for doctors and businesspeople, increasing numbers of medical and business schools are creating permanent positions for communication specialists.

Media Production, Analysis, and Criticism

Increasingly, students are attracted to careers in mass communication and technologies of communication. There are many careers paths in media production, all of which demand good communication skills (Gregory, Healy, & Mazierkska, 2007). News reporters need skill not only in presenting information clearly but also in conducting interviews and fostering trust so that people will open up to them. To be effective, broadcasters must speak clearly and engagingly, and they must communicate credibly. Script writing and directing also require solid understanding of human communication.

Analysis and criticism of media are valuable career paths. Because our society is media saturated, we rely on people with expertise in criticism and analysis to help us understand what media are doing: whether they are representing information fairly or not, whether they are biased, or whether they are offering messages that are healthy or harmful to us. One of my colleagues studies the ways that the connectedness made possible by social media affects our understandings of ourselves and our relationships. A former student of mine is now pursuing graduate study in mass and social media so that she can specialize in teaching media literacy to others.

Training and Consulting

Consulting is another field that welcomes people with backgrounds in communication. Businesses want to train employees in effective group communication skills, interview techniques, and group and team work. Some large corporations, such as IBM, have entire departments devoted to training and development. People with communication backgrounds often join these departments and work with the corporation to design and teach courses or workshops that enhance employees' communication skills.

This counselor's nonverbal communication suggests he is engaged, relaxed, and unhurried.

David Buffington/age fotostock/PhotoLibrary

Communication specialists may also join or form consulting firms that provide particular kinds of communication training to government and businesses. One of my colleagues consults with organizations to help them develop work teams that interact effectively. I sometimes prepare workshops for educators who want to learn how to use communication to stimulate students' interest and learning. Other communication specialists work with politicians to improve their presentation styles and sometimes to write their speeches. I consult with attorneys on cases involving charges of sexual harassment and sex discrimination: I help them understand how particular communication patterns create hostile, harassing environments, and I collaborate with them to develop trial strategy. Other communication consultants work with attorneys on jury selection and advise attorneys' courtroom communication strategies.

Human Relations and Management

Because communication is the foundation of human relations, it's no surprise that many communication specialists build careers in human development or human relations departments of corporations. People with solid understandings of communication and good personal communication skills are effective in careers such as public relations, human resources, grievance management, negotiations, customer relations, and development and fundraising (NCA, 2000). In each of these areas, communication skills are the primary requirement.

Communication degrees may also open the door to careers in management. The most important qualifications for management are not technical skills but the ability to interact with others and communicate effectively. Good managers are skilled in listening, expressing their ideas, building consensus, creating supportive work environments, and balancing task and interpersonal concerns in dealing with others. Developing skills such as these gives communication majors a firm foundation for effective management.

BEYOND THE CLASSROOM

Each chapter in this book concludes with suggestions for taking the material in the chapter beyond the classroom. We'll focus on three extensions: considering the chapter's relevance in the workplace, probing ethical issues raised in the chapter, and connecting chapter material to civic and social engagement with the broader world. For the first chapter, you'll learn what the National Communication Association (NCA) and the International Communication Association (ICA) have to offer relevant to all three of those foci. NCA's home page is available by clicking **WebLink 1.3**. Click **WebLink 1.4** to go to ICA's welcome page. I suggest more specific links that will allow you to become familiar with the impressive scope of the organization and the discipline it represents.

1. **Workplace.** Click **WebLink 1.3** to go to NCA's page on communication in the workplace. Follow links there to learn about multiple ways that communication intersects the workplace.

2. **Ethics.** Click **WebLink 1.5** to read NCA's Credo for Ethical Communication, a document that members voted to endorse in 1999. Click **WebLink 1.6** to access ICA's statement on ethics. Carefully consider what the documents advocate and condemn. Do you agree with the ethical principles identified in the documents?

3. **Engagement.** Click **WebLink 1.7** to learn about NCA's "Communicating Common Ground" program that was launched in 1999 to encourage faculty, students, and practitioners in the field of communication to work actively in their communities to reduce prejudice and hateful acts based on racial, ethnic, religious, and other human differences.

Ethics

CHAPTER SUMMARY

In this chapter, we took a first look at human communication. First, we defined communication, and then we discussed its value in our lives. Next we considered a series of models, the most accurate of which is transactional. The transactional model emphasizes that communication is a systemic process in which people interact to create and share meanings.

Like most fields of study, communication has developed over the years. Today, communication scholars and teachers are interested in a range of communication activities. This broad range

of areas is held together by abiding interests in symbolic activities, meanings, critical thinking, and ethics, which together form the foundation of personal, interpersonal, and social life.

In the final section of this chapter, we considered some career opportunities open to people who specialize in communication. The modern field of communication offers an array of exciting career paths for people who enjoy interacting with others and who want the opportunity to be part of a dynamic discipline that evolves to meet changing needs and issues in our world.

APPLYING COMMUNICATION IN OUR LIVES

The key concepts, For Further Reflection and Discussion questions, and Experiencing Communication in Our Lives case study that follow will help you review, reflect on, and extend the information and ideas presented in this chapter. These resources, and a diverse selection of additional study tools, are

also available online at the CourseMate for *Communication in Our Lives.* Your CourseMate includes a student workbook, interactive video activities, a book companion website, Speech Builder Express, and InfoTrac College Edition. For more information or to access this book's online resources, visit **www.cengage.com/login**.

KEY CONCEPTS

communication, 3
content level of meaning, 4
critical thinking, 18
feedback, 9

interpersonal communication, 12
intrapersonal communication, 11
noise, 10
organizational culture, 13

process, 3
relationship level of meaning, 4
symbol, 4
systemic, 3

FOR FURTHER REFLECTION AND DISCUSSION

1. Using each of the models discussed in this chapter, describe communication in your family. What does each model highlight and obscure? Which model best describes and explains communication in your family?

2. Interview a professional in the field you plan to enter to discover what kinds of communication skills she or he thinks are most important for success. Which of those skills do you already have? Which skills do you need to develop or improve? How can you use this book and the course it accompanies

to develop the skills you will need to be effective in your career?

3. Think critically about the impact of digital technologies of communication. In what ways do you think these technologies might improve professional, personal, and social communication? In what ways might they be counterproductive?

4. Check out the NCA's online magazine, *Communication Currents,* which was launched in November 2006. To read it, click **WebLink 1.8**.

CourseMate

SHARPEN YOUR SKILL

1. Giving a Speech of Self-Introduction

This exercise serves two purposes: It gives you a first experience in public speaking, and it allows you to introduce yourself to your classmates. You may choose to develop your speech on your own, or you may use criteria specified by your instructor. If you want a basic blueprint for your speech, try this:

Reflect on yourself and your life. Identify one interesting or unusual aspect of your identity of your life, and use that as the focus of your speech. Possible foci for your speech are experience living in another country, the origin of an unusual name, a unique event in your life, or an interesting hobby or skill. Use the following basic structure for your speech:

I.   My name is _____
     I want to tell you this about myself: _____
     _____

II. Describe the interesting or unusual aspects of yourself or your life. _____
     _____

III. Conclude by restating your main idea. _____
     _____

You may want to review the sample speech of intro-duction at the end of this chapter and via your Online Resources for *Communication in Our Lives*. (To learn how to get started with your Online Resources, see the inside front and back covers of this book.)

2. Your Mediated World

How do social media affect your interactions? If you use the Internet, how are your electronic exchanges different from face-to-face inter-actions? Have you made any acquaintances or friends through social media? Did those rela-tionships develop differently from ones formed through face-to-face contact? Do you feel differ-ently about people you have never seen and those you see?

EXPERIENCING COMMUNICATION IN OUR LIVES

CASE STUDY: *A Model Speech of Self-Introduction*

The following speech is featured in your Chapter 1 Online Resources for *Communication in Our Lives*. Select "Speech of Self-Introduction" to watch the video of Mona Bradsher's speech. Improve your own communica-tion skills by reading, watching, and evaluating this sample speech.

Speech of Self-Introduction

My name is Mona Bradsher. I'm a junior, although I'm older than most juniors at our school. In my speech, I want to introduce you to a very persuasive 6-year-old. Through her, you'll learn why I have come back to finish my college degree after a 10-year break from school.

When I was 18, I started college like many of you. But unlike most of you, I dropped out when I was 20—in the middle of my sopho-more year. I left school because I wanted to get married to a man

© Cengage Learning

named Jason. I'd met him the summer before, and we had fallen in love. Jason and I did get married, and we had a daughter, Sasha.

In my case, the fairy tales were wrong: Jason and I didn't live happily ever after. We divorced just before our fifth wedding anniversary. So there I was: a 25-year-old single mom with a child to raise. My income was pretty low because I didn't have enough education to get a job that paid well. It was hard to get by on what I could make and the small amount of child support that Jason paid each month. We didn't go out for dinners or movies, but we did eat healthy meals at home. We didn't have money for a nice car, so we used the bus system. When Sasha was sick, I'd have to work extra hours to pay the doctor's bill and the cost of prescriptions. So it was tough, and I worried that as my daughter got older, I wouldn't be able to support her on what I made. I felt really trapped.

Last year, Sasha started school. One day, she came home and told me her teacher had taught them about the importance of education. Sasha's teacher had put up a chart showing the difference between what high school graduates and college graduates make. Her teacher also talked about how education helps every person fulfill his or her individual potential and lead a fuller life. The teacher told all the children that education was the most important gift they could give themselves. So Sasha said to me, "Mommy, now that I'm going to school, why don't you go too?"

At first, I told Sasha that Mommy had to work to pay for our apartment and food, but Sasha would have none of that. She insisted that I should go to school. I don't know how many of you have tried to argue with a very insistent 6-year-old, but take my word for it: You can't win! Because my daughter was so persistent, I checked around and found out there is an educational loan program specifically for older students who want to return to school and complete their education. I qualified, and I'll keep getting the loan as long as I maintain a B average. So far, my average is above that because Sasha and I have a deal: We study together for 3 hours every night.

And that's why I'm here now. That's why I've come back to finish my degree after a 10-year break. I'm here because my daughter reminded me of the importance of education. If I can learn an important lesson from a 6-year-old, then I can learn other important lessons from the teachers at our university.

QUESTIONS FOR ANALYSIS AND DISCUSSION

You can also answer these questions and see my responses to them online via your Online Resources for Chapter 1.

1. Does Mona's speech give you a sense of who she is?

2. Did Mona's introduction catch your attention and give you a road map of what she covers in her speech?

3. How did Mona create identification between herself and listeners?

4. How did examples add to the speech?

5. Was the quotation from Sasha effective?

6. Did Mona's conclusion create closure by returning to the theme of her introduction?

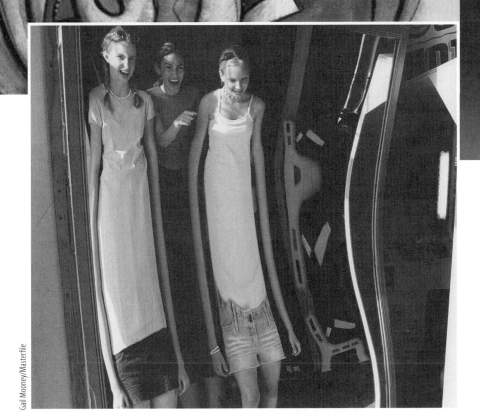

Gail Mooney/Masterfile

> We see the world as 'we' are, not as 'it' is; because it is the 'I' behind the 'eye' that does the seeing.
>
> **Anaïs Nin**

Perception and Communication

A few years ago, research that I was conducting involved interviewing male inmates in a medium-security prison. On the first day of interviewing, I arrived at the security station through which all visitors must pass. The guard looked at me and asked me to remove my necklace, a simple gold chain. "The inmates could use that to choke you," he explained. He then checked my purse, a standard procedure for visitors. He found my key ring, which is a two-inch piece of metal shaped like a cat's head with pointed ears. Pointing to the ears of the cat, he said, "This could be a weapon—they could put out your eyes." For the same reason, the guard confiscated my nail clipper and file. The guard also suggested that on future visits I not wear a belt.

The guard's experience with prisoners led him to perceive dangers that I didn't

SHARPEN YOUR SKILL

At the end of this chapter, refer to the Sharpen Your Skill features, Perceiving Others and Noticing Individualism, to apply concepts from Chapter 2.

notice. The necklace that I saw as a fashion accent he saw as a means of choking me. What I perceived as a key ring and manicure tools he saw as potential weapons. Our perceptions differed because we had different experiences and roles, which affected the meanings we assigned to things such as necklaces, key chains, and nail files and clippers.

This chapter focuses on **meaning,** which is the heart of communication. Meaning is the significance we attach to phenomena such as words, actions, people, objects, and events. To understand how humans create meanings for themselves and their activities, we need to explore the relationship between perception and communication. As we will see, these two processes interact so that each affects the other in an ongoing cycle of influence. In other words, perception shapes how we understand others' communication and how we ourselves communicate. At the same time, communication influences our perceptions of people and situations. The two processes are intricately intertwined.

To understand how perception and communication interact, we will first discuss the three-part process of perception. Next we'll consider factors that affect our perceptions. Finally we will explore ways to improve our abilities to perceive and communicate effectively.

HUMAN PERCEPTION

Perception is the active process of selecting, organizing, and interpreting people, objects, events, situations, and activities. The first thing to notice about this definition is that perception is an active process. Phenomena do not have intrinsic meaning that we passively receive. Instead, we actively work to make sense of ourselves, others, situations, and other phenomena. To do so, we focus on only certain things, and then we organize and interpret what we have selectively noticed. What something means to us depends on which aspects of it we attend to and how we organize and interpret what we notice.

Perception consists of three processes: selecting, organizing, and interpreting. These processes are overlapping and continuous, so they blend into and influence one another. They are also interactive, so each affects the other two.

Selection

Stop for a moment and notice what is going on around you right now. Is there music in the background? Is the room warm or cold, messy or clean, large or small, light or dark? Is there laundry in the corner waiting to be washed? Can you smell anything—food cooking, traces of cologne? Is anyone else in the room? Do you hear other conversations or music? Is the window open? Can you hear muted sounds of activities outside? What about this book—what do you notice about it? On what kind of paper is the book printed? Is the type large, small, easy to read? How do you like the size of the book, the colors used, the design of the text? Now think about what's happening inside you: Are you alert, sleepy, hungry, comfortable? Do you have a headache or an itch anywhere?

You probably weren't conscious of most of these phenomena when you began reading the chapter. Instead, you focused on reading and understanding the material in the book. You narrowed your attention to what you defined as important in that moment, and you were unaware of many other things going on around you. This is typical of how we live our lives. We can't attend to everything in our environment because there is simply far too much there, and most of it isn't relevant to us at any particular time.

Which stimuli we notice depends on a number of factors. First, some qualities of external phenomena draw attention. For instance, we notice things that **STAND OUT** because they are immediate, relevant, or intense. We're more likely to hear a loud voice than a soft one and to notice a bright shirt than a drab one. Second, our perceptions are influenced by the acuity of our senses. For

Image Source/Jupiter Images

We notice things that stand out or differ from their surroundings.

instance, if you have a good sense of smell, you're likely to notice a person's cologne or to be enticed by the smell of freshly baked bread. People whose vision or hearing is limited or nonexistent often develop greater sensitivity in their other senses.

Third, change or variation compels attention, which is why we may take for granted all the pleasant interactions with a friend and notice only the tense moments. Effective public speakers apply the principle that change compels notice to keep listeners focused on their speaking. For instance, they may raise or lower their voices or move to a different place in the room during a presentation.

Sometimes we deliberately influence what we notice. Self-indication occurs when we point out certain things to ourselves. Right now you're learning to indicate to yourself that you perceive selectively, so in the future you will be more aware of the selectivity of your perceptions. People who want to eat healthy diets deliberately notice fat, sodium, and protein content of food items.

What we select to notice is also influenced by who we are and what is going on inside us. Our motives and needs affect what we see and don't see. If you've just broken up with someone, you're more likely to notice attractive people at a party than if you are in an established romantic relationship. Motives also explain the oasis phenomenon, in which thirsty people stranded in a desert see an oasis although none really exists.

Our expectations further affect what we notice. We are more likely to perceive what we expect to perceive. This explains the phenomenon of the **self-fulfilling prophecy,** in which one acts in ways consistent with how one has learned to perceive oneself. Children who are told they are unlovable may perceive themselves that way and notice rejecting but not affirming communication from others. Recent research shows that lonely people tend to perceive others more negatively than non-lonely people (Tsai & Reis, 2009). There is a vicious cycle in which negative social judgments lead to unsatisfying interactions and perhaps alienate others (the ones who are judged negatively) so loneliness continues or increases. Click **WebLink 2.1** to learn more about self-fulfilling prophecies.

CourseMate

LEE TENG-HUI *Before I came to school here, I was told that Americans are very pushy, loud, and selfish. For my first few months here, I saw that was true of Americans just as I had been told it would be. It took me longer to see also that Americans are friendly and helpful because I had not been taught to expect these qualities.*

Organization

We don't simply string together randomly what we've noticed. Instead, we organize what we've selectively noticed to make it meaningful to us. The most useful theory for explaining how we organize what we've attended to is **constructivism**, the theory that we organize and interpret experience by applying cognitive structures called **schemata** (singular: *schema*). Originally developed by George Kelly in 1955, constructivism has been elaborated by scholars in communication and psychology. We use four kinds of cognitive schemata to make sense of phenomena: prototypes, personal constructs, stereotypes, and scripts (Burleson & Rack, 2008; Fehr, 1993; Hewes, 1995).

COMMUNICATION in Your Life

Who is your prototype for friend?

Prototypes A **prototype** is a knowledge structure that defines the best or most representative example of some category (Fehr, 1993). For example, you probably have prototypes of excellent teachers, true friends, great public speakers, and perfect romantic partners. Each of these categories is exemplified by a person who is the ideal case; that's the prototype.

We use prototypes to define categories: Jane is the ideal friend; Luke is the ideal romantic partner; Robin is the ideal work associate. Prototypes exemplify categories into which we place people and other phenomena. We may then consider how close a particular phenomenon is to the prototype for that category. As Alicia's commentary points out, our prototypes can be faulty, leading us to fail to perceive someone as belonging in the appropriate category because they don't match our prototype for the category.

COMMUNICATION HIGHLIGHT

Expectations and Perceptions

How we perceive others is influenced by past experiences and expectations. This has been demonstrated repeatedly in experiments (Bargh, 1997). In one study, two groups of research participants were asked to complete what was described as a language test. One group of participants worked with a list of words related to the personality, such as *honesty*. The other group of participants worked with a list of randomly selected words. Then both groups were asked to complete what they were told was a second, independent study, in which they read a short description of a person and then gave their impressions of the person. Participants who worked with the words related to honesty described the person they read about in the second study as more honest than did the participants who worked with words unrelated to honesty (Bargh, 1999).

CourseMate

ALICIA   *I was working with a male nurse. Every time he met a new patient, the patient would say, "Hi, doctor." Even when he told them he was a nurse, they treated him as a doctor. No one ever confused me with a doctor. I guess patients just assume that men in white are doctors and women in white are nurses.*

Personal Constructs   **Personal constructs** are mental yardsticks that allow us to position people and situations along bipolar dimensions of judgment. Examples of personal constructs are intelligent–not intelligent, responsible–not responsible, kind–not kind, and attractive–not attractive. To size up a person, we measure him or her by personal constructs that we use to think about people. How intelligent, kind, responsible, and attractive is this person? Whereas prototypes help us decide into which broad category a person or situation fits, personal constructs let us make more detailed assessments of particular qualities of phenomena we have selectively perceived. Our personal constructs shape our perceptions because we define something only in terms of how it compares to the constructs we use. Thus, we may not notice qualities of people that aren't covered by the constructs we apply.

Stereotypes   **Stereotypes** are predictive generalizations about people and situations. Based on the category in which we place a phenomenon and how the phenomenon measures up to the personal constructs we apply, we predict what it will do. For instance, if you define someone as conservative, you might stereotype the person as likely to oppose government-funded programs to help disadvantaged citizens, and so forth. You may have stereotypes of fraternity and sorority members, athletes, middle managers, and other groups of people.

Stereotypes may be accurate or inaccurate. They are generalizations, which are sometimes based on facts that are generally true of a group and sometimes on prejudice or assumptions. Even if we have accurate understandings of a group, they may not apply to particular individuals in it. Although most environmentalists don't smoke, a few do. Although college students as a group are more liberal than the population as a whole, some college students are very conservative. A particular individual may not conform to what is typical of his or her group as a whole. Ethical communicators keep in mind that stereotypes are generalizations that can be both useful and misleading.

COMMUNICATION
in Your Life

What are your stereotypes for faculty?

SCOTT   *The stereotype that really ticks me off is "dumb jock." I'm a fullback on the team, and I'm big just like any good fullback. But I'm also a good student. I study, and I put a lot into papers and homework for classes. But a lot of the professors here and the students, too, assume I'm dumb just because I'm an athlete. Sometimes I say something in class, and you can just see surprise all over everyone's faces because I had a good idea. When you think about it, athletes have to be smart to do all of their schoolwork plus practice and work out about 30 hours a week.*

David Madison/The Image Bank/Getty Images

What stereotypes do you have of the men in this photograph? Can you identify the basis of your stereotypes of them? What would change your stereotypes of these men?

Scripts To organize what we notice, we also use **scripts,** which are guides to action based on what we've experienced and observed. A script consists of a sequence of activities that define what we and others are expected to do in specific situations.

Many of our daily activities are governed by scripts, although we're often unaware of them. You have a script for greeting casual acquaintances: "Hey, how ya doing?" "Fine. See ya around." You have scripts for checking in with friends online: hi. where r u? gotta take a call. brb. (Carl, 2006). You also have scripts for managing conflict, talking with professors, interacting with superiors on the job, dealing with clerks, and relaxing with friends. Christine Bachen and Eva Illouz (1996) studied 184 people to learn about their views of romance. They found that people have clear scripts for appropriate sequences of events for first dates and romantic dinners. Similarly, Sandra Metts (2006b) has identified consistent scripts for heterosexual flirting.

It's important to realize that the four cognitive schemata interact. In his book *How Doctors Think* (2007), Dr. Jerome Groopman points out that doctors' stereotypes may lead them to follow inappropriate scripts with patients. For instance, a doctor who perceives a patient as a homeless man might, based on that stereotype, diagnose the patient's stumbling as a symptom of intoxication and follow a script of not checking for medical causes of stumbling. If the doctor had perceived the patient as middle class, the doctor would be more likely to assume that stumbling indicated a medical problem and follow a script that included talking with the man and performing tests.

COMMUNICATION HIGHLIGHT

More Complexity, More Categories

Tiger Woods may be in the news for more than his personal life. When asked what his race is, he replies, "I'm Cablinasian," a term he invented to describe his multiracial heritage: part Caucasian (*Ca*), Black (*bl*), Indian (*in*) and Asian (*asian*) (Strege, 1997). The U.S. Census Bureau seems to be following Tiger's lead. In 1860, the United States had only three categories for race: black, white, and quadroon. Today, the census allows people to check more than one racial category. As a result, there are many more recognized racial classifications (Armas, 2001; Schmitt, 2001b; U.S. Bureau of the Census, 2003; Zachary, 2002). Nearly 7 million Americans say they belong to more than one race. The majority of people who identify themselves as multiracial are young—children and teenagers.

The number of multiracial Americans is likely to rise in the years ahead because interracial marriages and domestic partnerships are growing (Nakazawa, 2003a, 2003b; Schmitt, 2001b). In 1970, there were 500,000 interracial unions in the United States; that number had swelled to well over a million by the turn of the century (Clemetson, 2000).

Go to **WebLink 2.2** to find out about current demographic statistics in the United States. Check the population reports for your state by using the search bar at the right of the screen.

CourseMate

Prototypes, personal constructs, stereotypes, and scripts are cognitive schemata that we use to organize the phenomena to which we selectively attend. They help us make sense of what we notice and help us anticipate how we and others will act in particular situations. Our cognitive schemata are not entirely individualistic. Rather, they reflect our membership in a culture and in specific social groups. As we interact with others, we internalize their ways of classifying, measuring, and predicting interaction in various situations. Each of us has an ethical responsibility to assess social perspectives critically before relying on them to organize our perceptions and direct our activities.

Interpretation

To assign meaning, we must interpret what we have noticed and organized. **Interpretation** is the subjective process of explaining perceptions to assign meaning to them.

Attributions   **Attributions** are explanations of why things happen and why people act as they do (Fehr, 1993; Fehr & Russell, 1991; Heider, 1958; Kelley, 1967). It's good to remind ourselves that the attributions we make aren't necessarily correct—they are our subjective ways of assigning meaning.

Attributions have four dimensions (Table 2.1). The first is *locus*, which attributes what a person does to either internal factors ("He's sick.") or external factors ("The traffic jam frustrated him."). The second dimension is *stability*, which explains actions as resulting either from stable factors that won't change ("She's a Type A person.") or from temporary, unstable factors ("She's irritable because

Table 2.1	Dimensions of Interpersonal Attributions	
Locus:	Internal	External
Stability:	Stable	Unstable
Scope:	Global	Specific
Responsibility:	Within personal control	Beyond personal control

she's just had a fight with the boss."). *Scope* (sometimes called *specificity*) is the third dimension, and it defines behavior as part of a global pattern ("He's a mean person.") or a specific instance ("He gets angry when he's tired."). Finally, the dimension of *responsibility* attributes behaviors either to factors people can control ("She doesn't try to control her outbursts.") or to ones they cannot ("She has a chemical imbalance that makes her moody.").

A student who was reading this book for a class at another university emailed me with a question about attributions. He and his classmates were debating whether scope and stability are really two different dimensions. This is a good question; most global attributions are also stable. However, there are exceptions. For example, you might say that someone is always efficient at work but inefficient during leisure time. In this case, the attribution is stable and specific. If the person were efficient in all spheres of life, the attribution would be stable and global.

Based on extensive research, Carol Tavris and Elliot Aronson (2007) conclude that "Happy and unhappy partners simply think differently about each other's behavior, even when they are responding to identical situations and actions" (p. 172). Investigations have shown that happy and unhappy couples have distinct attributional styles (Bradbury & Fincham, 1990; Fletcher & Fincham, 1991; Manusov & Harvey, 2001). Happy couples make relationship-enhancing attributions. Such people attribute nice things a partner does to internal, stable, and global reasons that the partner controls: "She got the film because she is a good person who always does sweet things." Unpleasant things a partner does are attributed to external, unstable, and specific factors and sometimes to influences beyond personal control: "He yelled at me because all the stress of the past few days made him irritable." Happy couples also tend to make benevolent attributions about partners' conflict styles (Segrin, Hanzal, & Domschke, 2009). For instance, it's more specific and positive to perceive that "she rarely screams" or "he seldom refuses to discuss problems" than to hold the more global perception that "she screams all the time" or "he stonewalls."

In contrast, unhappy couples make relationship-diminishing attributions. They explain nice actions as results of external, unstable, and specific factors: "She got the tape because she had some time to kill today." Negative actions are seen as stemming from internal, stable, and global factors: "He yelled at me because he is a nasty person who never shows any consideration for anybody else." Thus, we should be mindful of our attributions because they influence how we experience our relationships.

COMMUNICATION in Your Life

Make an internal and an external attribution for an action by a friend of yours.

The Self-Serving Bias   Research indicates that we tend to construct attributions that serve our personal interests (Hamachek, 1992; Manusov & Spitzberg, 2008; Sypher, 1984). Thus, we are inclined to make internal, stable, and global attributions for our positive actions and successes. We're also likely to claim that good results come about because of personal control we exerted. On the other hand, people tend to attribute negative actions and failures to external, unstable, and specific factors that are beyond personal control. In other words, we tend to attribute our misconduct and mistakes to outside forces that we can't help but attribute all the good we do to our personal qualities and effort. When it comes to judging others, we tend to be less charitable. If they make mistakes, we're likely to attribute the errors to internal, not external, forces beyond their control (Sedikides, Campbell, Reeder, & Elliot, 1998). If we have an argument with a romantic partner, we're likely to perceive that person's behaviors as unreasonable or wrong and to see ourselves as reasonable and right (Schütz, 1999). This **self-serving bias** can distort our perceptions, leading us to take excessive credit for what we do well and to abdicate responsibility for what we do poorly.

COMMUNICATION HIGHLIGHT

I'm Right; You're Wrong

When you are in conflict with a close friend or romantic partner, how do you see your role and the other person's? Do you often think you were being reasonable and the other person was being unreasonable? Do you tend to see yourself as having good intentions and the other person as having bad ones? If so, you're not alone. In 1999, Astrid Schütz separately asked husbands and wives to describe conflicts between them. Typically, each spouse described the problem as the other's fault. Each spouse saw his or her own behavior as justified and reasonable but described the partner's behavior as unfair, inconsiderate, inappropriate, or wrong. Participants also described their own intentions positively and their partners' intentions negatively—as unfair, irrational, mean-spirited, and so forth.

Schütz concluded that the self-serving bias is likely to affect how partners perceive themselves, each other, and conflicts between them. Resolution and positive feelings about each other are undermined when each partner perceives himself or herself as behaving well and the other as behaving wrongly.

In another experiment (Jaffe, 2004), peace proposals created by Israelis were labeled proposals created by Palestinians and proposals actually created by Palestinians were labeled proposals created by Israelis. Then Israeli citizens were asked to evaluate the proposals. The Israelis liked the proposal that was attributed to Israelis but actually authored by Palestinians better than they liked the proposal actually drafted by Israelis that was attributed to Palestinians. This displays how profoundly perceptions can be shaped by biases.

To explore your own experience with a conflict in which you were tempted to say "I'm right; you're wrong," complete the Communication Highlight Activity for Chapter 2 via your Online Resources for *Communication in Our Lives*.

MARGARET *Last summer, I worked at a day-care center for 4- to 6-year-olds. Whenever a fight started and I broke it up, each child would say the other one made them fight or the other one started it or they couldn't help hitting. They were classic cases of self-serving bias.*

We've seen that perception involves three interrelated processes. The first of these, selection, allows us to notice certain things and ignore others. The second process is organization, in which we use prototypes, personal constructs, stereotypes, and scripts to order what we have selectively noticed. Finally, we engage in interpretation by using attributions to explain what we have noticed and organized. Although we discussed these processes separately, in reality they interact continually.

INFLUENCES ON PERCEPTION

In opening this chapter, I mentioned an incident in which a prison guard's perceptions differed from mine. His experience and priorities as a guard who dealt with dangerous men led him to perceive that certain objects that I saw as harmless as potential weapons. Being unaccustomed to prison life, I didn't perceive the same things he did. Similarly, able-bodied people may not notice the lack of elevators or ramps in a building, but someone with a physical disability quickly perceives the building as inaccessible.

European American students at predominantly white schools often don't notice that few people of color are in their classes, but the ethnic ratio is very obvious to blacks, American Indians, students of Asian and Hispanic heritage, and others who are not European Americans. People who grew up in neighborhoods where everyone knew everyone else are more likely than people from urban areas to notice a lack of neighborliness in some big cities. As these examples illustrate, people differ in how they perceive situations and people. Let's consider some reasons for this.

Physiology

The most obvious reason perceptions vary is that people differ in sensory abilities and physiologies. Music that one person finds deafening is barely audible to another. Salsa that is painfully hot to one diner may seem mild to someone else. On a given day on my campus, students wear everything from shorts and sandals to jackets, indicating that they have different sensitivities to cold. Some people have better vision than others, and still others are color blind.

Our physiological states also influence perception. If you are tired, stressed, or sick, you're likely to perceive a comment from a co-worker as critical of you, but the comment wouldn't bother you if you felt good. If you interact with someone who is sick, you might attribute his or her irritability to temporary factors rather than to enduring personality. If you're a morning

person, you're most alert and creative early in the day; you're likely to notice things in the morning that you don't perceive when your energy level declines later in the day.

Age also influences our perceptions. The older we get, the more complex is our perspective on life and people. Perhaps you think nothing of paying seventy-five cents for a can of soda, but to a sixty-year-old person who recalls paying a nickel for a soda, the current prices may seem high. The extent of discrimination still experienced by women and minorities understandably discourages some young people. When I attended college, women weren't admitted on an equal basis with men, and almost all students of color attended minority colleges. The substantial progress made during my lifetime leads me to perceive current inequities as changeable.

Culture

A **culture** consists of beliefs, values, understandings, practices, and ways of interpreting experience that are shared by a number of people. It is a set of taken-for-granted assumptions that form the pattern of our lives and guide how we perceive as well as how we think, feel, and act.

Consider a few aspects of modern Western culture that influence our perceptions. One characteristic of our culture is an emphasis on technology and its offspring, speed. We expect things to happen fast—almost instantly. Whether it's instant photos, one-minute copying, or instant messaging, we live at an accelerated pace (Wood, 2000). We send letters by overnight mail, jet across the country, engage in instant messaging and texting, and microwave our meals. In countries such as Nepal and Mexico, life proceeds at a more leisurely pace, and people spend more time talking, relaxing, and engaging in low-key activity. Does Western culture's emphasis on speed diminish patience and thus our willingness to invest in long-term projects and relationships?

North America is also a fiercely individualistic culture in which personal initiative and independence are rewarded. Other cultures tend to be more communal, and identity is defined in terms of one's family rather than as an individual quality. In communal cultures, elders are given great respect and care, and children are looked after by the whole community.

In recent years, scholars have realized that we are affected not only by the culture as a whole but also by our particular location within the culture

Calvin and Hobbes

(Haraway, 1988; Harding, 1991; Wood 2005). **Standpoint theory** claims that a culture includes a number of social communities that have different degrees of social status and privilege. Each social community distinctively shapes the perceptions, identities, and opportunities of its members. If a member of a social group gains political insight into the group's social location, then he or she can develop a standpoint. For example, a Hispanic person has the social location of Hispanic. If that person learns about ways in which society discriminates against Hispanics, the person may develop a Hispanic standpoint. Without that political awareness, however, the person could not achieve a standpoint.

In the earliest writing on standpoint, philosopher Georg Wilhelm Friedrich Hegel (1807) pointed out that standpoints reflect power positions in social hierarchies. Hegel's original observations focused on the system of slavery, which, he noted, was perceived very differently by masters and slaves. Extending Hegel's point, we can see that those in positions of power have a vested interest in preserving the system that gives them privileges. Thus, they are unlikely to perceive its flaws and inequities or to notice how the system disadvantages others. On the other hand, those who have less power in a society are more able to discern inequities and discrimination (Collins, 1998; Harding, 1991).

CARL   *I'll admit that when Krista and I had a child, I expected Krista to stay home and take care of her. Actually, we both did, and that worked fine for three months. Then Krista got cancer, and she was in the hospital for weeks and then in and out for nearly a year for treatments. Even when she was home, she didn't have the energy to take care of little Jennie. I had to take over a lot of the child care. Doing that really changed me in basic ways. I had to learn to tolerate being interrupted when I was working. I had to tune into what Jennie needed and learn to read her. Before that experience, I thought women had a maternal instinct. What I learned is, anyone can develop a parental sensitivity.*

Gendered locations explain the difference between the amount of effort women and men, in general, invest in communication that maintains relationships. Socialized into the role of "relationship expert," women are often expected by others and themselves to take care of relationships (Tavris, 1992; Wood, 1994d, 2007a). This may explain why women tend to be more aware than many men of problems in relationships and to be more active in addressing them (Brehm, Miller, Perlman, & Campbell, 2001). It may also shed light on why many women exercise leadership in more personal and relationship-oriented ways than many men do (Helgesen, 1990; Natalle, 1996).

Social Roles

Our perceptions are also shaped by social roles that others communicate to us. Messages that tell us that we are expected to fulfill particular roles, as well as the actual demands of those roles, affect how we perceive and communicate.

Speakers are more likely than audience members to notice the acoustics of presentation rooms. Teachers often perceive classes in terms of how interested students seem, whether they have read material, and whether they engage in class discussion. On the other hand, many students perceive classes in terms of the number and difficulty of tests, whether papers are required, and whether the professor is interesting. In working on this book, I concentrated on ideas, information, and organization, and my editor focused on layout, design, and marketing issues that didn't occur to me.

The careers people choose influence what they notice and how they think and act. Doctors are trained to be highly observant of physical symptoms, and they may detect a physical problem before a person knows that he or she has it. For example, some years ago at a social gathering, a friend of mine who is

COMMUNICATION
in Your Life

To what extent do you act as relationship expert in your close relationships?

Inti St Clair/Photodisc/Getty Images

Some cultures are more communal than others.

a doctor asked me how long I had had a herniated disk. Shocked, I told him I didn't have one. "You do," he insisted, and sure enough, a few weeks later a magnetic resonance imaging examination confirmed a ruptured disk in my back. His medical training enabled him to perceive subtle changes in my posture and walk that I hadn't noticed.

Cognitive Abilities

In addition to physiological, cultural, and social influences, perception is also shaped by our cognitive abilities. How elaborately we think about situations and people, and the extent of our personal knowledge of others, affect how we select, organize, and interpret experiences.

Cognitive Complexity   People differ in the number and types of knowledge schemata they use to organize and interpret people and situations. **Cognitive complexity** refers to the number of constructs used, how abstract they are, and how elaborately they interact to shape perceptions. Most children have fairly simple cognitive systems. They rely on few schemata, focus more on concrete categories (tall–not tall) than on abstract ones (introspective–not introspective), and often don't perceive relationships between different perceptions. For instance, infants may call every man Daddy because they haven't learned more complex ways to distinguish among men.

Adults also differ in cognitive complexity. If you perceive people only as nice or mean, you have a limited range for perceiving others. Similarly, people who focus exclusively on concrete data tend to have less sophisticated understandings than people who also perceive psychological data. For example, you might notice that a co-worker is assertive, tells jokes, and contributes on task teams. These are concrete perceptions. At a more abstract, psychological level, you might infer that these concrete behaviors reflect a secure, self-confident personality. This is a more sophisticated cognition because it integrates three perceptions to develop an explanation of why the person acts as he or she does.

What if you later find out that the person is reserved in one-to-one conversations? Someone with low cognitive complexity would have difficulty integrating the new information into prior observations. Either the new information would be dismissed because it doesn't fit, or the most recent information would alter the former perception, and the person would be redefined as shy. A more cognitively complex person would integrate all the information into a coherent account. Perhaps a cognitively complex thinker would conclude that the person is confident in social situations but less secure in more personal ones.

Cognitively complex people tend to be flexible in interpreting complicated phenomena and integrating new information into their thinking about people and situations. Less cognitively complex people are likely to ignore information that doesn't fit neatly with their impressions or to use it to replace the impressions they had formed (Delia, Clark, & Switzer, 1974). Either way, they fail to recognize some of the nuances and inconsistencies that are part of human life.

The complexity of our cognitive systems affects the fullness and intricacy of our perceptions of people and interpersonal situations. Cognitively complex people also tend to communicate in more flexible and appropriate ways with a range of others. This probably results from their ability to recognize differences in people and to adapt their own communication accordingly.

Person-Centered Perception   **Person-centered perception** reflects cognitive complexity because it entails abstract thinking and a broad range of schemata. Person-centered perception is the ability to perceive another as a unique and distinct individual. Our ability to perceive others as unique depends both on the general ability to make cognitive distinctions and on our knowledge of particular others. As we get to know individuals, we gain insight into how they differ from others in their groups ("Rob's not like most campus politicos"; "Janet's more flexible than most managers."). The more we interact with one another and the greater variety of experiences we have together, the more insight we gain into other people. As we come to understand others, we fine-tune our perceptions of them in a process that continues throughout the life of relationships.

Person-centered perception is not the same as empathy. **Empathy** is the ability to feel with another person—to feel what he or she feels. Feeling with another is an emotional response. Because feelings are guided by our own experiences and emotions, it may be impossible to feel exactly and completely what another person feels. A more realistic goal is to try to recognize another's perspective and adapt your communication to how he or she perceives situations and people (Muehlhoff, 2006). With commitment and effort, we can learn a lot about how others see the world, even if that differs from how we see it.

Camille Tokerud/Stone/Getty Images

Taking the perspective of others is a foundation of effective communication.

When we take others' perspectives, we try to grasp what something means to them and how they perceive things. We can't really understand someone else's perspective when we're judging whether it is right or wrong, sensible or crazy. Instead, we have to let go of our own perspective and perceptions long enough to enter the thoughts and feelings of another person. Doing this allows us to understand issues from the other person's point of view so we can communicate more effectively (Servaty-Seib & Burleson, 2007). You might learn why your boss thinks something is important that you've been disregarding. You might find out how a friend interprets your behavior in ways inconsistent with what you intend to communicate.

At a later point in interaction, we may choose to express our own perspective or to disagree with another's views. This is appropriate and important in honest communication, but voicing our own views is not a substitute for the equally important skill of recognizing another's perspective. In sum, differences based on physiology, culture, standpoint, social roles, and cognitive abilities affect what we perceive and how we interpret others and experiences. In the final section of the chapter, we consider ways to improve the accuracy of our perceptions.

ENHANCING COMMUNICATION COMPETENCE

To be a competent communicator, you need to realize how perception and communication affect each other. We'll elaborate on the connection between perception and communication and then discuss guidelines for enhancing communication competence.

Perceptions, Communication, and Abstraction

Words crystallize perceptions. When we name feelings and thoughts, we create precise ways to describe and think about them. But just as words crystallize experiences, they can also freeze thought. Once we label our perceptions, we may respond to our own labels rather than to actual phenomena.

Consider this situation. Suppose you get together with five others in a study group, and a student named Andrea monopolizes the whole meeting with her questions and concerns. Leaving the meeting, one person says, "Gee, Andrea is so selfish and immature! I'll never work with her again." Another person responds, "She's not really selfish. She's insecure about her grades in this course, so she was hyper in the meeting." Chances are these two people will perceive and treat Andrea differently depending on whether they label her selfish or insecure. The point is that the two people respond not to Andrea herself but to how they label their perceptions of her.

Communication is based on a process of abstracting from complex stimuli. Our perceptions are not equivalent to the complex reality on which they are based because total reality can never be fully described or even apprehended. This means that what we perceive is a step removed from stimuli because perceptions are always partial and subjective. We move a second step from stimuli when we label a perception. We move even further from stimuli when we respond not to behaviors or our perceptions of them but to the judgments we

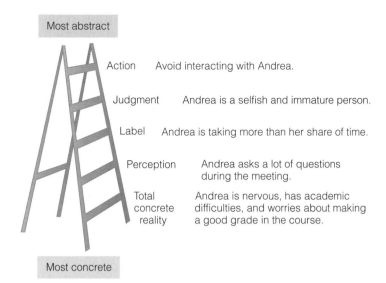

Figure 2.1
Perception, Communication, and Abstraction

associate with the label we have imposed. This process can be illustrated as a ladder of abstraction, as shown in Figure 2.1 (Hayakawa, 1962, 1964; Korzybski, 1948). To learn more about the abstraction process, visit the general semantics site by clicking **WebLink 2.3.**

Guidelines for Enhancing Competence

Thinking of communication as a process of abstracting suggests ways to enhance competence in interaction. Five guidelines help us avoid the problems abstraction may invite.

Recognize that All Perceptions Are Subjective   Our perceptions are partial and subjective because each of us perceives from a unique perspective. A class you find exciting may put another student to sleep. Writing is a creative, enjoyable activity for some people and a tedious grind for others. There is no truth or falsity to perceptions; they represent what things mean to individuals based on their individual social roles, cultural backgrounds, cognitive abilities, standpoints, and physiology. Effective communicators realize that perceptions are subjective and don't assume that their own perceptions are the only valid ones.

Avoid Mind Reading   One of the most common problems in communication is **mind reading**—assuming we understand what another person thinks or perceives. When we mind read, we act as if we know what's on another's mind, and this can get us into trouble. Marriage counselors identify mind reading as one of the behaviors that contributes to interpersonal tension (Gottman, 1993). According to communication scholar Fran Dickson (1995), one exception may be mind reading between spouses in long-lasting marriages. After living together for a long time, partners may be able to mind read with great accuracy.

For the most part, however, mind reading is more likely to harm than help communication. Mind reading invites problems when we say things such as "I know why you're upset" (has the person *said* he or she is upset?) or "You don't

COMMUNICATION in Your Life

Use the ladder of abstraction to describe your perceptions of a campus group you do or did belong to.

care about me" (maybe the other person is too preoccupied or worried to be as attentive as usual). We also mind read when we tell ourselves we know how somebody else will feel or react or what they'll do. The truth is we don't really know—we're only guessing. When we mind read, we impose our perceptions on others, which can lead to resentment and misunderstandings because most of us prefer to speak for ourselves.

PAT   *I got into a lot of trouble mind reading my girlfriend. When we first started dating, I made a lot of assumptions about what Anne would or wouldn't like and then acted as if what I assumed was a fact. For example, once I got tickets for a concert that I "knew" she'd want to go to, but she had to go out of town that weekend. Another time, I "knew" she'd want to take a study break during exam week, so I got a pizza and stopped by. She was really irritated because she had eaten early and was settled in for a heavy review session. I finally realized I should ask her what she wants instead of assuming I know. We've gotten along a lot better since I figured that out.*

Check Perceptions with Others   Because perceptions are subjective and mind reading is ineffective, we need to check our perceptions with others. Perception checking is an important communication skill because it helps people understand each other and their relationships. To check perceptions, you should first state what you have noticed. For example, a person might say, "Lately you've seemed less attentive to me." Second, the person should check to see whether the other perceives the same thing: "Do you feel you've been less attentive?" Third, it's appropriate to offer alternative explanations of your perceptions: "It might be that you're annoyed with me or that you're stressed out at work or that you're focused on other things." Finally, you may ask the other person to clarify how he or she perceives the behavior and the reasons for it: "What do you think is going on?" If the other person doesn't share your perceptions, ask him or her to explain the behaviors on which your perception is based: "Why have you wanted to be together less often and seemed distracted when we've talked lately?"

Speak tentatively when checking perceptions to minimize defensiveness and encourage open dialogue. Just let the other person know you've noticed something and would like him or her to clarify his or her perceptions of what is happening and what it means. It's also a good idea to check perceptions directly with the other person. It is more difficult to reach a shared understanding with another person when we ask someone else to act as a go-between or when we ask others whether they agree with our perceptions of a third person.

Distinguish between Facts and Inferences   Competent communicators know the difference between facts and inferences. A fact is a statement based on observation or other data. An inference involves an interpretation that goes beyond the facts. For example, it is a fact that my partner, Robbie, forgets a lot of things. Based on that fact, I might infer that he is thoughtless. Defining Robbie as thoughtless is an inference that goes beyond the facts. The "fact" of his forgetfulness could equally well be explained by preoccupation or general absentmindedness.

It's easy to confuse facts and inferences because we sometimes treat the latter as the former. When we say, "He is irresponsible," we make a statement that sounds factual, and we may then regard it that way ourselves. To avoid this tendency, substitute more tentative words for *is*. For instance, "Robbie's behaviors seem thoughtless" is more tentative than "Robbie is thoughtless." Tentative language helps us resist the tendency to treat inferences as facts.

Monitor the Self-Serving Bias   The self-serving bias exemplifies humans' broad tendency to protect self-image (Tavris & Aronson, 2007). We want to be competent, good, smart, and right. If we make dumb decisions, we're inclined to deny or justify them. A primary means of doing this is to engage in the self-serving bias, which distorts our perceptions. Monitoring the self-serving bias also has implications for how we perceive others. Just as we tend to judge ourselves generously, we may also be inclined to judge others too harshly. Monitor your perceptions to see whether you attribute others' successes and admirable actions to external factors beyond their control and their shortcomings and blunders to internal factors they can (should) control. If you do this, substitute more generous explanations for others' behaviors, and notice how that affects your perceptions of them.

Perceiving accurately is a communication skill that can be developed. Following the five guidelines we have discussed will allow you to perceive more carefully and accurately.

BEYOND THE CLASSROOM

Let's take the material in this chapter beyond the classroom by thinking about how what you've learned about perception might apply to the workplace, ethical choices, and engagement with the broader world.

1. **Workplace** This chapter discusses ways that culture and cultural values influence our perceptions. Think about how cultural values such as efficiency and individualism affect communication in your workplace or a former workplace. Continue this line of thinking by identifying other strong aspects of U.S. culture and tracing their impact on the workplace.

2. **Ethics** This chapter presents five guidelines for enhancing competence in perceiving. Each guideline has ethical implications and assumptions. For example, the first guideline is to recognize that all perceptions are subjective. This assumes that there are multiple ways of perceiving any phenomena; in turn, this implies that there is no automatic validity to any particular perception. If you accept those assumptions, the implication is that we can't assume others are wrong if their perceptions differ from our own. Thus, the guideline implies that ethical communication requires awareness of and respect for others' perceptions. Now you analyze the ethical assumptions and implications of the other four guidelines for increasing competence in perceiving.

Ethics

BEYOND THE CLASSROOM

3. **Engagement** Volunteer to work in a context that allows you to interact with a people you have not spent time with—for example, volunteer at a homeless shelter. Make a list of schemata (i.e., prototypes, personal constructs, stereotypes, and scripts) you have about these people before you interact with them. After spending time with them, review your list of schemata and evaluate how accurate they were.

CHAPTER SUMMARY

In this chapter, we've explored human perception, which involves selecting, organizing, and interpreting experiences. These three processes are not separate in practice; they interact such that each one affects the others. What we selectively notice affects what we interpret and evaluate. In addition, our interpretations act as lenses that influence what we notice in the world around us. Selection, interpretation, and evaluation interact continuously in the process of perception.

Perception is shaped by many factors. Our physiological abilities and conditions affect what we notice and how astutely we recognize stimuli around us. In addition, our cultural backgrounds and standpoints in society shape how we see and interact with the world. Social roles are another influence on perception. Thus, professional training and roles in families affect what we notice and how we organize and interpret it. Finally, perception is influenced by cognitive abilities, including cognitive complexity, person-centered perception, and perspective taking.

Thinking about communication as a process of abstracting helps us understand how perception works. We discussed five guidelines for avoiding the problems abstraction sometimes causes. First, realize that all perceptions are subjective, so there is no absolutely correct or best understanding of a situation or a person. Second, because people perceive differently, we should avoid mind reading or assuming we know what others are perceiving.

Third, it's a good idea to check perceptions, which involves stating how you perceive something and asking how another person perceives it. A fourth guideline is to distinguish facts from inferences. Finally, avoiding the self-serving bias is important because it can lead us to perceive ourselves too charitably and others too harshly.

When we label our selective perceptions, we abstract or notice only some of the stimuli around us. Consequently, we can't see aspects of ourselves and others that our labels don't highlight. Realizing this encourages us to be more sensitive to the power of language and to make more considered choices about how we use it.

Applying Communication in Our Lives

The key concepts, For Further Reflection and Discussion questions, and Experiencing Communication in Our Lives case study that follow will help you review, reflect on, and extend the information and ideas presented in this chapter. These resources, and a diverse selection of additional study tools, are also available as Online Resources for *Communication in Our Lives*. Your Online Resources include CourseMate, a student workbook, interactive video activities, audio study tools, a book companion website, Speech Builder Express, Speech Studio, and InfoTrac College Edition. For more information or to access this book's online resources, visit **www.cengage.com/login**.

KEY CONCEPTS

attribution, 33
cognitive complexity, 40
constructivism, 30
culture, 37
empathy, 41
interpretation, 33

meaning, 28
mind reading, 43
perception, 28
personal construct, 31
person-centered perception, 41
prototype, 30

schemata, 30
script, 32
self-fulfilling prophecy, 29
self-serving bias, 35
standpoint theory, 38
stereotype, 31

FOR FURTHER REFLECTION AND DISCUSSION

1. Identify an occasion when you engaged in the self-serving bias. Explain what you did, using the language of attributions.

2. Identify ethical issues involved in perceiving. What ethical choices do we make—perhaps unconsciously—as we selectively perceive, organize, and interpret others, particularly people whom we see as different from us in important ways?

3. Use the ladder of abstraction to analyze your perceptions and actions in a specific communication encounter. First, identify the concrete reality, what you perceived from the totality, the labels you assigned, and the resulting inferences and judgments. Second, return to the first level of perception and substitute different perceptions—other aspects of the total situation you might have perceived selectively. What labels, inferences, and judgments do the substitute perceptions invite? With others in the class, discuss the extent to which our perceptions and labels influence "reality."

Ethics

SHARPEN YOUR SKILL

1. Perceiving Others

Pay attention to the cognitive schemata you use the next time you meet a new person. First, notice how you classify the person. Do you categorize him or her as a potential friend, date, co-worker, or neighbor? Next, identify the personal constructs you use to assess the person. Do you focus on physical characteristics (attractive–not attractive), mental qualities (intelligent–not intelligent), psychological features (secure–not secure), or interpersonal qualities (available–not available)? Would different personal constructs be prominent if you used a different prototype to classify the person? Now note how you stereotype the person. What do you expect him or her to do, according to the prototype and personal constructs you've applied? Finally, identify your script: How do you expect interaction to unfold between the two of you?

2. Noticing Individualism

How do the individualistic values of our culture influence our perceptions and activities? Check it out by observing the following:

How is seating arranged in restaurants? Are there large, communal eating areas or private tables and booths for individuals, couples, and small groups? _____

How are living spaces arranged? How many people live in the average house? _____

Do families share homes? How many common spaces and individual spaces are there in homes? _____

How many people share a car in your family? How many cars are there in the United States? _____

How does the Western emphasis on individualism affect your day-to-day perceptions and activities? _____

EXPERIENCING COMMUNICATION IN OUR LIVES

Case Study: College Success

A video of the conversation scripted here is featured in your Chapter 2 Online Resources for *Communication in Our Lives.* Select "College Success" to watch the video of Jim's conversation with his dad. Improve your own communication skills by reading, watching, and evaluating this communication encounter.

CourseMate

Jason Harris/© Cengage Learning

    Your friend Jim tells you about a problem he's having with his parents. According to Jim, his parents have unrealistic expectations of him. He tends to be an average student, usually making Cs, a few Bs, and an occasional D in his courses. His parents are angry that his grades aren't better. Jim tells you that when he went home last month, his father said this: "I'm not paying for you to go to school so you can party with your friends. I paid my own way and still made Phi Beta Kappa. You have a free ride, and you're still just pulling Cs. You just have to study harder."

    Now Jim says to you, "I mean, I like to hang out with my friends, but that's got nothing to do with my grades. My dad's this brilliant guy, I mean, he just cruised through college, he thinks it's easy. I don't know how it was back then, but all my classes are hard. I mean, no matter how much studying I do, I'm not gonna get all As. What should I do? I mean, how do I convince them that I'm doing everything I can?"

QUESTIONS FOR ANALYSIS AND DISCUSSION

You can also answer these questions and see my responses to them online via your Online Resources for Chapter 2.

1. Both Jim and his parents make attributions to explain his grades. Describe the dimensions of Jim's attributions and those of his parents.

2. How might you assess the accuracy of Jim's attributions? What questions could you ask him to help you decide whether his perceptions are well founded or biased?

3. What constructs, prototypes, and scripts seem to operate in Jim's and his parents' thinking about college life?

4. What could you say to Jim to help him and his parents reach a shared perspective on his academic work?

Comstock

Go confidently in the direction of your dreams.

Henry David Thoreau

Communication and Personal Identity

Kate is a 35-year-old mother of two children. She is also an attorney, an aunt, and a sister. Once, she was a child, a student, and an engaged woman. One day, she may be retired and a grandmother. Like Kate, your identity changes over time. When you were five or six, you probably defined yourself as your parents' son or daughter. In doing so, you implicitly recognized sex, race, and social class as parts of your identity. In high school, you may have described yourself in terms of academic abilities ("I'm better at math than at history"), athletic achievements ("I'm on the soccer team"), leadership positions ("I'm president of the Drama Club"), your social circle ("I hang out with Cindy and Mike"), or future plans ("I'm going to study business when I go to college").

SHARPEN YOUR SKILL

At the end of this chapter, refer to the Sharpen Your Skill features, Reflecting on Your Identity Scripts and Your Looking-Glass Self, to apply concepts from Chapter 3.

If you entered college shortly after completing high school, you're probably starting to see yourself in terms of a major, a career path, and perhaps a relationship you hope will span the years ahead. If you worked or committed to a relationship before starting or returning to college, you may already have a sense of yourself as a professional and a family member, and you may see the role of student as only one of many in your life. By now, you've probably made some decisions about your sexual orientation, spiritual values, and political and social beliefs. Throughout your life, you'll continually create your personal identity.

As you think about the different ways you've defined yourself over the years, you'll realize that the self is not fixed firmly at one time and constant thereafter. Instead, the self is a process that evolves and changes throughout our lives. Communication with others is one of the greatest influences on our personal identities. In this chapter, we explore how the self develops continually through communication with others.

What Is the Self?

The **self** is a process of internalizing and acting from social perspectives that we learn in the process of communication. At first, this may seem like a complicated way to define the self. As we will see, however, this definition directs our attention to some important insights into what is complicated: the human self.

The Self Arises in Communication with Others

The most basic insight into the self is that it isn't something we are born with. Instead, the self develops only as we communicate with others and participate in the social world. From the moment we are born, we interact with others. We learn how they see us, and we internalize many of their views of the world and of who we are and should be. Through internal dialogues, or intrapersonal communication, we remind ourselves of others' perspectives and how others see us.

Communication with Family Members   For most of us, family members are the first important influence on how we see ourselves (Bergen & Braithwaite, 2009). Parents and other family members communicate who we are and what we are worth through *direct definition, identity scripts,* and *attachment styles.*

Direct definition, as the term implies, is communication that explicitly tells us who we are by labeling us and our behaviors. For instance, parents might say, "You're my little girl" or "You're a big boy" and thus communicate to the child what sex he or she is. Having been labeled *boy* or *girl,* the child then pays attention to other communication about boys and girls to figure out what it means to be a certain sex. Parents' own gender stereotypes typically are communicated to children, so daughters may also be told, "Don't play rough," "Be nice to your friends," and "Don't mess up your clothes." Sons, on the other hand, are more likely to be told, "Go out and get 'em," "Stick up for yourself," and "Don't cry." As we hear these messages, we pick up our parents' and society's gender expectations. Direct definition also takes place as family members respond to children's behaviors. If a child clowns around and parents respond by saying, "What a

RESEARCH IN OUR LIVES

"Half and Half"

"Half and Half" is the title of an article by Stephanie Young in which she considers how identity is expressed and negotiated in relationships between immigrant mothers and their second-generation interracial daughters. The method that Young employed for this study is autoethnography, which aims to provide a holistic, contextually rich examination of one's own life and experiences. In Young's case, she wanted to understand her experiences as the interracial daughter of a white U.S. father and an immigrant Korean American mother.

Young identified three factors that affect how she and her mother use communication to create, perform, and understand their hybrid racial identities. The first is location: Because Young's parents resided in the Midwest, they had limited access to an interaction with the larger Korean American community. If Young had grown up surrounded by other Korean Americans, it's likely that her self-concept would differ from what it is. The second factor is language: Her mother's English is hard for others to understand, so as a young child, Young often had to act as a translator for her mother—being the bridge between Korean and U.S. cultures. This type of incident also gave Young a keen sensitivity to discrimination such as when clerks treated her mother as "the other" and did not make serious efforts to understand her. The third factor is what Young labels the assimilation-preservation dialectic, which she describes as a tension in the relationship with her mother between a desire to assimilate to the values and traditions of U.S. culture and a desire to preserve and honor the values and traditions of Korean culture.

Young concludes by noting that the three factors her autoethnography identified—location, language, and the assimilation-preservation dialectic—are not necessarily the only influences on how interracial individuals create and enact their identities. She encourages others to explore hybrid identities and to discover other ways that they are defined, negotiated, and performed in everyday life.

Thinking Critically: What factors can you identify that have shaped your identity and your interaction with your mother?

Stephanie Young is a doctoral candidate in the School of Communication Studies at Ohio University. This research appeared in a 2009 article titled "Half and half: An (auto)ethnography of hybrid identities in a Korean American mother-daughter relationship" in Journal of International and Intercultural Communication, issue 2, pages 139–167.

Rob Gage/Taxi/Getty Images

Family members' communication shapes personal identity.

cutup; you really are funny," the child learns to see herself or himself as funny. If instead the parents respond by saying, "Quit fooling around and be serious," the child is likely to view playfulness as negative and may quit clowning around. If a child is praised for dusting furniture, being helpful is reinforced as part of the child's self-concept. Positive labels enhance our self-esteem: "You're so responsible," "You are smart," "You're sweet," "You're great at soccer." Negative labels can damage children's self-esteem: "You're a troublemaker," "You're stupid," and "You're impossible" are messages that can demolish a child's sense of self-worth (Brooks & Goldstein, 2001).

Parents also rely on direct definition to teach values to children. In my family, reading was highly valued and we were encouraged to read. I have vivid memories of being shamed for a B in reading on my first-grade report card. I recall just as keenly the excessive praise heaped on me when I won a reading contest in fourth grade. By then, I had learned how to get my parents' approval.

Identity scripts are another way family members communicate who we are and should be. Psychologists define identity scripts as rules for how we are supposed to live and who we are supposed to be (Berne, 1964; Harris, 1969). Like the scripts for plays, identity scripts define our roles, how we are to play them, and basic elements in the plot we are supposed to have for our lives. Usually, identity scripts reflect the values and heritage of our families. Think back to your childhood to identify some of the principal scripts that operated in your family. Did you learn, "We are responsible people," "Save your money for a rainy day," "Always help others," "Look out for yourself," or "Live by God's word"? These are examples of identity scripts people learn in families.

Children seldom coauthor, or even edit, initial identity scripts. In fact, children are generally not even conscious of learning identity scripts. As adults, however, we are no longer passive tablets on which others can write out who we are. We have the capacity to review the identity scripts that were given to us and to challenge and change those that do not fit the selves we now choose to be.

Finally, parents communicate who we are through **attachment styles,** which are patterns of parenting that teach us who we and others are and how to relate to others. From extensive studies of interaction between parents and children, John Bowlby (1973, 1988) developed the theory that most of us learn attachment styles in our first important relationship—usually with parents. They communicate how they see us, others, and relationships. In turn, we are likely to learn their views

COMMUNICATION in Your Life

What were two important identity scripts in your family?

and internalize them as our own. The first relationship is especially important because it forms expectations for later relationships (Rhodewalt, 2007; Trees, 2006). Four distinct attachment styles have been identified (Figure 3.1).

A child is most likely to develop a *secure attachment style* when the primary caregiver responds in a consistently attentive and loving way to the child. In response, the child develops a positive sense of self-worth ("I am lovable") and a positive view of others ("People are loving and can be trusted"). People with secure attachment styles tend to be outgoing, affectionate, and able to handle the normal challenges and disappointments of close relationships without

We learn attachment styles in our interactions with our parents.

losing self-esteem. Securely attached individuals tend to have more secure relationships (Rowe & Carnelley, 2005) and to have larger and more satisfying networks of friends (Anders & Tucker, 2000) than less securely attached individuals.

A child may develop a *fearful attachment style* if the primary caregiver communicates in negative, rejecting, or abusive ways to the child. Children who are treated this way often infer that they are unworthy of love and that others are not loving. Thus, they learn to see themselves as unlovable and others as rejecting. Not surprisingly, they are apprehensive about relationships. Although they may want close bonds with others, they fear that others will not love them and that they themselves are not lovable.

A caregiver who is disinterested, rejecting, or abusive may also lead a child to develop a *dismissive attachment style*, which makes the child tend to dismiss others as unworthy. People with dismissive attachment styles have a positive view

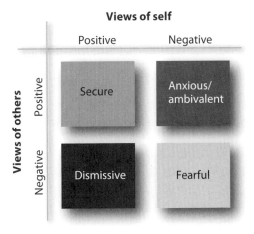

FIGURE 3.1
Styles of Attachment

of themselves and a low regard for others and relationships. This may lead them to regard relationships as unnecessary and undesirable.

ANNETTE *My sister and her husband adopted a daughter from China. When she first came here, Emma was very hard to interact with. She sometimes was very willing to be held and she would smile, but at other times she didn't respond at all to us. It took nearly a year before she would respond consistently to love like most babies do.*

Last is the *anxious/ambivalent attachment style*, which is the most complex of the four. Each of the other three styles results from a consistent pattern of treatment by a caregiver. However, the anxious/ambivalent style is fostered by *inconsistent* treatment from the caregiver. Sometimes the adult is loving and attentive, at other times indifferent or rejecting. The caregiver's communication is not only inconsistent but also unpredictable. He or she may respond positively to something a child does on Monday and react negatively to the same behavior on Tuesday. Naturally, this unpredictability creates anxiety in a child. Because children tend to assume that adults are right, they often believe they themselves are the source of any problem—that they are unlovable or deserve others' abuse.

In adult life, people who have anxious/ambivalent attachment styles know that others can be loving and affirming, but they also know that others can hurt them and be unloving. Reflecting the pattern displayed by the caregiver, people with anxious/ambivalent attachment styles often are inconsistent themselves. One day they invite affection; the next day they deny needing closeness. An interesting study by Tim Cole and Laura Leets (1999) found that people with anxious/ambivalent attachment styles often form relationships with television characters. Such people may feel that it is safer to be in relationships with television characters than with real people.

Unless we consciously work to change the attachment styles we learned in our first close relationships, they tend to affect how we communicate in our adult relationships (Bornstein & Languirand, 2003; Bowlby, 1988; Guerrero, 1996). However, we can modify our attachment styles by challenging unconstructive views of us communicated in our early years and by forming relationships that foster secure connections today (Banse, 2004). To learn more about attachment theory, use your Online Resources for *Communication in Our Lives* to access **WebLink 3.1.**

CourseMate

Communication with Peers A second major influence on our self-concepts is communication with peers. From childhood playmates to work associates, friends, and romantic partners, we interact with peers throughout our lives. As we do, we gain further information about how others see us, and this affects how we see ourselves. As we interact with peers, we engage in **social comparison,** which involves comparing ourselves with others to form judgments of our own talents, attractiveness, abilities, leadership skills, and so forth (Stapel & Blanton, 2006). We gauge ourselves in relation to others in two ways. First, we compare ourselves with others to decide whether we are like them or different from them. Are we the same age, color, or religion? Do we have similar backgrounds and social and political beliefs?

Peers are particularly strong in commenting directly on conformity to expectations of gender. Some college-age men think drinking and sexual activity embody masculinity. Men who are not interested in drinking and hooking up may be ridiculed and excluded for not being "real men" (Cross, 2008; Kimmel, 2008). Women who don't wear popular brands of clothing or who weigh more than what is considered ideal may be ridiculed and excluded for being unfeminine (Adler, 2007; Barash, 2006).

Assessing similarity and difference allows us to decide with whom we fit. Research has shown that people generally are most comfortable with others who are like them, so we tend to gravitate toward those we regard as similar (Amodio & Showers, 2006; Chen, Luo, Yue, Xu, & Zhaoyang, 2009; Lutz-Zois, Bradley, Mihalik, & Moorman-Eavers, 2006). However, this tendency can deprive us of the diverse perspectives of people whose experiences and beliefs differ from our own. When we interact only with people who are like us, we impoverish our understandings of ourselves and the world.

We also use social comparison to measure ourselves in relation to others. Am I as good a goalie as Jenny? Am I as smart as Sam? We continuously refine our self-image by comparing ourselves to others on various criteria of judgment. This is normal and necessary if we are to develop realistic self-concepts. However, we should beware of using inappropriate standards of comparison. It isn't realistic to judge our attractiveness in relation to that of movie stars and models or our athletic ability in relation to that of professional athletes (Buunk, Groothof, & Siero, 2007).

> **COMMUNICATION in Your Life**
>
> **To whom do you compare yourself when assessing your academic ability?**

KEVIN *I learned more about myself and about being white when I was assigned to room with a black guy my freshman year. I'd never interacted much with blacks, and I'd never had a black friend, but I got really close with my roommate. Carl helped me see a lot of things I take for granted that he can't because of his skin. For example, people assume I'm here because I earned a good record in high school, but a lot of people think Carl got in just because he's black and the college had to meet its minority quota. His SAT was higher than mine and so are his grades, but people believe I'm smart and he's a quota admission.*

Communication with Society A third influence on our self-concepts is interaction with society in general. As we observe and interact with others, we learn how society regards each sex, race, sexual orientation, and socioeconomic class. We also learn what others regard as effective public speaking, skillful group leadership, good managerial style, and so forth.

Western society encourages people to perceive themselves as individuals and to form separate families in adulthood. In contrast, traditional Indian culture emphasizes collective identity, and households under the same roof often include grandparents, aunts, uncles, and cousins (Lustig & Koester, 1999).

Who are your sources for social comparison? How do you assess yourself relative to them?

Dennis MacDonald/PhotoEdit

Western society also encourages competition, whereas many Asian societies teach children to place emphasis on cooperation and teamwork (Yum, 2000).

Social perspectives are also communicated to us through media. When we read popular magazines, watch films, and visit sites on the Web, we are inundated with messages about how women and men are supposed to look and act. Desirable women usually are thin, young, and beautiful, and attractive men are strong, in charge, and successful (Wood, 2011). Media shape teens' views of sex and sexuality—what is appropriate and "cool" (Bodey & Wood, in press; Brown, Steele, & Walsh-Childers, 2002).

The institutions that organize our society further communicate social perspectives by the values they uphold. For example, our judicial system reminds us that as a society we value laws and punish those who break them. The number of schools and the levels of education inform us that as a society we value learning. At the same time, institutions reflect prevailing social prejudices. For instance, we may be a lawful society, but wealthy defendants often can buy better "justice" than poor ones. Similarly, although we claim to offer equal educational opportunities to all, students whose families have money and influence often can get into better schools than students whose families lack such resources. These and other values are so thoroughly woven into the fabric of our culture that we learn them with little effort or awareness.

The Self-Fulfilling Prophecy   One particularly powerful way in which communication shapes the self is the self-fulfilling prophecy, which we discussed in Chapter 2. Self-fulfilling prophecies operate when we act in ways that bring about expectations or judgments of ourselves. If you have done poorly in classes in which teachers didn't seem to respect you and have done well with teachers who thought you were smart, then you know what a self-fulfilling prophecy is. The prophecies that we act to fulfill usually are first communicated to us by others. Because we often internalize others' perspectives, we may label ourselves as they do and then act to fulfill our own labels.

When I was 7 years old, my parents enrolled me in a 25-person swimming class. Unlike most of the other children, I didn't catch on quickly. The teacher modeled floating and then told us to try it. The other children floated; I sank. The teacher swam a lap and then told us to try it. The other children zipped across the water; I went under. After three weeks, the teacher told me I would never learn to swim. For 43 years, I believed that and didn't try to swim. When I was 50, my partner Robbie challenged my belief that I couldn't learn to swim. He said he could teach me if I wanted to learn. And he did, by giving me a few hours of one-on-one coaching, which the teacher had not given me at age 7. Now I can float with ease and swim well enough to go into the ocean or a pool. For 43 years, I internalized the label "nonswimmer," and it became a self-fulfilling prophecy for me.

> **TERRY**   *I can really identify with the self-fulfilling prophecy idea. In the second grade, my family moved from our farm to a city where my dad could find work. The first week of class in my new school, we had show and tell. When it was my turn, as soon as I started talking the other kids started laughing at me. I had been raised on a farm in the rural South, and the other kids were from the city. They thought I talked funny, and they made fun of my accent—called me "hillbilly" and "redneck." From then on, I avoided public speaking like the plague. I thought I couldn't speak to others. Last year, I finally took a course in public speaking, and I made a B. It took me a long time to challenge the label that I was a bad public speaker.*

Like Terry and me, many of us believe things about ourselves that are inaccurate. Sometimes labels that were once true aren't any longer, but we continue to believe them and act to fulfill them. In other cases, the labels were never valid, but we are trapped by them anyway. Unfortunately, children often are labeled "slow" or "stupid" when the real problem is that they have physiological difficulties such as impaired vision or hearing. Even when the true source of difficulty is discovered, it may be too late; the children may have already internalized a destructive self-fulfilling prophecy.

The Self Is Multidimensional

Although we use the word *self* as if it referred to a single entity, in reality the self has many dimensions. You have a physical self that includes your size, shape, skin, hair and eye colors, and so forth. In addition, you have a cognitive self that includes your intelligence, aptitudes, and education. You have an emotional self-concept. Are you interpersonally sensitive? Do you have a hot temper? Are you generally optimistic or pessimistic? You have a social self. Some people are extraverted, whereas others are more reserved. Our social selves also include our roles: daughter or son, student, worker, parent, volunteer, partner in a committed relationship. Each of us also has a moral self composed of ethical and spiritual principles we believe in and try to follow. As Carlyle points out, the different dimensions of ourselves sometimes seem at odds with one another.

COMMUNICATION in Your Life

Have you ever internalized a self-fulfilling prophecy?

> **CARLYLE**   *On my own, like with friends or family, I'm pretty quiet—even shy, you could say. But my job requires me to be real outgoing and sociable. I tend bar, and people expect me to kid around and talk with them and stuff. Believe me, if I were as quiet with my customers as I am with my friends, my tips would drop to nothing. It's like when I'm in my work role, I'm Mr. Hail-fellow-well-met, but away from work I'm pretty reserved.*

The Self Is a Process

The self develops over time; it is a process. A baby perceives no boundaries between its body and a nipple, a hand that tickles, or breeze. As an infant has a range of experiences and as others respond to him or her, the child gradually begins to develop **ego boundaries,** which define where the self stops and the rest of the world begins. This is the beginning of a self-concept: the realization that one is a separate entity.

In the first years of life, infants begin to differentiate themselves from the rest of the world, and the self starts to develop. They listen to and observe others to define themselves and to become competent in the identities others assign to them (Kohlberg, 1958; Piaget, 1932/1965). For instance, children work at being competent females or males. They identify females and males to use as models for their own performances of gender. In like manner, children figure out what it takes to be nice, tough, and responsible, and they work to become competent at displaying those qualities. The ways we define ourselves vary as we mature. Struggling to be a good mud-cake maker at age 4 gives way to striving for popularity in high school and succeeding in professional and family roles later in life.

Some people feel uneasy with the idea that the self is a process, not a stable entity. We want to believe there is some unwavering, enduring core that is our essence—our true, unchanging identity. Of course, we all enter the world with certain abilities and limits, which constrain the possibilities of who we can be. Someone without the genes to be tall and coordinated, for instance, probably is not going to be a star forward in basketball. Beyond genetic limits, however, we have considerable freedom to create who we will be.

We Internalize and Act from Social Perspectives

We've already noted that in developing a self, we internalize, or take inside ourselves, others' perspectives on us. To elaborate that idea, we will now explore how we internalize both the general perspective of our society and the perspectives of particular others who are significant in our lives.

Particular Others   We first encounter the perspectives of **particular others.** As the term implies, these are the viewpoints of specific people who are significant to us. Mothers, fathers, siblings, and often day-care providers are particular others who are significant to most infants. In addition, some people include as family members aunts, uncles, grandparents, and others who live together or nearby. Hispanic and black families, in general, are extended, so children in these families often have a great many particular others who affect how they come to see themselves (Gaines, 1995; Hecht, Jackson, & Ribeau, 2003).

SHENNOA   *My grandmother was the biggest influence on me. I lived with her while my mama worked, and she taught me to take myself seriously. She's the one who told me I should go to college and plan a career so that I wouldn't have to depend on somebody else. She's the one who told me to stand up for myself and not let others tell me what to do or believe in. But she did more than just tell me to be a strong person. That's how she was, and I learned just by watching her. A lot of who I am is modeled on my grandmother.*

The process of seeing ourselves through others' eyes is called **reflected appraisal.** It means that we see ourselves in terms of the appraisals reflected in others' eyes. The process has also been called the "looking-glass self" because others are mirrors who reflect who we are (Cooley, 1912). Reflected appraisals are not confined to childhood but continue throughout our lives. When a teacher communicates that a student is smart, the student may come to see himself or herself that way. In professional life, co-workers and supervisors reflect their appraisals of us when they communicate that we're on the fast track, average, or unsuited to our position. When we speak in public, audience responses reflect appraisals

Leigh M. Wilco

We see ourselves in the looking glass of others' eyes.

of our effectiveness. The appraisals that others communicate shape how we see ourselves. In turn, how we see ourselves affects how we communicate. Thus, if you see yourself as an interesting conversationalist, you're likely to communicate that confidence when you talk with others.

The Generalized Other   The second social perspective that influences how we see ourselves is called the **perspective of the generalized other.** The generalized other is the collection of rules, roles, and attitudes endorsed by the whole social community in which we live (Mead, 1934). In other words, the generalized other is overall society. In the process of socialization, most individuals internalize the perspective of the generalized other and thus come to share that perspective. The generalized other is culture specific; the values, codes of conduct, roles, rules, and so forth of the generalized other reflect the distinct history and character of a given culture at a particular time. Modern Western culture emphasizes gender, race, sexual orientation, and economic class as central to personal identity (Andersen & Collins, 2006; Wood, 1995b, 1996b, 2005). Each of these social groupings represents a standpoint, which we discussed in Chapter 2.

North American culture views race as a primary aspect of personal identity. The white race historically has been privileged in the United States. In the early years of this country, it was considered normal and right for white men to own black women, men, and children and to require them to work for no wages and in poor conditions. Later, it was considered natural that white men could vote but black men could not. White men had rights to education, professional jobs, ownership of property, and other basic freedoms that were denied to blacks. Clearly, racial prejudice has diminished substantially. Even so, the upper levels of government, education, and business are dominated by white men, whereas people of color continue to fight overt and covert discrimination in admission, hiring, and advancement. The color of one's skin makes a difference in how society perceives and treats us and, by extension, in how we may perceive ourselves and the opportunities open to us (Franklin, 2006; Lareau, 2003).

WEN-SHU *My family moved here when I was 9 years old. Because I look Asian, people make assumptions about me. They assume I am quiet (true), I am good at math (not true), and I defer to men and elders (true with regard to elders but not men). People also see all Asians as the same, but Taiwanese are as different from mainland Chinese as French Caucasians are from U.S. Caucasians. The first thing people notice about me is my race, and they make too many assumptions about what it means.*

Gender, another important facet of identity in Western culture, also is communicated through social practices and institutions. Historically, men— particularly white men—have been seen as more valuable than women and more entitled to privileges. In the 1800s, women weren't allowed to own property, attend college, or vote. Although there has been great progress in achieving equality between the sexes, in some respects women and men still are not considered equal or treated as such. From the pink and blue blankets that hospitals wrap around newborns to unequal salaries earned by women and men, gender discrimination is a persisting fact of modern life. Given the importance our society places on gender, it is no wonder that one of the first ways children learn to identify themselves is by sex (Wood, 1996b, 2011).

Western cultures have strong gender prescriptions. Girls and women are expected to be caring and cooperative, whereas boys and men are supposed to be independent, assertive, and competitive. Consequently, women who assert themselves or compete may receive social disapproval for violating gender prescriptions. Men who refuse to conform to social views of masculinity and who are gentle and caring risk being labeled "wimps." Gender prescriptions also specify ideal body images—tall and muscular for men; slender or thin and not too tall for women. Our sex, then, makes a great deal of difference in how others view us and how we may come to see ourselves.

A third aspect of identity that cultural communication establishes as salient is sexual orientation. Western culture's view that heterosexuality is normal and right is communicated not only directly but also through privileges given to heterosexuals but denied to gay men, lesbians, bisexuals, transsexuals, and transgendered people. For example, a woman and man who love each other can be married, and their commitment can be recognized religiously and legally. Two men or two women who love each other are not allowed to marry in most states, although domestic partnerships are increasingly recognized. Heterosexual spouses can obtain insurance coverage for their partners and can will them money tax free, but people with other sexual orientations often cannot. Although biases against sexual orientations are decreasing, they still very much affect how we are viewed and treated.

COMMUNICATION in Your Life

Are your personal views of masculinity and femininity consistent with those of the generalized other?

Jump Start reprinted by permission of United Feature Syndicate, Inc.

SANDI   *I've known I was lesbian since I was in high school, but only in the last year have I come out to others. As soon as I tell someone I'm lesbian, they see me differently. Even people who have known me a long time act like I've developed spots or something. Some of my girlfriends don't want to hug or touch me anymore, like they think I'm suddenly going to come on to them. Guys act as if I'm from another planet. It's really strange that sexual orientation makes so much difference in how others see you. I mean, relative to other things like character, personality, and intelligence, who you sleep with is pretty unimportant.*

A fourth dimension of identity, socioeconomic class, is also central to the generalized other's perspective in Western culture (Acker, 2005). Our socioeconomic class affects everything from the money we make to the schools, jobs, and lifestyles we see as possibilities for ourselves (Bornstein & Bradley, 2003; Langston, 2001; Lareau, 2003). Members of the middle and upper classes assume that they will attend college and enter good professions, yet people from the working class may be directed toward vocational training regardless of their academic achievements. In such patterns, we see how the perspective of the generalized other shapes our identities and our concrete lives.

ROCHELLE   *I got so mad in high school. I had a solid A average, and ever since I was 12 I had planned to go to college. But when the guidance counselor talked with me at the start of my senior year, she encouraged me to apply to a technical school that is near my home. When I said I thought my grades should get me into a good college, she did this double-take, like, "Your kind doesn't go to college." My parents both work in a mill and so do all my relatives, but does that mean that I can't have a different future? What really burned me was that a lot of girls who had average grades but came from "the right families" were told to apply to colleges.*

It's important to realize that social perspectives on race, sex, sexual orientation, and socioeconomic class interact. Race intersects gender, so women of color often experience double oppression and devaluation in our culture (Anzaldúa, 1999;

Social views of committed relationships between members of the same sex have changed over time.

Hernández & Rheman, 2002). Class and sexual orientation also interact: Homophobia tends to be pronounced among people in the working class, so a lesbian or gay person in a poor community may be socially ostracized. Socioeconomic class and gender are also interlinked; women are far more likely than men to live at the poverty level (Andersen & Collins, 2006). Intersections of race and class mean that minority members of the working class often are not treated as well as working-class whites (Rothenberg, 2006).

As we internalize the generalized other's perspective, we come to share many of the views and values of our society. Shared understandings are essential for collective life. If we all made up our own rules about when to stop and go at traffic intersections, the number of accidents would skyrocket. If each of us operated by our own inclinations, there would be no shared standards regarding rape, murder, robbery, and so forth.

Yet some social views are not as constructive as traffic rules and moral codes. The generalized other's unequal valuing of different races, genders, and sexual orientations fosters discrimination against whole groups of people just because they don't fit what society defines as normal or good. Each of us has an ethical responsibility to exercise critical judgment about which social views we personally accept and use as guides for our own behaviors, attitudes, and values. This suggests a fourth proposition about the self.

Social Perspectives on the Self Are Constructed and Changeable

The generalized other's perspectives are not fixed. They are constructed and therefore can be changed if members of a society challenge existing norms and values.

Constructed Social perspectives are constructed in particular cultures at specific times to support dominant ideologies, or the beliefs and traditions of those in power. When we reflect on social values, we realize that they are arbitrary and tend to serve the interests of those who benefit from prevailing values.

Individual and collective efforts change social perspectives.

Variable The constructed and arbitrary nature of social values becomes especially obvious when we consider how greatly values differ between cultures and within particular cultures over time. For example, in Sweden, Denmark, and Norway, marriages between members of the same sex are given legal and social recognition.

Prescriptions for femininity and masculinity also vary widely between cultures. In some places, men are emotional and dependent, and women are assertive and emotionally controlled (Wood, 2011). The meanings of femininity and masculinity also vary over time within a particular culture. In the 1700s and 1800s, women in the United States were defined as too delicate to engage in hard labor. During World Wars I and II, however, women were expected to do "men's work" while men were at war. When the men returned home, society once again decreed that women were too weak to perform in the labor market, and they were reassigned to home and hearth.

Social prescriptions for men also have changed. The rugged he-man who was the ideal in the 1800s used his six-shooter to dispose of unsavory rustlers and relied on physical strength to farm. After the Industrial Revolution, physical strength and bravado gave way to business acumen, and money replaced muscle as a sign of manliness. As women, men, and families change, ideals of femininity and masculinity continue to evolve.

Some cultures recognize more than two sexes and allow people to choose whether to live as women or as men (Brown, 1997; Nanda, 2004). In many countries south of the United States, mixed-race marriages are common and accepted. Even what counts as race has changed over times in societies ranging from America to South Africa (Manning, 2000). The individualistic ethic so prominent in the United States is discouraged in many countries, particularly Asian and African ones (Gudykunst & Lee, 2002; Hecht et al., 2003).

The meaning of homosexuality has also been revised over time in Western culture. Although much prejudice still exists, it is gradually diminishing. Laws have been enacted to protect lesbians and gays against housing and job discrimination. As social views of gender, race, class, and a range of sexualities evolve, individuals' views of others and their own self-concepts will also change.

Changeable Social perspectives are fluid. They change in response to individual and collective efforts to weave new meanings into the fabric of common life. From 1848 until 1920, many people fought to change social views of women, and they succeeded in gaining the right for women to vote, attend college, and own property, as well as other rights enjoyed by male citizens. In the 1960s, civil rights activism launched nationwide rethinking of actions and attitudes toward non-whites. The battle to recognize and respect gays and lesbians has begun to alter social perspectives. Changes in how we view sex, race, class, (dis)ability, and sexual orientation are negotiated in communication contexts ranging from one-to-one conversations to mass media. Each of us has an ethical responsibility to speak out against social perspectives that we perceive as wrong or harmful. By doing so, we participate in the ongoing process of refining social perspectives.

> **JANINE** My husband and I have really worked to share equally in our marriage. When we got married 8 years ago, we both believed women and men were equal and should have equal responsibilities for the home and family and equal power in making decisions that affect the family. But it's a lot harder to actually live that ideal than to believe in it. Both of us have struggled against our socialization that says I should cook and clean and take care of the kids and he should make big decisions about our lives. I think we've done a pretty good job of creating and living an egalitarian marriage. A lot of our friends see us as models.

ENHANCING THE SELF

So far, we've explained how the self forms in the process of communicating with others. Building on that knowledge, we'll now explore guidelines for encouraging personal growth as communicators.

Make a Strong Commitment to Improve Yourself

The first principle for enhancing who you are is to make a firm commitment to personal growth. This isn't as easy as it might sound. A firm commitment involves more than saying, "I want to listen better" or "I want to be less judgmental." Saying these sentences is simple, but actually investing the effort to change is difficult.

Changing ourselves takes persistent effort. Because the self is a process, it is not formed in one fell swoop, and it cannot be changed in one moment. We have to be willing to invest ongoing effort. In addition, we must realize at the outset that there will be setbacks, and we can't let them derail our resolve.

A second reason change is difficult is that the self resists change. If you realize in advance that you may struggle against change, you'll be prepared for the tension that accompanies personal growth. Because change is a process and the self resists change, a firm and continuing commitment to change is essential. It's also advisable to strive for incremental, gradual improvements rather than attempting to alter yourself radically all at once.

Gain Knowledge as a Basis for Personal Change

Commitment alone is insufficient to spur changes in who you are. In addition, you need several types of knowledge. First, you need to understand how the self is formed. In this chapter, we've discussed values and views of particular others and the generalized other. You may not want to accept all the views and values you were taught.

Second, you need to know how to develop goals you can achieve. Vague goals for self-improvement usually lead nowhere because they don't indicate concrete steps toward change. For instance, "I want to be better at intimate

COMMUNICATION in Your Life

Identify one aspect of yourself you would like to change.

COMMUNICATION HIGHLIGHT

Failure on the Way to Success

CourseMate

Who was Babe Ruth? If you know baseball history, you probably think of him as having hit 714 home runs. He did, but he also struck out 1,330 times. R. H. Macy, who founded Macy's department store, failed in his first seven efforts to start a business. Superstar Michael Jordan was cut from his high school basketball team because he wasn't good enough. Early in his career, Walt Disney was fired from a newspaper job because his editor thought he had no good or creative ideas. The Beatles finished 59 songs before they had their first hit.

Most people who succeed fail along the way; sometimes they fail many times. If Babe Ruth had let his strikeouts defeat him, he would never have been a champion batter. The same is true of most of us. Failures and defeats are inevitable. Letting them define who we are is not.

To consider what your life would be like if you were completely unafraid of failing, complete the Communication Highlight Activity for Chapter 3 via your Online Resources for *Communication in Our Lives*.

communication" is a very vague objective. You can't do anything to meet such an unclear goal until you know something about the talk that enhances and impedes intimacy. Books such as this one will help you pinpoint concrete skills that facilitate healthy intimate communication. For instance, Chapter 4 will help you develop listening skills, and Chapters 8 and 9 will explain how communication affects personal and social relationships.

Another important source of knowledge is other people. Perhaps you recall a time when you began a new job. If you were fortunate, you found a mentor who explained the ropes to you so that you could learn how to communicate effectively in your work context. Others can also provide useful feedback on your interpersonal skills and your progress in the process of change. Feedback from your supervisor helps you understand how she or he perceives your work and how you might improve your job performance. Finally, others can serve as models. If you know someone you think is particularly skillful in supporting others, observe him or her carefully to identify specific communication skills. Observing allows you to identify concrete skills that you can tailor to suit your personal style.

Set Realistic Goals

Changing ourselves is most likely when we set realistic goals. If you are shy and want to be more extraverted, it is reasonable to try to speak up and socialize more often. On the other hand, it may not be reasonable to try to be the life of every party. Realistic goals are based on realistic standards. In a culture that emphasizes perfection, it's easy to be trapped into expecting more than is humanly possible. If you set a goal to become a totally perfect communicator in all situations, you set yourself up to fail. It's more constructive to establish a series of realistic small goals. You might focus first on improving one communication skill. When you're satisfied with your ability at that skill, you can work on another one.

With regard to our discussion of social comparison, it's also important to select reasonable measuring sticks for yourself. It isn't realistic to compare your academic work with that of a certified genius. It is reasonable to measure your academic performance against that of others similar to you in intelligence and circumstances. It isn't realistic to compare your public speaking skill with that of someone who has made public presentations for years. It is reasonable to measure your public speaking ability against that of others who have speaking experience similar to yours. Setting realistic goals and selecting appropriate standards of comparison are important in bringing about change in yourself.

MIKE   *For a long time, I put myself down for not doing as well academically as a lot of my friends. They put mega-hours into studying and writing papers. I can't do that because I work 30 hours a week. Now I see that it's unfair to compare myself to them. When I compare myself to students who work as much as I do, my record is pretty good.*

Accept That You Are in Process

Previously in this chapter, we saw that one characteristic of the human self is that it is continually in process, always becoming. This implies that you need to accept who you are now as a starting point. You don't have to like or admire everything about yourself, but it is important to accept who you are today as a basis for going forward. The self that you are results from all the interactions, reflected appraisals, and social comparisons in your life. You cannot change your past, but you do not have to be bound by it forever. Only by realizing and accepting who you are now can you move ahead.

Accepting yourself as being in process also implies that you realize you can change. Because you are in process, you are always changing and growing. Don't let yourself be hindered by defeating self-fulfilling prophecies or the fallacy of thinking that you can't change (Rusk & Rusk, 1988). You can change if you set realistic goals, make a genuine commitment, and then work for the changes you want. Just remember that you are not fixed as you are; you are always in the process of becoming.

Create a Supportive Context for Change

Just as it is easier to swim with the tide than against it, it is easier to change our views of ourselves when we have some support for our efforts. You can do a lot to create an environment that supports your growth by choosing contexts and people who help you realize your goals. First, think about settings. If you want to lose weight, it's better to go to restaurants that serve healthful foods and offer light choices than to go to cholesterol castles. If you want to become more extraverted, go to parties, not libraries. But libraries are a better context than parties if your goal is to improve academic performance.

> **JAN** *I never cared a lot about clothes until I joined a sorority where the labels on your clothes are a measure of your worth. The girls compete with each other to dress the best and have the newest styles. When one of the sisters wears something out of style, she gets a lot of teasing, but really it's pressure on her to measure up to the sorority image. At first, I adopted my sisters' values, and I spent more money than I could afford on clothes. For a while I even quit making contributions at church so that I could have more money for clothes. When I finally realized I was becoming somebody I didn't like, I tried to change, but my sisters made me feel bad anytime I wasn't dressed well. Finally, I moved out rather than face that pressure all the time. It just wasn't a good place for me to be myself.*

Because how others view us affects how we see ourselves, you can create a supportive context by consciously choosing to be around people who believe in you and encourage your personal growth without being dishonest about your limitations. It's also important to steer clear of people who put you down or say you can't change. In other words, people who reflect positive appraisals of us enhance our ability to improve who we are.

Others aren't the only ones whose communication affects our self-concepts. We also communicate with ourselves, and our own messages influence how we see ourselves. One of the most crippling kinds of self-talk we can engage in is **self-sabotage**—telling ourselves we are no good, we'll never learn something, there's no point in trying to change. We may be repeating others' judgments of us, or we may be inventing negative self-fulfilling prophecies. Either way, self-sabotage undermines belief in ourselves.

Distinguished therapist Albert Ellis wrote a book titled *How to Stubbornly Refuse to Make Yourself Miserable About Anything—Yes, Anything* (1988). In it, he asserted that most of our negative feelings about ourselves result from negative messages we communicate to ourselves. His advice is to challenge negative statements you make to yourself and to replace them with constructive intrapersonal communication. Self-sabotage is poisonous; it destroys our motivation to change and grow. We can be as critical of ourselves as others can; in fact, we probably can do more damage to our self-concepts than others can because we are most aware of our vulnerabilities and fears.

Following Ellis' advice, we can affirm our worth, encourage our growth, and fortify our sense of self-worth. Positive self-talk builds motivation and belief in yourself. It is also a useful strategy to interrupt and challenge negative messages from yourself and others. The next time you hear yourself saying, "I can't do...," or someone else says, "You'll never change," challenge the self-defeating message with self-talk. Say out loud to yourself, "I can do it. I will change." Use positive self-talk to resist counterproductive communication about yourself. Of course, improving your self-concept is not facilitated by uncritical positive communication. None of us grows and improves when we listen only to praise, particularly if it is less than honest. The true uppers in our lives offer constructive criticism to encourage us to reach for better versions of ourselves.

In sum, to improve your self-concept you must create contexts that support growth and change. Seek out experiences and settings that foster belief in yourself and the changes you desire. Also, recognize uppers, downers, and vultures in yourself and others, and learn which people and which kinds of communication assist you in achieving your own goals for self-improvement.

If you'd like to try initiating changes in yourself related to the way you communicate interpersonally, complete the activity "Improving Self-Concept" via your Online Resources for *Communication in Our Lives*.

COMMUNICATION HIGHLIGHT

Uppers, Downers, and Vultures

CourseMate

Uppers are people who communicate positively about us and who reflect positive appraisals of our self-worth. They notice our strengths, see our progress, and accept our weaknesses and problems without discounting us. When we're around uppers, we feel more upbeat and positive about ourselves. Uppers aren't necessarily unconditionally positive in their communication; a true friend can be an upper by recognizing our weaknesses and helping us work on them.

Downers are people who communicate negatively about us and our self-worth. They call attention to our flaws, emphasize our problems, and deride our dreams and goals. When we're around downers, we tend to feel down about ourselves. Reflecting their perspectives, we're more aware of our weaknesses and less confident of what we can accomplish when we're around downers.

Vultures are extreme downers. They not only communicate negative images of us but also attack our self-concepts, like the birds that prey on their victims (Simon, 1977). Sometimes vultures harshly criticize us. They say, "You're hopeless." In other cases, vultures pick up on our own self-doubts and magnify them. They pick us apart by focusing on our weak spots. By telling us we are inadequate, vultures demolish our self-esteem.

BEYOND THE CLASSROOM

Let's take the material in this chapter beyond the classroom by thinking about how what you've learned about personal identity might apply to the workplace, ethical choices, and engagement with the broader world.

1. **Workplace.**   We discussed direct definition and identity scripts as two ways that others define who we are and who we are worth during the early years of life. Extend this by asking how those two factors influence identity development on the job. Recall examples of supervisors and co-workers' direct definitions of you or other employees. For example, were you defined as "a good worker" or "a quick learner"? Consider identity scripts that you were given in a particular workplace. What did others tell you about the company or workplace's identity and about how employees in this particular job were supposed to think and act?

2. **Ethics.**   How does what you learned in this chapter affect ethical choices about parenting? Reflect on the ethical implications of knowing that parents affect children's self-concepts by their choices of direct definitions, identity scripts and attachment styles. What ethical responsibilities, if any, do parents have regarding their impact on children's self-concepts and self-esteem?

   Ethics

3. **Engagement.**   Not all children have the fortune of having parents who are able to nurture them lovingly and help them develop positive self-concepts. In 1964 the United States launched the Head Start Program to help children and their families who have limited resources. Click **WebLink 3.2** to access the National Head Start Program's website. Spend some time reading this page and following links it provides. Can you identify ways that the program aims to enhance the self-concepts of underprivileged children and their families?

CHAPTER SUMMARY

In this chapter, we explored the self as a process that evolves as we communicate with others over the course of our lives. As we interact with others, we learn and internalize social perspectives, both those of particular others and those of the generalized other, or society as a whole. Reflected appraisals, direct definitions, and social comparisons are key communication processes that shape how we see ourselves and how we change over time. The perspective of the generalized other includes social views of key aspects of identity, including gender, race, and sexual orientation. However, these are arbitrary social constructions that we may challenge and resist once we are adults. When we resist social views and values that we consider unethical, we promote change in both society and ourselves.

In the final section of the chapter, we focused on ways to enhance communication competence by improving self-concept. Guidelines include making a firm commitment to personal growth, gaining knowledge about desired changes and the skills they involve, setting realistic goals, accepting yourself as in process, and creating contexts that support the changes you seek. We can make amazing changes in who we are and how we feel about ourselves when we commit to doing so.

APPLYING COMMUNICATION IN OUR LIVES

The key concepts, For Further Reflection and Discussion questions, and Experiencing Communication in Our Lives case study that follow will help you review, reflect on, and extend the information and ideas presented in this chapter. These resources, and a diverse selection of additional study tools, are also available as Online Resources for *Communication in Our Lives*. Your Online Resources include CourseMate, a student workbook, interactive video activities, audio study tools, a book companion website, Speech Builder Express, Speech Studio, and InfoTrac College Edition. For more information or to access this book's online resources, visit **www.cengage.com/login.**

KEY CONCEPTS

attachment style, 52
direct definition, 50
downer, 68
ego boundaries, 58
identity script, 52

particular others, 58
perspective of the generalized other, 59
reflected appraisal, 59
self, 50

self-sabotage, 67
social comparison, 54
upper, 68
vulture, 68

FOR FURTHER REFLECTION AND DISCUSSION

1. Set one specific goal for personal growth as a communicator. Be sure to specify your goal in terms of clear behavioral changes and make it realistic. As you study different topics during the semester, apply what you learn to your personal goal.

2. What ethical issues do you perceive in the process of developing and continuously refining self-concepts, both your own and those of people around you? Is it as important to be ethical in communicating with yourself (self-talk, or intrapersonal communication) as in communicating with others?

   Ethics

3. How do people you meet and get to know on the Internet affect your sense of who you are? Are they significant for you? Do they represent the generalized other to you? Is it useful to distinguish between the impact of face-to-face and online communication?

4. In what ways are your own experiences and your sense of identity consistent with generalizations about the effects on self-concept of race or ethnicity, economic class, sexual orientation, and sex? In what ways do your experiences and your sense of identity diverge from generalizations? What in your own life might account for the instances in which you do not fit generalizations?

5. Historically, India classified people according to caste, one of the most rigid systems of social class. To learn about how a person's caste affected his or her opportunities in life, click **WebLink 3.3.**

CourseMate

SHARPEN YOUR SKILL

1. Reflecting on Your Identity Scripts

Recall identity scripts your parents communicated about who you were or were supposed to become. Can you hear them saying, "Our people do . . ." or "Our family doesn't . . ."? Can you recall messages that told you what and who they expected you to be? As a youngster, did you hear, "You'll go to college" or "You're going to be a doctor"?

Now review key identity scripts. Which ones make sense to you today? Are you still following any that are irrelevant to your present life or that are at odds with your personal values and goals? If so, then commit to changing scripts that aren't productive for you or that conflict with values you hold. You can rewrite identity scripts now that you're an adult.

For additional insight into identity scripts that were communicated to you, complete the activity "Identifying Your Identity Scripts" **CourseMate** via your Online Resources for *Communication in Our Lives.*

2. Your Looking-Glass Self

Identify three people who have been or are particularly important to you. For each person, identify one self-perception you have that reflects the appraisal of you communicated by that person.

Now imagine that you'd never known each of the three people. Describe how you would be different. How would your self-image change? For instance, Shennoa (see commentary) might think she would be less independent had her grandmother not influenced how she sees herself.

Trace the way you see yourself to the appraisals that particular others have reflected.

Prepare a two-minute presentation in which you describe one of the people you've identified as a looking glass for yourself. Explain how this person has influenced the way you see yourself. You may want to look ahead to Part III of this book for guidelines on preparing a speech.

EXPERIENCING COMMUNICATION IN OUR LIVES

CASE STUDY: *Parental Teachings*

A video of the conversation scripted here is featured in your Chapter 3 Online Resources for *Communication in Our Lives.* Select "Parental Teachings" to watch the video. Improve your own communication skills by reading, watching, and analyzing this communication encounter.

CourseMate

© Cengage Learning

Kate McDonald is in the neighborhood park with her two children, 7-year-old Emma and 5-year-old Jeremy. The three of them walk into the park and approach the swing set.

KATE: Jeremy, why don't you push Emma so she can swing? Emma, you hang on tight.

Jeremy begins pushing his sister, who squeals with delight. Jeremy gives an extra-hard push that lands him in the dirt in front of the swing set. Laughing, Emma jumps off, falling in the dirt beside her brother.

KATE: Come here, sweetie. You've got dirt all over your knees and your pretty new dress.

Kate brushes the dirt off Emma, who then runs over to the jungle gym set that Jeremy is now climbing. Kate smiles as she watches Jeremy climb fearlessly on the bars.

KATE: You're a brave little man, aren't you? How high can you go?

Encouraged by his mother, Jeremy climbs to the top bars and holds up a fist, screaming, "Look at me, Mom! I'm king of the hill! I climbed to the very top!"

Kate laughs and claps her hands to applaud him. Jealous of the attention Jeremy is getting, Emma runs over to the jungle gym and starts climbing. Kate calls out, "Careful, honey. Don't go any higher. You could fall and hurt yourself." When Emma ignores her mother and reaches for a higher bar, Kate walks over and pulls her off, saying, "Emma, I told you that is dangerous. Time to get down. Why don't you play on the swings some more?"

Once Kate puts Emma on the ground, the girl walks over to the swings and begins swaying.

QUESTIONS FOR ANALYSIS AND DISCUSSION

You can answer these questions and see my responses to them online via your Online Resources for Chapter 3.

1. Identify examples of direct definition in this scenario. How does Kate define Emma and Jeremy?

2. Identify examples of reflected appraisal in this scenario. What appraisals of her son and daughter does Kate reflect to them?

3. What do Emma's and Jeremy's responses to Kate suggest about their acceptance of her views of them?

4. To what extent does Kate's communication with her children reflect conventional gender expectations in Western culture?

Jose Galvez/PhotoEdit

4

> The best way to understand people is to listen to them.
>
> **Ralph Nichols**

Listening Effectively

Do you have a minute to talk?" Joanne asks her friend Elly as she enters her dorm room.

"Sure," Elly agrees without looking up from the email she is writing to her mother. Lately her mother has been criticizing her for not studying enough, and Elly's trying to explain that college is more than academics.

"I'm worried about what's happening between Drew and me," Joanne begins. "He takes me for granted all the time. He never asks what I want to do or where I'd like to go. He just assumes I'll go along with whatever he wants."

"Yeah, I know that routine. Steve does it to me, too," Elly says with exasperation as she looks up from the computer. "Last weekend, he insisted we go to this stupid war movie that I wouldn't have chosen to see in a million years. But what I wanted didn't make a lot of difference to him."

"That's exactly what I'm talking about," Joanne agrees. "I don't like it

SHARPEN YOUR SKILL

At the end of this chapter, refer to the Sharpen Your Skill features, Improving Recall and Learn from the Pros, to apply concepts from Chapter 4.

when Drew treats me that way, and I want to know how to get him to be more considerate."

"What I told Steve last weekend was that I'd had it, and from now on we decide together what we're doing, or we don't do it together," Elly says forcefully. "We've had this talk before, but this time I think I really got through to him that I was serious."

"So are you saying that's what I should do with Drew?"

"Sure. You have to stand up for your rights, or he'll walk all over you," Elly says while typing on the keyboard. "Take it from me, subtlety won't work. Remember last year when I was dating Larry? Well, he started this routine, and I tried to be subtle and hint that I'd like to be consulted about things. What I said to him went in one ear and out the other. If you're not firm, they'll run over you."

"But Drew's not like Larry or Steve. He's not trying to run over me. I think he just doesn't understand how I feel when he makes all the decisions," Joanne says.

"Well, I really don't think Steve's 'like that' either. He's just as good a guy as Drew," Elly snaps.

"That's not what I meant," Joanne says. "I just meant that I don't think I need to hit Drew over the head with a two-by-four."

"And I suppose you think Steve does need that?"

"I don't know. I'm just thinking that maybe our relationships are different," Joanne says.

How would you describe the communication between Elly and Joanne? Is Elly a good listener? Usually, when we think about communication, we focus on talking. Yet talking is not the only part—or even the greatest part—of communication. Effective communication also involves listening. As obvious as this is, few of us devote as much energy to listening as we do to talking.

Poor listening is evident in the conversation between Elly and Joanne. The first obstacle to effective listening is Elly's initial preoccupation with the email she's writing to her mother. If she really wants to listen to Joanne, she should postpone the email. A second problem is Elly's tendency to monopolize the conversation by focusing on her own problems and boyfriends instead of on Joanne's concerns about the relationship with Drew. Third, Elly listens defensively, taking offense when Joanne suggests that their relationships may differ. Like Elly, most of us often don't listen as well as we could. When we listen poorly, we are not communicating well.

You spend more time listening—or trying to—than talking. Studies of people from college students to professionals indicate that the average person spends 45 to 75 percent of waking time listening to others (Nichols, 1995; Steil, 1997; Wolvin, 2009). If we don't listen effectively, we're communicating poorly much of the time.

When people don't listen well on the job, they may miss information that can affect their professional effectiveness and advancement (Darling & Dannels, 2003; Deal & Kennedy, 1999; Gabric & McFadden, 2001; Landrum & Harrold, 2003). In a survey, 1,000 human resource professionals ranked listening as the

Who Listens?

CourseMate

Dan Rather interviewed Mother Teresa shortly before her death (Bailey, 1998). She had this to say about listening.

Rather: "What do you say to God when you pray?"

Mother Teresa: "I listen."

Rather: "Well, what does God say?"

Mother Teresa: "He listens."

number one quality of effective managers (Windsor, Curtis, & Stephens, 1997). Skill in listening is also linked to resolving workplace conflicts (Van Styke, 1999). Doctors who don't listen fully to patients may misdiagnose or mistreat medical problems (Christensen, 2004; Scholz, 2005; Underwood & Adler, 2005). Ineffective listening in the classroom diminishes learning and performance on tests. In personal relationships, poor listening can hinder understanding of others, and listening ineffectively to public communication leaves us uninformed about civic issues. Learning to listen well enhances personal, academic, social, civic, and professional effectiveness.

This chapter focuses on listening. First, we'll consider what's involved in listening, which is more than most of us realize. Next, we'll discuss obstacles to effective listening and how to minimize them. Third, we'll consider common forms of nonlistening. The fourth section of the chapter explains different types of listening and the skills needed for each. In our discussion, we'll identify principles for improving listening effectiveness.

COMMUNICATION in Your Life

Describe the communication of the best listener you know.

THE LISTENING PROCESS

Although we often use the words *listening* and *hearing* as if they were synonyms, actually they're not. **Hearing** is a physiological activity that occurs when sound waves hit our eardrums. Hearing is passive; we don't have to invest any energy to hear. Listening, on the other hand, is an active process that requires energy (International Listening Association, 1995). Listening involves more than just hearing or receiving messages through sight, as when we notice nonverbal behaviors or when people with hearing impairments read lips or receive messages in American Sign Language (ASL).

Listening is an active, complex process that includes being mindful, physically receiving messages, selecting and organizing information, interpreting communication, responding, and remembering. The complexity of listening is represented in the Chinese character for listening, which includes symbols for eyes, ears, and heart (Figure 4.1). As the character suggests, to listen effectively, we use not only our ears, but also our eyes and hearts.

Eyes

Ears

Heart

FIGURE 4.1
The Chinese Character for
Listening

Listening

Being Mindful

The first step in listening is making a decision to be mindful. **Mindfulness** is being fully engaged in the moment. Your mind is focused on what is happening in the here and now. When you are mindful, you don't let your thoughts wander from what is happening in the present conversation. You don't think about what you did yesterday or about a message you want to text to a friend, and you don't think about your own feelings and issues. Instead, when you listen mindfully, you tune in fully to another person and try to understand that person without imposing your own ideas, judgments, or feelings on the message. You may later express your thoughts and feelings, but when we listen mindfully, we attend to another fully. You demonstrate mindfulness by paying attention, indicating interest, and responding to what another expresses (Deal & Kennedy, 1999).

Mindfulness enhances communication in two ways. First, attending mindfully to others increases our understanding of how they feel and think about what they are saying. In addition, when we mindfully attend, others engage us more fully, elaborate their ideas, and express themselves in greater depth.

Being mindful is a personal commitment to attend fully and without diversion to another person. No amount of skill will make you a good listener if you do not choose to attend mindfully to others. Thus, your own choice to be mindful or not is the foundation of how well you listen—or fail to.

Physically Receiving Messages

In addition to mindfulness, listening involves physically receiving oral messages. For many people, this happens through hearing. People who are deaf, however, receive messages by reading lips or by reading sign language (Carl, 1998). Our ability to receive messages may decline when we are fatigued or when we have to be attentive for extended periods without breaks. You may have noticed that it's harder to sustain attention in long classes than in shorter ones. Physical reception of messages may also be impeded by background noises, such as a blaring television, others talking nearby, or by competing visual cues. Thus, it's a good idea to control distractions that hinder listening.

> **JIMMY** *It's impossible to listen well in my apartment. Four of us live there, and at least two different stereos are on all the time. Also, a TV is usually on, and there may be conversations or phone calls, too. It's crazy when we try to talk to each other in the middle of all the racket. We're always asking each other to repeat something or skipping over whatever we don't hear. If we go out to a bar or something, the noise there is just as bad. Sometimes I think we don't really want to talk with each other and all the distractions protect us from having to.*

Selecting and Organizing Material

The third part of listening is selecting and organizing material. As we noted in Chapter 2, we don't perceive everything around us. Instead, we selectively attend to some messages and elements of our environments and disregard others. What we select to attend to depends on many factors, including our physiology, interests, cognitive structures, and expectations. For instance, our sex seems to affect how we listen. As a rule, men tend to focus, shape, and direct their hearing in instrumental ways, whereas women are more likely to attend to the whole of communication, noticing details and noises and activities surrounding the primary communication ("Men Use," 2000). The difference in listening styles can complicate interaction between women and men. Sometimes men think women's communication is unfocused and burdened with irrelevant details, but to many women, the details and sideline topics are part of the overall interaction (Johnson, 2000). Women, on the other hand, sometimes think the linear, direct communication that is more typical of men is too abbreviated to cultivate real connection.

We can compensate for our tendencies to attend selectively by remembering that we are more likely to notice stimuli that are intense, loud, or unusual. Thus, we may overlook communicators who don't call attention to themselves with strong volume and bold gestures. If we're aware of this tendency, we can guard against it. Once again, mindfulness comes into play. Choosing to be mindful doesn't necessarily mean that our minds won't stray when we try to listen, but it does mean that we notice when that happens and we refocus on what the other is saying.

Once we've selected what to notice, we organize what we've received. As you'll recall from Chapter 2, we use cognitive schemata to organize what we selectively notice. When others are talking, we make decisions—usually not consciously—about how to organize what they say: Does the communication fit the prototype of venting or problem solving or something else? We apply personal constructs to classify the message as rational or irrational, emotional or not emotional, and so forth. Based on how you construct what you are selectively attending to, you apply stereotypes to predict what the other person will do and expects you to do. Finally, based on the meanings you have constructed, you choose which script to follow in interaction.

When a friend is upset, you can reasonably predict that he may not want advice until he has first had a chance to express his feelings. On the other hand, when a co-worker comes to you with a problem that must be solved quickly, you assume she might welcome concrete advice or collaboration. Your script for responding to the distraught friend might be to say, "Tell me more about what you're feeling" or "You sound really upset—let's talk." With a work team that is facing a deadline, you might adopt a more directive script and say, "Here's what we need to do" or "Maybe we can work together and get it all done."

Interpreting Communication

The fourth part of listening is interpreting others' communication. When we interpret, we put together all that we have selected and organized to make sense of the overall situation. The most important principle in this process is to be person centered, which means interpreting others on their own terms. Certainly, you won't always agree with other people and how they see themselves, others, issues, and situations. However, if you want to listen well, you have an ethical responsibility to make an earnest effort to understand others' perspectives. To interpret someone with respect for their perspective is one of the greatest gifts we can give.

MAGGIE   *Don and I didn't understand each other's perspective, and we didn't even understand that we didn't understand. Once I told him I was really upset about a friend of mine who needed money for an emergency. Don told me she had no right to expect me to bail her out, but that had nothing to do with what I was feeling. He saw the situation in terms of what rights my friend had, but to me it was about feeling concerned for someone I like. Only after we got counseling did we learn to really listen to each other instead of listening through ourselves.*

Responding

Effective listening includes responding, which is communicating attention and interest as well as voicing our own views when that is appropriate (Purdy, 1997). Skillful listeners give outward signs that they are interested and involved not only when others finish speaking but throughout interaction. Indicators of engagement include attentive posture, head nods, eye contact, and vocal responses such as "um hmm," "okay," and "go on." This is what makes listening such an active process. When we respond with interest, we communicate that we care about the other person and what she or he is saying.

Remembering

The final part of effective listening is remembering, or retaining what you have heard. According to communication professors Ron Adler and Neil Towne (1993), we remember less than half of a message immediately after we hear it. As time goes by, retention decreases further; we recall only about 35 percent of most messages 8 hours after we hear them. Because we forget about two-thirds of what we hear, it's important to make sure we hang onto the most important third. Effective listeners let go of many details to retain basic ideas and general impressions (Cooper, Seibold, & Suchner, 1997; Fisher, 1987). Later in this chapter, we'll discuss strategies for increasing retention.

OBSTACLES TO EFFECTIVE LISTENING

There are two broad types of obstacles to good listening: those external to us and those inside us.

External Obstacles

There are many hindrances to effective listening in communication situations. Although we can't always control external obstacles, knowing what situational factors hinder listening can help us guard against them or compensate for the interference they create.

THE FAMILY CIRCUS   **By Bil Keane**

10-24
© 2003 Bil Keane, Inc.
Dist. by King Features Synd.
www.familycircus.com

"Sam's my best friend. He never talks about himself, and he listens while I talk about me."

Family Circus © 2003 Bil Keane, Inc. King Features Syndicate

Message Overload   The sheer amount of communication in our lives makes it impossible to listen fully to all of it. As communication technologies have grown, so has the amount of information we are expected to process. When we're not talking face-to-face with someone, we're likely to be texting, talking on a cell, listening to podcasts, or watching YouTube videos. We simply aren't able to listen mindfully all of the time. Instead, we have to screen the talk around us, much like we screen calls on our answering machines, to decide when to listen mindfully.

Message overload often occurs in academic settings, in which readings and class discussions are packed with content. If you're taking four or five classes, you confront mountains of information. Message overload may also occur when communication takes place simultaneously in two channels. For instance, you might suffer information overload if a speaker presents information verbally while also showing a graph with complex statistical data. It's difficult to know whether to focus your listening energy on the visual message or the verbal one.

Message Complexity   Listening is also impeded by the difficulty of some messages. The more detailed and complicated ideas are, the harder it is to follow and retain them. Many jobs today are highly specialized; hence much on-the-job communication is complex and increasingly rapid (Cooper, 1997; Hacker, Goss, & Townley, 1998). We need to guard against the tendency to tune out people who use technical vocabularies, provide lots of detail, and use complex sentences.

COMMUNICATION in Your Life

How do you manage message complexity in your classes?

Environmental Distractions   Distractions in the environment can interfere with listening. Perhaps you've been part of a crowd at a rally or a game. If so, you probably had trouble hearing the person next to you. Although most sounds aren't as overwhelming as the roar of crowds, there is always some noise in communication situations. Music, television in the background, side conversations in a class, or rings of cell phones and PDAs can hinder communication.

Good listeners try to reduce environmental distractions. It's considerate to turn off televisions, cells, and PDAs if someone wants to talk with you. In the example that opened this chapter, Elly should have put aside the email she was writing if she wanted to listen mindfully to Joanne. Professionals hold incoming phone calls when they want to give undivided attention to a client or business associate. It's also appropriate to suggest moving away from a noisy area to talk. Even if we can't always eliminate distractions, we can usually reduce them or change our location to one more conducive to good communication.

Increasingly, we are interrupted by the buzzes of pagers and the ring tones of cells and BlackBerry devices. Cognitive psychologists have found that email alerts, IMs, and notifications of text messages distract people and undermine their ability to listen or focus mindfully (Begley, 2009). Interruptions fragment concentration so we have trouble resituating ourselves in whatever we were doing before the interruption. We may miss something, particularly if we were interrupted while performing a sequential task. In the summer of 2008 an airliner taking off from Madrid crashed and 153 people died. Crash investigations revealed the error resulted from interruptions in the preflight check (Begley, 2009).

Environmental distractions interfere with effective listening.

David Young-Wolff/PhotoEdit

Internal Obstacles

In addition to external interferences, listening may be hindered by four psychological obstacles.

Preoccupation   When we are preoccupied with our own thoughts and concerns, we can't focus on what someone else is saying. Perhaps you've attended a class right before taking a test in another class and later realized you got almost nothing out of the first class. That's because you were preoccupied with the upcoming test. If you are preoccupied with a report you need to prepare, you may not listen effectively to what a colleague says.

> **ANDY**   *I've been really stressed about finding a job. I've had lots of first interviews, but no callbacks and no offers. Even when I'm not interviewing—like when I'm with friends or in class—getting a job is in the back of my mind. It just stays there so that it's hard for me to really focus on anything else happening around me.*

Prejudgments   Another obstacle to effective listening is prejudgment of others or ideas. Anna Deavere Smith, who teaches listening to students in law and medical school, says that to listen, "I empty out myself. While I'm listening, my own judgments and prejudices certainly come up. But I know I won't get anything unless I get those things out of the way" (Arenson, 2002, p. 25).

Sometimes we decide in advance that others have nothing to offer us, so we tune them out. If a co-worker's ideas have not impressed you in the past, you might assume he or she will contribute nothing of value to a present conversation. The risk is that you might miss a good idea simply because you prejudged the other person. A recent study (Levine, 2004) found that, on average, doctors interrupt patients 23 seconds after patients have started explaining their medical situation or need. When doctors stop listening, they risk not getting information that could help them diagnose and treat patients. It's also important to keep an open mind when listening to communication regarding issues about which you already have opinions. You might miss important new information and perspectives if you don't put your prejudgments aside long enough to listen mindfully.

Another kind of prejudgment occurs when we assume we know what another feels, thinks, and is going to say, and we then assimilate his or her message into our preconceptions. This can lead us to misunderstand what the person means because we haven't really listened on his or her own terms. When we impose our prejudgments on others' words, we express a disregard for them and what they say. It may also deprive us of information, which can be costly in the workplace.

> **KEITH**   *My parents need a course in listening! They are so quick to tell me what I think and feel, or should think and feel, that they never hear what I do feel or think. Last year I approached them with the idea of taking a year off from school. Before I could even explain why I wanted to do this, Dad was all over me about being responsible and getting ahead in a career. Mom jumped on me about looking for an easy out and not having the gumption to stick with my studies. The whole point was that I wanted to work as an intern to get some hands-on experience in media production, which is my major. It had nothing to do with wanting an easy out or not trying to get ahead, but they couldn't even hear me through their own ideas about what I felt.*

Lack of Effort   It takes a lot of effort to listen well, and sometimes we aren't willing to invest it. It's hard work to be mindful—to focus closely on what others are saying, try to grasp their meanings, ask questions, and give responses so they know we are interested and involved. In addition to these activities, we have to

Different cultures have different norms for listening. These Nepalese villagers have been socialized to be quiet and attentive when another person is talking.

control distractions inside ourselves, monitor external noise, and perhaps fight fatigue or hunger (Isaacs, 1999).

Because active listening takes so much effort, we're not always able or willing to do it well. Sometimes we make a decision not to listen fully, perhaps because the person or topic isn't important to us. There are also times when we really want to listen but have trouble marshaling the necessary energy. If you can't summon the effort to listen well, you might suggest postponing interaction until a time when you will be able to invest effort in listening. If you explain to the other that you want to defer communication because you really are interested and want to be able to listen well, she or he is likely to appreciate your honesty and commitment to listening.

Failure to Accommodate Diverse Listening Styles   A final internal obstacle to effective listening is not recognizing and adjusting to different listening styles that reflect diverse communities and cultures (Brownell, 2002). The more we understand about different people's rules for listening, the more effectively we can signal our attention in ways they appreciate. For example, in the United States it is considered polite to make frequent but not continuous eye contact in conversation. Yet in some cultures, continuous eye contact is normative, and in others almost any eye contact is considered intrusive.

Even within the United States, there are differences in listening rules based on membership in racial, gender, and other social communities. Some African Americans engage in a more participative listening style than is typical of European Americans. Blacks who grew up attending traditional black churches may have learned to call out responses to a speaker as a way of showing their interest. A speaker who doesn't understand that this is a compliment in some African American communities is likely to misinterpret such responses as interruptions (Houston & Wood, 1996). In general, men provide fewer verbal and nonverbal clues that they are interested in what another person is saying. They may also respond primarily to the content level of meaning and tune in less to the relationship level of meaning. If you understand these general differences, you can adapt your listening style to particular people with whom you communicate. In addition, understanding diverse listening styles will improve your accuracy in interpreting what others mean by the ways they listen and signal interest.

> **LAVONDA**   *My boyfriend is the worst listener ever. Whenever I try to tell him about some problem I have, he becomes Mr. Answer Man. He tells me what to do or how to handle a situation. That doesn't do anything to help me with my feelings or even to let me know he hears what I'm feeling.*

We have seen that there are many obstacles to effective listening. Obstacles inherent in messages and situations include message overload, message complexity, and environmental distractions. In addition, there are four potential interferences inside us: preoccupation, prejudgment, lack of effort, and failure to recognize and adapt to diverse expectations of listening.

FORMS OF NONLISTENING

Now that we've discussed obstacles to effective listening, let's consider some forms of nonlistening. As you read about these six types of nonlistening, they may seem familiar because you and others probably engage in them at times.

Pseudolistening

Pseudolistening is pretending to listen. When we pseudolisten, we appear to be attentive, but really our minds are elsewhere. Sometimes we pseudolisten because we don't want to hurt a friend who is sharing experiences, even though we are not really interested. We also pseudolisten when communication bores us but we have to appear interested. Superficial talk in social situations and boring lectures are two communication situations in which we may consciously choose to pseudolisten so that we seem polite even though we really aren't involved. On the job, we often have to appear interested in what others say because of their positions.

> **SOURYANA**   *I do a lot of pseudolistening in classes where the teachers are boring. I pretend I'm taking notes on my laptop, but really I'm checking email or visiting my favorite blogs. Every now and then, I look up and nod at the teacher so I look like I'm listening.*

Monopolizing

Monopolizing is hogging the stage by continually focusing communication on ourselves instead of on the person talking. Two tactics are typical of monopolizing. One is *conversational rerouting,* in which a person shifts the topic of talk to himself or herself. For example, if Ellen tells her friend Marla that she's having trouble with her roommate, Marla might reroute the conversation by saying, "I know what you mean. My roommate is a real jerk." Then Marla would go off on an extended description of her own roommate problems. Rerouting takes the conversation away from the person who was talking.

Another monopolizing tactic is *diversionary interrupting,* which is interrupting in ways that disrupt the person speaking. Often, interrupting occurs in

COMMUNICATION in Your Life

In which situations are you most likely to pseudolisten?

combination with rerouting, so that a person interrupts and then directs the conversation to a new topic. In other cases, monopolizers fire questions that express doubt about what a speaker says ("What makes you think that?", "How can you be sure?", "Did anyone else see what you did?") or prematurely offer advice to show how much they know ("What you should do is. . . ," "You really blew that," "What I would have done is . . ."). Both rerouting and diversionary interrupting are techniques for monopolizing a conversation. They are the antithesis of good listening.

It's important to realize that not all interruptions are monopolizing tactics. We also interrupt to show interest, voice support, and ask for elaboration. This type of interrupting usually takes the form of minimal communication such as "umm," "go on," and "really?" that shows interest in the person who is speaking. Some research indicates that women are more likely than men to use interruptions to show interest and support (Anderson & Leaper, 1998; James & Clarke, 1993). Although it has been claimed that men use interruptions to assert themselves and gain control of conversations, existing research doesn't provide a clear picture of men's reasons for interrupting (Aires, 1996; Goldsmith & Fulfs, 1999).

Selective Listening

Selective listening is focusing on only particular parts of messages. One form of selective listening is focusing only on aspects of communication that interest us or correspond with our values. Students often become highly attentive when teachers say, "This is important for the test." We might give only half an ear to a friend until the friend mentions spring break, and then we tune in fully. In the workplace, we may become more attentive when communication addresses topics such as raises, layoffs, and other matters that may affect us directly.

Selective listening also occurs when we reject communication that bores us or makes us uncomfortable. For instance, we may not listen when others criticize us because we don't like what they say or when others point out good qualities of public officials we don't like. Being mindful allows you to curb the tendency to tune out messages you find boring or uncomfortable.

"WE NEED TO TALK, DENNIS, SO SIT DOWN AND LISTEN!"

Defensive Listening

Defensive listening involves perceiving personal attacks, criticisms, or hostile undertones in communication when no offense is intended. When we listen defensively, we read unkind motives into whatever others say. Some people are generally defensive, expecting insults and criticism from all quarters (a global, stable attribution). They hear threats and negative judgments in almost anything said to them. Thus, an innocent remark such as "Have you finished your report yet?" may be perceived as suspicion that you aren't doing your work.

Ambushing

Ambushing is listening carefully for the purpose of attacking. Unlike the other kinds of nonlistening we've discussed, ambushing involves very careful listening, but it isn't motivated by interest in another. Instead, ambushers listen intently to gather ammunition, which they then use to attack a speaker. Political candidates routinely do this as do trial attorneys. Each person listens carefully to the other for the sole purpose of later undercutting the opponent. Ambushing may be common in organizations that have a competitive culture in which employees feel they must outdo one another. Ambushing is not advisable when openness and genuine dialogue are wanted.

COMMUNICATION in Your Life

Have you ever interacted with an ambusher?

ERIC *One of the brothers at my house is a real ambusher. He's a pre-law major, and he loves to debate and win arguments. No matter what somebody talks about, this guy just listens long enough to mount a counterattack. He doesn't care about understanding others, just about beating them. I've quit talking when he's around.*

Literal Listening

The final form of nonlistening is **literal listening**, which is listening only to the content level of meaning and ignoring the relationship level of meaning. When we listen literally, we attend only to the content meaning and overlook what's being communicated about the other person or our relationship with that person.

In summary, nonlistening comes in many forms, including pseudolistening, ambushing speakers, monopolizing the stage, responding defensively, attending selectively, and listening literally. Being aware of forms of nonlistening enables you to exercise control over how you listen and thus how fully and mindfully you participate in communication with others.

ADAPTING LISTENING TO COMMUNICATION GOALS

Effective listening is tailored to specific purposes. Informational listening, critical listening, and relational listening entail different listening styles and behaviors. We'll discuss the specific attitudes and skills that support each type of listening.

Informational and Critical Listening

Much of the time, we listen to gain and evaluate information. We listen for information in classes, at political debates, in professional meetings, when important news stories are reported, and when we need guidance on everything from medical treatment to directions to a new place. In all of these cases, the primary purpose of **informational listening** is to gain and understand information.

Closely related to informational listening is **critical listening**, in which we listen to form opinions, to make judgments, or to evaluate people and ideas. Critical listening goes beyond gaining information; it requires us to analyze and evaluate information and the people who express it. We decide whether a speaker is credible and ethical by judging the thoroughness of a presentation, the accuracy of evidence, and the carefulness of reasoning. In Chapter 15, we discuss ways to evaluate evidence. Both informational and critical listening require us to be mindful and to organize and retain information.

Be Mindful   Informational and critical listening begins with the decision to be mindful. Don't let your mind wander when information gets complicated or confusing. Avoid going off on tangents; instead, stay focused on gaining as much information as you can. Later, you may want to ask questions if material wasn't clear even though you listened mindfully.

Control Obstacles   You can also minimize distractions when listening for information or critically listening. You might shut a window to block out traffic noises and empty your mind of preoccupations and prejudgments that can interfere with effective listening.

A park ranger is communicating important information about safety. Visitors who listen well will gain the knowledge they need to enjoy a mishap-free visit to the park.

David R. Frazier Photolibrary, Inc./Alamy

Ask Questions   Asking speakers to clarify or elaborate on their messages allows you to understand information you didn't grasp at first and enhances insight into content that you did comprehend. Questions also compliment speakers because they indicate that you are interested and want to know more.

When listening critically, it's appropriate to ask probing questions of speakers: "What is the source of your statistics on the rate of unemployment?" "Have you met with any policymakers who hold a point of view contrary to yours? What is their response to your proposals?" It's especially important and appropriate for non-native speakers to ask questions if they don't understand language (Lee, 1994, 2000). The English language is ambiguous, and it contains many colloquial phrases and slang expressions. People whose native language is not English may not understand idioms such as *in a heartbeat* (instantly) or *not on your life* (very unlikely). Sensitive communicators avoid or explain idioms when non-native speakers are present. If speakers don't offer explanations, listeners should request them.

Use Aids to Recall   To understand and remember important information, we can apply the principles of perception we discussed in Chapter 2. For instance, we learned that we tend to notice and recall stimuli that are repeated. To use this principle in everyday communication, repeat important ideas to yourself immediately after hearing them. Repetition can save you the embarrassment of having to ask people you just met to repeat their names.

Another way to increase retention is to use mnemonic (pronounced "nemonic," rhymes with *demonic*) devices, which are memory aids that create patterns for what you've heard. You probably already do this in studying. For instance, you could create the mnemonic MPSIRR, which is made up of the first letter of one word for each of the six parts of listening (**m**indfulness, **p**hysically receiving, **s**electing and organizing, **i**nterpreting, **r**esponding, **r**emembering). You can also invent mnemonics to help you recall personal information in communication. For example, KIM is a mnemonic to remember that Kim from Iowa is going into medicine.

Organize Information   Another technique to increase retention is to organize information. For example, suppose a friend tells you he is confused about long-range goals, doesn't know what he can do with a math major, wants to locate in the Midwest, wonders whether graduate school is necessary, likes small

COMMUNICATION HIGHLIGHT

Between a Rock and a Hard Place

Most of us have had the experience of being frustrated by a speaker who used specialized language that we couldn't understand. That experience is common for people in the United States for whom English is a second language.

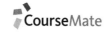

According to communication scholar Wen-Shu Lee (1994, 2000), phrases that often defy understanding for non-native speakers include *miss the boat* (Where is the boat? I don't see a boat.), *kick the bucket* (Who's kicking what bucket?), *chew the fat* (Why would you want to chew fat?), *between a rock and a hard place* (Why is someone in such a position?), and *hit the road* (Why would anybody hit a road?).

To learn more about English slang and people for whom English is a second language, use your Online Resources for *Communication in Our Lives* to access **WebLink 4.1**.

towns, needs some internships to try out different options, and wants a family eventually. You could regroup this stream of concerns into two categories: academic information (careers for math majors, graduate school, internship opportunities) and lifestyle preferences (Midwest, small town, family). Remembering those two categories allows you to retain the essence of your friend's concerns, even if you forget many of the specifics.

Relational Listening

Listening for information focuses on the content level of meaning in communication. Yet in some listening situations, we're as concerned or even more concerned with the relational level of meaning. We engage in **relational listening** when we listen to a friend's worries, let a romantic partner tell us about problems, counsel a co-worker, or talk with a parent about health concerns. Whenever supporting a person and maintaining a relationship are important, we should use skills that advance relational listening.

Be Mindful   The first requirement for effective relational listening is to be mindful. You'll recall that this was also the first step in informational and critical listening. When we're interested in relational meanings, however, a different kind of mindfulness is needed. Instead of focusing our minds on information, we need to concentrate on understanding feelings that may not be communicated explicitly. Thus, mindful relational listening calls on us to pay attention to what lies "between the words," the subtle clues to feelings and perceptions. As listening scholar Gerald Egan (1973, p. 228) notes, "Total listening is more than attending to another person's words. It is also listening to the meanings that are buried in the words and between the words and in the silences in communication."

Suspend Judgment   When listening to provide support, it's important to avoid highly judgmental responses. Although Western culture emphasizes evaluation, often we really don't need to judge others or what they feel, think, and do. Judgments add our evaluations to the others' experiences. When we do this, we move away from them and their feelings. To curb evaluative tendencies, ask whether you really need to pass judgment in the present moment.

Only if someone asks for our judgment should we offer it when we are listening to support. Even if our opinion is sought, we should express it in a way that doesn't devalue others. Sometimes people excuse strongly judgmental comments by saying, "You asked me to be honest" or "I mean this as constructive criticism." Too often, however, the judgments are not constructive and are harsher than candor requires. Good relational listening includes responses that support others.

JOSÉ   *My best friend makes it so easy for me to tell whatever is on my mind. She never puts me down or makes me feel stupid or weird. Sometimes I ask her what she thinks, and she has this way of telling me without making me feel wrong if I think differently. What it boils down to is respect. She respects me and herself, so she doesn't have to prove anything by acting better than me.*

Understand the Other Person's Perspective   One of the most important principles for effective relational listening is to grasp the other person's perspective. We can't respond sensitively to others until we understand their perspective and meanings. This means we have to step outside of our own point of view, at least long enough to understand how another person sees things.

Paraphrasing is a method of clarifying another's meaning or needs by reflecting our interpretations of his or her communication back to him or her. For example, a friend might confide, "I'm really scared my kid brother is messing around with drugs." We could paraphrase this way: "It sounds as if you think your brother may be experimenting with drugs." This paraphrase allows us to clarify whether the friend has any evidence of the brother's drug involvement. The response might be, "No, I don't have any real reason to suspect him, but I just worry because drugs are so pervasive in high schools now." This tells us that the friend's worries are more the issue than any evidence that his or her brother is trying drugs.

Another skill to help you understand others is the use of **minimal encouragers**. These are responses that express interest in hearing more and thus gently invite another person to elaborate. Examples of minimal encouragers are "Tell me more," "Really?" "Go on," "I'm with you," "Then what happened?" "Yeah?" and "I see." We can also use nonverbal minimal encouragers, such as a raised eyebrow to show we're involved, a nod to indicate we understand, or widened eyes to indicate we're fascinated.

Minimal encouragers indicate that we are listening, following, and interested. They encourage others to keep talking so that we can more fully understand what they mean. Keep in mind that these are *minimal* encouragers. Effective minimal encouragers are brief interjections that prompt, but do not interfere with, the flow of another's talk.

To enhance understanding of what another feels or wants from us we can ask questions. For instance, we might ask, "How do you feel about that?" or "Do you want to talk about how to handle the situation, or do you just want to air the issues?" Asking directly signals that we really want to help and allows others to tell us how we can best do that.

Express Support   Once you have understood another's meanings and perspective, then relational listening should focus on communicating support. This doesn't necessarily require you to agree with another's perspective or ideas. What it does call on you to do is to communicate support for the person. To illustrate how we can support a person even if we don't agree with his or her position, consider the following exchange between a son and his father.

SON: Dad, I'm changing my major from business to drama.
FATHER: Oh.
SON: Yeah, I've wanted to do it for some time, but I kept holding back because acting isn't as safe as accounting.
FATHER: That's certainly true.
SON: Yeah, but I've decided to do it anyway. What do you think about this?

**COMMUNICATION
in Your Life**

Practice paraphrasing and minimal encouragers when you are listening, and note how doing so affects interaction.

FATHER: It worries me. Starving actors are a dime a dozen. It just won't provide you with any economic security.

SON: I understand acting isn't as secure as business, but it's what I really want to do.

FATHER: Tell me what you feel about acting—why it matters so much to you.

SON: It's the most creative, totally fulfilling thing I do. I've tried to get interested in business, but I just don't love that like I do acting. I feel like I have to give this a try, or I'll always wonder if I could have made it. If I don't get somewhere in 5 or 6 years, I'll rethink my career options.

FATHER: Couldn't you finish your business degree and get a job and act on the side?

SON: No. I've got to give acting a full shot—give it everything I have, to see if I can make it.

FATHER: Well, I still have reservations, but I guess I can understand having to try something that matters this much to you. I'm just concerned that you'll lose years of your life to something that doesn't work out.

SON: Well, I'm kinda concerned about that too, but I'm more worried about wasting years of my life in a career that doesn't turn me on than about trying to make a go of the one that does.

FATHER: I can understand that. I wouldn't make the choice you're making, but I respect your decision and your guts for taking a big gamble.

This dialogue illustrates several principles of effective relational listening. First, notice that the father's first two comments are minimal encouragers that invite his son to elaborate thoughts and feelings. The father also encourages his son to explain how he feels. Later, the father suggests a compromise solution, but his son rejects that, and the father respects the son's position. Importantly, the father makes his own position clear, but he separates his personal stance from his respect for his son's right to make his own choices. Sometimes it's difficult to listen openly and nonjudgmentally, particularly if we don't agree with the person speaking, as in the example. However, if your goal is to support another person, then sensitive, responsive involvement without evaluation is important to effective listening.

Listening to discriminate is vital when doctors communicate with patients.

Fancy/Veer/Corbis/Jupiter Images

Other Purposes of Listening

Listening for information to evaluate critically and listening to support others are two major listening purposes. In addition, we will briefly discuss other listening goals.

Listening for Pleasure   Sometimes we listen for pleasure, as when we attend concerts or play CDs. Listening for enjoyment is also a primary purpose when we go to comedy shows or pay attention to jokes an acquaintance tells. When we are listening for pleasure, we don't need to concentrate on organizing and remembering as much as when we listen for information, although retention is important if you want to be able to tell a joke to someone else later. Yet listening for pleasure does require mindfulness, hearing, and interpretation.

Listening to Discriminate   In some situations, we listen to make fine discriminations in sounds to draw valid conclusions and act appropriately in response. For example, doctors listen to discriminate when they use stethoscopes to diagnose heart functioning or chest congestion. Parents listen to discriminate among a baby's cries for attention, food, or a diaper change. Subtle differences in crying signal distinct needs in infants, and parents need to be able to discriminate accurately. Skilled mechanics can distinguish between engine sounds that most people cannot detect. Mindfulness and keen hearing abilities are particularly important when listening to discriminate.

BEYOND THE CLASSROOM

Let's take the material in this chapter beyond the classroom by thinking about how what you've learned about listening might apply to the workplace, ethical choices, and engagement with the broader world.

1. **Workplace.** The chapter identified six forms of nonlistening. To what extent are any of these types of nonlistening evident in your current workplace or to what extent were they present in a former workplace? Reflect on particular instances of nonlistening in the workplace: Can you identify any causes or conditions that were common to them? Do you recognize any costs of the nonlistening in terms of productivity, relations among workers, and so forth? (You could apply this same analysis to a classroom or other campus location.)

2. **Ethics.** At the end of Chapter 1, I invited you to read NCA's Credo for Ethical Communication by clicking **WebLink 1.4.** Reread that now as **WebLink 4.2.** Using that credo as a guideline, develop a Credo for Ethical Listening that identifies both what listeners must do and what they cannot do if they wish to listen ethically.

3. **Engagement.** American Public Media developed a radio program called "The Story," which presents interviews with people who have interesting stories to tell about their lives. Most of the people interviewed are not celebrities; they aren't famous; and they aren't particularly heroic. In other words, many of them are regular people, but the interviewer uses excellent listening skills to bring the interviewees out and make their stories sing. Click **WebLink 4.3** to find the home page for "The Story." Listen to one podcast of a story. As you listen, pay particular attention to the interviewer: How does he demonstrate engagement with the interviewee? How does he encourage the interviewee to expand on points and to move along with the story?

CHAPTER SUMMARY

According to Zeno of Citium, an ancient philosopher, "We have been given two ears and but a single mouth, in order that we may hear more and talk less." Thousands of years later, we can still learn from his comment. Listening is a major and vital part of communication, yet too often we don't consider it as important as talking. In this chapter, we've explored the complex and demanding process of listening.

We began by distinguishing between hearing—physically receiving messages—and listening. The former is a straightforward physiological process that doesn't take effort on our part. Listening, in contrast, is a complicated and active process involving being mindful, hearing, selecting and organizing, interpreting, responding, and remembering. Listening well takes commitment and skill.

To understand what interferes with effective listening, we discussed obstacles in situations and messages and obstacles in us. Listening is hindered by message overload, complexity of material, and external noise in communication contexts. In addition, listening can be hampered by our preoccupations and prejudgments, lack of effort, and failure to recognize differences in listening styles. These obstacles to listening give rise to various types of nonlistening, including pseudolistening, monopolizing, selective listening, defensive listening, ambushing, and literal listening. Each of these forms of nonlistening signals that we aren't fully present in interaction.

We also discussed different purposes for listening and identified the skills and attitudes that advance each purpose. Informational listening and critical listening require us to adopt a mindful attitude and to think critically, organize and evaluate information, clarify understanding by asking questions, and develop aids to retention of complex material. Relational listening also requires mindfulness, but it calls for other, distinct listening skills. Suspending judgment, paraphrasing, giving minimal encouragers, and expressing support enhance the effectiveness of relational listening.

APPLYING COMMUNICATION IN OUR LIVES

The key concepts, For Further Reflection and Discussion questions, and Experiencing Communication in Our Lives case study that follow will help you review, reflect on, and extend the information and ideas presented in this chapter. These resources, and a diverse selection of additional study tools, are also available as Online Resources for *Communication in Our Lives*. Your Online Resources include CourseMate, a student workbook, interactive video activities, audio study tools, a book companion website, Speech Builder Express, Speech Studio, and InfoTrac College Edition. For more information or to access this book's online resources, visit **www.cengage.com/login.**

KEY CONCEPTS

ambushing, 85
critical listening, 86
defensive listening, 85
hearing, 75
informational listening, 86

listening, 75
literal listening, 85
mindfulness, 76
minimal encouragers, 89
monopolizing, 83

paraphrasing, 89
pseudolistening, 83
relational listening, 88
selective listening, 84

FOR FURTHER REFLECTION AND DISCUSSION

1. Select one type of nonlistening in which you engage, and work to minimize its occurrence.

2. How do you know whether someone is really listening to you when you are talking online? What signals mindful listening in these settings?

3. What ethical principles guide different listening purposes? What different ethical responsibilities accompany listening for information and listening relationally?

4. Who is your prototype of an excellent listener? Describe what the person does that makes him or her effective. Do the person's listening behaviors fit with the guidelines offered in this chapter?

5. Dave Isay set out to make an oral history of the United States by listening to the stories of everyday people—not politicians, celebrities, or CEOs, but regular people. By January of 2009, StoryCorps had recorded more than 40,000 stories of ordinary Americans—what they value and how they understand life. Isay gathered a number of these stories into a book, which he titled *Listening as an Act of Love* (2008).

6. If you want to work on your listening skills, you might be interested in Madelyn Burley-Allen's book *Listening: The Forgotten Skill* (1995). She provides a self-teaching guide for improving listening effectiveness.

7. A website that offers guidelines for listening better is available by clicking on **WebLink 4.4.** CourseMate

SHARPEN YOUR SKILL

1. Improving Recall

Apply the principles we've discussed to enhance memory.

- The next time you meet someone, repeat his or her name to yourself three times after you are introduced. Do you remember the name?
- After your next class, take 15 minutes to review your notes in a quiet place. Read them aloud so that you hear as well as see the main ideas. Does this increase your retention of material?
- Invent mnemonics to create patterns that help you remember basic information in a message.
- Organize ideas into categories. To remember the main ideas of this chapter, you might use major subheadings to form categories: listening process, obstacles to listening, and listening goals. The mnemonic LOG (i.e., listening, obstacles, goals) could help you remember those topics.

2. Learn from the Pros

One way to improve your listening skills is to observe people who are experts at effective listening. Watch a television program that features interviews—Sunday morning news shows and programs such as *20/20* and *60 Minutes*. Select one interview to observe, and answer the following questions about it:

- How does the interviewer phrase questions to encourage the interviewee to talk? Are questions open or closed, biased or unbiased?
- How is the interviewer seated in relation to the interviewee—how close, at what angle?
- Does the interviewer paraphrase the interviewee's responses?
- Does the interviewer make minimal responses?
- How, if at all, does the interviewer show that she or he understands and respects the interviewee's perspective?
- How, if at all, does the interviewer demonstrate attentiveness?

EXPERIENCING COMMUNICATION IN OUR LIVES

CASE STUDY: *Family Hour*

A video of the conversation scripted here is featured in your Chapter 4 Online Resources for *Communication in Our Lives*. Select "Family Hour" to watch the video. Improve your own communication skills by reading, watching, and evaluating this communication encounter.

© Cengage Learning

Over spring break, 20-year-old Josh visits his father. He wants to convince his family to support him in joining a fraternity that has given him a bid. On his second day home, after dinner Josh decides to broach the topic. His dad is watching the evening news on television when Josh walks into the living room. Josh sits down and opens the conversation.

JOSH: Well, something pretty interesting has happened at school this semester.

DAD: I'll bet you found a girlfriend, right? I was about your age when your mother and I started dating, and that was the best part of college. I still remember how she looked on our first date. She was young, and then she was very slender and pretty. I saw her and thought she was the loveliest thing I'd ever seen. Before long, we were a regular item. Yep, it was about when I was 20, like you are now.

JOSH: Well, I haven't found a girlfriend, but I did get a bid from Sigma Chi.

DAD: Sigma Chi. What is that—a fraternity?

JOSH: Yeah, it's probably the coolest fraternity on campus. I attended some rush parties this semester—mainly out of curiosity, just to see what they were like.

DAD: Why'd you do that? Before you ever went to college, I told you to steer clear of fraternities. They cost a lot of money, and they distract you from your studies.

JOSH: Well, I know you told me to steer clear of fraternities, but I did check a few out. I'd be willing to take a job to help pay the membership fee and monthly dues. Besides, it's not that much more expensive when you figure I'd be eating at the house, and . . .

DAD: Do you realize how much it costs just for you to go to that school? I'm paying $14,000 a year! When I went to school, I had to go to state college because my parents couldn't afford to send me to the school of my choice. You have no idea how lucky you are to be going to the school you wanted to go to and have me footing all the bills.

JOSH: But we could work it out so that a fraternity wouldn't cost you anything. Like I said, I . . .

DAD: If you want to take a job, fine. I could use some help paying your tuition and fees. But you're not taking a job just so you can belong to a party house.

JOSH: I thought they were just party houses too, until I attended rush. Now, I went to several houses that were that way, but Sigma Chi isn't. I really liked the brothers at Sigma Chi. They're interesting and friendly and fun, so I was thrilled when . . .

DAD: I don't want to hear about it. You're not joining a fraternity. I told you what happened when I was in college. I joined one, and pretty soon my Dean's List grades dropped to Cs and Ds. When you live in a fraternity house, you can't study like you can in your dorm room or the library. I should know. I tried it and found out the hard way. There's no need for you to repeat my mistake.

JOSH: But, Dad, I'm not you. Joining a fraternity wouldn't necessarily mean that my grades . . .

DAD: What do you mean, you're not me? You think I wasn't a good student before I joined the fraternity? You think you're so smart you can party all the time and still make good grades? Let me tell you something, I thought that too, and, boy, was I ever wrong! As soon as I joined the house, it was party time all the time. There was always music blaring and girls in the house and poker games—anything but studying. I wasn't stupid. It's just not an atmosphere that encourages academic work.

JOSH: I'd like to give it a try. I really like these guys, and I think I can handle being in Sigma Chi and still . . .

DAD: Well, you think wrong!

QUESTIONS FOR ANALYSIS AND DISCUSSION

You can also answer these questions and see my responses to them online via your Online Resources for Chapter 4.

1. What forms of ineffective listening are evident in this dialogue?

2. If you could advise Josh's father on listening effectively, what would you tell him to do differently?

3. Would you offer any advice to Josh on how he could listen to his father more effectively?

> A different language is a different vision of life.
>
> Federico Fellini

Polka Dot Images/Jupiter Images

The Verbal Dimension of Communication

Perhaps you are familiar with the story of Helen Keller. As an infant, she contracted an illness that left her deaf and blind. Trapped in her silent world, Helen behaved more like an animal than a human infant. She reacted to whatever stimuli were in her immediate environment but did not show any ability to self-reflect, grasp meanings, or communicate with others. Later in life, she achieved remarkable things: She graduated with honors from Radcliffe, authored nearly a dozen books, met 12 United States presidents, learned to read and write four languages other than English, and lectured throughout the United States, Europe, and Asia.

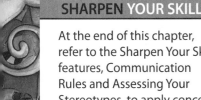

SHARPEN YOUR SKILL

At the end of this chapter, refer to the Sharpen Your Skill features, Communication Rules and Assessing Your Stereotypes, to apply concepts from Chapter 5.

What allowed Helen to move from reacting only to immediate stimuli to being an engaging, reflective person who connected with a wide range of people? Language. It was learning to use language that opened the human world of meaning for Helen. When Helen was 7, her life changed because Annie Sullivan became her teacher. Helen was smart, so Annie was able to teach her the manual alphabet quickly. In just a few weeks with Annie, Helen was able to use her hands to spell words, but she didn't understand what they meant. She didn't grasp that the actions of her or Annie's fingers were communicating meaning.

That changed in one electric moment. While one of Helen's hands was under the spout of a water pump, Annie spelled W-A-T-E-R into her other hand. Suddenly Helen got it; she understood that the actions of the fingers meant something; she realized she could actually communicate with others. Once Helen understood how to communicate, she was unstoppable and went on to accomplish amazing things in her life.

In this chapter, we take a close look at language. We begin by defining symbols, which are the basis of language. Second, we explore principles of verbal communication. Next, we consider what language allows us to do. The final section of the chapter focuses on guidelines for effective use of language.

copyright L.A. Holman 1907

Library of Congress Prints and Reproduction Division [LC-USZ62-69879]

Learning to use language opened the human world of meaning for Helen Keller.

SYMBOLS AND MEANING

Symbols are representations of people, events, and other phenomena. For instance, the word *house* is a symbol that stands for a type of building. *Total quality management* is a verbal symbol that represents a specific managerial philosophy. *Cyberspace, hyperlink, instant messaging,* and *blog* are words we have coined to represent phenomena that accompany computer technologies.

Language and much nonverbal behavior are symbolic. Art, music, company logos, and objects also can be symbols that stand for feelings, thoughts, and experiences. The key to understanding symbols is to realize that they are arbitrary, ambiguous, abstract ways of representing things.

Symbols Are Arbitrary

Symbols are **arbitrary**, which means they are not intrinsically connected to what they represent. For instance, the word *book* has no necessary or natural connection to what you are reading now. We could substitute a different word, as long as we agreed it would stand for what we now call a book. Certain words seem right because as a society we agree to use them in particular ways, but they have no natural correspondence to their referents.

COMMUNICATION **HIGHLIGHT**

Code Talkers

CourseMate

During World War II, a special group of soldiers serving on Iwo Jima developed a private code that was never broken by enemy intelligence. Because all the soldiers in this group were Navajo Indians, the code they devised was based on the Navajo language, an oral language that had never been written down and was not understood by non-Navajos. Dubbed "code talkers," these soldiers invented a 400-word code that was extremely secure. Drawing on the strong nature theme in Navajo life and language, the code included the Navajo words

AP Photo/The Gallup Independent, Jeffery Jones

for owl (observer), hawk (dive bomber), and egg (bomb).

To learn more about the code talkers, use your Online Resources for *Communication in Our Lives* to access **WebLink 5.1.** This site provides facts about the history and work of the Navajo code talkers, as well as related links, including a dictionary of terms used by the code talkers.

Because language is arbitrary, we can create private communication codes. For example, in most organizations employees use some specialized terms that are not understood by outsiders. Similarly, most couples have terms that are not understood, and are not meant to be understood, by people outside the relationship. This allows them to pass private messages in public settings. Coded language also allows people to communicate confidential information. Two primary tasks of military intelligence are to invent secret, unbreakable codes and to break the secret codes of others.

Because symbols are arbitrary, their meanings can change over time. In the 1950s, *gay* meant "lighthearted and merry;" today it is generally understood to mean men who are sexually oriented toward men. Until the 1980s, the word *apple* was assumed to refer to a fruit, but today it is equally likely to refer to a computer company and its products.

New words and terms were coined in response to changes in business and the professions. *Heads up* means "I'm giving you some information in advance so you'll be prepared for something that's coming later." Today, many people work out of *virtual offices*, a term nobody had heard 20 years ago. The word *downsize* didn't exist 15 years ago, yet today it is commonly used. We used to hear that companies laid people off; today we hear that companies have *downsized* or *rightsized*. The word *friend* was invariably a noun until people on social network sites such as Facebook and MySpace began using it as a verb—one person *friends* another on the site. Online communication is punctuated by terms that didn't exist even 10 years ago: *buddy list, IM, punt* (to cause another user's screen to freeze), *cobweb* (a website that is never updated), and *meatspace* (the physical world as distinct from the virtual world).

COMMUNICATION in Your Life

As a child, did you belong to a club that had a secret code?

Symbols Are Ambiguous

Symbols are also **ambiguous**, which means their meanings aren't fixed in an absolute way. The meanings of words vary based on the values and experiences of those who use them. *Government regulation* may mean positive assistance to citizens who are suffering from pollutants emitted by a chemical company. To owners of the chemical company, however, *government regulation* may mean costly and undesired requirements to reduce pollution. To one person, a *good friend* means someone to hang out with; to another person, it means someone to confide in. *Affirmative action* means different things to people who have experienced racial or sexual discrimination and to those who haven't. Although the words are the same, their meanings vary according to individuals' identities and experiences.

Although words don't mean exactly the same thing to everyone, many symbols have an agreed-on range of meanings within a culture. Thus, we all understand that *dog* means a four-footed creature, but each of us also has personal meanings for the word based on dogs we have known and our experiences with them. We've all experienced dynamic speakers, yet we may differ in our notions of what concrete attitudes and behaviors would lead us to label a speaker *dynamic* (remember the abstraction ladder we discussed in Chapter 2).

The ambiguity of symbols explains why misunderstandings so often occur. At work, team members may have different meanings for the same words. In personal relationships, too, the ambiguity of words is a source of frequent misunderstandings. Ambiguity often surfaces in friendships and romantic relationships. Martina tells her boyfriend that he's not being attentive, meaning that she wants him to listen more closely to what she says. However, he infers that she wants him to call more often. Similarly, spouses often have different meanings for "doing their share" of home chores. To most women, it means doing half of the work, but some men may see it as doing more than their fathers did (Hochschild & Machung, 2003; Wood, 1998).

To minimize the problems that ambiguity can cause, we should be as clear as possible in communication. In the previous example, Martina asked her boyfriend to be more attentive, but she and he had different ideas about what that meant. Thus, it's more effective to say, "I would like you to look at me and give feedback when I'm talking" than "I wish you'd be more attentive."

The ambiguity of language may also cause problems in groups, organizations, and public speaking. A team leader who asks members to be "more responsible" may get a variety of responses, depending on what the ambiguous term *responsible* means to different members. The term *restructuring* may be interpreted to mean firing employees, closing locations, or reducing bonuses and salaries. Your supervisor tells you it's important to be "a team player," which you assume means you should cooperate with co-workers. However, your supervisor may mean that you are expected to initiate and participate in project teams on the job. After you give a public presentation, someone suggests you should be "more forceful," but does that mean you should use more facial expressions, greater vocal inflection, stronger evidence, or more motion?

Symbols Are Abstract

Finally, symbols are **abstract,** which means not concrete or tangible. They stand for ideas, people, events, objects, feelings, and so forth, but they are not the things they represent. In Chapter 2, we discussed the abstraction ladder, whereby we move farther and farther away from concrete reality. The symbols we use vary in abstractness. *Managerial potential* is an abstract term. *Organizational and presentational skill* is less abstract. Even more concrete expressions are *experience in collaborating with others, speaking to large groups,* and *organizing project teams.*

> **ADIVA**   *My resident assistant told us we must observe "quiet hours" from 7 to 10 each night so that people can study. But everyone on my hall plays music and talks during quiet hours. My adviser told me I needed to take courses in social diversity, so I took a class in oral traditions of Asian cultures. Then my adviser told me that is a non-Western civilization course, not one in social diversity.*

As our symbols become increasingly abstract, the potential for confusion mushrooms. One way this happens is through overgeneralization. For example, the assertion that "environmentalists despise big business" is overly general. Few environmentalists dislike all big business; many respect the goals and the efforts to protect the environment made by a substantial number of big companies and industries, and Sierra Club, one of the premiere environmental groups, has even partnered with companies such as Clorox.

Overly abstract language can also complicate personal relationships. Couple counselor Aaron Beck (1988) reports that generalizations can distort how partners think about a relationship. Statements such as "You never go along with my preferences" or "You always interrupt me" are overgeneralizations that are not entirely accurate. Yet the symbols partners use frame how they think about their experiences. Thus, if one partner thinks the other always interrupts, she or he is likely to perceive the other as constantly interrupting. We are more likely to notice behaviors that are consistent with our labels for people than behaviors that are inconsistent (Fincham & Bradbury, 1987). When we say that a partner never listens, we're likely to notice the times he or she doesn't seem to listen and likely not to perceive all the times when he or she listens carefully.

To develop your ability to reduce the abstractness of language, complete the activity "Reducing the Abstractness of Language" via your Chapter 5 Online Resources for *Communication in Our Lives.*

Because symbols are arbitrary, ambiguous, and abstract, they can represent complex ideas and feelings in ways that allow us to share our ideas with others. At the same time, symbols have the potential to create misunderstandings. When we understand that symbols are ambiguous, arbitrary, and abstract, we can guard against their potential to hinder communication.

COMMUNICATION in Your Life

What is one overgeneralization that really annoys you?

CourseMate

COMMUNICATION HIGHLIGHT

Lost in Translation

Language doesn't always translate well. Consider these examples of English terms that turned out to mean something very different in other cultures (Leaper, 1999).

When the U.S. manufacturer of the soft drink Fresca decided to export the product to Mexico, sales were dismal. It turned out the word *fresca* in Spanish sometimes is used to describe a woman who is aggressive, brash, or unfeminine in her behavior—hardly an image that prompts buying a soft drink.

Don't say, "I'm a Pepper" in the United Kingdom. The manufacturer of the soft drink Dr. Pepper discovered that this didn't work because *pepper* is British slang for "prostitute."

When General Motors exported its popular Chevrolet Nova to South America, there were problems. In Spanish, *no va* means "does not go"—not a very good advertisement for a car!

For years, Allstate Insurance Company has run an ad that shows a person holding out his or her hands while the voice-over promises, "You're in good hands with Allstate." This ad didn't work in Germany; there, two hands held out signify begging, not offering security and protection.

PRINCIPLES OF VERBAL COMMUNICATION

Three principles clarify how we use verbal communication and how it affects us.

Interpretation Creates Meaning

Because symbols are abstract, ambiguous, and arbitrary, their meanings aren't self-evident or absolute. Instead, we have to interpret the meaning of symbols. We construct meanings in the process of interacting with others and through dialogues we carry on in our own heads (Duck, 1994; Shotter, 1993).

If a work associate says, "Let's go to dinner after work," the comment could mean a variety of things. It could be an invitation to explore transforming the work relationship into a friendship. It could be a veiled request for a strategy session regarding some issue in the workplace. It might also indicate that the person issuing the invitation is interested in a romantic relationship. Does "I'm sorry" mean I am sorry for something I did? Or does it mean I'm sorry about something that happened, even though it wasn't my fault? We have to invest effort to interpret words and assign meanings to them. By extension, effective communicators are alert to possible misunderstandings, and they check with others to see whether meanings match.

Communication Is Rule Guided

Verbal communication is patterned by unspoken but broadly understood rules (Argyle & Henderson, 1984; Shimanoff, 1980). **Communication rules** are shared understandings of what communication means and what kinds of

communication are and are not appropriate in various situations. For the most part, rules aren't explicit or intentionally constructed. In the course of interacting with our families and others, we unconsciously absorb rules that guide how we communicate and how we interpret others' communication.

Two kinds of rules guide communication (Cronen, Pearce, & Snavely, 1979; Pearce, Cronen, & Conklin, 1979). **Regulative rules** specify when, how, where, and with whom to talk about certain things. For instance, we follow regulative rules for turn taking in conversation. In formal contexts, we usually know not to interrupt when someone else is speaking, but in more informal settings interruptions may be appropriate. Talking during formal speeches is appropriate in some contexts, as in traditional black churches and public meetings. Some families have a rule that people can't argue at the dinner table or that conflict should be avoided (Honeycutt, Woods, & Fontenot, 1993; Jones & Gallois, 1989).

Regulative rules also define when, where, and with whom it's appropriate or necessary to communicate in particular ways. Some couples have the rule that it's okay to kiss in private but not in public. On the job, there are often unwritten regulative rules that specify that people with higher positions may interrupt subordinates but that subordinates may not interrupt organizational superiors. Regulative rules in the workplace may also stipulate that employees are expected to show interest and respect when higher-ups communicate.

Constitutive rules define what communication means by telling us how to count certain kinds of communication. We learn that paying attention counts as showing respect, hugging counts as affection, and interrupting counts as being rude. We learn it is appropriate to applaud when a speaker is introduced and after she or he finishes a presentation.

Social interactions tend to follow rules that are widely shared in a specific society. Interaction between intimates also follows rules, but these may not be shared by the culture as a whole. Intimate partners negotiate private rules to guide how they communicate and what certain things mean (Wood, 2000). Couples craft personal rules that specify how to argue, express love, make decisions, request favors, and spend time together (Beck, 1988; Fitzpatrick, 1988; Wood, 2006a).

In the process of interacting with others, we learn communication rules, usually without realizing it. New employees learn the rules for communicating with each other and with superiors as they interact with co-workers and internalize the organizational culture. They learn whether teamwork or individual initiatives are rewarded and what degree of socializing is expected on the job. We may not realize that rules exist until one is broken and we become aware that we had an expectation. A study by Victoria DeFrancisco (1991) revealed that husbands consistently interrupted wives and were unresponsive to topics wives initiated. The couples were unaware of the rules, but their communication nonetheless followed the pattern. Becoming aware of communication rules empowers you to change those that don't promote healthy interaction and relationships.

MILAN *There's this funny pattern with the guys I hang out with. It starts when one of us says, "Let's go get something to eat." Then somebody suggests Mexican food, and someone else says he hates it. Another guy says we should get a pizza, and someone else says they're too expensive. Somebody says burgers, and one of the others groans. Then we decide to fix something at the apartment. Honestly, we go through this routine two or three times a week, and it's always the same.*

Punctuation Affects Meaning

We punctuate communication to create meaning. In writing, we use periods to define where ideas stop and start. Similarly, in interpersonal communication, **punctuation** is the mental mark of the beginnings and endings of particular interactions (Watzlawick, Beavin, & Jackson, 1967). For example, when a teacher steps to the front of a classroom, that punctuates the beginning of the class. When the CEO enters a room, that punctuates the beginning of a meeting. When a speaker says, "Thank you for your attention" and folds notes, that punctuates the end of the formal speech.

When we don't agree on punctuation, problems may arise. A common instance of conflicting punctuation is the demand–withdraw pattern illustrated in Figure 5.1 (Bergner & Bergner, 1990; Caughlin & Vangelisti, 2000; Wegner, 2005). This occurs when one person tries to express closeness and the

What regulative and constitutive rules guided mealtime conversation in your family when you were growing up?

Kevin Laubacher/Taxi/Getty Images

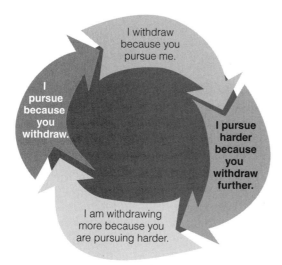

Figure 5.1
The Demand–Withdraw Pattern

other strives to maintain autonomy by avoiding interaction. The more one partner pushes for personal talk, the further the other withdraws. Each partner punctuates the beginning of the interaction with the other's behavior. Thus, the demander thinks, "I pursue because you withdraw," and the withdrawer thinks, "I withdraw because you pursue."

Effective communicators realize that people don't always agree on punctuation. When they punctuate differently, they ascribe different meanings to what is happening between them. To break out of destructive cycles such as demand–withdraw, partners need to discuss how each of them is punctuating the experience. This reminds us of a guideline discussed previously: Effective communication includes perspective taking. Steven's comment illustrates the demand–withdraw pattern and a lack of perspective taking between him and his parents.

> **STEVEN**   *My parents say I am irresponsible if I don't tell them about something I do. So then they probe me and call more often to check up on me. I hate that kind of intrusion, so I don't return their calls and I sidestep questions. That makes them call more and ask more questions. That makes me clam up more. And we just keep going in circles.*

SYMBOLIC ABILITIES

Because we use symbols, we live in a world of ideas and meanings. Instead of just reacting to our concrete environments, we think about them and sometimes transform them. In much the same way, we don't simply accept ourselves as we are but continuously work to change and grow. Philosophers of language have identified five ways symbolic capacities affect our lives (Cassirer, 1944; Langer, 1953, 1979). As we discuss each, we'll consider how to realize the constructive power of symbols and minimize the problems they can generate.

Symbols Define

We use symbols to define experiences, people, relationships, feelings, and thoughts. As we saw in Chapter 2, the definitions we impose on phenomena shape what they mean to us. When we label people, we focus attention on particular aspects of them, and we necessarily obscure other aspects of who they are. We might define a person as an environmentalist, a teacher, a gourmet cook, and a Republican. Each way of classifying the person directs our attention to certain, and not other, aspects of identity. We might discuss wilderness legislation with the environmentalist, talk about testing with the teacher, swap recipes with the cook, and discuss politics or not, depending on our own political stance, with the Republican. We tend to interact with people according to how we define and classify them.

Totalizing is using a single label to represent the totality of a person. We fixate on one symbol to define someone and fail to recognize many other aspects of who he or she is. Some people totalize gay men and lesbians as if sexual orientation were the only important facet of a person (Wood, 1998). Interestingly, we don't totalize heterosexuals on the basis of their sexuality. Totalizing also occurs when we dismiss people by saying, "He's a liberal," "She's old," "She's preppy," or "He's a jock." When we totalize others, we negate most of who they are by spotlighting a single aspect of their identity.

NANYA *I'm Indian, and that's all a lot of people here see in me. They see that my skin is dark and I wear a sari, and they put me in the category "foreigner" or, if they are observant, "Indian." They mark me off as different, foreign, not like them, and they can't see anything else about me. How would they feel if I categorized them as "Americans" and didn't see their individual qualities?*

The power of symbols to define and evaluate phenomena is evident in the nonverbal communication at public events, such as this one at President Ronald Reagan's funeral.

© Spencer Platt/Getty Images News/Getty Images

Symbols influence how we think and feel about experiences and people. In one study, colleagues and I asked romantic couples how they defined differences between them (Wood, Dendy, Dordek, Germany, & Varallo, 1994). We found that some people define differences as positive forces that energize a relationship. Others define differences as problems or barriers to closeness. There was a direct connection between how partners defined differences and how they dealt with them. Partners who labeled differences as constructive approached disagreements with curiosity and a belief that they would grow by discussing differences. On the other hand, partners who labeled differences as problems tended to deny differences or avoid talking about them.

COMMUNICATION HIGHLIGHT

Blaxicans

What do you call yourself when language has no name that fits you? That didn't stump a young woman from San Diego whose mother was Mexican and whose father was African. She coined the term *Blaxican* to describe her ethnicity (Rodriguez, 2003). We're likely to see more creative language as multiracial children decide how to name themselves.

How we think about relationships directly affects what happens in them (Duck, 1994; Honeycutt, et al., 1993). People who dwell on negative thoughts about relationships heighten awareness of relationship flaws and diminish perceptions of strengths (Cloven & Roloff, 1991). Conversely, partners who focus on good facets of their relationships are more conscious of positive qualities of partners and relationships and less aware of imperfections (Bradbury & Fincham, 1990; Fletcher & Fincham, 1991; Seligman, 2002).

> **CHERYL**   *About 3 years ago, my husband and I were seriously considering divorce. We decided to try marital counseling first, and that saved our marriage. The counselor helped us see that we noticed problems, aggravations, and faults in each other and didn't see all of the good qualities in each other and our relationship. Now we have a "warts-and-all" philosophy, which means we accept each other, warts and all. Changing how we think about our marriage really has changed what it is for us.*

As Cheryl's commentary indicates, our definitions of relationships can create self-fulfilling prophecies. Because verbal language is ambiguous, arbitrary, and abstract, there are multiple ways we can define any experience, person, relationship, policy, or idea. Once we select a label, we tend to see what our label spotlights and to overlook what it doesn't highlight. This suggests an ethical principle for using and interpreting language: We should consider what the language that we and others use includes as well as what it excludes.

Symbols Evaluate

Symbols are not neutral. They are laden with values. We tend to describe people we like with language that accents their good qualities and downplays their flaws. The reverse is generally true of descriptions of people we don't like. My friend is *casual*; someone I don't like is *sloppy*. Restaurants use language that is designed to heighten the attractiveness of menu items. "Tender lobster accented with drawn butter" sounds more appetizing than "crustacean murdered by being boiled alive and then drenched in saturated fat."

Of course, there are degrees of evaluation in language. We might describe people who speak their minds as *assertive, outspoken, straightforward, blunt,* or *rude*. Each word has a distinct connotation. In recent years, we have become more sensitive to how the evaluative nature of symbols can hurt people. Most people with disabilities prefer not to be called *disabled* because that tends to totalize them in terms of a disability (Braithwaite & Braithwaite, 1997). The term *African American* emphasizes cultural heritage, whereas *black* focuses on skin color. The word *Hispanic* emphasizes the Spanish language spoken in the home countries, whereas *Latino* and *Latina* highlight the geographic origin of Latin American men and women, respectively (Glascock, 1998). People with roots in Spanish-speaking Caribbean countries tend to refer to themselves as *Latinos* and *Latinas* or to use more specific labels such as *Cubano, Peruvian,* and *Mexican* (Rodriguez, 2003). An ethical guideline for using language is to try to learn and respect others' preferences for describing their identities.

Loaded language consists of words that strongly slant perceptions and thus meanings. For example, conservative television and radio commentators sometimes disparage people with liberal social and political values as *knee-jerk liberals* and call environmentalists *tree-huggers.* At the same time, liberal commentators sometimes describe people with conservative social and political values as *country club fat cats* and describe people who oppose environmental regulations as *maiming nature.* Loaded language also fosters negative views of older citizens. Terms such as *geezer* and *old fogey* incline us to regard older people with contempt or pity. Alternatives such as *senior citizen* and *elderly person* encourage more respectful attitudes.

A number of companies have message boards to allow employees to discuss issues relevant to their work. However, some employees have found other uses for the message boards: using loaded language to spread gossip and engage in hateful speech about co-workers (Abelson, 2001). If you'd like to understand arguments for and against allowing companies to regulate employees' communication while on the job, use your Online Resources for *Communication in Our Lives* to access **WebLink 5.2.**

COMMUNICATION
in Your Life

Identify an instance of loaded language that you find hurtful.

CourseMate

COMMUNICATION HIGHLIGHT

Language Shapes Our Realities

Language shapes our perceptions in ways that reflect a culture's values (Whorf, 1956). In one part of Australia, people speak Guugu Timithirr, a language that does not include the terms *right* and *left.* In Guugu Timithirr, special locations are described in relation to a compass. Thus, a person speaking this language might ask to have the pepper passed north (Monastersky, 2002). People recall colors more clearly if their language provides distinct terms, so English speakers do not remember shades of blue (light blue, dark blue) as precisely as Russian speakers who have different words for light blue *(goluboy)* and dark blue *(sinly)* (Gentner & Boroditsky, 2009).

CourseMate

To explore your own experience with how the language you speak influences your reality, complete the Communication Highlight Activity for Chapter 5 via your Online Resources for *Communication in Our Lives.*

Symbols Organize Perceptions

We use symbols to organize our perceptions. As we saw in Chapter 2, we rely on cognitive schemata to classify and evaluate experiences. How we organize experiences affects what they mean to us. For example, your prototype of a good friend affects how you judge particular friends. When we place someone in the category of friend, the category influences how we interpret that person's communication. An insult is likely to be viewed as teasing if made by someone we define as a friend but a call to battle if made by someone we classify as an enemy. The words don't change, but their meaning varies, depending on how we classify the person uttering them.

Because symbols organize thought, they allow us to think about abstract concepts such as the work ethic, democracy, morality, good citizenship, and healthy family life. We use broad concepts to transcend specific, concrete activities and to enter the world of conceptual thought and ideals. Thinking abstractly relieves us of having to consider every specific object and experience individually.

Our capacity to abstract can also distort thinking. A primary way this occurs is in stereotyping—thinking in broad generalizations about a whole class of people or experiences. Examples of stereotypes are "Sorority women are yuppies," "Ph.D.s are smart," and "Democrats tax and spend." Notice that stereotypes can be positive or negative.

> **REGGIE**   *People say racism no longer exists, but I know it does. If I'm out walking at night, white girls cross the street because they think I'll mug them. They don't cross the street if they see a white guy. One of the guys on my hall asked me whether I thought the Bridge Program was helpful. I didn't go through it because I had a good high school record. Does he think every black needs special help?*

Common to all stereotypes is classifying experiences or people into a single category based on general knowledge or beliefs about a group. When we do this, we obscure the uniqueness of the individual person or a specific experience. Clearly, we have to generalize. We can't think about each thing in our lives as a specific instance. However, stereotypes can discourage us from recognizing important differences among the phenomena we lump together. Thus, we have an ethical responsibility to stay alert to differences among the things and people that we place in a single category.

Symbols Allow Hypothetical Thought

Who was your best friend when you were 5 years old? What would you do if you won the lottery? To answer these questions, you must think hypothetically, which means thinking about experiences and ideas that are not part of your concrete, present situation. Because we can think hypothetically, we can plan, dream, remember, fantasize, set goals, and weigh alternative courses of action.

RESEARCH IN OUR LIVES

"I" versus "We" in IMs

Does it matter whether partners in a relationship use "I" or "we" more often in IMs? Does "we" indicate a stronger commitment to the relationship? Are couples who use more emotional words closer than couples who don't? Three psychologists interested in the link between language and relationship quality devised a study to answer those questions. Richard Slatcher, Simine Vazire, and James Pennebaker asked 68 heterosexual couples (136 total participants) that had been dating for at least 6 months to provide transcripts of their IMs to each other.

Trained researchers then hand-coded the IMs and also created a macro in Microsoft Word to identify all instances of first-person pronouns (i.e., I, me, we, our, us) and positive and negative emotion words. They also used a validated instrument to assess all participants' satisfaction with their relationship at the beginning of the study and again 6 months after the study was completed.

The researchers assessed relationship stability by finding out whether the relationships were still active 6 months after the study. Of the participants who responded to the inquiry 6 months after the study, 61 percent were still dating the same people.

The researchers found that the frequency of "we" in IMs was not related to relationship satisfaction or stability. However, for women frequency of the use of "I" was positively associated with relationship satisfaction and stability. The researchers reasoned that this is probably because I-statements are often disclosures, which are linked to intimacy, and because they reveal a comfortable level of autonomy within the couple relationship.

The researchers found that emotion words were related to relationship satisfaction and stability in some interesting ways. For men, genuine (not sarcastic) positive emotions were related to both their satisfaction with the relationship and the satisfaction of their partners. They also found that women's satisfaction with relationships and the stability of relationships declined when male partners expressed positive emotions sarcastically.

Thinking Critically: Do the patterns for responding to emotion words identified in this article apply to your close relationships?

Richard Slatcher is in the Department of Psychology at the University of California–Los Angeles. Simine Vazire is in the Department of Psychology at Washington University–St. Louis. James Pennebaker is in the Department of Psychology at the University of Texas. This research was presented in a 2008 article titled "Am 'I' more important than 'we'? Couples' word use in instant messages" in *Personal Relationships*, volume 15, pages 407–424.

Hypothetical thought is possible because we use symbols. When we symbolize, we name ideas so that we can hold them in our minds and reflect on them. We can contemplate things that currently have no real existence, and we can remember ourselves in the past and project ourselves into the future. Our ability to live simultaneously in all three dimensions of time explains why we can set goals and work toward them even though there is nothing tangible about them in the moment (Dixson & Duck, 1993). For example, you've invested many hours in studying and writing papers because you imagine having a college degree. The degree is not real now, nor is the self that you will become once you have the degree. Yet the idea is sufficiently real to motivate you to work hard for many years.

Close relationships rely on ideas of history and future. One of the strongest glues for intimacy is a history of shared experiences (Bruess & Hoefs, 2006; Cockburn-Wootten & Zorn, 2006; Wood, 2006a). Just knowing that they have weathered rough times in the past helps partners get through current trials. Belief in a future also sustains intimacy. We interact differently with people we don't expect to see again and people who are continuing parts of our lives. Talking about the future also enhances intimacy because it suggests that more lies ahead (Acitelli, 1993; Duck, 1990).

Hypothetical thought can help us grow personally. In Chapter 3, we noted that improving self-concept begins with accepting that you are in process. This requires you to remember how you were at a previous time, to appreciate progress you've made, and to create an image of how you want to be, to motivate your continued growth.

Symbols Allow Self-reflection

Just as we use symbols to reflect on what goes on outside of us, we also use them to reflect on ourselves. There are two aspects to the self (Mead, 1934). First is the *I*, which is the spontaneous, creative self. The *I* acts impulsively in response to inner needs and desires, regardless of social norms. The *me* is the socially conscious part of the self that monitors and moderates the *I*'s impulses. The *me* reflects on the *I* from the social perspectives of others. The *I* is impervious to social conventions and expectations, but the *me* is keenly aware of them. In an argument, your *I* may want to hurl a biting insult at a co-worker who has criticized you, but your *me* censors that impulse and reminds you that it's impolite to put others down and that doing so might create future problems with that co-worker.

The *me* is the reflective part of the self. The *me* reflects on the *I*, so we simultaneously author our lives and reflect on them. This means we can think about who we want to be and set goals for becoming the self we desire. We can feel shame, pride, and regret for our actions—emotions that are possible because we self-reflect. We can control what we do in the present by casting ourselves forward in time to consider how we might later feel about our actions.

Self-reflection also empowers us to monitor ourselves and our actions. When we monitor ourselves, we (the *me*) notice and evaluate our (the *I*'s) actions and may modify them based on our (the *me*'s) judgments. For instance, while

Self-reflection is a foundation of personal identity and communication.

PhotoAlto/Jupiter Images

giving a speech, you might notice that quite a few members of the audience are looking around or slouching. You think to yourself, "They seem bored. Perhaps I've been using too many statistics. Maybe I could regain their interest by mentioning some personal examples." In this case, monitoring allowed you to gauge your speaking effectiveness and make adjustments.

Self-reflection also allows us to manage our image, or the identity we present to others. Because we reflect on ourselves from social perspectives, we are able to consider how we appear in others' eyes. Our ability to manage how we appear sometimes is called *facework* because it involves controlling the face we present to others. When talking with teachers, you may consciously present yourself as a respectful, attentive student. When interacting with parents, you may repress some of the language that surfaces in discussions with your friends. When communicating with someone you'd like to date, you may choose to be more attentive and social than you are in other circumstances. In work situations, you may do facework to create an image of yourself as responsible, ambitious, and dependable. Continuously, we adjust how we present ourselves so that we sculpt our image to fit particular situations and people.

Summing up, we use symbols to define, evaluate, and organize experiences, think hypothetically, and self-reflect. Each of these abilities helps us create meaning in our lives.

ENHANCING EFFECTIVENESS IN VERBAL COMMUNICATION

We've explored what symbols are and how they may be used differently in distinct social communities. Building on these understandings, we can now consider ways to improve the effectiveness of our verbal communication.

Engage in Dual Perspective

The single most important guideline for effective verbal communication is to engage in **dual perspective**. Dual perspective involves recognizing another person's point of view and taking that into account as you communicate. Effective communication is not a solo performance but interaction between people. Awareness of others and their viewpoints should be reflected in how we speak. For instance, a person using dual perspective when talking with a woman who has a problem might realize that many women appreciate empathy and supportive listening more than advice (Wood, 1998, 2005). Public speakers should take listeners' values into consideration when planning and presenting speeches.

We don't need to abandon our own perspectives to recognize those of others. In fact, it would be just as unethical to stifle your own views as to dismiss those of others. Dual perspective, as the term implies, consists of two perspectives. It entails understanding both our own and another's point of view and acknowledging each when we communicate. For example, you and your supervisor may disagree about a performance review. It's important that you understand why your supervisor assigns the ratings he or she does, even if you don't share his or her perceptions. By understanding the supervisor's perceptions and ratings, you enhance your ability to have a good working relationship and to perform effectively on the job.

Dual perspective is a foundation of effective communication.

Own Your Feelings and Thoughts

We sometimes use language that obscures our responsibility for how we feel and what we think. For instance, people say, "You made me mad," "You made me feel inadequate about my job performance," or "You hurt me," as if what they feel is caused by someone else. On a more subtle level, we sometimes blame others for our responses to what they say. "You're so demanding" really means that you don't like what someone else wants or expects. The sense of feeling pressured by another's expectations is in you; it is not created by the other person. In reality, others seldom directly cause our feelings.

Our feelings and thoughts result from how we interpret others' communication, not from their communication itself. Others sometimes exert a great deal of influence on how we feel and how we see ourselves. Yet they do not directly cause our feelings. Although how we interpret what others say may lead us to feel certain ways, we can't hold them directly responsible for our feelings. In relationships with manipulative or hurtful people, you may find it useful either to communicate in ways that don't enable the other and that do preserve your integrity or to leave the relationship before it jeopardizes your own well-being.

Effective communicators take responsibility for themselves by using language that owns their thoughts and feelings. They own their feelings and do not blame others for what happens in themselves. To take responsibility for your own feelings, rely on *I*-language instead of *you*-language. Table 5.1 gives examples of the difference.

In my work with inmates who have violent histories, one of the key skills they learn is using *I*-language. At the outset, the inmates say things such as, "She made me hit her by what she did." Through instruction, exercises, and practice, they learn to change their *you*-language to *I*-language, saying, "I hit her because I didn't like how she was acting." The inmates tell me that learning *I*-language

Table 5.1	*You*-Language and *I*-Language

You-Language	*I*-Language
You hurt me.	I feel hurt when you ignore what I say.
You make me feel small.	I feel small when you tell me that I'm selfish.
My boss intimidates me.	When my boss criticizes my work, I feel intimidated.
You're really domineering.	When you shout at me, I feel dominated.
The speaker made me feel dumb.	I felt uninformed when the speaker discussed such complex information.
You humiliated me.	I felt humiliated when you mentioned my problems in front of our friends.

is empowering because it helps them see that they have more control over their actions than they had realized.

There are two differences between *I*-language and *you*-language. First, *I*-statements own responsibility, whereas *you*-statements project it onto another person. *You*-language tells others that they make you feel some way. This is likely to arouse defensiveness, which doesn't facilitate healthy communication. Second, *I*-statements offer more description than *you*-statements. *You*-statements tend to be abstract accusations, which is one reason they're ineffective in promoting change. *I*-statements, on the other hand, provide concrete descriptions of behaviors and feelings without directly blaming another person for how we feel.

Some people feel awkward when they first start using *I*-language. This is natural because most of us are accustomed to using *you*-language. With commitment and practice, however, you can learn to communicate using *I*-language. Once you feel comfortable using it, you will find that *I*-language has many advantages. It is less likely than *you*-language to make others defensive, so *I*-language opens the doors for dialogue.

I-language is also more honest. We deceive ourselves when we say, "You made me feel…" because others don't control how we feel. Finally, *I*-language is more empowering than *you*-language. When we say, "You hurt me," or "You made me feel bad," we give control of our emotions to others. This reduces our personal sense of agency and, by extension, our motivation to change what is happening. Using *I*-language allows us to own our feelings while also explaining to others how we interpret their behaviors.

To practice using *I*-language, complete the activity "Learning to Use *I*-Language" via your Online Resources for *Communication in Our Lives*.

COMMUNICATION in Your Life

The next time you use *I*-language, try changing it to *you*-language, and note how that affects your thoughts and the interaction.

CourseMate

ROTH   *I never realized how often I use* you-*language. I'm always saying my girlfriend makes me feel happy or my father makes me feel like a failure. What I'm beginning to see is that they really don't control my feelings. I do.*

Respect What Others Say About Their Feelings and Ideas

Has anyone ever said to you, "You shouldn't feel that way"? If so, you know how infuriating it can be to be told that your feelings aren't valid, appropriate, or acceptable. It's equally destructive to be told our thoughts are wrong. When someone says, "How can you think something so stupid?" we feel devalued. Effective communicators don't disparage what others say about what they feel and think. Even if you don't feel or think the same way, you can still respect another person as the expert on her or his perspective.

We also disrespect others when we speak for them instead of letting them speak for themselves. Recently, I had a conversation with a couple at a party in which one person spoke for another. In response to questions that I asked the man, the woman said, "He's having trouble balancing career and family responsibilities," "He's proud of sticking with his exercise program," and "He's worried about how to take care of his parents now that their health is declining." She didn't allow her husband to speak for himself. By automatically answering questions I addressed to him, she left him voiceless. Parents sometimes speak for children by responding to questions the children could answer. Generally, it's arrogant and disempowering to speak for others.

Just as we should not speak for others, we also should not assume that we understand how they feel or think. We called this mind reading in Chapter 2, and it is relevant to this discussion as well. As we have seen, our distinct experiences and ways of interpreting life make each of us unique. We seldom, if ever, completely grasp what another person feels or thinks. Although it is supportive to engage in dual perspective, it isn't supportive to presume that we fully understand someone else's feelings or thoughts, especially when he or she differs from us in important ways. It's particularly important not to assume we understand people from other cultures or social communities (Fussell, 2002; Houston, 2003).

Respecting what others say about what they feel and think is a cornerstone of effective communication. We also grow when we open ourselves to perspectives, feelings, and thoughts that differ from our own. If you don't understand what others say, ask them to elaborate. This shows you are interested and respect their expertise and experience.

Strive for Accuracy and Clarity

Because symbols are arbitrary, abstract, and ambiguous, the potential for misunderstanding always exists. In addition, individual and cultural differences may lead to misunderstandings. Although we cannot entirely eliminate misunderstandings, we can minimize them.

Used by permission of Mischa Richter and Harold Bakken

"Well, then, if 'commandments' seems too harsh to me, and 'guidelines' seems too wishy-washy to you, how about 'The 10 Policy Statements'?"

Be Aware of Levels of Abstraction Misunderstandings are most likely when language is very abstract. For instance, suppose a professor says, "Your papers should demonstrate a sophisticated conceptual grasp of the material and its pragmatic implications." Would you know how to write a paper to satisfy the professor? You might not, because the language is very abstract and unclear. Here's a more concrete description: "Your papers should include definitions of the concepts and specific examples that show how they apply in real life." With this less abstract statement, you would have a better idea of what the professor expected.

Abstract language is not always inadvisable. As we have seen, abstract language allows us to generalize, which is necessary and useful. The goal is to use a level of abstraction that suits particular communication objectives and situations. Abstract words are appropriate when speakers and listeners have similar concrete knowledge about what is being discussed. For example, a couple that has been dating for a year might talk about "light movies" and "heavy movies" as shorthand ways to refer to two kinds of films. Because they have seen many movies together, they have shared referents for the abstract terms *light* and *heavy*.

More concrete language is advisable when communicators don't have shared experiences and interpretations. For example, early in a friendship the suggestion to "hang out" would be more effective if it included specifics: "Let's hang out today—maybe watch the game and go out for pizza." Providing concrete examples for general terms clarifies meanings.

Abstract language is particularly likely to lead to misunderstandings when people talk about how they want one another to change. Concrete language and specific examples help people share understandings of which behaviors are unwelcome and which ones are wanted. For example, "I want you to be more responsible about your job" does not explain what would count as being more responsible. Is it arriving on time, taking on extra assignments, or something else? It isn't clear what the speaker wants unless more concrete descriptions are supplied. Likewise, "I want to be closer" could mean the speaker wants to spend more time together, talk about the relationship, do things together, or any number of other things. Vague abstractions promote misunderstanding if people don't share concrete referents.

Politicians are often criticized for using abstract language. Why might politicians prefer to speak in the abstract instead of using concrete language?

Courtney Perry/Dallas Morning News/CORBIS

Qualify Language Another way to increase the clarity of communication is to qualify language. Two types of language should be qualified. First, we should qualify generalizations so we don't mislead ourselves or others. "Politicians are crooked" is a false statement because it overgeneralizes. A more accurate statement would be, "A number of politicians have been shown to have accepted paybacks for favors." Qualifying reminds us of the limitations of what we say.

To develop your skill in using qualified language, complete the activity "Practicing Using Qualified Language" via your Online Resources for *Communication in Our Lives.*

CourseMate

We should also qualify language when describing and evaluating people. **Static evaluation** consists of assessments that suggest that something is unchanging or frozen in time. These are particularly troublesome when applied to people: "Ann is selfish.", "Don is irresponsible.", "Bob is generous." Whenever we use the word *is*, we suggest that something is inherent and fixed. In reality, we aren't static but continuously changing. A person who is selfish at one time may not be at another. A person who is irresponsible on one occasion may be responsible in other situations.

To develop skill in avoiding static language, complete the activity "Guarding against Static Language" via your Online Resources for *Communication in Our Lives.*

Indexing is a technique developed by early communication scholars that allows us to note that our statements reflect only specific times and circumstances (Korzybski, 1948). To index, we would say "Ann$_{June\ 6,\ 1997}$ acted selfishly," "Don$_{on\ the\ task\ committee}$ was irresponsible," Bob$_{in\ college}$ was generous." See how indexing ties description to a specific time and circumstance? Mental indexing reminds us that we and others are able to change in remarkable ways.

> **ROY**   *I had a couple of accidents right after I got my driver's license. Most teenagers do, right? But to hear my father, you'd think I am a bad driver today. Those accidents were 5 years ago, and I haven't even had a ticket since then. But he still talks about "reckless Roy."*

We've considered four principles for improving the effectiveness of verbal communication. Engaging in dual perspective is the first principle and a foundation for all others. A second guideline is to take responsibility for our own feelings and thoughts by using *I*-language. Third, we should respect others as the experts on what they feel and think and not speak for them or presume we know what they think and feel. The fourth principle is to strive for clarity by choosing appropriate degrees of abstraction, qualifying generalizations, and indexing evaluations, particularly ones applied to people.

BEYOND THE CLASSROOM

Let's take the material in this chapter beyond the classroom by thinking about how what you've learned about verbal communication might apply to the workplace, ethical choices, and engagement with the broader world.

1. **Workplace.** In this chapter, we discovered verbal interaction is guided by constitutive and regulative rules. Think about a place where you work or where you worked in the past. Identify two key rules of each type and analyze how they shaped communication in that work site.

Ethics

2. **Ethics.** Articulate the ethical basis for the third guideline presented in this chapter: Respect what others say about their feelings and ideas. Why might it be ethical to do so and unethical not to do so?

3. **Engagement.** Subordinate groups are often defined by others who have the power to name them. Yet subordinate groups may eventually challenge the names others confer on them. In the 1960s, blacks in the United States rejected names that had been applied to members of their race and advanced new names they chose for themselves: African American and Afro American. In the 1990s, people who are not heterosexual began resisting names that had been applied to them and using self-definitions. Thinking about these two examples, consider definitions others impose on groups that are currently subordinate in the United States. How do the labels define members of the group? If you want to extend this exercise, talk with members of these groups and ask how they would define themselves or what words they would like others to use when referring to them.

CHAPTER SUMMARY

In this chapter, we've discussed the world of words and meaning, which make up the uniquely human universe of symbol users. Because symbols are arbitrary, ambiguous, and abstract, they have no inherent meanings. Instead, we actively construct meaning by interpreting symbols based on perspectives gleaned through interaction with others and our personal experiences. We also punctuate to create meaning in communication.

We use symbols to define, evaluate, and organize our experiences. In addition, we use symbols to think hypothetically so we can consider alternatives and inhabit all three dimensions of time.

Finally, symbols allow us to self-reflect so we can monitor our own behaviors.

Because symbols are abstract, arbitrary, and ambiguous, misunderstandings can occur between communicators. We can reduce the likelihood of misunderstandings by being sensitive to levels of abstraction. In addition, we should engage in dual perspective, own our thoughts and feelings, respect what others say about how they think and feel, and monitor abstractness, generalizations, and static evaluations. In Chapter 6, we continue our discussion of the world of human communication by exploring the fascinating realm of nonverbal behavior.

APPLYING COMMUNICATION IN OUR LIVES

The key concepts, For Further Reflection and Discussion questions, and Experiencing Communication in Our Lives case study that follow will help you review, reflect on, and extend the information and ideas presented in this chapter. These resources, and a diverse selection of additional study tools, are also available as Online Resources for *Communication* *in Our Lives*. Your Online Resources include CourseMate, a student workbook, interactive video activities, audio study tools, a book companion website, Speech Builder Express, Speech Studio, and InfoTrac College Edition. For more information or to access this book's online resources, visit **www.cengage.com/login**.

KEY CONCEPTS

abstract, 101
ambiguous, 100
arbitrary, 98
communication rules, 102
constitutive rules, 103

dual perspective, 112
hypothetical thought, 111
indexing, 117
loaded language, 108
punctuation, 104

regulative rules, 103
static evaluation, 117
symbols, 98
totalizing, 106

FOR FURTHER REFLECTION AND DISCUSSION

1. Pay attention to *I*- and *you*-language in your own communication and that of others. What happens when you switch a *you*-statement to an *I*-statement? Does it change how you feel or what happens in interaction?

2. What is a good term for describing someone with whom you have a serious romance? *Boyfriend* and *girlfriend* no longer work for many people. Do you prefer *significant other*, *romantic partner*, *special friend*, or another term?

3. What ethical responsibilities should accompany the right to free speech? Do you think individuals have an unqualified right to say whatever they want or are there limits to what people should be allowed to say?

4. Identify communication rules for online conversations. What counts as joking (how do you indicate you're joking)? What counts as flaming? How is interaction regulated with rules for turn taking and length of comment?

SHARPEN **YOUR SKILL**

1. Communication Rules

Identify constitutive and regulative rules you follow when you are interacting on the job and when you are with your family.

Constitutive Rules

What counts as being attentive in a team meeting at work?

What counts as being attentive to a romantic partner?

What counts as being respectful of parents?

What counts as being responsible on the job?

What counts as showing affection to parents and stepparents?

Regulative Rules

When is it appropriate to interrupt parents, friends, or co-workers?

What topics are appropriate during family dinner conversation?

With which family members do you talk about personal issues?

With which family members do you talk about money problems?

2. Assessing Your Stereotypes

Identify a stereotype you use, and consider 10 people to whom you might apply it. Identify differences between the people. At first, this may be difficult because stereotypes gloss over differences. What do you discover as you look for individual variations in the people you lumped together under a single symbol?

EXPERIENCING COMMUNICATION IN OUR LIVES

CASE STUDY: *The Roommates*

A video of the conversation scripted here is featured in your Chapter 5 Online Resources for *Communication in Our Lives*. Select "The Roommates" to watch the video. Improve your own communication skills by reading, watching, and evaluating this communication encounter.

Bernadette and Celia were assigned to be roommates a month ago when the school year began. Initially, both were pleased with the match because they discovered commonalities in their interests and backgrounds. They are both sophomores from small towns, they have similar tastes in music and television programs, and they both like to stay up late and sleep in.

Lately, however, Bernadette has been irritated by Celia's housekeeping or lack of it. Celia leaves her clothes lying all over the room. If they cook in, Celia often leaves the pans and dishes for hours, and then it's usually Bernadette who cleans them. Bernadette feels she has to talk to Celia about this problem, but she hasn't figured out how or when to talk. When Celia gets in from classes, Bernadette is sitting and reading a textbook on her bed.

CELIA: Hey Bernie, how's it going?

Celia drops her book bag in the middle of the floor, flops on the bed, and kicks her shoes off on the floor. As Bernadette watches, she feels her frustration peaking and decides now is the time to talk to Celia about the problem.

BERNADETTE: You shouldn't do that. You make me nuts the way you just throw your stuff all over the room.

CELIA: I don't "throw my stuff all over the room." I just took off my shoes and put my books down, like I do every day.

BERNADETTE: No, you didn't. You dropped your bag right in the middle of the room, and you kicked your shoes where they happen to fall without ever noticing how messy they look. And you're right—that is what you do every day.

CELIA: There's nothing wrong with wanting to be comfortable in my own room. Are we suddenly going for the Good Housekeeping Seal of Approval?

BERNADETTE: Comfortable is one thing. But you're so messy. Your mess makes me really miserable.

CELIA: Since when? This is the first I've heard about it.

BERNADETTE: Since we started rooming together, but I didn't want to say anything about how angry you make me. I just can't stand it any more. You shouldn't be so messy.

CELIA: Sounds to me like you've got a problem—you, not me.

BERNADETTE: Well it's you and your mess that are my problem. Do you have to be such a slob?

QUESTIONS FOR ANALYSIS AND DISCUSSION

You can answer these questions and see my responses to them online via your Online Resources for Chapter 5.

1. Identify examples of *you*-language in this conversation. How would you change it to *I*-language?

2. Identify examples of loaded language and ambiguous language.

3. Do you agree with Celia that the problem is Bernadette's, not hers?

4. Do Celia and Bernadette seem to engage in dual perspective to understand each other?

6

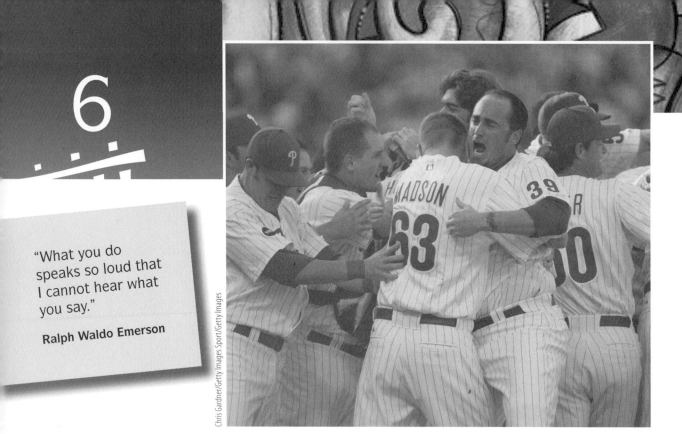

Chris Gardner/Getty Images Sport/Getty Images

The Nonverbal Dimension of Communication

Ben Thompson had traveled to Japan to negotiate a joint business venture with Haru Watanabe. They seemed to see the mutual benefit of combining their resources, yet Thompson felt something was wrong in their negotiations. Every time they talked, Watanabe seemed uneasy and refused to hold eye contact. Thompson wondered whether Watanabe was trying to hide something. Meanwhile, Watanabe wondered why Thompson was so rude if he wanted them to work together.

Maria noticed a nice-looking guy who was studying two tables away from her in the library. When he looked up at her, she lowered her eyes. After a

SHARPEN YOUR SKILL

At the end of this chapter, refer to the Sharpen Your Skill features, Communicating Closeness and Environmental Awareness, to apply concepts from Chapter 6.

moment, she looked back at him just for a second. A few minutes later he came over, sat down beside her, and introduced himself.

These examples illustrate the power of nonverbal communication. In the first case, Thompson and Watanabe have difficulty because of different nonverbal communication norms in Japan and the United States. Thompson has learned that eye contact is a sign of honesty and respect, so he looks directly at Watanabe when they talk. In Watanabe's culture, however, direct eye contact is considered rude and intrusive, so he doesn't meet Thompson's gaze and feels uncomfortable when Thompson looks directly at him.

In the library scene, we see a gendered pattern of nonverbal communication. Maria follows feminine communication norms by indirectly signaling her interest and waiting for the man to initiate contact. In turn, he enacts the rules of masculine communication culture by gazing directly at her and moving to her table.

Gender, ethnicity, sexual orientation, and socioeconomic class are identities that we create and sustain by performing them day in and day out. Candice West and Don Zimmerman (1987) note that we "do gender" all the time by behaving in ways that announce that we are feminine or masculine. We also communicate nonverbally to perform, or "do," race, class, and sexual orientation. In this sense, nonverbal communication, like language, is a primary way in which we announce who we are. The intricate system of nonverbal communication helps us establish identity, negotiate relationships, and create environments we enjoy.

Nonverbal behavior is a major dimension of human communication. The nonverbal system accounts for 65 to 93 percent of the total meaning of communication (Birdwhistell, 1970; Hickson, Stacks, & Moore, 2004; Mehrabian, 1981). One reason for the impact of nonverbal communication is its breadth: It includes everything from dress and eye contact to body posture and vocal inflection.

In this chapter, we explore the fascinating realm of nonverbal interaction. We will identify principles of nonverbal communication and then discuss types of nonverbal behavior and ways to improve our effectiveness in nonverbal communication.

PRINCIPLES OF NONVERBAL COMMUNICATION

Nonverbal communication is all aspects of communication other than words themselves. It includes how we utter words (i.e., inflection, volume), features of environments that affect interaction (i.e., temperature, lighting), and objects that influence personal images and interaction patterns (i.e., dress, jewelry, furniture). Five key points highlight the nature and power of nonverbal communication to affect meaning.

Similar to and Different from Verbal Communication

Nonverbal communication and verbal communication are similar in some ways and different in others. We'll identify both the similarities and the differences.

Similarities Like verbal communication, nonverbal behavior is symbolic, which means it is ambiguous, abstract, and arbitrary. Thus, we can't be sure

COMMUNICATION
in Your Life

**When verbal
and nonverbal
communication
are inconsis-
tent, which
do you tend
to believe?**

what a smile or a gesture means, and we can't guarantee that others understand the meanings we intend to express with our own nonverbal behaviors. Also like verbal communication, our nonverbal behavior and our interpretations of others' nonverbal behaviors are guided by constitutive and regulative rules.

A third similarity between the two communication systems is that both are culture bound. Our nonverbal communication reflects and reproduces values and norms of the particular culture and social communities to which we belong (Hickson et al., 2004). For instance, dress considered appropriate for women varies across cultures: Some women in the United States wear miniskirts; women in some other countries wear veils. Dress also reflects organizational identities: Bankers, attorneys, and many other professionals are expected to wear business suits or dresses; carpenters and plumbers usually wear jeans.

Lastly, both verbal and nonverbal communication may be either intentional or unintentional. Sometimes we carefully sculpt our appearance, just as we sometimes control our verbal communication. For instance, in a job interview we are highly conscious of our dress and posture as well as the words we use. At other times, our verbal and nonverbal communication may be unintentional. If the interviewer asks you a difficult question, your facial expression may reveal that you are caught off guard, or you may speak ungrammatically.

Differences   There are also differences between the two systems of communication. First, nonverbal communication is perceived as more honest. If verbal and nonverbal behaviors are inconsistent, most people trust the nonverbal behavior. There is little evidence that nonverbal behavior actually is more trustworthy than verbal communication; after all, we often control it quite deliberately. Nonetheless, it tends to be *perceived* as more trustworthy (Andersen, 1999).

Second, unlike verbal communication, nonverbal communication is multi-channeled. Verbal communication usually occurs within a single channel; oral verbal communication is received through hearing, and written verbal communication and sign language are received through sight. In contrast, nonverbal communication may be seen, felt, heard, smelled, and tasted. We often receive nonverbal communication simultaneously through two or more channels, as when we feel and see a hug while hearing a whispered "I love you."

Finally, verbal communication is discrete, whereas nonverbal is more continuous. Verbal symbols start and stop; we begin speaking at one moment and stop speaking at another moment. In contrast, nonverbal communication tends to flow continually. Before we speak, our facial expressions and posture express our feelings; as we speak, our body movements and appearance communicate; and after we speak our posture changes, perhaps relaxing.

Frans Lemmens/The Image Bank/Getty Images

Different cultures prescribe different styles of dress.

Supplements or Replaces Verbal Communication

Communication researchers have identified five ways in which nonverbal behaviors interact with verbal communication (Andersen, 1999; Richmond & McCroskey, 1995b). First, nonverbal behaviors may repeat verbal messages. For example, you might say "yes" while nodding your head. In making a public presentation, you might hold up first one, then two, and then three fingers to signal to listeners that you are moving from the first to the second to the third points of your speech.

Second, nonverbal behaviors may highlight verbal communication, as when you use inflection to emphasize certain words ("This is the *most* serious consequence of the policy that I oppose"). Third, nonverbal behaviors may complement or add to words. When you see a friend, you might say, "I'm glad to see you" and underline the verbal message with a smile. Public speakers often emphasize verbal statements with forceful gestures and increases in volume and inflection. Fourth, nonverbal behaviors may contradict verbal messages, as when a group member says, "Nothing's wrong" in a hostile tone of voice (Knapp & Hall, 2006). Finally, we sometimes substitute nonverbal behaviors for verbal

COMMUNICATION HIGHLIGHT

Cross-Cultural Nonverbal Clashes

Cross-cultural misunderstandings aren't limited to verbal communication, according to Siu Wa Tang, chair of the Department of Psychiatry at the University of California at Irvine (Emmons, 1998). When Dr. Tang and a colleague visited pharmaceutical plants in Changchun, China, Tang was well accepted, but his colleague was not. The Chinese took an immediate and strong dislike to the colleague. Tang says the problem was facial expressions. His U.S. colleague used facial expressions that Americans would interpret as showing honesty and directness but which the Chinese people interpreted as aggressive and rude.

Based on this experience, Tang conducted experiments to test the universality of facial expressions. He found that a few basic feelings and expressions were understood across cultures. Happiness and sadness, for example, were nonverbally expressed in similar ways. However, other facial expressions did not translate so well. Nine out of 10 Americans interpreted a photograph of a face as showing fear, yet 6 of 10 Japanese identified the same photograph as expressing surprise or sadness. A photo identified by 9 of 10 Americans as showing anger was interpreted by 75 percent of Japanese as expressing disgust or contempt. Another source of cross-cultural nonverbal misunderstandings is eye contact. Americans generally consider it polite to look another person in the eye when conversing, but Japanese look at each other's cheeks; to look another in the eyes is perceived as very aggressive.

Cross-cultural communication clashes may also occur over gift giving (Axtell, 2007). An American might offend a Chinese person with the gift of a clock because in China, clocks symbolize death. Giving a gift to an Arab person on first meeting would be interpreted as a bribe. Bringing flowers to a dinner hosted by a person from Kenya would puzzle the host because in Kenya flowers are given only to express sympathy for a loss. And the Swiss consider even numbers of flowers bad luck, so giving a dozen is inappropriate, and the recipient would probably interpret the gift as reflecting ill will.

ones. For instance, you might roll your eyes to indicate that you are exasperated by something.

Regulates Interaction

You generally know when someone else has finished speaking, when a professor welcomes discussion from students, and when someone expects you to speak. Seldom do explicit, verbal cues tell us when to speak and keep silent. Instead, conversations usually are regulated nonverbally (Guerrero & Floyd, 2006). When talking, friends don't say, "It's your turn to talk"; work associates don't point to one another to switch speaking roles; and professors don't hold up signs saying, "I am through now." We use our eyes and body posture to indicate that we want to enter conversations, and speakers step back from a podium to indicate that they have finished a speech. We invite people to speak by looking directly at them, often after asking a question (Drummond & Hopper, 1993; Knapp & Hall, 2006).

DARCY   *I know one guy who dominates every conversation. I'd never noticed this until we studied how nonverbal behaviors regulate turn taking. This guy won't look at others when he's talking. He looks out into space, or sometimes he gives you a hard stare, but he never looks at anyone like he's saying, "Okay, your turn now."*

Establishes Relationship-Level Meanings

In Chapter 1, we noted that there are two levels of meaning in communication. To review: The content level of meaning concerns actual information or literal meaning; the relationship level of meaning defines people's identities and relationships. Nonverbal communication is often more powerful than verbal language in conveying relationship-level meanings (Manusov & Patterson, 2006). For this reason, some communication scholars call nonverbal communication the "relationship language" (Richmond & McCroskey, 1995b; Sallinen-Kuparinen, 1992).

Nonverbal communication is used to convey three dimensions of relationship-level meanings: *responsiveness, liking,* and *power* (Mehrabian, 1981). Yet how we convey relationship meanings and what specific nonverbal behaviors mean depends on the communication rules we've learned in our particular cultures.

Responsiveness   One facet of relationship-level meaning is responsiveness. We use eye contact, facial expressions, and body posture to indicate interest in others, as Maria did in one of the examples that opened this chapter. We signal interest by holding eye contact and assuming an attentive posture. But as the example with Haru Watanabe and Ben Thompson reveals, eye contact doesn't mean the same thing in all cultures. Also, harmony between people's postures and facial expressions may reflect how comfortable they are with each other (Capella, 1991; Guerrero & Floyd, 2006; Trees, 2000). In cohesive groups, there is typically a great deal of nonverbal communication indicating responsiveness. Less cohesive groups include fewer nonverbal indicators of engagement.

MARYAM   *Americans do more than one thing at a time. In Nepal, when we talk with someone, we are with that person. We do not also write on paper or have the television on. We talk with the person. It is hard for me to accept the custom of giving only some attention to each other in conversation.*

As Maryam's observation indicates, different cultures teach members distinct rules for showing responsiveness. In the West, feminine speech communities emphasize sensitivity to others, so women generally display greater emotional responsiveness and interest in what others say than do men (Wood, 2011). In addition to communicating their own feelings nonverbally, women are generally more skilled than men in interpreting others' emotions (Burgoon & Le Poire, 1999; Noller, 1986, 1987). Decoding may be a survival strategy for people in subordinate standpoints. Their well-being and sometimes their physical safety depend on being able to decipher the feelings and intentions of those with greater power.

Ellen   *Secretaries are the best decoders. They can read their bosses' moods in a heartbeat. I am a secretary, part time now that I'm taking courses, and I can tell exactly what my boss is thinking. Sometimes I know what he feels or will do before he does. I have to know when he can be interrupted, when he feels generous, and when not to cross his path.*

Liking   A second dimension of relationship-level meaning is liking. Smiles and friendly touching usually indicate positive feelings, whereas frowns and belligerent postures express antagonism. Have you ever noticed how often political candidates shake hands, slap backs, and otherwise touch people whose votes they want? Happy couples sit closer together and engage in more eye contact than unhappy couples (Noller, 1986, 1987). Similarly, in work settings, people who like one another often sit together, exchange eye contact, and smile at one another.

Power   The third aspect of relationship-level meanings is power, or control. We use nonverbal behaviors to assert dominance, express deference, and negotiate status and influence (Andersen, 1999; Henley, 1977; Remland, 2000). In general, men assume more space and use greater volume and more forceful gestures than women (Hall, 1987; Major, Schmidlin, & Williams, 1990). Men are also more likely than women to move into others' space, as the man in the library moved to Maria's table in the example at the beginning of this chapter. In addition, men tend to use gestures and touch to exert control. Powerful people, such as bosses, touch those with less power, such as secretaries, more than those with less power touch those with more power (Hall, Coats, & Smith-LeBeau, 2004; Spain, 1992).

Posture and other nonverbal behaviors can indicate power relations.

Jonatan Fernstrom/Jupiter Images

As Ramona observes, the amount of space a person has often directly reflects his or her power. The connection between power and space is evident in the fact that CEOs usually have spacious offices, entry-level and mid-level professionals have smaller offices, and secretaries often have minuscule workstations, even though secretaries often store and manage more material than those higher in the organizational chain of command. Regulative communication rules also tacitly specify that people with status or power have the right to enter the space of people with less power, but the converse is not true. Space also reflects power differences in families. Adults usually have more space than children; like Ramona's father, men more often than women have their own rooms and sit at the head of the table.

> **RAMONA**   *In my home, my father sits at the head of the table, and he has his chair in the family room and his workroom. My mother does not have her chair anywhere in the house, and she has no room of her own either. This accurately reflects the power dynamics between them.*

Reflects Cultural Values

Like verbal communication, nonverbal patterns reflect communication rules of specific cultures and social communities (Andersen, Hecht, Hoobler, & Smallwood, 2002; Manusov & Patterson, 2006). This implies that most nonverbal behavior isn't instinctual but learned in the process of socialization. Nonverbal behaviors vary across cultures and social communities.

Have you ever seen the bumper sticker that says, "If you can read this, you're too close"? That slogan proclaims North Americans' fierce territoriality. We value our private spaces, and we resent—and sometimes fight—anyone who trespasses on what we consider our turf. We want to have private homes, and many people want large lots to protect their privacy. On the job, a reserved parking space and a private office with a door mark status; employees with lower status often park in satellite lots and share offices or have workstations without doors. In cultures where individuality is less valued, people are less territorial. For instance, Brazilians routinely stand close together in shops, buses, and elevators, and

COMMUNICATION in Your Life

How is power nonverbally communicated in classrooms?

> **SUCHENG** *In the United States, each person has so much room. Every individual has a separate room in which to sleep and sometimes another separate room in which to work. Also, I see that each family here lives in a separate house. People have much less space in China. Families live together, with sons bringing their families into their parents' home and all sharing the same space. At first when I came here it felt strange to have so much space, but now I sometimes feel very crowded when I go home.*

when they bump into each other, they don't apologize or draw back. Similarly, in countries such as Hong Kong people are used to living and working in very close quarters, so territoriality is uncommon (Andersen et al., 2002; Chan, 1999). In some cultures—Italy, for example—dramatic nonverbal displays of emotion are typical, but other cultures consider more reserved displays of emotion appropriate (Matsumoto, Franklin, Choi, Rogers, & Tatani, 2002).

Patterns of eye contact also reflect cultural values. In the United States, frankness and assertion are valued, so meeting another's eyes is considered appropriate and a demonstration of personal honesty. Yet, as we've noted, in many Asian and northern European countries, direct eye contact is considered abrasive and disrespectful (Axtell, 2007; Samovar & Porter, 2001).

In Brazil, eye contact often is so intense that people from the United States consider it rude staring. As the example with Mr. Watanabe and Mr. Thompson suggests, this cultural difference can cause misunderstandings in intercultural business negotiations.

Greeting behaviors also vary across cultures. In the United States and many other Western countries, the handshake is the most common way to greet. Arab men are more likely to kiss each other on both cheeks as a form of greeting. Embraces are typical greetings in Mexico. Bowing is the standard form of greeting in some Asian cultures (Samovar & Porter, 2001).

In sum, we've noted five important features of the nonverbal communication system. First, there are similarities and differences between nonverbal and verbal communication. Second, nonverbal behavior can supplement or replace verbal communication. Third, nonverbal behaviors regulate interaction. Fourth, nonverbal communication is often especially powerful in establishing and expressing relational meanings. Fifth, nonverbal behaviors reflect cultural values and are learned, not instinctive. We're now ready to explore the many types of behavior in the intricate nonverbal communication system.

TYPES OF NONVERBAL COMMUNICATION

In this section, we will consider nine forms of nonverbal behavior, noticing how we use each to communicate.

Kinesics

Kinesics is body position and body motions, including those of the face. Our bodies express a great deal about how we see ourselves. A speaker who stands erect and appears confident announces self-assurance, whereas someone who slouches and shuffles may seem to say, "I'm not very sure of myself." A person who walks quickly with a resolute facial expression appears more determined than someone who saunters along with an unfocused gaze. People whose nonverbal communication conveys vitality are less likely to be attacked than people whose nonverbal communication indicates less vigor (Gunns, Johnson, & Hudson, 2002). We sit rigidly when we are nervous and adopt a relaxed posture when we feel at ease. Audiences and groups indicate attentiveness and interest by body posture.

Body postures and gestures may signal whether we are open to interaction and how we feel about others. Someone who sits with arms crossed and looks downward seems to say, "Don't bother me." That's a nonverbal strategy students sometimes use to dissuade teachers from calling on them in classes. To signal that we'd like to interact, we look at others and sometimes smile. We use one hand gesture to say okay and another to communicate contempt.

Our faces are intricate messengers (Carroll & Russell, 1996). The human face is capable of more than 1,000 distinct expressions. Our eyes can shoot daggers of anger, issue challenges, express skepticism, or radiate love. With our faces, we can indicate disapproval (scowls), doubt (raised eyebrows), love (eye gazes), and challenge (stares). The face is particularly powerful in conveying responsiveness and liking (Gueguen & De Gail, 2003). Responsiveness is generally greater in women, who smile more than men, particularly during adolescence (Hall, 2006).

How we position ourselves relative to others may express our feelings toward them. On work teams, friends and allies often sit together, and competitors typically maintain distance. We communicate dissatisfaction by moving away from others and by decreasing smiles and eye contact (Walker & Trimboli, 1989).

Anna Gowthorpe/PA Wire/AP Photo

Look at the man at the left. What do his facial expression and kinesics tell you about how he relates to the homeless man at the right?

Americans often cross their legs, but this is perceived as offensive in Ghana and Turkey (Samovar, Porter, & McDaniel, 2009).

Our eyes communicate some of the most important and complex messages about how we feel. If you watch infants, you'll notice that they focus on others' eyes. As adults, we often look at eyes to judge emotions, honesty, interest, and self-confidence. This explains why strong eye contact tends to heighten the credibility of public speakers. Eye contact tends to make us feel closer to others and more positive about them. This may explain the research finding that customers leave larger tips when servers maintain eye contact with them (Davis & Kieffer, 1998).

Haptics

Haptics is physical touch. Touch is the first of our senses to develop, and many communication scholars believe that touching and being touched are essential to a healthy life (Whitman, White, O'Mara, & Goeke-Morey, 1999). Research reveals that mothers in dysfunctional families touch their babies less often and less affectionately than mothers in healthy families do. Conversely, research shows that massage helps babies thrive (Mwakalye & DeAngelis, 1995).

Touching also communicates power and status. People of high status touch others and enter others' spaces more than people with less status (Henley, 1977). Cultural views of women as more touchable than men are reflected in gendered patterns. Women tend to touch others to show liking and intimacy, whereas men more typically rely on touch to assert power and control (Andersen, 1999; Jhally & Katz, 2001; Le Poire, Burgoon, & Parrott, 1992).

> **YVETTE**   *When I was pregnant, total strangers would walk up to me and touch my belly. It was amazing—and disturbing. They seemed to think they had a right to touch me or that the baby wasn't me, so they could touch him. Amazing!*

Physical Appearance

Western culture places an extremely high value on **physical appearance**. For this reason, most of us notice how others look, and we form initial evaluations based on their appearance. We first notice obvious physical qualities such as sex, skin color, size, and features. What we notice about others' appearance leads us to form judgments of how attractive they are and to make inferences about their personalities. Although our judgments and inferences may be inaccurate, they can affect our decisions about friendships, dating, hiring, and promotion.

Cultures stipulate ideals for physical form. Currently, cultural ideals in the West emphasize thinness and softness in women and muscularity and height in men (Kilbourne, 2004; Lamb & Brown, 2006; Levin & Kilbourne, 2008). In an effort to meet these ideals, some men engage in excessive body building or use steroids, and many people—particularly women—develop eating disorders (Kilbourne, 2004). If you'd like to learn about eating disorders and ways to help people who have them, use your Online Resources for *Communication in Our Lives* to access **WebLink 6.1** and visit the National Eating Disorders Association's website.

COMMUNICATION in Your Life

How are cultural ideals for physical appearance communicated to us?

CourseMate

General Western standards for attractiveness are qualified by ethnic identity. African Americans generally admire fuller figures than European Americans, and this is especially true among African Americans who identify strongly with African American culture (Mernissi, 2004; Schooler, Ward, Merriwether, & Caruthers, 2004; Walker, 2007).

CASS   *I found out how much appearance matters when I was in an auto accident. It messed up my face so that I had scars all over one side and on my forehead. All of a sudden, nobody was asking me out. All these guys who had been so crazy about me before the accident lost interest. Some of my girlfriends seemed uneasy about being seen with me. When I first had the wreck, I was so glad to be alive that I didn't even think about plastic surgery. After a couple of months of seeing how others treated me, however, I had the surgery.*

Artifacts

Artifacts are personal objects with which we announce our identities and personalize our environments. We craft our image by how we dress, the jewelry we wear, and the objects we carry and use. Nurses and doctors wear white and often drape stethoscopes around their necks; professors travel with briefcases, whereas students more often tote backpacks. George W. Bush insisted on formal dress—coat and tie—at all times in the Oval Office. He once chewed out a staff person who dared to wear khakis and a buttoned down shirt on a Saturday, and the staff person was not allowed to enter the Oval Office (Stolberg, 2009). When he became President, Barack Obama created a less formal working culture in the White House. He sometimes takes off his jacket while working in the Oval Office, and he often skips the tie on weekends.

We also use artifacts to define settings and personal territories (Wood, 2006a). At annual meetings of companies, the CEO usually speaks from a podium that bears the company logo. In much the same manner, we claim our private spaces by filling them with objects that matter to us and reflect our experiences and values. Lovers of art adorn their homes with paintings and sculptures. Religious families display pictures of holy scenes and the Bible, the Koran, or another sacred text. Our artifacts also symbolize important relationships and experiences. Pictures of family members decorate many offices. I've personalized my writing desk with a photograph of my sister, Carolyn; an item that belonged to my father; the first card Robbie ever gave me; and a jar of rocks from my favorite beach.

NAOMI   *I've moved a lot since coming to college—dorm, apartment, another apartment, and another apartment. I never feel a place is home until I put a photograph of my grandmother holding me on my dresser. Then it's home.*

Artifacts can express personal identity. For instance, body piercing has become popular, particularly among people under 25. Because some people find it unattractive, however, restaurant chains such as Chili's have established policies to limit piercings that might offend customers: Ears are the only visible body part that employees may pierce ("Business Bulletin," 1996).

We also use artifacts to express ethnic identity. Kwanzaa is an African American holiday tradition that celebrates the centrality of home, family, and community. Hanukkah is a Jewish holiday tradition, and Christmas is a European American, Christian tradition. The kinara is a branched candle-holder that holds seven candles, one of which is lit during each day of Kwanzaa (Bellamy, 1996; George, 1995). The menorah is a candleholder used during Hanukkah, and Christmas trees and manger scenes are artifacts used in conjunction with Christmas. In recent years, marketers have offered more ethnic clothing and jewelry so people of color can more easily acquire artifacts that express their cultural heritage.

COMMUNICATION in Your Life

How do your artifacts define your personal environment?

COMMUNICATION HIGHLIGHT

Dress for Success

CourseMate

Does what you wear have anything to do with getting a job or promotion? According to image consultants, dress definitely affects both women's and men's success on the job (Bixler & Nix-Rice, 2005; Henderson & Henshaw, 2007). The colors most appropriate for business settings are black, brown, navy, gray, and beige. Darker colors usually are associated with higher status and greater authority, so wearing navy or black may increase others' perceptions of your rank. What about bolder colors, such as red or purple? A splash of color, such as a bright scarf on a navy dress or a red tie with a dark suit, can indicate confidence; others may assume that you are sure enough of yourself not to stick rigidly to the "safe" colors. However, wearing a bright red dress or a purple jacket may communicate just the opposite message: that you don't know what is appropriate in a work setting.

To learn more about norms for professional dressing, use your Online Resources for *Communication in Our Lives* to access **WebLink 6.2**.

Artifacts chosen by others can communicate about relationships. We give gifts to say, "You matter to me." Artifacts such as engagement rings and wedding bands signify commitment. We also symbolize that we're connected to others by wearing their clothes, as when women wear male partners' shirts.

Proxemics

Proxemics is space and how we use it. Every culture has norms for using space and for how close people should be to one another (Afifi & Burgoon, 2000). In a classic study, Edward Hall (1966) found that in the United States, we interact with social acquaintances from a distance of 4 to 12 feet but are comfortable with 18 inches or less between us and close friends or romantic partners. When we are angry with someone, we tend to move away from him or her and to resent it if he or she approaches us.

Space also signals status; greater space is assumed by those of higher status. Research shows that in our society women and minorities generally have less space than white men (Andersen, 1999; Spain, 1992). The prerogative of entering someone else's personal space is also linked to power; those with greater power are most likely to trespass into others' territory. Responses to invasions

Brad Perks Lightscapes/Alamy

What does this executive's space convey about his power and openness to others?

of space also reflect the relationship between gender and power: Many men respond aggressively when their space is invaded, whereas women are more likely to yield space to the aggressor (Le Poire et al., 1992).

How people arrange space reflects how close they are and whether they want interaction. Rigidly organized businesses may have private offices with doors and little common space. In contrast, more open businesses are likely to have fewer doors and more common space, to invite interaction between employees. Couples who are very interdependent tend to have greater amounts of common space and less individual space in their homes than do couples who are more independent (Fitzpatrick, 1988; Fitzpatrick & Best, 1979; Werner, Altman, & Oxley, 1985). Families that enjoy interaction tend to arrange furniture to invite conversation and eye contact.

Environmental Factors

Environmental factors are elements of settings that affect how we feel and act. For instance, we respond to architecture, colors, room design, temperature, sounds, smells, and lighting. Rooms with comfortable chairs invite relaxation, whereas rooms with stiff chairs prompt formality. Research shows that students perceive professors as more credible and approachable if the professors have attractively decorated offices (Taylor, Wiley, Kuo, & Sullivan, 1998). Dimly lit rooms can enhance romantic feelings, although dark rooms can be depressing. We feel solemn in churches and synagogues with their somber colors and sacred symbols, such as crosses and menorahs.

We tend to feel more lethargic on sultry summer days and more alert on crisp fall days. In settings where people work at night, extra lighting and even artificial skylights sometimes are installed to stimulate alertness. A study conducted by the Rocky Mountain Institute found that increased daylight in work spaces resulted in less absenteeism and fewer errors. Similarly, Wal-Mart discovered that in areas with skylights, customers bought more and employees were more productive than in artificially lit areas (Pierson, 1995).

Restaurants use environmental features to control how long people linger over meals. For example, low lights, comfortable chairs or booths, and soft music often are part of the environment in upscale restaurants. On the other hand, fast-food eateries have hard plastic booths and bright lights, which encourage diners to eat and move on. To make a profit, restaurants have to get people in and out as quickly as possible. Studies indicate that faster music in the background speeds up the pace of eating ("Bites," 1998).

Feng shui is the ancient Chinese art of placement that arranges furniture, objects, colors, and walls in harmony with the earth. Dating back more than 3,000 years, feng shui aims to balance life energy, called *chi*, so that a setting promotes a harmonious flow of energies. Many feng shui principles are consistent with research on nonverbal communication: Don't put large furniture in the path to a door; stairways should not be visible from the front door; use colors to stimulate feelings such as creativity and calmness (Cozart, 1996; O'Neill, 1997; Spear, 1995).

Ron Baker is an expert on classroom environments. He says that even when constructing new classroom buildings, planners are often "making the same kinds of stupid mistakes" (Bartlett, 2003, p. A36). What are those "stupid mistakes"?

COMMUNICATION **HIGHLIGHT**

Environmental Racism

According to Robert Cox (2009), president of the Sierra Club, the term *environmental racism* arose to describe a pattern whereby toxic waste dumps and hazardous industrial plants are located in low-income neighborhoods and communities of color. The pattern is clear: The space of minorities and poor people can be invaded and contaminated, but the territory of more affluent citizens cannot be.

To learn more about environmental racism (also called *environmental justice*), use your Online Resources for *Communication in Our Lives* to access **WebLink 6.4.** This site provides information on the Environmental Protection Agency's strategies for preventing environmental racism.

Lights that cause glare on laptop screens; chairs that are too small for some students; desks that won't accommodate a notebook, a laptop, and a textbook; and inadequate air conditioning or heating. To learn more about Ron Baker's ideas on ideal classrooms, visit his website by using your Online Resources for *Communication in Our Lives* to access **WebLink 6.3.**

Chronemics

Chronemics is how we perceive and use time to define identities and interaction. In an early study of how and what time communicates, Nancy Henley (1977) identified a cultural rule: Important people with high status can keep others waiting. Conversely, people with low status are expected to be punctual in Western society. More recent research validates Henley's finding that time and status are related (Levine & Norenzayan, 1999; Richmond & McCroskey, 1995b). It is standard practice to have to wait, sometimes a long while, to see a doctor, even if you have an appointment. This carries the message that the doctor's time is more valuable than ours. Professors can be late to class, and students are expected to wait, but students sometimes are reprimanded if they arrive after a class begins. Subordinates are expected to report punctually to meetings, but bosses are allowed to be tardy.

Chronemics express cultural attitudes toward time. In Western societies, time is valuable, so speed is highly valued (Calero, 2005; Hochschild, 1997; Honoré, 2005). Thus, we replace our computers and cell phones as soon as faster models hit the market. We often try to do several things at once to get more done. Many everyday expressions reflect the cultural view that time is like money, a valuable and limited resource to be used wisely: "You're *wasting* my time." "This will *save* some time." "I don't *have* any time to *give* you." "That mistake *cost* me 3 hours." "I've *invested* a lot of time in this class, and now I'm *running out of time.*"

Many other cultures have far more relaxed attitudes toward time and punctuality. In many South American countries it's not impolite to come late to meetings or classes, and it's not assumed that people will leave at the scheduled ending time (Levine & Norenzayan, 1999). Whether time is treated casually, or closely watched and measured out, reflects larger cultural attitudes toward living.

The amount of time we spend with different people reflects our interpersonal priorities. A manager spends more time with a new employee who seems to have executive potential than with one who seems less impressive. A speaker spends more time responding to a question from a high-status member of the audience than to a person of lower status. We spend more time with people we like than with those we don't like or who bore us. Increasing time together is one of the most important ways college students intensify relationships, and reducing time together signals decreasing interest (Baxter, 1985; Dindia, 1994; Tolhuizen, 1989).

Paralanguage

Paralanguage is vocal communication that does not involve words. It includes sounds, such as murmurs and gasps, and vocal qualities, such as volume, rhythm, pitch, and inflection. Our voices are versatile instruments that tell others how to interpret us and what we say. Vocal cues signal others to interpret what we say as a joke, threat, statement of fact, question, and so forth. Vocal cues also express irritation. Effective public speakers know how to modulate inflection, volume, and rhythm to enhance their verbal messages.

We use our voices to communicate feelings. Whispering, for instance, often signals secrecy, and shouting conveys anger. Depending on the context, sighing may communicate empathy, boredom, or contentment. Research indicates that tone of voice is a powerful clue to feelings between marital partners. Negative vocal tones are among the most important symbols of marital dissatisfaction (Gottman, 1994b; Noller, 1987). Negative intonation may also signal dissatisfaction or disapproval in work settings. The reverse is also true: A warm voice conveys liking, and a playful lilt suggests friendliness.

We use our voices to communicate how we see ourselves and wish to be seen by others. For instance, we use a firm, confident voice in job interviews or when explaining why we deserve a raise. We also know how to make ourselves sound apologetic, seductive, or angry when it suits us. In addition to the ways we intentionally use our voices to project an image, vocal qualities we don't deliberately choose can affect how others perceive us. Pace of speaking may influence perceptions. For instance, research shows that people who speak at a slow to moderate rate are perceived as having greater control over interaction than people who speak rapidly (Tusing & Dillard, 2000).

> **COMMUNICATION**
> **in Your Life**
>
> **With whom do you spend the most and least time?**

RAYNA *When I first moved to the United States, I didn't understand many words and idioms. I did not understand that "A bird in the hand is worth two in the bush" meant it is smart to hold on to what is sure. I did not understand that "hang a right" meant to turn right. So when I did not understand, I would ask people to explain. Most times they would say the very same thing over, just louder and more slowly, like I was deaf or stupid. I felt like saying to them in a very loud, slow voice, "I am Indian, not stupid. You are stupid."*

Paralanguage also reflects our cultural heritage. For example, many African Americans' speech has more vocal range, inflection, and tonal quality than that

Whispered secrets reflect special intimacy between people.

of most European Americans (Garner, 1994). In addition, among themselves some African Americans engage in highly rhythmic rapping and "high talk" to create desired identities (Ribeau, Baldwin, & Hecht, 1994). We also use paralanguage to perform gender. To perform masculinity, men use strong volume, low pitch, and limited inflection, all of which conform to cultural prescriptions for men to be assertive and emotionally controlled. To perform femininity, women tend to use higher pitch, softer volume, and more inflection. We also perform class by our pronunciation of words, our accents, and the complexity of our sentences.

Silence

A final type of nonverbal behavior is **silence,** which can communicate powerful messages. The assertion "I'm not speaking to you" actually speaks volumes. We use silence to communicate different meanings. For instance, silence indicates contentment when intimates are so comfortable they don't need to talk. Silence can also communicate awkwardness, as you know if you've ever had trouble keeping conversation going with a new acquaintance. We feel pressured to fill the void.

Silence can also disconfirm others. In some families, children are disciplined by being ignored. No matter what the child says or does, parents refuse to acknowledge his or her existence. In later life, the silencing strategy may also surface. You know how disconfirming silence can be if you've ever said hello to someone and gotten no reply. Even if the other person didn't deliberately ignore you, you felt slighted. We sometimes deliberately freeze out others when we're angry with them (Williams, 2001). In some military academies, such as West Point, silencing is a recognized method of stripping a cadet of personhood if he or she is perceived as having broken the academy code. Whistle-blowers and union-busters often are shunned by peers. Similarly, the Catholic Church excommunicates people who violate its canons.

The complex system of nonverbal communication includes kinesics, haptics, physical appearance, artifacts, proxemics, environmental features, chronemics, paralanguage, and silence. We use these nonverbal behaviors to announce our identities and to communicate how we feel about relationships with others. To explore using nonverbal communication to project an identity for yourself in various situations, complete the activity "Sculpting Personal Image with Nonverbal Communication" via your Online Resources for *Communication in Our Lives.*

In the final section of this chapter, we consider guidelines for improving the effectiveness of our nonverbal communication.

CourseMate

IMPROVING NONVERBAL COMMUNICATION

Nonverbal communication, like its verbal cousin, can be misinterpreted. You can reduce the likelihood of misunderstandings in nonverbal communication by following two guidelines.

Monitor Your Nonverbal Communication

The monitoring skills we have stressed in other chapters are also important for competent nonverbal communication. Think about the ways we use nonverbal behaviors to announce our identities. Are you projecting the image you desire? Do your facial and body movements represent how you see yourself and how you want others to perceive you? Do people ever tell you that you seem uninterested when they are talking to you? If so, you can monitor your nonverbal actions and modify them to more clearly communicate involvement and interest. You can also set up your spaces to invite the kind of interaction you prefer.

Interpret Others' Nonverbal Communication Tentatively

In this chapter, we've discussed findings about the meanings people tend to attach to nonverbal behaviors. It's important to realize that these are only generalizations about how we interpret nonverbal communication. We cannot state what any particular behavior means to specific people in a particular context. For instance, we've said that people who like each other tend to be physically closer when interacting. However, sometimes people prefer autonomy and want personal space. In addition, someone may maintain distance because she or he has a cold and doesn't want a partner to catch it. Also, the generalizations we've discussed may not apply to people from non-Western cultures. Ethical communicators qualify their interpretations of nonverbal behavior by considering personal and contextual considerations.

Personal Qualifications   Nonverbal patterns that accurately describe most people may not apply to particular individuals. Although eye contact generally indicates responsiveness, some people close their eyes to concentrate when listening. In such cases, it would be inaccurate to conclude that a person who doesn't look at us isn't listening. Similarly, people who cross their arms and condense into a tight posture may be expressing hostility or lack of interest in interaction. However, the same behaviors might mean a person is cold. Most people use less inflection, fewer gestures, and a slack posture when they're not really interested in what they're talking about. However, fatigue can result in the same behaviors.

To avoid misinterpreting others' nonverbal communication, you can check perceptions and use *I*-language, not *you*-language, which we discussed in Chapter 5. You can check perceptions to find out whether the way you interpret another's nonverbal behavior is what that other person means: "I sense that you're not really involved in this conversation; is that how you feel?" In addition, you can rely on *I*-language. *You*-language might lead us to inaccurately say of someone who doesn't look at us, "You're communicating lack of interest." A more responsible statement would use *I*-language to say, "When you don't look at me, I feel you're not interested in what I'm saying." Using *I*-language reminds us to take responsibility for our judgments and feelings. In addition, it reduces the likelihood that we will make others defensive by inaccurately interpreting their nonverbal behavior.

Contextual Qualifications Like the meaning of verbal communication, the significance of nonverbal behaviors depends on the contexts in which they occur. Most people are more at ease on their own turf than on someone else's, so we tend to be more friendly and outgoing in our homes than in business meetings and public spaces. We also dress according to context. When I am on campus or in business meetings, I dress professionally, but at home I usually wear jeans or running clothes.

In addition to our immediate physical settings, nonverbal communication reflects particular cultures. We are likely to misinterpret people from other cultures when we impose the norms and rules of our culture on them. An Arabic man who stands practically on top of others to talk with them is not being rude, according to his culture's standards, although Westerners might interpret him as such.

ELENI *I have been misinterpreted very much in this country. My first semester here, a professor told me he wanted me to be more assertive and to speak up in class. I could not do that, I told him. He said I should put myself forward, but I have been brought up not to do that. In Taiwan, that is very rude and ugly, and we are taught not to speak up to teachers. Now that I have been here for 3 years, I sometimes speak in classes, but I am still quieter than Americans. I know my professors think I am not so smart because I am quiet, but that is the teaching of my country.*

Even within a single culture, different social communities have distinct rules for nonverbal behavior. A man who doesn't make "listening noises" may be listening intently according to the rules of masculine speech communities. Similarly, when women nod and make listening noises while another is talking, men may misperceive them as agreeing. According to the rules typically learned in feminine social communities, ongoing feedback is a way of signaling interest, not necessarily agreement. We should adopt dual perspective when interpreting others, especially when they belong to cultures or communities that are different from ours.

BEYOND THE CLASSROOM

Let's take the material in this chapter beyond the classroom by thinking about how what you've learned about nonverbal communication might apply to the workplace, ethical choices, and engagement with the broader world.

1. **Workplace.** Visit a workplace of the type you imagine working in after you've completed your education. Analyze nonverbal communication and notice what it tells you about this particular workplace. How is space arranged? Are there individual offices or workstations that aren't isolated? If there are both, who gets the private offices? How are employees dressed? How much do employees rely on nonverbal communication such as touch and eye contact to signal friendliness?

2. **Ethics.** Ethical issues surround space and who does and doesn't have access to particular spaces. Some managers of stores do not want homeless citizens in their places of business. They think that these citizens' presence would hurt business by discouraging other citizens from patronizing their stores. Yet advocates for homeless citizens say that businesses are places that are open to the public, and business owners and managers can't allow only some of the public to enter their establishments. What do you think is the most ethical way to address the issue of whether businesses should allow homeless citizens into their establishments?

   Ethics

3. **Engagement.** Attend a gathering of people from a culture different from yours. It might be a meeting at a Jewish temple if you're Christian, a black church if you are white, or a meeting of Asian students if you are Western. Observe nonverbal behaviors of the people there: How do they greet one another? How much eye contact accompanies interaction? How close to one another do people sit? Can you make inferences about cultural values based on nonverbal communication that you observe?

CHAPTER SUMMARY

In this chapter, we've explored the world beyond words. We learned that there are similarities and differences between nonverbal communication and verbal communication. Next, we noted that nonverbal communication supplements or replaces verbal messages, regulates interaction, reflects and establishes relationship-level meanings, and expresses cultural membership.

We discussed nine types of nonverbal communication: kinesics, haptics, physical appearance, artifacts, proxemics, environmental features, chronemics, paralanguage, and silence. Each form of nonverbal communication reflects cultural understandings and values and also expresses our personal identities and feelings toward others.

Because nonverbal communication, like verbal communication, is symbolic, it has no inherent, universal meaning. Instead, we construct meaning as we notice, organize, and interpret nonverbal behaviors.

APPLYING COMMUNICATION IN OUR LIVES

The key concepts, For Further Reflection and Discussion questions, and Experiencing Communication in Our Lives case study that follow will help you review, reflect on, and extend the information and ideas presented in this chapter. These resources, and a diverse selection of additional study tools, are also available as Online Resources for *Communication in Our Lives*. Your Online Resources include CourseMate, a student workbook, interactive video activities, audio study tools, a book companion website, Speech Builder Express, Speech Studio, and InfoTrac College Edition. For more information or to access this book's online resources, visit **www.cengage.com/login**.

KEY CONCEPTS

artifacts, 132
chronemics, 136
environmental factors, 135
haptics, 131

kinesics, 129
nonverbal communication, 123
paralanguage, 137
physical appearance, 131

proxemics, 134
silence, 138

FOR FURTHER REFLECTION AND DISCUSSION

1. Attend a gathering of people who belong to a social community different from yours. Observe nonverbal behaviors of the people there: How do they greet one another, how much eye contact accompanies interaction, and how close to one another do people stand and sit?

2. Visit restaurants near your campus. Describe the kinds of seats, lighting, music (if any), and distance between tables. Do you find any connections between nonverbal patterns and expensiveness of restaurants?

3. Describe the spatial arrangements in the home of your family of origin. Was there a room in which family members interacted a good deal? How was furniture arranged in that room? Who had separate space and personal chairs in your family? What do the nonverbal patterns reflect about your family's communication style?

4. What ethical issues are entailed in interpreting others' nonverbal communication? What would be ethical and unethical interpretations?

Ethics

SHARPEN YOUR SKILL

1. Communicating Closeness

What do nonverbal behaviors say about how intimate people are? To find out, observe (a) a couple that you know is very close, (b) a clerk and a shopper in a store, and (c) a teacher and student who are talking. How closely do the people sit or stand to each other? How do their postures differ? What facial expressions and eye contact do they use in each situation?

2. Environmental Awareness

Think of one place where you feel rushed and one where you linger. Describe the following about each place:

How is furniture arranged?
What kind of lighting is used?
What sort of music is played, and what other sounds are there?
How comfortable is the furniture for sitting or lounging?
What colors and art are there?
Based on your observations, can you make generalizations about environmental features that promote relaxation and ones that do not?

EXPERIENCING COMMUNICATION IN OUR LIVES

CASE STUDY: *Nonverbal Cues*

A video of the conversation scripted here is featured in your Chapter 6 Online Resources for *Communication in Our Lives*. Select "Nonverbal Cues" to watch the video. Improve your own communication skills by reading, watching, and evaluating this communication encounter.

CourseMate

© Cengage Learning

A project team is meeting to discuss the most effective way to present its recommendations for implementing a flextime policy on a trial basis. Members of the team are Jason Brown, team leader; Erika Filene; Victoria Lawrence; Bill Williams; and Jensen Chen. They are seated around a rectangular table with Jason at the head.

JASON: So we've decided to recommend trying flextime for a 2-month period and with a number of procedures to make sure that people's new schedules don't interfere with productivity. There's a lot of information to communicate to employees, so how can we do that best?

VICTORIA: I think it would be good to use PowerPoint to highlight the key aspects of the new procedures. People always seem to remember better if they see something.

BILL: Oh, come on. PowerPoint is so overused. Everyone is tired of it by now. Can't we do something more creative?

VICTORIA: Well, I like it. It's a good teaching tool.

BILL: I didn't know we were teaching. I thought our job was to report recommendations.

VICTORIA: So what do you suggest, Bill? (*She nervously pulls on her bracelet as she speaks.*)

BILL: I don't have a suggestion. I'm just against PowerPoint. (*He doesn't look up as he speaks.*)

JASON: Okay, let's not bicker among ourselves. (*He pauses, gazes directly at Bill, then continues.*) Lots of people like PowerPoint, lots don't. Instead of arguing about its value, let's ask what it is we want to communicate to the employees here. Maybe talking about our goal first will help us decide on the best means of achieving it.

ERIKA: Good idea. I'd like us to focus first on getting everyone excited about the benefits of flextime. If they understand those, they'll be motivated to learn the procedures, even if there are a lot of them.

JENSEN: Erika is right. That's a good way to start. Maybe we could create a handout or PowerPoint slide—either would work—to summarize the benefits of flextime we've identified in our research.

JASON: Good, okay now we're cooking. Victoria, will you make notes on the ideas as we discuss them?

Victoria opens a notebook and begins writing notes. Noticing that Bill is typing into his PDA, Jason looks directly at Bill and speaks.

JASON: Are you with us on how we lead off in our presentation?

BILL: Sure, fine with me. (*He puts the PDA aside but keeps his eyes on it.*)

ERIKA: So maybe then we should say that the only way flextime can work is if we make sure that everyone agrees on procedures so that no division is ever missing more than one person during key production hours.

JENSEN: Very good. That would add to people's motivation to learn and follow the procedures we've found are effective in other companies like ours. I think it would be great if Erika could present that topic because she did most of the research on it. (*He smiles at Erika, and she pantomimes tipping her hat to him.*)

JASON: (*He looks at Erika with a raised brow, and she nods.*) Good. Okay, Erika's in charge of that. What's next?

VICTORIA: Then it's time to spell out the procedures and . . .

BILL: You can't just spell them out. You have to explain each one—give people a rationale for them—or they won't follow them.

Victoria glares at Bill, then looks across the table at Erika, who shrugs as if to say, "I don't know what's bothering Bill today."

JASON: Bill, why don't you lead off, then, and tell us the first procedure we should mention and the rationale we should provide for it.

BILL: (*Looks up from his PDA, which he's been using again, and shrugs.*) Just spell out the rules, that's all.

VICTORIA: Would it be too much trouble for you to cut off your gadget and join us in this meeting, Bill?

BILL: Would it be too much trouble for you to quit hassling me?

JASON: (*He turns his chair to face Bill squarely.*) Look, I don't know what's eating you, but you're really being a jerk. If you've got a problem with this meeting or someone here, put it on the table. Otherwise, be a team player.

QUESTIONS FOR ANALYSIS AND DISCUSSION

You can answer these questions and see my responses to them online via your Online Resources for Chapter 6.

1. Identify nonverbal behaviors that regulate turn taking within the team.
2. Identify nonverbal behaviors that express relational-level meanings of communication. What aspects of team members' nonverbal communication express liking or disliking, responsiveness or lack of responsiveness, and power?
3. How do artifacts affect interaction between members of the team?
4. If you were the sixth member of this team, what kinds of communication might you enact to help relieve tension in the group?

7

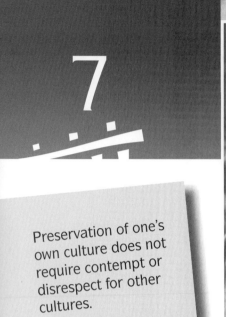

> Preservation of one's own culture does not require contempt or disrespect for other cultures.
>
> **Cesar Chavez**

Ira Block/National Geographic/Getty Images

Communication and Culture

Concha cradles his daughter in his arms and sings her to sleep while his village wife, Bishnu, plows the small field of vegetables outside their cottage. Later today, she will repair the walls on the cottage for the harsh winter ahead. Tomorrow Concha begins the 2-day walk to Kathmandu, where he will live with his city wife, Ran Maya, and their children. That will be his home for the next 6 months between treks he leads in the Himalayas.

Halfway across the globe, John returns home after a long day at his law office. He parks his Buick in the garage and walks into the kitchen, where his wife, Ginny, is nursing their son, Daniel. After dinner, she will bathe Daniel and put him to bed, and John will mow the lawn and repair a leaky faucet. Later, he'll pack a bag for tomorrow's flight to

SHARPEN YOUR SKILL

At the end of this chapter, refer to the Sharpen Your Skill features, Communicating Culture and Your Culture's Sayings, to apply concepts from Chapter 7.

a conference 2,000 miles away. He'll be gone a week, and the au pair will help Ginny with Daniel.

More than distance separates these two families. They have different understandings of what family means and how it operates. In Nepal, gender roles are not as distinct as they are in the United States: Both women and men, as well as extended families, care for children. Both sexes engage in physical labor. Having both a village family and a city family ensures a continuous home life for many Nepalese men, who often spend half of each year based in Kathmandu, from which mountain treks and expeditions originate. Having two families is acceptable in Nepal, but no Nepalese would hire an au pair because they believe that family and neighbors should participate in caring for children. What Concha, Bishnu, Ran Maya, John, and Ginny consider normal and right reflects the values and norms of their respective cultures.

In this chapter, we explore relationships between communication and culture. In our multicultural society, being an effective citizen and professional depends on understanding different heritages and the communication practices they foster. First, we'll define culture and discuss the intricate ways it is entwined with communication. Then, we'll focus on guidelines for increasing the effectiveness of communication between people of different cultures and social communities.

UNDERSTANDING CULTURE

Although the word **culture** is part of our everyday vocabulary, it's difficult to define. Culture is part of everything we think, do, feel, and believe, yet we can't point to a thing that is culture. Most simply defined, culture is a way of life. It is a system of ideas, values, beliefs, structures, and practices that is communicated by one generation to the next and that sustains a particular way of life. To understand cultures more fully, we now consider two key premises about them.

Cultures Are Systems

The first premise about cultures is that they are systems. A culture is not a random collection of ideas, beliefs, values, and customs; rather, it is a coherent system of understandings, traditions, values, communication practices, and ways of living. As anthropologist Edward T. Hall noted years ago, "You touch a culture in one place and everything else is affected" (1977, p. 14).

You'll recall that when we defined communication in Chapter 1, we noted that it is a systemic process. This means that communication can be understood only within its particular systems or contexts. Culture is one of the most important systems within which communication occurs. We are not born knowing how, when, and to whom to speak, just as we are not born with attitudes about different races, religions, sexual orientations, and other aspects of identity. We learn these as we interact with others, and we then tend to reflect cultural teachings in our own communication. For each of us, our culture directly shapes how we communicate, teaching us whether interrupting is appropriate, how much eye contact is polite, and whether argument and conflict are desirable in groups and personal relationships.

You'll recall from our previous discussion of systems that the parts of a system interact and affect one another. Because cultures are systems, aspects of a culture are interrelated and work together to create a whole. For example, one of the major changes in Western society was the Industrial Revolution. Before the mid-1800s, most families lived and worked together in one place. In agricultural regions, women, men, and children worked together to plant, tend, harvest, and store crops and to take care of livestock. In cities, family businesses were common. This preindustrial way of life promoted cooperative relationships and family togetherness. The invention of fuel-powered machines led to mass production in factories, where workers spent 8 or more hours each day. In turn, this provoked competition among workers to produce and earn more, and on-the-job communication became more competitive and individualistic. As men were hired for industrial jobs, women assumed primary responsibilities in the home, and men's roles in family life diminished. Thus, a change in work life produced reverberations throughout the culture.

The technological revolution that began in the 1970s and continues today has also had multiple and interrelated repercussions in cultural life. The Internet and cells allow people to maintain regular communication over great distances. Computer networking, virtual conferencing, and virtual offices allow many people to work at home. Today, many people sustain and form friendships and romantic relationships over the Internet. New technologies change how, where, and with whom we communicate, just as they change the boundaries we use to define work and personal life. Because cultures are holistic, no change is ever isolated from the overall system.

Multiple Social Communities in a Single Culture

When we speak of different cultures, we often think of geographically distinct regions. For instance, India, South America, Africa, and France are separate cultures. Yet geographic separation isn't what defines a culture. Instead, a culture exists when a distinct way of life shapes what a group of people believes, values, and does. Even within a single culture, however, there are numerous social communities with distinct ways of life.

Social communities are groups of people who live within a dominant culture yet also are members of another group or groups that are not dominant in a particular society. Social communities are distinct from dominant culture although not necessarily opposed to or entirely outside of it. In this book, I use the term *culture* to refer to the way of life that is dominant in a society. I use the term *social community* to refer to groups that are both distinct from and part of the larger culture.

Every culture has a dominant, or mainstream, way of life. Although many groups may exist within a single society, not all of them identify equally and exclusively with the dominant culture. Since the colonial days, mainstream Western culture has reflected the values and experiences of Western, heterosexual, young and middle-aged, middle- and upper-class, able-bodied White men who are Christian at least in heritage if not in actual practice.

Yet Western culture includes many groups that do not fully identify with the mainstream. People in their 70s, 80s, or 90s often feel devalued or erased

COMMUNICATION HIGHLIGHT

Life on the Color Line

Gregory Howard Williams began life as the white son in a middle-class family in Virginia. At age 10, however, he became a black living in Muncie, Indiana. His father, James Anthony "Buster" Williams, was an olive-skinned man with some African ancestry. Buster wanted desperately to escape racism and gain the privileges that whites have as a birthright. His son, Gregory, has pale skin, thin lips, and straight hair, which allowed others to perceive him as White.

In his autobiography, *Life on the Color Line: The True Story of a White Boy Who Discovered He Was Black* (1995), Gregory Williams provides a stunning account of the differences in how he was treated when he was considered white and black.

by the youth-oriented culture of the United States. Gay men, lesbians, intersexuals, transsexuals, transgendered people, and bisexuals experience difficulty in a society that defines them as marginal (Ekins & King, 2006). People who have disabilities encounter countless problems as they attempt to live and work in a society that is made for able-bodied people. Prevailing customs in the United States often ignore the traditions of people who follow religions such as Judaism and Buddhism. Bikers, skinheads, and punk rockers are other groups that do not fit—and often don't want to fit—within mainstream U.S. culture.

Mainstream ideology is evident in nonverbal communication. For example, Western culture often conveys the message that people without disabilities are normal and people with disabilities are not. Notice how many buildings have no ramps and how many public presentations don't include signers for people with impaired hearing. Most campus and business buildings feature portraits of white men, leaving people of color and women unrepresented.

Mainstream values may be in tension with those of particular social communities. As Sabrina notes in her commentary, misunderstanding can erupt when values and communication practices of social communities and mainstream culture clash.

COMMUNICATION in Your Life

Do you belong to any social groups that are outside of the cultural mainstream in the United States?

SABRINA   *I get hassled by a lot of white girls on campus about being dependent on my family. They say I should grow up and leave the nest. They say I'm too close to my folks and my grandparents, aunts, uncles, and cousins. But what they mean by "too close" is that I'm closer with my family than most whites are. It's a white standard they're using, and it doesn't fit most blacks. Strong ties with family and the black community have always been our way.*

Communication styles reflect cultures and social communities.

Collectivist cultures and social communities regard people as deeply connected to one another and to their families, groups, and communities. Thus, priority is given to harmony, group welfare, and interdependence (Jandt, 2006; Samovar, Porter, & McDaniel, 2009). Collectivist cultures and social communities tend to rely on a **high-context communication style**, which is indirect and undetailed. Because it is assumed that people are deeply interconnected, people do not feel the need to spell everything out in explicit detail (Jandt, 2009).

Individualistic cultures and social communities regard each person as distinct from others; individuality is more prominent than membership in groups, families, and so forth. Priority is given to personal freedom, independence, and individual rights. Members of individualist cultures and social communities generally use a **low-context communication style**, which is explicit, detailed, and precise. The emphasis on individuality means that communicators cannot presume others share their meanings and values (Jandt, 2009).

When people from different cultures and social communities interact, their different ways of communicating may cause misunderstandings. For instance, traditional Japanese people don't touch or shake hands to greet. Instead, they bow to preserve each person's personal space, which is very important in that culture. In Greece, however, touching is part of being friendly and sociable (Hargraves, 2001a, 2001b; Kohls, 2001). In the United States, Britain, and some other societies, people form orderly lines to buy tickets, enter buildings, and board buses and planes. In India, people don't form lines—they push and rush to get a place (Spano, 2003). An American might interpret pushing for a space as rude, but in India it is an acceptable way to get a place.

Gender as a Social Community   Of the many social communities that exist, gender has received particularly intense study. Because we know more about it than about other social communities, we'll explore gender as an extended example of a social community that shapes how members communicate.

Researchers have investigated how girls and boys usually are socialized primarily in sex-segregated groups so that they learn communication practices that society regards as appropriate for their respective sexes. For instance, women's talk generally is more expressive and focused on feelings and relationships, whereas men's talk tends to be more instrumental and competitive (Aries, 1987; Beck, 1988; Johnson, 1989, 1996; Walker, 2004; Wood, 1993b, 1995a, 1996b, 2005, 2011).

Another general difference lies in what each gender regards as the primary basis of relationships. For people who have internalized masculine identities, activities tend to be a key foundation of close friendships and romantic relationships (Inman, 1996; Metts, 2006a; Swain, 1989; Walker, 2004; Wood & Inman, 1993). Thus, men typically cement friendships by doing things together (i.e., working on cars, watching sports) and doing things for one another (i.e., trading favors, washing a car).

People who have internalized feminine identities tend to regard communication as the crux of relationships. Thus, women often regard talking about feelings, personal issues, and daily life as the way to build and enrich relationships (Braithwaite & Kellas, 2006; Duck & Wood, 2006; Johnson, 1996; Metts, 2006a).

Given the differences between how women and men, in general, use communication, it's hardly surprising that the sexes often misunderstand one another. One clash between gendered communication styles occurs when women and men discuss problems. When women talk about something that is troubling them, they are often looking first for empathy and connection. Yet, masculine socialization teaches men to use communication instrumentally, so they often offer advice or solutions (Tannen, 1990; Wood, 1998, 2011). Thus, women sometimes interpret men's advice as a lack of personal concern. On the other hand, men may feel frustrated when women offer empathy and support instead of advice for solving problems. In general, men also make fewer explicit personal disclosures, whereas women regard sharing confidences as an important way to enhance closeness (Aries, 1987; Johnson, 1996).

Men and women, in general, also have different styles of listening. Socialized to be responsive and expressive, women tend to make listening noises such as "um hm," "yeah," and "I know what you mean" when others are talking (Tannen, 1990; Wood, 2009, 2011). Sometimes women think men aren't listening to them because men who follow the communication rules of masculine social communities don't show attentiveness in the ways women have learned to expect.

COMMUNICATION in Your Life

Is your communication consistent with general tendencies for your gender?

Bonnie Kamin/PhotoEdit

Do the women in this photo appear to be communicating in ways consistent with research on feminine social communities?

Men may misinterpret women's listening noises as indicating agreement (rather than attention) and be surprised when women later disagree with them.

Perhaps the most common complication in communication between women and men occurs when a woman says, "Let's talk about us." To men, this often means trouble because they interpret the request as implying there is a problem in a relationship. For women, however, this is not the only—or even the main—reason to talk about a relationship. Within feminine social communities, talking is a primary way to celebrate and increase closeness (Acitelli, 1993; Wood, 2011). The instrumental focus of masculine social communities teaches that talking about a relationship is useful only if there is some problem to be resolved (Acitelli, 1988, 1993; Wood, 1998).

LARRY   *Finally, I see what happens between my girlfriend and me. She always wants to talk about us, which I think is stupid unless we have a problem. I like to go to a concert or do something together, but then she says that I don't want to be with her. We speak totally different languages.*

Other Social Communities   Gender isn't the only social community, and communication between men and women is not the only kind of interaction that may be plagued by misunderstandings. Research indicates that communication patterns vary between social classes. For example, working-class people tend to stay closer to and rely more on extended family than do middle- and upper-class Americans (Bornstein & Bradley, 2003; Cancian, 1987). Working-class men also tend to see physical strength and practical skills as more central to masculinity than middle- and upper-class men (Mumby, 2006a).

Race and ethnicity may also shape social communities and their distinct communication patterns. For example, research indicates that African Americans generally communicate more assertively than European Americans (Orbe & Harris, 2001; Ribeau, Baldwin, & Hecht, 1994). What some African Americans consider authentic, powerful exchanges may be perceived as antagonistic by people from different social communities. The rapping and styling that some African Americans engage in are not practiced (or understood) by most European Americans (Houston & Wood, 1996; Wood, 1998). African American communication also tends to reflect greater commitment to collective interests such as family and community, whereas European American communication tends to be more individualistic (Gaines, 1995). As a rule, African Americans also communicate more interactively than European Americans. This explains why some African Americans call out responses such as "Tell it," "All right," and "Keep talking" during speeches, church sermons, and other public presentations. What many Caucasians regard as interruptions, some African Americans perceive as participation in communication.

Notice that in discussing social communities and their communication patterns, I use qualifying words. For instance, I note that *most* women behave in certain ways and that *some* blacks *tend to* communicate more interactively than whites. This is to remind us that not all members of a social community behave

Cybercommunities

Are groups that form and operate on the Web and the Internet cultures or social communities? To answer that question, we need to know whether cybercommunities have shared values, beliefs, practices, and languages that are not understood by people outside the groups. Many ongoing chat rooms and cybergroups do share values and unique practices and language that newcomers must learn in order to participate effectively (Swiss, 2001). They develop specialized abbreviations and phrases that cannot be understood by people who are not members. Does this make them cultures or social communities?

To learn more, use your Online Resources for *Communication in Our Lives* to access **WebLink 7.1.**

in the same way. Although generalizations are useful and informative, they should not mislead us into thinking that all members of any social community think, feel, and communicate alike. We engage in stereotyping and uncritical thinking when we fail to recognize differences between individual members of social groups.

COMMUNICATION'S RELATIONSHIP TO CULTURE AND SOCIAL COMMUNITIES

Communication and culture cannot be separated because each influences the other. Culture is reflected in communication practices; at the same time, communication practices shape cultural life. We'll discuss five principles that apply to social communities and cultures.

Communication Expresses and Sustains Cultures

Patterns of communication reflect cultural values and perspectives. For example, many Asian languages include numerous words to describe particular relationships (my grandmother's brother, my father's uncle, my youngest son, my oldest daughter). This reflects the cultural emphasis on family relationships (Ferrante, 2009). There are fewer English words to describe specific kinship bonds.

The respect of many Asian cultures for elderly people is reflected in language. "I will be 60 tomorrow" is an Asian saying that means, "I am old enough to deserve respect." In contrast, Western cultures tend to prize youth and to have many positive words for youthfulness (*young in spirit, fresh*) and negative words for seniority (*has-been, outdated, old-fashioned, over the hill*) (Ferrante, 2009).

Communication simultaneously reflects and sustains cultural values. Each time we express cultural values, we also perpetuate them. When some Asian Americans veil emotions in interaction, they fortify and express the value of self-restraint and the priority of reason over emotion. When Caucasians argue, emphasize their ideas, and compete in conversations, they uphold the values of individuality and assertiveness. Beards worn by Orthodox and Hasidic Jews

COMMUNICATION HIGHLIGHT

Proverbs Express Cultural Values

Here are examples of sayings that reflect the values of particular cultures (Gudykunst & Lee, 2002; Samovar & Porter, 2001).

- "It is the nail that sticks out that gets hammered down." This Japanese saying reflects the idea that a person should not stand out from others but instead should conform.

- "No need to know the person, only the family." This Chinese axiom reflects the belief that individuals are less important than families.

- "A zebra does not despise its stripes." Among the African Masai, this saying encourages acceptance of things and oneself as they are.

- "The child has no owner." "It takes a whole village to raise a child." These African adages express the cultural beliefs that children belong to whole communities and that rearing and caring for children are the responsibility of all members of those communities, not just the children's biological parents.

To learn proverbs in other countries such as Turkey and Palestine, use your Online Resources for *Communication in Our Lives* to access **WebLink 7.2** and **WebLink 7.3**.

express reverence, whereas Buddhist monks often shave their faces and heads to express their spiritual commitments (Haught, 2003). Communication, then, is a mirror of a culture's values and a primary means of keeping them woven into the fabric of everyday life.

Cultures Consist of Material and Nonmaterial Components

Cultures include both material and nonmaterial elements. Material components are tangible objects and physical substances that have been altered by human intervention. The objects a culture invents reflect its values, needs, goals, and preoccupations. For example, a culture that creates an abundance of offensive weapons is likely to have goals of conquest. Material objects common in Western cultures include cars, phones, computers, pagers, shovels, and hammers. Each of these objects began with natural raw materials, such as metals, trees, and minerals, that were shaped into new forms for new uses. The numerous inventions to enhance speed and output in the United States reflect the Western emphasis on efficiency and productivity (Wood, 2000).

RAUL   *In Mexico, most people walk or take buses; if a bus is full, no problem—we wait for the next one or the one after that. Here, everybody has his or her own car, and people do not like to wait.*

Cultures also include nonmaterial components. These are intangible creations that reflect a culture's values and influence personal and social behavior. Four of the most important nonmaterial aspects of a culture are beliefs, values, norms, and language.

Beliefs   **Beliefs** are conceptions of what is true, factual, or valid. Beliefs may be rooted in faith ("God said that we will live forever if we accept Him"), experience ("Storing grain in elevated places keeps it dry during the monsoons"), or science ("Penicillin cures infections"). Cultural beliefs are regarded as truths even though they are sometimes false. At one point, it was widely believed that the earth was flat, so sailors did not venture beyond what they believed to be the edge of the earth. Even after that, people thought that the sun revolved around the earth. We now know that the earth is round and that it revolves around the sun. Cultural beliefs, even if inaccurate, influence how members of a culture think, act, and communicate.

The value placed on family life differs from culture to culture.

Values Values are generally shared views of what is good, right, worthwhile, and important with regard to conduct and existence. Whereas beliefs have to do with what people think is true, values are concerned with what should be or what is worthy in life. For example, cultures that value families and define individuals in terms of their connections with others create laws and social policies to support family life. Developed countries that value strong families provide paid, guaranteed family leave for all workers.

Cultures have different values toward the natural world. Many American Indian tribes valued living in harmony with nature, with other creatures, and with the earth. Thus, they adjusted their lives to the rhythms of seasons, created communication rituals to celebrate changes in the seasons, worked with the land, and hunted to meet needs for food and clothing but not for sport. Many American Indians performed rituals upon killing an animal to honor the animal's spirit and to express thanks to it for its life. Embracing a very different value, Europeans who settled in the United States saw nature as something to be conquered and made to serve humans.

Norms Norms are informal rules that guide how members of a culture act, as well as how they think and feel. Norms define what is considered to be normal, or appropriate, in particular situations. For instance, in China, defendants are presumed guilty, whereas in the United States they are presumed innocent until proven guilty. In the United States, children are expected to leave their families of origin to start their own families. In some Asian societies, however, children are expected to live with or near their parents and to operate as a single large family.

Norms reflect cultural values. In the United States, for instance, many norms reflect respect for individuals' privacy and property: knocking on closed doors,

COMMUNICATION
in Your Life

Identify two
strongly
held values
in Western
culture.

COMMUNICATION HIGHLIGHT

What's in a Name?

Long before the present era, some women resisted taking a man's name upon marriage. At the first Women's Rights Convention, held in 1848 at Seneca Falls, New York, Elizabeth Cady Stanton (Stanton, Anthony, & Gage, 1881/1969) said:

> When a slave escapes from a Southern plantation, he at once takes a name as the first step in liberty—the first assertion of individual identity. A woman's dignity is equally involved in a life-long name, to mark her individuality. We can not overestimate the demoralizing effect on woman herself, to say nothing of society at large, for her to consent thus to merge her existence so wholly in that of another.

Communication scholars Karen Foss and Belle Edson (1989) studied married women's reasons for choosing their birth names, their husbands' names, or hyphenated names. Foss and Edson reported that women who took their husbands' names place greater emphasis on relationships than on self. Those who retained their birth names valued self above relationships. Women who chose hyphenated names value self and relationships equally.

having separate utensils for serving food and individual places with separate eating utensils for each person, and moving from one residence to another without consulting any authorities. In countries with collectivist values, however, different communicative norms prevail. Koreans do not set individual places, and they use the same utensils for serving and eating. In China, no citizen would change jobs or move without first getting approval from the local unit of the Communist Party (Ferrante, 2009).

Language Language shapes how we think about the world and ourselves. As we saw in Chapter 5, language is packed with values. Consequently, in the process of learning language, we learn our culture's values. The importance that most Asian cultures attach to age is structured into Asian languages. For instance, the Korean language makes fine distinctions between different ages, and any remark to another person must acknowledge the other's age (Ferrante, 2009).

Language also reflects cultural views of personal identity. Western cultures tend to emphasize individuals, whereas many Eastern cultures place greater emphasis on family and community than on individuals. It's unlikely that an Eastern textbook on human communication would even include a chapter on self, which is standard in Western textbooks. If I were a Korean, I would introduce myself as Wood Julia to communicate the greater value placed on familial than personal identity.

Language, beliefs, values, and norms are cultural couriers that carry a way of life forward from day to day and generation to generation. These nonmaterial components, in combination with material ones, reflect and perpetuate cultures and social communities.

Cultures Are Shaped by Historical and Geographic Forces

Patterns of cultural life are not random or arbitrary. Many of them grow out of the history and geographic location of a society. Historically, the southern region of the United States has been more agrarian than the northern region because southern soil and climate are conducive to farming. Water is used freely in the United States but very sparingly in the hill country of Nepal, where it must be hand-carried into villages. The scarcity of oil, wood, and coal in Korea explains why Koreans use fuels conservatively. Similarly, the lack of grazing land in Korea means there are few sheep and cows for meat and dairy products. For food, Koreans rely on resources available in their country: rice and other grains, vegetables, fish, snakes, and soybeans. Many South American societies have siestas so that people's energy is not drained by the fierce midday heat. Cities and towns on seaboards develop maritime industries and have more seafood in their diets than inland areas do.

AIKAU *Americans say they like Asian food, but really they do not know what it is. At home, we use meat only to flavor. We have slivers of meat or chicken in a meal, but we do not have big pieces like in America. When my parents came here and opened a restaurant, they had to learn how to fix Asian food for American tastes, not like we fix it at home.*

Just as our family history shapes our identity, the traditions and history of a culture shape its character. Many American Indians are suspicious of whites because of a history of exploitation and betrayal. Similarly, some blacks may distrust whites because their ancestors were enslaved and exploited by whites. Jewish people have a painful legacy of persecution that explains why many are wary of non-Jews even today. In 1939, a ship transporting Jews from Nazi Germany docked in Miami, Florida, and was turned back. That incident is part of the history of Jewish people and helps us understand why they often distrust non-Jews and preserve their heritage within their own social communities.

Historical influences also shape the communication patterns of social groups. For instance, some blacks know how to use standard English to fit into the dominant culture; at the same time, they know how to use more colloquial language that is typical in some traditional black communities (Orbe & Harris, 2001). Members of other communities, such as Jewish, Hispanic, and gay groups, also become bilingual to be effective in both mainstream culture and their social communities.

Cultural practices that originally developed for functional reasons may persist simply because "that's how we've always done it." For example, thousands of years ago, women probably stayed near their homes (or caves) because they had to nurse babies, and men developed physical strength and stamina to provide for the family by hunting. Today, brains are more important than brawn for providing for a family, and infants can be fed with formula or with expressed and stored breast milk, so the mother's full-time presence is not essential. Although the original reasons for assigning women to homemaking and men to breadwinning are no longer valid, a traditionally gendered division of labor persists.

Cultural traditions shape daily activities and social life. Hindus believe that what a person is in this life reflects past lives and determines his or her fate in the next one. Thus, present behaviors are chosen with an eye toward what they are likely to bring about in the next incarnation. Cultures steeped in violence and war may regard death and battle as unremarkable parts of life. In cultures less accustomed to war and violence, elaborate communication rituals convey the extraordinariness of war and violent death.

The traditions of a culture also regulate and order life. Cultures develop traditions that dictate who does what kinds of work, where and how long people work, how much status various jobs have, and how work fits into overall life. These traditions are communicated through cultural institutions (i.e., schools, churches, synagogues) and practices (i.e., different dress for blue- and white-collar jobs, individual or team structures on the job). In the United States, for instance, people are encouraged to put in longer hours at the workplace than members of many other cultures. In a number of European countries, workers are required to take generous vacations, and extra jobs are discouraged. Hendrick, an exchange student from Germany, notes differences between U.S. and German views of work.

HENDRICK   *Americans are obsessed with work. Most students here work jobs too—sometimes 30 or 40 hours a week. I ask my American friends why they work so hard, and they tell me they need the money for their car or clothes or going out. But it seems to me that they need a car and nice clothes to go to work. If they did not work, they would not need so much of the money that they work to get.*

Calendars reflect cultural traditions and values by designating significant days. In the United States, the Fourth of July commemorates the United States' independence from Britain; Eastern societies have a day each year to honor the elderly. National holidays symbolize important moments in a culture's life and remind members of what the culture values. On a less obvious level, calendars define who is in the mainstream of a given society and who is not. Rachael, a young woman who took several of my classes, explains this point.

RACHAEL   *It is hard to be Jewish in a Christian society, especially in terms of holidays. For me, Rosh Hashanah and Yom Kippur are high holy days, but they are not holidays on the calendar. Some of my teachers give me grief for missing classes on holy days, and my friends don't accept that I can't go out on Saturday, which is our sacred day. At my job, they act like I'm being a slouch and skipping work because my holidays aren't their holidays. They get Christmas and New Year's Day off, but I celebrate Hanukkah and Rosh Hashanah. And I don't have to tell you why making Easter a national holiday offends Jewish people.*

We Learn Culture in the Process of Communicating

We learn a culture's views and patterns in the process of communicating. As we interact with others, we come to understand the beliefs, values, norms, and language of our culture. By observing how others communicate, we learn language (*dog*) and what it means (i.e., a pet, a work animal, or food to eat). This allows us to participate in a social world of shared meanings.

From the moment of birth, we begin to learn the beliefs, values, norms, and language of our society. We learn our culture's values in a variety of communication contexts. We learn to respect our elders, or not to, by how we see others communicate with older people and by what we hear others say about elders. We learn what body shape is valued by what we see in media and how we hear others talk about people of various physical proportions. Children enter the world without strong gender scripts, but socialization teaches most boys to be masculine and most girls to be feminine (Wood, 1996b, 1998, 2011). By the time we are old enough to appreciate the idea that culture is learned, our beliefs, values, language, and practices are already thoroughly woven into who we are and are almost invisible to us.

Bill Aron/PhotoEdit

Both verbal and nonverbal communication reflect cultural teachings. Here, an elder and a young boy wear traditional yarmulkes and partake of unleavened bread and wine as part of Passover seder.

Cultures Are Dynamic

The final principle of cultures is that they are **dynamic**, which means they evolve and change over time. To survive, cultures must adapt to the natural world (i.e., geographic location, available natural resources, climate changes) and to human activities (i.e., inventions, war). We'll discuss four sources of cultural adaptation, or change.

Invention   **Invention** is the creation of tools, ideas, and practices (Samovar et al., 2009). A frequently cited example of a tool is the wheel, which had far-reaching implications. Not only did its invention alter modes of transportation, but it is also the foundation of many machines and technologies. Other inventions that have changed cultural life are radio, television, the computer, the telephone, the airplane, and the automobile.

Inventions include more than machines. Medical inventions have dramatically extended the human life span, thereby altering our culture's views of age and of the timing of life events. For example, in the 1800s, when the average life span was around 40 years, people in the United States commonly married and had children while in their teens. Today, the average life span is around 70 years, and many people don't marry until their mid-twenties or early thirties and have children at later ages or not at all. The mid-twenties was considered middle age in 1900! When the average life span was 60 to 65 years, someone who retired at 65 didn't have a long life expectancy. Today, a person who retires at 62 or 65 may have many more years of active life.

ALAN   *I'm not working toward a degree but just taking classes out of interest. I retired 5 years ago at 63, and at first it was nice not to have anything I had to do or anywhere I had to go. But then I got bored. After 40 years of being active, I didn't like just sitting around. A lot of my friends feel trapped in retirement. As a society, we haven't figured out how to make the later years satisfying.*

Cultures also invent ideas that alter social life. For example, the United States was founded on the concept of *democracy*, which influenced laws, rights, and responsibilities. Another concept that has changed Western life is environmental responsibility. Information about our planet's fragility has infused cultural consciousness. Terms such as *environmental responsibility* and *environmental ethics* have entered our everyday vocabularies, reshaping how we see our relationship with the environment.

Diffusion   **Diffusion** is borrowing from another culture. Obvious examples of diffusion are borrowing language and foods from other cultures. What we call English or the American language includes a number of words imported from other cultures. Everyday conversations between Westerners are punctuated with terms such as *brocade*, *touché*, and *yin-yang*. The Japanese have traditionally enjoyed sushi. In recent years, many Westerners have tried and liked sushi, and sushi bars are not difficult to find in many U.S. cities. Taco Bells and pizza parlors dot Western cities, and McDonald's has franchises throughout the world.

There are also forms of diffusion that seriously alter a culture's way of life. Jagat Man Lama, a Nepalese man and village leader, studied in India and took back what he learned to his native country. He has taught Nepalese villagers how to build water systems that provide unpolluted water. He has also taught them how to farm without harming the land. There are also many U.S. businesses that have adopted Japanese systems of management to improve productivity.

Cultural Calamity   **Cultural calamity** is adversity that brings about change in a culture. For example, war may devastate a country, destroying land and people alike. Losing a war can alter a culture's self-image, reshaping it into that of conquered people. Cultural calamity may also involve disasters such as hurricanes, volcanic eruptions, and plagues, which can wipe out countless lives and alter patterns of life for the future.

The HIV/AIDS crisis is a recent example of a calamity that has transformed cultural life. Traditionally, many gay men were less monogamous than lesbians or heterosexual women and men, but the AIDS threat has increased long-term commitments between gay men (Huston & Schwartz, 1996). The HIV/AIDS crisis also has changed dating and sexual practices among some heterosexuals, especially college students.

COMMUNICATION in Your Life

Identify an adversity that brought about change in the United States.

Communication   A fourth source of cultural change is *communication*. Social communities in the United States have used communication to resist the mainstream's efforts to define their identity. Anytime a group says, "No, the way you describe Americans doesn't fit me," that group initiates change in the culture's views of itself and of the range of people who make up that culture.

A primary way in which communication propels change is by naming things in ways that shape how we understand them. For instance, the term *date rape* was coined in the late 1980s. Although historically, many women had been forced to have sex by men they were dating, until recently there was no term that named what happened as a violent invasion and a criminal act (Wood, 1992). Similarly, the term *sexual harassment* names a practice that is certainly not new but only lately has been labeled and given social reality (Wood, 1994c). As a primary tool of social movements, communication impels significant changes in cultural life. Thirty years ago, the civil rights movement in the United States used communication to transform laws and views of blacks. Powerful leaders such as the Reverend Martin Luther King Jr., and Malcolm X raised blacks' pride in their identity and heritage and inspired them to demand their rights in United States. Simultaneously, black leaders used communication to persuade the non-Black public to rethink its attitudes and practices.

Language also reflects changes in cultural attitudes and practices. For example, the term *homosexual* has been largely replaced by the terms *gay* and *lesbian*. The terms *boyfriend* and *girlfriend* are no longer the only ones people use to identify romantic interests; *partner, significant other,* and *special friend* are among the terms created to define romantic relations today.

In addition to bringing about change directly, communication also accompanies other sources of cultural change. Inventions such as antibiotics had to be explained to medical practitioners and to a general public that believed infections were caused by fate and accident, not viruses and bacteria. Ideas and practices borrowed from other cultures similarly must be translated into the language and culture of a particular society. Cultural calamities, too, must be defined and explained: Did the volcano erupt because of pressure in the earth or because of the anger of the gods? Did we lose the war because we had a weak military or because our cause was wrong? The ways a culture defines and communicates about calamities establish what these events mean and imply for future social practices and social life.

In sum, we've seen that cultures and social communities are distinct ways of life that order personal identity and social activities. Five principles about cultures capture the main points we've covered. First, communication is a primary way in which cultures are expressed and sustained. Second, cultures consist of material and nonmaterial components, including beliefs, values, norms, and language. Third, all cultures are shaped by historical and geographic forces that are carried forward through oral traditions and other forms of communication among members of a culture. The fourth principle emphasizes that we learn culture in the process of communicating with others; we are talked into membership in a society. Finally, we saw that cultures change continually in response to inventions, diffusion, calamities, and communication that challenges the status quo and argues for new ideas, roles, and patterns of life.

IMPROVING COMMUNICATION BETWEEN CULTURES AND SOCIAL COMMUNITIES

Each of us acts, speaks, and interprets others from the distinct perspective of the cultures and social communities with which we identify. As long as we interact with others in our own culture, we're likely to share understandings of how to communicate and interpret one another. However, when we interact with people from other cultures and social communities, we can't count on shared guidelines. Thus, misunderstandings often occur. Although we can't eliminate misunderstandings, we can minimize them and the damage they can cause.

Let's consider two principles for effective communication between members of different cultures and social communities.

Resist the Ethnocentric Bias

Most of us unreflectively use our home culture as the standard for judging other cultures. Some Japanese may regard many European Americans as rude for maintaining direct eye contact, whereas some European Americans may perceive some Japanese as evasive for averting their eyes (Jandt, 2009). Many Westerners' habitual self-references may appear selfish and egocentric to some Koreans, and many Koreans' unassuming style may seem passive to some Westerners. How we view others and their communication depends more on the perspective we use to interpret them than on what they say and do.

Although it is natural to use our own culture and social communities as the standard for judging other cultures, this tendency interferes with understanding and communication. **Ethnocentrism** is the use of one's own culture and its practices as the standard for interpreting the values, beliefs, norms, and communication of other cultures. Literally, ethnocentrism means to put our own ethnicity (*ethno*) at the center (*centrism*) of the universe. Ethnocentrism fosters negative judgments of anything that differs from our own ways. In extreme form, ethnocentrism can lead one group of people to think it has the right to dominate and exploit other groups and to engage in genocide.

To reduce our tendencies to be ethnocentric, we should first remind ourselves that culture is learned. What is considered normal and right varies between cultures. In place of ethnocentrism, we can adopt the perspective of **cultural relativism**, which recognizes that cultures vary in how they think, act, and behave as well as in what they believe and value. Cultural relativism reminds us that something that appears odd or even wrong to us may seem natural and right from the point of view of a different culture. That awareness facilitates understanding among people of different cultures and co-cultures.

Recognize That Responding to Diversity Is a Process

We don't move suddenly from being unaware of how people in other cultures communicate to being totally comfortable and competent interacting with them. Dealing with diversity is a gradual process that takes time, experience with a variety of people, and a commitment to learning about a range of people and communication styles. We will discuss five distinct responses to diversity, ranging from total rejection to complete acceptance.

Resistance   A common response to diversity is **resistance**, which occurs when we attack the cultural practices of others or proclaim that our own cultural traditions are superior. Without education or reflection, many people deal with diversity by resisting the practices of cultures and social communities different from their own. Some people think their judgments reflect universal truths about what is normal and right. They aren't aware that they are imposing the arbitrary yardstick of their own particular social communities and culture and ignoring the yardsticks of other cultures and social communities.

BRENDA   *I overheard three of my classmates complaining about all of the mess and noise in the building where we have a class. They were saying what an inconvenience it is. The construction is to install an elevator in the building so that students like me, who are in wheelchairs, can take classes in classrooms on the second and third floor. I don't think my classmates are mean, but I do think they've never put themselves in my shoes—or my wheelchair! Every semester they pick classes according to what they want to take and when they want to take it. My first criterion is finding classes that I can get to—either first floor or in buildings that are wheelchair accessible.*

Resistance may be expressed in many ways. Hate crimes pollute campuses and the broader society. Rejection of other cultures fuels racial slurs, anti-Semitic messages, and homophobic attitudes and actions. Resistance may also motivate members of a culture or social community to associate only with each other and to resist recognizing any commonalities with people from other cultures or social communities (Gitlin, 1995).

Members of a culture or social community may resist their own group practices in an effort to fit into the mainstream (Yamato, 2001). **Assimilation** occurs when people give up their own ways and adopt into the dominant culture. For many years, assimilation was the dominant response of immigrants who came to the United States. The idea of the United States as a "melting pot" encouraged newcomers to melt into the mainstream by surrendering anything that made them different from native-born Americans. More recently, the Reverend Jesse Jackson proposed an alternative metaphor, the family quilt. This metaphor portrays the United States as a country in which people's unique values and customs are visible, as are the individual squares in a quilt; at the same time, each group contributes to a larger whole, just as each square in a quilt contributes to its overall beauty.

Tolerance   A second response to diversity is **tolerance**, the acceptance of differences even though we may not approve of or even understand them. Tolerance involves respecting others' rights to their own ways even though you may think their ways are wrong, bad, or offensive. Judgment still exists, but it's not actively imposed on others. Tolerance accepts the existence of differences, but it does not necessarily respect the value of other cultures and social communities. Although tolerance is less actively divisive than resistance, it doesn't foster a world in which people appreciate diversity and learn to grow from encountering differences.

Understanding   A third response to diversity involves **understanding** that differences are rooted in cultural teachings and that no customs, traditions, or behaviors are intrinsically better than any others. This response grows out of cultural relativism, which we discussed previously. Rather than assuming that whatever differs from our ways is a deviation from a universal standard (ours), a person who understands realizes that diverse values, beliefs, norms, and communication styles are rooted in distinct cultural perspectives. A person who responds to diversity with understanding might notice that a Japanese person doesn't hold eye contact, but he or she wouldn't assume that the Japanese person was devious. Instead, he or she would try to learn what eye contact means in Japanese

Bill Aron/PhotoEdit

Communicating with people who differ from us fosters personal growth.

society to understand the behavior in its native cultural context. Curiosity, rather than judgment, dominates in this response to cultural diversity.

Respect   Once we move beyond judgment and begin to understand the cultural basis for practices that diverge from our own, we may come to **respect** differences. We can appreciate the value of placing family above self, of arranged marriage, and of feminine and masculine communication styles. We don't have to adopt others' ways to respect them on their own terms. Respect allows us to acknowledge differences yet remain personally anchored primarily in the values and customs of our own culture.

Participation   A final response to diversity is **participation**, in which we incorporate some of the practices and values of other groups into our own lives. More than other responses, participation encourages us to develop new skills and perspectives and to nurture a civic culture that celebrates both differences and commonalities.

Participation calls for us to be **multilingual**, which means we are able to speak and think in more than one language. Members of many social communities already are at least bilingual: Many blacks know how to operate in mainstream white society and in traditional black communities (Orbe & Harris, 2001). Most women know how to communicate in both feminine and masculine ways, and they adapt their

COMMUNICATION
in Your Life

Have you ever adopted a communication practice from a culture or social community to which you don't belong?

style to the people with whom they interact. Bilingualism is also practiced by many Asian Americans, Hispanics, lesbians, gay men, and members of other groups that are simultaneously part of a dominant culture and minority communities.

My partner, Robbie, and I have learned how to communicate in both conventionally feminine and masculine styles. Like many men, he was socialized to be assertive, competitive, and instrumental in conversation, whereas I learned to be more cooperative, relational, and expressive. When we were first married, we often frustrated each other with our different ways of communicating. I perceived him as domineering and sometimes insensitive to feelings. He perceived me as being too focused on relationship issues and inefficient in moving from problems to solutions. Gradually, each of us learned to understand the other's ways of communicating and to respect our differences without judging them by our own norms. Still later, we came to appreciate and participate in each other's style; now both of us are fluent in both ways of communicating. This not only has improved our relationship but also has made each of us a more competent communicator in a range of settings.

The different responses to cultural diversity that we've discussed represent a process of learning to interact with cultural groups other than our own. In the course of our lives, many of us move in and out of various responses as we interact with people from multiple cultures and social communities. At specific times, we may find we are tolerant of one cultural group and respectful of another, and those responses may change over time.

COMMUNICATION HIGHLIGHT

Attitudes Toward Differences Are Learned

Are racists born or made? Are sexists innately biased, or do they learn to be biased? Sociologist Phyllis Katz was so fascinated by those questions that she spent years studying children 6 months through 6 years old (Sommerville, 1999). Her research included both white and black children. Katz found that as early as 6 months babies notice differences in sex and skin color. They first notice these in much the same way they recognize differences in hair color, height, size, and other physical characteristics of people. But by the time children begin kindergarten, they have learned how to think about sex and race differences.

Children who are taught that differences are interesting but not unequal tend to be open to people of different races, sexes, and other qualities. On the other hand, children who are taught to associate differences with unequal worth tend to devalue women and minority races. To raise children who respect differences, Katz encourages parents to talk openly and nonjudgmentally with their children about differences; pretending there are no differences doesn't work because children can see them. She also advises parents to expose their children to other people of different races, sexes, religious backgrounds, and so forth. The more children experience diversity, the less likely they are to be ethnocentric.

To explore, and perhaps better appreciate, differences between you and people from different groups in your own community, complete the activity "Appreciating Differences Among People" via your Online Resources for *Communication in Our Lives*.

CourseMate

BEYOND THE CLASSROOM

Let's take the material in this chapter beyond the classroom by applying it to the workplace, ethical choices, and engagement with the broader world.

1. **Workplace.** Go to an office building (it could be one on your campus) and make note of the culture and social communities that it reflects. If there are portraits on the walls, what are the sexes, races, and nationalities of the subjects? What does employees' dress tell you about cultural norms in this workplace?

2. **Ethics.** This chapter encourages people to resist the ethnocentric bias, but doesn't offer a specific plan or set of guidelines for reaching that ethical goal. Based on what you've learned in Chapters 1 through 7, as well as your life experiences, what can you suggest as concrete steps people can take to resist or at least reduce the tendency to judge other cultures by the norms and values of their home culture?

3. **Engagement.** Check your campus calendar for meetings of various groups and select an event sponsored by an ethnic group other than your own. Attend the event and pay attention not only to the event itself but to the verbal and nonverbal communication patterns, including protocols for greeting, parting, and introducing speakers (if there is one or more).

CHAPTER SUMMARY

In this chapter, we've learned about the close connections between communication and cultures. Our communication reflects our culture's values and norms; at the same time, our communication sustains those values and norms and the perception that they are natural and right. In elaborating this view of culture, we saw that cultures consist of both material and nonmaterial components, that they are shaped by historical and geographic forces, that they are learned through socialization, and that they are dynamic, always evolving and changing.

The final section of the chapter emphasized the importance of learning to communicate effectively in a multicultural society. We need to understand and respect the ways in which we differ from one another if we are to communicate effectively and if we are to live and work together in a diverse social world. Moving beyond ethnocentric judgments based on our own culture allows us to understand, respect, and sometimes participate in a diverse world and to enlarge ourselves in the process.

But differences between us are only part of the story. It would be a mistake to be so aware of differences that we overlook our commonalities. We all have feelings, dreams, ideas, hopes, fears, and values. Our common humanness transcends many of our differences, an idea beautifully expressed in a poem by Maya Angelou (1990, p. 5).

Human Family

I note the obvious differences
between each sort and type,
but we are more alike, my friends,
than we are unalike.
We are more alike, my friends,
than we are unalike.

"Human Family" from *I Shall Not Be Moved* by Maya Angelou, copyright © 1990 by Maya Angelou. Used by permission of Random House, Inc.

APPLYING COMMUNICATION IN OUR LIVES

The key concepts, For Further Reflection and Discussion questions, and Experiencing Communication in Our Lives case study that follow will help you review, reflect on, and extend the information and ideas presented in this chapter. These resources, and a diverse selection of additional study tools, are also available as Online Resources for *Communication in Our Lives*. Your Online Resources include CourseMate, a student workbook, interactive video activities, audio study tools, a book companion website, Speech Builder Express, Speech Studio, and InfoTrac College Edition. For more information or to access this book's online resources, visit **www.cengage.com/login.**

KEY CONCEPTS

assimilation, 164
belief, 155
culture, 147
cultural calamity, 161
cultural relativism, 163
diffusion, 161
dynamic, 160
ethnocentrism, 163

high-context communication
  style, 150
invention, 160
low-context communication
  style, 150
multilingual, 165
norm, 156
participation, 165

resistance, 163
respect, 165
social community, 148
tolerance, 164
understanding, 164
values, 156

FOR FURTHER REFLECTION AND DISCUSSION

1. Some scholars claim that there are many distinct social communities in the United States. Examples are deaf people, people with disabilities, and elderly people. Do you agree that these groups qualify as distinct social communities? What is needed for a group to be considered a specific and distinctive social community?

2. Continue the exercise started on page 169 by listing common sayings or adages in your culture and social communities. Decide what each saying reflects about the beliefs, values, and concerns of your culture.

3. Are the different styles of communication typical of distinct social communities evident in online interaction? For instance, do

SHARPEN YOUR SKILL

1. Communicating Culture

Locate a standard calendar and an academic calendar used on your campus. Check each calendar to determine which of the following holidays of different cultural groups are recognized on the calendars and which are declared as holidays by suspension of normal operations in communities and on campuses:

Christmas
Hanukkah
Kwanzaa
Elderly Day
Passover
Easter
Yom Kippur
Ramadan
Hegira
Rosh Hashanah
Saka
Seleicodae
Martin Luther King Jr. Day

2. Your Culture's Sayings

What do common sayings and proverbs in the United States tell us about cultural values? What cultural values are expressed by these sayings:

"You can't be too rich or too thin."
"A stitch in time saves nine."
"What goes around comes around."
"A watched pot never boils."
"Penny wise, pound foolish."
"You can't take it with you."
"You've made your bed, now you have to lie in it."

What other sayings can you think of that express key Western values?

you see patterned differences between messages written by women and men? If you see differences, are they consistent with the generalizations about gendered social communities that we discussed in this chapter?

4. Think critically about how you do and do not fit generalizations about your racial or ethnic group. Identify three ways in which you reflect what is generally true of your group. Identify three ways in which you personally diverge

from generalizations about your group. Extend this exercise by thinking critically about how people in racial or ethnic groups other than your own do and do not fit generalizations about their group.

5. Reflect on the different responses to diversity that we discussed in the last section of this chapter. What ethical values do you perceive in each response?

Ethics

EXPERIENCING COMMUNICATION IN OUR LIVES

CASE STUDY: *The Job Interview*

A video of the conversation scripted here is featured in your Chapter 7 Online Resources for *Communication in Our Lives*. Select "The Job Interview" to watch the video. Improve your own communication skills by reading, watching, and evaluating this communication encounter.

CourseMate

Mei-ying Yung is a senior who has majored in computer programming. Mei-ying's aptitude for computer programming has earned her much attention at her college. She has developed and installed complex new programs to make advising more efficient and to reduce the frustration and errors in registration for courses. Although she has been in the United States for 6 years, in many ways Mei-ying reflects the Chinese culture into which she was born and in which she spent the first 15 years of her life. Today Mei-ying is interviewing for a position at New Thinking, a fast-growing tech company that specializes in developing programs tailored to the needs of individual companies. The interviewer, Barton Hingham, is 32 years old and a native of California, where New Thinking is based. As the scenario opens, Ms. Yung walks into the small room where Mr. Hingham is seated behind a desk. He rises to greet her and walks over with his hand stretched out to shake hers.

© Cengage Learning

HINGHAM: Good morning, Ms. Yung. I've been looking forward to meeting you. Your résumé is most impressive.

Ms. Yung looks downward, smiles, and limply shakes Mr. Hingham's hand. He gestures to a chair, and she sits down in it.

HINGHAM: I hope this interview will allow us to get to know each other a bit and decide whether there is a good fit between you and New Thinking. I'll be asking you some questions about your background and interests. And you should feel free to ask me any questions you have. Okay?

YUNG: Yes.

HINGHAM: I see from your transcript that you majored in computer programming and did very well. I certainly didn't have this many As on my college transcript!

YUNG: Thank you. I am very fortunate to have good teachers.

HINGHAM: Tell me a little about your experience in writing original programs for business applications.

YUNG: I do not have great experience, but I have been grateful to help the college with some of its work.

HINGHAM: Tell me about how you've helped the college. I see you designed a program for advising. Can you explain to me what you did to develop that program?

YUNG: Not really so much. I could see that much of advising is based on rules, so I only need to write the rules into a program so advisors could do their jobs more better.

HINGHAM: Perhaps you're being too modest. I've done enough programming myself to know how difficult it is to develop a program for something with as many details as advising. There are so many majors, each with different requirements and regulations. How did you program all of that variation?

YUNG: I read the handbook on advising and the regulations on each major and then programmed decision trees into an advising template. Not so hard.

HINGHAM: Well that's exactly the kind of project we do at New Thinking. People come to us with problems in their jobs, and we write programs to solve them. Does that sound like the kind of thing you would enjoy doing?

YUNG: Yes. I very much like to solve problems to help others.

HINGHAM: What was your favorite course during college?

YUNG: They are all very valuable. I enjoy all.

HINGHAM: Did you have one course in which you did especially well?

YUNG: (*blushing, looking down*) I would not say that. I try to do well in all my courses, to learn from them.

Later, Barton Hingham and Molly Cannett, another interviewer for New Thinking, are discussing the day's interviews over dinner.

CANNETT: Did you find any good prospects today?

HINGHAM: Not really. I thought I was going to be bowled over by this one woman—name's Mei-ying Yung—who has done some incredibly intricate programming on her own while in college.

CANNETT: Sounds like just the kind of person we're looking for.

HINGHAM: I thought so too, until the interview. She just didn't seem to have the gusto we want. She showed no confidence or initiative in the interview. It was like the transcript and the person were totally different.

CANNETT: Hmmm, that's odd. Usually when we see someone who looks that good on paper, the interview is just a formality.

HINGHAM: Yeah, but I guess the formality is more important than we realized—Yung was a real dud in the interview. I still don't know what to make of it.

QUESTIONS FOR ANALYSIS AND DISCUSSION

You can answer these questions and see my responses to them online via your Online Resources for Chapter 7.

1. How does Mei-ying Yung's communication reflect her socialization in Chinese culture?

2. How could Mei-ying be more effective without abandoning the values of her native culture?

3. What could enhance Barton Hingham's ability to communicate effectively with people who were raised in non-Western cultures?

8

Daniel Bosler/Stone/Getty Images

> A loving person lives in a loving world. A hostile person lives in a hostile world. Everyone you meet is your mirror.
>
> **Ken Keys Jr.**

Foundations of Interpersonal Communication

- You have scheduled a performance review with Jenette, an employee assigned to your project team. You need to call her attention to some problems in her work while also communicating that you support her and value her in the company.

- You know your neighbor is worried about losing his job because his company has announced substantial layoffs. You want to let him know that you are open to talking with him about his worries.

SHARPEN YOUR SKILL

At the end of this chapter, refer to the Sharpen Your Skill features, Using Descriptive Language and Assessing Climate, to apply concepts from Chapter 8.

- You're concerned about reports of drugs at the school your 13-year-old son attends. You want to warn him about the dangers of drugs without making him feel you're judging him. You also want to establish open lines of communication between the two of you so he feels free to talk with you about drugs and other issues.

In each of these situations, achieving your goals depends on your ability to create an effective climate for communication. Your goals—to offer criticism in a supportive manner, to make it comfortable for others to disclose private feelings, and to open lines of communication—are likely to be met only if you cultivate a climate that fosters openness and trust between people.

Do you feel more energetic and positive on sunny days than on rainy days? In much the same way that physical climates influence how we feel, interpersonal climates affect how we communicate with others. We feel on guard when a supervisor is manipulative, when a co-worker is in a stormy mood, or when a friend judges us. In each case, the interpersonal climate is cloudy.

Interpersonal climate is the overall feeling between people that arises largely out of the ways people communicate with each other. Interpersonal climate isn't something we can see or measure objectively, and it isn't just the sum of what people do together. Instead, it is the emotional mood between people.

Interpersonal climate is an important foundation of communication in all contexts. On the job, we need to know how to create supportive, productive climates that foster good work relationships and outcomes. In public contexts, speakers want to create climates that lead listeners to trust them and attend to what they say. In social relationships, we try to build climates that allow us and others to feel at ease. In personal relationships, we want to develop climates that nurture intimacy.

This chapter focuses on interpersonal climate as a cornerstone of effective communication in all contexts. We'll begin by discussing self-disclosure, a form of communication that, if used appropriately, can promote an open climate. Next, we'll explore how specific kinds of communication foster defensive and supportive climates. Third, we'll consider the role of conflict in relationships, and we'll see that creating healthy climates helps us manage conflict constructively. The final section of the chapter identifies guidelines for creating and sustaining healthy interpersonal climates.

COMMUNICATION
in Your Life

Describe the interpersonal climate in a close, healthy relationship in your life.

SELF-DISCLOSURE

Self-disclosure is the revelation of information about ourselves that others are unlikely to discover on their own. We self-disclose when we share private information about ourselves—our hopes, fears, feelings, thoughts, and experiences. Although we don't reveal our private selves to everyone and don't do it often even with intimates, self-disclosure is an important kind of communication.

Self-disclosure has notable values. First, sharing personal feelings, thoughts, and experiences often enhances closeness between people (Hendrick &

Hendrick, 1996, 2006; Samp & Palevitz, 2009; Stafford, 2009). By extension, when others understand our private selves, they may respond to us more sensitively, as unique individuals. Self-disclosing also tends to invite others to self-disclose, so we may learn more about them. Finally, self-disclosure can affect what we know about ourselves and how we feel about who we are. For example, if we reveal a weakness or an incident of which we're ashamed, and another person accepts the disclosure without judging us negatively, we may find it easier to accept ourselves.

Self-Disclosure and Personal Growth

A number of years ago, Joseph Luft and Harry Ingham created a model that describes different kinds of knowledge related to individual growth and the development of relationships (Luft, 1969). They called the model the Johari Window (Figure 8.1), which is a combination of their first names, Joe and Harry.

The Johari Window includes four types of information. Open, or public, information is known both to us and to others. Your name, height, academic major, and tastes in food and music are known by many people. Listeners usually are aware of a speaker's professional title and some of his or her accomplishments. Our co-workers often know our work patterns and dress style.

The *blind area* contains information that others know about us but we don't know about ourselves. For example, others may see that we are insecure in new situations, even though we don't realize we are. Co-workers and supervisors may recognize in us strengths and potentials of which we are unaware.

The *hidden area* includes information that we know about ourselves but choose not to reveal to most others. You might not tell many people about your vulnerabilities or about traumatic experiences. You might not reveal blemishes in your work history to employers. Politicians seldom reveal that their speeches were written mostly or completely by others.

The *unknown area* is made up of information about ourselves that neither we nor others know. This area includes our untapped resources, untried talents, and unknown reactions to experiences we've never had. Nobody knows how you will manage a crisis until you've been in one; nobody knows whether you have managerial aptitude until you are in a management role.

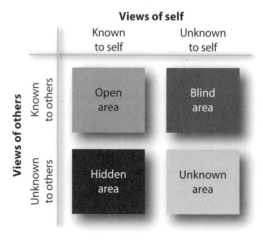

Figure 8.1
The Johari Window

AMANDA *Last summer I went with my church group on a building mission in Mexico. I'd never lived away from home, so I was nervous about whether I would feel homesick or scared or be awkward interacting with Mexicans. The first week there, I stayed with my group and just did the work. But then I met a woman who lived down the street, and we talked. I began to go out on my own to meet people. Pretty soon, I felt totally comfortable and accepted there.*

Because a healthy self-concept begins with knowing yourself, it's valuable to learn about what's in your blind area and to explore your unknown area. Some ways to do this are to enter unfamiliar situations, to try novel things, and to experiment with new kinds of communication. Another way to increase self-knowledge is to ask how others see you, and then reflect on what they say.

The areas in your Johari Window are neither static nor the same for all relationships. They may change over time. For example, if you enter new situations and see yourself doing things you've never done, your unknown area shrinks. If you do something you are ashamed of, or if something disturbing happens to you, your hidden area may expand. The size of the panes of the window may also vary across different relationships. For example, my hidden area in my relationship with Robbie is much smaller than with casual acquaintances. I also have a smaller blind area in the relationship with Robbie because he has given me lots of feedback on how he perceives me.

Self-Disclosure and Closeness

At least among Westerners, self-disclosure is a key gauge of closeness (Samp & Palevitz, 2009). Satisfaction with romantic relationships is closely tied to appropriate self-disclosure (Fitzpatrick & Sollie, 1999; Stafford, 2009; Vito, 1999). As people share their private selves with each other, trust and understanding tend to grow.

Self-disclosure should take place gradually and with appropriate caution. It's unwise to tell anyone too much about ourselves too quickly, especially if revelations could be used against us (Petronio, 2000). We begin by disclosing information that is somewhat private but not likely to make us too vulnerable ("I haven't had much experience in this kind of assignment"). If a person responds with acceptance to early and limited disclosures, and if the person keeps our confidences, we're likely to reveal progressively more intimate information as the relationship continues ("I was let go from my last job because I couldn't handle the stress."). If these disclosures are also met with understanding and confidentiality, trust and intimacy may grow.

In the early stages of relationships, disclosures are more frequent, and reciprocity is important. If you disclose to a new acquaintance, you'll be more comfortable if the other person responds by revealing private information about herself or himself (Cunningham, Strassberg, & Haan, 1986; Dindia, 2000). Sharing personal information also tends to foster an interpersonal climate of trust and comfort.

JAN *Josh and I have been married for 15 years. At first, we shared a lot of personal information and private thoughts with each other, but we don't do that much now. Yet I feel so close to Josh because he knows me in ways no one else does. All the experiences and feelings we shared earlier help us understand the significance of things that happen now. We don't even have to talk, because we know layers and layers of each other.*

The need to reciprocate disclosures recedes in importance once trust is established. Partners in established friendships and romances generally don't feel the need to reciprocate disclosures immediately. Further, in relationships that endure over time, disclosures make up very little of the total communication between partners (Duck & Wood, 2006; Wood & Duck, 1995a, 1995b). Of course, partners in established relationships continue to disclose new experiences and insights to one another; it's just that significant disclosures tend to be less frequent in long-term relationships. When closeness declines, so do disclosures (Baxter, 1987).

SID *For 3 years, Tom and I worked together, and we were really close. We'd even talked about starting up our own company and being partners. Tom and I knew everything about each other, and it was easy to talk about anything, even problems or failures, with him. But last year he stopped talking about himself. At first I didn't notice and just kept telling him what was going on with me, but then I got to feel kind of awkward, like it was one-way, and I was more exposed than he was. I asked Tom if anything was wrong, and he said no, but he didn't talk to me like he used to. Finally, I found out he was working with another guy to start a franchise. When he stopped talking openly with me, it was a signal that our relationship was over.*

COMMUNICATION TO BUILD SUPPORTIVE CLIMATES

One of the greatest influences on interpersonal climate is communication that is confirming and supportive. Philosopher Martin Buber (1957, 1970) believed that to be healthy and to grow, each of us needs confirmation. Recognizing the importance of Buber's insight, research on confirmation has been conducted by communication scholars (Anderson, Baxter, & Cissna, 2004; Arnett, 2004; Stewart, Zediker, & Black, 2004). The essence of confirmation is feeling valued. When others confirm us, we feel cherished and respected. When they disconfirm us, we feel disregarded and devalued.

Few relationships are purely confirming or disconfirming. In reality, most relationships include some communication that is confirming and other messages that are disconfirming. In healthy, positive relationships, confirming communication outweighs disconfirming communication.

Levels of Confirmation and Disconfirmation

Communication scholars (Cissna & Sieburg, 1986) have identified specific kinds of communication that confirm or disconfirm others on three levels.

The most basic form of confirmation is **recognition** that another person exists. We do this with nonverbal behaviors (i.e., offering a smile or handshake; looking up when someone enters our office) and verbal communication (i.e., "Hello," "Good to meet you"). We disconfirm others at a fundamental level when we don't acknowledge their

Disclosing private thoughts and feelings tends to enhance closeness.

existence. For example, you might not speak to or look at a person when you enter a room or look at a teammate who comes late to a meeting. Parents who punish a child by refusing to speak to him or her disconfirm the child's existence.

> **REGGIE**   *Any African American knows what it means to have your existence denied. The law may forbid segregation now, but it still exists. When I go to an upscale restaurant, sometimes people just look away. They ignore me, like I'm not there. I've even been ignored by waiters in restaurants. This is especially true in the South, where a lot of Whites still don't want us in their clubs and schools.*

A second level of confirmation is **acknowledgment** of what another feels, thinks, or says. Nonverbally, we acknowledge others by nodding our heads or using facial expressions to indicate that we are listening. Verbal acknowledgments are direct responses to others' communication. If a friend says, "I'm really worried that I blew the LSAT exam.", you could acknowledge that by responding, "So you're scared that you didn't test well on it, huh?" If a co-worker tells you, "I'm not sure I have the experience to handle this assignment.", you could acknowledge that disclosure by saying, "Sounds as if you feel this is a real challenge." These are paraphrasing responses, which we discussed in Chapter 4. We disconfirm others when we don't acknowledge their feelings or thoughts. For instance, if you responded to your friend's statement about the LSAT by saying, "Want to go out and throw some darts tonight?" that would be an irrelevant response that ignores the friend's comment. We also disconfirm

COMMUNICATION in Your Life

Have you ever tried to interact with someone who would not recognize you exist?

another when we deny the feelings he or she expresses: "You did fine on the LSAT." René Dailey (2006) reports that adolescents talk more openly with parents if they perceive the parents as acknowledging their feelings without judging them.

LISA   *I'm amazed by how often people won't acknowledge what I tell them. A hundred times, I've been walking across campus and someone's come up and offered to guide me. I tell them I know the way and don't need help, and they still put an arm under my elbow to guide me. I may be blind, but there's nothing wrong with my mind. I know if I need help. Why can't others acknowledge that?*

COMMUNICATION HIGHLIGHT

Guidelines for Communicating with People Who Have Disabilities

1. When talking with someone who has a disability, speak directly to the person, not to a companion or interpreter.
2. When introduced to a person with a disability, offer to shake hands. People who have limited hand use or who have artificial limbs usually can shake hands.
3. When meeting a person with a visual impairment, identify yourself and anyone who is with you. If a person with a visual impairment is part of a group, preface comments to him or her with a name.
4. You may offer assistance, but don't provide it unless your offer is accepted. Then ask the person how you can best assist. (Ask for instructions.)
5. Treat adults as adults. Don't patronize people in wheelchairs by patting them on the shoulder or head; don't use childish language when speaking to people who have no mental disability.
6. Respect the personal space of people with disabilities. It is rude to lean on a wheelchair because that is part of a person's personal territory.
7. Listen mindfully when talking with someone who has difficulty speaking. Don't interrupt or supply words to others. Just be patient and let them finish. Don't pretend to understand if you don't. Instead, explain what you understood and ask the person to respond.
8. When you talk with people who use a wheelchair or crutches, try to position yourself at their eye level and in front of them to allow good eye contact.
9. It is appropriate to wave your hand or tap the shoulder of people with hearing impairments as a way to get their attention. Look directly at the person and speak slowly, clearly, and expressively. Face those who read lips, face a good light source, and keep hands, cigarettes, and gum away from your mouth.
10. Relax. Don't be afraid to use common expressions, such as "See you later" to someone with a visual impairment or "Did you hear the news?" to someone with hearing difficulty. They're unlikely to be offended and may turn the irony into a joke.

Source: Adapted from AXIS Center for Public Awareness of People with Disabilities, 4550 Indianola Avenue, Columbus, OH 43214. To visit the Axis website, use your Online Resources for *Communication in Our Lives* to access **WebLink 8.1.**

Lisa makes an important point. We shouldn't assume we know more than others about what they want or need. When we don't acknowledge what another says, we disconfirm him or her. You may recall that in previous chapters we've cautioned against speaking for others. It is fundamentally disconfirming to have others deny us our own voices.

The final level of confirmation is **endorsement.** Endorsement involves accepting another's feelings or thoughts as valid. You could endorse the co-worker by saying, "It's natural to be a little anxious about a new assignment." We disconfirm others when we don't accept their thoughts and feelings. For example, it would be disconfirming to say, "How can you whine about whether you can do this assignment, when so many people are being laid off? You should be glad to have a job." This response rejects the validity of the other person's expressed feelings and is likely to close the lines of communication.

Disconfirmation is not mere disagreement. After all, disagreements can be productive and healthy, and they imply that people matter enough to each other to argue. It is disconfirming to be told that we or our ideas are crazy, wrong, stupid, or deviant. If you think about what we've discussed, you'll probably find that the relationships in which you feel most valued and comfortable are ones in which you feel confirmed.

DEFENSIVE AND SUPPORTIVE CLIMATES

Confirming and disconfirming messages are one important influence on the climate of relationships. Other kinds of communication also contribute to interpersonal climate. Communication researcher Jack Gibb (1961, 1964, 1970) studied the relationship between communication and interpersonal climates. He began by noting that in some relationships we feel defensive and on guard, whereas in others we feel safe and supported. Of course, the climate of many relationships is in between the extremes of defensive and supportive. Gibb, however, was interested in understanding the specific kinds of communication that foster defensive climates and supportive climates. He identified six types of communication that promote each kind of climate.

> **WAYNE** *I've gotten a lot of disconfirmation since I came out. When I told my parents I was gay, Mom said, "No, you're not." I told her I was, and she and Dad both said I was just confused, but I wasn't gay. They refuse to acknowledge I'm gay, which means they reject me. My older brother isn't any better. His view is that being gay is a sin against God. Now, what could be more disconfirming than that?*

Evaluation Versus Description

We tend to become defensive when we believe others are evaluating us. Few of us feel what Gibb called "psychologically safe" when we are the targets of judgments. This is true in both professional and personal relationships (Conrad & Poole, 2004; Reis, Clark, & Holmes, 2004). In his commentary, Wayne expressed feeling disconfirmed by his family when he told them he was gay. His parents and brother made evaluations—very negative ones—of him and of gayness. Yet even positive evaluations may provoke defensiveness because they imply that another person feels entitled to judge us. We may feel that if our supervisor makes positive judgments, he or she may also render negative ones. Examples of evaluative statements are "You have no discipline," "It's dumb to feel that way," "I approve," "You shouldn't have done that," "You did the right thing," and "That's a stupid idea."

An alternative to evaluation is description. Descriptive communication describes behaviors without passing judgment. *I*-language, which we learned about in Chapter 5, describes what the person speaking feels or thinks, but it doesn't evaluate. For example, "I wish you hadn't done that" describes your feelings, whereas "You shouldn't have done that" evaluates another's behavior. Descriptive language may describe another's behavior in a nonjudgmental way: "You seem to be sleeping more lately" (versus "You're sleeping too much"), "You've shouted three times today" (versus "Quit flying off the handle").

Certainty Versus Provisionalism

Language characterized by certainty is absolute and often dogmatic. It suggests there is one and only one right answer, point of view, or course of action. Because communication laced with certainty proclaims an absolutely correct position, it fosters a climate that is not conducive to collaboration (Wilmot & Hocker, 2001). A leader who expresses certainty about what a team should generate is likely to stifle creativity and openness. Similarly, supervisors who communicate that their minds are made up often miss critical feedback. There's no point in talking with people whose minds are made up and who demean any point of view other than their own. Certainty is also expressed by, "My mind can't be changed because I'm right," "Only a fool would vote for that person," or "There's no point in discussing it further." People who restate their own positions in response to others' ideas also express certainty.

One form of communication characterized by certainty is ethnocentrism, which we discussed in Chapter 7. Ethnocentrism is an attitude based on the assumption that our culture and its norms are the only right ones. For instance, someone who says, "It's disrespectful to be late" reveals a lack of awareness of cultures that are less concerned with speed and efficiency than the United States.

COMMUNICATION in Your Life

Describe your reaction to dogmatic communication.

MONIKA *My father is a classic case of close-mindedness. He has his ideas, and everything else is crazy. I told him I was majoring in communication studies, and he hit the roof. He said there was no future in learning to write speeches and told me I should go into business so that I could get a good job. He never asked me to describe communication studies. If he had, I would have told him it's a lot more than speech writing. He starts off sure that he knows everything about whatever is being discussed. He has no interest in exploring other points of view or learning something new. He just locks his mind and throws away the key. We've all learned just to keep our ideas to ourselves around him—there's no communication.*

An alternative to certainty is provisionalism, which expresses tentativeness about our own ideas and openness to other points of view. When we speak provisionally, we indicate that we have a point of view, yet our minds aren't closed. We signal that we're willing to consider alternative positions, and this encourages others to voice their ideas. Provisional communication includes statements such as "The way I tend to see the issue is …," or "One way to approach the problem is …." Notice how these comments signal that the speaker realizes there could be other positions that are also reasonable. Tentative communication reflects an open mind, which is why it invites continued conversation.

Strategy Versus Spontaneity

Most of us feel on guard when we think others are manipulating us or being less than upfront about what's on their minds. For instance, employees are likely to feel defensive if they think management is trying to trick them into doing extra work or giving up benefits (Conrad & Poole, 2004). An example of strategic communication is this: "Would you do something for me if I told you it really mattered?"

We're also likely to feel that another is trying to manipulate us with a comment such as "Remember when I helped you with your math last term and when I did your chores last week because you were busy?" With a preamble like that, we suspect a trap of some sort is being set. We also get defensive when we suspect others of using openness to manipulate how we feel about them. As Sandy points out in her commentary, people who disclose highly personal information early in a relationship may be trying to win our trust so that we will self-disclose in return.

SANDY   *This guy I dated last year was a real con artist, but it took me a while to figure that out. He would look me straight in the eye and tell me he really felt he could trust me. Then he'd say he was going to tell me something he'd never told anyone else in his life, and he'd tell me about fights with his father or how he didn't make the soccer team in high school. The stuff wasn't really that personal, but the way he said it made it seem that way. So I found myself telling him a lot more than I usually disclose and a lot more than I should have. He started using some of the information against me, which was when I started getting wise to him. Later on, I found out he ran through the same song and dance with every girl he dated. It was quite an act!*

Copyright PhotoDisc

Based on nonverbal behaviors, what kind of climate do you think is present in this photograph?

Spontaneity is a counterpoint to strategy. Spontaneous communication may be thought out, yet it is also open, honest, and uncontrived. "I really need your help with this computer glitch" is a more spontaneous comment than "Would you do something for me if I told you it really mattered?" Likewise, it is more spontaneous to ask for a favor in a straightforward way ("Would you help me?") than to preface a request with a recitation of all we've done for someone else.

Control Versus Problem Orientation

Controlling communication tends to trigger defensiveness (Wilmot & Hocker, 2001). A common instance of controlling communication is a person's insistence that her or his solution or preference should prevail. In the workplace, employees tend to feel defensive if supervisors are overly controlling or micromanaging (Conrad & Poole, 2004). The relational meaning is that the person exerting control thinks he or she has greater power, rights, or ideas than others. It's disconfirming to be told that our ideas are wrong or that we can't do our job without micromanagement by a supervisor.

A study by Escudero Valentin, Edna Rogers, and Emilio Gutierrez (1997) found that there were more attempts to dominate and control in unsatisfying marriages than in satisfying ones. For example, a wife who earns a higher salary than her husband might say to him, "I like the Honda more than the Ford you want, and it's my money that's going to pay for it." The wife not only pushes her preference but also tells her husband that she has more power than he does because she makes more money. This disconfirms and disrespects him.

Rather than imposing a preference, problem-oriented communication cooperatively focuses on finding answers that satisfy everyone. The goal is to come up with a solution that all parties find acceptable. Here's an example of problem-oriented communication: "It seems that we have really different preferences about a car. Let's talk through what we like and dislike about the two models and see if that helps us decide." Notice how this statement invites collaboration and confirms the other and the relationship by expressing a desire to meet both people's needs. Problem-oriented communication tends to reduce unproductive conflict and keep lines of communication open (McKinney,

Kelly, & Duran, 1997). One of the strengths of focusing on problems is that the relationship level of meaning emphasizes the importance of the relationship between communicators. In contrast, controlling behaviors aim for one person to triumph over the other, an outcome that undercuts relationships.

Neutrality Versus Empathy

People tend to become defensive when others act in a neutral, or detached, manner. It's easy to understand why we might feel uneasy with people who seem uninvolved, especially if we are talking about personal matters. Neutral communication implies a lack of regard and caring for others.

In contrast to neutrality, expressed empathy confirms the worth of others and our concern for their thoughts and feelings. Empathy is communicated when we say, "I can understand why you feel that way," or "I don't blame you for being worried about the situation." Empathy doesn't necessarily mean agreement; instead, it acknowledges others and their perspectives and demonstrates that we want to understand them (Hall & Bernieri, 2001).

Superiority Versus Equality

It's normal to feel on guard when talking with people who act as if they are better than we are. Consider several messages that convey superiority: "I know a lot more about this than you." "You just don't have my experience." "You really should go to my hairdresser." Each of these messages says, loud and clear, "You aren't as good (smart, savvy, competent, attractive) as I am." Predictably, the result is that we protect our self-esteem by defensively shutting out the people and messages that belittle us.

> **CARL**   *I am really uncomfortable with one of the guys on my team at work. He always acts like he knows best and all the rest of us aren't as smart or experienced or whatever. The other day, I suggested a way we might improve our team's productivity, and he said, "I remember when I used to think that." What a put-down! I feel uneasy saying anything around him.*

We feel more relaxed and comfortable communicating with people who treat us as equals. At the relationship level of meaning, expressed equality communicates respect and equivalent status between people. This promotes an open climate. Creating a climate of equality allows everyone to be involved without fear of being judged inadequate.

We've seen that specific kinds of communication express confirmation or disconfirmation and foster climates that are more or less defensive or supportive. Establishing a confirming, supportive climate is especially important as a foundation for managing conflict. Building on what we've discussed so far, let's now explore how communication allows us to manage it productively.

CONFLICT IN RELATIONSHIPS

Conflict exists when people who depend on each other have different views, interests, or goals and perceive their differences as incompatible. Conflict is a normal, inevitable part of all relationships. You like to eat meat, and your roommate is a strict vegetarian. You believe money should be enjoyed, and your partner believes in saving for a rainy day. You favor one way of organizing a work team, and your colleague thinks another is better. Again and again, we find ourselves seemingly at odds with others. When this happens, we either part ways or resolve the differences, preferably in a way that doesn't harm the relationship.

YIH-TANG LIN *I had a very bad conflict with my ex-girlfriend. When we disagreed, she wanted to argue about problems, but I couldn't do that. I was brought up to see conflict as bad. I learned to smooth over problems. So I would avoid conflict and say everything was okay when it was not. I think this kept us from working out problems.*

The presence of conflict doesn't indicate that a relationship is in trouble, although how people manage conflict does influence relational health. Conflict is a sign that people are involved with each other. If they weren't, it wouldn't matter if they differed, and they wouldn't need to resolve differences. This is a good point to keep in mind as we discuss four principles of conflict.

Conflict May Be Overt or Covert

Overt conflict exists when people express differences in a straightforward manner. They might discuss their disagreement, honestly identify their different points of view, argue about ideas, or engage in a shouting match. In each case, differences are out in the open.

Yet much conflict isn't overt. **Covert conflict** exists when partners deny or camouflage disagreement or anger and express it indirectly. For instance, if you're annoyed that your roommate left the kitchen a mess, you might play the stereo when she or he is sleeping. A man who is angry with his wife might deliberately be half an hour late to meet her when he knows she hates to be kept waiting. Covert aggression sidesteps the real problems and issues, which makes it almost impossible to resolve the problems.

CARLOTTA *My roommate will never say when she's mad or hurt or whatever. Instead, she plays games that drive me crazy. Sometimes she'll just refuse to talk to me and deny anything is wrong. Other times she forgets some of my stuff when she gets our groceries and pretends it was an accident. I have to guess what is wrong because she won't just come out and tell me. It really strains our friendship.*

Conflict May Be Managed Well or Poorly

Depending on how we handle disagreements, conflict can strengthen a relationship or poison it. We're most able to realize conflict's potential to enhance relationships when we understand the different parts of the conflict process. Clyde Feldman and Carl Ridley (2000) identify four components of conflict:

- *Conflicts of interest:* These are the seemingly incompatible opinions, viewpoints, goals, or interests that the conflict addresses.

- *Conflict orientations:* These include attitudes toward conflict, whether people think conflict is healthy, how people are characteristically inclined to regard conflict (e.g., win–win, win–lose, lose–lose).

- *Conflict responses:* These are each person's overt behavioral responses to conflict, methods of addressing conflict, and conflict strategies, which may sustain, escalate, defuse, or resolve conflict.

- *Conflict outcomes:* Included as outcomes are whether and how the conflict of interest is resolved, how mutual the process is, and how the conflict process affects emotional closeness in a relationship.

We've already discussed the first component of the conflict model. The second one refers to our typical ways of thinking about and approaching conflict. Do you tend to think conflict is bad, period? Do you typically think that everyone loses in conflict, or that one person wins and the other loses, or that both can win? Your orientations toward conflict can act as a self-fulfilling prophecy, shaping how you communicate and what happens in the situation.

To increase your awareness of how your family may have shaped your orientation to conflict, complete the activity "Understanding Your Conflict Script" via your Online Resources for *Communication in Our Lives*.

CourseMate

The third component of the conflict process is responses: how we actually respond when conflict occurs. Caryl Rusbult and her colleagues conducted a series of studies that allowed them to identify four distinct ways Westerners respond to relational distress (Rusbult, 1987; Rusbult, Johnson, & Morrow, 1986; Rusbult & Zembrodt, 1983; Rusbult, Zembrodt, & Iwaniszek, 1986). These are represented in Figure 8.2. According to this model, responses to conflict can be either active or passive, depending on how emphatically they address problems. Responses can also be constructive or destructive in their capacity to resolve tension and to preserve relationships.

The *exit* response is leaving a relationship, either by walking out or by withdrawing psychologically. Because exiting doesn't address problems, it is destructive. Because it is forceful, it is active. The *neglect* response occurs when a person denies or minimizes problems. "You're making a mountain out of a molehill" denies that a serious issue exists. The neglect response is also disconfirming because it fails to acknowledge and respect another person's opinion that the issue *is* serious. Neglect is destructive because it evades difficulties, but it does so passively, by avoiding discussion.

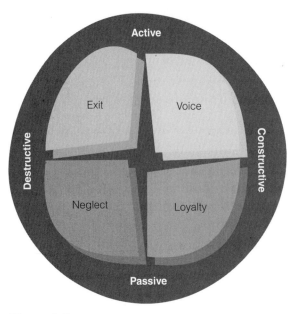

Figure 8.2
The Exit-Voice-Loyalty-Neglect Model

COMMUNICATION
in Your Life

On which response to conflict do you most often rely?

The *loyalty* response is staying committed to a relationship despite differences. Loyalty might be expressed by hoping that conflicts will blow over. Loyalty is silent allegiance, so it is a passive response. Because it doesn't end a relationship and preserves the option of addressing tension later, loyalty is considered constructive. Finally, *voice* is an active, constructive strategy that responds to conflict by talking about problems, offering sincere apologies, or trying to resolve differences so that a relationship remains healthy (Fincham & Beach, 2002).

The final component of the conflict process is outcomes. In addition to the obvious outcome of how the issue is resolved, another consequence is impact on the relationship between people. Our choices of how to communicate during conflict shape how conflict affects our feelings toward others and our relationships with them.

Although each of us has characteristic conflict orientations and responses, we can develop skill in other orientations and alternative ways of responding. Constructive strategies (i.e., voice and loyalty) are advisable for relationships that you want to maintain. Of those two, voice is preferable because it actively intervenes to resolve conflict. Loyalty may be useful as an interim strategy when partners need time to reflect or cool off before dealing with tension directly. Once you understand your current tendencies for responding to conflict, you can consider whether you want to develop skill in alternatives to them.

Conflict Reflects and Expresses Cultures and Social Communities

How we perceive conflict and how we act during conflict are shaped by our membership in particular cultures and social communities. For example, most Mediterranean cultures regard spirited conflict as a normal part of everyday life. In contrast, many Asian cultures discourage open expression of conflict or disagreement (Gangwish, 1999).

Our views of conflict and ways of dealing with it are also influenced by the social communities to which we belong. For instance, there are general differences between women's and men's responses to conflict. Although the generalizations don't apply to all women and all men, in general, women are more likely to adopt a voice or loyalty response to conflict, whereas men are more likely to choose the exit response, often by refusing to discuss problems (Jacobson & Gottman, 1998; Stafford, Dutton & Haas, 2000). Terri Orbuch and Joseph Veroff (2002) report that spirited verbal arguments can be harmful to white couples, but they aren't necessarily damaging to black couples.

Robert Glenn/DK Stock/Getty Images

What responses to conflict do the people in this photo seem to be employing?

Conflict May Be Good for Individuals and Relationships

Although many people think conflict is negative, it can benefit us and our relationships in several ways. When managed constructively, conflict can help us grow as individuals and strengthen our relationships. Conflict can also allow people to work through and resolve differences that have been interfering with their relationships.

How you act during conflict influences how others act toward you. Communication scholars Beth Le Poire and Stephen Yoshimura (1999) had research participants participate in a practice medical interview. They found that pleasant behaviors were consistently reciprocated. Reciprocity appears to be especially likely with positive behaviors. If you try to understand a partner's perspective during a conflict, it's likely your partner will also try to understand yours.

COMMUNICATION in Your Life

Describe a conflict that led to improvements in one of your relationships.

GUIDELINES FOR CREATING AND SUSTAINING HEALTHY CLIMATES

We've seen that communication plays a vital role in creating the climate of relationships in general, and the climate for dealing with conflict in particular. To translate what we've learned into practical information, we'll discuss five guidelines for building and sustaining healthy climates in social, professional, and personal relationships.

Actively Use Communication to Shape Climates

We have seen that communication influences the climate of relationships. Thus, we want to use communication to foster effective, supportive climates. Several principles suggest themselves. First, we want to recognize and acknowledge others and to endorse them when we honestly can. Two studies found that people felt

COMMUNICATION HIGHLIGHT

The Four Horsemen of the Apocalypse

Psychologist John Gottman has spent more than 20 years studying marriages and counseling couples (Gottman, 1994a, 1994b, 1999; Gottman & Silver, 1994). He concludes that there is no difference in the amount of conflict between happily married couples and couples who divorce or have unhappy marriages.

Healthy and unhealthy marriages do differ in two important respects. First, partners who are unhappy together and who often divorce tend to engage in what Gottman calls "corrosive communication patterns." Gottman views these destructive communication practices as "the four horsemen of the apocalypse":

complaint and criticism

defensiveness and denial of responsibility

expressions of contempt

stonewalling

These "four horsemen of the apocalypse" foster negative feelings, including anger, fear, sadness, and dissatisfaction. Gottman thinks the most corrosive of the four is **stonewalling**, which is relying on the exit response to conflict and refusing to discuss issues. When people stonewall, they block the possibility of resolving conflicts. In addition, on the relationship level of meaning they communicate that problems in the relationship aren't worth dealing with. Gottman has found that husbands are more likely than wives to stonewall.

The second major difference between marriages that succeed and those that fail is not bad moments but a predominance of good moments. Happy couples have as many conflicts and tensions as unhappy ones, but they have more enjoyable times together. Says Gottman, a positive balance is everything.

least validated and least able to express their authentic selves when their partners were self-focused and didn't acknowledge them. The people who felt most validated were in relationships with partners who balanced focus on self and others (Harter, Waters, Pettitt, Whitesell, & Kofkin, 1997; McKinney et al., 1997).

Second, we should use communication that fosters confirming, supportive climates. What you've learned about defensive and supportive climates should allow you to monitor your communication to make sure it contributes to open, positive interaction. You can identify and avoid disconfirming patterns of talk, such as evaluation and superiority. In addition, you can actively work to use supportive communication, such as problem orientation and tentativeness.

Third, use skills we've discussed in previous chapters to shape climates effectively. For example, being mindful, engaging in dual perspective, checking perceptions, using *I*-language, and paraphrasing are important skills when conflict arises.

To practice using communication to shape climates, complete the activity "Transforming Defensive Communication into Supportive Communications" via your Online Resources for *Communication in Our Lives.*

Accept and Confirm Others

Although we can understand how important confirmation is, it isn't always easy to give it. Sometimes we disagree with others or don't like certain things they do. Confirming others does not necessary require agreeing with them or withholding criticisms. Communication research indicates that people expect real friends to communicate honestly, even if it isn't always pleasant to hear (Rawlins, 1994). It is false friends who tell us only what we want to hear.

The same is true in professional relationships. To build good working relationships with subordinates, managers must give honest feedback (Fisher, 1998). The key is to communicate in ways that express respect for others as people, even if we disagree or have a criticism. As Aaron's commentary explains, we can offer honest feedback within a context that assures others that we value and respect them.

> **AARON**   *When I first came to school here, I got in with a crowd that drank a lot. At first I drank only on weekends, but then it got so I was drinking every night and drinking more and more. My classes were suffering, but I didn't seem able to stop on my own. Then my friend Betsy told me she was worried about me and wanted to help me stop drinking so much. I'd have been angry if most people had said that, but Betsy talked to me in a way that said she really cared about me. I saw that she was a better friend than all my drinking buddies because she cared enough not to stand by when I was hurting myself. All my other so-called friends just stood by and said nothing.*

In satisfying, healthy relationships, people feel confirmed. This doesn't mean that you always agree with others or that you defer your own needs. Instead, the point is to recognize and respect others' needs just as you want them to respect yours. Listening mindfully and engaging in dual perspective are primary ways to communicate respect and affirmation of others (McKinney et al., 1997; Weisinger, 1996).

Accept and Confirm Yourself

It is just as important to accept and confirm yourself as to do that for others. You are no less

Marc Oeder/Stock4B/Getty Images

Do these women seem to be engaged in supportive, confirming communication?

valuable; your needs are no less important; your preferences are no less valid than those of others. It is a misunderstanding to think that communication principles we've discussed concern only how we should behave toward others. They pertain equally to how we should treat ourselves. Ethical communicators respect both their own and others' needs, preferences, and ways of creating intimacy.

Although we can't always meet the needs of all parties in relationships, it is possible and desirable to give respect to everyone, including yourself. If you don't express your feelings, there's no way others can know them and thus no way they can confirm you.

LIZ   *Ever since I was a kid, I have muffled my own needs and concentrated on pleasing others. I thought I was taking care of relationships, but actually I was hurting them because I felt neglected. My resentment poisoned relationships in subtle ways, so it was really destructive. I've been developing my skills in telling others what I want and need, and that's improving my relationships.*

Unlike aggression, assertion doesn't involve putting your needs above those of others. But unlike deference, assertion doesn't subordinate your needs to those of others. Assertion is a matter of clearly and nonjudgmentally stating what you feel, need, or want. You should do this without disparaging others and what they want. You should simply make your feelings known in an open, descriptive manner. Table 8.1 illustrates aggressive, assertive, and deferential responses.

We can tolerate sometimes not getting what we want as long as we don't feel personally devalued. However, it is disconfirming when our needs and our worth are not acknowledged. Even when people disagree or have conflicting needs,

Table 8.1	Aggression, Assertion, and Deference	
Aggressive	**Assertive**	**Deferential**
We are going to spend the weekend together.	I'd like to spend the weekend together.	If you don't want to spend time together this weekend, it's okay.
Tell me what you're feeling.	I'd like to know what you are feeling.	If you don't want to talk about your feelings, it's okay.
I refuse to take the assignment.	That assignment doesn't interest me. Can we find another one for which I'm better suited?	If you want me to take that assignment, okay. I'll do it.

each person can state his or her feelings and express awareness of the other's perspective. Usually, there are ways to acknowledge both viewpoints, as Dan's comments illustrate.

DAN   *My supervisor did an excellent job of letting me know I was valued even when I got passed over for a promotion last year. I'd worked hard and felt I had earned it. Jake, my supervisor, came to my office to talk to me before the promotion was announced. He told me that both I and the other guy were qualified, but that the other person had seniority and also field experience I didn't have. Then Jake told me he was assigning me to a field position for 6 months so that I could get the experience I needed to get promoted the next time a position opened up. Jake communicated that he understood how I felt and that he was supporting me even if I didn't get the promotion. His talk made all the difference in how I felt about staying with the company.*

COMMUNICATION HIGHLIGHT

Responding to Anger in the Workplace

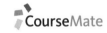

What should you do if you are the target of anger from a co-worker or supervisor? In his book *Anger at Work,* Dr. Hendrie Weisinger (1996) suggests two ways to respond.

First, try to defuse the conflict by improving the climate. Use your communication to relax the angry person and to foster a more relaxed, cooperative climate. For instance, you might offer the person a glass of water or invite the person to sit down and talk. Another strategy is to suggest a "time out"—tell the person that you want to discuss the issue but need 10 minutes to return a call or finish a report. It may also help to move to a different environment, out of the office or room where the conflict erupted. Strategies such as these interrupt the angry moment and the other person's tendencies to attack.

Second, says Dr. Weisinger, listen mindfully to the other person. Although this is difficult when someone seems to be attacking you, listening is a key way to acknowledge and affirm the other person. Make a sincere effort to understand what he or she is angry about. Don't interrupt when he or she is talking: Interruptions communicate that you are more interested in what you have to say than what the other person has to say. Also, avoid mind reading. Let the other person talk, concentrate on understanding his or her perspective, acknowledge what the other person says, and look for points of agreement. Only then should you think about responding with questions, paraphrases, and expressions of your own point of view.

To learn more about the problems of anger in the workplace and ways to manage it, use your Online Resources for *Communication in Our Lives* to access **WebLink 8.2,** which will take you to the website of the Centre for Conflict Resolution International. On that site, you can take an interactive quiz to assess your own style of managing conflict.

Self-Disclose When Appropriate

As we noted previously, self-disclosure allows people to know each other in greater depth. For this reason, it's an important communication skill, especially in the early stages of relationships. Research indicates that appropriate self-disclosure tends to increase trust and feelings of closeness (Dindia, 2000; Meeks, Hendrick, & Hendrick, 1998). In addition, self-disclosure can enhance self-esteem and security in relationships. Finally, self-disclosure is an important way to learn about ourselves. As we reveal our hopes, fears, dreams, and feelings, we get responses from others that give us new perspectives on who we are.

As we have seen, self-disclosures necessarily involve risk—the risk that others will not accept private information or that they might use it against us (Petronio, 2000). Appropriate self-disclosure minimizes these risks by proceeding slowly and establishing trust. It's wise to test the waters gradually before plunging into major self-disclosures. Begin by revealing information that is personal but not highly intimate or able to damage you if exploited. Before disclosing further, observe how the other person responds to your communication and what she or he does with it. You might also pay attention to whether the other person reciprocates by disclosing personal information to you.

Respect Diversity in Relationships

Just as individuals differ, so do relationships. There is tremendous variety in what people find comfortable, affirming, and satisfying in interpersonal interaction. You may have one friend who enjoys a lot of verbal disclosure and another who prefers less. There's no need to try to persuade the first friend to disclose less or the second one to be more revealing. Similarly, you may be comfortable with greater closeness in some of your relationships and more autonomy in others. The differences between people create a rich variety of relationships.

Research indicates that people vary in how they create closeness with others. Most of us enjoy talking intimately with close friends and romantic partners, and most of us enjoy doing things with and for people we care about. However, research suggests that people differ somewhat in the emphasis they place on talk and activity. Some people—women more often than men—rely primarily on talking to create closeness with others. This is called **closeness in dialogue.** Other people—men more often than women—see doing things

IPA/The Image Works

Men often prefer a side-by-side style of friendship in which closeness is expressed through doing things together, such as fishing.

with and for others as a primary (but not the only) means of creating close-ness (Inman, 1996; Johnson, 1996, 2000; Wood & Inman, 1993). This mode is called **closeness in the doing.** The two ways of expressing and experienc-ing closeness are different but not necessarily of different value. Most of us engage in and appreciate both modes, although we may differ in how much of each we prefer.

Because people and relationships are diverse, we should strive to respect a range of communicative choices and relationship patterns. In addition, we should be cautious about interpreting others' communication through our own perspectives. People from distinct cultures and social communities have learned different communication styles. What Westerners consider openness and healthy self-disclosure may feel offensive and intrusive to people from some Asian societies. To improve your understanding of others, ask them what they mean by certain behaviors. This conveys the relational message that they matter to you, and it allows you to gain insight into the interesting differences between us.

BEYOND THE CLASSROOM

Let's take the material in this chapter beyond the classroom by thinking about how what you've learned about foundations of interpersonal communication might apply to the workplace, ethical choices, and engagement with the broader world.

1. **Workplace.** Think of the place where you currently work or a place you worked in the past. How would you describe the interpersonal climate in that workplace? To what extent did communication nurture a supportive climate (provisional, empathic, spontaneous, etc.) or a defensive climate (evaluative, dogmatic, strategic, etc.)?

2. **Ethics.** Personal relationships are not closely regulated by laws and policies such as those that apply to public and professional life. That means that individuals have to develop their own codes of ethics for friendships and romantic relationships. What do you consider two of the most important ethical guiding principles for friendships and two of the most important for romantic relationships? Why do you consider these principles particularly imperative?

3. **Engagement.** Talk with someone—a student or not—who comes from a culture different than the one in which you were raised. Ask him or her what he or she considers the most important ethical guiding principles for friendships and the most important for romantic relationships. Without judging one as better than the other, compare your answers, probing how each of your principles reflects your respective culture and its values.

CHAPTER SUMMARY

In this chapter, we've explored self-disclosure and climates as foundations of interpersonal communication. A basic requirement for healthy communication climates is confirmation. Each of us wants to feel valued, especially by those for whom we care most deeply. When partners recognize, acknowledge, and endorse each other, they communicate, "You matter to me." Confirmation is also fostered by communication that fosters supportive climates and discourages defensive ones. Defensiveness is fueled by evaluation, certainty, superiority, strategies, control, and neutrality. More supportive climates arise from communication that is descriptive, provisional, equal, spontaneous, empathic, and problem oriented.

The communication skills that confirm others and build supportive climates also help us manage conflict constructively so that it enriches, rather than harms, relationships. By creating affirming, healthy climates, we establish foundations that allow us to deal with tensions openly and to communicate in ways that enhance the likelihood that we can resolve differences or find ways of accepting them with grace.

We closed the chapter by discussing five guidelines for building healthy communication climates. The first one is to use communication to create healthy climates. Second, we should accept and confirm others, communicating that we respect them, even though we may not always agree with them or feel the same as they do. The third guideline is a companion to the second one: We should accept and assert ourselves. A fourth guideline is to self-disclose when appropriate so that we increase our security in relationships and so that we add to the information we have about ourselves and others.

Finally, embracing diversity in relationships is a source of personal and interpersonal growth. People vary widely, as do the relationship patterns and forms they prefer. By respecting differences between us, we expand our insights into the fascinating range of ways in which humans form and sustain relationships. In Chapter 9, we'll continue to think about interpersonal communication by exploring how it influences friendships and romantic relationships.

APPLYING COMMUNICATION IN OUR LIVES

The key concepts, For Further Reflection and Discussion questions, and Experiencing Communication in Our Lives case study that follow will help you review, reflect on, and extend the information and ideas presented in this chapter. These resources, and a diverse selection of additional study tools, are also available as Online Resources for *Communication in Our Lives*. Your Online Resources include CourseMate, a student workbook, interactive video activities, audio study tools, a book companion website, Speech Builder Express, Speech Studio, and InfoTrac College Edition. For more information or to access this book's online resources, visit **www.cengage.com/login.**

KEY CONCEPTS

acknowledgment, 177	covert conflict, 184	recognition, 177
closeness in dialogue, 192	endorsement, 179	self-disclosure, 173
closeness in the doing, 193	interpersonal climate, 173	stonewalling, 188
conflict, 184	overt conflict, 184	

FOR FURTHER REFLECTION AND DISCUSSION

1. Develop ethical guidelines for building confirming, supportive climates in one relationship in your life. It might be a personal relationship or a workplace relationship. Identify the ethical values that communication should serve to build and maintain a healthy climate.

2. Using the six categories for defensive and supportive styles of communication, describe communication in a place where you have worked or currently work. Do the categories allow you to analyze why that workplace feels supportive or defensive?

3. How often do you rely on exit, voice, loyalty, and neglect styles when responding to conflict or tension in relationships? What does your response style achieve and prevent?

SHARPEN YOUR SKILL

1. Using Descriptive Language

To develop skill in supportive communication, translate the following evaluative statements into descriptive ones.

Evaluative	Descriptive
This report is poorly done.	This report doesn't include background information.
You're lazy.	_____
I hate the way you dominate conversations with me.	_____ _____ _____
Stop obsessing about the problem.	_____ _____
You're too involved.	_____

2. Assessing Climate

Use the behaviors we've discussed as a checklist for assessing climates. The next time you feel defensive, ask whether others are communicating superiority, control, strategy, certainty, neutrality, or evaluation. Chances are that one or more of these attitudes laces communication.

For a communication climate you find supportive, check to see whether others are communicating spontaneity, equality, provisionalism, problem orientation, empathy, and description.

If you find yourself in a defensive climate, try to resist the normal tendency to respond defensively. Instead, try to make the climate less defensive by being empathic, descriptive, and spontaneous, showing equality and tentativeness, and solving problems.

EXPERIENCING COMMUNICATION IN OUR LIVES

CASE STUDY: *Dan and Charlotte*

The following conversation is featured in your Chapter 8 Online Resources for *Communication in Our Lives*. Select "Dan & Charlotte" to watch the video. (Note that this scenario has two possible endings.) Improve your own communication skills by reading, watching, and evaluating this communication encounter.

CourseMate

Dan and Charlotte have been married for almost 5 years. They both have great careers and are very comfortable in their life and relationship. Dan is talking to his mom on the phone while Charlotte sits in the living room working on her laptop.

DAN: Yeah, that sounds good. We'll swing by after dinner.... Right.... No, Mom, we're still not sure.... Because we're still thinking about it.... about whether or not we're even going to have kids! I really don't want to get into right now, Mom.... Yeah, we'll see you then. Bye.

CHARLOTTE: How's Mom?

DAN: Oh, fine. Just really wondering when her grandkids are on the way!

CHARLOTTE: *(Laughing)* Your mom's funny. She's really got a one-track mind these days.

DAN: Well, we really should figure out if we're going to do it or not.

CHARLOTTE: What? Have kids?

DAN: Yeah, I mean we've been married 5 years. I'd say it's now or never.

CHARLOTTE: Well, what do you think?

DAN: Well, it's the ultimate commitment. I mean, if we're going to do it, we have to do it right. I know so many people—friends and co-workers—who just jumped right into it and really seem to resent their kids for being a burden. I don't want to be one of those parents, you know?

CHARLOTTE: Absolutely. And there are our careers to think about. I mean, we're both doing great right now, and we're really happy as a couple. I'd have to cut back to part-time, and I'd need help from you, too. No matter what, having a child would mean less time, money, energy for ourselves, you know?

DAN: Right. But do we really want to have kids?

CHARLOTTE: I'm not against it. What about you?

DAN: Yeah, I feel the same. I'm not against it, but do we really want to give up what we have now?

Ending 1

A few months later, Dan and Charlotte attend a friend's dinner party. A lot of their friends are there, most of whom have brought their children. As Charlotte mingles, Dan plays with the younger kids, throwing them over his shoulder and tickling them. Charlotte's friend Maggie is talking about her own child.

MAGGIE: It's hard work, but it's so much fun. I really don't know what my family did before we had a child. I mean, we all just sit and watch her do her thing, you know? She'll dance and sing, tell us stories. It's really so funny! . . . So when are you two going start trying?

(Dan approaches and hands Charlotte a drink.)

CHARLOTTE: Well, we really aren't planning on having kids.

MAGGIE: Haven't you guys been married for a long time? I mean, if you wait any longer, it could get complicated. There's really something to be said about having kids young, because the older you get, the less energy you'll have. I mean, how long are you going to wait?

DAN: We're not planning on having kids at all. We just decided that it's not something we want to do.

MAGGIE: But what about your parents? What did they say about it? I mean, aren't they expecting grandkids someday?

DAN: (*A little irritated*) It's really not up to them. We decided what's best for us, and that's it.

(Later that night at home, Dan and Charlotte discuss the party.)

CHARLOTTE: Geez, did everyone there have kids? It felt like the Inquisition, you know?

DAN: Yeah, that was weird. I actually felt a bit left out, you know? I mean, I love playing with everyone's kids, but it seems like the only topic of conversation was when we're going to have one.

CHARLOTTE: Do you still feel okay about our decision? You seemed to be having a lot of fun with the kids tonight.

DAN: I love playing with them! But I love where we are and what we do, and I don't want to change it. I absolutely stand by our decision. What about you?

CHARLOTTE: Definitely. We'll just have to deal with the fact that things have changed. Our relationships with our friends are going to be different from now on since everyone else has kids.

Ending 2

A year and a half later, Dan and Charlotte have had their own child. One night, Dan is putting the baby to bed in her crib. He tickles her and smiles at her before he turns off the light and goes into the living room to sit on the couch across from Charlotte. He sighs and picks up the checkbook to balance it.

DAN: Tired?

CHARLOTTE: I'm exhausted. She was up four times last night and wouldn't go back to sleep. I think she has a new tooth coming in, and it's keeping her up.

DAN: Well, I have tomorrow off. I'll get up with her, and you can sleep in.

CHARLOTTE: Thanks.

DAN: You seem a little distant tonight. What is it?

CHARLOTTE: Oh, there's just a lot happening at work that I'm missing—things I'd like to be involved with, but since I'm part time now, I can't really take them on.

DAN: Man, we really need to watch our spending this month. We're pretty tight here.

(The baby begins to cry. Dan starts to get up, but Charlotte stops him.)

CHARLOTTE: (*A little irritated*) Dan, didn't we agree to let her cry for a while? She has to get used to the crib sometime, right?

DAN: (*Confrontational*) Isn't it hard for you to hear her cry like that?

CHARLOTTE: (*Defensive*) Of course, but she has to learn to calm herself down. Trust me, this is what Maggie and John did with Katie, and it worked. *[She pauses before asking a question.]* Did you think it would be this hard?

DAN: I don't know. It's definitely harder than I expected. I do miss just the two of us hanging out. And the tight budget is something to get used to.

CHARLOTTE: You know, today, she was eating her oatmeal in her chair. I went outside for a second, and when I came back in, the entire bowl was on her head! (*Laughing*) She had dumped the whole thing on her head! She had blueberries in her nose! I wouldn't change any of this. I don't care how tight our budget is or how exhausted we are. I love her so much.

DAN: Yeah, me too. I really love being a dad. There's nothing more important than that.

QUESTIONS FOR ANALYSIS AND DISCUSSION

You can answer these questions and see my responses to them online via your Online Resources for Chapter 8.

1. To what extent do you think Dan and Charlotte felt listened to by the other?

2. Dan responded somewhat defensively to Maggie's questions. Based on what you have learned about communication that fosters defensiveness, explain why Dan might have felt this when talking with Maggie.

3. Identify communication in Dan's and Charlotte's exchange that fostered a supportive climate.

Peter Arnold, Inc./Alamy

9

Communication in Personal Relationships

It's been a rough semester. You're not doing well in your classes, and you're having trouble balancing work and school. You feel overwhelmed by all of it. Then you talk to your best friend about your problems. She listens and sympathizes with all the stress you feel. Even though you haven't solved your troubles, you feel better because you've shared your feelings with someone who cares about you.

Your partner graduated last term and took a job 500 miles away. You call and text a lot, but that's no substitute for seeing each other every day. After 8 weeks apart, you're finally together for a long weekend. Just being together

SHARPEN **YOUR SKILL**

At the end of this chapter, refer to the Sharpen Your Skill features, Faded Friendships and Private Language, to apply concepts from Chapter 9.

makes you feel more complete and happier. You can't imagine not having this person in your life.

This chapter builds on what we learned in Chapter 8 by focusing on communication in two special types of personal relationships: friendships and romantic relationships. To launch the discussion, we'll define personal relationships. Next, we'll consider how communication guides the development of friendships and romances over time. Finally, we'll examine some of the special challenges for personal relationships in our era.

DEFINING PERSONAL RELATIONSHIPS

You have many relationships, but only a few are personal. **Personal relationships** are unique commitments between irreplaceable individuals who are influenced by rules, relational dialectics, and surrounding contexts. We'll discuss each part of this definition.

Uniqueness

Most of our relationships are social, not personal. In social relationships, participants adhere to social roles rather than interacting as unique individuals. For instance, you might exchange class notes with a classmate, play racquetball each week with another person, and talk about politics with a neighbor. In each case, the other person could be replaced by someone else taking the same role. The value of social relationships lies more in what participants do than in who they are because a variety of people could fulfill the same functions.

In personal relationships, however, the particular people—who they are and what they think, feel, and do—define the value of the connection. For example, I am deeply committed to a particular man named Robbie and the unique ways in which we have fitted ourselves together. Nobody else could replace him. When one person in a personal relationship leaves the relationship or dies, that relationship ends. We may later have other intimates, but a new romantic partner or best friend will not replace the former one.

Commitment

For most of us, passion is what first springs to mind when we think about intimacy. **Passion** involves intensely positive feelings and desires for another person. The sparks and the emotional high of being in love or discovering a new friend stem from passion. It's why we feel "butterflies in the stomach" and fall "head over heels." Despite its excitement, passion isn't the primary building block of long-lasting personal relationships.

Passion is a feeling based on the rewards of involvement with a person. **Commitment**, in contrast, is a decision to remain in a relationship in spite of trouble, disappointments, sporadic boredom, and lulls in passion. The hallmark of commitment is the intention to share the future. Because a committed relationship assumes a future, partners are unlikely to bail out if the going gets rough. Instead, they weather bad times (Le & Agnew, 2003; Lund, 1985; Previti & Amato, 2003). Commitment tends to be high when partners have

COMMUNICATION
in Your Life

What have you invested in a significant friendship or romantic relationship?

high respect for each other (Hendrick & Hendrick, 2006).

Commitment grows out of **investments,** or that which we put into relationships that we could not retrieve if the relationship were to end. When we care about another person, we invest material things, such as money and possessions. Even more important, we invest time, energy, trust, and feelings. In doing this, we invest *ourselves.* We can't get back the feelings and energy and material investments. For good or ill, investments bind us to relationships. The more we invest in a relationship, the more difficult it is to end it (Dainton, 2006; Guerrero, Andersen, & Afifi, 2008).

Relationship Rules

All relationships have **rules** that guide how partners interact. As in other contexts, relationship rules define what is expected, what is not allowed, and when and how to do various things. Typically, relationship rules are unspoken understandings between partners. As you may recall from our discussion in Chapter 5, two kinds of

Jason Homa/The Image Bank/Getty Images

In personal relationships, partners invest themselves.

rules guide our communication. *Constitutive rules* define the meaning of various types of communication in personal relationships. For instance, women friends often count listening to problems as demonstrating care, whereas many men are more likely to count hanging out and doing things together as showing care (Tavris, 1992; Wood, 1998, 2005). Friends work out a number of constitutive rules to define what kinds of communication count as loyalty, support, rudeness, love, joking, and so forth.

Regulative rules influence interaction by specifying when and with whom to engage in various kinds of communication. For example, some friends have a regulative rule that says it's okay to criticize each other in private but not okay to do so in front of others. Many men regard interrupting as a normal part of conversation between friends, whereas women sometimes interpret interruptions as rude (Wood, 1998, 2005). Some romantic partners limit physical displays of affection to private settings.

Friends and romantic partners develop rules for what they want and expect of each other, as well as rules for what will not be tolerated. For example, you would probably consider it a betrayal if your best friend dated your romantic partner, and you would end one or both relationships. On the other hand, not interrupting may be a rule, but breaking it probably won't destroy a good friendship.

Affected by Contexts

Personal relationships are not isolated from the social world. Instead, the surroundings of relationships influence interaction between partners (Dainton, 2006; Duck, 2007; Klein & Milardo, 2000). Friendships and romances are affected by neighborhoods, social circles, family units, and society as a whole. For instance, Western culture values marriage, which means that men and women who marry generally receive more social support than do cohabiting gay, lesbian, or heterosexual couples. Our families of origin shaped what we look for in intimates—the importance we place on social status, faith, intelligence, and so on. Families may voice approval or disapproval of our choices of intimates or of how we run our private relationships. Our social circles establish norms for activities such as drinking, involvement with community groups, studying, and partying. In many ways, families, friends, and society shape the rules we form in our relationships.

KAYA   *I had never drunk much until I started going out with Steve. He was 10 years older than me. We usually spent time with his friends, who were also older and in business. All of them drank—not like a whole lot or anything, but several drinks a night. Pretty soon, I was doing that too—it was just part of the relationship with Steve.*

Changes in society and social norms go hand in hand with changes in relationship forms. The number of single-parent households is also expanding rapidly. In the decade from 1990 to 2000, the number of families headed by single women grew five times faster than the number of married couples with children. Some women are sure they want to bear and raise children but not sure they want to live with a man for life or haven't found the right relationship yet. Other women, as well as men, decide to adopt, feeling that they are ready to commit to raising a child but not to a serious relationship with a partner (Kantrowitz & Wingert, 2001). The emerging forms of relationships reflect changes in social values, priorities, gender roles, and resources.

Personal media such as cells and BlackBerrys, make it increasingly possible to sustain intimacy over distance (Carl, 2006; Sahlstein, 2006a, 2006b). The growing number of dual-career couples is revising traditional expectations about how much each partner participates in earning income, homemaking, and child care (Galvin, 2006). As our society becomes more culturally diverse, interracial, interreligious, and interethnic personal relationships become more common and more socially accepted. The number of interracial marriages tripled between 1970 and 2002, and interracial dating grew at an even higher rate (Troy & Laurenceau, 2006). Thus, our social circles and the larger society as well are contexts that influence the relationships we form and the how we communicate within them.

Relational Dialectics

A final feature of personal relationships is **relational dialectics**—the opposing and continual tensions that are normal in personal relationships. Scholars have identified three relational dialectics (Baxter, 1990, 1993; Baxter & Montgomery, 1996; Erbert, 2000).

Autonomy/Connection   Intimates experience tension between the desire for autonomy and the urge for connection. Because we want to be deeply linked to intimates, we cherish time with them and the sharing of experiences, thoughts, and feelings. At the same time, each of us needs some independence. We don't want our individuality to be swallowed up by relationships, so we seek some privacy and distance, even from the people we love most.

In most close relationships there is frequent—sometimes continuous—friction arising from the contradictory impulses for autonomy and connection (Erbert, 2000). Friends and romantic partners may vacation together and be with each other almost all the time for a week or more. Yet the intense closeness leads them to crave time apart once they return home. Both autonomy and closeness are natural human needs. The challenge is to preserve individuality while also creating intimacy.

> **STANLEY**   *For a long time, I've been stressed about my feelings. Sometimes I can't get enough of Annie, and then I feel crowded and don't want to see her at all. I never understood these switches, and I was afraid I was unstable or something. Now I see that I'm pretty normal after all.*

Novelty/Predictability   The second dialectic is a tension between wanting familiar routines and wanting novelty. We like a certain amount of routine to provide security and predictability in our lives. Friends often have standard times to get together, and they develop preferred interaction routines (Braithwaite & Kellas, 2006). Romantic couples develop preferred times and places for going out, and they establish patterns for interacting. Families have rituals to mark holidays (Bruess & Hoefs, 2006). Yet too much routine is boring, so friends occasionally explore a new restaurant, romantic couples periodically do something spontaneous to introduce variety into their customary routines, and families change established rituals.

Openness/Closedness   The third dialectic is tension between the desire for openness and the desire for privacy. Although intimate relationships sometimes are idealized as totally open and honest, in reality complete openness would be intolerable (Petronio, 2000; Petronio & Caughlin, 2006). We want to share our inner selves with our intimates, yet there are times when we don't feel like sharing and topics that we don't want to talk about. All of us need some privacy, and our partners need to respect that. Wanting some privacy doesn't mean that the relationship is in trouble. It means only that we need both openness and closedness in our lives.

Managing Dialectics   Leslie Baxter (1990) identifies four ways intimates deal with dialectical tensions. One response, called **neutralization,** negotiates a balance between dialectical needs. This involves striking a compromise in which both needs are met to an extent but neither is fully satisfied. A couple might agree to be somewhat open but not intensely so. The **separation** response favors one need in a dialectic and ignores the other. For example, friends might agree

COMMUNICATION in Your Life

Have you experienced the autonomy/ connection dialectic in your relationships?

RESEARCH IN OUR LIVES

Grieve with me; let me grieve alone

We all experience losses in our lives, but the loss of a child is especially devastating to the individual parents and often to marriages. How do parents experience grief and how do they communicate about it with each other? Those are the questions that communication scholars Paige Toller and Dawn Braithwaite asked in a recent investigation. Toller interviewed 37 bereaved parents and then transcribed the interviews, which she and Dr. Braithwaite then analyzed.

Toller and Braithwaite found that bereaved parents experienced a dialectical tension between desires to grieve together and grieve separately. In other words, most of the participants wanted to grieve with their spouses and also wanted to grieve alone. Mourning the loss of a child with a spouse provided comfort and support based on a shared history and shared love for the child. At the same time, most bereaved parents also felt a need to grieve privately. They felt that their grief was, in some ways, unique and their paths to healing were also unique in particular ways. Their different experiences of grief and different approaches to handling it required individual grieving.

The dialectical tension between wanting to connect by grieving together and wanting to be autonomous by grieving apart was accompanied by a second dialectical tension between wanting to be open with a spouse and wanting to keep some feelings and thoughts to oneself. Many bereaved parents wanted to keep some emotions private, even from their spouses. At the same time, they believed it was important to be open and honest with their spouse whenever possible.

Some bereaved couples experienced conflict, stemming from the belief that they should experience and express grief the same way. According to Toller and Braithwaite, "spouses who openly expressed their grief believed their partner needed to do the same. If their partner was not open with his or her grief, then their partner was perceived to be grieving incorrectly" (p. 265). However, most of the participants in this study were able to accept differences between their own and their partners ways of grieving and to allow their partners space to grieve as they needed to while also encouraging connection to grieve together. Communication to address the dialectical tensions between grieving together and grieving apart allowed parents to meet needs that were contradictory and concurrent.

Paige Toller is an Assistant Professor in the School of Communication at the University of Nebraska–Omaha. Dawn Braithwaite is the Willa Cather Distinguished Professor of Communication at the University of Nebraska–Lincoln. This research was presented in a 2009 article: "Grieving together and apart: Bereaved parents' contradictions of marital interaction, *Journal of Applied Communication Research, 37,* 257–277.

to make novelty a priority and suppress their needs for routine. Separation also occurs when partners cycle between dialectical poles to favor each pole alternately. For example, a couple could spend weekends together and have little contact during the week.

A third way to manage dialectics is **segmentation,** in which partners assign each need to certain spheres, issues, activities, or times. For instance, friends might be open about many topics but respect each other's privacy and not pry into one or two areas.

> **MARIANNE**   *Bart and I used to be spontaneous all the time. There was always room for something unexpected and unplanned. That changed when we had the twins last year. Now our home life is totally regulated, planned to the last nanosecond. If we get off schedule in getting the boys dressed and fed in the morning, then we're late getting to day care, which means we have to talk with the supervisor there, and then we're late getting to work. We try to have some spontaneity times when Bart's folks take the boys for a weekend, but it's a lot harder now that the boys are in our life.*

The final method of dealing with dialectics is **reframing.** This is a complex strategy that redefines apparently contradictory needs as not really in opposition. My colleagues and I found examples of reframing in a study of romantic partners (Wood, Dendy, Dordek, Germany, & Varallo, 1994). Some of the couples said that their autonomy enhanced closeness because knowing they were separate in some ways allowed them to feel safer being connected. Instead of viewing autonomy and closeness as opposing, these partners transcended the apparent tension between the two to define the needs as mutually enhancing.

Research suggests that separation in which only one need is fulfilled is generally the least satisfying response to dialectical tensions (Baxter, 1990). Repressing any natural human impulse diminishes us. The challenge is to find ways to honor and satisfy the variety of needs that humans have. Understanding that dialectics are natural and constructive allows us to accept and grow from the tensions they generate.

THE EVOLUTIONARY COURSE OF PERSONAL RELATIONSHIPS

Each relationship develops in unique ways. Yet there are commonalities in the evolutionary courses of personal relationships. We'll explore prototypical patterns for the evolution of friendships and romances.

Laurence Monneret/Riser/Getty Images

Partners in enduring, intimate relationships accept dialectics as natural and create constructive ways to respond to them.

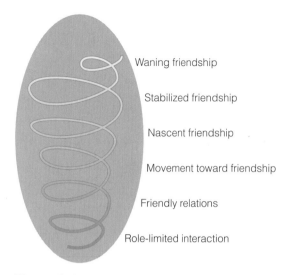

Waning friendship

Stabilized friendship

Nascent friendship

Movement toward friendship

Friendly relations

Role-limited interaction

Figure 9.1
Stages of Friendship

Friendships

Although friendships sometimes jump to life quickly, usually they unfold through a series of stages. Bill Rawlins (1981, 1994), an interpersonal communication researcher, developed a six-stage model of how friendships develop (Figure 9.1).

Role-Limited Interaction   Friendships begin with an encounter. We might meet a new person at work, through membership on an athletic team or in a club or on Facebook or MySpace. During initial encounters, we rely on standard social rules and roles. We tend to be polite and careful about what we disclose, and we are keenly alert to signs that interest in a relationship is not mutual (Snapp & Leary, 2001). One exception to this generalization is electronically conducted relationships, in which people often venture into more personal, disclosive communication in the early stages of acquaintance. Willingness to take some risks early in relationships may be greater when people aren't interacting face to face.

LEWIS   *I met Stan over the Internet. We were both in the same chat room, and it was like we were on the same wavelength, so we started e-mailing each other privately. After a couple of months, it was like I knew Stan better than any of my close friends here, and he knew me, too—inside and out. It seemed safer or easier to open up online than in person. Maybe that's why we got so close so fast.*

Friendly Relations   The second stage of friendship is friendly relations, in which each person checks the other out to see whether common ground and interests exist. Communication during this stage allows people to discover not only whether they have shared interests but also whether they have similar or compatible perspectives on life and ways of interacting (Monsour, 2006; Weinstock & Bond, 2000). Riddick tells Jason that he really likes adventure movies. If Jason says he does, too, then they've found a shared interest. A businessperson talks to an associate about running, to find out whether the associate is also a runner and might want to set up a running schedule. Although friendly exchanges are not dramatic, they are important in allowing us to explore the potential for a deeper relationship with another person.

Movement toward Friendship   Moving toward friendship involves stepping beyond social roles. To signal that we're interested in being friends, we could introduce a more personal topic than any we've discussed so far. We also move toward friendship when we set up times to get together. Maria might ask Raul to go to lunch after class. Sometimes we involve others to lessen the potential awkwardness of being with someone we don't yet know well. For instance, you might invite a new acquaintance to a party where others will be present. People who have gotten to know each other over the Internet may arrange a face-to-face meeting. As people interact more personally, they begin to form a foundation for friendship.

Nascent Friendship   During the stage of nascent friendship, people may begin to think of themselves as friends or as becoming friends. At this point, social norms and roles become less important, and friends begin to work out their own private ways of relating. When my friend Sue and I were in graduate school, we developed a ritual of calling each day between 5 and 6 o'clock to catch up while we cooked our dinners. Some friends settle into patterns of getting together for specific things (e.g., watching games, discussing books, walking, shopping). Other friends share a wider range of times and activities. The milestones of this stage are that people begin to think of themselves as friends and start to work out private roles and rules that establish basic patterns and climate for the friendship.

Stabilized Friendship   When friends feel established in each other's lives, friendship stabilizes. Typically, stabilized friendships are integrated into the larger social contexts of the friends' lives so that they become part of an overall social network (Spenser & Pahl, 2006). The benchmarks of this stage are the assumptions of continuity and trust. Whereas in previous stages the friends didn't count on getting together unless they made a specific plan, stabilized friends assume they'll keep seeing each other. They no longer have to ask whether they'll get together because they are committed to continuing the relationship. Stabilized friends communicate their assumption of ongoing closeness by asking, "Where do you want to have lunch this Friday?" instead of asking, "Do you want to have lunch on Friday?" The former question assumes they will see each other.

Stabilized friends tend to feel safe sharing even more intimate information and revealing vulnerabilities they normally conceal from others. As trust and knowledge of each other expands, friends become more deeply woven into each other's life. Stabilized friendships may continue indefinitely, in some cases lasting a lifetime.

COMMUNICATION
in Your Life

Describe one ritual in a close friendship of yours.

Waning Friendship   Friendship withers when one or both people cease to be committed to it. Sometimes friends drift apart because each is pulled in a different direction by personal or career demands (Guerrero, Jones, & Boburka, 2006). In other cases, friendships deteriorate because they've become boring. Breaking relationship rules can also end friendships. Telling a friend's secrets to a third person or being dishonest may violate the rules of the friendship.

When friendships deteriorate, communication changes in predictable ways. Defensiveness and uncertainty rise, causing people to be more guarded and less open. Communication may also become more strategic as people try to protect themselves from further exposure and hurt. Even when serious violations occur between friends, relationships can sometimes be repaired. For this to happen, both friends must be committed to rebuilding trust and talking openly about their feelings and needs.

Romantic Relationships

Like friendships, romances also have a typical—but not a universal—evolutionary path. For most of us, romance progresses through the stages of escalation, navigation, and deterioration. Within these three broad stages are a number of more specific moments.

Escalation   Six stages of interaction progressively move two people toward the point of commitment. At any point in this process, one or both people may decide to end the relationship. In the first stage, **independence,** we aren't interacting. We are individuals who are aware of ourselves as such, with particular needs, goals, experiences, and qualities that affect what we look for in others and relationships. Before forming romantic relationships, we also have learned a number of constitutive and regulative communication rules that affect how we interact with others and how we interpret their communication (Bachen & Illouz, 1996).

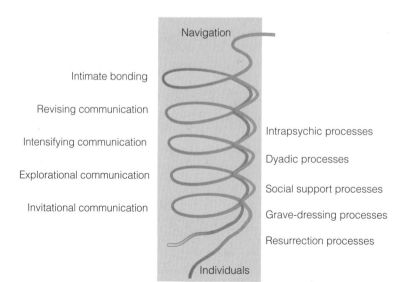

Figure 9.2
Typical Evolution of
Romantic Relationships

The second stage is **invitational communication,** in which people express interest in interacting. This stage involves both extending invitations to others and responding to invitations they extend to us (Metts, 2006b). "Hi, my name's Shelby," and "Did you just start working here?" are examples of invitations to interact. Invitational communication usually follows a conventional script for social conversation. The meaning of invitational communication is found on the relational level of meaning, not the content level. The relational level of meaning communicates "I'm available and possibly interested. Are you?"

Out of all the people we meet, we are attracted romantically to only a few. The three greatest influences on initial attraction are self-concept, proximity, and similarity. Our self-concept affects our choices of candidates for romance. How we define our sexual orientation, for example, is a primary influence on our consideration of potential romantic partners, as are race and social class. The myth that the United States is color blind and classless is disproven by the fact that most people pair with others of their race and social class. In fact, social prestige influences dating patterns now more than it did in the 1950s (Monsour, 2006).

In addition to self-concept, proximity influences initial attraction. We can interact only with people we meet, whether in person or in cyberspace. Social and economic class affects who we meet. For example, people in lower economic strata are less likely to use the Internet, so they have less opportunity to meet people and develop relationships online (Flanagin, Farinola, & Metzger, 2000). Consequently, the places in which we live, work, and socialize, as well as the electronic networks in which we participate, constrain the possibilities for relationships. Some contexts, such as college campuses, promote meeting potential romantic partners, whereas other contexts are less conducive to meeting and dating. Romantic relationships increasingly start and are maintained online. Ninety-three percent of young adults have Internet access, and most of them use the Internet daily (Lenhart, Madden, Macgill, & Smith, 2007). Increasingly, we rely on online and cell communication for quality contact (Peter & Valkenburg, 2006).

Similarity is also important in romantic relationships. In the realm of romance, "birds of a feather flock together" seems truer than "opposites attract" (Samp & Palevitz, 2009). Most of us are attracted to people whose values, attitudes, and lifestyles are similar to ours. In general, people also tend to match themselves with others who are about as physically attractive as they are. We may fantasize about relationships with movie stars and devastatingly attractive people, but when reality settles in, we're likely to pass them by in favor of someone who is about as attractive as we are. In general, we seek romantic partners who are similar to ourselves in many respects.

Explorational communication is a stage in which we explore the possibilities for a relationship. As in the early stages of friendship, potential romantic partners fish for common interests: "Do you like jazz?" "What's your family like?" "Do you follow politics?" As we continue to interact with others, both breadth and depth of information increase. Self-disclosure tends to escalate intimacy (Duck & Wood, 2006) because we perceive it as a sign of trust.

If early interaction increases attraction, then we may escalate the relationship. **Intensifying communication** increases the depth of a relationship by

COMMUNICATION in Your Life

What is your script for first communication with someone you'd like to date?

increasing the amount and intimacy of interaction. My students nicknamed this stage *euphoria* to emphasize the intensity and happiness it typically embodies. During this phase, partners spend more and more time together, and they rely less on external structures such as movies or parties. Instead, they immerse themselves in the budding relationship and may feel they can't be together enough. Additional and more personal disclosures are exchanged, and partners increasingly learn how the other feels and thinks.

Increasingly, people develop relationships online. Compared to face-to-face relationships, online relationships tend to form more rapidly and tend to involve a greater degree of idealization—partners have overly positive perceptions of one another (McQuillen, 2003; Walther & Parks, 2002).

Revising communication, although not part of escalation in all romantic relationships, occurs often enough to merit our consideration. During this stage, partners come down out of the clouds to talk about their relationship's strengths, problems, and potential for the future. With the rush of euphoria over, partners consider whether they want the relationship to be permanent or at least extended. If so, they work through problems and obstacles to long-term viability. In same-sex relationships, partners often have to resolve differences about openness regarding their sexual orientations. Couples may also need to work out differences in religions and conflicts in locations and career goals.

KYLE   *When Todd and I got together, I knew he was the one for me—the man I wanted to spend the rest of my life with. But we had a huge problem. He is totally out, and I'm not. If I came out at my job, I'd be off the fast track immediately, and I'd probably be fired. It was a huge issue between us because he wanted me to be as out as he is—like to take him with me to the holiday parties at my company. I can't do that. It's still a real tension between us.*

As you might expect, during this phase of romance, communication often involves negotiation and even conflict. Issues that weren't problems in a dating relationship may have to be resolved if partners are to commit to a long-term future. Many couples are able to revise their relationships in ways that make the long term possible. Other couples find they cannot resolve problems. It is entirely possible to love a person with whom we don't want to share our life.

Commitment is a decision to stay with a relationship permanently. This decision transforms a romantic relationship from one based on past and present experiences and feelings into one with a future. Before making a commitment, partners don't view the relationship as continuing forever. With commitment, the relationship becomes a given around which they arrange other aspects of their lives.

Romantic relationships escalate for different reasons and with different effects (Surra, Arizzi, & Asmussen, 1988). Some relationships are driven by external events and circumstances that push a couple toward commitment. Timing, approval from friends and family, good jobs, and so forth can drive relationships forward.

Other relationships seem to be driven by factors internal to the relationship. Trust, compatibility, history, shared values, and self-disclosure are examples of relationship factors that can drive romance forward. Long-term satisfaction with marriage is more positively associated with relationship-driven commitments than with event-driven ones. Here are examples of both escalation processes.

Emeka and Fred met and started dating in their senior year of college. Both families supported the relationship, and Emeka and Fred felt it was time to settle down. They married a month after graduation but separated a year later.

Tyrone and Ella dated for 3 years. By the time they walked down the aisle, they knew each other well, they shared the same values and faith, and they had developed trust. Three years later, they are very satisfied with the marriage.

Bizarro

Bizarro(NEW) © 1998 Dan Piraro. King Features Syndicate

Navigation Navigation is the ongoing process of communicating to sustain intimacy over time and in the face of changes in oneself, one's partner, the relationship, and surrounding contexts. Although navigation can be an extended stage in romantic intimacy, it is not stable but very dynamic (Canary & Dainton, 2003). Couples continuously work through new problems, revisit old ones, and accommodate changes in their individual and joint lives. To use an automotive analogy, navigating involves both preventive maintenance and periodic repairs (Stafford, 2009). Navigating communication aims to keep intimacy satisfying and healthy and to deal with problems and tensions. In her study of older couples who have stayed together, therapist Maggie Scarf (2008) found that the later years in very long-term marriages can be the happiest, in part because couples have learned to focus on what matters and not to sweat the small stuff. Other research (Parker-Pope, 2009b) confirms the finding that many couples find the "empty nest years" the happiest in their marriages because there are fewer stresses and more couple time.

The nucleus of intimacy is **relational culture,** a private world of rules, understandings, meanings, and patterns of interacting that partners create for their

COMMUNICATION HIGHLIGHT

Mixed Matches

Although similarity clearly is a major influence on romantic attraction, it isn't the whole story. As society becomes more ethnically diverse, people of different races and cultural heritages are finding each other and building relationships together (Crohn, 1995; Dicks, 1993; Moran, 2001; Schmitt, 2001b).

To create enduring and satisfying relationships, people with different cultural backgrounds need to understand each other and work out accommodations. A man from the United States who married an Italian woman reports that his greatest difficulty was adjusting to the closeness of Italian families. A German woman and a Portuguese man found it difficult to establish a mutually acceptable level of emotional expressiveness. In Mediterranean cultures, free and often dramatic expression of feelings is normal, but German culture emphasizes greater emotional restraint. A woman from the United States who married a Turkish man was astonished by his and his family's expectations that women should be highly deferential and should cater to husbands and in-laws.

relationship (Wood, 1982). Relational culture includes how a couple manages relational dialectics. Mei-Ling and Gregory may do a great many things together, whereas Lana and Kaya emphasize autonomy. Brent and Carmella may be open and expressive, whereas Marion and Senona prefer more privacy. There aren't right and wrong ways to manage dialectics, because individuals and couples differ in what they need. The unique character of each relationship culture reflects how partners deal with tensions between autonomy and connection, openness and privacy, and novelty and routine (Wood, 2006a).

Relational culture also includes communication rules, usually unspoken, about how to signal anger, love, sexual interest, and so forth. Couples also develop routines for contact. Robbie and I catch up while we're fixing dinner each evening. Other couples reserve weekends for staying in touch. Especially important in navigation is small talk, through which partners weave together the fabric of their history and their current lives, experiences, and dreams.

Not all intimately bonded relationships endure. Despite popular belief that love is forever, often it isn't forever and may not even be for very long. Tensions within a relationship, as well as pressures and problems in surrounding contexts, may contribute to the end of intimacy.

Deterioration Processes   Some years ago, Steve Duck (1982) proposed a five-phase model of relationship deterioration. Working with me (Duck & Wood, 2006) and Stephanie Rollie (Rollie & Duck, 2006), Duck recently revised his original model to emphasize the processual nature of relationship decline. Instead of representing relationship deterioration as a sequence of stages, Duck and his colleagues emphasize that relationships decline through a series of processes, each of which is complex and dynamic.

Intrapsychic processes launch relational deterioration. During these processes, one or both partners reflect and sometimes brood about dissatisfaction with the relationship. It's easy for intrapsychic processes to become self-fulfilling prophecies: As gloomy thoughts snowball and awareness of positive features

COMMUNICATION **HIGHLIGHT**

How Do I Love Thee?

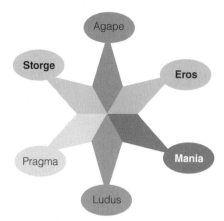

"How do I love thee? Let me count the ways." In opening one of her best-known poems with these lines, Elizabeth Barrett Browning foresaw what social scientists would later discover: that there are many ways of loving (Swidler, 2001). Just as people differ in their tastes in food and styles of dress, we differ in how we love. Researchers have identified six different styles of loving, each of which is valid in its own right, although not all styles are compatible with one another (Hendrick & Hendrick, 1996; Hendrick, Hendrick, Foote, & Slapion-Foote, 1984; Lee, 1973, 1988). See whether you can identify your style of loving in the descriptions given.

Figure 9.3
The Colors of Love

Eros is a style of loving that is passionate, intense, and fast moving. Not confined to sexual passion, eros may be expressed in spiritual, intellectual, or emotional ways.

Storge (pronounced "store-gay") is a comfortable, best-friends kind of love that grows gradually to create a stable and even-keeled companionship.

Ludus is a playful, sometimes manipulative style of loving. For ludic lovers, love is a challenge, a puzzle, a game to be relished but not one to lead to commitment.

Mania is a style of loving marked by emotional extremes. Manic lovers often are insecure about their value and their partners' commitment.

Agape is a selfless kind of love in which a beloved's happiness is more important than one's own. Agapic lovers are generous, unselfish, and devoted.

Pragma is a pragmatic and goal-oriented style of loving. Pragmas rely on reason and practical considerations to select people to love.

of the relationship ebbs, partners may actually bring about the failure of their relationship. There are some general sex and gender differences in what generates dissatisfaction (Duck & Wood, 2006). For women, unhappiness most often arises when communication declines in quality or quantity. Men are more likely to be dissatisfied by specific behaviors or the lack of valued behaviors or by having domestic responsibilities that they feel aren't a man's job. Because many women are socialized to be sensitive to interpersonal nuances, they are generally more likely than men to notice tensions and early symptoms of relationship problems.

Dyadic processes usually—but not always—come next. These processes first may involve the breakdown of established patterns, understandings, and rules that have been part of the relationship. Partners may stop talking after dinner, no longer bother to call when they are running late, and in other ways depart from rules and patterns that have defined their relational culture. As the relational culture weakens, dissatisfaction mounts.

Communication scholars report that many people avoid talking about problems, refuse to return calls from partners, and in other ways evade confronting the difficulties (Metts, Cupach, & Bejlovec, 1989). Although it is painful to talk about problems, avoiding discussion does nothing to resolve them and may make them worse. What happens during dyadic processes depends on how committed the partners are, on whether they perceive attractive alternatives to the relationship, and on whether they have the communication skills to work through problems constructively. Many college undergraduates follow a cyclical pattern when breaking up. They pull apart and get back together several times before actually ending the relationship (Battaglia, Richard, Datteri, & Lord, 1998).

If partners lack commitment or the communication skills they need to restore intimacy, they enter into **social support processes,** which involve telling others about problems in the relationship and seeking support from others. Friends and family members can provide support by being available and by listening. Partners may give self-serving accounts of the breakup to save face and secure sympathy from others. Thus, Vera may tell her friends all the ways in which Frank was at fault and portray herself as the innocent party. Each partner may criticize the other and expect friends to take sides. Although self-serving explanations of breakups are common, they aren't necessarily constructive. We have an ethical responsibility to monitor communication during this period so that we don't say things we'll later regret.

If partners decide they will definitely part ways, they move into **grave-dressing processes.** One important part of grave dressing is that either separately or in collaboration, partners decide how to explain their problems to friends, co-workers, children, in-laws, and social acquaintances. When partners don't craft a joint explanation for breaking up, friends may take sides, gossip, and disparage one or the other partner as the bad guy (La Gaipa, 1982). During grave dressing, each partner also works individually to make sense of the relationship: what it meant, why it failed, and how it affected him or her. Typically, partners mourn the failure to realize that which once seemed possible.

Yet mourning and sadness may be accompanied by other, more positive outcomes from breakups. Ty Tashiro and Patricia Frazier (2003) surveyed undergraduates who had recently broken up with a romantic partner. They found that people reported that breaking up gave them new insights into themselves, improved family relationships, and gave them more clear ideas about future partners. Grave-dressing processes allow partners to put the relationship to rest so they can get on with their individual lives.

The final part of relationship deterioration is **resurrection processes,** in which each former partner moves ahead to a future without the other. Each person prepares himself or herself to live without a partner, for either the short term or the long term, or to seek new romantic relationships.

The stages we've discussed describe how most people experience the evolution of romance (Figure 9.2 on p. 208). However, not all couples follow the standard pattern. Some couples skip one or more stages or cycle more than once through certain stages. For example, a couple might soar through euphoria, work out some tough issues in revising, then go through euphoria a second time. It's also normal for long-term partners to move out of navigation periodically as they experience both euphoric seasons and intervals of dyadic breakdown. In the ebb and flow of enduring romantic relationships, there is a great deal of movement. As long as intimacy exists, what remains constant is partners' commitment to a future and investments in the relationship.

CHALLENGES IN PERSONAL RELATIONSHIPS

To sustain fulfilling personal relationships, partners rely on communication to deal with internal tensions between themselves and external pressures. The skill with which we manage these challenges is a major influence on the endurance and quality of personal relationships. We'll consider five specific challenges that many friends and romantic partners face.

Adapting to Diverse Communication Styles

Personal relationships may be strained when friends and romantic partners have different ways of communicating that reflect their different cultures. A range of communication styles is common in a diverse society such as ours.

For instance, a native Japanese man might perceive a friend from Milwaukee as arrogant for saying, "Let's go out to celebrate my job offer." A Thai woman might not get the support she wants from a friend from Brooklyn because she learned not to assert her needs, whereas the Brooklyn friend was taught that people speak up for themselves.

In the United States, misunderstandings also arise from differences between social communities. Joe, who is white, might feel hurt if Markus, a black friend, turns down going to a concert to go home to care for an ailing aunt. Joe might interpret this as meaning that Markus really doesn't want to be with him. Joe would interpret Markus differently if he realized that, as a rule, blacks are more communal than whites, so taking care of extended family members is a priority (Gaines, 1995). Ellen may feel that her friend Jed isn't being supportive when, instead of listening to her problems, he offers advice or suggests they go out to take her mind off her troubles. Yet he is showing support according to masculine rules of communication. Jed, on the other hand, may feel that Ellen is intruding on his autonomy when she pushes him to talk about his feelings. According to feminine rules of communication, however, Ellen is showing interest and concern (Wood, 1998, 2011).

Differences themselves usually aren't the cause of problems between intimates. Instead, how we interpret and judge diverse communication styles is the root of much tension and hurt (remember the abstraction ladder we discussed in Chapter 2?). Jed interpreted Ellen according to his communication rules, not hers, and she interpreted Jed according to her communication rules, not his. The tension between them results from their interpretations of each other's behaviors, not from the behaviors themselves.

Dealing with Distance

Geographic separation can be difficult for friends and romantic couples. Fully 70 percent of college students are or have been in long-distance romances (Guldner, 2003), and even more have one or more long-distance friendships (Sahlstein, 2006a, 2006b).

One of the greatest problems for long-distance commitments is inability to share small talk face-to-face and to engage in daily routines is a major one. As we have seen, communication about the ordinary comings and goings of days helps partners keep their lives woven together. The mundane conversations of romantic partners and friends form the basic fabric of their relationship.

A second common problem is unrealistic expectations for time together (Stafford, 2005). Because friends and partners have so little time together physically, they often believe that every moment must be perfect. They may feel that there should be no conflict and that they should be with each other during all the time they have together. Yet this is a very unrealistic expectation. Conflict and needs for autonomy are natural in all relationships. They may be even more likely in long-distance relationships because friends and partners are used to living alone and have established independent rhythms that may not mesh well. In fact, Laura Stafford, Andy Merolla, and Janessa Castle (2006) report that loss of autonomy is a key reason some couples who have dated long-distance break up when they are reunited in the same place.

A third common challenge in long-distance relationships is idealization. Because partners are not physically together much of the time, they are more likely than geographically close partners to idealize each other, and this tendency is not lessened by computer-mediated communication (CMC) or phone calls (Stafford & Merolla, 2007). The unrealistic views of each other, which some long-distance partners have, explains why breakups are common for partners who transition to a geographically close relationship (Stafford & Merolla, 2007).

The good news is that these problems don't necessarily sabotage long-distance romance. Many people maintain satisfying commitments despite geographic separation. To overcome the difficulties of distance, many couples use cell phones and e-mail and engage in creative communication to sustain intimacy (Guldner, 2003). To learn more about long-distance relationships and ways to connect with people who are in them, use your Online Resources for *Communication in Our Lives* to access **WebLink 9.1** and **WebLink 9.2.** You can also use your InfoTrac College Edition to read the article on long-distance relationships that appeared in the May 21, 2001, issue of *Jet*. How does the advice in this article reflect and extend the concepts you've read in this chapter?

> **COMMUNICATION in Your Life**
>
> How do you communicate with long-distance friends?

CourseMate

Creating Equitable Romantic Relationships

Equity between partners affects satisfaction with relationships. On the job, we expect equity: to be treated the same as other employees at our level. If we are asked to do more work than our peers, we can appeal to a manager or supervisor. In romantic relationships, however, there is no supervisor to ensure equity. Researchers report that the happiest dating and married couples believe both partners invest equally (Buunk & Mutsaers, 1999; DeMaris, 2007). When we think we are investing more than our partner is, we tend to be resentful. When it seems our partner is investing more than we are, we may feel guilty (Guerrero, La Valley, & Farinelli, 2008).

Although few partners demand moment-to-moment equality, most of us want our relationships to be equitable over time (Dainton & Zelley, 2006). Equity has multiple dimensions. We may evaluate the fairness of financial, emotional, physical, and other contributions to a relationship. One area that strongly affects satisfaction of spouses and cohabiting partners is equity in housework and child care. Inequitable division of domestic obligations fuels dissatisfaction and resentment, both of which harm intimacy (DeMaris, 2007; Steil, 2000). Marital stability is more closely linked to equitable divisions of child care and housework than to income or sex life (Oakley, 2002; Risman & Godwin, 2001).

A majority of marriages today include two wage earners. Unfortunately, divisions of family and home responsibilities have not changed much in response to changing employment patterns. Even when both partners in heterosexual relationships work outside the home, in most dual-worker families women do most of the child care and homemaking.

How are domestic responsibilities managed in same-sex couples? Lesbian couples create more egalitarian relationships than either heterosexuals or gay

Amy Etra/PhotoEdit

Couples who share equitably in domestic responsibilities are happier than couples who don't.

men. More than any other type of couple, lesbians are likely to communicate collaboratively to make decisions about domestic work and parenting (Golberg & Perry-Jenkins, 2007). Consequently, lesbians are least likely to have negative feelings of inequity. In many gay couples, the man who makes more money has and uses more power, both in making decisions that affect the relationship and in avoiding housework (Huston & Schwartz, 1996).

As a rule, women assume **psychological responsibility** for relationships, which involves remembering, planning, and coordinating domestic activities (Hochschild with Machung, 2003; Steil, 2000). Parents may take turns driving children to the doctor, but it is usually the mother who remembers when checkups are needed, makes appointments, and reminds the father to take the child. Both partners may sign cards and give gifts, but women typically assume the burden of remembering birthdays and buying cards and gifts. Successful long-term relationships in our era require partners to communicate collaboratively to design equitable divisions of responsibility.

MOLLY   *It really isn't fair when both spouses work outside of the home but only one of them takes care of the home and kids. For years, that was how Sean's and my marriage worked, no matter how much I tried to talk with him about a more fair arrangement. Finally, I had just had it, so I quit doing everything. Groceries didn't get bought, laundry piled up and he didn't have clean shirts, he didn't remember his mother's birthday (and for the first time ever, I didn't remind him), and bills didn't get paid. After a while, he suggested we talk about a system we could both live with.*

Resisting Violence and Abuse Between Intimates

Intimate partner violence is widespread and it cuts across lines of socioeconomic status, race, and ethnicity (Johnson, 2008; Spitzack & Cupach, 2009). Violence is high not only in heterosexual marriages but also in dating and cohabiting relationships (Johnson, 2006, 2008). In addition to physical abuse, verbal and emotional brutality poison altogether too many relationships.

It is estimated that 10 percent of teenage dating relationships includes violence (Olson, 2009). Similarly, the Centers for Disease Control and Prevention found 1 in 11 teens are bruised by dates, and 8.9 percent of students in grades 9 through 12 reported experiencing physical violence from a date in the past year (Bowman, 2006). Among heterosexuals, intimate partner violence is inflicted primarily by men against women. Although a majority of perpetrators of intimate partner violence are men (Johnson, 2006, 2008), the vast majority of men do not inflict violence on girlfriends and wives, and they would not consider doing so.

A rising form of intimate partner violence is stalking, which is repeated, intrusive behavior that is uninvited and unwanted, that seems obsessive, and that makes the target afraid or concerned for his or her safety. In studies conducted on college campuses (Bazar, 2007, Spitzack & Cupach, 2009), 13 to 21 percent of students report having been stalked—approximately the same percentage of the general population that reports being stalked (Spitzack & Cupach, 2009). About half of female victims are stalked by ex-partners, and another 25 percent by men they have dated at least once (Meloy, 2006). Stalking is particularly easy on campuses because it isn't difficult to learn others' routines. Sending IMs and social networking sites such as MySpace and FaceBook give stalkers more ways to learn about (potential) victims' habits and patterns.

Intimate partner violence tends to follow a predictable cycle: Tension mounts in the abuser, the abuser explodes by being violent, the abuser then is remorseful and loving, the victim feels loved and reassured that the relationship is working, and then tension mounts anew and the cycle begins again. Too often, people don't leave abusive relationships because they feel trapped by economic pressures or by relatives and clergy who counsel them to stay (Foley, 2006; Jacobson & Gottman, 1998). Without intervention, the cycle of violence is unlikely to stop. Abusive relationships are unhealthy for everyone involved. They violate the trust that is a foundation of intimacy, and they jeopardize the comfort, health, and sometimes the lives of victims of violence.

Communication is related to intimate partner violence in two ways. Most obviously, patterns of communication between couples and the intrapersonal communication of abusers can fuel tendencies toward violence. Some partners deliberately annoy and taunt each other. Also, the language abusers use to describe physical assaults on partners includes denial, trivializing the harm, and blaming the partner or circumstances for "making me do it" (Johnson, 2006; Wood, 2001b). These intrapersonal communication patterns allow abusers to deny their offenses, justify violence, and cast responsibility outside themselves.

Intimate partner violence is also promoted by cultural communication practices that normalize violence, including violence against women (Herbert, 2009). From magazines to films to MTV, domination of women and violence against them are pervasive in media. News accounts that refer to "loving her too much" and "love that gets out of hand" camouflage the brutality and unloving nature of violence (Meyers, 1994, 1997).

Violent relationships are not the fault of victims. A person cannot earn battering, nor do victims encourage it. If you know or suspect that someone you care about is a victim of abuse, don't ignore the situation, and don't assume it's none of your business. It is an act of friendship to notice and offer to help. Victims of violence must make

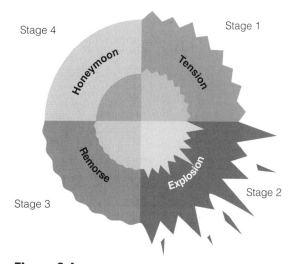

Figure 9.4
The Cycle of Abuse

the ultimate decisions about what to do, but the support and concern of friends can help them.

Negotiating Safer Sex

In our era, sexual activities pose serious, even deadly, threats to sexual partners—heterosexuals as well as gays and lesbians. To date, more than half a million people in the United States have died of AIDS (http://www.cdc.gov), and more than one and a quarter million people in the U.S. are living with HIV (Altman, 2008). Most of them contracted the virus through sex with a hookup, casual date, or serious romantic partner. New HIV and AIDS cases have actually increased since 1999 (Altman, 2008; Carey & O'Connor, 2004). Every single day, 68,000 people are infected with HIV (Schott, 2008). And HIV is not the only sexually transmitted disease (STD). One in four girls between the ages of 14 and 19 is infected with a common STD ("One in Four," 2008). If you'd like to learn more about the range of STDs and their consequences, use your Online Resources for *Communication in Our Lives* to access **WebLink 9.3**.

Researchers have identified three primary reasons many people don't practice safer sex. First, ironically, many people find it more embarrassing to talk about sex than to engage in it, especially when sex occurs in casual encounters such as hookups (McGinn, 2004; Paul, 2006). They find it awkward to ask direct questions of partners (i.e., "Have you been tested for HIV?" "Are you having sex with anyone else?") or to make direct requests of partners (i.e., "I want to wear a condom," "I would like you to be tested for HIV before we have sex"). Naturally, it's difficult to talk explicitly about sex and the dangers of HIV. However, it is far more difficult to live with HIV or the knowledge that you have infected someone else.

A second reason some people don't practice safer sex is that they hold erroneous and dangerous misperceptions. Among these are the assumptions that you are safe if you and your partner are monogamous, the belief that you can recognize "the kind of person" who might have HIV, and the idea that planning for sex destroys the spontaneity. Some of my students have told me that they think the new treatments for HIV reduce the seriousness of the disease and that soon a cure will be found. All of these are dangerous beliefs that can put you and your partners at grave risk. A third reason people sometimes fail to practice safer sex is that their rational thought and control are debilitated by alcohol and other drugs (McGinn, 2004).

Discussing and practicing safer sex may be awkward, but there is no sensible alternative. Good communication skills can help you negotiate safer sex. It is more constructive to say, "I feel unsafe having unprotected sex" than "Without a condom, you could give me AIDS." (Notice that the first statement uses *I*-language, whereas the second one relies on *you*-language.) A positive communication climate is fostered by using relational language, such as *we*, *us*, and *our relationship*, to talk about sex.

BEYOND THE CLASSROOM

Let's take the material in this chapter beyond the classroom by thinking about how what you've learned about communication in personal relationships might apply to the workplace, ethical choices, and engagement with the broader world.

1. **Workplace.** Apply the idea of investments and commitments to the employment context. Review the jobs that you have had in your life. Which ones did you invest most heavily in? Were you more committed to those jobs than ones in which you invested less?

2. **Ethics.** This chapter cites substantial research that shows equity between partners in romantic relationships is linked to satisfaction and relationship longevity. The chapter also presents research showing that men and women in heterosexual relationships are not contributing equitably. Are inequitable relationships unethical? Is it right or fair for one partner to do more of the work required to keep a relationship going? If not, what ways can you think of to change the long-standing pattern whereby women do more of the work involved in maintaining relationships?

Ethics

3. **Engagement.** Consider volunteering at a domestic violence shelter or helpline. The skills you've developed in your communication class will enhance your effectiveness in talking with victims of intimate partner violence.

CHAPTER SUMMARY

In this chapter, we've explored communication in personal relationships, which are defined by uniqueness, commitment, relational dialectics, relationship rules, and interaction with surrounding contexts. We traced the typical evolutionary paths of friendships and romances by noting how partners communicate during the escalating, stabilizing, and declining stages of personal relationships.

In the final section of the chapter, we considered five challenges that friends and romantic partners face. The communication principles and skills we have discussed in this and previous chapters can help us meet the challenges of adapting to diverse communication styles, sustaining intimacy across geographic distance, creating equitable relationships, resisting violence, and negotiating safer sex. Good communication skills enable us to meet these challenges so that we, our intimates, and our relationships survive and thrive over time.

APPLYING COMMUNICATION IN OUR LIVES

The key concepts, For Further Reflection and Discussion questions, and Experiencing Communication in Our Lives case study that follow will help you review, reflect on, and extend the information and ideas presented in this chapter. These resources, and a diverse selection of additional study tools, are also available as Online Resources for *Communication in Our Lives.* Your Online Resources include CourseMate, a student workbook, interactive video activities, audio study tools, a book companion website, Speech Builder Express, Speech Studio, and InfoTrac College Edition. For more information or to access this book's online resources, visit **www.cengage.com/login.**

KEY CONCEPTS

commitment, 200
dyadic processes, 213
explorational communication, 209
grave-dressing processes, 214
independence, 208
intensifying communication, 209

intrapsychic processes, 212
investment, 201
invitational communication, 209
neutralization, 203
passion, 200
personal relationship, 200
psychological responsibility, 218
reframing, 205

relational culture, 211
relational dialectics, 202
resurrection processes, 214
revising communication, 210
rules, 201
segmentation, 205
separation, 203
social support processes, 214

FOR FURTHER REFLECTION AND DISCUSSION

1. Think about the distinction between passion and commitment in personal relationships. Describe relationships in which commitment is present but passion is not. Describe relationships in which passion exists but not commitment. What can you conclude about the values of each?

2. Are you now or have you been involved in a long-distance personal relationship, either friendship or romance? How did you communicate to bridge the distance? Do your experiences parallel the chapter's discussion of challenges in long-distance relationships?

3. Does a person who wants to end a serious romantic relationship have an ethical responsibility to talk with his or her partner about why he or she is no longer interested in maintaining the relationship? Under what conditions are we ethically obligated to help a partner through a breakup?

Ethics

SHARPEN YOUR SKILL

1. Faded Friendships

Remember three friendships that were once very close but have faded away. Describe the reasons they ended. How did boredom, differences, external circumstances, or violations contribute to the decay of the friendships? How did communication patterns change as the friendships waned?

2. Private Language

What are the special words and nonverbal codes in a close relationship of yours? Do you have a way to signal each other when you're bored at a party and ready to leave? Do you use nicknames and private words? Would you feel any loss if you had no private language in your relationship?

The intensifying stage often involves idealizing and personalized communication. Just as private language within a group increases cohesiveness (Bolman & Deal, 1992; Fisher, 2000), private language between intimates increases the sense of "we-ness," or pair identity. Sometimes Robbie and I greet each other by saying, *"Namaste."* This is a Nepalese greeting that expresses good will. Saying it reminds us of our trek in the mountains of Nepal. Private language heightens partners' sense of themselves as a special couple. Partners make up words and nicknames for each other, and they develop ways to send private messages in public settings.

EXPERIENCING COMMUNICATION IN OUR LIVES

CASE STUDY: *Wedding Bells?*

A video of the conversation scripted here is featured in your Chapter 9 Online Resources for *Communication in Our Lives*. Select "Wedding Bells?" to watch the video. Improve your own communication skills by reading, watching, and evaluating this communication encounter.

    After meeting at a New Year's party in the winter of their senior year at Agora College, Trevor and Meg quickly developed an exclusive dating relationship. Now, 4 months later, they are trying to figure out what to do about their relationship.

TREVOR: Do you realize that half our friends are planning weddings? Maybe we should start thinking about ours.

MEG: Don't start this again. You know how I feel about that. It's just too soon. We need to know a lot more before we even think about marriage.

TREVOR: Why? I'm crazy in love with you, and you are with me, right?

MEG: *(Nods)*

TREVOR: So what's too soon? What else do we need to know?

MEG: First of all, I'll be starting law school in the fall, and that's a whole new thing for me. You haven't decided on a job yet. We don't even know if we'll be in the same city!

TREVOR: Sure we do. You'll be going to law school at State, and I can get a job near there. One good thing about being a business major is that I can get a job anywhere.

MEG: See, right there is a problem: I'm much more concerned about my career than you are about yours. Your whole attitude toward it is just so casual.

TREVOR: I am not casual about us. I love you enough to arrange the rest of my life around our relationship. So why aren't you willing to do the same?

MEG: 'Cause it's just too soon. Law school will be very demanding, and I don't want to try starting that and a marriage at the same time.

TREVOR *(grinning):* I'll help you study. Any other problems?

MEG: What about eating? We do okay now because we don't live together. But I'm a vegan, and you'll eat anything. I think we'd have problems if we lived together.

TREVOR: Just keep your tofu away from my chicken in the refrigerator, and we'll be fine.

MEG: I'm serious, Trevor.

TREVOR: So am I. I mean, just because we live together doesn't mean we have to eat the same things. That's not a problem.

MEG: You and I have different values and goals. You think I'm nuts to want a Mercedes, and I don't know how you can be happy with that old truck you drive. And you think I'm extravagant any time I buy anything for myself.

TREVOR: Okay, so we'll have separate accounts, and that way each of us can decide how to spend our own money. Next problem?

MEG: What about children?

TREVOR: What about children? I don't see any children. No problem there.

MEG: Quit kidding around, you know what I mean. You definitely want children; I don't know if I do. That's a big issue, one we should settle before we even think about marriage.

TREVOR: Meggie, if we wait until we've settled every issue, you know, solved every problem, we'll never get married. I totally love you, and I believe in us. I think that we can resolve any issue as it comes along. That's what love is.

MEG: I'm just not comfortable with that. I'd like a lot more of these issues settled before I marry anyone. Love is great, but it's not enough.

QUESTIONS FOR ANALYSIS AND DISCUSSION

You can answer these questions and see my responses to them online via your Online Resources for Chapter 9.

1. Based on the scenario, which styles of loving do you think Meg and Trevor have? What communication by each of them leads you to perceive particular styles of loving?

2. Based on their conversation, what do you perceive to be Meg's and Trevor's levels of commitment to the relationship?

3. What aspects of context seem to influence Meg's and Trevor's preferences for how the relationship should proceed?

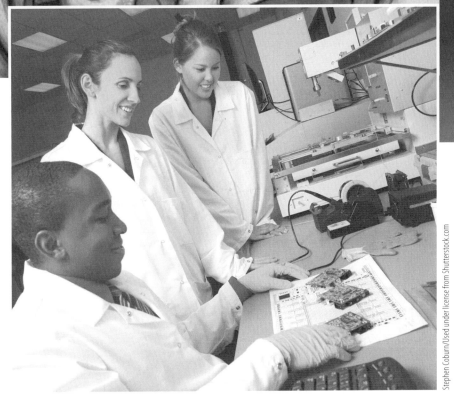

Stephen Coburn/Used under license from Shutterstock.com

> Never doubt that a small group of thoughtful, committed citizens can change the world; indeed, it's the only thing that ever has.
>
> **Margaret Mead**

Foundations of Group and Team Communication

"Teams take too much time to decide anything."
"Working in groups increases creativity and commitment."
"Groups suppress individuality."
"Teams make better decisions than individuals do."

SHARPEN YOUR SKILL

At the end of this chapter, refer to the Sharpen Your Skill features, Assessing the Values of Your Group and Your Communication in Groups, to apply concepts from Chapter 10.

With which of these statements do you agree? Actually, there's some truth to each statement. Groups generally do take more time to reach decisions than individuals, yet group decisions often are superior to those made by one person. Although group interaction stimulates creativity, it may also suppress individual opinions.

COMMUNICATION
in Your Life

List all of the groups to which you currently belong.

Communication is a major influence on whether groups and teams are productive and enjoyable or inefficient and unpleasant. Communication in groups and teams calls for many of the skills and understandings that we've discussed in previous chapters. For example, constructive group communication requires that members express themselves clearly, check perceptions, support others, respect differences between people, build good climates, and listen mindfully. This chapter and Chapter 11 will enhance your ability to participate in and lead groups and teams effectively.

The chapter opens by defining groups and teams. Next, we discuss potential weaknesses and strengths of groups. We then examine influences on interaction between members of groups and teams. Finally, we identify various kinds of group communication and consider how each affects collective climate and productivity.

WHAT ARE GROUPS AND TEAMS?

Pick up any newspaper or surf the Internet and you will see announcements and advertisements for social groups, volunteer service committees, personal support groups, health teams, focus groups sought by companies trying out new products, and political action coalitions. It is a rare person in the United States who hasn't had a wealth of group experiences.

The tendency toward group work is especially pronounced in the workplace. Although groups and teams have gained increased prominence in today's organizations, they actually have a long history in the workforce. Miners, seafarers, and other laborers rely on groups to accomplish their jobs and often to survive harsh and dangerous working conditions (Hodson & Sullivan, 2002).

Today groups and teams are an even greater part of work life (Barge, 2009; Rothwell, 2009). Whether you are an attorney working with a litigation team, a health-care professional who participates in health delivery teams, or a factory worker on a team assigned to find ways to reduce production time, working with others probably will be part of your career. It's likely that your raises and advancement will depend significantly on how well you work in groups. The reason for increasing reliance on groups and teams is that they often produce better results than individuals. As members of a team communicate, thinking is stimulated and creativity is stoked. Often, the outcomes are better ideas and greater personal satisfaction with work. In this chapter, we'll cover some of the foundations for participating in many types of groups and teams; in Chapter 11, we'll focus in greater depth on communication within task teams.

Thus far in this chapter, we've mentioned *groups* and *teams* several times. But what are groups and teams? Are six people standing together on a street corner waiting to cross the street a group? Are five people studying independently in a library a group? Are four students standing in line to buy books a group? The answer is *no* in each case. These are collections of individuals, but they are not groups.

For a group to exist, there must be interaction and interdependence between individuals, a common goal, and shared rules of conduct. Thus, we can define a **group** as three or more people who interact over time, depend on one another, and follow some shared rules of conduct to reach a common goal. To be a group, members must perceive themselves as interdependent—as somehow needing one another and counting on one another (Lumsden & Lumsden, 2009; Rothwell, 2009).

A **team** is a special kind of group that is characterized by different and complementary resources of members and a strong sense of collective identity (Cobb, 2006; Rothwell, 2009). Like all groups, teams involve interaction, interdependence, shared rules, and common goals. Yet a team is distinct in two respects. First, teams consist of people with diverse skills. Whereas group members may have similar backgrounds and abilities, a team consists of people who bring different resources to a common project (Kelley & Littman, 2001; Wheelan, 2005). Second, teams tend to develop greater interdependence and a stronger sense of collective identity than most groups (Lumsden & Lumsden, 2009).

Teams and other groups consist of individuals who are interdependent and who interact over time. People who are in one place but do not interact are not a group and a group does not exist if contact is limited to a fleeting exchange that is insufficient to generate cohesion or interdependence. Groups and teams also develop rules that members understand and follow. You'll recall from previous chapters that constitutive rules state what counts as what. For example, in some groups, disagreement counts as a positive sign of involvement, whereas other groups regard disagreement as negative. Regulative rules regulate how, when, and with whom we interact. For instance, a group might have regulative rules stipulating that members don't interrupt each other and that it's okay to be a few minutes late but more than 10 minutes is a sign of disregard for other group

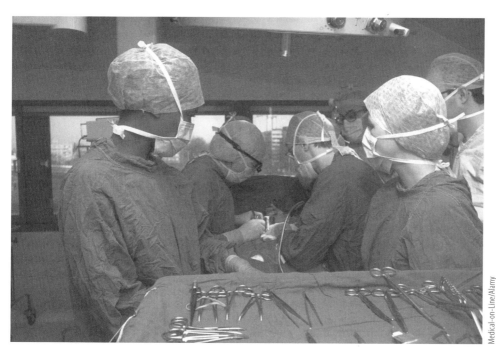

Medical-on-Line/Alamy

Teams have become increasingly popular in today's business world. Team members must communicate continuously and well to meet their shared goals.

members. Groups generate rules over time in the process of interacting and figuring out what works for them.

Groups are also characterized by shared goals. Some common objective or objectives bring and hold members together. Citizens form groups to accomplish political goals, establish social programs, protest zoning decisions, and protect the security of neighborhoods. Workers form teams to develop and market products, evaluate and refine company programs, and improve productivity. Other groups form around goals such as promoting personal growth (therapy groups), sharing a life (families), socializing (singles clubs), having fun and fitting in (peer groups), or participating in sports (intramural teams). As Mieko explains in her commentary, without a common goal, a group doesn't exist. Groups end if the common objective has been achieved or if it ceases to matter to members. To better understand small groups, we'll now consider their potential values and limits, features that affect participation, and the influence of culture on group communication.

MIEKO *When I first came here to go to school, I felt very alone. I met some other students from Japan, and we formed a group to help us feel at home in the United States. For the first year, that group was most important to me and the others because we felt uprooted. The second year, it was good but not so important because we'd all started finding ways to fit in here, and we felt more at home. When we met the first time of the third year, we decided not to be a group anymore. The reason we wanted a group no longer existed.*

POTENTIAL LIMITATIONS AND STRENGTHS OF GROUPS

A great deal of research has compared individual and group decision making. As you might expect, the research identifies both potential weaknesses and potential strengths of groups.

Potential Limitations of Groups

Two significant disadvantages of group discussion are the time needed for the group process and the potential for pressure to conform; both can interfere with high-quality work from groups.

Time If you've ever worked in a group—and who hasn't?—you know that a group takes much longer to decide something than an individual does. Operating solo, an individual can think through ideas efficiently and choose the one she or he considers best. In group discussion, however, all members must have an opportunity to voice their ideas and to respond to the ideas others put forward.

It takes substantial time for each person to present ideas, clarify misunderstandings, and respond to questions or criticisms. In addition, groups need time to deliberate about alternative courses of action. Thus, group discussion probably is not a wise choice for routine policy making and emergency tasks. When

creativity and thoroughness are important, however, the values of groups may outweigh the disadvantage of time.

Conformity Pressures Groups also have the potential to suppress individuals and encourage conformity. This can happen in two ways. The most obvious is that conformity pressures may exist when a majority of members has an opinion different from that of a minority of members or a single member. It's hard to hold out for your point of view when most of your peers have a different one. In effective groups, however, all members understand and resist conformity pressures. They realize that the majority is sometimes wrong, and the minority, even a minority of one, is sometimes right. This implies that group members should encourage expression of diverse ideas and open debate about different viewpoints. The Chapter 8 discussion of communication that creates an open climate can be applied to group contexts to help you create climates that are sufficiently open and supportive to encourage expression of differences.

Conformity pressures may also arise when one member is extremely charismatic, has high prestige, or has greater power than other members. Even if that person is all alone in a point of view, he or she may have sufficient status to sway others. Sometimes a high-status member doesn't intend to influence others and may not overtly exert pressure. For example, President John F. Kennedy often tried not to shape the views of his advisers, but they regarded him so highly that in some cases they suspended their individual critical thinking and agreed with whatever he said (Janis, 1977). As this example illustrates, often neither the high-status person nor others are conscious of conformity pressures. Effective discussion occurs when members guard against the potential to conform uncritically.

COMMUNICATION in Your Life

Have you ever experienced conformity pressures in a group?

LANCE *I used to belong to a creative writing group where all of us helped each other improve our writing. We were all equally vocal, and we had a lot of good discussions and even disagreements when the group first started. But then one member of the group got a story of hers accepted by a big magazine, and all of a sudden we thought of her as a better writer than any of us. She didn't act any different, but we saw her as more accomplished, so when she said something, everybody listened and nobody disagreed. It was like a wet blanket on our creativity because her opinion just carried too much weight once she got published.*

Potential Strengths of Groups

In comparison to individuals, groups generally have greater resources, are more thorough and more creative, and generate greater commitment to decisions.

Greater Resources   A group obviously exceeds any individual member in the number of ideas, perspectives, experiences, and expertise it can bring to bear on solving a problem. Especially on teams, the different resources of individual members are a key to effectiveness (Kelley & Littman, 2001). One member knows the technical aspects of a product, another understands market psychology, a third has expertise in cost analysis, and so forth. When my father was hospitalized, his health-care team included a neurologist, a cardiologist, a physical therapist, a social worker, and a registered nurse. Each member of the team had distinct expertise, and they coordinated their specific skills and knowledge to provide integrated care.

Greater Thoroughness   Groups also tend to be more thorough than individuals, probably because members act as a check-and-balance system for each other (Rothwell, 2009; Salazar, 1995). The parts of an issue one member doesn't understand, another person does; the details of a plan that bore one person interest another; and the holes in a proposal that one member overlooks are recognized by others.

The greater thoroughness of groups isn't simply the result of more people. It also reflects interaction among members. Discussion itself promotes more critical and more careful analysis because members propel each other's thinking. **Synergy** is a special kind of energy that combines and goes beyond the energies, talents, and strengths of individual members (Lumsden & Lumsden, 2009).

COMMUNICATION HIGHLIGHT

Einstein's Mistakes

That's the title of a book by Hans Ohanian (2008). As brilliant as Einstein may have been, he didn't make his great discoveries alone. He is most famous for $E = mc^2$, the equation expressing the law of relativity. However, math wasn't Einstein's strong suit and his proof of the law contained a number of mathematical errors. Another physicist, Max Von Laue worked out a complete and correct proof, at which point $E = mc^2$ was on scientifically solid ground.

The myth of the individual genius is popular in Western societies, in part because they place high value on individualism. However, great innovations, discoveries, and inventions usually reflect the work of many people (Rae-Dupree, 2008). In his book *Group Genius*, Keith Sawyer (2008) shows that most creativity is the product of groups and teams. One person may get the credit—the raise, the patent, or the Nobel prize—but it took many to do the work.

CourseMate

LAURA *The first time I heard about brainstorming was on my job, when the supervisor said all of us in my department were to meet and brainstorm ways to cut costs for the company. I thought it was silly to take time to discuss cost saving when each person could just submit suggestions individually. But I was wrong. When my group started, each of us had 1 or 2 ideas—only that many. But the six of us came up with more than 25 ideas after we'd talked for an hour.*

Greater Creativity A third value of groups is that they are generally more creative than most individuals. Again, the reason seems to lie in the synergetic communication in groups. When members know how to communicate effectively, they interact in ways that spark good ideas, integrative thinking, and creativity. Any individual eventually runs out of new ideas, but groups seem to have almost infinite generative ability. As members talk, they build on each other's ideas, refine proposals, see new possibilities in each other's comments, and so forth. Often, the result is a greater number of ideas and more creative final solutions.

Greater Commitment Finally, an important strength of groups is their ability to generate stronger commitment to decisions. The greater commitment fostered by group discussion arises from two sources. First, participation in the decision-making process enhances commitment to decisions, which is especially important if members are to be involved in implementing the decision. Second, because groups have greater resources than the individual decision maker, their decisions are more likely to take into account the points of view of various people whose cooperation is needed to implement a decision. This is critical because a decision can be sabotaged if the people it affects dislike it or believe their perspectives weren't considered.

Greater resources, thoroughness, creativity, and commitment to group goals are powerful values of group decision making. To realize these values, however, members

David Purdy/Getty Images

Interaction between team members often heightens commitment to collective goals.

must be aware of the trade-off of time needed for group discussion and must resist pressures to conform, or to induce others to conform, without critical thought.

FEATURES OF SMALL GROUPS

The group strengths we've identified are realized only if members participate effectively. If members don't participate or lack the communication skills to participate effectively, a group can't achieve its potential for creativity, thoroughness, resourcefulness, and commitment. Thus, we need to know what influences communication in small groups and how communication itself influences the nature and quality of group work. We'll consider five features of small groups that directly affect participation.

Cohesion

Cohesion is the degree of closeness, esprit de corps, and group identity. In highly cohesive groups, members see themselves as linked tightly together and unified in their goals. This increases members' satisfaction with the group and, in turn, their productivity (Forsyth, 2009; Gammage, Carron, & Estabrooks, 2001). High cohesion and the satisfaction it generates tend to increase members' commitment to a group and to common goals (Langfred, 1998; Wech, Mossholder, Streel, & Bennett, 1998).

How members communicate can foster or inhibit a group's cohesiveness. Communication that cultivates cohesion emphasizes the group or team and the common objectives of all members. Comments that stress pulling together to promote collective interests build cohesion by reinforcing group identity. Cohesion is also fostered by communication that highlights similarities between members: the interests, goals, experiences, and ways of thinking that are common to different people in the group (Donnellon, 1996; Wilmot & Hocker, 2001). A third way to enhance cohesion is by expressing affection, respect, and inclusion so that all members feel valued and part of the group.

Cohesion and participation influence each other reciprocally. Cohesion is promoted when all members participate. At the same time, because cohesion generates a feeling of identity and involvement, once it is established, it fosters participation. Thus, high levels of participation tend to build cohesion, and strong cohesion generally fosters vigorous participation. Encouraging all members to be involved and attending responsively to everyone's contributions generally foster cohesion and continued participation.

Although cohesion is important for effective group communication, too much cohesion can undermine sound group work (Mullen, 1994). When members are extremely close, they may be less critical of each other's ideas and less willing to engage in the analysis and arguments necessary to the best outcomes. When groups are too cohesive, they may engage in **groupthink**; that is, members may cease to think critically and independently about ideas generated by the group. Groupthink has occurred in such high-level groups as presidential advisory boards and national decision-making bodies (Janis, 1977, 1989; Young, Wood, Phillips, & Pedersen, 2001). Members perceive their group so positively that they share the illusion that it cannot make bad decisions. Consequently, they are less careful in evaluating ideas generated in the group. The predictable result is inferior group outcomes.

Group Size

The sheer number of people in a group affects the amount of communication. Consider the difference between communication between two people and among five people. When only two individuals talk, two people send and receive messages. In a group of five, each idea that's expressed must be understood by four others, each of whom may choose to respond. Consequently, the greater the number of people in a group, the fewer the contributions any individual may make. Because participation is linked to satisfaction and commitment, larger groups may generate less satisfaction and commitment to decisions than smaller ones. Groups with nine or more members may form cliques and may be less cohesive than smaller ones (Benenson, Gordon, & Roy, 2000).

Because of the disadvantages of large groups, you might assume that small groups would be the most effective. However, groups can be too small as well as too large. With too few members, a group has limited resources, which eliminates a primary advantage of groups. Also, in very small groups, members may be unwilling to disagree or criticize each other's ideas because alienating one person in a three- or four-person group would dramatically diminish the group. Most researchers agree that five to seven members is the ideal size for a small group (Hamilton & Parker, 2001; Lumsden & Lumsden, 2009).

YOLANDA *The worst group I was ever in had three members. We were supposed to have five, but two dropped out after the first meeting, so there were three of us to come up with proposals for artistic programs for the campus. Nobody would say anything against anybody else's ideas, even if we thought they were bad. For myself, I know I held back from criticizing a lot of times because I didn't want to offend either of the other two. We came up with some really bad ideas because we were so small we couldn't risk arguing.*

Power Structure

Power structure is a third feature that influences participation in small groups. **Power** is the ability to influence others (Rothwell, 2009; Young et al., 2001). There are different kinds of power, or ways of influencing others.

Power over is the ability to help or harm others. This form of power usually is expressed in ways that highlight the status and visibility of the person wielding influence. A group leader might exert positive *power over* a member by providing mentoring, positive reports to superiors, and visibility in the group. A leader could also exert negative *power over* a member by withholding these benefits, assigning unpleasant tasks, and responding negatively to the member's communication during group meetings.

Power to is the ability to empower others to reach their goals (Boulding, 1990; Conrad & Poole, 2004). *Power to* is expressed in creating opportunities for others, recognizing achievements, and arranging circumstances to facilitate others in accomplishing their goals. In small groups, *power to* involves the capacity to create community, inspires loyalty, and builds team spirit so that members are productive and satisfied (Boulding, 1990). Group members who use *power to* help each other foster a win–win group climate in which each member's success is seen as advancing collective work.

STANLEY *The different kinds of power we discussed make me think of my high school. The principal came over the intercom to make announcements or lecture us on improper behaviors and threaten us about what was going to happen if we misbehaved. The teachers were the ones with power to. Most of them worked to empower us. They were the ones who gave us encouragement and praise. They were the ones who helped us believe in ourselves and reach our goals.*

The power structure of a group refers to the distribution of power among various members. Power may result from position (i.e., CEO, president, professor) or it may be earned (i.e., demonstrated competence or expertise). Ideally, a person who holds a powerful position will have earned that position through competence. If all members of a group have equal power, the group has a *distributed power structure*. On the other hand, if one or more members have greater power than others, the group has a *hierarchical power structure*. In some cases, hierarchy takes the form of one person who is

Aspects of nonverbal communication, such as seating patterns, both reflect and shape the power structure of groups.

more powerful than all others, who are equal in power to each other. In other cases, hierarchy may be more complicated, with more than two levels of power. A leader might have the greatest power, three others might have power equal to each other's but less than the leader's, and two other members might have little power.

How are individual power and group power structures related to participation? First, members with high power tend to be the centers of group communication: They talk more, and others talk more to them. **Social climbing** is the attempt to increase personal status in a group by winning the approval of high-status members. If social climbing doesn't work to increase the status of the climber, he or she may become a marginal participant in the group. In addition, members with a great deal of power often have greater influence on group decisions. Not surprisingly, high-power members tend to find group discussion more satisfying than members with less power (Young et al., 2001). This makes sense because those with power get to participate more and get their way more often.

Power not only influences communication but also is influenced by communication. In other words, how members communicate can affect the power they acquire. People who demonstrate expertise in the group's task tend to acquire power quickly (Hawkins, 1995). This is an example of *earned power*, which is gained when a member provides skills valued by the group.

Interaction Patterns

Another important influence on participation is the group's interaction patterns. Some groups are centralized; one or two people have key positions, and most or all communication is funneled through them (Figure 10.1). Other groups

COMMUNICATION in Your Life

Have you more often encountered people who use *power over* or *power to*?

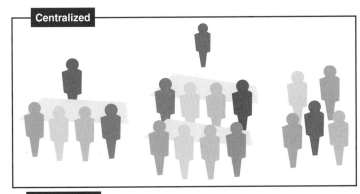

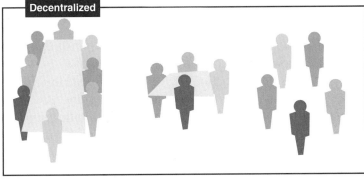

Figure 10.1
Group Interaction Patterns

COMMUNICATION HIGHLIGHT

Five Bases of Power

What is power? How does a person get it? There is more than one answer to each of these questions because there are different sources of power (Arnold & Feldman, 1986).

Reward power	The ability to give people things they value, such as attention, approval, public praise, promotions, and raises
Coercive power	The ability to punish others through demotions, firing, and undesirable assignments
Legitimate power	The organizational role, such as manager, supervisor, or CEO, that results in others' compliance
Expert power	Influence derived from expert knowledge or experience
Referent power	Influence based on personal charisma and personality

To explore your own preferences regarding power—your own and your supervisor's at work—complete the Communication Highlight Activity for Chapter 10 via your Online Resources for *Communication in Our Lives*.

have decentralized patterns, in which communication is more balanced and thus more satisfying to everyone. As you might suspect, the power of individual members and the power structure of the group often affect interaction patterns. If one or two members have greater power than others, a centralized pattern of interaction is likely to emerge.

Decentralized patterns are more typical when members have relatively equal power. One strategy for controlling communication in groups is to manage nonverbal influences on interaction. If you want a centralized communication structure (and hierarchical power), you might arrange chairs so that one person is more central than the others. On the other hand, if you want a decentralized structure, you would arrange chairs so that no one person was more central than any other.

Group Norms

A final small-group feature that affects communication is **norms.** Norms are standardized guidelines that regulate how members act and how they interact with each other. Our definition of a small group, in fact, emphasizes that individuals must share understandings about their conduct to be a group. Like rules in relationships, a group's norms define what is allowed, what is not allowed, and what kind of participation is rewarded.

Group norms regulate all aspects of a group's life, from the trivial to the critical. Fairly inconsequential norms may regulate how members dress, whether they take breaks during meetings, and whether interruptions are allowed when members are speaking. More substantive norms govern how carefully members prepare for meetings, how critically they analyze ideas, how well they listen to one another, and how they deal with differences and conflict.

Norms grow directly out of interaction. For example, at a group's initial meeting, one person might dismiss another's idea as dumb, and several members might not pay attention when others are speaking. If this continues for long, a norm of disrespect will develop, and members will form the habit of unproductive communication. On the other hand, when one member says an idea is dumb, another person might counter by saying, "I don't think so. I think we ought to consider the point." If others then do consider the idea, a norm of respectful communication may develop.

Because norms become entrenched, it's important to pay attention to them from the outset of a group's existence. By noticing patterns and tendencies, you can exert influence over the rules that govern conduct in a group.

> **COMMUNICATION in Your Life**
>
> Identify two norms in one group to which you currently belong.

CULTURAL INFLUENCES ON GROUP DECISION MAKING

In Chapter 7, we noted that communication reflects culture; that principle pertains to groups as well as to individuals and relationships. Although Western society is increasingly diverse, work groups in the United States still tend to reflect primarily Western values and styles of communicating. For example, the democratic ideology of our society is reflected in the widespread tendency toward democratic leadership in groups. Let's consider several pronounced Western values that shape group communication in the West.

Individualism

One of the most strongly held values of Western society is **individualism,** which holds that each person is unique and important and should be recognized for his or her personal activities (Hofstede, 1980; Samovar, Porter, & McDaniel, 2009a,b; Triandis, 1990). It means that individual achievement and personal freedom are greatly respected. In group discussions, individualism is evident in the extent to which Western groups acknowledge the individuals who make contributions, and in the assumption that each individual has the right to express himself or herself freely and fully. Contrast this with the greater emphasis on collectivism found in countries such as Japan, Pakistan, Nepal, and Colombia.

Assertiveness

Perhaps because most Westerners place such high value on individualism, they also tend to admire assertiveness. People are expected to speak up, to assert their ideas, and to stand up for their rights. Like other cultural values, this one is not universal. In Thailand, the Philippines, and Japan, assertiveness not only is not admired but may also be considered offensive. Filipinos regard bluntness as extremely rude and disrespectful (Gochenour, 1990) and instead admire *pakikisma*, or harmonious interaction. A person from Chicago may argue forcefully for her position and offend a Japanese member of the group. The American may regard the Japanese member as uninterested because he won't take a firm position.

BETSY   *I think I really misjudged a guy in a class project group I was in last term. No matter what anyone said, Park Jin Kean nodded and praised the idea. When we asked him what he thought, he would say stuff like "I do not have an opinion to advance" or "I will support whatever others want." I just thought he was a real wimp, but now I see that he just had a different point of view on how to communicate as a good group member.*

Equality

A second strong Western value is equality. The United States was founded on the belief that all people are created equal. Even though there are clear status markers and much class division in the United States, the idea of equality is strongly endorsed in Western society, and this value influences communication in small groups. In small groups, the value placed on equality is reflected in the assumption that every member has an equal right to speak and that no member is better than others. In a number of other cultures, hierarchies are used to order people according to particular criteria. Even in Western society, the ideal of equality is qualified in specific ways. For example, men often are more assertive and more likely to put themselves forward than women, so male members of groups may speak more, and their comments may be given greater respect (Mapstone, 1998).

Progress, Change, and Speed

Westerners also tend to value progress, change, and speed, especially in the area of technology. We like a quick pace, rapid answers, and fast action. The Western emphasis on progress is not a specific belief or activity but a basic mind-set by which Westerners operate (Samovar et al., 2009a,b). Valuing change and progress leads Westerners to focus on the future and to believe they can (and should) control almost all things. The typical Western decision-making committee would be likely to feel it had accomplished nothing if it did not recommend changes in existing policies. The goal is to produce change and move forward. In societies such as Japan and China, history is more revered, and traditions are more likely to be affirmed and left in place by group decisions.

Risk and Uncertainty

The importance Westerners place on progress also explains why they tend to be more tolerant of risk than members of many other cultures. Embarking on new paths, trying bold innovations, and experimenting with untested ideas take daring and willingness to take risks. Associated with risk is acceptance of uncertainty as a normal part of life and of moving forward. Countries such as the United States, Sweden, Ireland, and Finland accept uncertainty more easily than do countries such as Greece, Germany, Peru, and Japan (Samovar et al., 2009a).

One implication of the value placed on risk taking is that Western groups are more likely to accept new ideas if such ideas promise to contribute to what

Speeding Along

CourseMate

David Brooks is a writer and an observer of social trends. One that has caught his attention lately is Americans' growing love affair with technology and its offspring, speed. Brooks thinks that communication technologies are teaching us to crave speed and to be impatient with even the slightest delays in getting information or service. "Wireless Man," says Brooks, "craves his next data fix. He's a speed freak" (2001b, p. 71). Brooks also notes that 21st-century Westerners are addicted to whatever is new, cool, and on the cutting edge (2001a). We want to do more and do it faster. But the quest for speed may undermine real creativity. When we're accustomed to doing everything in high gear, reflection and the time for thinking in fresh ways become rare.

To learn more about Americans' addiction to speed, use your Online Resources for *Communication in Our Lives* to access **WebLink 10.1**.

they regard as progress. Ironically, valuing newness and change doesn't always translate into appreciating people or ideas that depart from Western cultural values. Westerners' generally high regard for change is in tension with resistance, sometimes quite strong, to people and ideas that challenge Western conventions.

Informality

Another Western cultural value is informality. People generally treat each other directly and in a relaxed way. How often have you heard someone say, after a formal introduction, "Please call me by my first name"? College classes tend to feature informal interaction between professors and students. In contrast, classes in a number of cultures are rigidly organized, with the teacher at the center and perhaps on a stage or raised platform; sometimes the teacher's voice is almost the only one to be heard. Once initial introductions have been made, Americans largely avoid titles and the formal rituals of conduct followed in other countries such as Japan, Egypt, Turkey, and Germany.

COMMUNICATION IN SMALL GROUPS

We've seen that effective small group discussion entails knowing when groups are likely to be superior to individuals and understanding how group features affect participation. We're now ready to consider the variety of ways in which members communicate within groups. We'll discuss ways group members contribute, decision-making methods, and communication responsibilities of leadership.

Forms of Group Communication

Because communication is the heart of all groups, the ways members communicate are extremely important to the effectiveness of group process. There are four kinds of communication in groups (Mudrack & Farrell, 1995; see Table 10.1). The first three— *task communication, procedural communication,* and *climate communication*—are

Table 10.1	Types of Communication in Groups

Task Communication	Climate Communication
Initiates ideas	Establishes and maintains healthy climate
Seeks information	Energizes group process
Gives information	Harmonizes ideas
Elaborates ideas	Recognizes others
Evaluates, offers critical analysis	Reconciles conflicts
	Builds enthusiasm for group
Procedural Communication	
Establishes agenda	**Egocentric Communication**
Provides orientation	Aggresses toward others
Curbs digressions	Blocks ideas
Guides participation	Seeks personal recognition (brags)
Coordinates ideas	Dominates interaction
Summarizes others' contributions	Pleads for special interests
Records group progress	Confesses, self-discloses, seeks personal help unrelated to the group's focus
	Disrupts tasks
	Devalues others
	Trivializes group and its work

constructive because they foster good group processes and outcomes. The fourth kind of communication is *egocentric*, or *dysfunctional, communication*. It tends to detract from group cohesion and effective decision making.

These forms of communication shape group climate and productivity for groups and teams that meet face to face as well as those that interact by videoconferencing. As technologies become increasingly sophisticated, videoconferencing is becoming more popular, especially for group discussions between people who do not work in the same area.

Task Communication   Task communication focuses on the problems, issues, or information before a group. It provides ideas and information, ensures members' understanding, and uses reasoning to evaluate ideas and information. Task contributions may initiate ideas, respond to others' ideas, or provide critical evaluation of information before the group. Task contributions also include asking for ideas and evaluation from others. Task comments emphasize the content of a group's work.

Procedural Communication   If you've ever participated in a disorganized group, you understand the importance of **procedural communication,** which helps a group get organized and stay on track in its decision making. Procedural contributions establish an agenda, coordinate the comments of different members, and record group progress. In addition, procedural contributions may curb digressions and tangents, summarize progress, and regulate participation so that everyone has opportunities to speak and nobody dominates.

COMMUNICATION HIGHLIGHT

Virtual Groups

Technologies are allowing more and more groups and teams to work without getting together in the same physical space. Increasingly, businesses are holding virtual conferences, in which people who are separated by distance interact in simultaneous time in videoconferences or computer-mediated conferences (Cragan, Wright, & Kasch, 2004). All that's needed is the correct software, a computer with a video monitor, and a modem hooked to a telephone line.

One gauge of the growth of virtual teams is the increasing number of workers who work off-site, usually in homes. In 1991, only 1.4% of U.S. workers were telecommuters. In 1999, 5% were, and that number is expected to increase to 40% by 2020 (Stroup, 2001).

Communication researchers Erik Timmerman and Craig Scott (2006) point out that the degree of virtualness varies. Some teams work face-to-face part of the time and online part of the time. Some teams rely entirely on videoconferencing, whereas other teams never even see each other but communicate via e-mail and groupware.

If you have a group or team and want to create a virtual conference room, try researching web conferencing software and service-providers on the Internet. Visit your Online Resources to access **WebLink 10.2**, which includes a link to WebEx, one such web conferencing application.

Climate Communication   A group is more than a task unit. It also includes people who are involved in a relationship that can be more or less pleasant and open. **Climate communication** focuses on creating and maintaining a constructive climate that encourages members to contribute cooperatively and evaluate ideas critically. Climate comments emphasize a group's strengths and progress, encourage cooperative interaction, recognize others' contributions, reconcile conflicts, and build enthusiasm for the group and its work.

Egocentric Communication   The final kind of group communication is not recommended but does sometimes surface in groups. **Egocentric communication,** or dysfunctional communication, is used to block others or to call attention to oneself. It detracts from group progress because it is self-centered rather than group centered. Examples of egocentric talk are devaluing another member's ideas, trivializing the group's efforts, aggressing toward other members, bragging about one's own accomplishments, dominating, disrupting group work, and pleading for special causes that aren't in a group's interest. Another form of egocentric communication is making cynical remarks, which undermines group cohesion and enthusiasm.

Task, procedural, and climate communication work together to foster productive, organized, and comfortable group discussion. Egocentric communication, on the other hand, does not contribute to enjoyable group interaction or high-quality outcomes. Egocentric participation can sabotage a group's climate and hinder its progress. If it occurs, others in the group should intervene to discourage it. Communicating clearly that egocentric behavior will not be tolerated in your

COMMUNICATION
in Your Life

To what extent does your communication in groups contribute to task, procedure, and climate?

group fosters norms for effective interaction.

The following excerpt from a group discussion will give you concrete examples of each type of group communication. Each comment is coded as one of the four types of communication we have identified.

ED: We might start by discussing what we see as the goal of this group. *(procedural)*

JAN: That's a good idea. *(climate)*

BOB: I think our goal is to come up with a better meal plan for students on campus. *(task)*

ED: What do you mean by "better"? Do you mean cheaper or more varied or more tasteful? *(task)*

ANN: I think we need to consider all three. *(task)*

ED: Well, we probably do care about all three, but maybe we should talk about one at a time so that we can keep our discussion focused. *(procedural)*

BOB: Okay, I vote we focus first on taste—like it would be good if there were some taste to the food on campus! *(task and climate [humor])*

JAN: Do you mean taste itself or quality of food, which might also consider nutrition? *(task)*

BOB: Pure taste! When I'm hungry, I don't think about what's good for me, just what tastes good. *(task)*

JAN: Well, maybe that's a reason why we might want the food service to think about nutrition—because we don't. *(task)*

BOB: If you're a health food nut, that's your problem. I don't think nutrition is something that's important in the food service on campus. *(task; possibly also egocentric if his tone toward Jan was snide)*

ED: Let's do this: Let's talk first about what we would like in terms of taste itself. *(procedural)* Before we meet next time, it might be a good idea for one

What can you infer about this group from members' dress, physical arrangement, and postures?

John Zoiner/Workbook Stock/Getty Images

of us to talk with the manager of the cafeteria to see whether they have to meet any nutritional guidelines in what they serve. *(task)*

ANN: I'll volunteer to do that. *(task)*

ED: Great. Thanks, Ann. *(climate)*

BOB: I'll volunteer to do taste testing! *(climate [humor])*

JAN: With your weight, you'd better not. *(egocentric)*

BOB: Yeah, like you have a right to criticize me. *(egocentric)*

ANN: Look, none of us is here to criticize anyone else. We're here because we want to improve the food service on campus. *(climate)* We've decided we want to focus first on taste *(procedural)*, so who has an idea of how we go about studying that? *(task)*

This dialogue includes all four kinds of communication that we've discussed. It's particularly noteworthy to recognize how skillfully Ann communicates to defuse tension between Bob and Jan before it disrupts the group. You might also notice that Ed provides the primary procedural leadership for the group, and Bob is effective in interjecting humor. Several members recognize contributions to the discussion.

P.S.I. Prisma/age fotostock/PhotoLibrary

The most effective work teams spend a good deal of time on task communication; however, they also find time to laugh and enjoy interaction.

In effective group discussion, communication meets the task, procedural, and climate demands of teamwork and avoids egocentrism that detracts from group progress and cohesion. By understanding how varied types of communication affect collective work, you can decide when to use each type of communication in your own participation in groups. Although you may not be proficient in all three valuable kinds of group communication right now, with commitment and practice, you can develop skill.

BEYOND THE CLASSROOM

Let's take the material in this chapter beyond the classroom by thinking about how what you've learned about the foundations of group and team communication might apply to the workplace, ethical choices, and engagement with the broader world.

1. **Workplace.** Interview a professional in the field you hope to enter after college. Ask him or her to identify how various groups and teams discussed in this chapter are used on the job. If you are already employed in a career, reflect on your experiences with groups on the job.

2. **Ethics.** Ask several people who have lived in non-Western cultures whether the cultural values that affect group communication in the United States are present in the countries where they lived. In your conversation, explore how differences in cultural values affect group interaction.

Ethics

3. **Engagement.** This chapter points out that groups exist within cultural contexts that affect how they operate. Talk with classmates or other students who were raised in a non-Western culture. Ask them what values of their home culture are reflected in the ways groups operate.

CHAPTER SUMMARY

In this chapter, we've considered what small groups are and how they operate. We defined groups as three or more people who meet over time, share understandings of how to interact, and have a common goal. The potential weaknesses of group discussion, notably conformity pressures and time, must be recognized and managed to realize the important advantages of group decision making.

Communication in groups and teams is influenced by cohesion, group size, power, norms, interaction patterns, and cultural values. Each of these features shapes the small-group system within which communication transpires. At the same time, how members communicate affects the nature and functioning of groups by encouraging or inhibiting cohesion, power, and norms. Effective communication in groups and teams requires that members be aware of and exert control over features that make up the group system.

By managing these influences, you should be able to enhance the content and climate of communication, the outcomes of group deliberation, and members' feelings about participation.

The final section of the chapter focused on the kinds of communication that occur in small groups. We saw that effective group interaction includes task, climate, and procedural contributions and is hindered by egocentric communication. Developing skill in the three constructive types of communication and avoiding egocentric comments will make you a valuable member of any group.

In Chapter 11, we will build on what we have learned in this chapter. We will identify the kinds of task teams that dot the contemporary landscape, and we will discuss leadership, organization of group discussion, and ways of managing conflict so that it benefits group work.

APPLYING COMMUNICATION IN OUR LIVES

The key concepts, For Further Reflection and Discussion questions, and Experiencing Communication in Our Lives case study that follow will help you review, reflect on, and extend the information and ideas presented in this chapter. These resources, and a diverse selection of additional study tools, are also available as Online Resources for *Communication in Our Lives.* Your Online Resources include CourseMate, a student workbook, interactive video activities, audio study tools, a book companion website, Speech Builder Express, Speech Studio, and InfoTrac College Edition. For more information or to access this book's online resources, visit **www.cengage.com/login.**

KEY CONCEPTS

climate communication, 241
cohesion, 232
egocentric communication, 241
group, 226
groupthink, 232

individualism, 237
norm, 236
power, 233
power over, 233
power to, 233

procedural communication, 240
social climbing, 235
synergy, 230
task communication, 240
team, 227

FOR FURTHER REFLECTION AND DISCUSSION

1. Talk with several people who have lived in non-Western cultures. Ask them whether the cultural values that affect group communication in the United States are present in the countries where they lived. In your conversation, explore differences in cultural values and ways in which these differences affect small group interaction.

2. What ethical responsibilities accompany having power in a group? What are ethical and unethical uses of power in group and team situations?

3. Observe a group discussion on your campus or in your town. Record members' contributions by classifying them as task, climate, procedural, or egocentric. Does the communication you observe explain the effectiveness or ineffectiveness of the group?

4. To learn more about groupthink, use your Online Resources for *Communication in Our Lives* to access **WebLink 10.3.**   CourseMate

SHARPEN YOUR SKILL

1. Assessing the Values of Your Group

Select one group to which you belong that has existed for an extended period of time. Identify communication that reflects the values discussed in this section:

Communication that reflects individuality:

_____

Communication that reflects assertiveness:

_____

Communication that values risk taking:

_____

Communication that expresses equality:

_____

Communication that fosters informality:

_____

2. Your Communication in Groups

Draw on your own perceptions to answer the following four questions. After you have responded, ask one or two people who have worked with you in groups to answer these questions about your participation.

1. How do you contribute to small group discussions? _____

2. Do you specialize in task, procedural, or climate communication?

   _____

3. Observe yourself in a small group setting, and record the focus of your comments.

   _____

4. Which kinds of group communication do you do well? In which areas do you want to develop greater skill?

   _____

EXPERIENCING COMMUNICATION IN OUR LIVES

CASE STUDY: *The Class Gift*

A video of the conversation scripted here is featured in your Chapter 10 Online Resources for *Communication in Our Lives*. Select "The Class Gift" to watch the video. Improve your own communication skills by reading, watching, and evaluating this communication encounter.

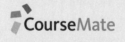

   Andy, Erika, Camilla, Vernon, and Jenn are in charge of deciding what their graduating class will give to their university as the class gift. This is the second meeting of their group.

© Cengage Learning

VERNON (*looking around at the other members*): Hey, hey—good to see you all again.

CAMILLA: The most awesome group on campus!

ANDY: We're looking fine, for sure.

VERNON (*glances at watch*): Okay, all of you fine-looking people (*smiles at Andy*), it's 10 minutes after. Has anyone heard from Jenn?

   Erika, Camilla, and Andy shake their heads and shrug.

VERNON: Okay, well, let's get started and hope she joins us in a couple of minutes. I want to get rolling on this project!

ERIKA: Hear, hear! I'm really psyched about doing this. We have the coolest class ever, and I want us to come up with a gift that's as cool as we are.

ANDY: That would have to be waaaaaaaaaaaay cool!

The four slap hands, laugh, and chorus: Waaaaaaaaaaaaaay cool!!

VERNON: Okay, since we're so cool, what are our cool ideas for our class gift? Anybody have a suggestion?

CAMILLA: When we met last week, one idea we all kind of liked was giving a sculpture—you know, an outdoor one that could go in the main quad where everyone would see it.

ANDY: Yeah, I agree; that's the best idea we came up with.

CAMILLA: The image I have is a sculpture of a student studying—like maybe reading a book.

ERIKA: Hold on. Studying is not waaaaaaaaaaaay cool.

ANDY: Definitely not. Maybe we could have a sculpture of players on our basketball team. Now *that* would be cool!

ERIKA: Oh, please, that's even worse.

Jenn walks in and pulls a chair into the circle with the others. Erika and Vernon smile at her as she joins them. Camilla gives her a quick hug.

ANDY: Hey, Jenn. Glad you made it.

JENN: Sorry I'm late. I was meeting with a study group for my Econ exam tomorrow.

CAMILLA *(smiling mischievously):* I rest my case. Jenn was studying, which *is* what students do!

ERIKA: Yeah, but it's not waaaaaay cool.

VERNON: Wait a minute, let's give Camilla's idea a chance. A sculpture. I kind of like the idea of a sculpture.

JENN: That would be unique. I don't think any other class has given a sculpture.

ERIKA: I'm not against a sculpture. I just don't think a student studying is the most exciting thing.

VERNON: Maybe not the most exciting, but it really gets at what being at this school is about.

ANDY: I'm beginning to agree. I mean, the sculpture should celebrate this school and its values.

VERNON: What about you, Erika. Is this idea working for you yet?

ERIKA: Personally, I'm not wild about a sculpture of a student studying. But the most important thing is that we come up with something we can all support, and the other four of you seem to like this idea.

CAMILLA: I don't think any of us is settled on the idea yet. We may come up with a different kind of sculpture that we'd all love. Does anyone have a different idea for the sculpture?

Erika, Vernon and Andy shrug no.

JENN: How about a sculpture of a student in regalia—as if the student is graduating? Isn't that the goal of being here?

ERIKA: That's interesting—instead of symbolizing studying to get to the goal, we could symbolize achieving it.

ANDY: I don't know. Those regalia are pretty weird looking, and they're not what students wear, except for one day. I don't think students would identify with that as much as a sculpture of a student in regular dress, like we're wearing.

JENN: Good point. You could be right.

CAMILLA: Yeah, but we do identify with the goal that the regalia symbolize. I don't know that students wouldn't identify with a sculpture of a student wearing the regalia.

VERNON: I think they might.

ERIKA: I'm not convinced.

CAMILLA: We're just speculating and stating our own opinions. Let's do some research to find out what students think. Why don't we do a couple of sketches—one of a student studying and one of a student in regalia—and poll students as to which they like better?

JENN: Good idea, but let's not move to that just yet. We might come up with more ideas for the sculpture if we talk longer.

QUESTIONS FOR ANALYSIS AND DISCUSSION

You can answer these questions and see my responses to them online via your Online Resources for Chapter 10.

1. Apply material from Chapter 10 (pages 232–237) to analyze the features of this small group.

2. Drawing on the discussion of confirmation in Chapter 8, analyze the extent to which members of this group confirm one another by communicating recognition, acknowledgment, and endorsement.

3. How effective is the climate communication in this group?

Bill Bachmann/PhotoEdit

11

Individual commitment to a group effort—that is what makes a team work, a company work, a society work, a civilization work.

Vince Lombardi

Effective Communication in Task Groups and Teams

SHARPEN YOUR SKILL

At the end of this chapter, refer to the Sharpen Your Skill features, Brainstorming and Clarifying Questions, to apply concepts from Chapter 11.

There are many kinds of groups, and each kind has distinctive goals and communication patterns. Social groups provide us with recreation and the stimulation of conversation with people we enjoy. Communication in social groups tends to be relaxed, informal, and more focused on interpersonal climate than on task goals. Personal growth groups enable people to deal with significant issues and worries in a context of interpersonal support. In personal growth groups, communication generally is personal in topic and tone, and its goals are to support members and to help them clarify and address issues in their lives. Task groups, such as project teams and decision-making groups, focus on accomplishing a particular objective, such as improving the quality of work, generating policy, or resolving problems.

Although groups differ in their primary purposes and foci, most groups include interaction that goes beyond their basic purpose. For example, social groups often move into task discussion, as when one friend asks another for advice in solving a problem. Groups that exist to accomplish a task typically include some social communication, and therapy groups usually involve both task and social dimensions that contribute to the primary goal of personal growth.

Because task groups and teams are extensively relied on in professional and civic life, this chapter concentrates on communication in task-oriented groups and teams that manage projects, develop ideas, and make decisions or recommendations. We'll begin by identifying types of task groups. Next, we'll discuss leadership in task groups. We'll then consider a method of organizing efficient and productive discussion. In the fourth section of this chapter, we'll consider alternative methods of making decisions in groups. Finally, we'll return to the topic of conflict, which we first discussed in Chapter 8. We will focus on the constructive potential of conflict and ways to manage it effectively in task groups and teams.

TASK GROUPS

The task group, which often is a team, has emerged as a major feature of modern life. The prominence of task groups is due to increased awareness of the advantages of groups compared to individuals (Levi, 2007). We'll discuss six common types of task groups here.

Project Teams

Project teams consist of people who have special expertise in relation to some project and who work together over a period of time to accomplish a common goal. Typically, project teams exist to deal with one-time tasks (Jossi, 2001), such as establishing a training system for a company, creating a public relations campaign for a new product, or determining the public image of a corporation in a community.

Communication in project teams allows each member to draw on the resources of other members and coordinate their different areas of experience and talent. To launch a new product, pharmaceutical companies often compose product teams that include scientists who understand the technical character of the new drug, and personnel from marketing, product design, advertising, and customer relations. Working together, these people develop a coherent plan for testing, packaging, advertising, and marketing the new product to the public. If the individuals worked separately in their specific areas, they would generate a less well-coordinated, less effective plan: Marketing wouldn't know what advertising was planned, advertising wouldn't understand the overall image of the product, and customer relations wouldn't have informed advertising and marketing of salient issues in the product's target market.

Focus Groups

Also popular in the workplace is the focus group, which is used to find out what people think about a specific idea, product, issue, or person. Focus groups are a mainstay of advertisers, who want to understand the attitudes, preferences, and responses of the people most likely to buy their product: What do 21- to 25-year-olds think of a new light beer? How do retirees respond to a draft advertising campaign for cruises? Focus groups are also popular in political life: What do middle-class women and men think of a politician's record on social issues? Do Latinos and Latinas regard Candidate Y as trustworthy?

Comstock/Jupiter Images

Members of a project team bring specialized expertise that allows them to approach a task in an integrated manner.

A focus group is guided by a leader or facilitator, who encourages members to communicate their ideas, beliefs, feelings, and perceptions relevant to the topic. The facilitator offers no personal judgments or opinions but guides group members to express themselves, respond to each other's communication, and elaborate the reasons for their thoughts, feelings, and responses.

Brainstorming Groups

Brainstorming groups harness group discussion's creative potential. Brainstorming groups—or a brainstorming phase in other types of groups—are used to generate ideas and to stimulate "outside-the-box" thinking.

Non Sequitur

Table 11.1	Rules for Brainstorming

- Do not evaluate ideas that are volunteered. Criticism—both verbal and nonverbal—is inappropriate.
- Record ideas on a blackboard or easel pad so that all members of the group can see them.
- Go for quantity. The more ideas, the better.
- Build on ideas. An idea presented by one member of the group may stimulate an extension by another member. This is desirable.
- Encourage creativity. Wild, even preposterous, ideas should be welcomed. An idea that seems wacky may lead to other ideas that are more workable.

COMMUNICATION
in Your Life

With four classmates, brainstorm assignments for your communication class.

In **brainstorming**, the goal is to come up with as many ideas as possible. Because criticism tends to stifle creativity, no criticism is allowed while brainstorming is in progress. Creativity and even wild thinking are encouraged to come up with the most imaginative ideas possible. Table 11.1 lists the rules for brainstorming.

Perhaps you're concerned that brainstorming can produce unrealistic ideas or ideas that are not well analyzed. That's not really a problem because brainstorming is followed by evaluative discussion. During evaluation, members work together to appraise all the ideas that were generated in brainstorming. At that point, impractical ideas are discarded, weak or undeveloped ideas are improved, related ones are consolidated, and promising ones are discussed further.

The leader or facilitator of a brainstorming group should set a tone for creative communication. To do this, leaders should show energy, respond enthusiastically to members' ideas, and communicate excitement. Leaders may also need to stoke members' imaginations if they hit a dry spell. This can be done by making encouraging comments, such as, "Who can add to the list of ideas?" "Imagine that we have unlimited money and time. What else might be possible under those conditions?"

Advisory Groups

As the name suggests, advisory groups provide advice to others. Advisory groups do not actually make policies or decisions. Instead, they inform and recommend to others who make the actual decisions. Advisory groups are formed when a person wants to be briefed by experts on a topic about which he or she must make a decision.

Advisory groups may also consist of peers who advise each other. The Young Presidents Forum is a system of peer advisory groups, each consisting of 8-10 business presidents. By conferring regularly with peers, these presidents advise each other on common problems, practices, and goals. The members pool experience, coach each other, and collaboratively solve problems.

In business and civic affairs, executives are seldom experts on the range of issues relevant to decisions they must make. The solitary manager, president, or senator who relies only on his or her own ideas is seldom effective on the whole range of issues he or she needs to handle. Advisory groups allow individuals to use other experts' information and advice in developing effective policies and making informed decisions.

Quality Improvement Teams

A **quality improvement team** (also called a *continuous quality improvement team*) is three or more people from different areas of an organization who work together to improve quality in the organization (Lumsden & Lumsden, 2009). Originally, small working groups, or *quality circles*, were part of a management approach called *total quality management* (Deming, 1982), in which intensive teamwork was used to maximize the quality of an organization's output. The original quality circles have evolved into quality improvement teams, which are used in a variety of organizations whether or not they embrace total quality management as an overall organizational philosophy.

Typically, quality improvement teams mix not just people from different areas of expertise but also people from different levels of an organization's hierarchy. Thus, a secretary may contribute as much as a managing partner to a discussion of ways to improve office productivity. A line worker in a cafeteria may have a better understanding of waste and ways to reduce it than the manager of the cafeteria does.

The first few meetings of a quality improvement team typically involve a lot of complaining about problems. This is natural, and it helps members become comfortable with one another because they create common ground over shared frustrations. After initial venting of frustrations, discussion focuses on solving problems.

To be effective, quality improvement teams must be given the power to solve problems (Hyatt & Ruddy, 1997). Nothing is more frustrating than to be asked to work on a problem but to be denied the authority to implement changes or the assurance that others will implement them. When given appropriate authority, quality improvement teams often generate impressive and creative solutions to such organizational concerns as lowering expenses, improving safety, and recognizing accomplishments. To learn more about quality improvement teams, use your Online Resources for *Communication in Our Lives* to access **WebLink 11.1**.

CourseMate

Decision-Making Groups

A sixth kind of task group exists to make decisions. In some cases, decision-making groups and teams are formed to render a specific decision or policy: What should be Corporation X's policy on family leave? What operations should we reduce or eliminate to achieve a 15% decrease in annual expenses? In other cases, ongoing groups are charged with making decisions and solving problems in particular areas. Many organizations have standing committees that assume responsibility for budget, public relations, external communication, and other matters.

Task groups are becoming more and more prominent in professional and civic life. They allow diverse people with varying experience, expertise, interests, and talents to interact and generate ideas, understandings, plans, and decisions that often are more creative and better informed than those an individual could devise.

LEADERSHIP COMMUNICATION

For decades, it was assumed that leaders were born, not made. In following this assumption, researchers attempted to identify the traits of effective leaders. Personal qualities ranging from intelligence and height to emotional balance and physical energy were studied in an effort to understand the traits of born leaders. This line of study was unsuccessful in discovering any consistent traits that mark leaders (Northouse, 2006). However, it was effective in shifting our understanding of leadership. The lack of identifiable leader traits led researchers to realize that leadership is not a person or a set of personal qualities. Instead, leadership is a set of functions that assists groups in accomplishing tasks efficiently while maintaining a good climate.

Leadership, Not Leader

Leadership may be provided by one individual or by several members who contribute to guiding the process and ensuring effective communication within the group. Leadership exists when one or more members communicate to establish a good working climate, organize group processes, and focus discussion productively on the task at hand. Recalling our discussion in Chapter 10, you may realize that the functions of leadership we've just identified parallel the three types of constructive communication that group members make in discussions. A fourth function of leadership is to control disruptive members who engage in egocentric communication.

When one person provides leadership, he or she performs the functions necessary for effective group discussion. When leadership is not vested in one person, several members share responsibilities (Lumsden & Lumsden, 2009; McCauley & Van Velsor, 2003). Whether there is one leader or shared leadership, the primary responsibilities are to organize discussion, to ensure critical thinking, to create a productive working climate, to build group morale, to promote effective communication between members, and to discourage egocentric communication that detracts from group efforts.

KRYSTAL   *The most effective group I've ever been in had three leaders. I was the person who understood our task best, so I contributed the most to critical thinking about the issues. But Belinda was the one who kept us organized. She really knew how to see tangents and get us off of them, and she knew when it was time to move on from one stage of work to the next. She also pulled ideas together to coordinate our thinking. Kevin was the climate leader. He could always tell a joke if things got tense, and he was the best person I ever saw for recognizing others' contributions. I couldn't point to any one leader in that group, but we sure did have good leadership.*

When we realize that leadership is a series of functions that move groups along, it becomes clear that more than one person may provide leadership for a group or team. Sometimes, one member provides guidance on tasks and procedures and another member focuses on building a good group climate.

A group needs both climate and task leadership to be maximally effective. It is also possible for various people to provide leadership at different times in a group's life. The person who is most active in organizing at the outset may not be the one who keeps the group on track in later phases.

Depending on what a group needs at any given time, different leadership functions are appropriate and may come from different members. Even when an official leader exists, other members may contribute much of the communication that provides leadership for a group. Although the official leader has the responsibility for a group's decision (and gets the credit or blame), others often contribute to running a group.

Styles of Leadership

Although leadership can't be reduced to a set of traits, it can be understood as an overall style of communication. The different styles of leadership differently impact group productivity and climate (Lewin, Lippitt, & White, 1939). Styles may be enacted by a single group leader or by several members. Researchers have identified three primary styles of leadership, each of which involves distinctive forms of communication and each of which has a unique impact on group climate and productivity. In many cases, a group's leadership cannot be classified neatly into one of the three styles. Instead, leadership may be a blend of the styles, and the blend may change over time.

Laissez-Faire Leadership   *Laissez-faire* is a French phrase that is roughly translated "do nothing." **Laissez-faire leadership** is laid-back and nondirective.

COMMUNICATION in Your Life

Which leadership functions do you contribute to groups?

COMMUNICATION HIGHLIGHT

Honest Abe's Leadership Lessons

According to David Herbert Donald, the Charles Warren Professor of American History at Harvard University, Abraham Lincoln's ability to lead well resulted largely from his skills as a communicator (Donald, 1996). Donald concludes that two principles were especially prominent in Lincoln's leadership:

- *Encourage criticism from others and listen carefully to it.* Without the public opinion polls that are common today, Lincoln stayed in touch with citizens and learned what mattered to them and what they thought of his actions and plans. Nearly every day of his presidency, Lincoln opened the doors to the White House for what he called his "public opinion baths." Ordinary citizens poured in to voice their opinions, and Lincoln listened intently.

- *Communicate clearly and concisely.* Lincoln believed that any effective leader had to be able to speak and write clearly in ways that ordinary citizens could understand. He abhorred jargon, preferring to speak naturally and informally. He worked to create language that brought ideas alive: vivid words and phrases, concrete analogies, everyday examples.

In seeking feedback, Lincoln followed a principle that is central to contemporary leadership training—to actively encourage feedback from peers, subordinates, and supervisors (McCauley & Van Velsor, 2003). It's vital to understanding how others perceive your effectiveness as a leader.

The laissez-faire leader doesn't provide guidance or suggest directions in which the group should move. Laissez-faire leaders allow groups to set their own goals and move at their own speed. If problems develop in a group, the laissez-faire leader is unlikely to intervene to get the group back on track.

When a group consists of members who are mature, experienced, and self-directed, there may be little need for control by one or more leaders. Yet this is more the exception than the rule. Most groups need guidance, at least at times, to develop and sustain a good climate and to be productive. For this reason, laissez-faire leadership generally is not recommended (Bass, 1990). Inefficiency is perhaps the most common characteristic of laissez-faire leadership (White & Lippitt, 1960).

Authoritarian Leadership   As the term suggests, **authoritarian leadership** is directive. This style of leadership tends to be used by a lone leader rather than by several members who share leadership. Authoritarian leaders may announce directions for discussion, assign specific tasks to members, make decisions without consulting others in the group, and otherwise exert control over the group process. As you might suspect, groups that have authoritarian leadership often are very efficient, but members' morale and work quality may not be optimal (Van Oostrum & Rabbie, 1995).

Highly authoritarian leadership tends to foster a centralized pattern of leader-to-member, member-to-leader communication. Although groups with authoritarian leaders sometimes produce good decisions, this style of leadership seldom promotes satisfaction and cohesion among members. Dependence, apathy, low cohesion, and resentment are common responses to highly authoritarian leadership (Kouzes & Posner, 1999; Lewin et al., 1939).

Before you dismiss authoritarian leadership altogether, you should realize that it can be effective, even ideal, in some circumstances (Yanes, 1990). The movie *Vertical Limit* is an adventure tale about high-risk mountain climbers. In the film, one group of climbers falls into a crevasse while attempting to reach the summit of K2 in the Himalayas. Another group of climbers decides to mount a rescue effort. When disagreement about how to proceed breaks out among the rescuers, the most seasoned and expert climber tells the others, "This is not a democracy. You'll do what I say." This autocratic style of leading was appropriate for two reasons. First, the leader had the most experience and probably the best judgment about how to proceed. Second, the first group of climbers could have died from edema, hypothermia, or other conditions if the rescue team had taken the time to democratically decide what to do.

DOUG   *It took me a while to learn that my boss doesn't want any of us to take initiative or state our ideas unless we agree with him. He is a classic authoritarian leader who tells us what to do as well as what answers and decisions he wants us to produce. He blasts anyone who doesn't play "yes man" to him. By now, none of us cares what happens in our project group. We don't even try to think of ways to improve our work. He's taught us not to take any initiative by penalizing us anytime we depart from his agenda and his prejudgments.*

Democratic Leadership **Democratic leadership** provides direction and guidance but does not impose rigid authority. Democratic leadership, whether provided by one individual or by several members, fosters members' development by encouraging them to take responsibility within a group. This style of leadership tends to generate high, generally balanced communication among members who have been socialized in democratic cultures. In turn, high participation fuels group cohesion and members' satisfaction with belonging to a group (Gastil, 1994; Gibb, 1969). Finally, democratic leadership tends to yield high-quality task outcomes that are generally more original and creative than those produced by groups with authoritarian or laissez-faire leadership (Blanchard, Carlos, & Randolph, 1998; White & Lippitt, 1960).

Research that has found the democratic style of leadership is linked to good group climate and productivity was conducted in societies committed to democratic values. In societies that place higher value on authoritarian structures, an autocratic style of leadership might well be more acceptable and effective (Connerley & Pedersen, 2005). Like other forms of communication, good leadership is responsive to particular members, situations, circumstances, and cultures.

Effective leadership often changes over time. What a group needs to be productive varies at different points in a group's life cycle and in relation to the maturity of members. When a group first begins to work, direction in framing the issues and determining the group's objectives is vital, and the person who supplies this is performing the critical leadership at that time. As a group continues to work, however, it often matures and no longer needs strong task guidance. At that point, the most effective leadership communication may focus on consideration or climate contributions.

As members invest in group work, the person or persons who initially provided leadership may delegate more and more responsibility. This acknowledges group members' abilities, increases satisfaction, and heightens their loyalty to the group and its decisions (Johnson & Johnson, 1991).

In sum, leadership is a dynamic process of meeting the changing and multiple needs of effective communication in small groups. Whether provided by one member or several, effective leadership involves communication that advances a group's task, organizes deliberations, builds group morale, controls disruptions, and fosters a constructive climate.

Stephen Agricola/The Image Works

What leadership style seems to be operating in this group? Identify aspects of nonverbal communication that affect your perceptions of leadership style.

COMMUNICATION HIGHLIGHT

Empowering Leadership

In recent years, the term *empowerment* has gained increasing currency in the workplace. Leaders and managers are realizing that employees tend to be maximally productive, satisfied, and committed when they feel empowered in their jobs, which happens when they believe that they have the ability to accomplish things and that they and their work matter. What makes employees feel empowered? That's the question addressed in two books by highly accomplished leadership scholars and consultants.

CourseMate

Ken Blanchard, John Carlos, and Alan Randolph wrote *Empowerment Takes More Than a Minute* (1998) to give working tools to people who want to be empowering leaders. The book is organized in story form, relying on an extended case study to provide hands-on advice, tools, and exercises to increase employees' sense of empowerment. The authors emphasize the importance of personal contact, encouragement, and feedback between leaders and employees. James Kouzes and Barry Posner wrote *Encouraging the Heart: A Leader's Guide to Recognizing and Rewarding Others* (1999). Their book aims to guide leaders in building skills for empowering others. Kouzes and Posner think that employees are empowered by stretching to meet high goals and standards. At the same time, leaders must provide appropriate support if they want employees to stretch. Appropriate support includes being clear about goals, giving continuous feedback (more feedback early in a new stretch, less later), and recognizing progress and accomplishments privately and publicly. When leaders are effective in empowering others, eventually those people become self-empowering.

To explore your own experiences with empowerment, complete the Communication Highlight Activity for Chapter 11 via your Online Resources for *Communication in Our Lives*.

DECISION-MAKING METHODS

Task groups make decisions; they develop plans for new products, generate recommendations for others, create policies, and solve problems. To accomplish these objectives, task groups must have methods of making decisions. Four common methods of group decision making have been identified. Each involves distinct communication styles and has particular strengths and limitations (Wood & Phillips, 1990). We'll describe each method and consider when it is most likely to be constructive and appropriate.

Consensus

Perhaps the most popular decision-making method in Western societies is **consensus**, in which all members of a group express their ideas and agree on a decision. Members may differ in how enthusiastically they support a decision, but everyone agrees to it. Communication to achieve consensus involves wide participation and often prolonged discussion. For everyone to support the decision, everyone must be involved in crafting it.

COMMUNICATION HIGHLIGHT

Emotionally Intelligent Leadership

Psychologist Daniel Goleman (1995, 1998, 2007) says that one aspect of intelligence that standard IQ tests don't measure is *emotional intelligence*. Goleman defines **emotional intelligence** as the ability to recognize which feelings are appropriate in which situations and the ability to communicate those feelings effectively. Goleman's research indicates that people who have high emotional intelligence are comfortable with themselves and are able to create satisfying personal relationships.

But that's not all. According to Goleman (1998; Goleman, McKee, & Boyatzis, 2002) and other researchers (Ciarrochi & Mayer, 2007; Niedenthal, Krauth-Gruber, & Ric, 2006), emotionally intelligent people are also more effective leaders. They have keen awareness of their own feelings and can recognize and respond to the feelings of others. Thus, they are both self-confident and sensitive—a winning combination, particularly when groups are under stress. Does this mean we have finally found a leadership "trait"? Not according to Goleman. He maintains that emotional intelligence is learned, just as leadership is. Both are skills that can be acquired with commitment and practice.

The strength of the consensus method is that it involves all members; thus, consensus decisions tend to have strong support. In addition, consensus tends to increase cohesion and member satisfaction because the method generates commitment to both the process and its outcome. As you probably realize, the greatest disadvantage of the consensus method is the time needed to hear all members and to secure everyone's commitment to a single decision. This makes consensus inappropriate for trivial decisions, emergency issues, or decisions on which members cannot agree even after extended discussion (Wood & Phillips, 1990).

Voting

A second method of making decisions is **voting**, by which a decision is made based on the support of a certain number of group members. Some groups have simple majority rule; others require two-thirds or three-fourths support before

Non Sequitur

a decision can be accepted. Voting has the potential to foster dissatisfaction, reduce group cohesion, and generate low commitment in members. Also, voting may preclude thorough analysis, clarification of issues, and evaluation of different possibilities. Yet voting also has advantages, notably its efficiency and resolution. Thus, when time is short, when a decision is not major, or when a group needs to move on, voting may be advisable.

Compromise

A third method of decision making is **compromise**, in which members work out a solution that satisfies each person's minimum criteria but may not fully satisfy all members. Compromise decisions often involve trading and bargaining—"I'll give on this point if you'll give on that one" (Wood & Phillips, 1990). Sometimes compromise results in an effective decision that combines the strong points advocated by different members. In other cases, members hammer out a decision that meets each person's bottom line but may not inspire great enthusiasm from anyone.

The shortcomings of the compromise method are obvious. One is that decisions may not be coherent. Because compromise may involve a series of separate considerations designed to satisfy particular members, the parts of a decision may not come together into a fully integrated whole. Yet sometimes compromise is the only way to make a decision. If members are deadlocked even after extensive discussion, they may be unable to reach consensus. Also, if members represent outside constituencies, as in labor–management negotiations, they are likely to have conflicting interests and goals that make consensus unlikely.

Authority Rule

A final method of group decision making actually doesn't involve a decision made by a group. In **authority rule**, an individual or group with power tells a group what to do, and the group ratifies the authority's decision. In some cases, the authority is a high-status member of the group (e.g., the group leader). In other cases, the authority is someone outside the group who appoints the group to give the appearance of a democratic method and to distribute responsibility for what may be an unpopular decision.

You probably can guess the drawbacks of this decision-making method. It can generate resentment in members, who may dislike being forced to ratify a decision of which they don't approve or being used to camouflage an autocratic process. Equally important, this method short-circuits the potential of group discussion to generate outcomes superior to those of individuals. Exerting authority over a group undermines the special values of group discussion such as increased resources, creativity, and thoroughness. Finally, authority rule can dampen participation in the long run if members think their ideas make no difference in decisions made. On the other hand, authority rule, like autocratic leadership, has advantages in some situations (Yanes, 1990). Obviously, this method is very efficient, so it has the virtue of saving time. Also, it may be useful for routine decisions that could take more time to discuss than their importance justifies.

COMMUNICATION in Your Life

Describe a compromise decision reached by a group to which you belong(ed).

CEDRIC   *I wish someone would teach my work group about authority rule. There are eight of us who meet as a group to decide everything that affects our department. Each of us likes to have our say and to talk things through, and that makes a lot of sense for big decisions like how to assign projects or evaluate subordinates or design new policies. But we talk just as long about trivial decisions. Last week we had a 40-minute discussion about whether to give our secretary individual gifts or pool our money to buy one large gift for the holidays. Forty minutes! We talked just as long about new carpeting for our office. Everyone had a different color preference, and we never did agree. We should let one person make a decision on these things.*

There is no single best method of making group decisions. Instead, the appropriate method varies according to factors such as the nature of the decision, preferences of group members, time available for reaching decisions, and cultural values and norms. Many ongoing groups rely on multiple methods of decision making and attempt to use the method most appropriate in each particular situation.

ORGANIZING GROUP DISCUSSION

One of the most frequent complaints about group work is that it is disorganized. Groups often are disorganized, primarily because members don't know how to move efficiently through decision making. One particularly effective method of organizing group discussion is the *standard agenda* (Rothwell, 2009; Young, Wood, Phillips, & Pedersen, 2001). The **standard agenda** is a logical, seven-step method for making decisions. In our discussion, we'll focus on the kinds of communication that occur during each of the stages in the standard agenda. Figure 11.1 summarizes the stages.

Stage One: Define the Problem

One of the most common errors groups make is to assume that all members agree on the problem or issue to be resolved and turn immediately to discussing possible solutions. This is a mistake because in reality people often don't agree on what the problem is or what they must decide upon. For instance, I once served on a group that was instructed to review the undergraduate curriculum in my department.

AP Photos/Mario Lopez

This group is voting. Reaching consensus on each issue would be difficult and extremely time consuming with a group this large.

I. Define the problem
   A. Define terms
   B. Phrase a question to guide deliberation

II. Analyze the issues
   A. Gather information on history, how issues have been addressed elsewhere, and so on
   B. Analyze causes of problem or need
   C. Discuss desired outcomes of decision

III. Establish criteria

IV. Generate possible solutions
   A. Review research
   B. Brainstorm

V. Evaluate possible solutions

VI. Select and implement solution

VII. Develop an action plan to monitor solution

Figure 11.1
Stages in the Standard Agenda

I assumed this meant we were to consider whether the courses we offered reflected the communication field. Another member thought our job was to decide on the requirements for a major. A third person believed we were to evaluate whether we offered courses sufficiently often. Each of these views of the task made sense, but they weren't equivalent. Our first task was to define exactly what we were to do.

Decision-making groups often find it useful to decide whether they are dealing with issues of fact, value, or policy. Each type of issue necessitates a different sort of analysis and decision, so groups need to agree on their focus (Lumsden & Lumsden, 2009). Factual tasks involve finding out what is the case, what is true or untrue, and what exists. Usually, factual group reports are descriptive. For instance, the group I mentioned previously could address the factual question, "What are the undergraduate courses taught in our department?" The answer would be a list of undergraduate courses taught.

Value questions have to do with the worth, ethicality, or importance of a policy, procedure, concept or action—for example, "Which courses offer the most valuable educational experiences to undergraduates?" Answering this question would require members to consider and evaluate the alternative values of education (i.e., broadening the mind, developing skills, increasing understanding). What are the standards for judging educational value: national trends, student evaluations of courses, faculty competencies, or the overall mission of a particular college (e.g., liberal arts)? Deciding how to define valuable educational experiences allows a group to proceed with common understandings.

A policy focus requires a group to decide what actions or positions to take and who will be responsible for taking them. For example, my group might have concentrated on recommending what courses should be offered each term and which ones should be offered only yearly. Policy issues revolve around questions of viability, feasibility, need, and responsibility for implementation. Groups must identify the needs at stake, evaluate the viability of different ways to meet needs, and determine who can most effectively implement their recommendations (Young et al., 2001).

Although each group should decide whether its primary purpose is to make a factual, value, or policy decision, most task deliberations involve all three types of questions. We often need facts to design policy (e.g., how many students currently enroll in each class we offer?), and values are at stake in almost every decision, no matter how objective or factual it may appear.

Whether a group is dealing with facts, values, or policies, part of the work in stage one is to define all terms in the group's question. As we learned in Chapter 5, language is ambiguous. Because meanings vary among people, it's unwise to assume that key words in a group's mission mean the same thing to all members. We've already seen that a word such as *should* must be clarified by identifying the standards for what ought to be. Other ambiguous words also must be defined in the initial meetings of a group. For example, "What is the most meaningful way to structure a curriculum?" cannot be answered until the word *meaningful* is defined clearly.

In clarifying its focus, a group should attempt to minimize bias. Asking, "How can we give students the classes they want?" is obviously biased toward students' perspectives. Likewise, "How can we let faculty teach the courses they want?" is biased toward faculty interests. Once members have decided whether they are dealing with issues of fact, value, or policy, clarified key terms, and minimized bias, they are ready to move to stage two.

Stage Two: Analyze the Issues

The focus of this stage is gathering and analyzing information about the issues confronting a group. Initially, members must decide what information they need: Reports from prior groups dealing with this issue, existing records, opinion polls, interviews with experts, information about how others handle the problem, and research are all valuable sources of information that may shed light on issues before the group. (Chapter 15 discusses ways to gather and evaluate research.)

During this phase, communication between members focuses on presenting and evaluating information. Members should be critical of information to screen out what isn't accurate or helpful. Asking about the credentials and biases of any interviewee or source is important, as is questioning the methods used to conduct opinion polls. To do a good job of analyzing information, members may want to consult books that cover principles of logic and reasoning.

Stage Three: Establish Criteria

What would a good decision look like? That's the question members deal with during stage three of the standard agenda. **Criteria** are standards members use to evaluate alternative solutions or decisions. Without clear criteria, it's easy for groups to make decisions that don't meet needs or that create new problems. Establishing clear criteria before considering solutions helps a group avoid these pitfalls.

The curriculum group on which I served established four criteria: The recommended curriculum had to (a) allow all majors to meet requirements for the major within 4 years, (b) include only courses that our faculty were qualified to

COMMUNICATION in Your Life

How much time did your last task group devote to defining the problem?

teach, (c) offer courses that have high student demands most often, and (d) conform to the university's requirements for an undergraduate major and for faculty teaching loads. These criteria provided us with a blueprint for evaluating possible decisions in the next phase of our work.

Stage Four: Generate Solutions

Once a group understands the issues surrounding its topic and has agreed on criteria for assessing resolutions, the group's focus turns to generating possible decisions. The research conducted during stage two often uncovers a number of possible solutions. My curriculum group's research revealed how curricula were designed in communication departments around the country, so all of those were possible solutions for us. We also learned about prior curricular reforms in the department and why they hadn't worked, so we were spared the embarrassment of repeating past mistakes.

A second source of alternative solutions is brainstorming, which encourages the free flow of ideas without immediate criticism. In brainstorming, the goal is to generate as many and as creative solutions as possible. Members should volunteer any ideas that occur to them, even ones that seem outrageous. Also, they should prompt each other to think imaginatively. For brainstorming to work, members must refrain from criticizing ideas when they are contributed. Evaluation is appropriate later, but at this point it can inhibit participation. One member records all the ideas so that the group has a complete list of possibilities.

Stage Five: Evaluate Solutions

Once members have a good list of solutions based on research and brainstorming, the goal is to evaluate each one against the criteria established in stage three of the standard agenda. Solutions that don't meet all criteria are discarded. Remaining are those that satisfy all of the standards members consider important for a good decision. Sometimes only a single solution meets all criteria. In other cases, members must decide which one of several solutions most fully meets the criteria.

Ideally, by this point members can arrive at a consensus on the best decision. Sometimes consensus doesn't develop, however, and members must rely on other methods of decision making. If there is

Members of a zoning board analyze information pertinent to reaching a sound decision about future growth in their community. What can you tell from the members' nonverbal communication? Do they look involved in the task and responsive to one another?

/Comstock/Jupiter Images

sufficient time, it's worthwhile to keep talking in the hope of reaching a consensus. If time is limited or extensive discussion indicates that consensus is not possible, then voting and compromise are viable options. Occasionally, rule by authority is exercised, although this should be a last resort.

Stage Six: Choose and Implement the Best Decision

In stage six, the group implements its decision. Implementation may involve announcing its decision—perhaps a new policy or set of procedures. More often, implementing a decision involves writing a formal report to the individual or body that initially charged the group.

Many groups who effectively work through the first five stages of the standard agenda stumble in the final stage by saying, "We recommend that such-and-such decision be implemented." A vague recommendation such as this does not specify what is necessary to ensure that a decision will be implemented effectively. Because group members are the experts on the issues, they need to make very specific recommendations about who is to do what when and by what means. Should the decision be implemented by the CEO, the department chair, the group itself, or some other person or group? When should the decision take effect, and how should those affected be notified of the decision? Specifying the logistics of implementation is an important group responsibility.

Stage Seven: Develop an Action Plan to Monitor the Solution

The final responsibility of decision-making groups is to develop an action plan for monitoring the effectiveness of their solution and, if necessary, modifying it. This involves designating ways to assess the impact of a decision and ways to determine whether the decision achieves the intended result without creating any new problems. The point here is to check on the effectiveness of the solution once it has been put into effect.

Members should specify how they will measure the success of their decision. My curricular group recommended that it conduct a poll of majors and faculty 1 year after the new curriculum was implemented to find out whether students were able to get the courses they needed and whether faculty thought teaching assignments were fair. Without monitoring, even a sound decision can go awry or produce side effects nobody envisioned. By specifying monitoring provisions and who is to implement them, a group ensures that what seems like a good decision in theory actually works in practice. If it doesn't work, modifications must be made to achieve the desired goal. Thus, the action plan should identify a person or group to make modifications, if any are needed.

SIBBY   *A student group I was in came up with a great plan for printing student evaluations of all courses so that students could decide which ones to take. We got funding for the project, collected the data, and printed up the booklets. It wasn't until a year later that we figured out most students weren't reading the booklets because we weren't distributing them to the places students are likely to be when they sign up for courses—advisers' offices, for instance. If we had monitored our solution from the start, it would have worked better.*

The standard agenda guides groups through the stages and issues that allow members to develop, implement, and assess decisions. Many groups use the standard agenda to schedule meetings. One or more meetings are devoted to each stage, which allows members to think ahead and to keep focused.

UNDERSTANDING AND MANAGING CONFLICT IN GROUPS

Conflict exists when people who are interdependent have different views, interests, or goals that seem incompatible. In Chapter 8, we learned that conflict is a natural and productive part of relationships. Likewise, conflict is normal and can be productive in groups. Conflict stimulates thinking, ensures that different perspectives are considered, and enlarges members' grasp of issues involved in making decisions and developing policies.

To achieve the potential values of conflict, however, members must manage it carefully. In this section, we build on the discussion of conflict in Chapter 8 to consider how to manage it constructively so that it enriches the processes and outcomes of collective endeavors.

TREY   *I used to think conflict was terrible and hurt groups, but last year I was a member of a group that had no—I mean, zero—conflict. A couple of times, I tried to bring up an idea different from what had been suggested, but my idea wouldn't even get a hearing. The whole goal was not to disagree. As a result, we didn't do a very thorough job of analyzing the issues, and we didn't subject the solution we developed to critical scrutiny. When our recommendation was put into practice, it bombed. We could have foreseen and avoided the failure if we had been willing to argue and disagree in order to test our idea before we put it forward.*

Trey's commentary is instructive. Although many of us do not enjoy conflict, we can nonetheless recognize its value—even its necessity—to effective group work. Just as conflict in relationships can enlarge perspectives and increase understanding, conflict in groups can foster critical, thorough, and insightful deliberations.

Types of Conflict

Depending on how it is handled, conflict may be disruptive or constructive. Effective leadership helps groups communicate in ways that allow constructive conflict about the substance of the group's work. At the same time, effective leadership helps group members avoid or control communication that fosters disruptive conflict over personal differences or matters not relevant to the task. Table 11.2 summarizes the differences between these two basic forms of group conflict.

Table 11.2	Characteristics of Group Conflict
Disruptive Conflict	**Constructive Conflict**
Competition	Cooperation
Self-interest	Collective focus
Win–lose approach	Win–win approach
Screens out opposing ideas	Listens to opposing ideas
Closed climate	Open climate
Defensive communication	Supportive communication
Personal attacks	Issue focus

Disruptive Conflict Disruptive conflict exists when disagreements interfere with the effective work and healthy communication climate of a group. Typically, disruptive conflict is marked by communication that is domineering, rigid, and competitive (Wilmot & Hocker, 2001). Accompanying the competitive tone of communication is a self-interested focus in which members talk only about their own ideas, their own solutions, or their own points of view. The competitive and self-centered communication in disruptive conflict fosters a win–lose orientation. Members express the belief that only one or some members can win, and others will lose.

Disruptive conflict harms group climate and undercuts members' satisfaction (Anderson & Martin, 1995). A closed atmosphere often develops in which members feel defensive and apprehensive. They may feel it's unsafe to volunteer ideas because they might be harshly evaluated or scorned by others. Personal attacks may occur as members criticize one another's motives or attack one another personally.

Disruptive conflict results from communication that produces defensiveness and draws members' attention from collective concerns and goals. In Chapter 8, we saw that defensive climates are promoted by communication that expresses evaluation, superiority, control orientation, neutrality, certainty, and closed-mindedness. Just as these forms of communication undermine personal relationships, they also interfere with group climate and productivity.

Constructive Conflict Constructive conflict occurs when members understand that disagreements are natural and can help them achieve their goals. This attitude is reflected in collaborative communication. Each person listens respectfully to others' opinions and voices her or his own ideas. Members also emphasize shared interests and goals. Collaborative communication encourages a win–win orientation. Discussion is open and supportive of differences, and disagreements focus on issues, not personalities.

Communication that fosters constructive conflict expresses interest in hearing differing ideas, openness to others' points of view, willingness to alter opinions, and respect for the integrity of other members and the views they express. As we learned in Chapter 8, these forms of communication build supportive communication climates in which individuals feel free to speak.

COMMUNICATION in Your Life

Use the material in this chapter to describe the last group conflict you experienced.

To extend this discussion by examining different orientations to conflict in group and team situations, complete the activity "Orientations to Conflict" in your Online Resources for *Communication in Our Lives*.

CourseMate

Constructive conflict allows members to broaden their understandings, generate a range of possible decisions or solutions, and subject all ideas to careful, cooperative analysis. Constructive conflict is most likely to occur when the appropriate groundwork has been established by creating a supportive, open climate. Group climate is built throughout the life of a group, beginning with the first meeting. Thus, it's important to communicate in ways that build a strong climate from the start so that it is established when conflict arises.

BEYOND THE CLASSROOM

Let's take the material in this chapter beyond the classroom by thinking about how what you've learned about effective communication in groups and teams might apply to the workplace, ethical choices, and engagement with the broader world.

1. **Workplace.** Interview a professional in the field you hope to enter after college. Ask him or her to identify the different work groups and teams he or she has been part of in the past year. How many of the types of groups and teams described in this chapter does your interviewee name?

2. **Ethics.** To what extent do you think the different styles of leadership identified in this chapter reflect different ethical values? How would you describe the ethical framework of democratic, autocratic, and laissez-faire leadership?

   Ethics

3. **Engagement.** Read a local newspaper and notice the number of community groups and teams that are mentioned both for contributing to the community and for efforts to attract new members.

CHAPTER SUMMARY

In this chapter, we focused on task teams, groups that communicate to provide responses to ideas, people, and products; to inform and advise; to improve work continually; to generate ideas; and to make decisions. Task teams are increasingly popular in modern professional life because they are often more effective than individuals in producing creative, high-quality decisions.

To be effective, task teams need leadership. As we have seen, leadership may be provided by a single person or by a group of members. What matters is that one or more members communicate to organize discussion, ensure careful work on the task, and build cohesion, morale, and an effective climate for collective work. Meeting the task and climate responsibilities of leadership may be achieved by different styles of leadership. After discussing the laissez-faire, authoritarian, and democratic styles of leading, we noted that effective leadership style depends on the particular circumstances of a group, including the values of the culture and organization in which the group exists.

We also examined the advantages and limitations of consensus, voting, negotiation, and authority rule as methods of making decisions. No one decision-making method is best for all situations because what will be effective varies according to particular group circumstances, tasks, and members. Thus, groups should consider their situations and needs to choose the most effective decision-making methods.

In this chapter, we also discussed the standard agenda, a well-tested and effective way of organizing discussion so that it is thorough, efficient, and effective. The standard agenda also allows groups to break down decision making into units that can be managed in a series of separate meetings. What we covered in this chapter should give you a good general understanding of how task teams work and how to be an effective member of groups in which you participate. Finally, we considered the role of conflict in enhancing group work, and we identified communication that fosters constructive conflict and improves the quality of group decision making. Constructive conflict in groups, as we have seen, grows out of a supportive communication climate that is built over the course of a group's life.

APPLYING COMMUNICATION IN OUR LIVES

The key concepts, For Further Reflection and Discussion questions, and Experiencing Communication in Our Lives case study that follow will help you review, reflect on, and extend the information and ideas presented in this chapter. These resources, and a diverse selection of additional study tools, are also available as Online Resources for *Communication in Our Lives*.

Your Online Resources include CourseMate, a student workbook, interactive video activities, audio study tools, a book companion website, Speech Builder Express, Speech Studio, and InfoTrac College Edition. For more information or to access this book's online resources, visit **www.cengage.com/login.**

KEY CONCEPTS

authoritarian leadership, 256
authority rule, 260
brainstorming, 252
compromise, 260

consensus, 258
criteria, 263
democratic leadership, 257
emotional intelligence, 259

laissez-faire leadership, 255
quality improvement team, 253
standard agenda, 261
voting, 259

FOR FURTHER REFLECTION AND DISCUSSION

1. Interview a professional in the field you hope to enter after college. Ask him or her to identify ways in which the various task groups and teams discussed in this chapter are used on the job. What can you conclude about the prevalence of task teams in modern professional life?

2. Reread the Communication Highlight on page 255. Do you think all leaders should follow Lincoln's practice of taking "public opinion baths"? What ethical responsibility do leaders have to listen to the views and ideas of subordinates?

Ethics

3. Form groups of five to seven members in your class to use the standard agenda to work on a problem. You might address the question, "What is the best method of testing in this course?" or another question that you and your instructor select. Move through the standard agenda, and record your key ideas and conclusions for each stage. For example, if you addressed the suggested question, in stage one you would need to define *best* and *knowledge*. After the process is completed, assess the value of the standard agenda as a problem-solving method.

4. Review guidelines for creating effective climates in personal relationships that we discussed in Chapter 8. How would you modify the guidelines to apply them to group and team work?

SHARPEN YOUR SKILL

1. Brainstorming

To discover the value of brainstorming, try this: First, write down as many ideas as you can think of to make your campus more environmentally sensitive. Then, with four to six other students in your class, spend 10 minutes generating responses to the same question. Be sure to follow the rules for brainstorming that appear in Table 11.1.

What do you conclude about the value of brainstorming as a method of promoting creative communication in groups?

2. Clarifying Questions

Phrase a question of fact, a question of value, and a question of policy for each of the following topics:

Class Attendance
Fact _____
Value _____
Policy _____

Graduation Requirements at Your School
Fact _____
Value _____
Policy _____

Allowing Students to Take Grades of Incomplete in Courses
Fact _____
Value _____
Policy _____

EXPERIENCING COMMUNICATION IN OUR LIVES

CASE STUDY: *Teamwork*

A video of the conversation scripted here is featured in your Chapter 11 Online Resources for *Communication in Our Lives*. Select "Teamwork" to watch the video. You'll recognize this video because you watched it before in Chapter 6. When you view it this time, focus on group dynamics and communication.

A project team is meeting to discuss the most effective way to present its recommendations for implementing a flextime policy on a trial basis. Members of the team are team leader Jason Brown, Erika Filene, Victoria Lawrence, Bill Williams, and Jensen Chen. They are sitting around a rectangular table with Jason at the head.

JASON: So we've decided to recommend trying flextime for a 2-month period and with a number of procedures to make sure that people's new schedules don't interfere with productivity. There's a lot of information to communicate to employees, so how can we do that best?

VICTORIA: I think it would be good to use PowerPoint to highlight the key aspects of the new procedures. People always seem to remember better if they see something.

BILL: Oh, come on. PowerPoint is so overused. Everyone's tired of it by now. Can't we do something more creative?

VICTORIA: Well, I like it. It's a good teaching tool.

BILL: I didn't know we were teaching. I thought our job was to report recommendations.

VICTORIA: So what do you suggest, Bill? *(She nervously pulls on her bracelet as she speaks.)*

BILL: I don't have a suggestion. I'm just against PowerPoint. *(He doesn't look up as he speaks.)*

JASON: Okay, let's not bicker among ourselves. *[He pauses, gazes directly at Bill, then continues.]* Lots of people like PowerPoint, lots don't. Instead of arguing about its value, let's ask what it is we want to communicate to the employees here. Maybe talking about our goal first will help us decide on the best means of achieving it.

ERIKA: Good idea. I'd like us to focus first on getting everyone excited about the benefits of flextime. If they understand those, they'll be motivated to learn the procedures, even if there are a lot of them.

JENSEN: Erika is right. That's a good way to start. Maybe we could create a handout or PowerPoint slide—either would work—to summarize the benefits of flextime that we've identified in our research.

JASON: Good, okay, now we're cooking. Victoria, will you make notes on the ideas as we discuss them?

Victoria opens a notebook and begins writing notes. Noticing that Bill is typing into his personal digital assistant (PDA), Jason looks directly at Bill.

JASON: Are you with us on how we lead off in our presentation?

BILL: Sure, fine with me. *(He puts the PDA aside but keeps his eyes on it.)*

ERIKA: So maybe then we should say that the only way flextime can work is if we make sure that everyone agrees on procedures so that no division is ever missing more than one person during key production hours.

JENSEN: Very good. That would add to people's motivation to learn and follow the procedures we've found are effective in other companies like ours. I think it would be great if Erika could present that topic, because she did most of the research on it. *(He smiles at Erika, and she pantomimes tipping her hat to him.)*

JASON: *(He looks at Erika with a raised brow, and she nods.)* Good. Okay, Erika's in charge of that. What's next?

VICTORIA: Then it's time to spell out the procedures and . . .

BILL: You can't just spell them out. You have to explain each one—give people a rationale for them, or they won't follow them.

   Victoria glares at Bill, then looks across the table at Erika, who shrugs, as if to say, "I don't know what's bothering Bill today."

JASON: Bill, why don't you lead off, then, and tell us the first procedure we should mention and the rationale we should provide for it.

BILL: *(Looks up from his PDA, which he's been using again, and shrugs.)* Just spell out the rules, that's all.

VICTORIA: Would it be too much trouble for you to cut off your gadget and join us in this meeting, Bill?

BILL: Would it be too much trouble for you to quit hassling me?

JASON: *(He turns his chair to face Bill squarely.)* Look, I don't know what's eating you, but you're really being a jerk. If you've got a problem with this meeting or someone here, put it on the table. Otherwise, be a team player.

QUESTIONS FOR ANALYSIS AND DISCUSSION

You can answer these questions and see my responses to them online via your Online Resources for Chapter 11.

1. Identify leadership behaviors on the team. Is Jason the single leader, or do other team members contribute leadership to the group?

2. Is the conflict on this team constructive, disruptive, or both? If you were a member of the team, how might you communicate to enhance the constructiveness of disagreements?

3. Judging from Jason's comments, what leadership style does he seem to use?

Left: Michael Newman/PhotoEdit; right: Pete Jenkins/Alamy

Find a job you like
and you add five
days to every week.

H. Jackson Brown, Jr.

Communication in Organizations

SHARPEN YOUR SKILL

At the end of this chapter, refer
to the Sharpen Your Skill features,
Noticing Stories and the Work They
Do and Noticing Rituals in Your
Organization, to apply concepts
from Chapter 12.

Josh is a senior systems analyst at MicroLife, an innovative technology firm in Silicon Valley. Although he typically works more than 40 hours a week, Josh's schedule varies according to his moods and his responsibilities for caring for his daughter, Marie. Some days, Josh is at his desk by 8 a.m., and on other days he gets to the office around noon. Life on the job is casual, as is dress. Sneakers, T-shirts, and jeans are standard attire for all employees at MicroLife. People drop by each other's offices without appointments and sometimes even without specific business to conduct.

When Josh first joined MicroLife, drop-by chats with longer-term employees gave him insight into the company. He can still remember hearing stories about Wayne Murray—fondly called "Wild Man Wayne"—who launched the company from a makeshift workstation in his garage. He also heard tale after tale of oddball ideas the company backed that became highly profitable. Josh really enjoys the creative freedom at MicroLife: Everyone is encouraged to think innovatively, to try new ways of doing things. Weekly softball games provide friendly competition between the Nerds (the team of systems analysts) and the Words (the team of software writers).

Jacqueline slips her shoes off under her desk, hoping nobody will see, because Bankers United has a strict dress code requiring suits, high heels (for women), and clean-shaven faces (for men). On her first day at work, a manager took her out to lunch and mentioned two recent hires who "just didn't work out" because they didn't dress professionally. Jacqueline got the message. From other employees, she heard about people who had been given bad performance reviews for being late more than once in a 6-month period. When Jacqueline suggested a way to streamline mortgage applications, she was told, "That isn't how we do things here." She quickly figured out that at Bankers United the operating mode was rigid rules rigidly enforced. Although she sometimes feels constrained by the authoritarian atmosphere of Bankers United, Jacqueline also likes having clear-cut rules to follow. For her, rules provide a kind of security.

Would you rather work for MicroLife or Bankers United? If you're a relaxed person who enjoys informality and does well in unstructured environments, MicroLife may appeal to you. On the other hand, if you like clear rules and a traditional working environment, Bankers United may be more attractive to you. Neither company is better in an absolute sense. Some businesses and professions can be flexible about dress and hours. As long as the work gets done—programs debugged, products developed—it doesn't matter how people dress and when they work. Other organizations must accommodate a time clock and must follow inflexible procedures to meet their objectives. For instance, hospitals must schedule operating rooms, and doctors, nurses, and anesthesiologists must be on time for surgery. Although organizations differ in many ways, common to them is the centrality of communication.

Communication in organizations is the topic of this chapter. In the first section, we'll identify key features of organizational communication. Next, we'll discuss the overall culture of the organization, which is what creates the interpersonal and task climate for its members. As we will see, organizational culture is created and expressed in communication. Every organization has a distinct culture that consists of traditions, structures, and practices that reflect and reproduce a particular form of work life and on-the-job relationships. In the third section of the chapter, we'll discuss three guidelines for communicating in organizations in our era.

KEY FEATURES OF ORGANIZATIONAL COMMUNICATION

Much of what you've learned in previous chapters applies to communication in organizations. For instance, successful communication on the job requires listening skills, verbal and nonverbal competence, and the abilities to build supportive climates and manage conflict. In addition, organizational communication has three distinct features: structure, communication networks, and links to external environments.

Structure

As Charles Conrad and Marshall Scott Poole (2004) point out, the very word *organization* means "structure." **Structure** is a set of procedures, relationships, and practices that provides predictability for members so that they understand roles, procedures, and expectations and so that work gets done.

Most modern organizations rely on a hierarchical structure, which assigns different levels of power and status to different members and specifies the chain of command that specifies who is to communicate with whom about what. Although hierarchies may be more or less rigid,

"I've never actually seen a corporate ladder before."

a loose chain of command doesn't mean there isn't one. My department, like many academic units, has a fairly loose structure in which members generally interact as equals. However, faculty are ultimately responsible to the chair of the department. He can reprimand or assign tasks to any faculty member, but we can't do the same to him.

Communication Networks

A second characteristic of organizational communication is that it occurs in **communication networks**, which are formal and informal links between people. In most organizations, people belong to multiple networks (Conrad & Poole, 2004). For example, in my department I belong to a social network that includes colleagues, students, and staff with whom I have personal relationships; task networks consisting of people with whom I discuss teaching, research, and departmental issues; and ad hoc networks that arise irregularly in response to specific crises or issues. I also belong to networks outside my department yet within the university. Overlaps between networks to which we belong ensure that we will communicate in various ways to many people in any organization.

In addition to networks in physical places of work, an increasing number of workers are part of virtual networks. The growth in telecommuting is striking. In 1991, only 1.4% of U.S. workers were telecommuters. In 1999, 5% were, and by 2020 it's expected that 40% of workers will telecommute (Stroup, 2001). Made possible by new technologies, telecommuting allows millions of people to work from their homes or mobile offices. Using computers, e-mail, BlackBerrys, and faxes, telecommuters do their work and maintain contact with colleagues without going to the physical job site. Results so far show that telecommuting raises the productivity and morale of employees while also saving organizations the expense of providing office space.

COMMUNICATION HIGHLIGHT

Blogging to Improve Communication with the Community

In May 2006, the Los Angeles Police Department became the first police force in the United States to have a blog. Chief William J. Bratton thought a blog would improve communication between police and community. Well—it increased communication, at least. One response to Chief Bratton's initial message inviting dialogue with the public was this: "Good luck with your cesspool of crime, disease and victimhood" (Glazer, 2006). Despite that and a few other less-than-friendly posts, the majority of posts have been positive. And it has definitely become a communication hub—more than 24,000 visitors in the first week of its existence! To visit the LAPD blog, use your Online Resources for *Communication in Our Lives* to access **WebLink 12.1**.

Electronic brainstorming groups are increasingly effective because members can remain anonymous and so are more willing to risk venturing creative ideas (Harris, 2002). And electronic brainstorming, also called virtual conferencing, isn't necessarily a one-time event. Virtual teams are becoming more and more common in the workplace (Godar & Ferris, 2004; Rothwell, 2009).

Links to External Environments

In Chapter 1, we discussed systems as interdependent, interacting wholes. Like other communication systems, organizations are embedded in multiple contexts that affect how they work and whether they succeed or fail. In other words, an organization's operation cannot be understood simply by looking within the organization. We must also look outside it to grasp how the organization is related to and affected by its contexts.

Consider the impact on a few U.S. organizations of the sharp rise in gasoline prices that began in the summer of 2005:

> Tourist attractions saw drops in attendance because people were driving less.
>
> Sales of hybrid cars and conventional cars with high miles-per-gallon ratings rose, whereas sales of low-mpg vehicles slumped.
>
> People who did travel by car spent less on hotels and meals on the road, to compensate (they said) for the high cost of gasoline.
>
> Transportation companies raised prices to offset the higher costs of gasoline for transporting merchandise.

Although internal factors may have contributed to the sales losses and gains of these businesses, clearly many organizations suffered because of factors outside their organizational boundaries. When economic times are good, when war is not a threat, and when inflation is in check, even mediocre companies survive and sometimes thrive. When external conditions are bad, even good companies can be hurt or driven out of business.

ORGANIZATIONAL CULTURE

In Chapter 7, we noted that cultures are characterized by shared values, behaviors, practices, and communication forms. Extending the idea of culture to organizations, communication scholars focus on **organizational culture**, which consists of ways of thinking, acting, and understanding work that are shared by members of an organization and that reflect an organization's distinct identity.

Just as ethnic cultures consist of meanings shared by members of the ethnic groups, organizational cultures consist of meanings shared by members of organizations. Just as new members of ethnic cultures are socialized into preexisting meanings and traditions, new members of organizations are socialized into pre-existing meanings and traditions (Mumby, 2006a, 2006b). Just as a culture's way of life continues even though particular people leave or die, an organization's culture persists despite the comings and goings of particular workers.

Scholars have gained insight into the ways in which communication creates, sustains, and expresses the culture of organizations (Pacanowsky, 1989; Pacanowsky & O'Donnell-Trujillo, 1983; Scott & Myers, 2005). The relationship between communication and organizational culture is reciprocal: Communication between members of organizations creates, sustains, and sometimes alters the culture. At the same time, organizational culture influences patterns of communication between members.

As employees interact, they create, sustain, and sometimes change their organization's culture. Four kinds of communication that are particularly important in developing and conveying organizational culture are vocabularies, stories, rites and rituals, and structures.

Vocabulary

Just as the language of an ethnic culture reflects and expresses its history, norms, values, and identity, the *vocabulary* of an organization reflects and expresses its history, norms, values, and identity.

Hierarchical Language   Many organizations and professions have vocabularies that distinguish levels of status among members. The military, for example, relies on language that continually acknowledges rank (i.e., *Yes, sir; chain of command*), which reflects the close ties between rank, power, and privilege. Salutes, as well as stripes and medals on uniforms, are part of the nonverbal vocabulary that emphasizes rank and honors. In a study of police, researchers noted the pervasiveness of

Ivan Hunter/Jupiter Images

Interaction among employees creates and sometimes changes an organization's culture.

derogatory language for suspects and informants. Officers routinely referred to *creeps*, *dirtbags*, and *maggots* to draw a clear distinction between upstanding citizens and criminals (Pacanowsky & O'Donnell-Trujillo, 1983).

Unequal terms of address also communicate rank. For instance, the CEO may use first names ("Good morning, Jan") when speaking to employees. Unless given permission to use the CEO's first name, however, lower-status members of an organization typically use *Mr.*, *Ms.*, *Sir*, or *Ma'am* in addressing the CEO. Colleges and universities use titles to designate faculty members' rank and status: instructor, assistant professor, associate professor, full professor, and distinguished (or chaired) professor. Faculty generally use students' first names, whereas students tend to use titles to address their teachers: Dr. Armstrong or Professor Armstrong, for example.

Masculine Language Because organizations historically have been run by men, and men have been the primary or exclusive members of them, it's not surprising that many organizations have developed and continue to use language more related to men's traditional interests and experiences than to women's (Ashcraft & Mumby, 2004; Mumby, 2006a, 2006b). Consider the number of phrases in the working world that are taken from sports (i.e., home run, ballpark estimate, touchdown, develop a game plan, be a team player, take a time out, the starting lineup), from military life (i.e., battle plan, mount a campaign, plan of attack, under fire, get the big guns, defensive move, offensive strike), and from male sexual parts and activities (i.e., a troublesome person is a *prick*; you can *hit* on a person, *screw* someone, or *stick it to* them; bold professionals have *balls*).

Less prevalent in most organizations is language that reflects traditionally feminine interests and experiences (i.e., put something on the back burner, percolate an idea, stir the pot, give birth to a plan). Whether intentional or not, language that reflects traditionally masculine experiences and interests can bind men together in a community in which many women may feel unwelcome or uncomfortable (Murphy & Zorn, 1996).

Similarly, many organizations in the United States reflect Caucasian and Christian values and experiences more than those of other ethnic and religious groups (Allen, 2006). For instance, most portraits are of white people; official holidays generally include Christmas but not Kwanzaa or Yom Kippur. This may be unconscious and unintended, but it can nonetheless make organizations feel more familiar and comfortable to Christians and whites than to other groups.

Stories

Scholars of organizational culture recognize that humans are storytellers by nature. We tell stories to weave coherent narratives out of experience and to create meaning in our lives. Furthermore, the stories we tell do some real work in establishing and sustaining organizational cultures. In a classic study, Michael Pacanowsky and Nick O'Donnell-Trujillo (1983) identified three kinds of stories within the organizational context.

Corporate Stories Corporate stories convey the values, style, and history of an organization. Just as families have favorite stories about their histories and

---

COMMUNICATION in Your Life

To what extent is masculine language present in an organization to which you belong(ed)?

COMMUNICATION HIGHLIGHT

Language in Left Field

The prevalence of sports-related terms in U.S. business culture can pose challenges for international business conversations. Consider these foul balls that only Americans understood (Jones, 2007):

While at a global leadership meeting in Italy, William Mitchell, CEO of Arrow Electronics, wanted to change the agenda, so he said, "I'm calling an audible."

At a meeting with Indian executives, Alan Guarino, CEO of Cornell International, tried to change a contractual clause by demanding "a jump-ball scenario."

AFLAC CEO Dan Amos baffled Japanese executives when he told them that using the AFLAC duck for ads in Japan would be a "slam dunk."

identities that they retell often, organizations have favorite stories that reflect their collective visions of themselves (Conrad & Poole, 2004; Mumby, 1993, 2006a).

One important function of corporate stories is to socialize new members into the culture of an organization. Newcomers learn about the history and identity of an organization by listening to stories of its leaders as well as its trials and triumphs. For example, both Levi Strauss and Microsoft are known for their informal style of operation. Veteran employees regale new employees with tales about the laid-back character of the companies. These stories socialize new employees into the cultures of the companies.

When retold among members of an organization, stories foster feelings of connection and vitalize organizational ideology. You've heard the term *war stories*, which refers to frequently retold stories about key moments such as crises, successes, and takeovers. When long-term members of organizations rehash pivotal events in their shared history, they cement the bonds between them and their involvement with the organization. Jed's commentary provides a good example of how stories express and reinforce organizational culture.

> **JED**   *I sing with the Gospel Choir, and we have a good following in the Southeast. When I first joined the group, the other members talked to me. In our conversations, what I heard again and again was the idea that we exist to make music for God and about God, not to glorify ourselves. One of the choir members told me about a singer who had gotten on a personal ego trip because of all the bookings we were getting, and he started thinking he was more important than the music. That guy didn't last long with the group.*

Personal Stories   Members of organizations also tell stories about themselves. Personal stories are accounts that announce how people see themselves and how they want to be seen by others (Cockburn-Wootten & Zorn, 2006). For example, if Sabra perceives herself as a supportive team player, she could simply tell new employees this: "I am a supportive person who believes in teamwork." On the

How would this photograph of professionals be different if it had been taken 20 years ago?

other hand, she could define her image by telling a story: "When I first came here, most folks were operating in isolation, and I thought a lot more could be accomplished if we learned to collaborate. Let me tell you something I did to make that happen. After I'd been on staff for 3 months, I was assigned to work up a plan for downsizing our manufacturing department. Instead of just developing a plan on my own, I talked with several other managers, and then I met with people who worked in manufacturing to get their ideas. The plan we came up with reflected all of our input." This narrative gives a concrete, coherent account of how Sabra sees herself and wants others to see her.

Collegial Stories The third type of organizational story offers accounts of other members of the organization. When I first became a faculty member, a senior colleague took me out to lunch and told me anecdotes about people in the department and the university. At the time, I thought he was simply sharing some interesting stories. As time went on, however, I realized he had told me who the players were so that I could navigate my new context.

Collegial stories told by co-workers forewarn us what to expect from whom. "If you need help getting around the CEO, Jane's the one to see. A year ago, I couldn't finish a report by deadline, so Jane rearranged his calendar so he thought the report wasn't due for another week." "Roberts is a real stickler for rules. Once when I took an extra 20 minutes on my lunch break, he reamed me out." Whether positive or negative, collegial stories assert identities for others in an organization. They are part of the informal network that teaches new members of an organization how to get along with various other members of the culture.

Rites and Rituals

Rites and rituals are verbal and nonverbal practices that express and reproduce organizational cultures. They do so by providing standardized ways of expressing organizational values and identity.

Rites Rites are dramatic, planned sets of activities that bring together aspects of an organization's culture in a single event. Harrison Trice and Janice Beyer (1984) identified six kinds of organizational rites. Rites of passage are used to mark membership in different levels or parts of organizations. For example, a nonverbal symbol of change may be the moving of an employee's office from the

COMMUNICATION in Your Life

Recall one story you were told by a co-worker shortly after taking a new job.

second to the fourth floor after a promotion. Special handshakes are nonverbal rites that symbolize communality among members of clubs and other groups. A desk plaque with a new employee's name and title is a rite that acknowledges a change in identity. *Rites of integration* affirm and enhance the sense of community in an organization. Examples are holiday parties, annual picnics, and graduation ceremonies.

Organizational cultures also include rites that blame or praise people. Firings, demotions, and reprimands are common blaming rites—the counterpart of which are enhancement rites, which praise individuals and teams that embody the organization's goals and self-image. Campuses bestow awards on faculty who are especially gifted teachers and chaired professorships on outstanding scholars. Many sales companies give awards for productivity (i.e., most sales of the month, quarter, or year). Many organizations use listservs or organizational newsletters to congratulate employees on accomplishments. In my department, faculty meetings always open with announcements about honors and achievements of faculty members. This recognition rite gives each of us moments in the limelight. Audrey describes an enhancement rite in her sorority.

> **AUDRY**   *In my sorority, we recognize sisters who make the dean's list each semester by putting a rose on their dinner plates. That way everyone realizes who has done well academically, and we can also remind ourselves that scholarship is one of the qualities we all aspire to.*

Organizations also develop rites for managing change. Renewal rites aim to revitalize and update organizations. Training workshops serve this purpose, as do periodic retreats at which organizational members discuss their goals and the institution's health. Organizations also develop rituals for managing conflicts between members of the organization. Conflict resolution rites are standard methods of dealing with differences and discord. Examples are arbitration, collective bargaining, mediation, executive fiat, voting, and ignoring or denying problems. The conflict resolution rite that typifies an organization reflects the values of its overall culture.

COMMUNICATION in Your Life

Identify two rites on your campus.

Rituals   **Rituals** are forms of communication that occur regularly and that members of an organization perceive as familiar and routine parts of organizational life. Rituals differ from rites in that rituals don't necessarily bring together a number of aspects of organizational ideology into a single event. Rather, rituals are repeated communication performances that communicate a particular value or role definition.

Organizations have personal, task, and social rituals. *Personal rituals* are routine behaviors that individuals use to express their organizational identities. In their study of organizational cultures, Pacanowsky and O'Donnell-Trujillo (1983) noted that Lou Polito, the owner of a car company, opened all the company's mail every day. Whenever possible, Polito hand-delivered mail to the divisions of

Commencement ceremonies are key rites of passage at colleges and universities. Which aspects of university life are brought together in commencement ceremonies?

Jürgen Schulzki/Alamy

his company to communicate his openness and his involvement with the day-to-day business.

Social rituals are standardized performances that affirm relationships between members of organizations (Mokros, 2006; Mumby, 2006a). Some organizations have a company dining room to encourage socializing among employees. In the United Kingdom and Japan, many businesses have afternoon tea breaks. E-mail chatting and forwarding jokes are additional examples of socializing rituals in the workplace. Tamar Katriel (1990) identified a social ritual of griping among Israelis. *Kiturim*, the name Israelis give to their griping, most often occurs during Friday night social events called *mesibot kiturim*, which is translated as "gripe sessions." Unlike griping about personal concerns, kiturim typically focuses on national issues, concerns, and problems. Some Jewish families engage in ritualized *kvetching*, which is personal griping that aims to air frustrations but not necessarily to resolve them. The point of the ritual is to complain, not to solve a problem. Sharon provides an example of an office griping ritual.

SHARON *Where I work, we have this ritual of spending the first half-hour or so at work every Monday complaining about what we have to get done that week. Even if we don't have a rough week ahead, we go through the motions of moaning and groaning. It's kind of like a bonding ceremony for us.*

Task rituals are repeated activities that help members of an organization perform their jobs. Perhaps a special conference room is used for particular tasks, such as giving marketing presentations, holding performance reviews, or making sales proposals. Task rituals are also evident in forms and procedures that members of organizations are expected to use to do various things. These forms and procedures standardize task performance in a manner consistent with the organization's view of itself and how it operates. In their study of a police unit, Pacanowsky and O'Donnell-Trujillo (1983) identified the routine that officers are trained to follow when they stop drivers for violations. The questions officers are taught to ask ("May I see your license, please?" "Do you know why I stopped you?" "Do you know how fast you were going?") allow them to size up traffic violators and decide whether to give them a break or a closer look. The Sharpen Your Skill exercise on page 292 allows you to notice rituals in an organization to which you belong.

Structures

Organizational cultures are also represented through structural aspects of organizational life. As the term implies, structures organize relationships and interaction between members of an organization. We'll consider four structures that express and uphold organizational culture: roles, rules, policies, and communication networks.

Roles Roles are responsibilities and behaviors that are expected of people because of their specific positions in an organization. Most organizations formally define roles in job descriptions:

> Training coordinator: Responsible for assessing needs and providing training to Northwest branches of the firm; supervises staff of 25 professional trainers; coordinates with director of human relations.

A role is not tied to any particular person. Rather, it is a set of functions and responsibilities that could be performed by any number of people who have particular talents, experiences, and other relevant qualifications. If one person quits or is fired, another can be found as a replacement. Regardless of who is in the role, the organization will continue with its structure intact. The different roles in an organization are a system, which means they are interrelated and interacting. Each role is connected to other roles within the system. Organizational charts portray who is responsible to whom and clarify the hierarchy of power among roles in the organization.

Rules Rules, which we discussed in Chapter 5, are patterned ways of interacting. Rules are present in organizational contexts just as they are in other settings of interaction. As in other contexts, organizational rules may be formal (in the contract or organizational chart) or informal (norms for interaction).

Within organizations, constitutive rules specify what various kinds of communication symbolize. Some firms count working late as evidence of commitment. Socializing with colleagues after work may count as showing team spirit. Taking on extra assignments, attending training sessions, and dressing like upper management may communicate ambition. The Communication Highlight on page 284 discusses systemic and deliberate corporate operations that were illegal or immoral and suggests that, in some of these organizations, going along with unethical practices and not blowing the whistle counted as company loyalty. Lyle's commentary points out what counted as violating the chain of command in his company.

COMMUNICATION
in Your Life

Write a job description for the job you hope to get after graduating.

LYLE *I found out the hard way that a company I worked for was dead serious about the organizational chart. I had a problem with a co-worker, so I talked with a guy in another department I was friends with. Somehow my supervisor found out, and he blew a gasket. He was furious that I had "gone outside of the chain of command" instead of coming straight to him.*

COMMUNICATION HIGHLIGHT

Organizations and Ethics—Or Lack Thereof

In 2002, the Enron scandal was a huge news story. According to news reports, the accounting firm Arthur Andersen had knowingly misrepresented Enron's financial condition in ways that misled investors, many of whom lost substantial funds they had invested in Enron. Investigations revealed that knowledge of the misrepresentation was widespread, although not universal, among both Enron and Andersen employees. Shortly after the Enron story broke, companies such as Adelphia Communications and WorldCom were charged with illegal practices. Americans expressed shock and disbelief at the scandals.

Two years later, in 2004, news broke of U.S. soldiers' abuse of prisoners at Abu Ghraib prison in Iraq. Initially, the U.S. administration claimed the problem was a "few bad apples," who didn't represent what the U.S. military was about. As the story grew, however, it became clear that higher-ranking military personnel and members of the administration were aware of the abuses and did not intervene to stop them. Once again, Americans expressed shock that such a thing could happen.

Shock and outrage are legitimate responses to unethical behavior. However, perhaps Americans shouldn't have been shocked because illegal activities are hardly new. Scandals in government are not unfamiliar to us—Watergate is a prime example of egregiously unlawful behavior at the highest levels of U.S. government. Between 1975 and 1990, fully two-thirds of the *Fortune 500* companies were convicted (not just accused) of crimes including price fixing, illegal dumping of toxic waste, and accounting violations (Conrad & Poole, 2004).

What should we conclude from these reports? Are organizations unethical, or is it simply that certain individuals (a few "rotten apples") in some organizations act illegally and unethically (Lefkowitz, 2003)? Although individuals are responsible for their ethical choices, it would be naive to assume that organizations aren't also blameworthy. Two organizational communication scholars, Charley Conrad and Marshall Scott Poole (2004), assert that the power structures, norms, and cultures in many organizations allow or even encourage unethical activities and punish those who resist or blow the whistle. One example of the systemic nature of unethical behavior is that, in 1996, 29 of 30 Harvard MBAs contacted for a study reported they had been ordered by superiors at their places of work to violate their personal ethics at least once (Barlow, 1996).

Regulative rules specify when, where, and with whom communication occurs. Organizational charts formalize regulative rules by showing who reports to whom. Other regulative rules may specify that problems should not be discussed with people outside the organization and that social conversations are (or are not) permitted during working hours. Some organizations have found that employees spend so much time online that productivity suffers, so rules regulating online time are instituted.

Policies Policies are formal statements of practices that reflect and uphold the overall culture of an organization. For example, my university's mission statement emphasizes the importance of teaching. Consistent with the organizational identity reflected in that mission statement, we have policies that require teaching evaluations and policies that tie good teaching performance to tenure,

COMMUNICATION HIGHLIGHT

Keeping Track of Employees

More and more companies are instituting systems to monitor employees' online communication. One popular system, Worktrack, is used by employers to track workers who make home calls (e.g., technicians who repair heating and air conditioning). In addition to verifying that workers are actually at job sites, Worktrack monitors driving speed (Levy, 2004). During a random check of employees' online activities, a chapter of the American Heart Association discovered that an employee repeatedly had visited a pornographic website. He was dismissed (Jones, 1999).

A number of employers also routinely screen employees' e-mail to filter out profanity, pornography, and sexist and racist jokes and language (Jones, 1999). Employees who protest that this is an invasion of privacy are learning that the courts regard e-mail and web access as company resources that employees are allowed to use. Court rulings do not support any expectation of privacy in e-mail or web communication on the job (Monmonier, 2002).

On the other hand, in a recent court case, Judge John Spooner ruled that surfing the web at work is not necessarily inappropriate in the workplace because it is no different from reading a newspaper or talking with co-workers. Judge Spooner said, "The Internet has become the modern equivalent of a telephone or daily newspaper" ("Surfing Web," 2006, p. 3A).

---

promotion, and raises. Most organizations codify policies governing such aspects of work life as hiring, promotion, benefits, grievances, and medical leave. The content of policies in these areas differs among organizations in ways that reflect the distinct cultures of diverse work environments.

Organizational policies also reflect the larger society within which organizations are embedded. For example, as public awareness of sexual harassment has increased, most organizations have developed formal policies that define sexual harassment, state the organization's attitude toward it, and detail the procedure for making complaints. Because of the prevalence of dual-career couples, many organizations have created departments to help place the spouses of people they want to hire.

Communication Networks   As we noted previously in this chapter, communication networks link members of an organization together through formal and informal forms of interaction and relationship. These networks play key roles in expressing and reinforcing the culture of an organization.

Job descriptions and organizational charts, which specify who is supposed to communicate with whom about what, are formal networks. Formal networks provide the order necessary for organizations to operate. They define lines of upward communication (i.e., subordinates to superiors; providing feedback, reporting results), downward communication (i.e., superiors to subordinates; giving orders, establishing policies), and horizontal communication (i.e., peer to peer; coordinating between departments).

The informal communication network is more difficult to describe because it is neither formally defined nor based on fixed organizational roles. Friendships, alliances, carpools, and nearby offices can be informal networks through which a great deal of information flows. Most professionals have others within their organization with whom they regularly check perceptions and past whom they run certain ideas.

Communication outside the formal channels of an organization is sometimes called the *grapevine*, a term that suggests its free-flowing quality. Grapevine communication, although continual in organizational life, tends to be especially active during periods of change. This makes sense because we engage in communication to reduce our uncertainty and discomfort with change. New information (a fresh rumor) activates the grapevine. Although details often are lost or distorted as messages travel along a grapevine, the information conveyed informally has a surprisingly high rate of accuracy: 75 to 90% (Hellweg, 1992). If details are important, however, the grapevine may be a poor source of information.

GUIDELINES FOR COMMUNICATING IN ORGANIZATIONS

We'll discuss three guidelines that are particularly relevant to organizational communication in our era.

Adapt to Diverse Needs, Situations, and People

Consider the following descriptions of people who work in one company in my community:

> Eileen is 28, single, Jewish, fluent in English and Spanish, and the primary caregiver for her disabled mother.
>
> Frank is 37, a father of two, and a European American married to a full-time homemaker. He is especially skilled in collaborative team building.
>
> Denise is 30, single, European American, an excellent public speaker, and mother of a 4-year-old girl.
>
> Sam is 59, African American, father of two grown children, and married to an accountant. He is widely regarded as supportive and empathic.
>
> Ned is 42, divorced, European American, and recovering from triple bypass surgery.
>
> Javier is 23, a Latino, and married to a woman who works full time. They are expecting their first child in a few months.

These six people have different life situations, abilities, and goals that affect what they need and want to be effective on the job. Eileen and Denise need flexible working hours so that they can take care of family members. Eileen may also expect her employer to respect Rosh Hashanah, Yom Kippur, Hanukkah, and other holidays of her religion. Ned may need extended disability leave and a period of part-time work while he recuperates from his heart surgery. Javier may want to take family leave when his child is born, a benefit that wouldn't be valued by Frank or Sam. These six people are typical of the workforce today. They illustrate the diversity of people, life situations, and needs that characterize the modern workplace. The variety of workers is a major change, one that requires organizations to adapt.

Workers increasingly expect organizations to tailor conditions and benefits to their individual needs and circumstances. Many organizations have a cafeteria-style benefits package that allows employees to select benefits from a range of options that includes family leave, flexible working hours, employer-paid education, telecommuting, onsite day care, dental insurance, and personal days. Someone with primary caregiving responsibilities might sacrifice vacation time for additional family leave. A person nearing retirement might want maximum insurance and medical coverage but little family leave time.

The organizations that survive and thrive in an era of diversity will be those that adapt effectively to meet the expectations and needs of diverse workers (see the Communication Highlight on page 288). Flexible rules and policies, rather than one-size-fits-all formulas, will mark the successful workplaces of the future. By extension, the most competent, most effective professionals will be those who are comfortable with a stream of changes in people and ways of working. You might work closely with a colleague for several years and then see little of that person if he or she modifies working hours to accommodate changes in family life. If you choose to telecommute, you will need to develop new ways to stay involved in the informal network (which may operate largely on the Internet) and have the amount of social contact you enjoy. Managers will need to find ways to lead employees who work in different locations and at different hours.

Expect to Move In and Out of Teams

Effective communication in today's and tomorrow's organizations requires interacting intensely with members of teams that may form and dissolve quickly. Whereas autonomous workers—single leaders, mavericks, and independent

COMMUNICATION
in Your Life

Which benefits do you consider most important in your first postcollege job?

COMMUNICATION HIGHLIGHT

Tomorrow's Organizations

Increasingly, work groups and teams will work virtually; their members will connect from different places and even different countries (Rothwell, 2009). Technologies such as text messaging, audio- and videoconferencing, and webcasts allow groups to work across time and distance. In future years, we're sure to see additional technologies that further facilitate virtual group work.

CourseMate

One of the best ways to learn about social and organizational trends that are reshaping the world of work is to read online magazines. *Entrepreneurial Edge* discusses emerging trends and resources for entrepreneurs. Another savvy site is an idea café created by business owners, where you'll find advice on starting and running a business, using technologies, and networking. To check out *Entrepreneurial Edge* and the idea café online, use your Online Resources for *Communication in Our Lives* to access **WebLink 12.2** and **WebLink 12.3**.

professionals—were prized in the 1940s, the team player is most highly sought today (Rothwell, 2009). John, who returned to school in his mid-forties, describes the changes in his job over the past 13 years.

The skills we discussed in Part I of this book will help you perceive carefully, listen well, use verbal and nonverbal communication effectively, promote constructive climates, and adapt your style of interacting to the diverse people on your teams. The challenge is to be able to adjust your style of communicating to the expectations and interaction styles of a variety of people and to the constraints of a range of situations. The greater your repertoire of communication skills, the more effectively you will be able to move in and out of teams on the job.

JOHN *My job is entirely different today than when I started it 13 years ago. When I came aboard, each of us had his own responsibilities, and management pretty much left us alone to do our work. I found authors and helped them develop their ideas, Andy took care of all art for the books, someone else was in charge of marketing, and so forth. Each of us did our job on a book and passed the book on to the next person. Now the big buzzword is team. Everything is done in teams. From the start of a new book project, the author and I are part of a team that includes the art editor, marketing director, manuscript designer, and so forth. Each of us has to coordinate with the others continually; nobody works as a lone operator. Although I had reservations about teams at first, by now I'm convinced that they are superior to individuals working independently. The books we're producing are more internally coherent, and they are developed far more efficiently when we collaborate.*

COMMUNICATION HIGHLIGHT

Employee Mistreatment in Culturally Diverse Organizations

We hear a lot about the increasing diversity of the workforce in the United States and elsewhere. What we hear less about is emerging as a serious problem that seems more prevalent in culturally diverse workplaces than in culturally homogeneous ones. The problem is employee mistreatment. Research (Namie, 2000) shows that 23% of mistreated employees were from minority groups, and 77% of mistreated employees were women.

Mistreatment ranges from unlawful activities, such as harassment and inequitable benefits, to more subtle activities, such as stereotyping, ridicule, and intergroup conflict (Allen, 2006; Harlos & Pinder, 1999; Mumby, 2006a; Vardi & Weitz, 2004). A majority of male employees (61%) and European Americans (56%) report that they are treated fairly in their work life, but a significant minority of females (30%) and members of minority groups (33%) report being treated equitably (Meares, Oetzel, Torres, Derkacs, & Ginossar, 2004).

Individuals who are treated unfairly in the workplace tend to withdraw, leave, become resentful, or experience anger, which may be expressed in a variety of ways. Clearly, these consequences are not limited to individual employees—they affect organizations' health and productivity. If employees are not contributing constructively on the job, then the entire organization suffers.

Manage Personal Relationships on the Job

A third challenge of organizational life involves relationships that are simultaneously personal and professional. You probably will be involved in a number of such relationships during your life. In a 1995 study titled "Bosses and Buddies," Ted Zorn described his long friendship with a colleague who became his supervisor. Zorn described tensions that arose because of conflicts between the role of friend and those of supervisor and subordinate. Although management has traditionally discouraged personal relationships between employees, the relationships develop anyway. The goal, then, is to understand these relationships and manage them effectively.

Friendships between co-workers or supervisors and subordinates often enhance job commitment and satisfaction (Allen, 2006; Mokros, 2006; Mumby, 2006a; Zorn, 1995). This is not surprising, as we're more likely to enjoy work when we work with people we like. Yet workplace friendships also have drawbacks. As Zorn's story illustrates, on-the-job friendships may involve tension between the role expectations for friends and for colleagues. A supervisor may have difficulty rendering a fair evaluation of a subordinate who is also a friend. The supervisor might err by overrating the subordinate–friend's strengths or might try to compensate for personal affection by being especially harsh in judging the friend–subordinate. Also, workplace friendships that deteriorate may create stress and job dissatisfaction (Sias, Heath, Perry, Silva, & Fix, 2004).

> **ANNA**   *It's hard for me now that my best friend has been promoted over me. Part of it is envy, because I wanted the promotion too. But the hardest part is that I resent her power over me. When Billie gives me an assignment, I feel like as my friend she shouldn't dump extra work on me. But I also know that as the boss she has to give extra work to all of us sometimes. It just doesn't feel right for my best friend to tell me what to do and evaluate my work.*

Romantic relationships between people who work together are also increasing. Most women and men work outside the home, sometimes spending more hours on the job than in the home. In Chapter 9, we learned that proximity is a key influence on the formation of romantic relationships. It's no surprise, then, that people who see each other almost every day sometimes find themselves attracted to each other. Workplace romances are likely to involve many of the same tensions that operate in friendships between supervisors and subordinates. In addition, romantic relationships are especially likely to arouse co-workers' resentment and discomfort. Romantic breakups also tend to be more dramatic than breakups between friends. To learn more about personal relationships in the workplace, use your Online Resources for *Communication in Our Lives* to access **WebLink 12.4.**

EUGENE *Once, I got involved with a woman where I was working. We were assigned to the same team and really hit it off, and one thing led to another, and we were dating. I guess it affected our work some, since we spent a lot of time talking and stuff in the office. But the real problem came when we broke up. It's impossible to avoid seeing your "ex" when you work together in a small office, and everyone else acted like they were walking on eggshells around us. She finally quit, and you could just feel tension drain out of everyone else in our office.*

It's probably unrealistic to assume that we can avoid personal relationships with people on the job. The challenge is to manage those relationships so that the workplace doesn't interfere with the personal bond, and the intimacy doesn't jeopardize professionalism. Friends and romantic partners may need to adjust their expectations and styles of interacting so that personal and work roles do not conflict. It's also advisable to make sure that on-the-job communication doesn't reflect favoritism and privileges that could cause resentment in co-workers. It's important to invest extra effort to maintain an open communication climate with other co-workers.

BEYOND THE CLASSROOM

Let's take the material in this chapter beyond the classroom by thinking about how it might apply to the workplace, ethical choices, and engagement with the broader world.

1. **Workplace.** Think about the place where you work or a place you worked in the past. What stories—collegial, personal, and corporate—did you hear during the initial stage of your employment? How did those stories shape your early understandings of that workplace and your understandings of what was expected of you as an employee?

2. **Ethics.** In recent years, we've discovered instance after instance of egregiously unethical behavior by leaders of organizations. Between 2006 and 2008, loan officers in banks were told to sign people up for mortgages they didn't understand and couldn't afford. As a result, many of these people lost their homes to foreclosure. Bernie Madoff lied to thousands of people, taking their money in a giant Ponzi scheme that left many penniless. Incidents such as these have led some to recommend that ethical training of some sort be required for all professionals. Do you think it should be part of the curriculum in business and law schools?

3. **Engagement.** Watch the film *Remember the Titans*. It provides a dramatic account of a man who was assigned to coach a group of football players in a recently integrated school high school. The players didn't work together well, largely because of ethnic differences and ethnocentric attitudes. This film provides rich insights into leadership and the development of a cohesive organizational culture for the team.

CHAPTER SUMMARY

In this chapter, we've seen the importance of daily performances, such as rituals and storytelling, in upholding an organization's identity and a shared set of meanings for members of the organization. The culture of an organization is created, sustained, and altered in the process of communication between members of an organization. As they talk, interact, develop policies, and participate in the formal and informal networks, they continuously weave the fabric of their individual roles and collective life.

Organizations, like other contexts of communication, involve a number of challenges. To meet those challenges, we discussed three guidelines.

One is to develop a large repertoire of communication skills so you can adapt effectively to diverse people, situations, and needs in the workplace. A second guideline is to be prepared to move in and out of teams rapidly, which is required in many modern organizations. Finally, we discussed ways to manage personal relationships in the workplace. It's likely that you and others will form friendships and perhaps romantic relationships with people in the workplace. The communication skills we've discussed throughout this book will help you navigate the tensions and challenges of close relationships on the job.

APPLYING COMMUNICATION IN OUR LIVES

The key concepts, For Further Reflection and Discussion questions, and Experiencing Communication in Our Lives case study that follow will help you review, reflect on, and extend the information and ideas presented in this chapter. These resources, and a diverse selection of additional study tools, are also available as Online Resources for *Communication in Our Lives*. Your

Online Resources include CourseMate, a student workbook, interactive video activities, audio study tools, a book companion website, Speech Builder Express, Speech Studio, and InfoTrac College Edition. For more information or to access this book's online resources, visit **www.cengage.com/login.**

KEY CONCEPTS

communication network, 275	rite, 280	role, 283
organizational culture, 277	ritual, 281	structure, 275
policy, 284		

FOR FURTHER REFLECTION AND DISCUSSION

1. Locate a copy of your college's policies governing students. From its policies concerning class attendance, drug use, and dishonorable conduct, what can you infer about the culture the college wants to promote? (Note how dishonorable conduct is defined; this differs among schools.)

2. Reflect on the corporate, personal, and collegial stories you heard during your first few weeks on a new job. What did these stories say about the organizational culture?

3. Think about a group to which you belong. It may be a work group or a social group, such as a fraternity or interest club. Describe some common rites and rituals in your group. What do these rites and rituals communicate about the group's culture?

4. How can organizational rites and rituals normalize discrimination against particular groups? Identify examples of organizational rites and rituals that encourage or allow unequal treatment based on factors such as race, sex, sexual orientation, or economic class. When, if ever, are such uses of rites and rituals ethical?

Ethics

SHARPEN YOUR SKILL

1. Noticing Stories and the Work They Do

Think about an organization to which you belong, perhaps one in which you have worked or one that you have had many opportunities to observe. Identify corporate, personal, and collegial stories you were told when you first entered the organization. How did these stories shape your understandings of the organization?

Extend the concept of organizational stories to your family's culture. What family stories taught you your family's history and values? What personal stories did your parents tell you to define who they are and what they stand for? Did family members talk about others? If so, what collegial stories did you hear about other relatives? Do the stories told in your family form a coherent account of its identity?

2. Noticing Rituals in Your Organization

Think of an organization to which you belong. It could be your school or a more specific group such as a sports team, club, or workplace. Describe one ritual (i.e., personal, social, or task) and explain what it does for the organization and its members. What would be missing if this ritual were abandoned?

EXPERIENCING COMMUNICATION IN OUR LIVES

CASE STUDY: *Ed Misses the Banquet*

A video of the scenario featured here is included in your Chapter 11 Online Resources for *Communication in Our Lives*. Select "Ed Misses the Banquet" to watch the video. Improve your own communication skills by reading, watching, and evaluating this communication encounter.

© Cengage Learning

Ed recently began working at a new job. Although he's been in his new job only 5 weeks, he likes it a lot, and he's told you that he sees a real future for himself with this company. But last week, a problem arose. Along with all other employees, Ed was invited to the annual company banquet, at which everyone socializes and awards are given for outstanding performance. Ed's daughter was in a play the night of the banquet, so Ed chose to attend his daughter's play rather than the company event. The invitation to the banquet had stated only, "Hope to see you there" and contained no RSVP, so Ed didn't mention to anyone that he couldn't attend. When he arrived at work the next Monday morning, however, he discovered he should have rearranged his plans to attend or, at the very least, should have told his supervisor why he would not be at the event. That Monday, Ed talked with several co-workers who had been around a few years, and he discovered that top management sees the annual banquet as a "command performance" that signifies company unity and loyalty. Later in the day, Ed had the following exchange with his manager.

ED'S MANAGER: You skipped the banquet last Saturday. I had really thought you were committed to our company.

ED: My daughter was in a play that night.

ED'S MANAGER: I don't care why you didn't come. We notice who is really with us and who isn't.

QUESTIONS FOR ANALYSIS AND DISCUSSION

You can answer these questions and see my responses to them online via your Online Resources for Chapter 12.

1. How does the concept of constitutive rules, which we first discussed in Chapter 5, help explain the misunderstanding between Ed and his manager?

2. How might Ed use the informal network in his organization to learn the normative practices of the company and the meanings they have to others in the company?

3. How do the ambiguity and abstraction inherent in language explain the misunderstanding between Ed and his manager?

4. How would you suggest that Ed repair the damage done by his absence from the company banquet? What might he say to his manager? How could he use *I*-language, indexing, and dual perspective to guide his communication?

5. Do you think the banquet is a ritual? Why or why not?

13

> Reality is wrong.
> Dreams are for real.
>
> **Tupac Shakur**

age fotostock/SuperStock

Media and Media Literacy

On April 16, 2007, at Virginia Tech, Cho Seung-Hui gunned down 32 people, most of whom were students. By mid-morning, when the massacre ended, television crews were on site and filming. For the rest of that day, coverage of the killings at Virginia Tech dominated television programming. As soon as the news broke, students on my campus started contacting friends at Virginia Tech via cell phone and IM to make sure they were okay (most were), and they went to blogs to discuss the incident. Just 1 day later, on April 17, students at Virginia Tech began posting memorials to slain classmates on MySpace and other social networking sites. A video that Cho had sent to national television stations was aired on television. Starting on April 16 and continuing for several weeks, I called and texted with colleagues around the

SHARPEN YOUR SKILL

At the end of this chapter, refer to the Sharpen Your Skill features, Media Literacy in Action and Detecting Dominant Values in Media, to apply concepts from Chapter 13.

country as we tried to understand how such senseless killing could be part of campus life.

Mass media and social media allowed people who were separated in time and space to connect quickly. We relied on media to get news about the tragedy. At least as important, we relied on media to plug us into our networks and virtual communities.

People today are, in fact, the most media saturated and media engaged in history (Kung-Shankleman, Towse, & Picard, 2007). How does our intense engagement with media affect our lives? How do we use media to develop and negotiate identity, participate in relationships, and form opinions and perspectives? These are questions we'll consider in this chapter. We'll begin by defining and distinguishing between mass media and social media. Next, we'll explore how mass media and social media affect our lives. The last part of this chapter focuses on media literacy, a critical skill in our era.

THE NATURE AND SCOPE OF MEDIA

Media is a broad term that includes both mass media and social media. In this section, we define and distinguish between mass media and social media and explore their prevalence in our lives.

Defining Mass Media and Social Media

Mass media are electronic or mechanical channels of delivering one-to-many communication—in other words, the means of transmitting messages to large audiences. Mass media broadcast messages to a large group of people who generally are not in direct contact with the source of the messages. Mass media include television, newspapers, magazines, radios, books, and so forth. Television programs such as *Desperate Housewives*, *The Oprah Show*, *American Idol*, and *Queer Eye for the Straight Guy* attract millions of viewers; mass-mailed advertisements reach millions of people each week; millions of people rely on newspapers and the web for daily news updates. Each of these media reaches a mass audience.

Social media are means of connecting and interacting actively. In other words, as Mark Nunes (2006) puts it, "technology produces social space" (p. xx). Allison Fine (2006), author of *Momentum: Igniting Social Change in the Connected Age*, explains: "Combine the intimacy of the telephone with the reach of broadcast media and you have social media, the collection of tools used to connect people to one another" (p. xvi). Social media include cell phones, email, PDA, iPods, MP3s, the web, and other tools that allow us to interact actively, collaborate, and participate in self-organizing, fluid communities. Personal and social media are seamlessly integrated into our routines and identities (Bohil, Owen, Jeong, Alicea, & Bocca, 2009; Potter, 2009).

The primary difference between mass media and social media is digitalization. Three key implications of digitization are ease of manipulation, convergence, and nearly instant speed (Steele, 2009; Turow, 2008). Manipulation is not new; it was possible with analog film and video and film photography. For instance, a photo could be retouched and video could be edited. However,

COMMUNICATION in Your Life

In an average day, how many text messages do you send?

COMMUNICATION HIGHLIGHT

Generations Online

Many people think that new technologies are favored far more by younger than older people. That's not what the latest surveys show. Consider these findings (Jones & Fox, 2009):

- Between 2005 and 2008, 70- to 75-year-olds increased Internet usage more than any other group (26% used the Internet in 2005; 45% did in 2008).
- 80% of 33- to 44-year-olds shop online.
- Both teens and people aged 18 to 32 go online for videos, games, virtual worlds, and music downloads.
- 67% of 33- to 44-year-olds bank online.

manipulating analog media took a high level of skill that few people had. In contrast, most people who have grown up using digital media know how to manipulate them—for instance, using Photoshop's clone stamping and despeckle filter allow a person to alter a photo. The line that divided production and consumption of media in the analog era is blurred, if not erased in the digital era.

Digital media also cultivate convergence. Just a few years ago, it was very difficult and expensive to have a voice-over Internet phone call. Today, soldiers in Iraq routinely have voice-over Internet phone conversations with family members. This is possible because the technology for transmitting sound and the technology for transmitting visual images are both digital and, thus, they can be managed on a single network.

The third feature of digital media is nearly instant speed. The speed of information dissemination jeopardizes accuracy. Rayford Steele (2009), who studies digital media, points out that "in a world of instant access where everyone can be published or viewed, the time pressure and the volume increase make careful vetting that much harder" (p. 494).

RICH *Before I became a full-time student here, I took three online courses. It was great to be able to do the classes at home when I could make time. But the content of the class was only part of the experience. What I really loved was talking with other students who were also taking the class online. We set up discussion boards, and some of us put each other on our IM lists so we could talk even when we weren't on the course site. I really loved the interaction with other students.*

But the lines between social and mass media are not really clear cut. For instance, if you send a video to a friend who then posts it on YouTube, have you engaged in personal communication or mass communication or both? Stanley Baran and Dennis Davis (2003) believe it is more appropriate to think of media as a continuum that ranges from clearly interpersonal, or social, to clearly mass, with a lot of in-between media between those two extreme ends (Figure 13.1).

Interpersonal   **Mass**   **FIGURE 13.1**
                                                                                             The Media Continuum

Telephone and Cell   IM   PDA   Email   Listservs   MySpace   Blogs   YouTube   TV

UNDERSTANDING HOW MEDIA WORK

How do mass media and social media work? How do they affect our lives? In this section of the chapter, we'll first consider the ways we use mass media and ways they affect us. Then we'll explore the ways in which social media shape our lives.

Understanding Mass Media

Researchers have spent decades studying and theorizing about mass media. From their work, we can identify four key ways in which mass media influence—or *attempt* to influence—our lives.

Mass Media Provide Gratification   Think about the last time you went to a film. Did you go because the story mattered to you? Were you using the movie to escape from problems and worries? Did you attend because it featured stars you like? According to **uses and gratification theory**, we choose to attend to mass communication to gratify ourselves (Reinhard & Dervin, 2009). If you are bored and want excitement, you might watch an action film, whereas if you are stressed and want some lighthearted diversion, perhaps you choose a comedy or fantasy film. If you are interested in national affairs, you might most often listen to National Public Radio. If you are concerned that a game may be rained out, you might tune in to the Weather Channel. Uses and gratification theory says we use mass media to fulfill our needs and desires.

This theory assumes that people are active agents who make deliberate choices among media to gratify themselves. We use media to gain information, to alleviate loneliness, to divert us from problems, and so forth. In other

COMMUNICATION HIGHLIGHT

Burkas and BlackBerrys

In 1999, the ruler of Kuwait declared that women would have full political power, including the right to vote. Yet nothing changed—Kuwaiti women still didn't have political rights because the legislature had not passed legislation to enact the Sheikh's decree. But that changed in 2005. In May of that year, the Kuwaiti legislature passed legislation that gave women the right to vote and the right to hold elected office. What changed? While the legislature was meeting, women across Kuwait pulled out their BlackBerrys and cell phones, which they kept inside their burkas, to inundate legislators with messages encouraging them to vote for women's rights. The women in this tiny Arab country used social media to make social change happen!

Adapted from: Fine, A. (2006). *Momentum: Igniting Social Change in the Connected Age*. San Francisco: Jossey-Bass.

words, uses and gratification theory assumes that people exercise control over their interaction with mediated mass communication. As we look at the next theory, we'll see that not everyone agrees that people are active, deliberate consumers of mass communication.

Mass Media Set Agendas Mass media spotlight some issues, events, and people and downplay others. This affects our perceptions of what is (and is not) happening in the world and what is (and is not) important. **Agenda setting** is selecting and calling to the public's attention ideas, events, and people (Agee, Ault, & Emery, 1996; Bryant & Oliver, 2008; McCombs, Ghanem, & Chernov, 2009; Robinson, 2009).

Mass media exercise considerable control over the events, people, and issues that reach public consciousness (McCombs et al., 2009). For instance, television and newspaper reports make us aware of the sexual activities (real or rumored) of public figures, especially politicians. Historical accounts have documented the extramarital sexual activities of many past presidents, but at the time, those activities were not put on the public agenda. In our era, mass media call the sexual lives of public figures to our attention, making us more aware of this issue than the public was in previous times. Mass media also give prominence to celebrities; anyone who reads a newspaper or watches television news gets the latest updates on Paris Hilton's antics, real or suspected steroid use by athletes, and Britney Spears's activities.

Within agenda-setting theory, the **gatekeeper** is a key concept. A gatekeeper is a person or group who decides which messages pass through the gates of media to reach consumers. Gatekeepers are people who manage mass media—producers, editors, webmasters, and so forth. Gatekeepers screen messages, stories, and perspectives to create messages (i.e., programs, interviews, articles) and to shape our perceptions of what is happening and what is and is not significant. Which stories make the front page of a newspaper, and which are placed on a back page of Section C? Which stories get prime coverage in online newspapers such as *The Huffington Post*? Which stories lead nightly television news broadcasts, which are appended to the end of the program, and which are not covered at all? Which stories are the cover stories for such national magazines as *Newsweek* and *U.S. News & World Report*? When a controversial issue is covered, do spokespeople for all sides get equal time or space to present their points of view, or are spokespeople for some points of view given more or all of the time or space devoted to the story? Each of these gatekeeping decisions shapes what we perceive to be significant and the information to which we do and do not have access. The media have many gatekeepers:

Jochen Tack/imagebroker.net/PhotoLibrary

Social media allow ongoing contact with others.

- Reporters and program hosts decide whose perspectives on a story to present and whose to ignore.

- Editors of newspapers, books, and magazines screen the information that gets to readers and decide where to place stories and other material.

- Owners, executives, and producers filter information for radio and television programs.

- Government agencies may put pressure on the press and television and radio stations not to broadcast certain information.

- Advertisers and political groups may influence which messages get through.

There is evidence of racial bias in media accounts of crime stories. According to some media scholars (Devereux, 2007; Dixon, 2006; Dixon, Azocar, & Casas, 2003), newspapers and television programs present minority citizens as violent criminals more often than they present European Americans as violent criminals and more often than they present minorities in positive stories. This pattern may lead us to inaccurate perceptions of the extent to which members of different races perpetrate violent crimes. Latino and Latina actors are underrepresented in commercial programming. When Latina and Latino actors do appear, often they are typically portrayed as low-level workers, criminals, or other undesirable characters. Latino and Latina actors who are presented positively usually appear to have assimilated into mainstream white culture, and their racial and ethnic heritage is seldom evident in story lines.

Historically, gays and lesbians have been virtually invisible in mass media. One interesting change in commercial programming is the increased presence of gays and lesbians who are portrayed positively in prime-time shows and major films. In *Philadelphia*, Tom Hanks gave a compelling and positive portrayal of a gay man. Other films such as *As Good as It Gets*, *Midnight in the Garden of Good and Evil*, and *Brokeback Mountain* prominently featured characters who demonstrated the complexity and humanity of gays and lesbians. Since Ellen DeGeneres came out on her television program, *Ellen*, in 1997, more gay and lesbian characters have been included and sometimes featured as lead characters in popular television programs. *Will & Grace* and *Queer Eye for the Straight Guy* (a runaway success with viewers of all sexual orientations) are two good examples.

Mass Media Cultivate Worldviews Cultivation theory claims that television promotes a worldview that is inaccurate but that viewers nonetheless assume reflects real life. This theory is concerned exclusively with the medium of television, which it claims creates a synthetic reality that shapes heavy viewers' perspectives and beliefs about the world (Gerbner, 1990; Shanahan & Jones, 1999; Signorielli, 2009).

Many Americans rely on nightly news programs, even satirical ones, to understand major issues and events.

Cultivation is the cumulative process by which television shapes beliefs about social reality. According to the theory, television fosters particular and often unrealistic understandings of the world as more violent and dangerous than statistics on actual violence show it is. Thus, goes the reasoning, watching television promotes distorted views of life. The word *cumulative* is important to understanding cultivation. Researchers don't argue that a particular program has a significant effect on viewers' beliefs. However, they claim that watching a lot of television over a long period of time affects viewers' overall views of the world. By extension, the theory claims that the more television people watch, the more distorted their views of the world are likely to be. Simply put, the theory claims that television cumulatively cultivates a synthetic worldview that heavy viewers are likely to assume represents reality.

Cultivation theorists identify two means by which cultivation occurs: *mainstreaming* and *resonance*. **Mainstreaming** is a process by which mass communication stabilizes and homogenizes social perspectives. For example, if commercial programming consistently portrays Hispanics as unambitious, African Americans as criminals and uneducated, and European Americans as upstanding citizens, viewers may come to accept these representations as factual (Dixon, 2006). If television programs, from Saturday morning cartoons to prime-time dramas, feature extensive violence, viewers may come to believe that violence is common. As they interact with others, heavy viewers communicate their attitudes and thus affect the attitudes of others who watch little or no television.

The world of television teems with violence. Media scholar Glenn Sparks (2006) reports that nearly 60% of all television programs include violence. This raises particular concerns about young children, who are particularly heavy viewers of television. By the age of 6, the average child in the United States has watched 5,000 hours of television; by the age of 18, the average person has watched 19,000 hours and seen 100,000 acts of violence, including 40,000 murders (Kirsh, 2006; Palmer & Young, 2003; Valkenburg, 2004). To read a study of violence on children's TV, use your Online Resources for *Communication in Our Lives* to access **WebLink 13.1.**

CourseMate

The second explanation for television's capacity to cultivate worldviews is **resonance**, the extent to which media representations are congruent with personal experience. For instance, a person who has been robbed or assaulted is likely to identify with televised violence when watching shows that feature it. When media representations correspond with our personal experiences, we are more likely to assume that they accurately represent the world in general.

KELLY   *I didn't think much about sex and violence on TV until my daughter was old enough to watch. When she was 4, I found her watching an MTV program that was absolutely pornographic. What does seeing that do to the mind of a 4-year-old girl? We don't let her watch TV now unless we can monitor what she sees.*

The high incidence of violence in news programming reflects in part the fact that the abnormal is more newsworthy than the normal. It isn't news that 99.9% of couples are either getting along or working out their problems in nonviolent ways; it was news when Lorena Bobbitt amputated her husband's penis and when O.J. Simpson's wife was murdered. It isn't news that most of us grumble about big government but refrain from violent protest; it is news when someone blows up the federal building in Oklahoma City and cites dissatisfaction with big government as a motive. Simply put, violence is news.

Perhaps you are thinking that few people confuse what they see on television with real life. Research shows that this may not be the case. Children who watch a lot of violence on television tend to be less sensitive to actual violence than children who do watch less (Sparks, 2006). It's also the case that children who watch a lot of television violence score higher on measures of personal aggression than children who watch less television violence (Huesmann, Moise-Titus, Podolski, & Eron, 2003).

Mass media also cultivate unrealistic views of romantic relationships. MTV programming strongly emphasizes eroticism and sublime sex, and people who watch a lot of MTV have been shown to have higher expectations for sexual perfection in their relationships (Shapiro & Kroeger, 1991). A related finding is that people who read a lot of self-help books tend to have less realistic views of relationships than people who read few or no self-help guides. Investigations have also shown that both males and females who watch sexually violent MTV are more likely to regard sexual violence as normal in relationships (Dieter, 1989; Weimann, 2000).

KASHETA   *To earn money, I babysit two little boys four days a week. One day they got into a fight, and I broke it up. When I told them that physical violence isn't a good way to solve problems, they reeled off a list of TV characters that beat up on each other. Another day, one of them referred to the little girl next door as a "ho." When I asked why he called her that, he started singing the lyrics from an MTV video he'd been watching. In that video women were called "hos." It's scary what kids absorb.*

Mass Media Exercise Ideological Control

Critical media scholars focus on identifying and challenging the ways that media function as tools that represent the dominant ideology as normal and right (Hesmondhaigh, 2007; Potter, 2001). In other words, critical media scholars study how cultural elites use media to maintain their dominant positions and to advance their interests (Baran & Davis, 2003). Because individuals and groups that have benefited from the existing social structure tend to control mass media, they have a vested interest in promoting their own views and values as normal and right. Thus, it is unsurprising that mass media are more likely to portray white men as good, powerful, and successful than it is to describe white women or minority men or women in those ways.

Francois Duhamel/©Weinstein Company/Everett Collection

The prevalence of violence in mass media programs and movies can make the world seem more violent than it is.

Mass media are particularly powerful in representing the ideology of privileged groups as natural and good (Hall, 1986; McChesney, 2004, 2008). Television programs, from children's shows to prime-time news, represent white, heterosexual, able-bodied males as the norm in the United States, although they are actually not the majority. Magazine covers and ads, as well as billboards, portray young, able-bodied, attractive white people as the norm. Minorities continue to be portrayed most often as criminals, victims, subordinates, or otherwise less-than-respectable people (Dixon, 2006; Dixon, et al., 2003).

Think about the ways in which mass media tend to represent social movements. When college students protested the Communist government in China at Tiananmen Square, they were portrayed as "heroes of democracy," but when people protested the World Trade Organization in Seattle, Washington, they were portrayed as "extremists" and "radical anarchists" (Baran & Davis, 2003, p. 226; FAIR, 2000). In the first case, the protesters' views were consistent with elites who control media; in the second case, the protesters' views challenged elite interests.

We've considered four theories that offer insight into how mass media affect us. Probably each view has some validity. Surely, we make some fairly conscious choices about how to use mass media, as uses and gratification theory claims. At the same time, mass media probably influence us in ways we don't notice, as agenda setting and cultivation theories assert. And critical scholars probably are correct in describing mass media as a conservative force that supports dominant ideologies.

Understanding Social Media

Theories that emphasize mass media's ability to set agenda, cultivate worldviews, and maintain ideological control do not easily apply to social media. There is no mainstream view that dominates the web; there is no single form of music or broadcast that people load onto iPods; there is not one privileged group that controls content on the Internet or blogs.

Yet one theory about mass media, uses and gratification theory, does seem applicable to social media. In fact, social media offer us considerably more options for gratifying ourselves than mass media do. With social media, we have nearly infinite choices for pleasure, information, conversation, collaboration, and the like. We can load our iPods with the songs and podcasts that we like, put people we like on our IM lists, and participate in communities that gratify our various needs and desires. Blogs open up new possibilities for interacting and building community.

SKINNYGIRL   *Skinnygirl was the name I used when I belonged to a pro-ana blog. When I was anorexic I couldn't get any support or understanding from my family or ftf friends. It was only when I joined the pro-ana blog that I found people who were like me and who accepted me as I was. A lot of people say pro-ana sites are bad because they encourage girls to be unhealthy, but that's not true. The one I belonged to gave me support when I was anorexic and also when I decided I wanted to get better. It was a safe space to work out who I was and to evolve at my own pace.*

Five characteristics of social media help us understand how they fit into our lives and how they may change those lives.

Social Media Blur Production and Consumption   Unlike mass media, social media are increasingly produced and consumed by the same people, and most of them are not media executives. Rather, they are ordinary people who get to know social media by participating in their actual construction. Media scholar Henry Jenkins (2006, 2007) observes that production and consumption are not rigidly separated in social media. Rather, the lines between them have become blurred as people create personal blogs and podcasts, record their daily activities on LiveJournal, and post videos they've made on YouTube. The popularity of these sites suggests that the blurring of media production and consumption is widely embraced.

Today many people, particularly teens, learn how media work is by making media themselves. Jenkins says that young people today figure out how social media work by "taking their culture apart and remixing it" (2007, p. B10). Jenkins goes on to point out that those who think about and theorize media are also integrating theory and practice. This is a departure from the past. Think about the theories of mass media that we've just discussed. These theories were developed by scholars who have limited, if any, experience in actually producing media. But many of the people who are theorizing social media are engaging in producing what they theorize. As a result of this integration, we may see media theories that are more grounded in the everyday experiences and inclinations of nonacademics.

COMMUNICATION in Your Life

To what extent are you engaged in media production?

Social Media Alter Conceptions of Space   Social media change how we create and participate in communities by redefining our sense of space. Prior to the invention of computers, we understood space as something that was abstract, an inert container—"an emptiness awaiting objects" (Nunes, 2006, p. 22). We viewed space as distinct from the people, objects, and events that happened within it. It was something we could enter, send messages through, and put things into. It was something that existed independent of our actions.

Prominent media scholars (Hillis, 1999, 2006, in press; Lefebvre, 1994, 2003; Nunes, 2006), however, challenge that view of space. They argue that cyberspace ushers in new

Jose Luis Pelaez Inc/Blend Images/Jupiter Images

The line between producers and consumers of media has become blurred as an increasing number of people are both.

RESEARCH IN OUR LIVES

Sex and Second Life

We often hear that cyberspace allows people freedom to express themselves in unique ways and, specifically, that gender and sexual identities are less stereotyped in cyberspace than in offline life. At the same time, we also know that many online games rely on the most traditional stereotypes, particularly those that objectify women. Communication scholars Robert Brookey and Kristopher Cannon decided to conduct a case study of the norms for gender expression in one online community, Second Life.

Although Second Life is like many massive multiplayer online role-play games, it differs from them in key ways: Second Life doesn't specify clear goals and it allows—even encourages—players to alter the environment of the game by constructing buildings, creating clothing, and so forth.

Brookey and Cannon's in-depth analysis of Second Life led them to conclude that although the Second Life suggests users have nearly boundless choices for constructing their online identities, there are actually fairly strong constraints on how players can create identities. For instance, a player constructs an avatar by using the appearance editor provided by Second Life. Your options for avatars are limited to those that the editor allows. Players are also told they can select their own clothes, but they may do so only at stores created by Second Life. As Brookey and Cannon point out, "Many of the stores in SL offer clothing, swimwear and lingerie which accentuate feminine sexual attractiveness" (p. 150). Players may shop in stores that offer clothing and other supplies related to sexual fetishes and may see clothes modeled by the Post 6 Grrls who pose for pictures nude or provocatively dressed.

Although Brookey and Cannon concluded that Second Life is highly sexist, they also point out that there are challenges to this ideology. An art installation that provides a critical look at Second Life's objectification of women was positively reviewed in *The Second Life Herald*.

They concluded their article with this statement: "While SL may appear new and exciting, where gender and sexuality are concerned, too often it is the same old game" (p. 160).

Should sexism and other attitudes (for instance, homophobia, racism) be regulated in online communities or should they operate as members like?

Robert Brookey is an Associate Professor in the Department of Communication at Northern Illinois University, Kristopher Cannon is a doctoral student in the Department of Communication at Georgia State University. This research appeared in a 2009 article titled "Sex lives in Second Life" in *Critical Studies in Media Communication*, volume 26, pages 145–164.

understandings of space as a set of relations that is produced through the process of interacting. Rather than an empty container, cyberspace is a fluid, emergent process of connecting that grows out of interactions, not merely the context in which they occur. Cyberspace is social space in which dynamic actions and interactions actually constitute the environment. In other words, cyberspace is not something that exists prior to our interactions. It is not "out there" awaiting us. Instead, it comes into being only as a result of what we do. It is what we do in cyberspace that defines space—the space is produced by what we do.

Consider how we produce the spaces (and the possibilities of relations) in which we interact online. A blog, for instance, is created by bloggers. If some of the original bloggers leave and new ones participate, the blog itself—that cyberspace world—will change. When you set up a buddy list or list of IM members, you produce a set of relations, a community, that exists until and unless you delete or add names. Once you do that, you produce a different community—a different cyberspace that reflects the interactions and lived experience that now take place and that serve to establish new sets of relations.

This view of space exemplifies the blur between production and consumption that we just discussed because the space that we are in (e.g., a blog) is produced—brought into being—by what we do in that space. Cyberspaces are emergent and fluid, continuously open to change and reconfiguration as a result of the dynamic interactions of those who simultaneously inhabit and produce them. As Nunes (2006) explains, "[C]yberspace is not where these relations take place, it is the *'where' enacted by these relations*" (p. 28).

COMMUNICATION HIGHLIGHT

Video Résumés

Ten years ago, a person submitted a written résumé when he or she was applying for a job. Today, job seekers are as likely to prepare video résumés. Many employers now welcome these, and some require them from job applicants. Online services such as WorkBlast.com and ResumeBook.tv have sprung up to prepare video résumés, but not everyone needs a service. Increasingly, people are preparing their own video résumés, sometimes posting them on sites such as YouTube and emailing links to potential employers.

If you are thinking about preparing a video résumé, here are a few tips (Jesdanun, 2007):

1. Don't include unprofessional email addresses. Many students have email addresses that are "cool" among their friends but that would quickly turn off potential employers.
2. Keep the video professional. It's not an audition for *American Idol.* One job seeker showed himself lifting weights, playing tennis, and skiing. None of that established his qualifications for the job he was seeking in investment banking!
3. Don't be too casual. In the video, you should look like someone who belongs in the position for which you are applying—let that guide your choices of dress, speech, and nonverbal behaviors.

Social Media Invite Supersaturation   Today's social media give us unprecedented access to information. Media scholar Todd Gitlin (2005) refers to the never-ending flow of information as a "media torrent" that leads to supersaturation. We are saturated with information; at times we may feel overwhelmed by information overload. The sheer amount of information we receive can cause stress and confusion.

But it's not just information that saturates us—it's also people. Social media allow us nearly instant contact with other people. At the same time, these media give others greater access to us than ever before. Jane Brown and Joanne Cantor (2000) use the term *perpetual linkage* to refer to the state of continuous connection to others.

Maybe we should take a lesson from tech-savvy David Levy, a professor of information and the man in charge of planning the Center for Information and the Quality of Life. If anyone knows social technologies, it's David Levy. And Levy knows when to log off. Each week, he takes a full day off from technology—computers, cells, PDAs, every type of social media (Young, 2005). He thinks doing this is important to keeping himself balanced and making sure that he controls the media in his life rather than allowing them to control him.

JORDANN   *I really love my cell and my IM buddies—most of the time. But sometimes I want to be totally away from others, and that's really hard when everyone knows how to reach me 24-7. I know I can choose not to answer my cell or an IM, but I feel almost pressured to answer because everyone expects to be able to get me, and they'd be worried or hurt if I didn't answer. Being in touch sometimes feels like I can't ever be out of touch.*

COMMUNICATION HIGHLIGHT

Everyware Is Everywhere

How would you like it if your refrigerator told you when your milk had turned bad or when you were running low on cereal? How about a bathtub that alerts you in another room when the water is at the temperature you like? Or maybe you'd like floors that can detect a fall and call emergency services, or detect an intruder and alert you. These and more products will soon be available (Foster, 2007). They are part of a future defined by "ubiquitous computing."

Before you celebrate a refrigerator that keeps better track of your food than you do, you may want to recognize other ways in which ubiquitous computing—or *everyware*—may find its way into our lives. Radio frequency identification (RFID) tags can be put in cars, on knapsacks, or on people so that parents can know where children are at any moment and employers can keep track of employees. Adam Greenfield, who teaches a course in urban computing at New York University, warns that the development of everyware means that nearly every aspect of our lives is open to scrutiny, surveillance, and manipulation—by marketers, among others. In his book, *Everyware: The Dawning Age of Ubiquitous Computing* (2006), Greenfield argues that we need to weigh the convenience offered by technology against the losses of privacy and personal autonomy.

Social Media Encourage Multitasking Multitasking is doing multiple tasks at the same time or in rapid sequence. During classes, students often take notes while also sending and receiving email and checking favorite websites. When online, many people play games or visit blogs while also sending and responding to IMs. Many people also study while listening to iPods and visiting friends on Facebook. A recent report from the Kaiser Foundation found that 65% of the time, students who are studying are also doing something else (Aratani, 2007).

Actually, social media may encourage multitasking, but we don't actually do it. Despite widespread acceptance of the term *multitasking*, people do not really do multiple tasks at once. Neither do computers, for that matter—they do one task at a time; they just do each one very, very quickly. A slow computer can implement a million instructions in less than a second (Harmon, 2002), but it executes each one individually, in sequence. What about humans? Can we multitask? Neuroscientist Jordan Grafman says that people who try to do multiple tasks simultaneously tend to do all of them superficially (Aratani, 2007). This may explain why one former Microsoft and Apple executive refers to multitasking as "continuous partial attention" (Levy, 2006). There's also evidence that people

AP Photo/The Elyria Chronicle Telegram, Chuck Humel

Some media scholars believe that multitasking leads to partial attention and superficial learning.

COMMUNICATION HIGHLIGHT

Do u txt whl drvng?

Perhaps the only thing more popular than cell phones is arguments about whether using them distracts drivers. At first, those who want to talk while driving argued that talking on a cell was no different than talking to a passenger. Once that argument was discredited, the new defense was that it was safe to drive and talk if you used a hands-free cell. Now that argument has also collapsed. Substantial research demonstrates that talking on phones—hands-free or not—while driving is dangerous. The problem isn't that "your hands aren't on the wheel. It's that your mind isn't on the road" (Parker-Pope, 2009a, p. D5). Researchers tested drivers' concentration when talking on a hands-free phone, talking with other passengers, and listening to radio or audio books. The results were clear-cut: Phone conversations are more distracting than any of the other activities. Accident statistics bear this out: drivers talking on cells are four times as likely to have an accident as drivers who are not talking on cells. That's the same level of risk—four times—as driving while legally drunk.

who attempt to do several things at once make more mistakes and actually take longer than people who do one task at a time (Guterl, 2003).

Social Media Promote Visual Thinking Many of the media, both mass and social, that have become routine parts of our lives are highly visual, and consumers have pushed them to become more and more visual. When personal computers were first widely available in the late 1970s and early 1980s, monitors displayed content in black and white. Today, nearly all displays are in color because consumers want the visual stimulation. The first cell phones were like their land-line counterparts: tools for exchanging audio messages. Today, cameras and screens for text messages are standard on cell phones. Computers were developed as information tools, but quickly computer games were created. From the start, the games were highly visual, and they have become ever more so.

The continuously shifting images in computer games and other programs, as well as pop-up ads and IM announcements, shape our neural maps so that we grow to expect a steady diet of visual stimulation. Some media scholars (Guterl, 2003; Tufte, 2003) suggest that heavy use of social media may train people to have short attention spans and to be easily distracted by new visual stimuli that appear on screens.

There is a second way in which constant visual stimulation affects how we think. The right lobe of the brain specializes in parallel processing and spatial and visual tasks, whereas the left lobe specializes in sequential thought and analytic thinking. The highly visual nature of social media stimulates the right side of the brain (so does television) and cultivates development of that side. Given this, we should not be surprised to learn that children who are heavy computer users often have difficulty with tasks that require analytic thinking (Guterl, 2003).

Social media affect our lives in profound ways. According to prominent media scholars, they blur the traditional distinction between those who produce and those who consume media, alter our understanding of space, invite supersaturation, encourage multitasking, and promote visual activity and development. As social media become even more seamlessly woven into our lives, we may discover additional ways they influence our lives.

DEVELOPING MEDIA LITERACY

Because media, both mass and social, pervade our lives, we need to be responsible and thoughtful about how we use them—and how they use us. This requires us to develop **media literacy**, which is the ability to understand the influence of mass media and to access, analyze, evaluate, and respond actively to mass media in informed, critical ways. Figure 13.2 shows the components of media literacy. Just as it takes work to become literate in written and oral communication, it takes effort to develop literacy in interacting with media. Instead of passively absorbing media, you should cultivate your abilities to access, analyze, evaluate, and respond thoughtfully to media. How literate you become, however, depends on the extent to which you work to develop and apply critical skills.

Understand the Influence of Media

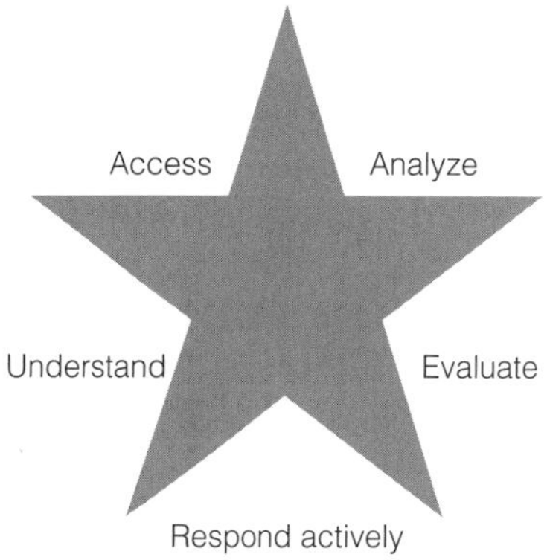

Media literacy begins with determining the extent to which social and mass media influence us. Do they determine individual attitudes and social perspectives, or are they two of many influences on individual attitudes and social perspectives? The first view is both naive and overstated. It obscures the complex, multiple influences on how we think as individuals and how we organize social life. It also assumes that media are linear—that we passively receive whatever mass media's gatekeepers send us and that we don't exercise thought as we engage social media.

The second view represents a thoughtful, qualified assessment of the influence of media and our ability to exercise control over their effects. Media, individuals, and society interact in complex ways. We are not unthinking sponges that absorb whatever is poured on us. Instead, we can interact thoughtfully and critically with media to mediate their impact on us and our assent—or resistance—to how they affect our identities and what they encourage us to believe, think, feel, and do.

If we choose to interact thoughtfully with media to control their impact on us and society, then we embrace questions about access to media and deliberate choices of how to engage them.

Access   Analyze

Understand   Evaluate

Respond actively

Figure 13.2
The Components of Media Literacy

Access to Media

Access is the capacity to own and use televisions, radios, computers, cell phones, and so forth. You may be thinking that access is not an issue. After all, you probably have a television, radio, and computer (among other products that allow you to access mass communication), and you know how to use them. But not everyone does.

Democratic Access   People do not have equal access to media. Existing social divisions will increase if some people have better access than others to new technologies (Nunes, 2006). Some media scholars (Doyle, 2008; McChesney, 2008; van Dijk, 2005) believe that an information elite already exists because access to media, especially social media, requires both knowledge and resources that not everyone has.

The term **digital divide** refers to the gap between people and communities with access to media, especially social media, and people and communities with less or no access. As citizens, workers, and voters, we have an ethical responsibility to identify, and work to realize, the potential of media to enrich us as individuals and as members of a common world. If access to new and converging technologies is limited to individuals and groups that are already privileged by their social, professional, and economic status, we will see an increasing chasm between the haves and the have-nots. In the short run, it would be expensive to provide access and training for people who cannot afford to purchase it for themselves. In the long run, however, it might be far less costly than the problems of a society in which a small technology elite is privileged and many citizens are excluded from full participation.

People who can afford the newest technology will be the first to own multiple computerized devices, some of which will soon be connected to each other (e.g. when your computerized alarm clock rings, your computerized coffee maker will start) and all of which will be linked to the Internet (e.g. the Internet will automatically reset your alarm clock and all other timing devices when you go on and off daylight savings time or after a power outage).

But a huge question remains: Who will have access to converging technologies, and who will not? If access is based on wealth, **convergence**—the integration of mass media, computers, and telecommunications—will increase the divide between haves and have-nots.

COMMUNICATION HIGHLIGHT

The Digital Divide

When communication technologies first gained widespread popularity, some critics and scholars worried about what they called "the digital divide," a term for the gap between people and communities that do and do not have access to technologies. As the costs of technologies and linking systems such as cable have declined, concern over the digital divide has lessened. Yet, recent data (Jones & Fox, 2009) indicate that access is not uniform. If we consider just Internet use, we see significant differences among groups:

Group	Percentage using Internet
Women	73
Men	73
18–29 year olds	90
30–40 year olds	85
50–64 year olds	70
65+ year olds	35
White, non-Hispanic	75
Black, non-Hispanic	59
English-speaking Hispanic	80
Less than $30,000 income	53
$50,000–$74,999 income	85
More than $75,000 income	95
Did not complete high school	44
Completed high school	63
Completed college	91

The full reports from which the above findings came are available via **WebLink 13.2**, which you can access through your Online Resources for *Communication in Our Lives*.

Expose Yourself to a Range of Media Sources In addition to the issue of democratic access to mass communication, each of us faces a personal challenge in deciding which media to access. Many people limit their exposure, choosing to access only media that support the views they already hold. For instance, if you are conservative politically, you might visit politically conservative blogs and listen to conservative radio and television programs. The problem with that is that you don't expose yourself to criticisms of conservative policies and stances, and you don't give yourself the opportunity to learn about more liberal policies and positions. The same is true if you are politically liberal—you cannot be fully informed if you engage only media that have liberal leanings. If you listen only to popular music, you'll never learn to understand, much less appreciate, classical music, jazz, or reggae. You cannot be truly informed about any issue unless you deliberately expose yourself to multiple, and even conflicting, sources of information and perspectives.

Exposing yourself to multiple media also means attending to more than entertainment. Television focuses primarily on entertainment, trends, and celebrities and officials in popular culture. One study of children ages 9 to 12 found that 98% of respondents knew who Michael Jordan was, but only 21% knew the names of leaders of major countries ("Names and Faces," 1997). Tuning into celebrity culture is not sufficient for media literacy. So the access component of media literacy includes both the ability to access media and the choice to expose yourself to varied sources of information, opinion, and perspective.

> **COMMUNICATION in Your Life**
>
> **How often do you engage media that do not support your perspectives?**

Analyze Media

When we are able to analyze something, we understand how it works. If you aren't aware of the grammatical structure and rules of the English language, you can't write, read, or speak English effectively. If you are unaware of the patterns that make up basketball, you will not be able to understand what happens in a game. In the same way, if you don't understand patterns in media, you can't understand fully how music, blogrings, advertising, programming, and so forth work. Learning to recognize patterns in media empowers you to engage media in critical and sophisticated ways.

James Potter (2009) points out that there are a few standard patterns that media use repeatedly. Most stories, whether in print, film, or television, open with some problem or conflict that progresses until it climaxes in final dramatic scenes. Romance stories typically follow a pattern in which we meet a main character who has suffered a bad relationship or has not had a serious relationship. The romance pattern progresses through meeting Mr. or Ms. Right, encountering complications or problems, resolving the problems, and living happily ever after (Riggs, 1999).

Just as media follow a few standard patterns for entertainment, they rely on basic patterns for presenting news. There are three distinct but related features by which media construct the news (Potter, 2001).

- Selecting what gets covered: Only a minute portion of human activity is reported in the news. Gatekeepers in the media decide which people and events are newsworthy. By presenting stories on these events and people, the media make them newsworthy.

- Choosing the hook: Reporters and journalists choose how to focus a story, or how to "hook" people into a story. In so doing, they direct people's attention to certain aspects of the story. For example, in a story about a politician accused of sexual misconduct, the focus could be the charges made, the politician's denial, or the increase in sexual misconduct by public figures.

- Choosing how to tell the story: In the aforementioned story, media might tell it in a way that fosters sympathy for the person who claims to have been the target of sexual misconduct (i.e., interviews with the victim, references to other victims of sexual misconduct); or media might tell it in a way that inclines people to be sympathetic toward the politician (i.e., shots of the politician with his or her family, interviews with colleagues who proclaim the politician's innocence). Each way of telling the story encourages people to think and feel distinctly about the story.

Critically Evaluate Media Messages

When interacting with mass communication, you think critically to assess what is presented. Rather than accepting news accounts unquestioningly, you should be thoughtful and skeptical. It's important to ask questions such as these:

- Why is this story getting so much attention? Whose interests are served, and whose are muted?

- What is the source of the statistics and other forms of evidence? Are the sources current? Do the sources have any interest in taking a specific position? (For example, tobacco companies have a vested interest in denying or minimizing the harms of smoking.)

- What's the hook for the story, and what alternative hooks might have been used?

- Are stories balanced so that a range of viewpoints are given voice? For example, in a report on environmental bills pending in Congress, do news reports include statements from the Sierra Club, industry leaders, environmental scientists, and so forth?

- How are different people and viewpoints represented by gatekeepers (e.g., reporters, photographers, experts)?

It's equally important to be critical in interpreting other kinds of mass communication, such as music, magazines, newspapers, and billboards. When listening to a piece of popular music, ask what view of society, relationships, and so forth it portrays, who and what it represents as normal, and what views of women and men it fosters. Raise the same questions about the images in magazines and on billboards. When considering an ad, ask whether it offers meaningful evidence or merely puffery. Asking questions such as these allows you to be critical and careful in assessing what mass communication presents to you.

You should also keep a critical eye on online "news" and, more generally, claims. Tim Clydesdale (2009) says claims and reports grounded in fact appear side-by-side with opinions those that have no basis. Communication professor

Rayford Steele (2009) extends this thinking one step further. He believes that newer media tempt people to rely on peer authority rather than expert authority. Many online sites allow postings by anyone; the editor may or may not be vigilant in checking the postings and their accuracy. As a result, the "information" we find online may be flawed or just plain wrong. According to Steele, "the democratization of information can quickly degenerate into an intellectually corrosive radical egalitarianism" (p. 493). Everyone may state opinions, make claims, etc. The problem is that not everyone is equally qualified, and not every opinion is equally well grounded. But if we are distrustful of steadfast authority, as Clydesdale argues, we may treat every opinion as equally valuable. We sacrifice our ability to think independently and to make reasoned judgments about which opinions really are supported and good.

The popular online encyclopedia, Wikipedia, illustrates both the advantages and drawbacks of open-source architecture on the Internet. The good news is that anyone can add, delete, or edit entries in Wikipedia. More than 350,000 people have participated in creating three-quarters of a million articles now on Wikipedia, and more than 14 million people visit the site each day (Fine, 2006).

The bad news is that anyone can add, delete, or edit entries in Wikipedia—yep, in this case, the bad news is the same as the good news. You or I can access Wikipedia and edit entries on cyberspace, baseball, or paragliding, regardless of whether we have any expertise on those topics. Further, someone who particularly admires or dislikes a public figure can edit that person's biography. John Siegenthaler, a journalist and assistant to former attorney general Robert F. Kennedy, found that out the hard way: When he checked his Wikipedia biography, he found it included a number of inaccuracies as well as attacks on his character (Fine, 2006). When anyone can contribute to a site, we need to exercise more than usual critical thinking about what we find on that site.

To practice thinking critically about what you watch on TV for entertainment, complete the activity "Critical Media Literacy" via your Online Resources for *Communication in Our Lives.*

COMMUNICATION HIGHLIGHT

Puffery: The Very Best of Its Kind!

One of the most popular advertising strategies is **puffery,** superlative claims that seem factual but are actually meaningless. For instance, what does it mean to state that a particular juice has "the most natural flavor"? Most natural in comparison to what? Other juices? Other drink products? Who judged it to have the most natural flavor: The corporation that produces it? A random sample of juice drinkers? What is the meaning of an ad that claims a car is "the new benchmark"? Who decided this was the new benchmark? To what is this car being compared? It's not clear from the ad, which is only puffery. And media-literate people don't buy the claim or the product!

Respond Actively

People may respond actively or passively to mass communication and the world-views that it portrays, depending on how media literate they are. If we respond passively, we mindlessly consume messages and the values implicit in them. On the other hand, if we respond actively, we recognize that the worldviews presented in mass communication are not unvarnished truth but partial, subjective perspectives that serve the interests of some individuals and groups while disregarding or misrepresenting the interests of others. Responding actively to mass communication includes choosing consciously how and when to use it, questioning what is presented, and involving yourself in controversies about media, particularly the newer technological forms.

Use Mass Communication Consciously   Do you ever just turn on the TV and watch whatever is on? Do you ever get on the web and spend an hour or more surfing with no particular goal in mind? Do you ever visit MySpace just to update your profile and wind up reading the updates of 15 or more other profiles? If so, you're not making a deliberate choice that allows you to select media to suit your needs and goals. Sophisticated media users realize that media serve many purposes, and they make deliberate choices that serve their goals and needs at particular times. For example, if you feel depressed and want to watch television, it might be better to watch a comedy or action drama than a television movie about personal trauma and pain. If you have used all the money you budgeted for entertainment, don't check out pop-up ads for new CDs.

You can also use media to respond to media. Since the 1970s, the Guerrilla Girls have used media-savvy techniques to critique sexism and racism, particularly in the art world (Köllwitz & Kahlo, 2003). Some organizations now rely on viral email to get their messages out to large numbers of people. A viral email is not a virus that infects a computer; rather, it's an email that is so provocative or interesting that receivers are eager to send it to others, thus getting the message out. People from all walks of life call in to talk radio shows to express their opinions and to challenge those of others. And letters to the editor remain a way for people to respond to newspaper coverage.

Don't succumb to thinking there's nothing you can do to affect media. Believing that we are powerless to control how mass communication affects us can become a self-fulfilling prophecy. Therefore, not recognizing your agency could induce you to yield the degree of control you could have. Each of us can do a great deal on both the personal and the cultural levels (Potter, 2002). To assume an active role in interacting with media, recognize that you are an agent who can affect what happens around you.

COMMUNICATION HIGHLIGHT

Responding Actively

If you want to learn more about gender and media, or if you want to become active in working against media that foster views of violence as normal, girls and women as subordinate, and buying as the route to happiness, visit these websites:

Action Coalition for Media Education: http://www.acmecoalition.org

Center for Media Literacy: http://www.medialit.org

Children Now: http://www.childrennow.org

Media Watch: http://www.mediawatch.com

National Association for Family and Community Education: http://www.nafce.org

TV Parental Guidelines Monitoring Board: http://www.tvguidelines.org

Participate in Decision Making About Media   Responding actively is not just looking out for ourselves personally. It also requires us to become involved in thinking about how media influence social life and how, if at all, media should be regulated. We've already discussed the escalation of violence in media, which can affect how people view violence and its appropriateness. But there are other issues, particularly in the context of the Internet and the web, which reach mass audiences. What guidelines are reasonable? What guidelines infringe on freedom of speech and the press? We need to think carefully about what kinds of regulations we want and how to implement them.

Who should control the Internet and web (Dennis & Merrill, 2006; McGrath, 2002)? In his book *Silent Theft: The Private Plunder of Our Common Wealth*, David Bollier (2002) claims that the Internet belongs to the public and should not be controlled by wealthy, monopolistic companies. Should private companies profit from regulating technologies whose development was supported by public funds? Are private companies correct in their claim that government regulation stifles innovation?

Privacy is a key issue for those interested in regulation of social media. Many online advertisers rely on *cookies*, small electronic packets of information about users that the advertisers store in users' personal browsers. *Spyware* is a means by which a third party (neither you-the-user nor the site you are visiting) tracks your online activity and gains personal information about you. Because spyware is implanted on users' computers, it can monitor a range of online activities in which users engage. Should cookies, spyware, and similar tools be regulated? Should users have the right to control who monitors their online communication and with whom it is shared?

Much of the media, particularly social media, remains unregulated. We have an ethical responsibility to become involved in questions of whether regulations should be developed and, if so, who should develop and implement them.

**COMMUNICATION
in Your Life**

Are you entitled to privacy when using social media?

BEYOND THE CLASSROOM

Let's take the material in this chapter beyond the classroom by thinking about how what you've learned about the media might apply to the workplace, ethical choices, and engagement with the broader world.

1. **Workplace** How have technologies altered the operation of groups in the workplace? Reflect on your own experience or talk with others who have belonged to work groups that operate face-to-face and to work groups that operate virtually. Are the two types of groups equally effective? Do they cultivate equal commitment from group members? Are there particular advantages and disadvantages of each type?

Ethics

2. **Ethics** Increasingly everything from attending school to communicating with co-workers to maintaining ties with friends and family depends on technologies of communication. Does the increasing importance of these technologies mean that we should ensure that everyone has equal access to them? Is there an ethical responsibility to prevent the digital divide?

3. **Engagement** Technologies of communication have vastly increased our ability to learn about and even participate in cultures other than our own. Identify an issue that interests you—the election and voting process, a human rights issue, education—and use technologies such as PDA or computer to learn about that issue in the context of a specific culture other than your own.

CHAPTER SUMMARY

In this chapter, we have examined mass and social media. We've explored ways in which these media influence our lives. They affect what we know and think about the world around us, and they affect how we think and act in our lives, both on- and offline.

The second section of the chapter focused on developing media literacy so that we can be informed, critical, and ethical citizens in a media-saturated world. To be responsible participants in social life, we need to think critically about what is included—and what is made invisible—in mass and social media.

Media-literate people do not accept media messages unthinkingly. Instead, they analyze and evaluate the messages and respond actively by participating thoughtfully in considerations about the extent of regulation of media and the people who should exercise that regulation.

APPLYING COMMUNICATION IN OUR LIVES

The key concepts, For Further Reflection and Discussion questions, and Experiencing Communication in Our Lives case study that follow will help you review, reflect on, and extend the information and ideas presented in this chapter. These resources, and a diverse selection of additional study tools, are also available as Online Resources for *Communication in Our Lives*. Your

Online Resources include CourseMate, a student workbook, interactive video activities, audio study tools, a book companion website, Speech Builder Express, Speech Studio, and InfoTrac College Edition. For more information or to access this book's online resources, visit **www.cengage.com/login.**

KEY CONCEPTS

agenda setting, 298
convergence, 310
cultivation, 300
cultivation theory, 299
digital divide, 309

gatekeeper, 298
mainstreaming, 300
mass media, 295
media literacy, 308
puffery, 313

resonance, 300
social media, 295
uses and gratification theory, 297

FOR FURTHER REFLECTION AND DISCUSSION

1. Would it be ethical to exercise control over the violence presented in media? Do you think viewers, especially children, are harmed by the prevalence of violence in media? If you think there should be some controls, what groups or individuals would you trust to exercise them?

2. Choose "PowerTrac" on your InfoTrac College Edition, then select "Key Word" in the search index. Type "Women and Weight and Magazine Covers." Read the article "Women and Weight: Gendered Messages on Magazine Covers" by Amy Malkin, Kimberlie Wornian, and Joan Chrisler, which was published in a 1999 issue of the journal *Sex Roles*.

How well do the different theories of mass media that we've discussed explain their findings about the influence of magazine covers on women's feelings about weight?

3. Susan Crawford is a legal scholar with particular expertise on Internet law and issues of privacy, intellectual property, and advertising. Her blog gives her opinions on a range of legal issues entailed by cyberspace. To read her blog, use your Online Resources *for Communication in Our Lives* to access **WebLink 13.3.**

CourseMate

SHARPEN YOUR SKILL

1. Media Literacy in Action

In this chapter, you have learned about some of the ways that gatekeepers shape understanding, perspective, and attitudes. Apply what you've learned by identifying ways that I, as the author of this chapter, shaped the information presented to you.

- *Gatekeeping*: Whose points of view do I emphasize in discussing mass communication and media literacy? Are there other involved groups that I neglect or ignore?
- *Agenda setting*: Which aspects of mass communication did I call to your attention? Which aspects of mass communication did I not emphasize or name?

2. Detecting Dominant Values in Media

Watch 2 hours of prime-time commercial television. Pay attention to the dominant ideology that is represented and normalized in the programming. Who are the good and bad characters? Which personal qualities are represented as admirable, and which are represented as objectionable? Who are the victims and victors, the heroes and villains? What goals and values are endorsed?

EXPERIENCING COMMUNICATION IN OUR LIVES

CASE STUDY: *Social Media and Future Employers*

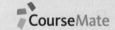

An audio recording of the scenario scripted here is featured in your Chapter 13 Online Resources for *Communication in Our Lives*. Select "Social Media and Future Employers" to listen. Improve your own communication skills by reading, watching, and evaluating this communication encounter.

Matthew Leone, a college senior, is a technology junkie who is currently looking for a job to take after he graduates in the spring. After sending out several résumés but receiving no response, he emails his friend Anna and they communicate via email.

As long as he could remember, Matthew Leone loved computers. When he was little, he'd had a Game Boy, and as he'd gotten older, his father had let him use his office computer so Matthew could download pictures of antique cars, one of his favorite things to do. Throughout college, Matthew not only emailed nearly everyone in his life, but also had a MySpace page where he uploaded pictures of such diverse events as his sister's wedding and his dog's birthday party. It was clear that Matthew loved computers, and as a cell phone junkie, iPod user, and DVD collector, he was also a lover of technology in general.

Matthew was graduating in the spring, so he was busy spending the month of February putting his résumé together and applying for jobs. He knew that his degree in economics and his 3.4 GPA would help him secure a good job, and he felt rather confident about his prospects after reading a glowing recommendation letter from one of his professors. Clearly, Matthew Leone was looking forward to a good-paying job with a great company.

Although Matthew credentials were outstanding, he couldn't figure out why he wasn't being contacted for interviews. He sent his résumé and cover letter to all sorts of companies—large and small, public and private—but never scored even one interview. He was confused and concerned, and it wasn't long before he emailed his best friend, Anna, to ask her what she thought.

Anna wrote that she was also surprised that Matthew hadn't been contacted for any interviews. As she rambled on in her email, she made one observation that stopped Matthew in his tracks. She told Matthew that she'd read a newspaper article about how "controversial" material on MySpace had prevented a man in Florida from getting a job. Apparently, the company the man had applied to had seen some damning pictures of the him in a neo-Nazi jacket. Matthew immediately thought of the pictures he'd put on his website of his spring break vacation in Cancun, Mexico. He didn't finish reading the rest of Anna's email. He went immediately to his MySpace page and saw that, indeed, there were provocative pictures of him drinking—and drinking, and drinking. In one picture taken in a bar, his friend Damien poured beer down Matthew's throat.

Matthew sat motionless in front of his computer. He thought the pictures were harmless, and couldn't believe that someone would take them seriously. Certainly, Matthew thought, plenty of potential employers have been drunk and must know that these pictures were taken for fun. He no longer wondered why he wasn't being called for interviews. Over his lifetime, Matthew Leone had loved technology. But now this technology was influencing his life in ways he had never imagined or considered.

QUESTIONS FOR ANALYSIS AND DISCUSSION

You can answer these questions and see my responses to them online via your Online Resources for Chapter 13.

1. According to the gratification theory, in what ways do you imagine Matthew was gratified by posting photos of himself on Myspace?

2. Matthew might initially appear to demonstrate media literacy because he uses cell phones, iPods, and DVDs, and posts on Myspace, but in what ways does Matthew not fully understand how media work?

3. How might Matthew's experiences with social media have altered his conception of space?

PictureNet/Corbis/Jupiter Images

> There are three things to aim at in public speaking: first, to get into your subject, then to get your subject into yourself, and lastly, to get your subject into the heart of your audience.
>
> **Alexander Gregg**

Planning Public Speaking

- Hank is a commercial artist at a public relations firm. On Thursday, Hank's supervisor asks him to prepare a 10-minute presentation for a client whose million-dollar account the firm hopes to get.

- Bonnie belongs to a student group that opposes a tuition hike. At a meeting of the college president's advisory committee, a member of the committee turns to Bonnie's group and asks, "Can you explain why you oppose the tuition increase?" Bonnie realizes that someone in the group needs to present their reasons for opposing the increase, and she rises to speak.

SHARPEN YOUR SKILL

At the end of this chapter, refer to the Sharpen Your Skill features, Selecting and Narrowing Your Topic and Defining Your Purpose and Thesis Statement, to apply concepts from Chapter 14.

- Miranda volunteers at the local animal protection society. The staff person who was scheduled to present an outreach program at a local high school calls in sick, and Miranda is asked to fill in.

- Juan is a software designer who has created a number of innovative programs. Today, he is giving a 20-minute talk about a new program to people who have little experience with technologies.

- At a public hearing on the location of a toxic waste dump, a representative of a chemical company claims that chemicals stored in the dump are safer than they really are. Kelly feels compelled to speak up so that listeners know the truth about the danger of the chemicals.

Although these people aren't professional speakers, each of them is called on to speak in public. If you are competent at public speaking, you increase your opportunities for professional effectiveness and advancement and your influence in civic life. Freedom to express our ideas in public is so basic to a democratic society that it is guaranteed by the First Amendment to the Constitution.

The role of public speaking in professional life is more obvious in some occupations than in others. If you plan to be an attorney, a politician, a salesperson, or an educator, it's easy to see that speaking in public will be a routine part of your life. The importance of public speaking is less obvious, yet also present, in other careers. If you intend to be an accountant, a city planner, a counselor, a doctor, or a businessperson, you will have many opportunities to speak to small and large groups. Whatever profession you enter, public speaking skills will be an asset.

The ability to present ideas effectively in public situations will also enhance your influence in civic, social, and political contexts. You'll have opportunities to voice your ideas at zoning meetings, neighborhood planning groups, and school boards. Public speaking is a basic communication skill that we all need if we want to have a voice in what happens in our workplaces, our communities, and our society.

Like other communication skills, effectiveness in public speaking can be developed with commitment and practice. Although some people may have more experience and perhaps more aptitude for public speaking than others,

COMMUNICATION HIGHLIGHT

The First Amendment: Freedom of Religion, Speech, and Press

Congress shall make no law respecting an establishment of religion, or prohibiting the free exercise thereof; or abridging the freedom of speech, or of the press; or the right of people peaceably to assemble, and to petition the Government for a redress of grievances."

—Amendment I, The Constitution of the United States

Jeff Greenberg/PhotoEdit

The ability to make effective presentations is critical to career development.

everyone can learn to make effective presentations. As we will see, many of the skills we've discussed in previous chapters are relevant to effective public communication.

This chapter and the four that follow lead you through the process of planning, developing, and presenting informative and persuasive speeches. In this chapter, we'll first note similarities between public speaking and other kinds of communication we've studied. Next, we'll discuss foundations of effective public speaking: selecting and limiting topics, defining a general purpose and a specific purpose, and developing a thesis statement. The third section of the chapter emphasizes adapting speeches to particular speaking occasions and to particular listeners' orientations to topics and speakers.

The next four chapters build on material presented in this one. Chapter 15 identifies types of support for public speeches and discusses methods of conducting research. In Chapter 16, we'll learn about ways to organize and present public speeches, and we'll discuss the widespread concern of communication anxiety and ways to manage it. If you feel anxious about giving a public speech, you may want to read that section of Chapter 16 now. Chapter 17 focuses on informative public speeches, and Chapter 18 focuses on persuasive public speeches. As we discuss these topics, I'll show you partial and complete sample speeches to illustrate how the principles we discuss apply in actual speaking situations. After reading these five chapters, you should be able to plan, develop, and present an effective speech.

PUBLIC SPEAKING AS ENLARGED CONVERSATION

Years ago, James Winans (1938), a distinguished professor of communication, remarked that effective public speaking is really enlarged conversation. Winans meant that the skills of successful public speaking are not so different from those we use in everyday conversations. As Michael Motley and Jennifer Molloy (1994, p. 52) explain, "Except for preparation time and turn-taking delay, public speaking has fundamental parallels to everyday conversation." Ethical considerations, such as honesty and avoidance of loaded and abusive language, are important in public speaking just as they are in social conversations. Furthermore, minor mistakes, such as stumbling over a phrase or forgetting a word, generally don't impair credibility (Motley, 1990). We make mistakes in everyday conversation and public speaking, and in neither case do they necessarily undercut our effectiveness.

Effective public communication uses and builds on skills and principles we've discussed in previous chapters. Whether we are talking with a couple of friends or speaking to an audience of 500, we need to consider listeners' perspectives, create a good climate for communication, express our ideas clearly, organize what we say so that others can follow our thinking, explain and support our ideas, and present our thoughts in an engaging manner. Whether in social conversation or public speaking, we should use language and nonverbal behaviors that present our ideas clearly and ethically, and we should be sensitive to diversity in age, sex, race–ethnicity, religion, and so forth. In public speaking, as in everyday conversation, these are the skills of effective communication.

> **TRINA**   *What I love about Oprah is that she always seems to be talking to me personally. I watch her show all the time, and I've been to see her in person twice. She's always the same. No matter how many people are in an audience—even thousands—you feel like she's having a chat with you.*

Thinking of public speaking as enlarged conversation reminds us that good public speaking is rarely stiff or exceedingly formal. In fact, the most effective public speakers tend to use an informal, personal style that invites listeners to feel as if they were being talked with, not lectured to. For the first 10 years of my career, I taught classes of 20 to 35 students, and I relied on an interactive communication style that involved all of us. When I decided to teach a class of more than 100 students, I worried that I couldn't develop a teaching style that would be effective with a large class. For half of that semester, I lectured in a fairly formal style because I thought that was appropriate for a class with so many students. One day, a student asked a question that I answered by asking a question in return. He replied, then another student added her ideas, and an open discussion was launched. Both the students and I were more engaged with each other and the course material than we had been when I lectured formally. That's when I realized that effective teaching in large classes was enlarged conversation in which all present are engaged. With this background, we're now ready to consider the first steps in designing effective public presentations.

David Young-Wolff/PhotoEdit

Often, the most engaging public presentations are conversational in style.

CHOOSING AND REFINING A TOPIC

A well-crafted speech begins with a limited topic, a clear purpose, and a concise thesis statement that listeners can grasp quickly and retain.

Choosing Your Topic

The first step in preparing a public speech is to select a topic. If you don't already have a topic in mind, you might consult sources such as *The Readers' Guide to Periodical Literature*, newspapers and news magazines, current events programs on TV, and online news sites. To visit online sites, use your Online Resources for *Communication in Our Lives* to access WebLink 14.1.

Select a Topic That Matters to You   When you are asked to speak, seize the chance to speak on a subject that matters to you. When we care about a topic, we have a head start in that we already know a fair amount about it. In addition, personal interest in the subject will make your delivery more engaging and more dynamic. Perhaps you are a vegetarian and want to inform others of the moral, health, and economic reasons for vegetarianism. If you are committed to environmental issues, you might want to persuade your classmates to be more environmentally responsible. Maybe you have strong beliefs about the death penalty, inner-city crime, or other important social topics. A speech is the ideal opportunity to influence how others feel and think about issues that matter to you.

Select a Topic Appropriate to the Speaking Occasion   Personal knowledge and interest aren't the only criteria for selecting a topic. We should also consider the speaking occasion or situation (Ferguson, 2008). What are the expectations, demands, and constraints of particular speaking situations? Some contexts virtually dictate speech topics. For example, a rally for a political candidate demands speeches that praise the candidate, a ceremony honoring a person requires speakers to pay tribute to the person, a keynote speech at a professional conference should address the concerns of that profession, and a funeral demands a speech that honors the person who has died and his or her life.

PAT   *When we had our Phi Beta Kappa induction last spring, we had a very well-known scholar give the speech. He began by talking about how great our basketball team is and how we may win the championship this year. He talked about the team for about 5 minutes before he said anything else. It's not like I'm against sports or anything. I mean, I go to games and I think our team is way cool. But Phi Beta Kappa is the highest academic honor society on campus. It didn't seem the right situation to be leading a rally for the team.*

Physical setting is also part of the speaking occasion. You know what your classroom is like and the time of day you will speak. In other speaking situations,

COMMUNICATION in Your Life

To what extent do your professors communicate conversationally?

COMMUNICATION in Your Life

Identify three issues that really matter to you.

it's appropriate to ask in advance about the physical setting. Is the room in which you will speak large or small? Is it well lit or dim? Are chairs comfortable or not? Will you present your speech at 10 A.M., after a heavy lunch, or in mid-afternoon? Will listeners have sat through a long day of meetings and speeches? Each of these factors influences listeners' ability to listen and pay attention.

If possible, check the room yourself in advance. You might be able to control some possible hindrances, such as temperature or seating arrangement. If undesirable aspects of the setting are beyond your control (i.e., uncomfortable seating, speaking after listeners have had a big meal), you must do your best to compensate for them. A dynamic and engaging delivery can do much to surmount listeners' lethargy or discomfort.

Sometimes, you won't know the physical setting in advance or won't be able to control it. In that case, you must adapt as best you can on the spot. Once, my partner, Robbie, was asked to give a keynote speech after dinner at a meeting of the North Carolina Student Sierra Club. In the past, he had given many keynote speeches at Sierra Club meetings. Based on past events, Robbie assumed that the dinner would be in a banquet room and that people would be dressed somewhat formally. He prepared a 30-minute speech, which he planned to deliver from a speaking podium. He dressed in a good suit and tie. When he got to the meeting, he discovered that the dinner was a cookout—certainly appropriate for a Sierra Club group, but not what he was expecting!

Robbie quickly adapted his appearance by taking off his jacket and tie and rolling up his shirtsleeves. He then adapted the content of his speech and his delivery to the informal speaking situation in which he found himself. He decided to eliminate some of the quotations from environmental leaders because the light from the campfire would not be sufficient for him to read the quotations from note cards, and he didn't want to risk misquoting others. And he adapted his planned, forceful, podium delivery to a more conversational, story-telling style. Robbie would have been ineffective had he not adapted himself and his speech to the physical setting.

COMMUNICATION
in Your Life

Describe the situation in which you will give your speech.

COMMUNICATION HIGHLIGHT

Connecting Yourself with Your Topic

One of the most powerful ways for speakers to enhance impact is to demonstrate personal involvement with their topics. Some good examples of speakers who show their personal involvement with topics come from acceptance speeches at Academy Awards ceremonies (Robinson, 2001). When Tom Hanks won the best actor award for his portrayal of an attorney with AIDS in *Philadelphia,* he used his speech to honor the millions of people who have died of HIV-related illnesses. He also paid tribute to a former teacher who was gay and who inspired his performance. That same year, Gerda Weisman Klein won an award for her documentary film about the Holocaust, *One Survivor Remembers.* Accepting the award, Weisman said, "I've been in a place for 6 incredible years where winning meant a crust of bread and to live another day" (p. 16).

Select a Topic Appropriate to Your Audience   Effective speakers also select topics that will appeal to the needs, interests, and situations of listeners. A public speech is not primarily a chance to showcase yourself by showing how smart, clever, funny, or knowledgeable you are. Rather, it is first and foremost a chance to affect others—that's the reason for speaking. And if you want to affect others, you begin by thinking about them in the first stages of planning a speech.

In selecting a topic, ask how topics that matter to you are or can be relevant to your listeners, what knowledge they have, and what experiences and concerns they are likely to share with you. Later in this chapter we'll discuss in depth how you can take listeners into consideration.

Narrow Your Topic   Effective speakers limit their speeches to a manageable focus (McGuire, 1989). A speech on the broad topic of interpersonal communication could be narrowed to a more specific focus on managing conflict, listening effectively, or creating supportive climates. Any of these three topics could be discussed in a 10- to 20-minute speech. If you're interested in the general topic of health-care reform, you might narrow that to reducing the costs of drugs or increasing preventive medicine (wellness). You can't competently discuss the broad topic of health-care reform in a single speech, but you can cover a particular aspect of it.

Another way to narrow your speaking purpose is to use a *mind map* (Jaffe, 2007). A **mind map** is a holistic record of information on a topic, which many visual thinkers prefer to an outline. You create a mind map by free-associating ideas in relation to a broad area of interest. For example, perhaps you want to speak on the general topic of the environment. To narrow that broad topic to a manageable focus for a single speech, you could brainstorm issues related to the topic. Figure 14.1 shows many specific issues that might occur to someone who creates a mind map on the topic of environment. If you would like to use a software program to map your ideas, use your Online Resources for *Communication in Our Lives* to access **WebLink 14.2.**

Defining Your General and Specific Purposes in Speaking

The second step in designing an effective speech is to define your purpose for speaking. This involves two steps. First, you should decide whether your general purpose is to persuade, to entertain, or to inform listeners. Second, you should refine your general purpose into a specific purpose.

General Purposes of Speaking   Traditionally, three general speaking purposes have been recognized: informing, persuading, and entertaining (Table 14.1). You probably realize that these purposes often overlap. For example, informative speeches routinely include humor or interesting comments that aim to entertain listeners. Persuasive speeches typically contain much information about issues and solutions. Speeches intended to inform may also persuade listeners to adopt new beliefs, attitudes, or actions. Although speeches often involve more than one purpose, usually one purpose is primary.

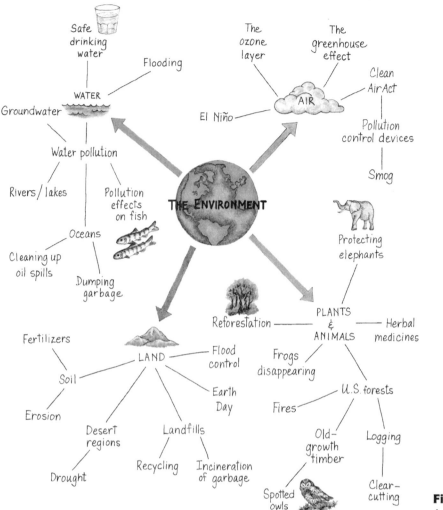

Fig ure 14.1
A Mind Map

One speaking goal is to entertain. In **speeches to entertain**, the primary objective is to engage, interest, amuse, or please listeners. You might think that speeches to entertain are presented only by accomplished comics and performers. Actually, in the course of our lives many of us will be involved in speaking to entertain. You might be asked to give an after-dinner speech, to present a toast at a friend's wedding, or to make remarks at a retirement party for a colleague. In each case, the primary goal is to entertain, although the speech might include information about the occasion, the couple being married, or the colleague who is retiring.

Even when your primary purpose in speaking is not to entertain, you'll want to interest listeners whom you intend to inform or persuade. If you want to include some entertainment in your speech, it's a good idea to test your jokes or amusing comments in advance. Don't assume that others will find humor in something you think is funny, and don't rely exclusively on close friends' judgment; after all, friends often think alike and have similar senses of humor.

Table 14.1	Speaking Purposes		
General Purposes			
To Inform		**To Persuade**	**To Entertain**
Speaking to define, instruct, explain, clarify, demonstrate, teach, or train		Speaking to influence attitudes, beliefs, or actions; to convince, motivate to action, inspire, or sell	Speaking to create interest, amusement, warm feelings; to celebrate, remember, or acknowledge others or events; to create or fortify ties between people
Specific Purposes			
To help listeners understand the balloting procedure used in the 2000 presidential elections in Florida		To persuade listeners to sign a petition demanding new voting systems for all districts in the United States	To have listeners laugh at my jokes in the after dinner speech at the retreat.

It's also a good idea to avoid jokes and remarks that might offend some people. Even if you find them funny, they could alienate listeners.

Humor isn't the only means of entertaining. We also entertain by telling stories to share experiences, build community, pass on history, and teach lessons. Storytelling is prominent in cultures that emphasize oral, more than written, communication. In some countries and in some social communities in the United States, individual and collective histories are kept alive through storytelling. Oral traditions tend to be particularly strong among traditional Native Americans (Einhorn, 2000), African Americans (Fitch, 2000), and Jewish people (Schram & Schwartz, 2000). In traditional West African culture, storytellers, who are called *griots*, tell stories that blend words, song, and dance, and audience members respond as a chorus (Cummings, 1993).

Storytelling, or narrative speaking, often occurs in families as parents share stories about their courtship, discuss their childhoods, and tell children about relatives. As we noted in Chapter 12, stories also recount significant moments in an organization's life, they introduce new members to key players in the organization and socialize the newcomers in the organization's history and core values. Notice that although narrative speaking is considered primarily entertaining, it may also serve to inform or persuade.

Speaking to inform is a second presentational goal. **Speeches to inform** have the primary goal of increasing listeners' understanding, awareness, or knowledge about some topic. When you speak to inform, your goal is to tell listeners something they don't already know. Consider several purposes for informative speaking:

- To make listeners aware of a new way of thinking about a familiar topic.
- To teach listeners how to do something new.
- To correct listeners' misconceptions.

- To increase listeners' understanding of a topic about which they know only a little.

- To make listeners aware of issues or problems.

- To inform listeners about important events.

- To describe a new procedure or policy.

A speaker might give an informative speech if he or she wants listeners to understand the philosophy of the Republican Party or existing programs for recycling. In both cases, the general purpose is to inform listeners. Speeches to inform may also take the form of demonstrations. For instance, a demonstration speech might show listeners how to distinguish poisonous from nonpoisonous mushrooms. Speeches to inform may also aim to teach listeners something entirely new. Sasha, a student in one of my classes, gave a speech on arranged marriages, which still occur in her native country. Her goal was for students to understand the history of arranged marriages and the reasons why they work for many people.

Speeches to persuade aim to change people's attitudes, beliefs, or behaviors or to motivate people to act. Persuasive goals are to influence attitudes, to change practices, to alter beliefs, and to motivate action. Rather than an entertainer or teacher, the persuasive speaker is an advocate who argues for a cause, issue, policy, attitude, or action. Persuasive speeches aim to change how listeners think, feel, or act. To do so, they must do more than provide information, although information typically is part of persuasive speaking as well. The key goal of persuasive speeches is to strengthen listeners' existing attitudes, beliefs, or actions or to actually change what they think, believe, and do. Persuasive purposes include these:

Storytelling is a powerful way to pass on history and strengthen familial and community bonds. It plays a central role in oral cultures.

- To convince listeners to do something they are not currently doing.

- To show listeners they should believe in or support a specific policy, law, or organization.

- To convince listeners to stop doing something they are currently doing.

- To convince listeners to buy a product.

- To motivate listeners to vote for a candidate.

- To inspire listeners to volunteer time or donate to a worthy cause.

In one of my classes, a student named Chris gave a speech to persuade other students to donate blood. He began by telling us that he was a hemophiliac and that his life depended on blood donations. This self-disclosure increased his credibility with listeners. He then informed listeners about the procedures for donating blood (a subordinate informational purpose) so that they would not be deterred by fear of the unknown. Next, he described the cases of several people who died because adequate supplies of blood weren't available. In the

COMMUNICATION
in Your Life

Recall a speech to inform that was excellent. What made it so impressive?

2 weeks after his speech, more than one-third of the students who had been in the audience donated blood!

Specific Purposes of Speaking Once you have decided on your general speaking purpose, you will want to define a **specific purpose**, which is a behavioral objective or observable response that will indicate that you have been effective in achieving your communication goal. Here are some examples of specific speaking purposes:

- I want 25% of listeners to sign up to donate blood.

- I want listeners to be able to give correct answers to questions about how HIV is and is not spread.

- I want listeners to know this candidate's stand on free trade.

Developing a Thesis Statement

Once you have selected and narrowed your speaking topic and defined your general and specific purpose, you're ready to develop the thesis statement of your speech. A **thesis statement** is the main idea of an entire speech. It concisely states the heart of your speech. It should capture the key message in a short, precise sentence that listeners can remember easily (Table 14.2).

A good thesis statement is one that listeners can grasp at the beginning of your talk and remember after you have finished. They may forget the specific details and evidence you present, but you want them to remember the main idea. They are most likely to retain it if you create a concise thesis statement and repeat it several times during your talk. Chris's thesis statement for his informative speech was this: "Donating blood is painless, quick, and life saving for others." Although Chris's listeners may have forgotten many of the specific points in his speech, they remembered his main idea: the thesis statement. When Chris gave his persuasive speech, his thesis statement was, "You should donate blood."

Speech Builder Express, which you can access via your Online Resources for *Communication in Our Lives*, includes a section on developing thesis statements that are appropriate and effective for the type of speech you're preparing.

In sum, the first steps in planning a public speech are to select and narrow a topic that matters to you and your listeners, to define your general and specific speaking purposes, and to develop a clear, concise thesis statement (Table 14.3). Now we're ready to consider the key process of adapting your speaking goals, content, and delivery to specific listeners and speaking contexts.

Table 14.2	Sample Thesis Statements
Ineffective	**Effective**
Think twice before you decide you're for gun control.	Gun control jeopardizes individuals' rights and safety.
Vegetarianism is a way of life.	Vegetarian diets are healthful and delicious.
Big business should get breaks.	Tax breaks for businesses are good for the economy.

Table 14.3	Steps in Planning Public Speaking
Step	**Example**
1. Identify the broad topic.	Education
2. Narrow the topic.	Continuing education
3. Define a general purpose.	To persuade
4. Determine a specific purpose.	To motivate listeners to take courses after graduating from college
5. Develop a thesis statement.	"Taking courses after you graduate can enrich your personal life and your professional success."

ANALYZING YOUR AUDIENCE

A student named Harold gave a persuasive speech to convince listeners to support affirmative action. He was personally compelling and dynamic in his delivery, and his ideas were well organized. The only problem was that his audience had little background on affirmative action, and he didn't explain exactly what it does and does not involve. He assumed listeners understood how affirmative action works, and he focused on its positive effects. His listeners weren't persuaded because Harold failed to give them information that might have secured their support. Harold's speech also illustrates our previous point that speeches often combine more than one speaking purpose; in this case, giving information was essential to Harold's larger goal of persuading listeners.

Another student named Christie spoke passionately about vegetarianism. She provided dramatic evidence of the cruelty animals suffer as they are raised and slaughtered. When we polled listeners after her speech, only 2 of 30 had been persuaded to consider vegetarianism. Why was Christie ineffective? Because she didn't recognize and address listeners' beliefs that vegetarian foods are unhealthy and tasteless. Christie mistakenly assumed that listeners would know that it's easy to get sufficient protein, vitamins, and minerals without consuming meat, and she assumed they understood that vegetarian foods can be delicious. However, her listeners didn't know that, and they weren't about to consider a diet that they thought was neither nutritious nor appetizing.

COMMUNICATION HIGHLIGHT

What Do People Think About . . .?

Speakers often want to know what the general public thinks about issues related to their topics. Tracking down information on opinions about specific issues can be time consuming, but there's a shortcut.

CourseMate

The People & the Press website, sponsored by the Pew Charitable Trusts, presents the results of public opinion surveys on a variety of topics, such as the present administration, national health care, and biological warfare. To check it out, use your Online Resources for *Communication in Our Lives* to access **WebLink 14.3**.

Christie and Harold made the mistake of not adapting to their audiences. It's impossible to entertain, inform, or persuade people if we don't understand and accommodate their perspectives, interests, attitudes, beliefs, and experiences (Griffin, 2008). Speakers need to know what listeners already know and believe as well as what reservations they might have about a topic (McGuire, 1989). To paraphrase the advice of an ancient Greek rhetorician, "The fool persuades me with his or her reasons, the wise person with my own." That is, effective speakers understand and work with listeners' reasons, values, knowledge, and concerns.

Demographic Audience Analysis

Demographic audience analysis identifies general features common to a group of listeners. Demographic characteristics include age, sex, religion, cultural heritage, race, occupation, political allegiances, and educational level. Demographic information about listeners is useful in two ways.

First, demographic information can help you adapt your speech to your listeners. For example, if you know the age or age range of listeners, you know what experiences are likely to be part of their history. You could assume that 60-year-old listeners know a fair amount about the Vietnam War but that 20-year-olds might not. You can assume that 60-year-olds remember President John F. Kennedy and Martin Luther King Jr., but that 18-to-22-year-old listeners will not remember them. In planning a speech, references to events, people, music, and so forth should be appropriate to the ages of listeners. In many speaking situations, you will have listeners of different ages—sometimes of several generations. In those cases, you'll want either to restrict your references to ones that will be familiar to listeners of all ages or to explain any references that might not be understood by some listeners.

Age is also linked to persuadability. In general, as people age, they are less likely to change their attitudes, perhaps because they've held their attitudes longer than younger people or because they've acquired knowledge that supports their attitudes (Meyers, 1993). Thus, it's generally reasonable to expect to move older listeners less than younger listeners toward new beliefs, attitudes, or actions.

Other demographic information can also guide speakers in preparing presentations that will interest and involve particular listeners. Because we live in a multicultural world, effective speakers must be careful not to use examples that exclude some groups. For instance, the use of generic male language (*chairman*, the pronoun *he* to refer to a doctor) is likely to offend some listeners. Similarly, referring to the winter break from school as "the Christmas holiday" disregards listeners who are not Christian.

The educational background of listeners can suggest what kinds of language may be appropriate. Once, when I was serving as an expert witness in a trial, I was asked about an instrument that had been used to measure an employee's effectiveness. I had reviewed the instrument in advance and determined that it was invalid and unreliable. I stated that as my opinion in court. One of the attorneys then asked me what validity and reliability were. The judge and jury didn't have statistical training, so I couldn't explain the technical meaning of convergent, predictive, internal, and external validity, and I couldn't explain specialized indexes of reliability. After a few moments of thought, I answered that validity is a matter of whether an instrument measures what it claims to measure, and reliability is a matter of whether the instrument consistently measures what it claims to measure over time. Had I been speaking to a group of researchers, I would have offered a more technical answer tailored to their greater statistical expertise.

We also know that people who have cognitively complex thinking styles want to understand things. For them, it's not enough to know that something is the case. They also need to know *why* it's the case—what makes it so (Meyers, 1993). Cognitive complexity tends to increase with age and education, so we can make predictions about listeners' cognitive complexity based on these other factors. When preparing a speech for cognitively complex listeners, we should provide more detailed evidence and explanations for our assertions than might be appropriate for a less cognitively complex group of listeners.

Speakers also use demographic information to make inferences about listeners' likely beliefs, values, and attitudes. For example, assume you plan to give a speech on the general topic of health-care reform. If your listeners' average age is 68, they are likely to be more interested in containment of drug costs and in reasonable options for long-term care of older adults than in preventive care and vaccines for children. Listeners in their twenties, on the other hand, would be likely to perceive preventive health care as more immediately relevant than ensuring reasonable options for long-term care of older adults.

Knowing something about the general characteristics of listeners may also suggest what type of evidence and which authorities will be effective. Statistics bore many listeners, especially if presented in a dull manner, but they might be interesting to an audience of economists or mathematicians. A quotation from George W. Bush is more likely to be effective with a Republican audience than with a Democratic one. Citing Justice Sonja Sotomayor might impress a group of women attorneys more than citing Clarence Thomas would. Although both are Supreme Court justices, they have different degrees of credibility with different groups.

Speakers may also draw on demographic information to create connections with their listeners. Politicians create points of identification with voters in diverse regions. In the South, a candidate might tell stories about growing up in southern towns; in New England, the candidate might reminisce about college years at Harvard or Dartmouth; in the Midwest, the candidate might speak about friends and family who live there. It is unethical for a speaker to disguise or distort his or her background, ideas, or positions to build common ground with listeners. However, understanding the demographic characteristics of listeners helps a speaker decide which aspects of his or her life and interests to emphasize in a particular situation.

LAMONT   *A big filmmaker came to talk to our class, and I figured he was in a world totally different from ours. I mean, the man makes multimillion-dollar movies and knows all the big stars. But he started his talk by telling us about when he was in college, and he talked about his favorite classes, about a bar he went to on Fridays, and about the special friends he'd made at college. I felt like he understood what my life is about, like he wasn't so different from me after all.*

COMMUNICATION
in Your Life

Identify
demographic
characteristics
of the audience
for your speech.

Demographic analysis can provide useful general information about listeners. However, it's important to guard against stereotypes of groups of people. Although many college students are between 18 and 22 years old, some are older than 22. Thus, it would be inadvisable to design a speech to college students for an exclusively 18-to-22-year-old audience. Although many women work outside the home, not all do, so an audience of women should not be addressed as if no homemakers were present. Similarly, speakers shouldn't stereotype an audience of men as uninterested in child care because many men are involved parents.

Situational Audience Analysis

A second method of audience analysis is **situational audience analysis,** which seeks information about specific listeners that relates directly to the speaker's topic and purpose. Situational audience analysis allows a speaker to discover what listeners already know and believe about a topic, speaker, and occasion so that the speaker can adapt to his or her listeners.

Listeners' Orientation toward the Topic   Effective speakers develop their speeches with attention to their specific listeners' interest, knowledge, and attitudes toward the speech topic. In many cases, listeners are already interested in the speech topic—that's why they attend. However, if listeners do not begin with interest in your topic, your job is to pique their interest. You might make them aware of how the topic relates to them: How does it, or how will it, affect them? What's at stake for them? Why should they care about what you have to say? Emma, a student of mine, began an informative speech about breast cancer this way: "Looking around the room, I see there are 16 women here. According to statistics, 2 of you—1 in every 8 women—will develop breast cancer in her lifetime."

You also want to analyze listeners' knowledge about your topic so that you can adapt appropriately. What do they already know about the topic? How much information (or misinformation) do they have? Once you have assessed listeners' knowledge about your topic, you can decide how much information you need to provide and how detailed and technical you can be.

Finally, in assessing your listeners' orientation toward your topic, you want to know what attitudes they hold. If they already favor something you are proposing, you don't need to persuade them to adopt a positive attitude. Instead, you may want to move them to action—to motivate them to act on what they already favor. On the other hand, if your listeners are against or indifferent to something you are proposing, your persuasive goal is to convince them to consider your point of view. You will need to provide more evidence than you will if they already favor your position.

Listeners' Orientation toward the Speaker   Listeners' perceptions of a speaker shape how they respond to the message. The more credibility a speaker has with listeners, the more likely they are to believe what the speaker says and to consider her or his proposals. Do the listeners already know who the speaker is?

Do they respect the speaker's expertise on the topic? Do listeners believe the speaker cares about what is good for them? If not, the speaker needs to give listeners reasons to trust him or her and to believe that he or she is interested in their welfare.

If you do not have credentials that establish you as an expert on a topic, you will want to demonstrate to listeners that you know what you are talking about. Explain how you learned about it. Describe your experiences with the topic. Include research that shows you are knowledgeable. Similarly, you will want to convince listeners that you care about what is good for them. Connect what you are talking about with listeners, as Emma did in opening her speech on breast cancer. Show that you have thought about them. Demonstrate that what you say will benefit them—how will it affect their health or success?

Because a speaker's credibility is critical to effectiveness, we'll return to this topic when we discuss using evidence (Chapter 15), building a strong introduction to a speech (Chapter 16), and increasing credibility (Chapter 18).

Listener's Orientation toward the Speaking Occasion   In the fall of 2002, Paul Wellstone, a Democratic senator from Minnesota, was killed in a plane crash. In addition to grieving for his tragic loss, Democrats were worried about the elections coming up in just a month. Wellstone had seemed assured of reelection. His sudden death meant that the Republican candidate might win his seat in the United States Senate. After late-night strategy sessions, the Democrats announced that Walter Mondale, a former vice president from Minnesota, was the Democratic candidate and would carry on Wellstone's legacy.

The nationally televised memorial service for Senator Wellstone and those of his family who also died in the plane crash began with speeches honoring the fallen senator, as was expected on this occasion. However, after the opening speeches, the memorial service turned into a political rally for Mondale, the new Democratic candidate. Although many of the people at the service joined in the spirit of the rally, the reaction from the broader public was decidedly unfavorable. Viewers were shocked and offended by what they perceived as disrespect for Wellstone and his family and a blatant exploitation of a memorial service for political purposes. Mondale was defeated, and most political analysts cited the voting public's negative reaction to the memorial service as the key reason.

This example illustrates the importance of considering what listeners expect in a particular speaking situation and what they will consider appropriate and inappropriate. An effective speech is not something that can be canned and presented the same way in every situation. Instead, an effective speech respects the particular situation in which it occurs, as well as listeners' expectations and their sense of what is and is not proper.

Adapting to particular occasions also requires speakers to consider what length of speech is appropriate. At a wedding reception I once attended, guests were toasting the newlyweds. One old friend of the groom got up to "say a few words" and then spoke for 15 minutes! That's much too long for a toast, and other guests were clearly uncomfortable with what they perceived as stage hogging. A speech introducing a main speaker should be short. Listeners will be displeased if a speech of introduction drags on because they came to hear the main speaker. On the other hand, the main speaker generally speaks at length; listeners would be disappointed by a 6-minute speech from a featured speaker.

Occasion also influences the type of speech. In the example of the memorial service for Wellstone, the occasion demanded speeches honoring Wellstone. Endorsement speeches for Mondale violated what listeners considered appropriate for the occasion. After-dinner speeches generally should include some entertainment—jokes, stories, and so forth—and should not be overly somber or information packed.

Whereas politicians and corporations can afford to conduct sophisticated polls to discover what people know, want, think, and believe, most of us don't have the resources to do that. So how do ordinary people engage in situational audience analysis? One answer is, by observation. Often, a speaker has some experience interacting with his or her listeners. Drawing on past interactions, a speaker may be able to discern a great deal about the knowledge, attitudes, and beliefs of listeners.

It's also appropriate to gather information about listeners through conversations, interviews, or surveys. You might conduct a survey to learn about your classmates' knowledge of and attitudes toward your thesis statement. The results of your survey should give you sufficient insight into the opinions of students on your campus to enable you to adapt your presentation to the students in your class.

Demographic and situational audience analysis provides you with direct knowledge of listeners and information from which you can draw additional inferences. Taking listeners into consideration allows you to build a speech that is adapted to your particular listeners and thus likely to have impact.

CHAPTER SUMMARY

In this chapter, we considered the nature of public speaking and the first steps in designing effective presentations. We began by noting that, rather than differing radically from other kinds of communication, public speaking is enlarged conversation, in which a speaker interacts personally with listeners. To do this effectively, it's important to select and limit your topic, to define your general and specific purposes, and to develop a clear thesis statement. In addition, designing an effective presentation requires consideration of listeners. Effective speakers take into account what listeners know, believe, value, think, and feel about the topic, speaker, and occasion. When a speaker adapts to listeners, they are likely to be more receptive to the speaker's ideas.

In the next chapter, we'll discuss ways to conduct research and use research in public speaking. Building good arguments increases a speaker's credibility and enhances the power of ideas presented. Before proceeding to Chapter 15, complete the checklist to make sure you've done the preliminary work to create a strong foundation for your speech.

CHECKLIST FOR PLANNING A PUBLIC SPEECH

If you prefer, you may complete this checklist online under your Chapter 14 Online Resources for *Communication in Our Lives*.

In addition, you may want to use Speech Builder Express, which you can access through your Online Resources. At the end of this chapter, I've included a specific suggestion for using Speech Builder Express to begin planning your speech.

My speech topic is _____

_____

My general purpose is _____

_____

My specific purpose is _____

_____

My thesis statement is _____

_____

1. I know the following demographic information about the people who will listen to my speech:

   Age: _____

   Education: _____

   Political position: _____

Sex ratio: _____

Ethnicities: _____

Other: _____

2. I know the following information about my particular listeners:

   Listeners' interest in my topic: _____

   _____

   Listeners' knowledge about my topic: _____

   _____

   Listeners' personal experience with my topic: _____

   _____

   Listeners' beliefs about my topic: _____

   _____

   Listeners' attitudes about my thesis: _____

   _____

   Listeners' expectations of the speaking occasion:

   _____

   _____

   Listeners' orientation toward me as a speaker: _____

   _____

APPLYING COMMUNICATION IN OUR LIVES

The key concepts, For Further Reflection and Discussion questions, and Experiencing Communication in Our Lives case study that follow will help you review, reflect on, and extend the information and ideas presented in this chapter. These resources, and a diverse selection of additional study tools, are also available as Online Resources for *Communication in Our Lives*. Your

Online Resources include CourseMate, a student workbook, interactive video activities, audio study tools, a book companion website, Speech Builder Express, Speech Studio, and InfoTrac College Edition. For more information or to access this book's online resources, visit **www.cengage.com/login.**

KEY CONCEPTS

demographic audience
    analysis, 332
mind map, 326

situational audience analysis, 334
specific purpose, 330
speech to entertain, 327

speech to inform, 328
speech to persuade, 329
thesis statement, 330

SHARPEN YOUR SKILL

1. Selecting and Narrowing Your Topic

Identify three broad topics or areas that you care about.

Topic 1: _____

Topic 2: _____

Topic 3: _____

Now list three subtopics for each one. The subtopics should be narrow enough to be covered well in a short speech.

Topic 1: 1. _____

2. _____

3. _____

Topic 2: 1. _____

2. _____

3. _____

Topic 3: 1. _____

2. _____

3. _____

Select one of the nine subtopics for your upcoming speech.

2. Defining Your Purpose and Thesis Statement

Write out the general purpose of your speech.
I want my speech to _____

_____

Define the specific purpose of your speech by specifying the observable response that will indicate you have succeeded:
At the end of my speech, I want listeners to _____

_____

Does your specific purpose require you to meet subordinate goals, such as including information in a persuasive speech?
To achieve my specific purpose I need to [entertain, inform, and/or persuade]. _____

_____

For additional practice in developing thesis statements, complete the activity "Developing Effective Thesis Statements" in your Chapter 14 Online Resources for *Communication in Our Lives.* CourseMate

FOR FURTHER REFLECTION AND DISCUSSION

1. Think about one presentation that you recently attended—perhaps a lecture in a class or a speech at a campus event. To what extent did the speaker seem to take the audience into consideration? Identify specific factors that affect your perception of the speaker's knowledge of you and other listeners. Did this make a difference in the speaker's effectiveness?

2. In this chapter, we discussed the importance of adapting to particular listeners. What ethical considerations apply to the process of adapting speeches to particular listeners? Is it ethical for a speaker not to disclose certain experiences with a topic? Is it ethical for a speaker to leave out evidence that is contrary to his or her speaking goal?

3. Check two databases for sources on a topic that interests you. Track down two sources from each database to read in detail.

4. Use your Online Resources for *Communication in Our Lives* to access **WebLink 14.4** to review commonly believed myths about public speaking.

EXPERIENCING COMMUNICATION IN OUR LIVES

CASE STUDY: A Model Speech of Introduction

The following speech is featured in your Chapter 14 Online Resources for *Communication in Our Lives*. Select "Speech of Introduction" to watch the video of Dan's speech. Improve your own public speaking skills by reading, watching, and evaluating this sample speech.

Dan's assignment was to present a speech of introduction in which he introduces his classmates to Dr. Evelyn Horton. Dr. Horton is a doctor who specializes in family medicine, the profession that Dan hopes to enter.

"If you don't listen to your patients, you'll never be able to provide them with good medical care." That was the first thing Dr. Evelyn Horton said to me when I asked her what kinds of communication are essential to her work. Last Monday, I interviewed her because I hope one day to be a doctor. I want to introduce you to Dr. Horton and to describe the role of communication in her work as a doctor. I'll focus on the importance of two communication skills that Dr. Horton emphasized: listening and building a supportive, trusting relationship.

The first communication skill that Dr. Horton emphasized is listening. She told me that one of the reasons she wanted to become a doctor is that she had encountered too many doctors who didn't listen to her when she was a patient. "How can a doctor treat you if he or she doesn't listen to you?" asked Dr. Horton. Dr. Horton isn't alone in feeling that many doctors don't listen. The *Journal of the American Medical Association* reported last year that patients' biggest dissatisfaction with doctors is that they don't listen.

I asked Dr. Horton to explain what was involved in effective listening. She said, and I quote, "To be a good listener, I have to let my patients know I really want to hear what's going on with them. I have to give them permission to tell me how they are feeling and if anything is bothering them." Some of the ways that Dr. Horton does this are to repeat what patients tell her so that they will elaborate, and to keep eye contact with them when they are speaking.

So focusing on patients and encouraging them to talk openly with her are the keys to effective listening in Dr. Horton's practice. The second communication skill that Dr. Horton emphasized is building a supportive, trusting relationship with her patients. She told me about one of her patients who had an eating disorder. Dr. Horton suspected the problem, but she couldn't do much to treat it until her patient, a 19-year-old woman, was willing to admit she had a problem.

How did Dr. Horton gain the patient's trust? She told me that she showed the patient she wasn't going to judge her—that it was okay to say anything, and it would be confidential. When the patient made a small disclosure about being afraid of gaining weight, Dr. Horton recalled, and I quote, "I told her many women have that fear, and there are healthy ways to control weight." Later, the patient told her that sometimes she skipped meals. Dr. Horton responded, and again I quote her, "That's an understandable thing to do when you're afraid of gaining weight, but there are healthier ways to maintain a good weight." As Dr. Horton responded without judgment to the patient, the young woman gradually opened up and told Dr. Horton about her excessive dieting and exercise. Together, they worked out a better plan for managing the patient's weight.

Being nonjudgmental, then, is a key to building a trusting doctor-patient relationship. Now you've met Dr. Evelyn Horton, a doctor who knows the importance of communication to her work. For her, listening and building a supportive, trusting relationship with patients are the keys to being a good doctor. Let me close with one last statement Dr. Horton made. She told me, "To treat people, you have to communicate well with them."

QUESTIONS FOR ANALYSIS AND DISCUSSION

You can answer these questions and see my responses to them online via your Online Resources for Chapter 14.

1. Does Dan's speech give you a sense of who Dr. Horton is?

2. Did Dan's introduction catch your attention and give you a road map of what he would cover in his speech?

3. How did Dan move you from one part of his speech to the next?

4. How did quotes and examples from Dr. Horton add to the speech?

5. Was Dan's conclusion effective?

6. Which model of communication presented in Chapter 1 best describes Dr. Horton's communication with patients?

SPEECH STUDIO

Access Speech Studio via your Online Resources. You can view other students' speeches, listen critically, and identify their speaking purposes, thesis statements, and selections of topics.

SPEECH BUILDER EXPRESS

This is a good time to get to know Speech Builder Express. It offers tools to help you complete your speech assignment. You can access Speech Builder Express through your Online Resources for *Communication in Our Lives*. Once you have accessed Speech Builder Express, select the "Create a New Speech" section.

If you have a title for your speech, type that in as the name of your file. If not, type a temporary name, such as "My First Speech." Next, select the Speech Timeline section on Speech Builder Express. Type in the date on which you will give your speech. Next, select "Goal/Purpose," and type in the specific purpose of your speech. Next, select "Thesis Statement," and type in the thesis statement for your speech (if you have developed it).

Save your file (Speech Title or "My First Speech") to your desktop, or email it to your instructor if that is requested. You'll be adding to this file as you develop your speech throughout this course.

15

Handle them carefully, for words have more power than atom bombs.

Pearl Strachan

Image Source/Getty Images

Researching and Developing Support for Public Speeches

You are four times more likely to have a traffic accident when using a cell phone than when not.

This isn't a hearing; it's a public lynching designed to persecute a black man.

Chief Seattle believed that human life is a web. He said, "Whatever we do to the web, we do to ourselves. All things are bound together."

Drivers shouldn't use cell phones.

This hearing isn't fair.

People are connected to one another.

SHARPEN YOUR SKILL

At the end of this chapter, refer to the Sharpen Your Skill features, Background on Experts and Bringing Statistics Alive, to apply concepts from Chapter 15.

The second statements have impact. They pack a punch and catch our attention. In contrast, the first statements are flat and unmemorable. One difference between the sentences is that the first ones include support for ideas, whereas the second ones simply advance claims without developing them. Critical listeners will not accept unsupported claims, so speakers must fortify the ideas they advance.

In the first statement, statistical evidence supports the claim that the chances of being in a traffic accident increase when drivers use cell phones. The second statement was made by Clarence Thomas in the 1991 Supreme Court confirmation hearings, regarding Anita Hill's charges that he had sexually harassed her. By using a metaphor equating the hearings with a lynching, Thomas induced some people to perceive the hearings not as an orderly judicial process but as a racist vendetta. The third statement quotes a widely admired Native American to argue that humans are deeply interconnected. Each of these statements relies on support, or evidence. Effective use of such supporting materials as statistics, analogies, and quotations enhances the impact of speeches and the credibility of speakers.

In this chapter, we focus on conducting research and weaving support into a presentation. Throughout the process of researching and building support for a speech, it's important to conduct research and select evidence adapted to particular listeners. A speaker's success is tied directly to whether listeners understand, believe, and accept what the speaker says. Your goal is not simply to use good evidence; rather, it is to use supporting materials that are ethical and that will be effective with your particular listeners.

CONDUCTING RESEARCH

At the outset of developing a speech, you may already have a definite point of view and know a good deal about your topic. Mining your own knowledge and conducting further research will help you find additional information to increase your effectiveness. Initial research includes reading, thinking, talking with others, and perhaps conducting surveys. All these activities help you discover the range of information available on your topic. Then, you are ready to evaluate all the evidence you've found and decide which materials most effectively support the specific claims in your speech.

Research continues throughout the development of the speech. In the early stages of research, you may unearth information that leads you to modify your original thesis statement. As you continue, you may find evidence that convinces you to add additional points. We'll discuss four types of research in which speakers engage as they develop informative and persuasive presentations: library and online research, personal knowledge, interviews, and surveys.

Library and Online Research

Libraries and online services hold a wealth of information that can help you develop and support the ideas in your speech. Begin your research by paying a visit to the reference librarian at your library. Describe your speech topic to your reference librarian, and ask for suggestions on relevant print and electronic sources of information.

The Internet   Although the Internet offers a lot of information, that information isn't necessarily credible or reliable. Most magazines and newspapers have staff who check all information in articles before they go to press. Before this textbook was published, references were checked by a researcher, and proofreaders verified cross-references. Claims and evidence were evaluated by independent reviewers. In contrast, there is no systematic procedure for checking the accuracy of information posted on the Internet. Anyone can create a website and put any content on it. People who create or contribute to sites may not have sound backing for their claims. They may have vested interests in particular viewpoints. They may be trying to sell a product. Information on the Internet may be out-of-date or presented out of context.

Indexes   Libraries have indexes, some of which are online, that summarize publications and backgrounds of individuals. Indexes of articles published in academic journals are important resources. *Psychological Abstracts*, for

---

COMMUNICATION HIGHLIGHT

Evaluating Online Sources for Speeches

Material found online is not necessarily trustworthy. Anyone can set up a website, and anyone can make claims on the Internet. Because Internet content is unregulated, you should be especially critical when evaluating it. **CourseMate**

To assess information found on the Internet, begin by applying the five standard tests for evidence summarized in Table 15.4 on page 362. In addition, ask the following questions:

1. Can you verify the material independently (by checking another source or consulting an expert)?
2. Does the source have the experience, position, or other credentials to be an authority?
3. Does the source have any vested interest in making the claim or presenting the alleged information?
4. Does the source acknowledge other sources, including ones that advance different points of view?

If you decide the online material is sound, you should cite it in your bibliography as well as your text, using the following format:

Hulme, M. & Peters, S. (2001). *Me, my phone, and I: The role of the mobile phone.* Workshop: Mobile communications: Understanding users, adoption, and design, Seattle WA. Retrieved January 3, 2002, from http://www.cs.colorado.edu/~palen/chi_workshop.

Basic principles for evaluating material found on the web, as well as links to multiple sites that discuss the credibility of web information, can be found at **WebLink 15.1.** You can access this link via your Online Resources for *Communication in Our Lives*.

example, surveys articles published on psychological topics. If you want to know what research has been done on self-concept, simply look up "self-concept" in *Psychological Abstracts*, and you will find a list (probably a very long one) of published research on the topic. In addition, indexes of government documents summarize laws, policies, and regulations related to many topics.

There are several good sources of background information on experts you may cite in your speech. Some of the more popular ones are *Who's Who in America*, *Who's Who in American Women*, *Biography Index*, and *Directory of American Scholars*. You enhance your own credibility and that of sources you cite when you provide detailed information about their qualifications and accomplishments.

Databases and Search Engines Databases allow you to search a library's or service's holdings from a computer terminal. One widely used database is Dialog Information Retrieval Service (DIRS), which includes more than a million records from popular and academic publications and news services. Two other superior information retrieval systems are Bibliographic Retrieval Service (BRS) and Wilsonline. InfoTrac is a fully searchable, online database that provides access to more than 20 years of complete articles published in more than 8,000 different periodicals. InfoTrac is updated daily, so it is also current.

InfoTrac College Edition is included in your Online Resources for *Communication in Our Lives*. InfoTrac College Edition is a version of the full database designed specifically for college. It features millions of full-text articles from 5,000 scholarly and popular sources. There are also specialized databases for fields such as medicine and law.

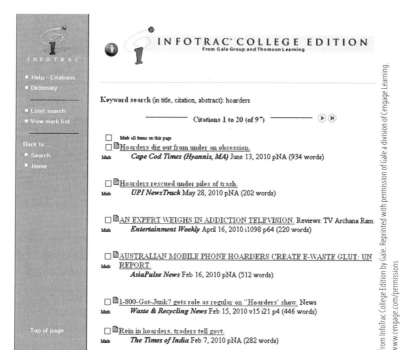

Figure 15.1
Using an Online Database to Research Your Speech Topic.

Online research includes sites such as the U.S. Census Bureau, which provides information on demographics and many facets of American life.

Reference Works Specialized references can save you hours of work by directing you to materials specifically on your topic. The *Reader's Guide to Periodical Literature* summarizes articles published in popular magazines, including *Newsweek*, *Ebony*, and *Fortune*. The *Public Affairs Information Service Bulletin* indexes books, pamphlets, and other materials pertinent to public affairs. *American Demographics* is an amazing reservoir of information on Americans' patterns, behaviors, possessions, and so forth. It's the resource to check if you want to know how many televisions the average household has, how much sugar the average person consumes in a year, or how often most people eat out. *Facts on File* is a weekly publication that provides factual information and background on world news.

Personal Knowledge

Another source of information is yourself. What do you already know about your topic? How are you involved with it? What experiences have you had that qualify you to speak on the topic? Why does this topic matter to you? You will probably be comfortable and engaging when you talk about experiences you have had and knowledge you have gained through personal involvement with a topic.

A second reason to include personal content in a speech is that it tends to enhance your credibility. When you draw on your own experiences and knowledge, listeners are likely to perceive you as more credible than someone who is not personally involved with the topic.

Interviews

Interviews allow you to gather information, to check the accuracy of ideas you have, and to understand the perspective of people who are experts or who have special experience with your topic. Many community organizations have experts who can provide you with a wealth of information on specific topics. For example, the American Lung Association has chapters in most communities, and a staff person could furnish recent information on the causes and frequency of lung disease and ways to reduce the toll on health and life. Other organizations, such as the Parent–Teacher Association, the Animal Protection Society, the Nature Conservancy, Habitat for Humanity, and Alcoholics Anonymous can provide up-to-date information and background in their respective areas.

You need to plan ahead for interviews because experts often have busy schedules. When you call to request an interview, identify yourself, explain the purpose of the interview, and state the approximate length of time you expect the interview to take. Prepare a list of questions in advance to increase the productivity of an interview and to ensure that you don't forget important

COMMUNICATION in Your Life

What personal knowledge do you have relevant to your speech topic?

questions. You may include both closed-ended questions, which ask for specific information (e.g., "How long have you held this position?" "How much does this program cost annually?"), and open-ended questions, which allow interviewees to give more elaborate responses (e.g., "What do you think would improve the system here?" "Can you describe how your organization identifies priorities?").

In addition to questions you prepare, you'll want to invite interviewees to initiate ideas. As experts, they may be aware of information and dimensions of a topic that haven't occurred to you. Furthermore, you have an ethical responsibility to respect an interviewee's priorities, concerns, and perspective. If an interviewee gives permission, it's acceptable to take notes during interviews. However, you should be careful to keep your primary attention on the interviewee. Taping interviews is appropriate only if the interviewee agrees.

Conducting interviews often increases a speaker's credibility. Quoting interviewees shows that a speaker has invested personal effort in researching a topic. In addition, listeners often find experts' opinions persuasive (Olson & Cal, 1984). To maximize the impact of testimony, speakers should identify the source's credentials and explain why the source qualifies as expert. You may credit your sources in several ways:

"Chris Brenner is the chief of police on our campus. He says, and I quote, . . . "
"After 10 years in the position of chief of campus police, Chris Brenner says, and I quote, . . . "
"In an interview I conducted with Chris Brenner, longtime chief of campus police, I learned that . . . "
"To find out about crime on our campus, I interviewed the chief of campus police. According to Chief Brenner, . . . "

> **COLE** *It was really effective when Joel told us he had interviewed police officers to find out their views about drivers who use cell phones. He had lots of good information from other sources, but what really impressed me was that he took the time to talk with police officers himself. I felt like that showed he cared enough to really learn about his topic in a personal way.*

Surveys

Survey research involves asking a number of people about their opinions, views, values, actions, or beliefs. Surveys are useful in two situations. First, sometimes there's no published research on something important to your speech. Yumiko, a student taking his first speaking course, was concerned that many of his peers at the university had misperceptions about Japanese people and their traditions. He decided to use his speech as an opportunity to correct misperceptions. After 2 weeks of research, he was discouraged because he couldn't find any studies

COMMUNICATION in Your Life

Identify three experts on the subject of your speech.

of U.S. college students' views of Japanese people. We developed a short questionnaire on views of Japanese people that was handed out to 100 students on campus. This gave Yumiko some information about local students' perceptions. Another student surveyed her peers to find out how often they attended women's and men's basketball games. For a speech about the dangers of drinking, Justin surveyed his peers to find out how often and how much they drank each week. By gauging the attitudes and patterns of behavior of people like your listeners, you gain valuable insight into ways to adapt your presentation to your listeners' views, beliefs, and habits. The more directly your speech relates to your listeners and their lives, the more effective you will be (Table 15.1).

Table 15.1	Guidelines for Constructing Surveys

The following guidelines will help you construct a survey that will provide you with solid information.

1. Respondents should be chosen to reflect the population (or larger group) whose opinions you seek to understand. (Students may reflect students' opinions. However, students generally would not reflect homeowners' opinions.)

2. Respondents should be qualified to answer the questions. (Only people who are informed about inflation and living expenses have the information to answer this question: "How much should the cost-of-living adjustment be for Social Security recipients?")

3. Questions should be worded to avoid bias. ("You favor gun control, don't you?" is a leading question that biases respondents toward answering affirmatively. The question "Do you favor gun control?" is not biased. You will get different responses if you ask people if they favor "helping the poor" and if they favor "welfare.")

4. Each question should focus on only one issue. ("Do you favor Medicare and Medicaid?" asks respondents' opinions on two distinct issues. This question should be split into two separate questions.)

5. Questions should allow for all possible responses. (It would not be accurate to ask respondents whether they are Democrats or Republicans because those two responses don't include other possible choices, such as Libertarians and Independents.)

6. Questions should rely on language that will be clear to respondents. (For years, the U.S. Bureau of the Census asked people whether they worked "full-time," which the bureau defined as 35 hours a week or more. However, many respondents interpreted "full-time" to mean 40 hours a week or more. The bureau revised the wording of the question to remove the ambiguity.)

7. Avoid negative language in survey items; it tends to be confusing. (Respondents are likely to misunderstand the question "Do you agree or disagree that the United States should not have socialized medicine?" The question is clearer when phrased this way: "Do you agree or disagree that the United States should have socialized medicine?")

For practice in determining effective survey strategies and questions, complete the activity "Survey Construction Guidelines" via your Online Resources for *Communication in Our Lives.*

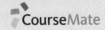

Adapted from Babbie, 2009.

RESEARCH IN OUR LIVES

What counts as evidence?

"What's your evidence?" "Prove it!" These are common challenges when people make claims. We insist that they support their claims with evidence. But what counts as evidence? According to communication researchers Jos Hornikx and Has Hoeken, there are cultural differences in what is perceived as effective evidence.

In one study Hornikx and Hoeken devised an experiment to measure the effectiveness of different types of evidence in two cultures. They asked 600 students from various universities in France and The Netherlands to read claims. All participants read the same claims, but they were given different types of evidence to support the claims: anecdotal, causal, statistical, and expert. The participants then indicated the extent to which they agreed with the claims. Using statistical tests, Hornikx and Hoeken determined that both the French and Dutch participants perceived anecdotal evidence as weaker than the other three types of evidence. They also found that the French participants perceived causal, statistical, and expert evidence as equally persuasive whereas the Dutch participants regarded statistical evidence as more persuasive than causal or expert evidence.

To follow up on this study, Hornikx and Hoeken conducted a second experiment. In this case, they tested whether the strength of expert and statistical evidence affected its effectiveness. They divided 600 students from The Netherlands and France into four groups. Group 1 read claims supported by strong statistical evidence. Group 2 read claims supported by weaker statistical evidence. Group 3 read claims supported by strong expert evidence. Group 4 read claims supported by weaker expert evidence. After conducting statistical tests of the data, Hornikx and Hoeken reported that the Dutch participants more clearly distinguished between strong and weak evidence than the French participants. Regardless of whether the evidence was statistical or expert, the Dutch participants were more persuaded by strong evidence. The French participants, however, were equally susceptible to strong and weak expert evidence.

Thinking Critically: What type(s) of evidence do you find most persuasive? Can you explain why?

Jos Hornikx is an Assistant Professor and Hans Hoeken is a Professor in the Department of Business Communication Studies at Radboud University Nijmengen (The Netherlands). This research was presented in an article titled "Cultural differences in the Persuasiveness of Evidence Types and Evidence Quality" in Communication Monographs, volume 74, pages 443–463.

A second use of surveys is to learn about your audience's knowledge of and attitudes toward your topic. Although it isn't always feasible to survey your listeners, when it is possible this helps you find out what listeners know. Based on what you learn, you can include information they don't have and avoid boring them by telling them what they already know. Surveys of listeners also allow you to discover what personal experience they have pertinent to your topic. Attitudes based on direct experience are more difficult to change (Wu & Shaffer, 1988).

If you plan to speak on gun control, you might want to know whether your listeners are aware of existing legislation, whether they hunt, and whether they or members of their families own firearms for protection. For a speech on family leave practices, it would be helpful to find out whether listeners understand the limits of the Family Medical Leave Act and whether they are aware that the United States is the only industrialized nation that doesn't have guaranteed family leave for all workers.

Audience surveys can also help you learn what attitudes your listeners hold. At a minimum, you'll want to know whether your listeners agree or disagree with your position and how strong their attitudes are. If you want to argue for more severe sentences for convicted felons, and your listeners are strongly against that, then you might choose to limit your persuasive goal to reducing the strength of listeners' resistance to stronger sentencing. On the other hand, if they already agree with your position, you might try to move them toward action by asking them to write letters to senators or to vote for candidates who share their attitudes. What you can achieve in a given speech depends to a large extent on the starting beliefs and knowledge of your listeners (Wu & Shaffer, 1988).

Now that we have discussed ways to conduct research, we're ready to consider specific forms of support, or evidence.

USING EVIDENCE TO SUPPORT IDEAS

Evidence is material used to support claims a speaker makes. You support an idea when you include material to clarify, prove, or demonstrate it. In addition, support may enhance interest and emotional response to ideas. Evidence serves a number of important functions in speeches. First, it can be used to make ideas clearer, more compelling, and more dramatic. Second, evidence fortifies a speaker's opinions, which are seldom sufficient by themselves to persuade intelligent listeners. Finally, evidence heightens a speaker's credibility. Speakers who use good evidence show that they are informed and prepared. Thus, including strong evidence allows speakers to build credibility.

The effectiveness of evidence depends directly on whether listeners understand and accept it. This reinforces the importance of audience analysis, which we discussed in Chapter 14. Remember that even if you quote a leading authority in support of your ideas, the evidence won't be effective if your listeners don't know the authority or don't find the authority credible (Olson & Cal, 1984). Consequently, your goal is to include support that your particular listeners will find credible, interesting, and convincing while also making sure your evidence is valid.

MARTEL   *We had a guest speaker in my econ class. He quoted Nobel Prize-winning economists and the findings of a report that was just done and hasn't even been published yet. All of us felt he was highly informed and credible.*

To decide when to use evidence in a speech, ask yourself, "Will my listeners understand and believe this claim on my say-so alone?" If not, then you'll want to include evidence.

Speech Builder Express, which you can access via your Online Resources for *Communication in Our Lives*, includes a section focused on selecting the amount and types of supporting material you may need, based on the main points of your speech.

The next decision you need to make is what type of evidence to use. Five forms of support are widely recognized, and each tends to be effective in specific situations and for particular goals. Before including any form of evidence in a speech, the speaker should check the accuracy of the material and the credibility of the source. When presenting evidence to listeners, speakers have an ethical responsibility to give credit to the source (an oral footnote) and tell listeners the date of the evidence.

Statistics

Statistics are numbers that summarize many individual cases or demonstrate relationships between phenomena. Statistics allow us to state quickly a large amount of information. For example, a speaker could demonstrate the prevalence of injuries caused by drivers who are under the influence of alcohol by stating, "According to the American Automobile Association, one in four people injured in traffic accidents is the victim of a driver who had been drinking." Statistics can also be used to document connections between two or more things. For instance, a speaker could tell listeners, "According to the Highway Patrol, you are 50% more likely to have an accident if you drink before driving." This draws listeners' attention to the link between drinking and automobile accidents.

Statistics can enhance a speaker's credibility (Crossen, 1997). For that to happen, you must translate statistics into information that is meaningful to listeners. A National Geographic program (*National Geographic*, 1994) on environmental responsibility forcefully made the point that Americans overconsume natural resources: It was stated that "North Americans make up only 6% of the world's population, yet they consume 40% to 60% of the planet's resources." To describe a million homeless people in terms listeners will immediately understand, a student speaker said, "That's fifty times the number of students on our campus."

Here's how another student speaker translated the statistic that one in four college-age women will be raped in her lifetime: "Of the seventeen women students in this room today, four will probably be raped some time during their lives." Statistics aren't boring, but they can be poorly presented. With imagination and effort, you can make statistics interesting and powerful.

Cartoon by Signe Wilkinson. Reprinted by permission of Cartoonists & Writers Syndicate/cartoonweb.com

Table 15.2	Guidelines for Using Statistics Effectively

Used unimaginatively, statistics are likely to bore listeners. To avoid this fate when you are speaking, follow these guidelines for using statistics effectively.

- Limit the number of statistics you use in a speech. A few well-chosen numbers mixed with other kinds of support can be dramatic and persuasive, whereas a laundry list of statistics can be monotonous and ineffective.

- Round off numbers so that listeners can understand and retain them. We're more likely to remember that "approximately a million Americans are homeless" than that "987,422 Americans are homeless."

- Select statistics that are timely. Occasionally, an old statistic is still useful. For example, the number of people who died in the Great Plague is not likely to change over the years. In most cases, however, the most accurate statistics are recent. Remember that statistics are a numerical picture of something at a specific time. But things change, and speakers should get new snapshots when they do.

- Make statistics interesting to listeners by translating statistics into familiar and relevant information.

Examples

Examples are single instances used to make a point, dramatize an idea, or personalize information. We'll consider four types of examples.

Undetailed Examples   When speakers want to make a point quickly, undetailed examples are useful. These are brief references that quickly recount specific instances of something. In this chapter, I've used a number of undetailed examples of student speeches to give you a concrete idea of conceptual points we're discussing. Undetailed examples may also be used to remind listeners of information with which they're already familiar. One student opened a speech on the costs of textbooks by saying, "Remember standing in the long lines at the bookstore and paying for more than your tuition at the start of this term?" His listeners immediately identified with the topic of the speech.

Detailed Examples   Detailed examples provide more elaborate information than undetailed ones, so they are valuable when listeners aren't familiar with an idea. A student included this detailed example in her speech on environmental justice:

> Most of you haven't lived near a toxic waste dump, so you may not understand what's involved. In one community, the incidence of cancer is 150% higher than in the country as a whole. The skin on one man's hands was eaten away when he touched the outside of a canister that stored toxic waste. His skin literally dissolved when it came in contact with the toxin.

Detailed examples create vivid pictures that can be moving and memorable. However, they take time to present, so they should be used sparingly.

COMMUNICATION in Your Life

What are two undetailed examples that might help listeners identify with your topic?

Hypothetical Examples Sometimes a speaker has no real example that adequately makes a point. In such cases, a speaker can create a hypothetical example, which is not factual but can add clarity and depth to a speech. To be effective, hypothetical examples must be realistic illustrations of what you want to exemplify. Hypothetical examples often are used to portray average cases rather than to represent a single person or event. If you use a hypothetical example, you have an ethical responsibility to inform listeners that it is not a factual, real example.

Stories A final kind of example is the story, or anecdote. Stories included in speeches often are based on personal experiences. Presidents Ronald Reagan and Bill Clinton routinely included several personal stories in their speeches to personalize their ideas and create identification with listeners. Religions rely on stories—parables in Christianity, *teichos* in Buddhism—to teach values and persuade people to follow them. Attorneys rely on stories to persuade judges and jurors, taking all the known facts in a case and weaving them together in a way that makes sense and supports their clients' accounts of events. The attorneys with whom I consult tell me that the key challenge in trial court is to create a story that covers all the facts and is more believable than the story created by the opposing counsel.

Speakers often tell a story to put a human face on abstract issues. To help middle-class listeners understand the personal meaning of poverty, a student told this story of a woman he interviewed to prepare his speech:

> To start her day, Annie pours half a glass of milk and mixes it half and half with water so that the quart she buys each week will last. If she finds day-old bread on sale at the market, she has toast, but she can't afford margarine. Annie coughs harshly and wishes this throat infection would pass. She can't afford to go to a doctor. Even if she could, the cost of drugs is beyond her budget. She shivers, thinking that winter is coming. That means long days in the malls so that she can be in heated places. It's hard on her and the kids, but the cost of heat is more than she can pay. Annie is only 28 years old, just a few years older than we are, but she looks well into her forties. Like you, Annie grew up expecting a pretty good life, but then her husband left her. He doesn't pay child support, and she can't afford a detective to trace him. Her children, both under 4, are too young to be left alone, so she can't work.

The story about Annie puts a human face on poverty. A story that has depth takes time, so speakers have to consider whether the point they want to make justifies the time a story will take. When developed with care, stories can provide valuable support to speakers' claims.

Comparisons

Comparisons are associations between two things that are similar in some important way or ways. **Similes** are explicit comparisons that typically use the words *like* or *as* to link two things: "A teacher is like a guide." "Smoking is like giving away years of life." **Metaphors** are implicit comparisons that suggest likeness

COMMUNICATION HIGHLIGHT

The Typical American Family

John F. Kennedy was a powerful public speaker. He wove many kinds of support into his speeches to strengthen his credibility and increase the impact of his ideas.

On May 19, 1962, President John F. Kennedy used the following hypothetical example in his speech at the rally for the National Council of Senior Citizens at Madison Square Garden:

Diamond Images/Getty Images

> Let's consider the case of a typical American family—a family which might be found in any part of the United States. The husband has worked hard all of his life, and now he has retired. He might have been a clerk or a salesman or worked in a factory. He always insisted on paying his own way. This man, like most Americans, wants to care for himself. He has raised his own family, educated his children, and he and his wife are drawing Social Security now. Then his wife gets sick, not just for a week, but for a very long time. First the savings go. Next, he mortgages his home. Finally, he goes to his children, who are themselves heavily burdened. Then their savings begin to go. What is he to do now? Here is a typical American who has nowhere to turn, so he finally will have to sign a petition saying he's broke and needs welfare assistance.

between two things that have something in common. A student speaker used this metaphor in her speech about the college experience: "College is a journey from the known to the unknown. Each step in the process takes us farther from what we knew before and leads us to new understandings."

Comparisons can be powerful rhetorical devices because they invite listeners to see something familiar in a new light.

Quotations

Quotations, or testimony, are exact citations of statements made by others. Speakers often use quotations to clarify ideas or to make them more credible. If someone has stated a point in an especially effective manner, then you may want to quote that person's words. In a speech on homeless citizens, a student quoted a metaphor used by a social worker: "Homelessness is a cancer that eats away at the vitality and decency of our society."

Quotations may also be used to substantiate ideas. Using an expert's testimony may be persuasive to listeners, but only if they respect the expert who is quoted. Thus, it's important to provide "oral footnotes" in which you identify the name, position, and qualifications of anyone you quote, as well as the date of the quoted statement. For example, in a speech advocating tougher laws for driving under the influence, you might say, "Speaking in 2008, our senior state senator,

COMMUNICATION HIGHLIGHT

I Have a Dream

In 1963, the Reverend Martin Luther King Jr., delivered his eloquent "I Have a Dream" speech to more than 200,000 listeners. In it, he compared the unfulfilled promises of the United States to African American citizens to a check for which funds must now be provided. This was a compelling metaphor that used the familiar idea of a check to explain civil rights promises that had been made but not yet kept by the country.

AP Photo

> We've come to our nation's capital to cash a check. When the architects of our republic wrote the magnificent words of the Constitution and the Declaration of Independence, they were signing a promissory note to which every American was to fall heir. The note was a promise that all men—yes, Black men as well as White men—would be guaranteed the unalienable rights of life, liberty and the pursuit of happiness.

It is obvious today that America has defaulted on this promissory note insofar as her citizens of color are concerned…America has given the Negro people a bad check; a check which has come back marked "insufficient funds." But we refuse to believe that there are insufficient funds in the great vaults of opportunity of this nation. So we've come to cash this check—a check that will give us upon demand the riches of freedom and security of justice.

To search for more information about Martin Luther King Jr.'s "I Have a Dream" speech, use your Online Resources for *Communication in Our Lives* to access **WebLink 15.2.**

Ben Adams, observed that if we had enacted the proposed law three years ago, 23 people killed by drunk drivers would be alive today."

Whenever you quote another person, you are ethically obligated to give credit to that person, just as you credit the sources of all forms of evidence. This can be done by changing your tone of voice after stating an authority's name, or by telling listeners, "This authority stated that…" It is also acceptable to say "quote" at the beginning of a quotation and "end quote" at the end of it, although this method of citing sources becomes boring if it is used repeatedly in a speech.

Effective and ethical quotations meet four criteria. First, as we've already noted, sources should be people whom listeners know and respect or whom they will respect once you identify credentials. You won't convince politically liberal listeners of anything by quoting Rush Limbaugh, and you'll never convince politically conservative listeners by quoting Barack Obama or Hillary Rodham Clinton. This point reinforces our previous discussion of the importance of keeping your listeners in mind at each step in the process of designing and delivering a speech.

A second criterion is that a quotation should come from someone who is qualified to speak on the issue (Olson & Cal, 1984). Michael Jordan is an awesome athlete. However, his expertise on the court has no relevance to Hanes underwear, which uses him in its ads. Hanes is counting on the **halo effect**, the tendency to assume that an expert in one area is also an expert in other areas. Although some people may fall prey to the halo effect, discerning listeners will not. Ethical speakers rely on authorities who are qualified, and they identify authorities' qualifications to enhance their credibility in listeners' minds.

Ethical quotations must also meet the criterion of accuracy. For instance, you should respect the context in which comments are made. It is unethical

Pepper . . . and Salt

THE WALL STREET JOURNAL

"He's a great field dog, and is much in demand as a motivational speaker."

From The Wall Street Journal. Reprinted by permission of Cartoon Features Syndicate.

COMMUNICATION HIGHLIGHT

Avoiding Plagiarism

CourseMate

The word *plagiarism* comes from the Latin word *plagiare*, which means "to kidnap." Plagiarism is the unattributed use of the language or ideas of another person. If you use the actual words or ideas of someone else, you must give credit to that person. Also, if you only slightly modify another's words or ideas, you must attribute the words or ideas to that person.

There is a distinction between paraphrasing and plagiarism. Paraphrasing is putting another person's ideas in your own words. Paraphrasing does not mean changing a word or two in someone else's sentence, changing the sentence structure while maintaining the original words, or changing a few words to synonyms. If you are tempted to rearrange a sentence in any of these ways, you are writing too close to the original. That's plagiarizing, not paraphrasing.

In the academic world, plagiarism by students is a very serious academic offense that can result in punishments such as a failing grade on the particular assignment, a failing grade for the course, suspension, or even expulsion from school. To learn more about what plagiarism is and how to avoid it, use your Online Resources for *Communication in Our Lives* to access **WebLink 15.3.**

to take a statement out of context to make it better support your ideas. Also, it's unethical to alter a direct quotation by adding or deleting words. Sometimes, writers omit words and indicate the omission with ellipses: "Noted authority William West stated that 'there is no greater priority . . . than our children.'" In oral presentations, however, it is difficult to indicate omitted words smoothly. When using quotations, speakers have an ethical responsibility to be accurate and fair in representing others and their ideas.

Finally, quotations should come from unbiased sources. It's hardly convincing when scientists paid by the tobacco industry tell us cigarettes don't cause cancer. For the same reason, it's not persuasive when spokespeople for Microsoft assure us that they are not trying to create a monopoly. These two sources are biased because they have a vested interest in a particular viewpoint. Their bias limits their credibility as believable authorities on tobacco and Microsoft products, respectively.

Visual Aids

Support also is provided by **visual aids**, such as charts, graphs, photographs, transparencies, computer graphics, and physical objects. Visual aids can increase listeners' understanding and retention of ideas presented in a speech (Hamilton, 2008; Hamilton & Parker, 2001). Visual aids also tend to increase listeners' interest in a presentation because they add variety to the message (Hamilton, 2005; Hamilton & Parker, 2001). Further, visual aids provide content cues to speakers, which reduces reliance on notes.

By using widely available computer technologies, it's often possible to prepare sharp, effective visual aids. You may have software programs that allow you to design charts, graphs, and other visuals. Computer-generated visual aids can be transformed easily into transparencies, which are the most commonly used visual aid in most professional presentations (Hamilton, 2008). Visual aids can be used either to reinforce ideas presented verbally or to provide information. For example, Figure 15.2 is a bar graph that could effectively strengthen the statistics on juvenile reform we discussed previously. Pie charts can forcefully emphasize contrasts and proportions (Figure 15.3). You can also use technologies to create visual aids. You may want to use part of a film or create a videotape to dramatize a point in your speech. A student speaker showed parts of the Disney film *Pocahontas* to support her claim that the main character was different from the historical figure.

Diagrams or models help speakers explain complex concepts and unfamiliar topics. Especially in speeches of demonstration, a model or physical diagram can be useful. One of my students prepared a diagram to show listeners how a nuclear reactor works. Maps help listeners understand geographic relationships and issues.

Photographs can reinforce verbal messages, or they can be messages in their own right. To fortify her argument that development is eroding coastal land, a student showed enlarged pictures

This speaker maintains eye contact with listeners while using a well-designed visual aid.

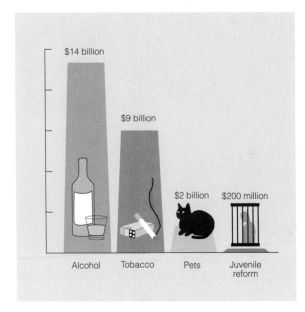

Figure 15.2
Bar Graphs Dramatize Statistics.

Figure 15.3
Pie Charts Clarify Proportions.

of an island community before development, when healthy sand dunes existed, and after development, when the dunes had eroded. In a speech urging listeners to contribute to an organization that provides food to starving people in undeveloped countries, a student showed pictures of women, men, and children who were so starved they looked like skeletons. The old adage, "A picture is worth a thousand words," was true in this case because the student's picture spoke more compellingly about hunger than words ever could have.

Handouts are also useful visual aids. Because listeners can take handouts with them, they are particularly valuable when a speaker wants information to remain with listeners. After a speech encouraging students to vote for a bill currently under consideration by the state legislature, a student gave every listener a handout with the names, addresses, and phone numbers of their representatives. Another student, who spoke on the topic of the dangers of drinking, concluded her speech by handing out a list of agencies and phone numbers that could be called by people who thought they might have problems with alcohol. In both cases, the handouts ensured that listeners had critical information long after the speech was over. You may have noticed that in both examples of students who used handouts, the written materials were passed to listeners at the end of the speeches. This was an effective choice on the speakers' parts because it avoided breaking up a speech to pass out paper and listeners reading the handout while the speaker was talking. Because handouts may distract listeners, it's wise to save them until you have finished speaking.

Visual aids don't need to be complex to have impact. Even simple ones can be effective. For example, President Reagan often held up letters from which he read to audiences. He could have simply summarized what the letter said, but he added force by holding the actual sheet of paper (Spaeth, 1996).

COMMUNICATION
in Your Life

What is one visual aid that would enhance your speech?

COMMUNICATION HIGHLIGHT

Making PowerPoint Work for You

Because computerized presentations can enhance speeches, many public speaking courses require students to learn PowerPoint or other presentational software. Communication scholars Joe Downing and Cecile Garmon (2001) wanted to know whether hands-on instruction and online learning differed in effectiveness. They had one group of students learn PowerPoint through a users' guide available online. A second group of students were taught PowerPoint in the classroom. There was no difference in the two groups of students' confidence and competence in using PowerPoint. You can access an online guide to using PowerPoint at **WebLink 15.4.** Use your Online Resources for *Communication in Our Lives* to access this link.

CourseMate

Guidelines for Using Visual Aids For visual aids to be effective, speakers should observe several guidelines (Williams, 1994). First, a visual aid should be large enough and clear enough to be seen clearly by all listeners. As obvious as this advice is, speakers routinely violate it by showing photographs, graphs, or PowerPoint slides that can be seen only by listeners in the front of the room. Make sure any numbers, words, or emblems can be seen clearly by listeners in the back of the room. Make sure that letters in major headings are at least 3 inches high and that letters in subpoints are at least 2 inches high. By using an overhead projector, a speaker can present transparencies and other material in enlarged form.

Second, visuals should be simple and uncluttered. Visuals with a great deal of information are more likely to confuse than clarify. Especially if you are presenting a series of slides (computerized or not), simplicity is important. You can create effective slides by following the guidelines in Table 15.3. A good basic rule is to use visual aids to highlight key information and ideas, not to summarize all content.

Third, visual aids should be safe and nondistracting. Some visual aids are not appropriate for use in any circumstances. For example, a real, functional firearm is dangerous in public situations. In addition to the fact that "there's no such thing as an unloaded gun," firearms may frighten listeners, distracting them from listening to the speech. Other visual aids that are risky and should be avoided include live animals, illegal substances, and chemicals that could react with one another. It's also unwise to use visual aids that might seriously upset or disgust listeners. The purpose of visuals is to enhance your speech, not to be so sensational that they take attention away from your ideas.

Many visual aids are verbal texts—main ideas of a speech, major points in a policy, or steps to action. When visual texts are used, certain guidelines apply. As a general rule, a visual text should have no more than six lines of words, should use phrases more than sentences, and should use a simple typeface. Color and variations in type size can be used to add emphasis to visual texts. This applies to handouts, overhead transparencies, and large visuals displayed at the front of a room. For practice identifying effective slides, complete the activity "Slide Construction Guidelines" via your Online Resources for *Communication in Our Lives*.

CourseMate

Although visual aids can be effective, it's possible to have too much of a good thing. When speakers use too many visuals or too much variation in type color and style, listeners may experience visual overload. As a guideline for deciding how many visuals to use in a speech, Cheryl Hamilton (2005) suggests this formula:

$$\frac{\text{Length of speech}}{2} + 1 = \text{Maximum number of visuals}$$

Table 15.3	Guidelines for Using Slides in a Speech

To create effective slides, including PowerPoint presentations for speeches, follow these guidelines:

1. Each slide should focus on a single concept or point and key information to support that concept or point (phrases or key words generally are preferable to whole sentences or lengthy text).

2. Fonts should be large enough to be read by listeners at the back of the speaking room. Generally, main points should appear in 36-point type, supporting ideas should appear in 24- or 28-point type, and text should appear in type no smaller than 18 points.

3. Typefaces should be clean and clear. Avoid script styles, *overuse of italics*, or **TRENDY TYPEFACES**. They are distracting and can detract from clarity.

4. Mix uppercase and lowercase lettering. ALL CAPITAL LETTERS CAN BE HARD TO READ.

5. Use art to provide visual relief from text and enhance interest. If using a computerized presentation program, consider using clip art or pictures imported from the web.

6. Use one design consistently. Computerized programs such as PowerPoint have design templates. Stick with one design to provide visual continuity and transitions.

7. Select a color scheme that is visually strong but not overpowering. Especially if you are showing a series of slides, avoid glaring colors that can tire listeners. Occasionally, you may violate this guideline to adapt to your particular listeners. For instance, if you are speaking at the banquet of a company whose logo is teal and white, you might want a teal and white color scheme.

8. Use special effects sparingly. It may be effective to have text zoom in from the right with a blaring sound on one slide, but it would be tiring and ineffective for text to zoom in on slide after slide.

9. Use visual highlighting sparingly. It can be effective to **boldface** or highlight one particularly important idea. However, the impact of visual highlighting is lost when it is overdone.

10. Give credit to those who created material you use. Acknowledge authors of quotations or other material. You should also get permission to use any materials that are not in the public domain.

11. Don't sacrifice content for flashy visuals. Visuals aids, including computerized ones, should enhance your content, not substitute for it.

12. Make slides bright enough that you do not have to darken the room fully.

If you are preparing a 10-minute speech, you should include no more than six visual aids ($10/2 + 1 = 6$). Note that each slide in a series of slides counts as one visual aid.

Perhaps the biggest mistake speakers make with visual aids is giving them higher priority than they give the speech itself. You should develop the content of your presentation before you even consider visual aids. After developing your ideas, if you do want to use visual aids, focus on creating ones that reinforce content. They should never eclipse content or compensate for the lack of careful development of ideas (Zukerman, 1999).

There are also some mechanical guidelines for using visual aids effectively. First, remove or cover visual aids before and after you use them. A visual aid that's strong enough to be effective in supporting ideas will distract listeners' attention from what you are saying if it is left in view when not in use. Also, maintain visual contact with listeners when using visual aids. Novice speakers often make the mistake of facing their charts or pictures when discussing them. This breaks the connection between speaker and listeners.

It's a good idea to keep an ongoing record of evidence you discover during the research process. There are two ways to do this. The traditional method is to write out each piece of evidence, preferably on separate note cards. By the time you have finished researching your speech, you should have a deck of cards that contain evidence you might use in the final speech.

A mind map is an alternative method of keeping track of information you find while you are researching a speech. In Chapter 14, we discussed mind maps as a way to narrow the focus of a broad topic. The same method can also help you record information. A mind map is a more holistic, less linear way to record information than the conventional note card system. To construct a mind map for your speech, begin by writing the subject of your presentation in the center of a blank page. Then, draw a line from the center to each piece of evidence that you discover as you conduct your research. At this stage, you shouldn't try to determine which evidence you will use; for now, write down all the information you find. Once you have a complete record of information you've gathered, you can decide which evidence to include in your presentation. Figure 15.4 shows a mind map record of information for a speech on Hawaiian sovereignty.

Statistics, examples, comparisons, quotations, and visual aids support your ideas in different ways. Whereas evidence such as statistics, examples, and quotations can provide strong logical support, visual aids and analogies often are more powerful in adding clarity, interest, and emotional appeal to a speech. All forms of evidence, when carefully chosen and ethically used, tend to increase the credibility listeners confer on a speaker and the extent to which they retain the speaker's ideas (Table 15.4).

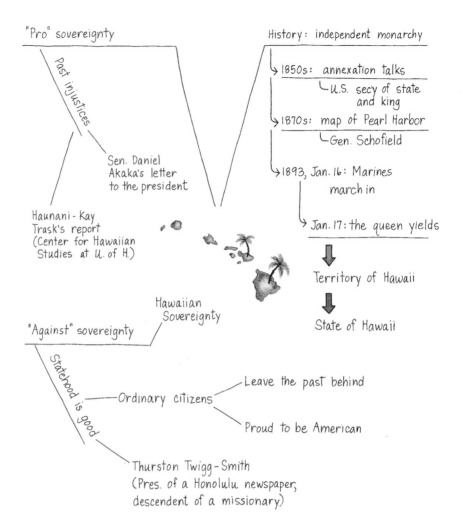

Figure 15.4
Mind Map of Evidence.
Source: Jaffe, C. (2007). Public *Speaking: Concepts and Skills for a Diverse Society,* Fifth Edition, Belmont, CA: Wadsworth.

Table 15.4	Testing Evidence

Five questions help speakers test whether evidence is ethical and effective. Each question addresses a specific criterion for assessing the worth of evidence:

1. Is there enough evidence to support a claim? (sufficiency)

2. Is the evidence accurately presented—quotations are verbatim, nothing is taken out of context? (accuracy)

3. Does the evidence relate directly to the claim it is intended to support? (relevance)

4. Is the evidence appropriately timely—are statistics, quotations, examples, and comparisons current or appropriate for the time discussed? (timeliness)

5. Is the evidence free of biases such as vested interest? (impartiality)

CHAPTER SUMMARY

This chapter focused on ways to research speeches and support ideas to be presented. Just as they do when you are first planning a speech, your listeners should influence how you research and support it. Therefore, you need to ask yourself what kinds of research and what forms of support your particular listeners are most likely to find interesting and credible.

The process of researching a speech includes reviewing your personal experiences and knowledge about your topic, interviewing experts who can expand your insight into the subject, scouting libraries for evidence, and conducting surveys to find out about others' beliefs, practices, and knowledge relevant to your topic. It isn't unusual for speakers to revise the focus of a speech in the course of conducting research. This is appropriate when information you discover modifies or alters your knowledge or even your position.

Research for a speech provides speakers with different kinds of evidence that they can use to clarify, dramatize, and energize a speech. The five types of evidence we discussed are statistics, examples, comparisons, quotations, and visual aids. These are effective forms of support when they are used thoughtfully and ethically and when they are adapted to the interests, knowledge, attitudes, and experiences of listeners.

Now that you've gone through the phases of planning, researching, and finding support for speeches, we're ready to consider the final steps in designing effective presentations. Chapter 16 explains how to organize and present public speeches. Before you move on to Chapter 16, take a moment to fill in this chapter's checklist for researching and supporting your speech.

CHECKLIST FOR RESEARCHING AND SUPPORTING A PUBLIC SPEECH

CourseMate If you prefer, you may complete this checklist online under your Chapter 15 Online Resources for *Communication in Our Lives*.

1. I conducted the following research: _____
   _____
   A. Review of my personal experience showed that _____
   B. I interviewed (name/title): _____
   _____
      (name/title): _____
      (name/title): _____
   C. I checked these three indexes: _____
   _____
   D. I checked these three online sources: _____
   _____
   E. I surveyed on the following issues: _____
   _____

2. I found the following key evidence for my speech:
   A. Statistics: _____
   B. Authorities I will quote: _____
   C. Examples: _____
   D. Comparisons: _____
   E. Visual aids: _____

3. I have all the information to identify my sources appropriately and to explain why they are qualified and relevant to the ideas I will present.

If you have not completed all items on this checklist, do so now before moving on to Chapter 16. You may want to use Speech Builder Express to complete some of these tasks, which you can access through your Online Resources.

APPLYING COMMUNICATION IN OUR LIVES

The key concepts, For Further Reflection and Discussion questions, and Experiencing Communication in Our Lives case study that follow will help you review, reflect on, and extend the information and ideas presented in this chapter. These resources, and a diverse selection of additional study tools, are also available as Online Resources for *Communication in Our Lives*.

Your Online Resources include CourseMate, a student workbook, interactive video activities, audio study tools, a book companion website, Speech Builder Express, Speech Studio, and InfoTrac College Edition. For more information or to access this book's online resources, visit **www.cengage.com/login**.

KEY CONCEPTS

comparisons, 353
evidence, 350
examples, 352
halo effect, 356

metaphors, 353
quotations, 354
similes, 353
statistics, 351

survey research, 347
visual aids, 357

FOR FURTHER REFLECTION AND DISCUSSION

1. After you've interviewed two experts on your topic, reflect on what you learned. What did they explain, reveal, or show you that added to your knowledge of the topic?

2. How did the process of researching your speech affect your understandings, beliefs, and speaking goal? Explain what changed and why.

3. Use your InfoTrac College Edition to find current evidence to support your speech. If you plan to speak on a health-related topic, use publications such as World Health, Health News, or Healthfacts. If you plan to speak on a public policy issue, check out publications such as Public Welfare, Weekly Compilation of Presidential Documents, and Public Interest. Type in the keywords relevant to your topic.

4. Pay attention to evidence in a speech on campus. Evaluate the effectiveness of evidence. Are visuals clear and uncluttered? Does the speaker explain the qualifications of sources cited, and are those sources adequately unbiased? What examples and comparisons are presented, and how effective are they? Evaluate the ethical quality of the evidence used. Did the speaker provide enough information for you to assess the expertise of any sources cited? Did the speaker show that the sources were not biased?

   Ethics

5. Experiment with PowerPoint or other computerized software. Notice how different designs, colors, and special effects affect the clarity and impact of your slides.

SHARPEN YOUR SKILL

1. Background on Experts

Research the credentials of three authorities you plan to cite in your speech. Below, write important information that contributes to their credibility.

1. _____holds the following titles: _____ and has the following experiences and qualifications: _____

2. _____holds the following titles: _____ and has the following experiences and qualifications: _____

3. _____holds the following titles: _____ and has the following experiences and qualifications: _____

2. Bringing Statistics Alive

Practice translating statistics into interesting and meaningful information. Here's an example.

Statistic: Americans annually spend $14 billion on alcohol, $9 billion on tobacco, $2 billion on pets, and $200 million on juvenile reform.

Translation: For every $1 spent on juvenile reform in the United States, $70 are spent on alcohol, $45 on tobacco, and $10 on pets.

Statistic: Children under 10 watch television an average of 50 hours each week.

Translation: _____

Statistic: The Stealth bomber program cost $40 billion and produced a total of 20 aircraft.

Translation: _____

Statistic: The number of working poor, people who make $13,000 or less a year, rose from 12% of the workforce in 1989 to 18% in 2008.

Translation: _____

Now, apply what you've learned to your own speech. Select three statistics you could use in your speech, and translate them into meaningful, interesting terms.

Statistic 1: _____
can be translated this way _____
Statistic 2: _____
can be translated this way _____
Statistic 3: _____
can be translated this way _____

For additional practice in bringing statistics alive, complete the activity "Translating Statistics" in your Chapter 15 Online Resources for *Communication in Our Lives.* **Course**Mate

EXPERIENCING COMMUNICATION IN OUR LIVES

CASE STUDY: *Understanding Hurricanes*

The following speech is featured in your Chapter 15 Online Resources for *Communication in Our Lives.* Select "Understanding Hurricanes" to watch the video of speech titled "Understanding Hurricanes." Improve your own public speaking skills by reading, watching, and evaluating this sample speech.

CourseMate

© Cengage Learning

Think about a time you've been absolutely terrified—whether it was by a person, event, or situation, and all you wanted to do was go home and be with your family and friends.

Now imagine the feeling you might have if you were that afraid, but you had no idea if your home would even be there when you arrived. This is the reality for many people living on the coastlines of the United States. Hurricanes affect the lives of those living in their direct paths, but they can also affect the entire country.

I have lived about forty-five minutes from the Gulf Coast of Texas my entire life and have seen and experienced the destruction caused by hurricanes first hand, especially in the past three years. (*Slide 1: picture of hurricane that hit my hometown last year.*) This is a picture of my hometown when a hurricane hit it last year.

Today I'd like to speak with you about the way hurricanes work, the ways they affect our whole country and, most importantly, the toll they have on the people who live in their direct paths.

To begin, let's discuss how hurricanes form and the varying degrees of intensity of them so we can be better informed when we watch news broadcasts and read newspaper reports about them.

Several basic conditions must be present for a Hurricane to form. According to award-winning Discovery Communications website, HowStuffWorks.com, hurricanes form "when an area of warm low-pressure air rises and cool, high pressure seizes the opportunity to move in underneath it." This causes a center to develop. This center may eventually turn into what is considered a hurricane. The warm and moist air from the ocean rises up into these pressure zones and begins to form storms. As this happens, the storm continues to draw up more warm moist air and a heat transfer occurs because of the cool air being heated causing the air to rise again. "The exchange of heat creates a pattern of wind that circulates around a center," (the eye of the storm), "like water going down a drain." The "rising air reinforces the air that is already" being pulled up from the surface of the ocean, "so the circulation and speeds of the wind increase."

Classifications of these types of storms help determine their intensity so we can prepare properly for them. Winds that are less than 38 miles per hour are considered Tropical Depressions. Tropical Storms have winds that range from 39 to 73 miles per hour. And lastly, Hurricanes are storms with wind speeds of 74 miles per hour and higher.

When storms become classified as a Hurricane, they become part of another classification system that is displayed by the Saffir-Simpson Hurricane Scale. Hurricanes are labeled as Categories 1-5 based on their wind intensity level or speed. (*Slide 2: hurricane scale chart*) Hurricane Ike was labeled differently at different places. (*Slide 3: Map showing the different places Ike was labeled in the different categories*)

Knowing how and where hurricanes occur help us determine how our daily lives, even here in Kentucky, may be affected when one hits.

A hurricane can affect more than just those living in its direct path and these effects can actually be seen across the country in terms of the environment and the economy.

Hurricanes affect wildlife in negative ways. According to the Beaumont Enterprise on October 7, 2008, Christine Rappleye reported that the storm surge, which is basically a wall of water, Hurricane Ike brought in across some parts of Southeast Texas—about 14 feet in some places—dolphins were swept inland with the surge and then, when the waters flowed back out to sea, dolphins were left stranded in the marsh. Some were rescued, but not all. This dolphin was rescued from a ditch. (*Slide 4: Dolphin being rescured*)

Hurricanes also affect the economy. Prices climb close to all time highs when hurricanes hit. According to economist Beth Ann Bovino, quoted in the September 29, 2005 issue of The Washington Post, gas prices sky-rocket when a hurricane like Katrina, Rita, or Ike hits. Paul Davidson said, in a September 12, 2008 article in USA Today, that in the anticipation of Hurricane Ike, 12 refineries in Texas were shut down. "This is 17% of the U.S. refining capacity" he said. That's why even residents here in Lexington saw a dramatic spike in gas prices immediately following Ike's landfall.

Energy costs to heat and cool our homes also rise. When consumers have to pay more to heat and cool our homes, we also have less to spend eating out at restaurants. And we have less to spend on non-essentials at the mall. So, economically we all feel the ripple effect when hurricanes hit.

So, yes, we all feel the effects of hurricanes, but we should not overlook the dramatic ways in which people who live in the direct path of a hurricane are affected.

When a hurricane hits, many of these people become homeless, at least for a while, and suffer emotionally and financially as they evacuate to places all over the country, including Kentucky!

People who go through Hurricanes suffer extreme emotional effects. Evacuation is stressful because people have to pack up what they can and have no way of knowing if their home will still be standing or inhabitable when they return (*Slides 5 and 6: Before and after pictures from Hurricane Ike*).

Even returning home is emotionally taxing because returning home means rebuilding homes, neighborhoods, and even memories. Though we try to get back to a "normal" life, it can never really be the same as it once was. Instead, it's what Silicon Valley venture capitalist and invester, Roger McNamee, calls the "new normal" in his book, *The New Normal: Great Opportunities in a Time of Great Risk*.

Because they have to rebuild their homes and lives, people also go through financial difficulties. People battle with insurance companies about whether a home has wind or water damage as they seek financial assistance. Insurance companies will often claim that it is the one (wind or water) the homeowner is uninsured for.

Price gouging is another financial challenge hurricane victims face. When families and businesses begin the process of rebuilding, people come from outside areas to help with labor and materials and will charge exorbitant fees. An example of this is when my father needed people to help remove two trees from our home in September 2005 after Hurricane Rita.

To close, I'd like to remind you that hurricanes affect victims who live in their direct path and the country as a whole. To understand some of these effects, we talked about how hurricanes work, how they affect our country and daily lives, and the impacts they have on the lives of people who live through them. Maybe knowing some of these facts will help each of us appreciate our homes and our families just a little bit more. (*Handout: Hurricane tracking charts*)

REFERENCES

Associated Press. (2008, October 8). Windstorm costs insurers $550M. *Newark Advocate*, p. x.

Bovino, B. A. (2005, September 29). Hurricanes impact national economy. *The Washington Post*, Retrieved online at: http://washingtonpost.com/wp-dym/content/discussion/2005/09/28/D12005092801431.html

Davidson, P. (2008, September 12). Ike blows gasoline prices higher." *USA Today*, p. x.

Marshall, B., Freudenrich, C., & Lamb, R. How hurricanes work. Retrieved October 8, 2008, from: http://www.howstuffworks.com/hurricanes.htm

McNamee, R. (2004). *The new normal: Great opportunities in a time of great risk*. New York: Penguin.

Rappleye, C. (2008, October 7). Hurricane strands marine mammals, damages facility for the stranded. *Beaumont Enterprise*.

QUESTIONS FOR ANALYSIS AND DISCUSSION

You can answer these questions and see my responses to them via your Online Resources for Chapter 15.

1. Identify the types of evidence that the speaker used to develop the point in this excerpt from a speech.

2. Was the evidence effective? Did it meet the five tests for evidence?

3. Was the evidence ethical?

SPEECH STUDIO

Access Speech Studio via your Online Resources. You can view other students' speeches and evaluate how they support claims, make statistics interesting to listeners, credit sources, and use visual aids.

SPEECH BUILDER EXPRESS

Access Speech Builder Express. Pull up the file you created after reading Chapter 14 (Speech Title or "My First Speech"). If you didn't give your speech a title previously, do so now.

Select the "Supporting Material" section on Speech Builder Express. Type in evidence that you plan to use in your speech. Next, select "Works Cited," and type in the complete reference information for each source of evidence.

Save your file to your hard drive, or e-mail it to your instructor if that is requested. You'll add to this file as you develop your speech, using Chapters 16 to 18.

Jacobs Stock Photography/Digital Vision/Getty Images

Organizing and Presenting Public Speeches

> As long as there are human rights to be defended; as long as there are great interests to be guarded; as long as the welfare of nations is a matter for discussion, so long will public speaking have its place.
>
> **William Jennings Bryan**

Millions of people have back problems in this country. It's hard to recover from back problems, particularly ruptures of discs. A lot of problems result from strains caused by lifting heavy objects. People could save themselves a lot of pain if they avoided doing things that hurt backs. It's important to take care of your back because a disc rupture can immobilize you for up to 2 weeks.

SHARPEN YOUR SKILL

At the end of this chapter, refer to the Sharpen Your Skill features, Designing Your Introduction and Rehearsing Your Speech, to apply concepts from Chapter 16.

Another way discs rupture is from unhealthy everyday habits such as sitting too long in one position or not using chairs that provide good support.

Millions of people in this country who suffer from back problems could save themselves a lot of pain by avoiding the two primary causes of back injury. One major cause is excessive strain, for example, from lifting heavy objects. A second cause is unhealthy everyday habits, such as sitting too long in one position. Avoiding strain and unhealthy habits can save weeks of recuperation.

Which of these paragraphs was easier for you to understand and follow? Which one made more sense to you? If you're like most people, the second paragraph seemed more logical and coherent. The content of the two paragraphs is the same. What differs is how they are organized. In the first paragraph, the speaker doesn't tell us that he or she is going to focus on two causes of back problems. Instead, the speaker wanders from discussing one cause (strain) of back problems, to noting the length of recuperation time, and then back to discussing a second cause (unhealthy habits) of back problems.

In contrast, in the second paragraph the speaker tells us that there are two primary causes of back problems, so we're prepared at the outset to learn about two causes. The speaker next explains both causes, and only then does the speaker discuss the recuperation time we're in for if we don't take care of our backs. The organization of the second paragraph makes it easier to follow and retain the information presented.

This chapter guides you through the process of organizing your speech and practicing your delivery. In the pages that follow, we'll consider alternative ways to organize ideas, styles of delivery, and ways to practice effectively.

ORGANIZING SPEECHES

We've all sat through speeches in which speakers seemed disorganized. They rambled or moved from one idea to the next in a way that was hard to follow. Perhaps they didn't tell us in advance what to expect, so we couldn't follow their thinking. Perhaps they submerged main ideas instead of making them stand out so that we'd retain them. Without strong organization, a speech will fail, no matter how good the ideas are and no matter how thoroughly they are researched and supported. If listeners cannot follow a presentation, they won't be informed, persuaded, or impressed. They also won't remember the ideas in the speech.

Organization increases speaking effectiveness for several reasons. First, people like structure, and they expect ideas to come to them in an orderly way. Second, organization influences comprehension of ideas. Listeners can understand and remember a speech that is well organized because they grasp connections between ideas. Listeners are less likely to retain the key ideas in a poorly organized speech. Third, listeners are persuaded better by an organized speech than by a disorganized one. Finally, organization enhances a speaker's credibility, probably because a carefully structured speech reflects well on a speaker's preparation and respect for listeners. Listeners may perceive a speaker as incompetent or unprepared if a speech is disorganized.

Organizing an effective speech is not the same as organizing a good paper, although the two forms of communication benefit by some similar structural principles. Effective organization for oral communication differs from organization for written communication in three key ways:

1. **Oral communication requires more explicit organization.**
2. **Oral communication benefits from greater redundancy within the message.**
3. **Oral communication should rely on less complex sentence structures.**

Unlike readers, listeners can't refer back to a previous passage if they become confused or forget a previous point. To increase listeners' comprehension and retention, speakers should use simple sentences, provide signposts to highlight organization, and repeat key ideas (Woolfolk, 1987). Consistent with the need for redundancy in oral communication, good speeches follow the form of telling listeners what you're going to tell them, presenting your message, then reminding them of your main points. This translates into preparing an introduction, a body, and a conclusion for an oral presentation.

Effective organization begins with a good outline. We'll discuss different kinds of outlines and how each can help speakers organize their ideas. Next, we focus on organizing the body of a speech because that is the substance of a presentation. After considering various methods of structuring the body of a speech, we'll discuss how to build an introduction and a conclusion and how to weave in transitions to move listeners from one point to another.

Outlining Speeches

Beginning speakers often think that an outline is unnecessary, but they're mistaken. A good outline helps you organize your ideas and make sure that you have enough evidence to support your claims. A good outline also provides you with a safety net in case you forget what you intend to say or in case you are interrupted by some unforeseen event, such as a question or a disturbing noise. Speakers who wing it without outlines can be undermined if they have a lapse of memory; there's nothing to guide them back on track. There are three kinds of outlines: working, formal, and key word.

The Working Outline

Speakers usually begin organizing their ideas by creating a **working outline** to give themselves a basic map of the speech. The working outline is just for the speaker; it is his or her sketch of the speech. In it, the speaker usually jots down main ideas to see how the ideas fit together. Once ideas are laid out in a basic structure, the speaker can tell where more evidence is needed, where ideas don't seem well connected, and so forth. Working outlines usually evolve through multiple drafts as speakers see ways to improve speeches. Because working outlines aren't meant for others' eyes, they often include abbreviations and shorthand that make sense only to the speaker.

The Formal Outline   A **formal outline** includes all main points and subpoints, supporting materials, and transitions, along with a bibliography of sources. It should not be the whole speech unless you are giving a manuscript speech, which we will discuss later in this chapter. In most cases, speakers who write out entire speeches sound canned, and they tend to read the speech instead of communicating interactively with listeners.

An effective formal outline has main headings for the introduction, body, and conclusion. Under each main point are subpoints, references to supporting material, and abbreviated transitions. If your speech includes quotations, statistics, or other evidence that must be presented with absolute accuracy, you should write the evidence in full, either on your outline or on separate index cards. Your written evidence should include the source and date of the evidence so that you can provide oral footnotes to listeners. Full references should be listed as your bibliography, or **Works Cited.** Table 16.1 presents guidelines for constructing formal outlines. Figure 16.1 shows a sample formal outline prepared by a student.

Table 16.1	**Principles for Preparing a Formal Outline**

1. Use full sentences for each point.

2. Each point or subpoint in a speech should have only one idea.

3. Use standard symbols and indentation for outlines.

  I. Roman numerals are used for main points.

   A. Capital letters are used for subpoints that support main points.

    1. Arabic numbers are used for material that supports subpoints.

      a. Lowercase letters are used for material that amplifies supporting material.

4. A point, subpoint, or supporting material should never stand alone. If you have a point I, you must have a point II (and possibly III). If you have a subpoint A, there must be a subpoint B (and possibly C). Outlines show how ideas are developed and related. If there is only one subpoint, you don't need to outline it—it's the main point.

5. Strive for parallelism when wording main points and subpoints. This adds to the coherence of a speech and makes it easier for listeners to follow. Here's an example of parallel wording of main and subpoints in a speech:

  I. Poor advising diminishes students' academic experiences.

   A. Students lose out by taking courses that don't interest them.

   B. Students lose out by missing courses that would interest them.

  II. Poor advising delays students' graduation.

   A. Some students have to return for a fifth year to graduate.

   B. Some students have to take extension courses to graduate.

   C. Some students have to attend summer school to graduate.

6. Include all references in your outline. These should be written as full citations according to the guidelines of a standard style manual, such as those published by the Modern Language Association (MLA) or the American Psychological Association (APA), or *The Chicago Manual of Style*. Your instructor may specify the style guidelines that you should follow.

7. Cite sources using accepted style guidelines for research reports. Three widely used systems for citing sources in papers and speech outlines are APA , MLA, and Council of Biology Editors (CBE). You can learn how to cite your sources using each set of guidelines by visiting these websites:

  APA: http://owl.english.purdue.edu/handouts/research/r_apa.html

  MLA: http://library.osu.edu/sites/guides/mlagd.php

  CBE: http://library.osu.edu/sites/guides/cbegd.html

Figure 16.1
A Formal Outline.

I. Introduction
   A. **Attention:** Would you vote for a system in which half of us work only one job, the other half of us work two jobs, and everyone gets equal rewards? No? Well that's the system that most families in this country have today.
   B. **Thesis statement:** Women's double shift in the paid labor force and the home has negative effects on them personally and on marriages.
   C. **Preview:** In the next few minutes, I will show that the majority of married women work two jobs: one in the paid labor market and one when they get home. I will then trace the harmful effects of this inequitable division of labor.

II. Body
   A. The majority of married women today work two jobs: one in the paid labor market and a second one when they get home each day.
      1. Most families today have two wage earners.
         a. Only 17% of contemporary families have one earner.
         b. As married women have taken on full-time jobs outside of the home over the past three decades, husbands of working wives have increased the amount of housework and child care they do from 20% to 30%.
      2. Working wives do more "homework" than working husbands.
         a. Research shows that husbands tend to do the less routine chores while wives do most of the daily chores.

Continued

The Key Word Outline   Some speakers prefer a less detailed formal outline, called a **key word outline.** As the term implies, a key word outline includes only key words for each point. Its purpose is to trigger the speaker's memory of each point. Like the working outline, a key word outline is intended for the speaker's use. Therefore, it may include abbreviations and shorthand that make sense only to the speaker. For instance, to prompt your memory of a quotation by Quincy Grady on the values of college sports, you might write this: "Grady—college sports." Although those three words might not make sense to anyone else, they would jog your memory of the quotation you want to share with listeners. Figure 16.2 (page 376) shows a key word outline for a student speech.

Organizing the Body of a Speech

The body of a speech develops and supports the central idea, or thesis statement, by organizing it into several points that are distinct yet related. In short speeches of 5 to 10 minutes, no more than three points can be developed well, and two

Figure 16.1
(Continued)

> b. Husbands' reasons for not doing more work in the home are that they are tired after work, they don't feel men should do many home chores, and their wives don't expect them to help out more.
> 3. Working wives tend to do more homemaking and child care chores, regardless of which spouse earns more in the job outside the home.
>   a. Consider Jeremy and Nancy. She earns 65% of the family's income, and she does 80% of the child care and home chores.
>   b. Sociologist Arlie Hochschild found that 2 out of 10 husbands in two-worker families do 50% of the work involved in homemaking and child care.
> **Transition:** Now that we've seen what the double shift is, let's consider its effects.
> B. The double shift harms women's health and creates marital stress.
>   1. The double shift harms women's physical and psychological health.
>   a. Research shows that women who work outside of the home and do most of the homemaking and child care suffer sleep deprivation, reduced immunity to infections, and increased susceptibility to illnesses.
>   b. A recent study by the American Medical Association found that working women who do the majority of "homework" are more stressed, depressed, and anxious.
>   2. The double shift also erodes marital satisfaction.
>   a. Women resent husbands who don't contribute a fair share to home life.

Continued

are often adequate. In longer speeches of 11 to 20 minutes, more points can be developed.

We'll discuss eight organizational patterns. As we discuss each pattern, you'll have the opportunity to think about how you might use it in your speech. Experiment with each structure for your presentation so that you see how the different patterns uniquely sculpt your ideas and their impact. In Chapter 18, we'll discuss one additional pattern that can be especially effective for persuasive speaking.

The Time Pattern   Time patterns (also called temporal and chronological patterns) organize ideas on the basis of temporal relationships. Listeners find it easy to follow a time pattern because we often think in terms of temporal order: what follows what, what comes first, and what comes next. Because time patterns emphasize progression, development, or change, they encourage listeners to perceive topics as a process.

Figure 16.1
(Continued)

          b. Inequitable division of "homework" is linked to
             separations and divorces.
      Transition: Let me now pull together what the double shift
         is and how it harms women and marriages.
  III. Conclusion
      A. **Summary:** I've shown you that the majority of wives
         today work a double shift while their husbands do not.
         This is not only unfair, it is also harmful to women's
         health and to marriages.
      B. **Final appeal:** Each of us who chooses to marry can
         create an equitable marriage. As I've shown you, the
         reward for making that choice is healthier wives and
         happier, more enduring marriages. That's a pretty good
         return on the investment of creating an equitable
         marriage.

Time patterns are useful for describing processes that take place over time, for explaining historical events, and for tracing sequences of action. Time patterns are also effective for presentations that create suspense and build to a climax. One student speaker led his listeners through the detective work of pharmaceutical research to develop a new drug for treating mood disorders. Another student traced how the Industrial Revolution changed domestic roles in the United States. In a persuasive speech opposing strip mining, a student described the progressive environmental damage strip mining causes.

> *Thesis:* Immigration has been part of America since the time of Columbus.
> *Main Point 1:* Columbus is credited with having brought the first immigrants
>   to America in 1492.

Figure 16.2
A Key Word Outline.

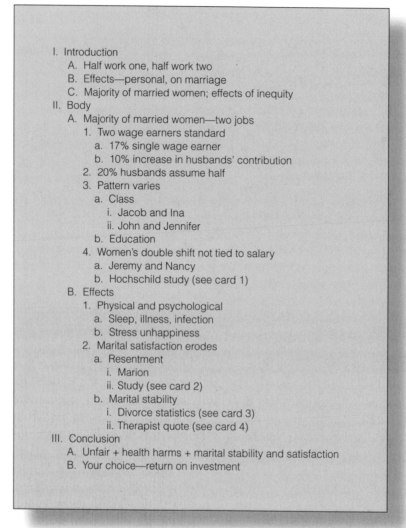

I. Introduction
   A. Half work one, half work two
   B. Effects—personal, on marriage
   C. Majority of married women; effects of inequity
II. Body
   A. Majority of married women—two jobs
     1. Two wage earners standard
       a. 17% single wage earner
       b. 10% increase in husbands' contribution
     2. 20% husbands assume half
     3. Pattern varies
       a. Class
          i. Jacob and Ina
          ii. John and Jennifer
       b. Education
     4. Women's double shift not tied to salary
       a. Jeremy and Nancy
       b. Hochschild study (see card 1)
   B. Effects
     1. Physical and psychological
       a. Sleep, illness, infection
       b. Stress unhappiness
     2. Marital satisfaction erodes
       a. Resentment
          i. Marion
          ii. Study (see card 2)
       b. Marital stability
          i. Divorce statistics (see card 3)
          ii. Therapist quote (see card 4)
III. Conclusion
   A. Unfair + health harms + marital stability and satisfaction
   B. Your choice—return on investment

Main Point 2: In the 1700s and 1800s, people from Europe and Asia came to America to make it their home.

Main Point 3: Today, the largest group of immigrants comes from South America.

COMMUNICATION in Your Life

Organize your speech using the time pattern.

The Spatial Pattern Spatial patterns organize ideas according to physical relationships. This structure is especially appropriate for speeches that describe or explain layouts, geographic relationships, or connections between objects or parts of a system. Listeners find it natural to think in terms of left to right, top to bottom, north to south, and back to front.

Spatial patterns can be used to structure both informative and persuasive speeches. Student speakers have successfully used spatial patterns to inform listeners about the relationships between components of nuclear reactors, the layout of a new library, and the four levels of forest vegetation. In persuasive speeches, students have relied on spatial patterns to argue that solar energy is sufficient to heat homes, that urban sprawl is increasing in the United States, and that global climate change will have devastating effects on the Antarctic, Africa, and Asia.

> *Thesis:* Our campus includes spaces for learning, socializing, and living.
> *Main Point 1:* At the center of our campus are the classroom buildings.
> *Main Point 2:* Surrounding the classroom buildings are places for students to eat and socialize.
> *Main Point 3:* The south part of campus consists of dormitories and apartments for students with families.

The Topical Pattern   Topical patterns order a presentation into several categories, classes, or areas of discussion. The classification pattern is appropriate when your topic breaks down into two or three areas that aren't related temporally, spatially, causally, or otherwise. Although topical patterns don't have the organic power of structures that highlight relationships, they can effectively order points in a speech.

Using topical patterns, speakers have given informative speeches on the three branches of government, the social and academic activities funded by student fees, and the contributions of students, faculty, and staff to campus life. Notice how each of these informative topics can be logically divided into two or three subtopics that serve as the main points of a speech.

Topical patterns can also be effective for persuasive speeches. In a speech urging students to vote for a candidate, one student focused on the candidate's personal integrity, experience in public service, and commitment to the community. Another student designed a persuasive speech that extolled the value of studying the humanities, the natural sciences, and the social sciences.

> *Thesis:* Student fees fund extracurricular, intellectual, and artistic activities on campus.
> *Main Point 1:* Fully 40% of student fees is devoted to extracurricular organizations.
> *Main Point 2:* Another 30% of student fees pays for lectures by distinguished speakers.
> *Main Point 3:* The final 30% of fees supports concerts and art exhibits.

The Star Pattern   The star pattern includes several main points that work together to support a speech's overall theme. As you might have noticed, the star pattern is a variation on the topical structure. Yet the star pattern is more organic (Jaffe, 2007) in tying each point to an overriding theme. The star pattern is also more flexible. A standard topical organization has two or three points that a speaker covers in the same order and to the same extent each time the speech is given. With a star pattern, however, a speaker might start with different points and give more or less attention to specific points when speaking to different audiences.

One of the more common uses of the star pattern is in political speeches. Most candidates for office have a standard stump speech that includes their key positions and proposals. The order in which a candidate presents points and the extent to which each point is developed varies from audience to audience. For example, a candidate's platform might include strong support for the environment, enhancing the fiscal security of the United States, and ensuring adequate care for elderly citizens. When the candidate speaks to environmental activists, he or she would lead with the stand on the environment and elaborate it in detail. When the candidate speaks to older citizens, he or she would begin by emphasizing his commitment to their health and to shoring up Medicare and Medicaid. When the candidate speaks to young and middle-aged audiences, the first point would be ensuring the fiscal security of the United States so young people aren't strapped with debt. Using the star pattern, the candidate could adapt the order of points and the emphasis placed on each one. It would not be ethical to misrepresent positions to suit different audiences, but it was both ethical and effective to adapt the order and emphasis on different points.

> *Thesis:* Our campus reflects contributions of administrators, faculty, students, and staff.
> *Main Point 1:* Administrators are in charge of planning and coordinating all aspects of campus life.
> *Main Point 2:* Faculty take the lead in charting the academic character of college life.
> *Main Point 3:* Students are the primary designers of extracurricular life on campus.
> *Main Point 4:* Staff make sure that the initiatives of administrators, faculty, and students are implemented consistently.

ANNE   *I'm an orientation counselor, and I think I've been using the star pattern to talk to new students, but I didn't know you called it that. With each new group, I have to tell them about the campus and town and school policies and so forth. With first-year students, I start off by talking about school policies because not knowing them can get the kids in trouble. With junior transfers, I get to that last and just spend a little time on it. With out-of-state students, I spend more time talking about the town and even the region—how the South is, which some of them don't understand. I pretty much cover everything with each group, but how I do it varies a lot, depending on who is in the group.*

The Wave Pattern   Like waves in an ocean, the wave pattern consists of repetition. Each wave, or main idea, builds up from evidence and then crests in a main point. Then more evidence follows, leading to the crest of another wave (Jaffe, 2007; Zediker, 1993). Each crest repeats the main theme, using the same words or variations on them. Look again at the excerpt from Martin Luther King's "I Have a Dream" speech. King gave examples of injustices and then crested with the statement, "I have a dream." He then gave more examples, and crested again by repeating the key line. Between each crest in a speech using the wave pattern,

COMMUNICATION HIGHLIGHT

Creating a Sense of Time

The Reverend Martin Luther King Jr. relied on a time pattern in his "I Have a Dream" speech (Cox, 1989). He opened with a reference to "today," then traced the history of African Americans in the United States. Next, he returned to the present to argue that the government's promises to African Americans should be kept. He concluded by quoting a Negro spiritual that envisioned a future when all people of all races would be free. Throughout the speech, he fortified the time structure by using words such as *now, today,* and *urgency* and by repeating the key phrase "Now is the time." Read the following excerpts from his speech to appreciate how King crafted his speech around a temporal theme.

> I am happy to join with you today in what will go down in history as the greatest demonstration in the history of our nation. . . .
>
> Five score years ago, a great American, in whose symbolic shadow we stand today, signed the Emancipation Proclamation. . . .
>
> But one hundred years later, the Negro is still not free. One hundred years later, the life of the Negro is still sadly crippled by the manacles of segregation and the chains of discrimination. . . .
>
> We have come to this hallowed spot to remind Americans of the fierce urgency of now. . . . Now is the time to make real the promises of Democracy. Now is the time to rise from the dark and desolate valley of segregation to the sunlight of racial justice. Now is the time to lift our nation from the quicksands of racial injustice to the solid rock of brotherhood. Now is the time to make justice a reality for all of God's children. . . .
>
> Nineteen-sixty-three is not an end, but a beginning . . .
>
> And as we walk, we must make a pledge that we shall always march ahead. We cannot turn back . . .
>
> I say to you today, my friends, so even though we face the difficulties of today and tomorrow, I still have a dream. . . . I have a dream that one day this nation will rise up and live out the true meaning of its creed: "We hold these truths to be self-evident; that all men are created equal." This will be the day . . . This will be the day when all of God's children will be able to sing with new meaning, "My country 'tis of thee, sweet land of liberty, of thee I sing." . . .
>
> We allow freedom to ring, when we let it ring from every village and every hamlet, from every state and every city, we will be able to speed up that day when all of God's children, black men and white men, Jews and Gentiles, Protestants and Catholics, will be able to join hands and sing in the words of the old Negro spiritual, "Free at last! Free at last! Thank God Almighty, we are free at last!"

Source: Reprinted by arrangement with The Estate of Martin Luther King Jr., c/o Writer's House, Inc., as agent for the proprietor, New York, NY. Copyright 1963 Martin Luther King Jr., copyright renewed 1991 Coretta Scott King.

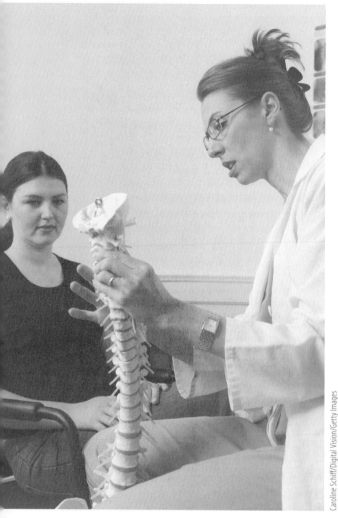

Caroline Schiff/Digital Vision/Getty Images

Good visual aids reinforce the organization of a presentation.

speakers should present listeners with a flurry of evidence: multiple undetailed examples, a few well-chosen detailed examples, statistics, quotations, and so forth. The wave pattern is effective because it moves organically, pulling listeners into its rhythm.

Thesis: The key mission of higher education is complete literacy.
Main Point 1: All students who graduate should be literate in speaking, reading, and writing.
Main Point 2: All students who graduate should be literate in communication technologies.
Main Point 3: All students who graduate should be literate in cultural life.

The Comparative Pattern   As the term suggests, comparative patterns compare two or more objects, people, situations, events, or other phenomena. This structure is also called *comparison/contrast* and *analogical organization.* It encourages listeners to be aware of similarities or differences between two or more things. It is particularly effective in helping listeners understand a new idea, process, or event in terms of one with which they're already familiar. Appropriate for both informative and persuasive presentations, the comparative pattern highlights likeness or difference. Notice that in organizing her speech, Mayumi relied on comparison as her overall pattern and created three topical areas that compared Japanese and U.S. views.

Informative speeches using the comparative structure might explain how computers are like (or not like) human brains, how research for new drugs is like a detective's investigation, or how fission and fusion are different means of creating energy. Students giving persuasive speeches have used the comparative pattern to argue that socialized medicine is inferior to or superior to the U.S. system, that computer literacy is as important as oral and written literacy, and that undergraduate education is different from career preparation. In each case, the comparative structure invites listeners to perceive how two or more phenomena are alike or different.

MAYUMI   *I selected comparative organization for my informative speech about American and Japanese marriages because I wanted the class to understand how people from my country think differently about marriage than Americans do. I divided my speech into courtship, division of household work, and meaning of divorce to show the difference between Americans and Japanese in each area.*

Thesis: Health maintenance organizations are inferior to private medical practices.

Main Point 1: Health maintenance organizations provide less individualized patient care than private practices do.

Main Point 2: Health maintenance organizations are less likely than private practices to authorize important diagnostic tests.

Main Point 3: Health maintenance organizations place less emphasis on preventive care than private medical practices do.

The Problem–Solution Pattern   This pattern divides a topic into two major areas: a problem and a solution. Usually, a speaker begins by describing a problem and its severity and then proposes a solution. Occasionally, this sequence is inverted when a speaker begins by discussing a solution and then explains the problem it solves. The problem–solution structure can be used for informative presentations with thesis statements, such as "The increased cost of running a university (problem) explains the rise in tuition costs (solution)" or "Deregulation (solution) is designed to prevent monopolies that are unfair to consumers (problem)."

The problem–solution pattern is also effective for persuasive speeches because it lends itself naturally to advocating policies, answers, and practices. Students have used this pattern effectively to persuade others that vegetarianism (solution) can reduce cruelty to animals and world hunger (problems), that thousands of injuries and deaths on the highway (problem) could be prevented if there were stronger sentences for people convicted of driving under the influence of alcohol and other drugs (solution), that many people who are severely ill or dying (problem) could be helped if more people were organ donors (solution), and that the overcrowding of jails and the backlog of court cases (problems) could be decreased if all victimless crimes were made misdemeanors (solution).

The power of this pattern derives from the sequential involvement it invites from listeners. If they accept a speaker's description of a problem and believe the problem is important or urgent, they hunger for a solution. The speaker who presents a solution that addresses the problem they've already acknowledged has a good chance of convincing listeners to endorse the recommended proposal.

Thesis: Victimless crimes should be reclassified as misdemeanors.

Main Point 1: Currently, courts across the nation are overwhelmed by cases in which there is no victim.

Main Point 2: Reclassifying victimless crimes as misdemeanors would dramatically ease the burden on our courts.

The Cause–Effect and Effect–Cause Patterns   This pattern is used to argue a direct relationship between two things: a cause and an effect. In some instances, speakers want to inform people that a situation, policy, or practice (effect) results from certain previous choices or events (causes). In other cases, speakers argue that a specific action (cause) will lead to a desired or undesired effect.

Cause–effect and effect–cause patterns are appropriate for both informative and persuasive speeches. We use them for informative presentations when our goal is to explain why something is the case (this effect results from this cause).

The cause–effect structure is effective for persuasive speeches when the goal is to advocate some course of action (cause) that will have a particular effect.

You should be aware that it is extremely difficult to prove direct causation. Even scientific researchers who are convinced that smoking leads to cancer, emphysema, and other serious conditions cannot conclusively verify that smoking is *the* cause. What they can prove is that smoking is related to higher mortality and debilitating medical conditions. There is ample evidence to establish a relationship between smoking (or chewing tobacco) and the likelihood of developing cancer and other diseases. Although other factors, such as lifestyle and heredity, may increase or decrease the likelihood of developing dreaded diseases, smoking is one factor that is strongly related. However, the relationship between smoking and disease does not definitively prove that smoking causes diseases. Thus, although speakers can seldom, if ever, prove direct causation, they can demonstrate relationships, or correlations, between two things, and this is often persuasive to listeners.

> *Thesis:* Raising the minimum wage would be bad for our economy.
> *Main Point 1:* Raising the minimum wage would reduce worker productivity.
> *Main Point 2:* Raising the minimum wage would lead to greater unemployment.
> *Main Point 3:* Raising the minimum wage would decrease profits for businesses.

CourseMate

The eight patterns we've discussed represent different ways to organize public presentations. No one pattern is inherently superior to any other. Each one can be effective for certain speaking goals, topics, and listeners. To structure your speech effectively, you should consider how each of the eight patterns might shape the content and impact of your presentation.

For practice identifying organizational patterns for various speech topics and thesis statements, complete the activity "Identifying Clues to Organization" in your Online Resources for *Communication in Our Lives*.

Designing the Introduction

The introduction to a speech is the first thing listeners hear. A good introduction accomplishes four goals: (a) It gets listeners' attention and motivates them to listen; (b) it presents a clear thesis statement; (c) it enhances the speaker's credibility; and (d) it previews how the speech will be developed. That's a lot to accomplish in a short time, so careful thought is required to design a strong introduction.

Getting Listeners' Attention and Motivating Them to Listen
The first objective of an introduction is to gain listeners' attention and give them a reason to listen. Often, speakers accomplish those objectives simultaneously because listeners are motivated to listen when something catches their attention.

There are many ways to gain listeners' attention and interest. You might begin with a dramatic piece of evidence, such as a stirring quotation, a striking visual aid, or a startling statistic or example. Each of these forms of evidence can capture listeners' interest and make them want to hear more.

COMMUNICATION in Your Life

Organize your speech using the cause–effect or effect–cause pattern.

You may also open with a question that invites listeners to become involved with the topic. Rhetorical questions are ones that do not require a response from listeners, yet they get listeners thinking about a topic: "Do you know the biggest cause of death among college students?" "Would you like to know how to double your chances of getting a job offer?" Action questions do require listeners to respond in some fashion, perhaps by nodding their heads or raising their hands: "How many of you wear seat belts when you drive?" "How many of you went home over fall break?" Both rhetorical and action questions engage listeners personally at the outset of a speech.

There are other ways to capture listeners' attention. For example, speakers sometimes refer to current events or experiences of listeners that are related to the topic of a speech. A student who spoke on homelessness immediately after fall break opened this way: "If you're like me, you went home over the break and enjoyed good food, a clean bed, and a warm, comfortable house—all the comforts that a home provides. But not everyone has those comforts."

When preparing a speech, build connections between your ideas and listeners' expectations, attitudes, and knowledge.

Another effective way to capture listeners' attention is to provide them with direct experience, which is a highly effective foundation for persuasion (Baron & Berne, 1994). For example, in a speech advocating a low-fat diet, a speaker began the presentation by passing out low-fat cookies he had baked. All the listeners then had an immediate experience with delicious and healthful food.

When appropriate to the speaking situation, humor can also be an effective way to open a speech—but only if it succeeds in amusing listeners. Unless you're sure a joke will be funny to listeners, it's better to avoid using humor to open a speech. Thus, it's a good idea to try jokes out on people who are similar to your listeners.

COMMUNICATION in Your Life

How will you gain the attention of your listeners?

Presenting a Clear Thesis Statement   The second function of an introduction is to state the main message of your speech, which is the thesis statement we discussed in Chapter 14. Your thesis should be a short, clear sentence that directly states the overall theme of your presentation. Remember that the thesis is not a full description of the content of your speech. Your thesis statement should only announce the key idea of your speech so that listeners have a clear understanding of your focus:

- "I will describe problems with advising on our campus and ask your help in solving them."

- "Today, I want to persuade you that we should protect the Arctic National Wildlife Refuge from development."

COMMUNICATION HIGHLIGHT

Gaining Listeners' Attention

Here are examples of ways in which students have captured audiences' initial attention:

Question to create suspense: "Have you ever wondered what life would be like if there were no deadly diseases?"

Startling evidence: "Nearly two-thirds of people over 60 who are poor are women."

Personal involvement: "Many of you have to work extra hours to make the money for your textbooks so that the student store can make its 35% profit—that's right, 35% profit just for selling you a book."

Inviting listeners' participation: "Imagine that you could design the undergraduate curriculum at this university. What would you recommend for all students who attend?"

Quotation: "Mahatma Gandhi said, 'You must be the change that you wish to see in the world.'"

Dramatic example: "My brother Jim and I grew up together, and we were best friends. He taught me to play basketball; I gave him advice on girls he was dating; we went to California together one summer. Jim would be 22 today if he had not been killed last summer by a drunk driver."

- "I will inform you of your legal rights when interviewing for a job."
- "I will show you that the death penalty is ineffective and discriminatory."

Building Credibility The third function of an introduction is to establish a speaker's credibility. Listeners regard a speaker as credible if he or she seems qualified to speak on a topic, shows goodwill toward them, and demonstrates dynamism or involvement with the topic.

To show that they are qualified to speak on a topic, speakers may mention their personal experience with a topic to establish initial credibility: "I've spent the last three summers working with inmates in a prison." "I am a hemophiliac." Speakers may also explain how they gained expertise on their topics. "For the past 2 years, I have volunteered at the homeless shelter here in town." If you do not have personal experience with a topic, let listeners know that you have gained knowledge in other ways. "I interviewed 10 people who work with abused children." "I learned about the problem of homelessness in two sociology classes that I took last year."

In addition to letting your listeners know that you are qualified to speak on your topic, you want to demonstrate that you have goodwill and are trustworthy. Doing so increases the likelihood that listeners will trust you and what you say. You might do this by explaining why you think your speech will help them. "What I'm going to tell you might save a life, perhaps your own." "My speech will give you information vital to making an informed choice when you vote next week."

Speakers confront a particular problem in establishing goodwill if they are advocating an unpopular position. They need to demonstrate that they respect listeners' possible objections. One way to do this is to show that you once held their attitudes. "Some of you may think homeless people are just lazy and don't want to work. I thought so, too, before I volunteered at the local shelter and got to know some of them."

Rebecca Ewing gave a speech favoring graduated licensing, a system that gives new drivers incremental driving freedom. She knew that many of her listeners, who were students, would not initially agree with her position. To defuse potential hostility or resistance, Rebecca explained that she understood many of them would disagree with her—a statement that showed she understood how they might feel. In turn, many of the students who were listening were willing to hear why she advocated graduated licensing. If you'd like to see how Rebecca did this, read her speech or view the video that appears at the end of Chapter 18.

Previewing the Body   The final purpose of an introduction is to tell listeners about coming attractions. You want to preview your major points so that listeners understand how you will develop ideas and can follow you. The preview announces the main points of your speech. Typically, a preview enumerates or lists the main points. Here are examples from student speeches:

- "I will show you that there has been a marked decrease in advisors' accessibility and helpfulness to students. Then I will ask you to sign a petition that asks our provost to hire more advisors and provide ongoing training to them."

- "In discussing the Arctic National Wildlife Refuge, I will describe the Coastal Plain, which is the biological heart of the refuge, and then tell you about the Porcupine caribou that come there each year to calve."

- "To convince you that the death penalty should be abolished, I will first provide evidence that it is ineffective as a deterrent to crime. Second, I will demonstrate that the death penalty discriminates against minorities and people who are poor."

Crafting the Conclusion

The next step in organizing a speech is to craft a strong conclusion. As you may recall, we noted that effective public speaking includes deliberate redundancy to enhance listeners' retention of key ideas. The conclusion is a speaker's last chance to drive home the main points of a presentation. An effective conclusion summarizes content and provides a memorable final thought. As you may realize, these two functions are similar to the attention and preview in introductions. In repeating key ideas and leaving the audience with a compelling final thought, a speaker provides psychological closure on the speech. Like introductions, conclusions are short, generally taking less than 5% of total speaking time. Thus, it's important to accomplish the two objectives of a conclusion very concisely.

To summarize the content of your speech, it's effective to restate your thesis and each major point. You can do this in a sentence or two. Here are examples from student speeches:

- "Today I've identified two key problems with advising: an insufficient number of advisers and inadequate training of advisers. Both of these problems can

COMMUNICATION in Your Life

Identify the two or three main points of your speech.

be solved if you will join me in urging our president to increase the number of advisers and the training they get."

- "If you believe, as I do, that Alaska's Arctic Wildlife Refuge should be protected from drilling, then please write or call your congressional representatives."

- "I hope my speech has informed you of your legal rights in interviews and what you can do if an interviewer violates them."

- "I've shown you that the death penalty doesn't prevent crime and that it discriminates against minorities and the poor."

After reviewing main points, a conclusion should offer listeners a final idea, ideally something particularly memorable or strong or an ending that returns to the opening idea to provide satisfying closure. In a speech on environmental activism, the speaker began with "'One earth, one chance' is the Sierra Club motto" and ended with "We have one chance to keep our one earth. Let's not throw it away." This was effective because the ending returned to the opening words but gave them a slightly different twist. A student who argued that the death penalty should be abolished ended the speech with this statement: "We need to kill the death penalty before it kills anyone else." A third example, again from a student speaker, is this memorable closing: "I've given you logical reasons to be a blood donor, but let me close with something more personal: I am alive today because there was blood available for a massive transfusion when I had my automobile accident. Any one of us could need blood tomorrow." Effective conclusions are short and focused. They highlight central ideas one last time and offer listeners a powerful or compelling concluding thought.

Speech Builder Express, which you can access through your Online Resources for *Communication in Our Lives,* includes extensive prompts and a clear framework for organizing and outlining different types of speeches.

Building in Transitions

The final organizational issue is **transitions**—words and sentences that connect ideas and main points in a speech so that listeners can follow a speaker. Transitions signal listeners that you are through talking about one idea and are

ready to connect it to the next one. Effective transitions are like signposts for listeners. They tell listeners where you have been, where you are, and where you are heading (Wilson & Arnold, 1974).

Transitions may be words, phrases, or entire sentences. Within the development of a single point, it's effective to use transitional words or phrases such as *therefore, and so, for this reason, as this evidence suggests*, and *consequently*. To make transitions from one point to another in a speech, phrases can be used to signal listeners that you are starting to discuss a new idea:

- "My second point is…"

- "Now that we have seen how many people immigrate to the United States, let's consider what they bring to us."

- "In addition to the point I just discussed, we need to think about…"

To move from one to another of the three major parts of a speech (i.e., introduction, body, and conclusion), you can signal your audience with statements that summarize what you've said in one part and point the way to the next. For example, here is an internal summary and a transition between the body of a speech and the conclusion:

- "I've now explained in some detail why we need stronger educational and health programs for new immigrants. Let me close by reminding you of what's at stake."

Transitions also may be nonverbal. For example, you might hold up one, two, and three fingers to reinforce your movement from the first to the second to the third main point in the body of your speech. Changes in vocal intensity, eye contact, and inflection can effectively mark movement from one idea to the next. For instance, you could conclude the final point of the body of your speech with strong volume and then drop the volume to begin the conclusion. Silence is also effective in marking transitions. A pause after the introduction signals listeners that a speaker is going to a new place. Visual aids also help listeners move with a speaker.

Transitions are vital to effective speaking. If the introduction, body, and conclusion are the bones of a speech, the transitions are the sinews that hold the bones together. Without them, a speech may seem more like a laundry list of unconnected ideas than like a coherent whole.

COMMUNICATION APPREHENSION: NATURAL AND OFTEN HELPFUL

There are very few people who don't sometimes feel apprehensive about talking with others (Bostrom, 1988; Richmond & McCroskey, 1992). Virginia Richmond and James McCroskey (1995a) reported that almost 95% of Americans surveyed said they had some degree of anxiety about communicating in some situations. As you prepare to present your speech, it's important for you to understand **communication apprehension** and how to manage it so that it doesn't detract from your effectiveness.

I'd Rather Lose Than Have to Give a Speech

Bob Daemmrich/PhotoEdit

Have you ever seen an interview with pro golfer Annika Sorenstam? If so, you've probably noticed that she seems at ease speaking in public. That wasn't always the case. As a high school student, she was so afraid of speaking that she often deliberately played to win second place so that she wouldn't have to give the winner's speech (Morreale, 2003). Her confidence today reminds us that communication apprehension can be managed.

CourseMate

To explore any anxiety you may feel about public speaking, complete the Communication Highlight Activity for Chapter 16 via your Online Resources for *Communication in Our Lives*.

A degree of anxiety may actually improve communication. It makes us more alert, largely because our bodies produce adrenaline and extra blood sugar, which increase energy. You can channel the extra energy into purposeful gestures and movement when you are speaking. The energy produced in response to communication anxiety allows politicians, teachers, and journalists to be more dynamic and interesting.

Although a degree of anxiety about speaking is natural, too much can interfere with effectiveness. Anxiety strong enough to hinder our ability to interact with others is communication apprehension. The apprehension may be about real or anticipated communication encounters.

Causes of Communication Apprehension

There are two types of communication apprehension: situational and chronic. For many of us, certain situations spark anxiety. For instance, if you are scheduled to speak to a group that is known to be hostile to you or your ideas, anxiety is to be expected. In other cases, we feel apprehensive because real or imagined features of a situation worry us. Before a performance review, it's natural to be a little anxious about what your supervisor might say about areas in which you need to improve.

Research indicates that five situational factors often generate apprehension. First, we tend to be more anxious when communicating with people who are unfamiliar to us or who we think are different from us. Apprehension is also likely to be present in new or unusual situations, such as your first job interview.

A third situational cause of apprehension is being in the spotlight. When we are the center of attention, we tend to feel self-conscious and anxious that we might embarrass ourselves. Fourth, we may feel apprehensive when we're being evaluated (Motley & Molloy, 1994).

A final situational reason for apprehension is a past failure or failures in a particular speaking situation. For example, my doctor called me one day to ask me to coach her for a speech she had to give to a medical society. Eleanor had last given a public speech 8 years ago in medical school. Just before the speech, her first patient had died, and she was badly shaken. As a result, she was disorganized, flustered, and generally ineffective. That single incident, which followed a history of successful speaking, was so traumatic that Eleanor developed acute speaking anxiety.

Communication apprehension is more difficult to manage when it is chronic. Rather than feeling anxious in specific situations, which is often appropriate, some people are generally apprehensive about communicating. People who have chronic communication anxiety learn to fear communication, just as some of us learn to fear heights or water (Beatty, Plax, & Kearney, 1985; DeFleur & Ball-Rokeach, 1989).

Reducing Communication Apprehension

Communication apprehension is learned. Therefore, it's reasonable to think it can also be unlearned—at least in many cases. Communication scholars have developed four methods of reducing communication apprehension. If you do not have significant communication apprehension, reading this section may help you understand people who do. If you have more communication apprehension than you would like, reading this section will give you ways to reduce your anxiety.

Systematic Desensitization **Systematic desensitization** is a method of treating many fears, from fear of flying to fear of speaking. It focuses on reducing the tension that surrounds the feared event (Beatty & Behnke, 1991; Daly & McCroskey, 1984). Systematic desensitization teaches people how to relax and thereby reduce the physiological features of anxiety. The goal is to learn to associate feeling relaxed with images of oneself in communication situations.

Cognitive Restructuring **Cognitive restructuring** is a method of helping people change how they think about speaking situations (Motley & Molloy, 1994). According to this method, speaking is not the problem; rather, the problem is how we use irrational beliefs to interpret speaking situations. For example, if you think you must be perfect, totally engaging, and liked by everyone who hears you, then you've set yourself up for failure. You've created expectations that are impossible to meet, which might be why you feel emotionally uneasy about communicating. A key part of cognitive restructuring is teaching apprehensive people to identify and challenge negative self-statements, which we discussed in Chapter 3.

Positive Visualization **Positive visualization** aims to reduce anxiety by guiding apprehensive speakers through imagined positive speaking experiences

(Hamilton, 2008). Researchers report that positive visualization is especially effective in reducing chronic apprehension (Ayres & Hopf, 1990; Bourhis & Allen, 1992; Lau, 1989). In professional life, managers are coached to visualize successful negotiations and meetings. In the world of sports, athletes are taught to imagine playing well, and those who engage in positive visualization improve as much as athletes who physically practice their sport. To read about positive visualization and other ways of reducing speaking anxiety, use your Online Resources for *Communication in Our Lives* to access **Weblink 16.1**.

COMMUNICATION in Your Life

Visualize yourself giving your speech and the audience being engaged.

Skills Training   **Skills training** assumes that lack of speaking skills causes us to be apprehensive about speaking. This method focuses on teaching people skills such as how to start conversations, organize ideas, build strong introductions, and support claims (Phillips, 1991).

You may be thinking that each of these methods seems useful. If so, your thinking coincides with research that indicates that a combination of all three methods is more likely to relieve speaking anxiety than any single method (Allen, Hunter, & Donahue, 1989). If you experience serious communication apprehension that interferes with your ability to express your ideas, ask your instructor to direct you to professionals who can work with you.

PRESENTING PUBLIC SPEECHES

We turn now to the final aspect of public speaking. Delivery, or oral style, affects every aspect of speaking effectiveness, from listeners' interest to listeners' judgments of a speaker's credibility. We'll first discuss oral style, pointing out how it differs from written style. Then, we'll consider alternative styles of delivery.

Oral Style

Oral style refers to speakers' visual, vocal, and verbal communication with listeners. *Visual delivery* concerns a speaker's appearance, facial expressions, eye contact, posture, gestures, movement during a presentation, and visual aids. *Vocal delivery* includes volume, pitch, pronunciation, articulation, inflection, pauses, and speaking rate. *Verbal delivery* consists of word choices and sentence structure.

A common mistake of speakers, both new and experienced, is to use written style rather than oral style. But a speech is not a spoken essay. There are three primary qualities of effective oral communication (Wilson & Arnold, 1974). First, it is usually more informal than written communication. Thus, speakers use contractions and sentence fragments that would be inappropriate in a formal written document. Informality may also be evident in speaker's dress and posture—for instance, sitting on the edge of a table to talk to an audience. The informal character of oral style also means it's appropriate for speakers to use colloquial words and even slang in informal speaking contexts. However, speakers shouldn't use slang or jargon that might offend any listener or that might not be understood by some listeners.

Second, effective oral style also tends to be more personal than written style. It's generally effective for speakers to include personal stories and personal pronouns, referring to themselves as "I" rather than "the speaker." In addition, speakers should sustain eye contact with listeners and show that they are approachable. If you reflect on speakers you've found effective, you'll probably realize that they seemed personal and open to you.

Third, effective oral style tends to be more immediate and more active than written style. This is important because listeners must understand ideas immediately as they are spoken, whereas readers can take time to comprehend ideas. In oral presentations, simple sentences ("I have three points") and compound sentences ("I want to describe the current system of selling textbooks, and then I will propose a less costly alternative") are more appropriate than complex sentences ("There are many reasons to preserve the Arctic National Wildlife Refuge, some of which have to do with endangered species and others with the preservation of wilderness environment, yet our current Congress is not protecting this treasure").

Immediacy also involves moving quickly instead of gradually to develop ideas. Rhetorical questions, interjections, and redundancy also enhance the immediacy of a speech. Reread the excerpts from Martin Luther King Jr.'s speech on page 379, and notice his skill in repeating key phrases, such as, "Now is the time." Also note Dr. King's use of simple sentences and his emphasis on personal language (*I* and *we*). Contrast the communication style of speakers you find effective with the style of speakers you judge to be less effective. The latter group is likely to adopt a formal, impersonal, abstract style of communication.

Styles of Delivery

Throughout this book, we've seen that communication occurs in contexts that influence what will be effective and ineffective. This basic communication principle guides a speaker's choice of a style of presentation. The style of delivery that's effective at a political rally is different from the style appropriate for an attorney's closing speech in a trial; delivering a toast at a wedding requires a style different from that required in testifying before Congress. There are four presentational styles.

Impromptu Style   **Impromptu speaking** involves little preparation. Speakers speak off the cuff, organizing ideas as they talk and working with evidence that is already familiar to them. You use an impromptu style when you make

Effective oral style is generally informal, personal, and immediate.

a comment in a class, answer a question you hadn't anticipated in an interview, or respond to a request to share your ideas on a topic. There is no time to prepare or rehearse, so you have to think on your feet.

Impromptu speaking is appropriate when you know a topic well enough to organize and support your ideas without a lot of advance preparation. For instance, the president of a company could speak off the cuff about the company's philosophy, goals, and recent activities. Similarly, politicians who have worked out their positions and familiarized themselves with evidence often speak in an impromptu style.

Impromptu speaking tends to be highly informal, personal, and immediate—the best qualities of oral style. Yet impromptu speaking has the disadvantage of allowing less time to research and organize. Consequently, this is not an effective style when speakers are not highly familiar with topics and at ease in speaking in public.

Extemporaneous Style Probably the most common presentational style today, **extemporaneous speaking** relies on preparation and practice, but actual words and nonverbal behaviors aren't memorized. Extemporaneous speaking (also called *extemp*) requires speakers to do research, organize ideas, select supporting evidence, prepare visual aids, outline the speech, and practice delivery. Yet the speech itself is not written out in full. Instead, speakers construct an outline—usually a key word outline.

Effective extemporaneous speaking requires a fine balance between too little and too much practice. Not rehearsing enough may result in stumbling, forgetting key ideas, and not being at ease with the topic. On the other hand,

Table 16.2	Guidelines for Effective Delivery

1. Adapt your appearance to your listeners. It's often effective for speakers to look similar to their listeners, probably because this suggests common ground.

2. Adapt your appearance to the speaking situation. Formal dress is likely to be appropriate for a speech to executives that is given in an office or board room. However, if that same speech were given at a company retreat by the ocean, casual dress would be more appropriate.

3. Use gestures to enhance impact. Gestures can reinforce ideas and complement verbal messages. Moving your arm in an arc motion can suggest progression to reinforce a time pattern.

4. Adopt a confident posture. Stand erect, with your shoulders back and your feet slightly apart for optimum balance.

5. Use confident, dynamic body movement to communicate your enthusiasm and confidence. Walk to the speaking podium (or wherever you will speak) with assurance: head up, arms comfortably at your side, at a pace that is neither hurried nor halting. As you speak, move away from the podium to highlight key ideas or to provide verbal transitions from one point to the next.

6. Maintain good eye contact with listeners. Try to vary your visual zone so that you look at some listeners at one moment and then move your gaze to a different segment of listeners.

7. Use volume that is strong but not overpowering. The appropriate volume will vary, depending on the size of your audience. You need to speak louder to an audience of 200 than to an audience of 25. You also need to adapt your volume to the environment. If a noisy air conditioner is running, you'll need to increase your volume to be heard. Be careful not to let your volume drop off at the end of sentences, a common problem for beginning speakers. At the same time, avoid excessive volume; listeners don't appreciate feeling that a speaker is shouting at them.

8. Use your voice to enhance your message. Pitch, rate, volume, and articulation are vocal qualities that allow you to add emphasis to important ideas. As you practice your speech, decide which words and phrases you want to emphasize.

9. Use pauses for effect. It is often effective to pause for a second or two after stating an important point or presenting a dramatic example or statistic.

10. Do not let accent interfere with clarity. Most of us speak in ways that reflect our ethnic and regional heritage. For everyone but professional broadcasters, regional dialects are acceptable. However, your accent must be understandable to listeners.

11. Articulate clearly. Speakers lose credibility when they mispronounce words or when they add or delete syllables. Common instances of added syllables are *cohabitate* for *cohabit*, *orientated* for *oriented*, *preventative* for *preventive*, and *irregardless* for *regardless*.

too much practice tends to result in a speech that sounds canned. The idea is to prepare and practice just enough to be comfortable with the material yet still natural and spontaneous in delivery. Extemporaneous speaking involves a conversational and interactive manner that is generally effective with listeners. This

Dr. Carberry has been showing much more originality in his sermons lately, hasn't he?

probably is why the extemporaneous style is the most popular presentational mode.

Manuscript Style As the term suggests, **manuscript speaking** involves speaking from the complete manuscript of a speech. After planning, researching, organizing, and outlining a presentation, a speaker then writes the complete word-for-word text and practices the presentation using that text or that text transferred to a teleprompter. The clear advantage of this style is that it provides security to speakers. Even if a speaker gets confused when standing before an audience, he or she can rely on the full text.

There are also disadvantages to manuscript speaking. First, this style limits a speaker's ability to adapt on the spot to listeners. If someone looks puzzled, the extemporaneous speaker can elaborate an idea, but the manuscript speaker may be locked into the written text. This points to a second hazard of manuscript speaking: the tendency to read the speech. It's difficult to be animated and visually engaged with listeners when reading a manuscript.

BRAD   *Most of my professors are pretty good. They talk with us in classes, and they seem to be really involved in interacting with students. But I've had several professors who read their notes—like, I mean, every day. They'd just come in, open a file, and start reading. I had one professor who almost never looked at us. It didn't feel like a person was communicating with us. I'd rather have read his notes on my own.*

A third disadvantage is that it's difficult to adopt oral style when relying on a written manuscript. Only veteran manuscript speakers or speech writers can write a speech that has oral flavor. More often, a manuscript speech adopts written style, so it isn't immediate, personal, and informal.

Manuscript speaking is appropriate, and perhaps necessary, in a few specific situations. When the content of a speech must be precise and there is no room for adapting or rewording ideas, then a manuscript is advisable. The situations that require this are few and not part of most people's everyday lives. Official declarations, diplomatic agreements, and formal press statements are examples of contexts in which manuscript speaking may be advisable.

Memorized Style   The final presentational style is **memorized speaking,** which carries the manuscript style one step further. After going through all the stages of manuscript speaking (i.e., preparing, researching, organizing, outlining, writing out the full text, and practicing), a speaker commits the entire speech to memory and speaks from a manuscript that is in his or her head. The advantages of this style are the same as those for manuscript speaking: An exact text exists, so everything is prepared in advance. However, there are serious disadvantages to memorizing. Because memorized speaking is based on a full written speech, the presentation may reflect written rather than oral style. In addition, memorized speaking is risky because a speaker has no safety net in case of memory lapses. Speakers who forget a word or phrase may become rattled and unable to complete the presentation. Whereas a speaker using extemporaneous style and an outline would simply substitute a different word if the desired one didn't come to mind, a speaker who has memorized a speech may get stuck and be unable to continue if she or he forgets anything. Memorized style also can limit effective delivery. It is difficult for a speaker to sound spontaneous when she or he has memorized an entire speech. Because the speaker is preoccupied with remembering the speech, she or he can't interact fully with listeners. These drawbacks of memorized speaking explain why it isn't widely used or recommended.

Knowing the benefits and liabilities of each presentational style provides you with alternatives. For most speaking occasions, extemporaneous style is effective because it combines good preparation and practice with spontaneity. Although this style tends to be the most effective in the majority of speaking situations, there are exceptions. When deciding which style to use, carefully consider your own needs and speaking preferences, the nature of your presentation, the context in which you will deliver it, and your particular listeners. For additional tips for effective delivery, use your Online Resources for *Communication in Our Lives* to access **WebLink 16.2**.

 **Course**Mate

Practice

Whichever presentational style you choose, practice is important. Ideally, you should begin practicing your speech several days before you plan to deliver it. During practice, you should rely on the outline you will use when you actually deliver the speech. This ensures that you will be familiar with its layout and will know where various materials are on the outline. You should also practice with visual aids and any other materials you plan to use in your speech so that you are comfortable working with them.

There are many ways to practice a speech. Usually, speakers prefer to practice alone initially so that they gain some confidence and comfort in presentation. You may find it helpful to practice in front of a mirror to see how you look and to keep your eyes focused away from the outline. Practicing before a mirror

Sven Hoogerhuis/United Archives GmbH/Alamy

Even in formal situations, openness and conversational style are appropriate. Notice the nonverbal behaviors of the speaker, actor Richard Gere.

is especially helpful in experimenting with different nonverbal behaviors that can enhance your presentational impact.

You may want to tape yourself during practice so that you can see and hear yourself and make decisions about how to refine your delivery. If the videotape shows you pulling your hair, scratching your face, or not keeping eye contact, you can monitor these behaviors in additional practice. If you see that you look at your notes too much, you can work to increase your eye contact when speaking. Take breaks between practices so that you don't wind up memorizing the speech inadvertently.

When you've rehearsed enough to feel comfortable with the speech, it's time to practice in front of others. Ask friends to listen, and invite their feedback on ways you can refine your presentation. Ask whether they can follow your organization; whether they find your evidence convincing; and whether they perceive your delivery as personal, immediate, and informal. Also ask your listeners to give you feedback on your nonverbal communication: Are you maintaining good eye contact? Are your gestures, facial expressions, and movements appropriate? Do you use vocal inflections, changes in volume, and pauses effectively to accent your ideas? Is it hard to understand any words you use in your speech?

Practice until you know your material well but haven't memorized it. Then stop! Overrehearsing is just as undesirable as not practicing enough. You want to preserve the freshness and spontaneity that are important in oral style.

CHAPTER SUMMARY

In this chapter, we focused on ways to organize and present public communication. We discussed different types of outlines that assist speakers in organizing material. Next, we considered eight patterns for ordering the ideas in a speech and explored how each pattern affects the residual message of a presentation. Which organizational structure is best depends on a variety of factors, including the topic, your speaking goal, and the listeners with whom you will communicate.

We also noted that communication apprehension is common, natural, and often helpful to speakers. If you understand why it occurs and how to manage any apprehension you have, you can be effective in making public presentations. We identified different presentational styles and saw that each one has potential advantages and liabilities. Effective delivery cannot be reduced to a universal formula. What is effective depends on particular speakers, contexts, listeners, and speaking goals. To make sure that you've thought through all important aspects of organizing, outlining, and delivery, review the checklist at the end of this chapter. Then you'll be ready to proceed to Chapter 17, in which we analyze the full text of a student speech to see how organization, evidence, and other facets of public speaking work in an actual presentation.

CHECKLIST FOR ORGANIZING AND PRESENTING A SPEECH

Complete this checklist to help you organize your next speech.

If you prefer, you can complete this checklist online via your Chapter 16 Online Resources for *Communication in Our Lives*.

In addition, you can use Speech Builder Express to help you organize your speech. At the end of this chapter, I've included a suggestion for using Speech Builder Express to help you with your next speech.

1. How could you structure your speech using each of the organizational patterns we discussed? Write out a thesis statement for each pattern.
   A. time: _____
   B. spatial: _____
   C. topical: _____
   D. star: _____
   E. wave: _____
   F. comparative: _____
   G. problem–solution: _____
   H. cause–effect: _____
   I. effect–cause: _____

2. Which pattern have you decided to use?
   A. List the two or three main points into which you've divided your topic:
      _____, _____
      _____, and _____
      _____

3. Describe the three parts of your introduction:
   A. I will gain attention by _____
   B. My thesis statement is _____
   C. My preview is _____

4. Describe the transitions you've developed to move listeners from idea to idea in your speech.
   A. My transition from introduction to the body of the speech is _____
   B. My transitions between major points in the body are _____
   C. My transition from the body to the conclusion of the speech is _____

5. Describe the two parts of your conclusion:
   A. Restatement of thesis and major points:

   _____

   B. Concluding emphasis: _____

   _____

6. The delivery style I will use is _____
   because _____

   _____

7. I've practiced my speech
   A. on my own
   B. in front of others
   C. in front of a mirror
   D. in the room where I will deliver it
   E. on videotape

APPLYING COMMUNICATION IN OUR LIVES

The key concepts, For Further Reflection and Discussion questions, and Experiencing Communication in Our Lives case study that follow will help you review, reflect on, and extend the information and ideas presented in this chapter. These resources, and a diverse selection of additional study tools, are also available as Online Resources for *Communication in Our Lives*. Your Online Resources include CourseMate, a student workbook, interactive video activities, audio study tools, a book companion website, Speech Builder Express, Speech Studio, and InfoTrac College Edition. For more information or to access this book's online resources, visit **www.cengage.com/login.**

KEY CONCEPTS

cognitive restructuring, 389
communication apprehension, 387
extemporaneous speaking, 392
formal outline, 371
impromptu speaking, 391

key word outline, 373
manuscript speaking, 394
memorized speaking, 395
oral style, 390
positive visualization, 389
skills training, 390

systematic desensitization, 389
transitions, 386
working outline, 371
Works Cited, 372

FOR FURTHER REFLECTION AND DISCUSSION

1. Do you think a speaker has an ethical responsibility to organize a speech well, or is organization strictly a strategic matter—something to help a speaker have impact? Does careful organization reflect ethical issues, such as respect for listeners?

2. Attend a public presentation and keep notes on how the speaker organizes the speech. What is the overall pattern of the presentation? Did the speaker make a wise choice? Identify transitions in the speech, and evaluate their effectiveness. Do the introduction and conclusion serve the appropriate speaking goals?

3. Give a 1- to-2-minute impromptu speech on your favorite activity or some other topic with which you are already familiar. Next, spend two days preparing an extemporaneous speech on the same topic. How do the two speeches differ in quality and effectiveness?

SHARPEN YOUR SKILL

1. Designing Your Introduction

Apply the principles we've discussed to develop an introduction to a speech you plan to give. Using the following outline, fill in full sentences for each element of your introduction.

I. Introduction
   A. Attention and motivation: _____
   B. Thesis: _____
   C. Credibility: _____
   D. Preview: _____

   To further enlarge your awareness of the elements in a good introduction, view the sample speech by Mariah Morgan, "Hate Crimes," in your Chapter 16 Online Resources for *Communication in Our Lives.* **CourseMate**

2. Rehearsing Your Speech

You'll need three 20-minute periods at different times to complete this activity.

   a. After you have prepared the outline and note cards that you will use when you present your speech, find a quiet place where you will not be disturbed. Present the speech as you intend to deliver it to your class. As you rehearse, practice looking at different parts of the room as you will later engage in eye contact with your classmates.

   b. Wait at least a few hours after your first practice to do the second one. This time, practice in the same room, but stand in front of a mirror; ideally it should be a full-length mirror so that you can see yourself as listeners will see you. Give your speech as you plan to deliver it to your classmates. As you speak, notice your posture and nonverbal communication. Are you using effective hand gestures, facial expressions, and changes in body posture and position?

   c. Wait at least a few hours after your second practice to do the third one. You may want to invite several friends or classmates to join you in this practice session so that you have an audience. For this rehearsal, go to your classroom or another classroom that is set up similarly to yours. Sit down in the room as you would sit in your class. Imagine the teacher announcing that it is your turn to speak. Get up from your seat, go to the podium or front of the classroom, and present your speech as you plan to deliver it to your classmates. Practice looking at different areas of the room or at your friends as you will later engage in eye contact with classmates. If you have access to a video camera, you may tape this third rehearsal and then analyze your presentation.

EXPERIENCING COMMUNICATION IN OUR LIVES

CASE STUDY: *Analyzing Delivery: Speech of Self-Introduction*

A video of the speech introduced here is featured in your Chapter 16 Online Resources for *Communication in Our Lives.* Select "Delivery" to watch the video of Adam Currier's speech of introduction. Improve your own public speaking skills by reading, watching, and evaluating this speech. **CourseMate**

Every year since I've remembered, we've gone back to Iowa and spent a week of that summer just being with my dad's parents, my grandparents. And each year, as I grew, I grew closer and closer to my grandfather. And it got to the point where I no longer just knew him as a relative but I knew him as a human being. Sitting outside on his porch one day, right before he died, he told me about his life. We were talking about what he had done, being in World War II, being a dentist, being a community leader, all the things he had ever achieved in his life—and it all sounded so perfect. I said, "Grandfather, what do you regret most in your life?" He said, "Adam, I regret not seeing more sunsets."

A couple months later, he passed on, and I realized that I didn't enjoy every single minute with him as much as I could've, and I didn't have the time with him that I thought that I had. So I look at my wall now, and I see the quotes on it and see the stories on it and the pictures on it and I realize that everyone I've come into contact with, everyone I've ever met, everything I've done, has all contributed to shaping the person that I am.

QUESTIONS FOR ANALYSIS AND DISCUSSION

You can answer these questions and see my responses to them online via your Online Resources for Chapter 16.

1. Was the speaker dynamic—excited about the topic?

2. Was the speaker's language clear, immediate, and vivid?

3. Did the speaker use nonverbal communication to enhance effectiveness?

4. What style of speaking did the speaker use? Was this an appropriate choice for this speech, this occasion, and the particular listeners?

SPEECH STUDIO

Access Speech Studio via your Online Resources. You can upload a video of your practice speech, share it with your instructor and other students, view other students' speeches, and read feedback on your speech.

SPEECH BUILDER EXPRESS

Access Speech Builder Express via your Online Resources for Chapter 16. If you'd like to continue working on an outline you've already started, click "Resume" to pull up the file for your speech.

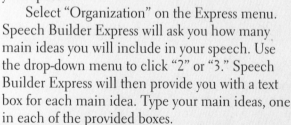

Select "Organization" on the Express menu. Speech Builder Express will ask you how many main ideas you will include in your speech. Use the drop-down menu to click "2" or "3." Speech Builder Express will then provide you with a text box for each main idea. Type your main ideas, one in each of the provided boxes.

You will then be asked to select an organization pattern for your speech. As you learned in this chapter, there is no single best organizational pattern for all speeches. Review your thesis and main points to decide which organizational pattern

will be most effective for your speech. Click that pattern on the list provided.

Now select "Outline" on the Express menu. Speech Builder Express will prompt you through the steps in outlining your speech: developing sub-points, designing internal summaries, creating transitions, developing the introduction and conclusion.

You're nearly done. Select "Completing the Speech Outline" on the Express menu. You can now review what you did in each of the preparation steps. You may also check for errors in spelling and formatting.

Save your file to your hard drive, and print it out so that you can work with it offline. You may also e-mail it to your instructor if that is requested. As you continue to think about your speech, you may return to Speech Builder Express at any time to modify your outline and notes.

Bernhard Lang/Photodisc/Getty Images

> Information is
> the currency of
> democracy.
>
> **Thomas Jefferson**

Informative
Speaking

Our era has been called "the information age." To live and work effectively in this time, we need to know how to share information—in the workplace, in social situations, and in community and civic contexts. Skill at informative speaking is critical if you want to be effective personally, professionally, and socially. To learn more about the role of informational speaking in professional life, use your Online Resources for *Communication in Our Lives* to access **WebLink 17.1**.

CourseMate

This chapter focuses on informative speaking. Much of what you've learned from previous chapters applies to your study of informative speaking. In Part I of this book, you studied principles of effective verbal and nonverbal communication, how to understand and adapt to cultural differences, and how to foster friendly, supportive

SHARPEN YOUR SKILL

At the end of this chapter, refer to the Sharpen Your Skill features, Informative Speaking in Your Life and Organizing Your Informative Speech, to apply concepts from Chapter 17.

climates for interaction. In addition, Chapters 14, 15, and 16 introduced you to the basics of planning, researching, supporting, organizing, and delivering speeches.

Building on what you've already learned, this chapter will guide you through the process of developing and presenting an informative speech. We will first highlight the importance of informative speaking in everyday life and note how it differs from persuasive speaking, which we will cover in the next chapter. Next, we'll discuss guidelines for effective informative speaking. At the end of the chapter, you'll find a sample informative speech.

THE NATURE OF INFORMATIVE SPEAKING

An **informative speech** is a presentation that aims to increase listeners' knowledge, understanding, or abilities. Competence in informative speaking is important if you plan to coach sports, to be part of neighborhood and civic groups, and to succeed in your profession (Morreale, Osborn, & Pearson, 2000).

Informative Speaking in Everyday Life

It's likely that you'll give a number of speeches in your life. Many of them—probably the majority—will be informative speeches. Some will be formal, many will be informal, but all will focus on conveying information to others. Consider these examples of everyday informative speaking:

- Explaining a new procedure to co-workers.
- Teaching Boy Scouts how to start a fire without matches.
- Informing your neighbors about a community watch program that's decreased burglaries in other neighborhoods.
- Briefing stake holders on the new strategic plan your firm is implementing.
- Describing a new offensive strategy to the Little League team you coach.
- Telling a civic group about traditions in your culture.

Table 17.1	Types of Informative Speeches
Type	**Sample Specific Purpose**
Demonstration	To show listeners how to construct a speech outline
Instruction	To teach listeners how to perform CPR
Description	To describe the people and land of Nepal
Explanation	To explain why (or how) hurricanes form
Briefing	To summarize the results of a new marketing strategy
Reporting	To provide detailed information on the results of a new marketing strategy

- Teaching a group of friends how to prepare a complicated dessert.
- Reporting to your co-workers on what you learned at a conference so that they understand new developments in your field.

Comparing Informative and Persuasive Speaking

Informative speaking and persuasive speaking differ, yet they also have much in common. Both require research, organization, supporting material, and delivery. There are also overlaps between informative and persuasive goals. For example, in an informative speech, you are trying to persuade listeners to attend to what you say and to care about learning. In persuasive speeches, you need to inform listeners about certain issues to influence their values, attitudes, or behaviors.

Four differences between informative and persuasive speaking are particularly important and are outlined in Table 17.2.

The Controversial Nature of the Purpose   The purposes of informative speeches tend to be less controversial than the purposes of persuasive speeches. Something is controversial when it can be debated or argued—in other words, when not everyone is likely to agree or accept it. Typically, informative presentations don't present highly controversial ideas. They generally aim to give listeners new information: to teach, explain, or describe a person, object, event, process, or relationship. Persuasive speeches, on the other hand, aim to change listeners' attitudes, beliefs, or behaviors.

Obviously, information can have persuasive impact, so it can be controversial. Yet the degree to which a purpose is controversial is much greater in persuasive speeches. An informative speech might have the specific purpose of describing the historical conditions that led to establishment of affirmative action policies. A persuasive speech on the same topic might have the specific purpose of persuading listeners to support or oppose affirmative action policies. Clearly, the latter purpose is more controversial than the former.

The Response Sought   Related to their differing purposes are the responses informative and persuasive speeches seek from listeners. In the affirmative action example, the speaker giving an informative speech wants listeners to understand certain historical conditions. The speaker giving a persuasive speech wants listeners to believe that affirmative action is right or wrong, justified or not justified, beneficial or harmful. The persuasive speaker might even want to persuade listeners to take specific actions to oppose or support affirmative action at local,

> **COMMUNICATION**
> **in Your Life**
>
> **What is the last informative speech you heard?**

Table 17.2	Informative versus Persuasive Speaking
1. Persuasive speeches tend to have more controversial purposes.	
2. Persuasive speeches seek more powerful responses from listeners.	
3. Persuasive speeches need more and better proof.	
4. Persuasive speeches require the speaker to earn greater credibility.	

This chef engages in informative speaking to instruct chef trainees in how to prepare a dish.

regional, or national levels. In seeking to change listeners in some way, persuasive speeches seek a more powerful response: change rather than acceptance of new information.

The Evidence Needed   Because persuasive speeches tend to be more controversial and seek to convince listeners to change in some way, they generally need stronger supporting material than informative speeches do. This does not mean that informative speeches don't need proof; they do. However, an effective persuasive speech generally must include more supporting material. Why? Because listeners expect more evidence when they are asked to think, feel, or act differently than when they are asked only to understand something. Listeners will want convincing evidence not only that discrimination exists and is wrong but also that affirmative action policies are an effective response to the problem.

In persuasive speeches, speakers also have a responsibility to anticipate and address their listeners' reservations. To do this effectively requires evidence. Perhaps, in researching public opinions on affirmative action, you learn that the most common objection is based on the assumption that it lowers standards for admission to schools and professions. To persuade listeners to support affirmative action, you should present evidence that shows that standards have not declined in institutions that follow affirmative action policies.

> **VINCE** *Last week, I went to hear a speaker on capital punishment. He was trying to convince us that we should abolish it, but I wasn't convinced. What he mainly did was to inform us that there are cases where innocent people are convicted or even put to death. But he never showed us—or me, anyway—that abolishing capital punishment is the answer. Why can't we just reform it, like, require absolute proof of guilt before someone can be sentenced to die? And what about all the people who really are guilty of horrible things, like school killings or the Oklahoma bombing? Shouldn't they be sentenced to death? He never talked about that.*

The Importance of Credibility Credibility is important to any speaker's effectiveness. As with evidence, however, the credibility a speaker needs varies with the speaking purpose. In general, a speaker who attempts to change people needs more credibility than a speaker who seeks only to inform them. The reason is simple: Because the persuasive speaker asks more of listeners than the informative speaker does, the listeners expect more credibility of the speaker.

Whereas an informative speech usually presents noncontroversial information, a persuasive speech asks listeners to think, feel, or act differently. Thus, persuasive speakers have a greater responsibility to convince listeners that they (the speakers) have the personal integrity and expertise to merit listeners' belief in them and the positions they advocate. Because credibility is so important in persuasive speaking, we will discuss it in depth in Chapter 18.

GUIDELINES FOR EFFECTIVE INFORMATIVE SPEAKING

Eight guidelines are particularly important for informative speeches.

Provide Listeners with a Clear Thesis Statement

As we noted in Chapter 14, listeners want to know why they are listening—what they are supposed to get out of the informative speech. Only then can they focus their listening. When giving an informative presentation, the speaker should state a simple, clear thesis that tells listeners what the speech will provide or do. The thesis should motivate listeners by alerting them that the information to come will be useful to them. As you'll recall from previous chapters, a good thesis is clear and direct: "At the end of my talk, you will understand the different citizen responsibilities and effects of three popular Neighborhood Watch programs used in our county." Upon hearing this thesis, listeners know exactly what the speaker plans to give them and what they should get out of listening.

Connect with Listeners' Values and Experiences

As with all communication, informative speeches should build connections with listeners. Speakers should learn what listeners know about a topic. This allows a speaker to avoid telling them what they already know and to connect

Digital Vision/Jupiter Images

This speaker uses nonverbal behaviors to connect with listeners.

the topic with listeners' values and experiences. For instance, in a speech with the specific purpose of describing alternative Neighborhood Watch programs, a speaker might open by saying, "I know we share a concern for safety in our neighborhood. What I want to do is describe the three Neighborhood Watch programs in our county so that we can make an informed choice about what is right for our community." This opening establishes common ground between the speaker and listeners by noting that they "share a concern" and by using *we* language: "our neighborhood," "we can make," "our community." Another way the speaker could open the speech is by saying, "I know several of you have been burglarized in the last year." To connect with listeners' values, the speaker might say, "We all want to feel that our homes are safe from intrusion. We have a right to that."

Motivate Listeners to Want Information

Information is so pervasive today that we screen much of it out. For an informative speech to be effective, listeners must be motivated to want what the speaker is providing. In some cases, listeners are motivated for their own reasons. For instance, listeners will attend a nonrequired cardiopulmonary (CPR) class because they want to learn how to perform CPR. They are already motivated.

In other cases, the speaker may need to motivate people to want information. For example, a supervisor may need to fuel employees' hunger for information on a new procedure the company wants them to follow. In this situation, the supervisor might say, "I know we all get tired of learning new procedures, but the one I'm going to explain today will make your jobs easier and increase your productivity." This statement motivates employees to listen, especially if their pay is based on their productivity. Notice that the statement also recognizes that listeners have been asked to learn numerous procedures and that it can get tiring.

> **MANDY** *I went to the placement office the other day for a workshop on interviewing. I wasn't really interested, but I thought I should go, so I was just kind of there but not really paying attention. Then the facilitator got us started. The first thing she said was that students who attend these workshops tended to get more and better job offers than students who don't. That definitely got my attention! From then on, I was listening very carefully and taking lots of notes.*

Build Credibility with Listeners

As we've noted, for the speaker to be effective, listeners must perceive him or her as credible. When giving an informative speech, you should demonstrate that you have some expertise relevant to your topic. You may show you have personal experience ("I took a CPR course"). You may also demonstrate to listeners that you have gained information in other ways ("To prepare to talk to you today, I spoke with emergency department doctors about people who died but could have been saved with CPR").

You'll also want to show listeners that you care about them or that the information you are offering will help them in some way. You might say, "This information will come in handy when you start interviewing for jobs." You might also show goodwill by explaining how the information you are presenting has helped you, and let your listeners infer that it might help them too ("My sister would have drowned last year if I hadn't known how to give CPR. It can help any of us save lives").

Adapt to Diverse Listeners

In our diverse society, few audiences are homogeneous. For the informative speaker, this implies that it is important to speak in ways that include and respect diverse experiences, values, and viewpoints. People whose homes have been burglarized have had a different experience from those whose homes have not been burglarized. People who believe in nonviolence as a way of life differ in key respects from people who believe that everyone has a right to use violence to protect themselves and their property. Citizens who were raised in highly communal cultures are likely to be more inclined toward communal efforts to protect a neighborhood than are people who were raised in highly individualistic cultures. Families without children may have different security concerns from families with children, especially young ones.

DIMITRI *I am looking for a new car, so I went to a dealership. I was looking at a model that Consumer Reports said has the highest safety rating. Then the salesman came over and started talking about the car I was looking at. His pitch was that it was cheap and fuel efficient. I asked him a couple of questions about safety issues, which are my primary concerns with cars, and he just brushed them back and kept telling me how economical it was. He lost that sale.*

A quotation from Jesus will have more impact with Christians than with Muslims. A quotation from Bill Clinton will carry more weight with Democrats than Republicans. Some people think more visually than others, so it's wise to include both visual aids and nonvisual supporting materials.

Organize So Listeners Can Follow Easily

From our discussion in Chapter 4, we know that listening is hard work. When giving an informative talk, a speaker should do all that she or he can to reduce the amount of work listeners have to invest. Applying the principles we discussed in Chapter 16, this means that you should structure your speech clearly. As we learned, your introduction should capture listeners' attention ("Would you like

Arch White/Alamy

Few audiences today are homogeneous.

to increase your productivity and paychecks by 10%?"), provide a clear thesis ("I'm going to explain a new procedure that will increase your efficiency and income"), and preview what will be covered ("I will demonstrate a new method of sorting and routing stock and show how much faster and more accurate it is than the method we've been using").

Transitions should be woven throughout the speech to assist listeners in following the flow of ideas. The conclusion should summarize key points ("I've shown you how to increase your paycheck") and end with a strong idea or punch ("In this case, what's good for the company is also good for you").

The body of an informative speech should also be organized clearly (see Table 17.3). Some of the patterns we discussed in Chapter 16 are especially well adapted to informative speeches. The time and spatial patterns can be effective for speeches that aim to demonstrate, describe, explain, or teach ("In my speech, I will describe how fetuses develop in the first, second, and third trimesters"; "I want to explain how leg and arm positions at the keyboard affect the back and neck"). Topical patterns are commonly used for reports and briefings that address several areas of a topic ("I want to summarize developments in our sales and marketing divisions").

When introducing new or alternative ideas or procedures, the comparative pattern can be effective ("The new method of sorting and routing stock differs from our current method in two key ways").

Table 17.3	**Organizing Informative Speeches**	
Specific Purpose	**Thesis**	**Organizational Patterns**
Listeners will learn how to recognize differences between poisonous and nonpoisonous plants.	I will teach you how to tell which plants are safe to eat.	Comparison/contrast
Team members will know management's response to our strategic plan.	I will summarize the feedback from management on our goals and implementation strategies.	Topical
To teach friends how I make crème brûlée.	I am going to take you through the steps involved in making a perfect crème brûlée.	Time
Employees will understand the reasons for a new procedure for sorting and routing stock.	I want to explain how the new procedure we're going to start using solves problems that have frustrated us for years.	Problem–solution

Although they are less commonly used in informative presentations, problem–solution and cause–effect or effect–cause patterns can be good choices. For instance, an informative speech might explain how a new procedure for sorting and routing stock solves a problem. The same topic might be organized using a cause–effect pattern to show that the new procedure (cause) will increase productivity (effect).

Like all other types of speeches, effective informative presentations highlight key points so they stand out to listeners. Also, smooth transitions should be developed to connect points in a speech.

Speech Builder Express, which you can access via your Online Resources for *Communication in Our Lives*, includes extensive prompts and a clear framework for organizing and developing speeches that incorporate a variety of informative strategies.

Design Your Speech to Enhance Learning and Retention

Much of the information we need to do our jobs and live our lives is not particularly interesting. This poses a challenge for you when you give an informative speech. The informative speaker is responsible for making material interesting to listeners. In addition, information can be complex and difficult to grasp, particularly in oral presentations. This creates a second challenge for informative speakers: You must do all you can to increase the clarity of the information. Five strategies can help you make your information interesting and clear.

Limit the Information You Present Most of us can understand and remember only so much information at a time. By the time you are ready to give an informative speech, you know a great deal about the topic. It's your job to sort through all your knowledge to choose wisely the two or three points you want to make. You may think five points are important. If you try to present all five, however, you risk having listeners remember none or the less important ones.

If you must cover more than two or three points to inform listeners fully, then you have two choices. You may give multiple informative talks, separated by time to allow listeners to absorb and apply the information you've provided before they get more. A second option is to rely on other principles of increasing clarity and interest that we discuss later in this chapter.

Move from Familiar to Unfamiliar It's normal to feel uneasy when you are asked to understand new information or learn a new process or skill. Speakers can reduce this anxiety by starting with what is familiar to listeners and moving to what is new. For instance, the supervisor in our example might open an informative speech by saying, "All of you know the sorting and routing procedure we've used for years. The new procedure extends what you already know. What you've done in the past is to sort incoming stock into three piles. From now on, you'll be sorting it into four. It's the same process—just one more pile." Upon hearing this, listeners realize that their basic sorting process is not being abandoned; it is only getting more complex. The skills they already have will transfer.

COMMUNICATION
in Your Life

What material in your speech is likely to be unfamiliar to your listeners?

Repeat Important Ideas Repetition is a powerful way to increase retention (Thompson & Grundgenett, 1999). Have you ever been introduced to someone and not been able to remember the person's name 5 minutes later? That's because you heard it only once. The introduction probably was like this: "Pat, I'd like you to meet Leigh." If the person doing the introduction had wanted to help you remember Leigh's name, it would have been better to say this: "Pat, I'd like you to meet Leigh. Leigh and I go way back; we met in our sophomore year. We got together when Leigh and I were trying out for the chorus, and Leigh got a place when I didn't." In that short introduction, Leigh's name was mentioned four times. You'll probably remember it. You're more likely to remember something you hear four times than something you hear only once.

The same principle applies to informative speaking. As an illustration, let's return to our supervisor. It's important that employees retain the new classifications into which they will be sorting stock, so these bear repeating: "In the past you've sorted stock into new, returns, and used. As most of you know, the stock we've been putting in the return pile has really been of two types: stock that was missing something and stock that was defective. Now we're breaking returns into two separate piles: ones with missing parts and ones with defective parts. So we have missings and defects. The missing pile is for stock that is missing a part. We can fix these items by adding the missing part. The defect pile is for stock that has something wrong with it, usually a defective part. So missings and defects are the new piles we want to use." The repeated references to *missings* and *defects* increase listeners' ability to understand and retain the new classifications for stock.

Highlight Key Material Do you become more attentive in class when a teacher says, "This next point is really important" or "You're likely to see this on the test"? Probably you do. That's what the teacher intends. He or she is highlighting key material to get your attention. In this example, the teacher highlighted by framing. "This material is important" is a frame that calls your attention to important material.

"This material is important."

MATERIAL

There are other ways to highlight key material. You might say something direct, such as, "Listen up. This is important." Or you might say, "I hope you'll really tune in to this next point." You could also say, "If you remember only one thing from my talk, it should be this:..." All of these statements give verbal clues to listeners that you are presenting especially important material.

You can also provide nonverbal clues to highlight key material. Raising volume or changing inflection tends to capture interest, so listeners are likely to listen more carefully when a speaker alters volume or inflection. Gestures can also emphasize the importance of key ideas. You can change your position—move from behind a podium to in front of it, move from sitting to standing—to draw listeners' attention.

Rely on Multiple Communication Channels If a speaker says, "Red berries often are poisonous," you might get the point. You'd be more likely to get it and

COMMUNICATION in Your Life

What parts of your speech are most important to highlight?

retain it if the speaker made that statement and also showed you pictures of red berries or gave you red berries. When we use multiple channels to communicate, we increase the likelihood that listeners will learn and retain new information.

When you're presenting a lot of information or complex information, handouts can greatly increase listeners' retention and ability to use new information. Listeners both hear the talk and see the notes summarizing key points. Visual aids can also highlight information. The supervisor in our example might develop a visual aid to show the two new classifications that grow out of the one former one (Figure 17.1). Showing this while also talking about the two new classifications lets listeners learn and retain through two senses: eyes and ears. The visual aid would be especially effective if the two new classifications stood out visually. They might be larger or a different, striking color.

Involve Listeners

Have you ever been a passenger when someone else was driving and later been unsure how to get back to where the two of you went? If you drive yourself, there's a greater likelihood that you'll learn how to get to the place. This common experience reminds us that we learn best when we do something ourselves rather than just hear about it. Involvement generates active learning, and that's critical to effective informative speaking. There are many ways to involve listeners in informative speeches. We'll highlight four of the most effective.

Call for Participation   You might give sticks to Boy Scouts and get them to try rubbing the sticks together as you demonstrate how to do this to start a fire (but only if fire codes allow this and if you can control possible danger). You might let people try a new procedure at a demonstration stand you set up. You might bring plants that are poisonous and nonpoisonous so that listeners can see, smell, and touch them as you describe how they differ.

COMMUNICATION in Your Life

Identify one way to invite your listeners to participate in your speech.

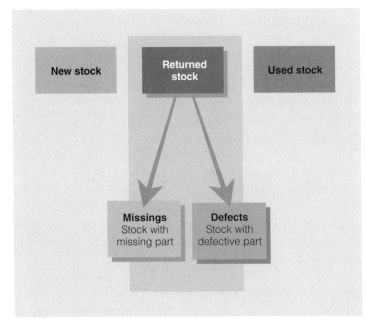

Figure 17.1
A Visual Aid to Illustrate a New Procedure.

Table 17.4	**Generating a Sense of Listener Participation**

Specific Informative Purpose: To Teach Listeners How to Recognize Poisonous Plants

Method	Example
Direct participation	I want each of you to smell the berries I'm handing out.
Rhetorical question	If you were stranded on a camping trip, would you know how to survive?
Poll listeners	How many of you have ever pulled a ripe berry off a bush and wondered if it was safe to eat?
Refer to specific listeners	Jane, remember when you watched Tom Hanks in *Castaway* and wondered how he knew what was safe to eat on the island?

Sometimes speakers can't have listeners participate directly. Perhaps it isn't feasible to set up a model for the new sorting and routing procedure. Perhaps you can't let Boy Scouts try making fire because the fire code prevents this. In such cases, effective speakers involve listeners in other ways (Table 17.4).

Ask Rhetorical Questions   One way to involve listeners when direct participation is impossible is to ask rhetorical questions. These are questions that a speaker doesn't actually expect listeners to answer. By asking them, however, a speaker invites listeners' mental participation: They are likely to answer rhetorical questions silently in their heads. This allows listeners to feel as if they are interacting with the speaker and are personally involved with the topics. "How many of you have ever wished you had an extra $100?" "What would you do if you made 20% more each week? Would you take a vacation, buy a new car, or pay some bills?"

Poll Listeners   Another way to involve listeners is to poll them to find out what they think, feel, or want or what experiences they have had. This allows you as a speaker to motivate them to want the information you are going to present. "How many of you have ever left your home for a vacation and worried about

"Hard to believe he flunked public speaking."

whether someone was going to break into it?" "How many of you would like to earn $100 more a week?" Speakers can ask for audible responses ("If you have had this experience, say yes") or a show of hands ("Let me see the hands of everyone who has had this experience").

Refer to Specific Listeners   To involve listeners, you may also speak directly to or about particular members of your audience. Ethically, you must be careful not to speak to or about others in ways that could embarrass them or reveal information they consider private. In many cases, you can honor this ethical principle and still speak to or about specific listeners to generate a sense of participation and community. "Bill and Sally, we've all heard about the break-in at your house." "Just the other day, I overheard Ed talking about what he'd do if he won the lottery. Well, Ed, I've got good news for you: You may not win the lottery, but you can get more money." Comments such as these create a sense of participation and interaction.

CourseMate

To practice involving listeners for various speech topics, complete the activity "Involving Listeners" in your Online Resources for *Communication in Our Lives.*

USE EFFECTIVE AND ETHICAL SUPPORTING MATERIALS

To be effective in informing listeners, speeches must include supporting material that is both effective and ethical. Effective supporting materials add interest and clarity to a speech. Ethical supporting materials present accurate information fairly and without distortion (Lehman & DuFrene, 1999).

Returning to our previous example, the supervisor might create a bar graph to provide a vivid visual comparison of productivity using the current and new procedures for sorting and routing stock. Quotes from employees at other firms that use the new procedure would add additional support, particularly because listeners are likely to believe what peer workers say about a new procedure. Statistics also can be effective if they are made interesting to listeners.

In our example, the speaker might take the average employee's salary and show how much it should go up using the new procedure. The speaker might develop a visual aid to show how that increase would multiply over a period of time (Figure 17.2). This would add interest and motivate listeners to pay close attention and learn the new procedure.

To be ethical, supporting material should meet the criteria we discussed in Chapter 15 (see Table 15.4 on page 362). To review, supporting material should be

- Sufficient to achieve the speaking purpose, such as teaching or describing (sufficiency).
- Accurate, correct and complete, with sources cited, presented in its original context (accuracy).
- Relevant to the topic and claims made (relevance).
- Timely, usually current or in some cases historically situated (timeliness).
- Free of biases, such as vested interests (impartiality).

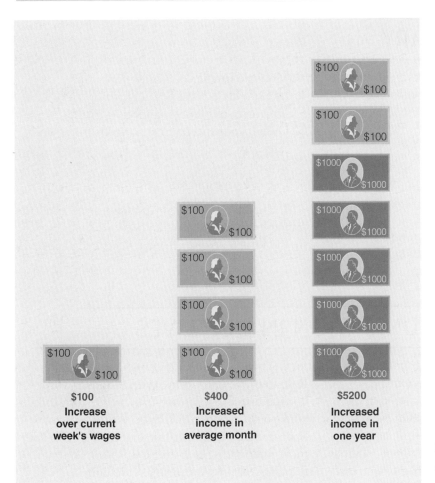

Figure 17.2
A Visual Aid to Motivate Employees.

Using these criteria, it would be ethical for the speaker to tell employees that their wages should increase an average of 20% only if the speaker had adequate data to support that claim (the criterion of accuracy). If only 25% of employees who have used the new procedure increase their productivity, it would not be ethical to state that they could expect to increase their wages because only one in four could reasonably expect that. If most employees do increase their productivity by 20% but only after 4 to 6 months of adjusting to the new procedure, the speaker would be ethically obligated to inform them of the time lag (the criterion of timeliness). If employees who use the new procedure at other plants have different working conditions and tools, the change in their productivity might not generalize to the listeners in this case (the criterion of relevance).

CHAPTER SUMMARY

In this chapter, we've focused on informative speaking, which is part of most people's lives. We described the many types of informative speeches and noted how informative speaking differs from persuasive speaking. We then highlighted eight guidelines for effective informative speaking. Because these guidelines are at the heart of the impact of your informative presentations, we summarize them here:

1. Provide listeners with a clear thesis statement.
2. Connect with listeners' values and experiences.
3. Motivate listeners to want information.
4. Incorporate diverse perspectives.
5. Organize so listeners can follow easily.
6. Design your speech to enhance learning and retention.
7. Involve listeners.
8. Use effective and ethical supporting materials.

If you follow these eight guidelines and apply the principles we've discussed in previous chapters, you should be able to give effective informative speeches.

APPLYING COMMUNICATION IN OUR LIVES

The key concepts, For Further Reflection and Discussion questions, and Experiencing Communication in Our Lives case study that follow will help you review, reflect on, and extend the information and ideas presented in this chapter. These resources, and a diverse selection of additional study tools, are also available as Online Resources for *Communication in Our Lives*. Your Online Resources include CourseMate, a student workbook, interactive video activities, audio study tools, a book companion website, Speech Builder Express, Speech Studio, and InfoTrac College Edition. For more information or to access this book's online resources, visit **www.cengage.com/login**.

KEY CONCEPTS

informative speech, 402

FOR FURTHER REFLECTION AND DISCUSSION

1. Attend an informative speech on campus or in the community. Identify the thesis and the organizational pattern. Evaluate the ethical and strategic quality of the speaker's evidence.

2. To find quotations that are relevant to your speech, use your Online Resources for *Communication in Our Lives* to access WebLink 17.2 and visit the Quotations Home Page.

3. Use the evaluation form on page 417 to evaluate Michael Daniels's speech on black boxes.

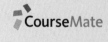

Informative Speech Outline

General Purpose: _____
Specific Purpose: _____

Introduction
I.   Attention device _____
II. Motivation for listening _____
III. Thesis statement _____
IV. Preview of speech _____

Body
I.   First main point _____
     A. Supporting material _____
     B. Supporting material (You may have only two main points) _____
     C. Transition _____
II. Second main point (You may have more than two kinds of supporting materials for main points)
     _____
     A. Supporting material _____
     B. Supporting material _____
     C. Transition _____
Transition to conclusion _____

Conclusion _____
I.   Summary of main points _____
II. Strong closing statement _____

References _____

Evaluation Form for Informative Speeches
Speaker's Name: _____ Date: _____
Speech Topic: _____

_____

1. Did the speaker capture listeners' initial attention? _____

   _____

2. Did the speaker motivate listeners to want information? _____

   _____

3. Did the speaker state a clear thesis? _____

   _____

4. Did the speaker preview the body of the speech? _____

   _____

5. Was the speech structured clearly and appropriately? _____

   _____

6. Were strong transitions provided between parts of the speech and main points in the body of the speech? _____

   _____

7. Did the speaker provide effective supporting material? _____

   _____

8. Did the speaker use ethical supporting material? _____
_____

9. Did the speaker involve listeners directly by polling them, asking rhetorical questions, or speaking to or about particular listeners? _____
_____

10. Did the speaker use strategies to enhance listeners' learning and retention? _____
_____

11. Did the speaker connect the topic to listeners' experiences and values? _____
_____

12. Did the conclusion summarize main points of the speech?_____
_____

13. Did the speech end on a strong note? _____
_____

SHARPEN YOUR SKILL

1. Informative Speaking in Your Life

How common is informative speaking in your everyday life? For the next week, keep a record of the informative speeches you hear (those given by others), grouped into the four categories listed here. Remember that an informative speech need not be long—it may be just a couple of minutes in which someone teaches you how to do something or explains a new procedure, describes a rule or policy, or tells you the background of an issue.

   a. Informative speaking in classes
   b. Informative speaking on the job
   c. Informative speaking with friends
   d. Other informative speaking

2. Organizing Your Informative Speech

Apply the principles of effective organization as you develop your informative speech. Provide the following information for your speech:

Introduction
   To capture listeners' attention and motivate them to listen, I will _____

   My thesis statement is _____
   To establish my initial credibility, I will _____
   To preview my speech, I will say _____
   My transition from the introduction to the body is _____

Body
   My organizational pattern is _____
   To provide transitions from one main point to the next, I will say
   A. Points one to two: _____
   B. Points two to three: _____
   C. Point three to conclusion: _____
   My transition from body to conclusion is
   _____

Conclusion
   I will summarize the key points in my speech by saying_____
   I will close with this strong statement:
   _____

EXPERIENCING COMMUNICATION IN OUR LIVES

CASE STUDY: *Informative Speech*: *Anytown USA*

A video of the speech described here is featured in your Chapter 17 Online Resources for *Communication in Our Lives*. Select "Informative Speech" to watch the video of Enriques Ruiz's speech. Improve your own public speaking skills by reading, watching, and evaluating this speech.

© Cengage Learning

I would not be the person I am today if it was not for Anytown. I would not be in this room if it was not for this organization. You're probably wondering what I'm talking about. What can so dramatically change someone's life?

Anytown is a summer leadership camp. Now there are thousands of summer leadership camps all around the world. You have science camps, young life camps, all kinds of camps—camps that change our lives in positive ways.

The summer before my junior year, I attended Anytown. Before camp, I was a deviant young man. After camp I was never the same. So what exactly is Anytown? What is its history and what goes on at camp that's so powerful? Today I'll discuss these three things with you.

According to the website, Anytown Arizona is a youth development program that focuses on diversity awareness, social justice, and personal empowerment. Its mission is to be a catalyst and facilitator for social change. This camp brings together people from different backgrounds and different cultures.

The Anytown USA organization has several types of programs: Anytown Junior is for junior highers; Unitowns are for weekend programs; Beyond Anytown is for people who have attended Anytown; and Powertown focuses for parents and community members.

The weeklong camp is filled with activities geared towards understanding diversity through a great deal of educational activities that have emotional impact. Typically the counselors act out different levels of violence that are seen everywhere. They start with verbal violence—someone saying an inappropriate comment to somebody just because they are a different color. They continue to physical violence, ganging up and pummeling another counselor because they are a different color. They finish with genocide. Genocide consists of four or six counselors acting out being Jewish, killed by two counselors acting out being Nazis. This is only one of the activities and there are many others.

So where did Anytown come from? What's its history? According to the Anytown website, Anytown began in 1957 known as the National Conference for Christians and Jews, now better known as the National Conference for Community and Justice. The goal then and now was to bring together a group of diverse young youth from a variety of different backgrounds, empower them to understand each other, and learn from each other.

In one cabin you will have a young man who has been very wealthy growing up and a young man who has had a very dysfunctional past. Together, throughout the week, they come together and they learn about each other and where they're from and what they've lived. Towards the end of the week they become kind of like brothers.

The staff, in a way, tests the students. They segregate them. Each day as a different theme, such as "know yourself," "know your friends," and "know your family." During the week in the end, when they become segregated they either continue to stay segregated or they desegregate themselves. These students never fail the test of desegregating themselves.

Each camp reacts differently to the segregation. Some break it and integrate to the camp. Some stay segregated until one specific student speaks up.

I hope you have learned a thing or two about this great organization that has been around for years. I'm sure that Anytown will be around for the future, helping our youth understand diversity, and understand each other. Jared Cohan, an Anytown alumni, quotes, "One person can achieve wonders by helping one person—an individual. Then that individual passes those things to another and so on and so on." This is the power Anytown has, changing the world one person at a time.

QUESTIONS FOR ANALYSIS AND DISCUSSION

You can answer these questions and see my responses to them online via your Online Resources for Chapter 17.

1. Did Enriques Ruiz effectively capture your attention at the beginning of his speech?
2. Did the preview forecast coverage adequately?
3. Did he provide effective and ethical evidence to support his ideas?
4. Were there good transitions between main points?
5. Did the conclusion summarize main points in the speech?

SPEECH STUDIO

Access Speech Studio via your Online Resources. You can upload a video of your informative speech, share it with your instructor and other students, view other students' informative speeches, and read feedback on your speech.

SPEECH BUILDER EXPRESS

Access Speech Builder Express via your Online Resources for *Communication in Our Lives*. If you'd like to continue working on an outline you've already started, click "Resume" to pull up the file for your speech.

Review your speech outline, and refine it to reflect your ongoing work on the speech. Also review your references. Be sure to check for errors in spelling and formatting. You're ready to print out your outline and begin practicing your informative speech. As you practice, you may find you want to make further revisions. Just return to Speech Builder Express, type in the changes, and print out the new outline.

Comstock Images/Getty Images

> Whatever words we utter should be chosen with care for people will hear them and be influenced by them for good or ill.
>
> **Buddha**

Persuasive Speaking

- You want to convince others to vote for a candidate in whom you believe deeply.

- You need to persuade your staff to embrace a new management philosophy.

- As the coach of a soccer team, you want to talk to the teenage players about the dangers of drugs and persuade them not to experiment.

- You want members of your fraternity to commit to a community service project.

- You want to persuade your friends to become organ donors.

- You want to convince the town council not to build a commercial center on the edge of your neighborhood.

SHARPEN YOUR SKILL

At the end of this chapter, refer to the Sharpen Your Skill features, Using the Motivated Sequence Pattern and Deciding Whether to Present One or Two Sides, to apply concepts from Chapter 18.

Although most of us won't give persuasive speeches regularly, nearly all of us will do so at times. In some cases, we'll be asked to make persuasive presentations. For instance, your manager might want you to persuade a potential client that your firm can provide the best service. In other cases, your values and commitments will compel you to speak in an effort to persuade others to ideas or actions that you think are right or desirable.

This chapter focuses on persuasive speaking. As you'll discover, much of what you've learned in previous chapters applies to persuasive speaking. Building on that knowledge, in this chapter we'll begin by defining persuasive speaking. Second, we'll discuss three cornerstones of persuasion and ways to build your credibility as a speaker. Next, we'll identify organizational patterns that are particularly effective for persuasive speeches. Fourth, we'll identify guidelines for effective persuasive speaking.

UNDERSTANDING PERSUASIVE SPEAKING

Persuasive speeches aim to change others by prompting them to think, feel, believe, or act differently. You may want to change people's attitudes toward policies, candidates for office, or groups of people. You may want to alter the strength of others' attitudes for or against particular issues. You may want to convince people to feel differently about the customs of immigrants. You may want to change how people act, perhaps convince them to quit smoking, to use seatbelts, to donate blood, or to volunteer for community service. In each case, your goal is persuasive: You aim to change the people with whom you speak.

In thinking about persuasive speaking, it's important to keep three characteristics in mind. First, like all other communication, persuasive speaking involves multiple communicators. The transactional model of communication we discussed in Chapter 1 is as relevant to persuasive speaking as it is to other kinds of communication. Effective persuasion is not something speakers do to listeners. Instead, it is engagement between a speaker and listeners. Although the speaker may be in the spotlight, the listeners are part of effective persuasive speaking, from planning to delivery. Speakers should consider listeners' experiences, expectations, values, and attitudes when they first think about topics and how to approach them.

In developing strong persuasive speeches, speakers need to keep listeners in mind: What kinds of evidence will they find impressive? Which experts will they respect? What is likely to lead these particular listeners to respect the speaker? In delivering persuasive speeches, speakers need to establish and maintain visual and personal connections with listeners and respond to feedback. After a persuasive speech, listeners may ask questions. Effective speakers respond in an open-minded manner that demonstrates respect for listeners. Throughout persuasive speaking, then, speakers and listeners are engaged in transactional communication.

Second, remember that persuasion is not coercion or force. The great rhetorical scholar Aristotle distinguished between what he called inartistic proofs and artistic proofs. An inartistic proof requires no art or skill on our part. We don't have to consider or respect others to get what we want using inartistic proofs. For instance, if you hold a gun to someone's head and say, "Give me your money or I'll shoot you," you may get the money. In that sense, you've been effective in getting the money (although you might wind up in jail). However, you haven't been artistic, and you haven't engaged in persuasion. To do that, you would need to give the other person convincing reasons to give you the money. You would use reasons and words to motivate, not force, the other person to do what you want. Persuasion relies on artistic, not inartistic, proofs.

Third, persuasive impact usually is gradual and incremental. Although people's positions occasionally change abruptly, usually we move gradually toward new ideas, attitudes, and actions. When we hear a persuasive speech, we compare its arguments with our experience and knowledge. If the speaker offers strong arguments, good evidence, and coherent organization, we may shift our attitudes or behaviors to some degree. If we later encounter additional persuasion, we may shift our attitudes further. Over time and with repeated persuasion, we may change our attitudes or behaviors.

Because persuasion tends to happen gradually and incrementally, speakers should understand the attitudes and behaviors of listeners and adapt their persuasive goals accordingly. For example, assume you believe that the role of the Electoral College in national elections should be abandoned, and you want to persuade others to your point of view. How would an effective persuasive speech differ if you knew in advance that listeners strongly favored the current Electoral College system or if you knew that they already had reservations about it?

In the first case, it would be unrealistic and ineffective to try to persuade listeners to support abolition of the Electoral College. A more realistic initial speaking goal would be to persuade listeners that there are some disadvantages to the current electoral system. In this instance, you would be effective if you could reduce the strength of their position favoring the Electoral College. Because the second group of listeners already has reservations, you can build on those and lead them closer to supporting abolition of the Electoral College.

Flying Colours Ltd/Digital Vision/Getty Images

Visual aids and dynamic extemporaneous delivery increase persuasive impact.

THE THREE PILLARS OF PERSUASION

Teachers in ancient Greece and Rome understood that effective speaking, especially persuasive speaking, is essential to democratic societies. Thus, learning to speak effectively and persuasively was central to the education of Greek and Roman citizens. These ancient teachers recognized three cornerstones of persuasion, which are also called three forms of proof, or reasons people are persuaded: These are *ethos*, *pathos*, and *logos* (Kennedy, 1991). Although these three forms of proof are also important in other kinds of speaking, they assume special prominence when we engage in persuasion (Figure 18.1).

Ethos

Ethos refers to the perceived personal character of the speaker. We are more likely to believe the words of people whom we trust. We tend to attribute high ethos to people if we perceive that

- They have integrity.
- They can be trusted.
- They have goodwill toward us.
- They know what they are talking about.
- They are committed to the topic (show enthusiasm, dynamism).

Listeners will have confidence in you and your words if they think you care about their welfare, are trustworthy, have relevant expertise, care about your topic, and have good character (Stiff, 1994). Conversely, listeners are likely not to place confidence in speakers they think are uninformed, uninvolved with the topic, untrustworthy, manipulative, or otherwise of poor character.

Figure 18.1
The Three Pillars of Persuasion.

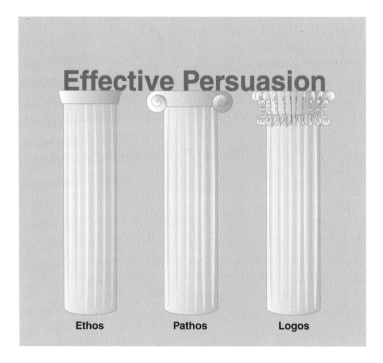

> **Carl**   *Last year, I had a teacher who didn't know anything about the subject. She made a lot of really vague statements, and when we tried to pin her down on specifics, she would blow off hot air—saying nothing at all. Nobody in the class thought she had any credibility.*

Because ethos is critical to persuasive impact, you should do what you can to demonstrate to your listeners that you are of good character. Table 18.1 identifies specific ways that you can influence listeners' perceptions of your ethos.

Table 18.1	Demonstrating Ethos
Dimensions of Ethos	**Ways to Demonstrate**
Goodwill	Identify common ground between you and listeners.
	Show respect for listeners' attitudes and experiences.
	Show that what you're saying will benefit them.
Expertise	Provide strong support for your claims.
	Document sources of support.
	Address concerns about or objections to your position.
	Demonstrate personal knowledge of the topic.
Trustworthiness	Use supporting materials ethically.
	Address other points of view fairly.
	Demonstrate that you care about your listeners.
Dynamism	Use appropriate volume and vocal emphasis.
	Assume a confident posture.
	Use gestures and kinesics to enhance forcefulness.
	Be energetic in presentation.

Pathos

Pathos refers to emotional reasons for attitudes, beliefs, or actions. Logic is not the only thing that affects what we believe. We are also influenced by our feelings: passions, fears, love, desire, personal values, shame, compassion, and so forth. Emotional proofs address the more subjective reasons for our beliefs in people, ideas, causes, and courses of action.

In preparing your persuasive presentation, develop ways to help your listeners not just to understand your ideas but also to feel a certain way about them. You may want them to feel positively about what you advocate. You may want them to feel negatively about some problem you are seeking to solve. You may want them to feel outraged about an injustice, compelled to help others, or afraid of a

Table 18.2	Enhancing Pathos

Ways to Enhance Pathos in Persuasive Speaking	Example
Personalize the issue, problem, or topic.	Include detailed examples.
	Tell stories that give listeners a sense of being in situations, experiencing problems.
	Translate statistics to make them interesting and personal.
Appeal to listeners' needs and values.	Show how your position satisfies listeners' needs, is consistent with their values.
	Use examples familiar to listeners to tie your ideas to their values and experiences.
	Show listeners how doing or believing what you advocate helps them live up to their values.
	Include quotations from people whom listeners respect.
Bring material alive.	Use visual aids to give listeners a vivid, graphic understanding of your topic.
	Use striking quotes from people involved with your topic.
	Use active, concrete language to paint verbal pictures.

Melanie   *Last night, I saw an ad on television that asked viewers to help children who were starving in other countries. At first, I paid attention, but it just went over the top. The pictures were so heartbreaking that I just couldn't watch. I felt disgusted and guilty and mainly, what I really felt was turned off.*

COMMUNICATION in Your Life

Recall a speech that relied strongly on pathos.

policy or possibility. Feelings such as these add to the persuasive impact of your speech. Table 18.2 shows particular ways to enhance pathos.

As Melanie notes, appeals to emotions are powerful—and dangerous. They can easily alienate listeners instead of involving them. Fear and guilt are uncomfortable emotions, so speakers should be cautious in arousing them. You may want your listeners to fear what will happen if they don't do what you advocate, but you don't want them to be so overwhelmed by fear that they are paralyzed and thus unable to act or to listen to you. Also, fear appeals can decrease a speaker's ethos if listeners are skeptical of the claimed dangers. If you appeal to listeners' fears, do so in moderation. Guilt, too, can be both aversive and disabling.

Generally, it's more effective to encourage listeners to do something they will feel good about (e.g., send money to help starving children overseas) than to berate them for what they are or aren't doing (e.g., eating well themselves while others starve). You want to appeal to listeners' emotions to persuade them, not to arouse their emotions for the sake of arousal itself.

Logos

The third reason for belief is **logos,** which is rational or logical proof. In persuasive speeches, logical proofs are arguments, reasoning, and evidence to support claims.

Forms of Reasoning   Most reasoning can be classified as one or the other of two basic forms. **Inductive reasoning** begins with specific examples and uses them to draw a general conclusion (Faigley & Selzer, 2000). **Deductive reasoning** begins with a general claim that is widely accepted and familiar to listeners. Following this, the speaker then offers a specific claim. The conclusion follows from the general claim combined with the specific claim. Suppose you want to present a speech arguing that climate change is damaging our environment. To reason inductively, you would start by citing specific places where global climate change has demonstrable impact and document the harm in each case. Then you would advance the general conclusion that global climate change threatens life on our planet. Reasoning deductively, you would start by stating a commonly accepted claim (i.e., "Climate change is having a negative impact on the entire world.") and then advance a specific claim (i.e., "Our region is part of the world."). From these two claims, it naturally follows that "Climate change is having negative impact on our region" (your conclusion).

The Toulmin Model

Another way to think about reasoning was originated by philosopher Stephen Toulmin (1958; Toulmin, Rieke, & Janik, 1984). Toulmin explained that logical reasoning consists of three primary components: claims, grounds for the claims, and warrants that connect the claims to the grounds for them. In addition to these three basic parts of logical reasoning, Toulmin's model includes qualifiers and rebuttals. Figure 18.2 shows the **Toulmin model of reasoning.**

The first component of Toulmin's model is the **claim,** which is an assertion. For instance, you might advance this claim: "The death penalty doesn't deter crime." On its own, that claim is not convincing.

To give persuasive impact to a claim, you need to provide some *grounds* for believing it. **Grounds** are evidence or data that support the claim. As we saw in Chapter 15, evidence includes examples, testimony, statistics, and analogies. Visual aids may be used to graphically represent examples, statistics, and so forth. For example, you might cite statistical evidence showing that crime did not diminish when certain states enacted the death penalty or that crime did not rise when certain states repealed the death penalty.

Consider a second example. You assert, or claim, that global climate change is harming the planet. Grounds, or evidence, to support that claim might include statistics to document the occurrence of global climate change, detailed examples of people whose lives have been negatively affected by changes in the earth's temperature, the testimony of distinguished and unbiased scientists, or visual aids that show changes over time. All these kinds of evidence support your claim that global climate change is harming our planet.

Grounds are necessary to support claims. However, they aren't sufficient; the grounds must be justified. That justification is a **warrant**—an explanation

COMMUNICATION in Your Life

What are the grounds for each claim in your speech?

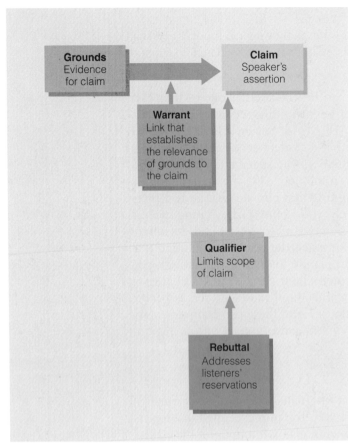

Figure 18.2
The Toulmin Model of Reasoning.

of the relevance of the grounds to the claim. You've probably heard the word *warrant* in connection with law enforcement. If a police officer wants to search the home of Pat Brown, the officer must obtain a search warrant from a judge. The officer shows the judge evidence suggesting that Brown has engaged in criminal activity. If the judge agrees that the evidence links Brown to criminal activity, a search warrant is issued. However, if the judge thinks the evidence is insufficient to link Brown to criminal activity, a warrant is not issued. Warrants operate the same way in persuasive speaking. If listeners perceive your evidence as relevant to and supportive of the claim, they're likely to believe your claim.

Let's return to a previous example. To support your claim that the death penalty does not deter crime, you provide statistics showing that crime rates did not increase when certain states repealed the death penalty. If the statistics were compiled by the Department of Justice, your listeners may perceive them as justifying the claim. On the other hand, if the statistics were compiled by an organization that opposes the death penalty, your listeners might perceive the source of the evidence as biased and therefore untrustworthy. In that case, there would be no warrant to justify linking the evidence to the claim.

A **qualifier** is a word or phrase that limits the scope of your claim. "Women are more interpersonally sensitive than men" is a very broad claim—so broad that it is difficult to support. A more supportable claim would be qualified: "In general, women are more interpersonally sensitive than men," or "Some women are more sensitive than some men," or "In many situations, women tend to be more interpersonally sensitive than men." The three qualified claims are more supportable.

Finally, Toulmin's model includes **rebuttal,** which anticipates and addresses reservations that listeners are likely to have about claims. As we've noted repeatedly, effective speakers consider listeners. When you analyze your listeners, try to anticipate their reservations about or objections to your claims. You demonstrate respect for listeners when you acknowledge their reservations and address them in your speech.

In our example, the speaker might realize that listeners could say to themselves, "The death penalty may not deter all crimes, but it deters serious crimes like homicide." If the speaker has reason to think listeners may resist the claim on this basis, the speaker would offer a rebuttal to the reservation. It would be effective for the speaker to cite the *New York Times* 2000 investigative report that shows that since 1976, states without the death penalty have had homicide rates no higher than those of states with the death penalty.

Careful reasoning and good evidence allow you to offer logical appeals that are sound, effective, and ethical. Later in this chapter, we'll discuss some of the most common kinds of logical fallacies so that you can avoid them when you make persuasive presentations.

BUILDING CREDIBILITY

We've already introduced the term *ethos* and noted its importance to effectiveness in persuasive speaking. Now, we want to consider ethos in more depth because of its critical role in persuasion.

Understanding Credibility

Another word for ethos is **credibility,** which a speaker earns by convincing listeners that he or she has personal integrity, is positively disposed toward them, and can be trusted. Notice that credibility is tied to how others perceive a speaker. This means that a speaker's credibility doesn't reside in the speaker. Instead, it is conferred by listeners or withheld if they find a speaker untrustworthy, uninformed, or lacking in goodwill.

In recent years, we've heard a lot about credibility gaps and the lack of credibility of some national figures. Many people have lost confidence in many politicians and other public figures. It's easy to understand why citizens don't find some national leaders credible. When a senator campaigns on a promise to restrict illegal immigration and then is found to employ an undocumented alien, credibility withers. Likewise, when congressional representatives proclaim the importance of fiscal responsibility and themselves bounce checks, they lose credibility as advocates of government financial responsibility. We believe in people who practice what they preach, and we grant credibility to people whose words and actions are consistent.

> **Soyana**   *The greatest teacher I ever had taught a class in government policies and practices. Before coming to campus, he had been an adviser to three presidents. He had held a lot of different offices in government, so what he was teaching us was backed up by personal experience. Everything he said had so much more weight than what I hear from professors who've never had any practical experience.*

Credibility arises from the three pillars of persuasion: ethos, pathos, and logos. Listeners are likely to find speakers credible if they demonstrate their personal integrity, establish emotional meaning for their topics, and present ideas logically and with good evidence.

COMMUNICATION HIGHLIGHT

Goodwill and Credibility

More than 2,000 years ago, the Greek rhetorician Aristotle wrote that a speaker's credibility depended on listeners' perceptions of the speaker's intelligence, character, and goodwill. Since Aristotle's time, research has established empirical support for strong links between credibility and perceived intelligence and character. But what about goodwill?

In a 1999 investigation, Jim McCroskey and Jason Teven found that perceived goodwill is positively linked to perceptions of likableness and believability. In other words, when listeners think a speaker cares about them and has ethical intentions toward them, they are likely to trust and like the speaker. The practical implication of this study is that speakers who want to be judged credible should establish goodwill toward listeners.

According to McCroskey and Teven (1999), goodwill tends to be established in three ways: showing understanding of listeners' ideas, feelings, and needs; demonstrating empathy, or identification, with listeners' feelings; and being responsive to listeners while speaking.

Types of Credibility

Credibility is not static; it can change in the course of communication (Figure 18.3). Have you ever attended a public speech by someone you respected greatly and found the presentation disappointing? Did you think less of the speaker after the speech than before it? Have you ever gone to a presentation without knowing much about the speaker and found it so impressive that you changed an attitude or behavior? If so, then you know from personal experience that credibility can increase or decrease as a result of a speech.

Developing Credibility

Initial Credibility   Some speakers have high **initial credibility,** which is the expertise and trustworthiness recognized by listeners before a presentation begins. Initial credibility is based on titles, positions, experiences, or achievements that are known to listeners before they hear a speech. For example, most listeners would grant General Colin Powell high initial credibility on issues of military goals and strategies. A former inmate of a state prison would have high initial credibility in a speech on prison conditions.

Derived Credibility   In addition to initial credibility, speakers may also gain **derived credibility,** which is the expertise and trustworthiness that listeners confer on speakers as a result of how speakers communicate during presentations. Speakers earn derived credibility by organizing ideas clearly and logically, by including convincing and interesting evidence that connects with listeners, and by demonstrating energy and involvement. Speakers who are not well known tend not to have high initial credibility, so they must derive credibility from the quality of their presentations.

Many Americans perceive Michelle Obama as highly credible on issues involving children.

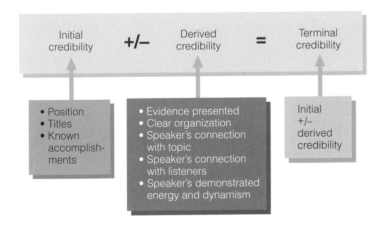

Figure 18.3
Developing Credibility.

Terminal Credibility   The credibility of speaker at the end of a presentation is **terminal credibility**. It is the cumulative expertise, goodwill, and trustworthiness listeners attribute to a speaker—a combination of initial and derived credibility. Terminal credibility may be greater or less than initial credibility, depending on how effectively a speaker has communicated.

ENHANCING CREDIBILITY

COMMUNICATION in Your Life

How can you build your credibility in the process of presenting your speech?

As you plan, develop, and present a persuasive speech, you should aim to enhance listeners' perceptions of your credibility. To summarize what we've discussed about credibility, here are ways to establish initial credibility and build derived and terminal credibility:

- State your qualifications for speaking on this topic: experiences you have had, titles or jobs you hold, research you have done.

- Show listeners that you care about them—that your speech is relevant to their welfare.

- Appeal to listeners' emotions, but be careful of overwhelming or alienating listeners with excessively dramatic appeals.

- Reason carefully, and avoid reasoning fallacies.

- Use effective, ethical supporting materials.

- Communicate both verbally and nonverbally that you care about the topic and are involved with it.

- Respond to questions fairly and with an open mind.

ORGANIZING SPEECHES FOR PERSUASIVE IMPACT

In Chapter 16, we discussed ways to organize speeches. The principles you learned in that chapter apply to persuasive speaking:

- Your introduction should capture listeners' attention, provide a clear thesis statement, establish your credibility, and preview your speech.

- Your conclusion should summarize main points and end with a strong closing statement.

- You should provide internal summaries of main points.

- You should provide smooth transitions between points and the parts of your speech.

- The body of your speech should be organized to reinforce your thesis and show listeners how your ideas cohere.

To build on these general principles for organizing public communication, we want to focus on special organizational concerns relevant to persuasive speaking. We will discuss two topics: the motivated sequence pattern, which is particularly well adapted to persuasive goals, and the relative merits of one-sided and two-sided presentations.

The Motivated Sequence Pattern

Any of the organizational patterns that we discussed in Chapter 16 can be used to structure persuasive speeches. Table 18.3 shows how each of the eight patterns we discussed could support a persuasive thesis.

In addition to the eight patterns we have already discussed, there is a ninth structure that can be highly effective in persuasive speaking. In the 1930s, public speaking scholar Alan Monroe developed the **motivated sequence pattern** for

Table 18.3	Organizing for Persuasion

Lloyd Bennett works for a public relations firm that wants to convince Casual Cruise Lines to become a client. Lloyd could use any of the eight basic organizational patterns to structure his speech to persuade the cruise line to hire his firm.

Pattern	Thesis and Main Points
Time	Our firm can move Casual Cruise Lines into the future. I. Originally, Casual Cruise Lines attracted customers whose average age was 58. II. In recent years, that customer base has shrunk. III. To thrive in the years ahead, Casual Cruise Lines needs to appeal to younger customers.
Spatial	Our proposal focuses on redesigning the space on cruise ships to appeal to the 30-to-45-year-old market. I. In the staterooms, we propose replacing the conventional seafaring motif with abstract, modernistic art. II. In the public area of the lower deck, we propose replacing the current coffee shops with sushi and espresso bars and adding fitness rooms. III. On the upper deck, we propose building hot tubs beside the pool.
Topical	Our firm has the most experience advertising cruise lines and the most innovative staff. I. Our firm has increased revenues for three other cruise lines. II. Our firm has won more awards for innovation and creativity than the other firms Casual Cruise Lines is considering for this account.
Star	Let's consider how younger customers might be attracted if we revamped ship décor, activities, and cuisine. I. Younger customers like modern décor. II. Younger customers want youthful activities. III. Younger customers want trendy food.
Wave	The theme we propose is: "No shuffleboard and no kids—Casual Cruise Lines." I. If you're too young for shuffleboard, you're ready for Casual Cruise. II. If you're too old to babysit, you're ready for Casual Cruise.

Continued

Comparative	Casual Cruise Lines needs to adapt to younger customers whose needs and interests differ from those of older customers.
	I. We recommend 3-, 5-, and 7-day cruises because, although older people have the time for extended cruises, 30-to-45-year-olds can usually spare only a week or less at a time.
	II. Casual Cruise Lines should get rid of bingo and shuffleboard and add dancing and nightclubs, which are favorite leisure activities of 30-to-45-year-olds.
	III. We recommend adding 24-hour espresso bars and onboard fitness rooms to meet the preferences of 30-to-45-year-olds.
Problem–solution	We have a solution to Casual Cruise Lines' inability to attract younger customers.
	I. Casual Cruise Lines hasn't been able to get a substantial share of the lucrative 30-to-45-year-old market.
	II. Our advertising campaign specifically targets this market.
Cause–effect	The advertising campaign we propose will attract young, affluent customers by appealing to their interests and lifestyles.
	I. Our proposal's emphasis on luxury features of the cruise caters to this market's appreciation of extravagance.
	II. Our proposal to feature adults-only cruises caters to this market's demonstrated preferences.
	III. Our proposal to offer 2-day to 4-day cruises meets this market's interest in long weekend getaways.

organizing speeches (Monroe, 1935). It has proven quite effective in diverse communication situations (Gronbeck, McKerrow, Ehninger, & Monroe, 1994; Jaffe, 2007). The primary reason for the effectiveness of the motivated sequence pattern is that it follows a natural pattern of human thought by gaining listeners' attention, demonstrating a need, offering a solution, and then helping them visualize and act on the solution. This pattern progressively increases listeners' motivation and personal involvement with a problem and its solution. The motivated sequence pattern includes five sequential steps, summarized in Table 18.4.

In the first step, listeners' attention is drawn to the subject. Here, a speaker makes a dramatic opening statement (e.g., "Imagine this campus with no trees whatsoever"), shows the personal relevance of the topic (e.g., "The air you are breathing right now exists only because we have trees"), or otherwise catches listeners' attention. Later in this chapter, we'll discuss additional ways to capture listeners' initial attention.

The second step establishes need by showing that a real and serious problem exists (e.g., "Acid rain is slowly but surely destroying the trees of this planet"). Next is the satisfaction step, in which a speaker recommends a solution (e.g., "Stronger environmental regulations and individual efforts to use environmentally safe products can protect trees and thus the oxygen we breathe"). The

Table 18.4	**The Motivated Sequence Pattern**

1. Attention: Focus listeners' attention.
2. Need: Demonstrate that a real problem exists.
3. Satisfaction: Propose a solution to the demonstrated problem.
4. Visualization: Give listeners a vision of the impact of the solution.
5. Action: Ask listeners to think, feel, or act to bring the proposed solution into being.

fourth step, visualization, increases listeners' commitment to the solution identified in the satisfaction step by helping them imagine the results that would follow from adopting the recommended solution (e.g., "You will have ample air to breathe, and so will your grandchildren. Moreover, we'll all have the beauty of trees to enrich our lives").

Speech Builder Express, which you can access via your Online Resources for *Communication in Our Lives*, includes extensive prompts and a clear framework for organizing and developing speeches that incorporate a variety of persuasive strategies.

CourseMate

Finally, speakers move to the action step, which involves a direct appeal for concrete action on the part of listeners (e.g., "Refuse to buy or use any aerosol products," "Sign this petition that I am sending to our senators in Washington, D.C."). The action step calls on listeners to take action to bring about the solution the speaker helped them visualize.

> **Velma** *I've heard a lot of speeches on discrimination, but the most effective I ever heard was Cindy's in class last week. Other speeches I've heard focused on the idea that discrimination is wrong, but that's something I already believe, so they weren't helpful. Cindy, on the other hand, told me how to do something about discrimination. She showed me how I could act on what I believe.*

Velma's commentary explains why the motivated sequence pattern is especially suited to persuasive speaking: It goes beyond identifying a problem and recommending a solution. In addition, it intensifies listeners' desire for a solution by helping them visualize what it would mean and gains their active commitment to being part of the solution. When listeners become personally involved with an idea and with taking action, they are more enduringly committed.

One-Sided and Two-Sided Presentations

Perhaps you are wondering whether it's more effective to present only your own point of view or both sides of an issue in a persuasive speech (the question generally is not relevant to informative speeches). That's an important question, and it's one that communication scholars have studied in depth.

Motivating Smokers to Quit

Have you ever tried to quit smoking? If so, you know it's difficult to do so, and most smokers don't succeed on the first attempt. Communication researchers Norman Wong and Joseph Cappella wanted to know what kind of messages are most likely to motivate smokers to decide to quit. They recruited 555 adults who smoked regularly in the United States. Wong and Cappella exposed all of the participants in their study to public service announcements (PSAs) urging smokers to quit. These PSAs were ones that had been broadcast on television. However, Wong and Cappella manipulated the level of threat and efficacy in the PSAs. Some ads featured low-level threats (e.g., social rejection) whereas other ads featured higher-level threats (e.g., disease, death). The ads also varied in the level of efficacy, which involves power or ability to produce an effect—in this case to quit smoking. Some ads encouraged smokers to use products that replace the nicotine in cigarettes whereas other ads encouraged smokers to call a quit line for support and tips on how to quit and featured ex-smokers who had used the quit line and succeeded in quitting. Thus, participants were divided into four groups based on which PSAs they saw: high threat and high efficacy, high threat and low efficacy, low threat and high efficacy, or low threat and low efficacy.

They found that the most effective PSAs included both a high level of threat and a high level of efficacy, giving participants confidence that they could succeed in quitting. They also found that smokers who were more ready to quit responded better to PSAs that gave them confidence that they could quit. Finally, they found that although participants perceived the high efficacy PSAs as more efficacious than the low efficacy PSAs, they did not perceive even the high efficacy PSAs as maximally efficacious. Based on these results, Wong and Cappella spelled out the implications for those who design health campaigns aimed at smoking cessation: (a) Design messages that convey a strong threat from smoking and build smokers confidence that they can succeed in quitting. (b) Strengthen the efficacy of anti-smoking messages beyond the level in current PSAs. Even if smokers are really scared (the high threat message), they're unlikely to try to quit if they aren't convinced they can succeed.

Thinking Critically: Using the information from Wong and Cappella's study, how would you design a campaign to persuade students on your campus to adopt healthy eating habits?

Norman C. H. Wong is an Assistant Professor in the Department of Communication at the University of Oklahoma. Joseph N. Capella is the Gerald R. Miller Distinguished Chair in the Annenberg School for Communication at the University of Pennsylvania. This research was presented in a 2008 article titled "Antismoking threat and efficacy appeals: Effects on smoking cessation intentions for smokers with low and high readiness to quit" in the *Journal of Applied Communication Research*, volume 37, pages 1–20.

Research conducted to discover whether one-sided or two-sided presentations are more effective suggests that the answer is, "It depends." More specifically, it depends on the particular audience a speaker addresses, which reminds us again that good audience analysis is critical to effective public speaking. Decisions of whether to present one side of an issue or more than one side depend on the particular listeners for whom a speech is intended.

Listeners' Expectations   As we've noted before, effective speakers always try to learn what listeners expect so they don't fail to meet expectations. In educational settings, listeners are likely to expect speakers to discuss more than one side of an issue (Lasch, 1990). On the other hand, at campaign rallies candidates often present only their own side because they are speaking to committed supporters. Expectations may also be shaped by prespeech publicity. Imagine that you decide to attend a speech after seeing a flyer for a presentation on the pros and cons of requiring all students at your school to purchase computers. You might be irritated if the speaker presented only the pros or only the cons of the proposed requirement.

Listeners' Attitudes   It makes a difference whether listeners are likely to be favorably disposed toward your ideas (Griffin, 2008). If they already favor your position, you may not need to discuss alternative positions in depth. However, if listeners favor a position different from yours, then it's essential to acknowledge and deal with their views. If your listeners oppose what you propose, it's unlikely that you will persuade them to abandon their position and adopt yours. With an audience hostile to your views, it's more reasonable to try to lessen their hostility to your ideas or to diminish the strength of their commitment to their present position (Trenholm, 1991).

Failure to consider listeners' opposing ideas diminishes a speaker's credibility because listeners may assume that the speaker either is uninformed about another side or is informed but trying to manipulate them by not discussing it. Either conclusion lessens credibility and the potential for impact on listeners. Speakers have an ethical responsibility to give respectful consideration to listeners' ideas and positions. Doing so encourages reciprocal respect from listeners for the ideas you present. R. J.'s commentary illustrates this.

> **R. J.**   *In my ROTC unit, there's a lot of bad will toward the idea of gays in the military. Some of the guys have really strong feelings against it, so I was interested in what would happen at a required seminar last week with a guest speaker who was arguing that gays should be allowed in the services. He was really good! He spent the first 10 minutes talking about all of the concerns, fears, and reasons why officers and enlisted personnel disapprove of having gays in the military, and he showed a lot of respect for those reasons. Then he presented his own ideas and showed how they answered most of the concerns people had. I won't say everyone was persuaded 100% that gays should be allowed in, but I will say he managed to get a full hearing with a group that I thought would just turn him off from the word go. Since he talked to us, I've heard some of the guys saying that maybe gays wouldn't be a problem.*

Listeners' Knowledge What an audience already knows or believes about a topic should influence decisions on whether to present one or more sides of an issue. Listeners who are well informed about a topic are likely to be aware of more than one side, so your credibility will be enhanced if you include all sides in your presentation (Jackson & Allen, 1990). Also, highly educated listeners tend to realize that most issues have more than one side, so they may be suspicious of speakers who present only one point of view.

In some instances, speakers know that later on listeners will be exposed to *counterarguments*—arguments that oppose those of a speaker. In such cases, it's advisable to inoculate listeners. **Inoculation** in persuasion is similar to inoculation in medicine. Vaccines give us limited exposure to diseases so that we won't contract them later. Similarly, persuasive inoculation "immunizes" listeners in advance against opposing ideas and arguments they may encounter in the future. If listeners later hear the other side, they have some resistance to arguments that oppose your position (Kiesler & Kiesler, 1971). For example, in political campaigns, candidates often make statements such as this: "Now, my opponent will tell you that we don't need to raise taxes, but I want to show you why that's wrong." By identifying and dispelling the opposing candidate's ideas in advance, the speaker improves the chance that listeners will agree with and later vote for him or her.

Listeners may be persuaded by arguments that oppose yours if you haven't inoculated them against those arguments. In fact, research indicates that of the three options—one-sided only, two-sided, or two-sided with refutation of the other side—generally the most persuasive strategy is to present both sides and refute arguments for the other side (Allen et al., 1990).

There is no quick and easy formula for deciding whether to present one-sided or two-sided discussions of a topic. Like most aspects of public speaking, this decision involves judgment on the speaker's part. That judgment should be informed by ethical considerations of what listeners have a right to know and what content is necessary to represent the issues fairly. In addition, judgments of whether to present more than one side should take into account listeners' expectations, attitudes, and knowledge and the likelihood that listeners have been or will be exposed to opposing arguments.

> **COMMUNICATION in Your Life**
>
> Given what you have read, should your speech be a one-sided or two-sided argument?

GUIDELINES FOR EFFECTIVE PERSUASIVE SPEECHES

In this chapter, we've already discussed some guidelines for effective persuasive speaking. For instance, we discussed the importance of developing a speech that includes the three pillars of persuasion: ethos, pathos, and logos. We also emphasized the importance of speaker credibility, and we identified specific ways to build yours when you speak. We extended our previous discussion of organizing speeches to discuss the motivated sequence pattern and the merits of presenting one or two sides of arguments. In addition to these guidelines, three other principles are important for effective persuasive speaking.

Create Common Ground with Listeners

In any communication context, common ground is important. That general principle has heightened importance in persuasive speaking. A persuasive speaker tries to move listeners to a point of view or action. It makes sense that they will be more likely to move with the speaker if they perceive some common ground with him or her. Listeners may think, "If we share all of these values and concerns, then maybe I should rethink my position on this one issue we disagree on."

Kenneth Burke (1950), a distinguished theorist of language, believed that people are divided from one another: They differ in experiences, attitudes, values, and so forth. At the same time, there is overlap between people: We share some experiences, values, language, and so forth. Burke viewed communication as the primary way in which people transcend their divisions and enlarge what is common to them. Burke saw finding common ground as a process of **identification,** or recognizing and enlarging commonalities between communicators.

Effective persuasive speakers seek out similarities between themselves and their listeners and bring those similarities into listeners' awareness. A few years ago, a student of mine wanted to persuade his listeners that fraternities are positive influences on members' lives. From polling students on campus, Steve knew that many held negative stereotypes of "frat men." He reasoned that most of his listeners, who did not belong to Greek groups, would be likely to view him both negatively and as different from them. This is how he established common ground in opening his speech:

> You've probably heard a lot of stories about wild fraternity parties and "frat men" who spend most of their time drinking, partying, and harassing pledges. I confess, I've done all of that as a brother in Delta Sigma Phi. I've also spent every Sunday for the last semester volunteering in the Big Brother Program that helps underprivileged kids in the city. And I've built friendships with brothers that will last my entire life. Like many of you, I felt a little lost when I first came to this campus. I wanted to find a place where I belonged at college. Like you, I want to know people and be involved with projects that help me grow as a person. For me, being in a fraternity has done that.

This is an effective opening. Steve began by showing listeners that he realized they might hold some negative views of fraternity men. He went further and acknowledged that he personally fit some of those stereotypes. But then Steve challenged the adequacy of the stereotypes by offering some information that didn't fit with them. Volunteering as a Big Brother isn't part of the "party guy" image. Having recognized and challenged stereotypes his listeners were likely to hold, Steve then began to create common ground. Most of his listeners could remember feeling lost when they first came to college. Most of them could identify with wanting to belong and to grow as people. Steve's opening successfully identified similarities between himself and his listeners, so they were open to considering his argument that fraternities are valuable.

Adapt to Listeners

Effective persuasion focuses on particular listeners. A good persuasive speech is not designed for just anyone. Instead, it is adapted to specific listeners' knowledge, attitudes, motives, experiences, values, and expectations. The methods of audience analysis that we discussed in Chapter 14 should help you learn who your listeners are and what they know, believe, and expect in relation to your topic.

As a speaker, your job is to apply what you learn about your listeners as you develop and present your speech. In his speech on the values of fraternities, Steve adapted to his listeners by showing that he understood common stereotypes of "frat men" and that there was some truth to them. This enhanced Steve's credibility and his listeners' willingness to open their minds to what he had to say.

In 1998, Raymond W. Smith, chairperson of Bell Atlantic, spoke about hate speech on the Internet. Smith spoke at the Simon Wiesenthal Center, which is dedicated to human rights (Smith, 1998). Although Smith spoke against censoring hate speech on the Internet, he realized that his largely Jewish listeners had acute knowledge of the dangers of hate speech. In his opening remarks Smith said,

> Neo-Nazis and extremists of every political stripe who once terrorized people in the dead of night with burning crosses and painted swastikas are now sneaking up on the public—especially our kids—through the World Wide Web.

Although Smith went on to argue against censorship, he let his listeners know that he was well aware of hate speech and the harms it can cause. Within his speech, Smith further adapted to his listeners by quoting Jewish leaders, who had high credibility with listeners.

Knowing that many of his listeners favored censorship, Smith presented a two-sided speech. He began by considering the arguments of those who favor censorship, treating them thoroughly and respectfully. He then turned to the other side (the one he favored): not censoring hate speech on the Internet. Smith argued that censorship will not get to the source of the problem, which is hate. Instead, he said the solution is to teach tolerance and respect. In making this argument, Smith adapted to his listeners at the Wiesenthal Center by saying,

> While cyberhate cannot be mandated or censored out of existence, it can be countered by creating hundreds of chat lines, home pages, bulletin boards, and websites dedicated to social justice, tolerance, and equality for all people. . . . Moral leadership can have a tremendous impact. Quite simply, we need more Simon Wiesenthal Centers.

To adapt to his listeners, Smith acknowledged their cultural history, quoted authorities they respected, and thoughtfully considered the argument for censorship. Therefore, his listeners were then willing to give an equally thoughtful hearing to Smith's argument against censorship.

Avoid Fallacious Reasoning

A **fallacy** is an error in reasoning. The word *fallacy* is derived from the Latin word *fallacia*, which means "deceit." Fallacies present false, or flawed, logic. Despite the original meaning, deceit, fallacies may be intentional or unintentional.

Effective speakers find common ground with listeners.

Either way, they are not effective with educated or thoughtful audiences. They detract from a speaker's credibility because they suggest that the speaker is not ethical. To be effective and ethical, you should avoid using fallacies in your speeches. To be a critical listener, you should be able to recognize fallacies used by others. We'll discuss eight of the most common fallacies in reasoning. This should allow you to avoid these fallacies in your speaking and to identify and resist them if they are part of others' communication.

Ad Hominem Arguments   In Latin, the word *ad* means "to," and *hominem* means "human being." Thus, **ad hominem** arguments are ones that go to the person instead of the idea. It is not ethical to argue for your point of view by attacking the integrity of someone who has taken a stand opposing yours.

"You can't trust what George Boxwood says about the importance of a strong military. After all, he never served a day in the military." Although it may be true that Boxwood didn't serve in the military, that doesn't necessarily discredit his argument about the importance of a strong military. Boxwood may have researched the topic vigorously, interviewed military personnel, and studied historical effects of strong and weak military forces. Boxwood's own service—or lack thereof—is not directly relevant to the quality of his argument for a strong military. Unethical speakers sometimes try to undercut people whose positions oppose their own by attacking the people, not the arguments. Critical listeners recognize this fallacy and distrust speakers who engage in it.

Post Hoc, Ergo Propter Hoc   *Post hoc, ergo propter hoc* is a Latin phrase meaning "after this, therefore because of this." Sometimes when one thing follows another, we mistakenly think the first thing caused the second. Unethical speakers sometimes try to persuade us to think that a coincidental sequence is causal. For instance, the U.S. economy faltered and verged on recession after George W. Bush became president. Does that mean Bush and his administration caused the economic slowdown? Not necessarily. To support the claim that Bush caused the economic slowdown, a speaker would need to demonstrate that specific policies implemented by Bush hurt the economy.

The Bandwagon Appeal   When I was a child, I often tried to persuade my parents that I should be allowed to do something because all of my friends were doing it. Invariably, my parents rejected that reason and replied, "If all of your friends jumped off the roof, would you do that?" At the time, that answer exasperated me. But my parents were right. They rejected the **bandwagon appeal**, which argues that because most people believe or act a particular way, you should too. Widely held attitudes are not necessarily correct, as Christopher Columbus and Galileo proved. Thoughtful listeners won't be persuaded to your point of view just because lots of other people have been. It's more ethical and more effective to give them good reasons why they should agree with you.

Slippery Slope   The **slippery slope** fallacy claims that once we take the first step, more and more steps inevitably will follow until some unacceptable consequence results. For example, an unethical speaker who wanted to argue against a proposal to restrict logging in a protected environmental area might state, "Restricting logging is only the first step. Next, the environmentalists are likely to want to prohibit any timber cutting. Pretty soon, we won't be able to build homes or furniture." The idea that we won't have lumber to build homes and furniture is extreme. It has little to do with the question of whether we should restrict logging in one particular area.

Hasty Generalization   A **hasty generalization** is a broad claim based on too-limited evidence. It is unethical to assert a broad claim when you have only anecdotal or isolated evidence or instances. Consider two examples of hasty generalizations based on inadequate data:

- Three congressional representatives have had affairs. Therefore, members of Congress are adulterers.

- An environmental group illegally blocked loggers and workers at a nuclear plant. Therefore, environmentalists are radicals who take the law into their own hands.

In each case, the conclusion is based on limited evidence. In each case, the conclusion is hasty and fallacious.

Red Herring Argument   Years ago, fox hunters sometimes dragged a dead fish across the trail of a fox to see whether the dogs would be diverted in the wrong

direction (Gass, 1999). They were trying to train the dogs not to let the smell of the fish, originally a herring, deflect them from hunting the fox. Speakers who try to deflect listeners from relevant issues engage in **red herring arguments**. They say something that is irrelevant to their topic or that doesn't really respond to a listener's question. The point is to divert the listener from something the speaker can't or doesn't want to address.

Either–Or Logic   What is wrong with the following statement: "Either abolish fraternities on our campus or accept the fact that this is a party school where drinking is more important than learning." The fallacy in this statement is that it implies there are only two options: either get rid of fraternities altogether or allow partying to eclipse academics. Are there no other alternatives? Might it be possible to work with fraternities to establish policies limiting parties to weekends? Might it be possible to increase the quality of academics so that students are motivated to be more involved with learning? In most instances, **either–or** thinking is simplistic and fallacious.

Reliance on the Halo Effect   The **halo effect** occurs when we generalize a person's authority or expertise in a particular area to other areas that are irrelevant to the person's experience and knowledge. It is fallacious to think that because a person is knowledgeable on particular topics, he or she is knowledgeable on all topics. It's also unethical to quote someone you think the audience will respect when that person has no qualification as an expert on your topic. Heather Locklear urges women to use L'Oréal hair coloring "because I'm worth it." Michael Jordan urges us to buy a particular brand of underwear. William Shatner and Leonard Nimoy, who played Captain Kirk and Mr. Spock on *Star Trek,* encourage us to use priceline.com. Well-known people appear in the mustache advertisements promoting milk. Are any of these people experts on the products they are urging us to buy and use?

To be effective and ethical, persuasive speakers should avoid fallacies in reasoning (Table 18.5). Likewise, effective critical listeners should be able to detect fallacies in reasoning and to resist being persuaded by them.

To practice identifying fallacies in various statements, complete the activity "Recognizing Fallacies" in your Online Resources for *Communication in Our Lives.*

Table 18.5	Fallacies in Reasoning
Ad hominem attack	You can't believe what Jane Smith says about voting because she doesn't vote.
Post hoc, ergo propter hoc	The new flextime policy is ineffective because more people have been late getting to work since it went into effect.
Bandwagon appeal	You should be in favor of the new campus meal plan because most students are.
Slippery slope	If we allow students to play a role in decisions about hiring and tenure of faculty, pretty soon students will be running the whole school.
Hasty generalization	People should not be allowed to own Rottweilers because there have been three instances of Rottweilers attacking children.
Either–or	Tenure should be either abolished or kept exactly as it is.
Red herring argument	People who own Rottweilers should own cats instead. Let me tell you why cats are ideal pets.
Reliance on the halo effect	World-famous actor Richard Connery says that we should not restrict people's right to own firearms.

CHAPTER SUMMARY

This chapter focused on persuasive speaking. After noting the many situations in which persuasive speaking occurs, we identified ethos, pathos, and logos and the cornerstones of effective persuasion, and we highlighted ways in which speakers can incorporate each into presentations. Extending this, we discussed credibility, which is especially important in persuasive speaking. We identified three types of credibility—initial, derived, and terminal—and discussed ways in which speakers can build their credibility during the process of planning, developing, and presenting persuasive speeches. The next section of the chapter reviewed general organizational principles and highlighted organizational concerns that are particularly relevant to persuasive speaking.

We introduced the motivated sequence pattern, which can be powerful in moving listeners to accept and act on persuasive appeals. We also discussed the merits of one-sided and two-sided presentations, and we identified criteria for choosing which will be most effective in particular situations and with particular listeners.

The last section of the chapter provided guidelines for persuasive speaking. The first is to build common ground between a speaker and listener. The second is to adapt to particular listeners by tailoring a persuasive speech to their expectations, knowledge, experiences, motives, values, and attitudes. The third is to avoid fallacies in reasoning, which are usually ineffective and always unethical.

APPLYING COMMUNICATION IN OUR LIVES

The key concepts, For Further Reflection and Discussion questions, and Experiencing Communication in Our Lives case study that follow will help you review, reflect on, and extend the information and ideas presented in this chapter. Your Online Resources include

CourseMate, a student workbook, interactive video activities, audio study tools, a book companion website, Speech Builder Express, Speech Studio, and InfoTrac College Edition. For more information or to access this book's online resources, visit **www.cengage.com/login.**

KEY CONCEPTS

ad hominem argument, 441
bandwagon appeal, 442
claim, 427
credibility, 429
deductive reasoning, 427
derived credibility, 430
either–or logic, 443
ethos, 424
fallacy, 440
grounds, 427

halo effect, 443
hasty generalization, 442
identification, 439
inductive reasoning, 427
initial credibility, 430
inoculation, 438
logos, 427
motivated sequence
    pattern, 433
pathos, 425

persuasive speech, 422
post hoc, ergo propter hoc, 442
qualifier, 428
rebuttal, 428
red herring argument, 443
slippery slope, 442
terminal credibility, 431
Toulmin model of
    reasoning, 427
warrant, 427

FOR FURTHER REFLECTION AND DISCUSSION

1. Reread this chapter's discussion of one-sided and two-sided persuasive speeches. When is it ethical to present only one side of a topic? When is it unethical? In answering this question, remember that ethical considerations are not necessarily the same as strategic ones. A speaker who uses unethical arguments or evidence might be effective in convincing listeners to think or do something.

2. If you would like to see and hear famous speeches, go to **WebLink 18.1**.

SHARPEN YOUR SKILL

1. Using the Motivated Sequence Pattern

Think about how you might organize a speech using the motivated sequence pattern. Write a thesis and five main points for a motivated sequence appeal.

Thesis _____

1. Attention: _____

2. Need: _____

3. Satisfaction: _____

4. Visualization: _____

5. Action: _____

2. Deciding Whether to Present One or Two Sides

Apply what you have learned to decide whether you should present one or two sides in your persuasive speech.

1. Are your listeners likely to expect to hear more than one side of the issue?
   _____

   A. How much education do they have?
      _____

   B. Has there been any prespeech publicity?
      _____

   C. Is there any reason to think that listeners do or do not care about hearing both sides? _____

2. What are your listeners' attitudes toward your topic?
   _____

   A. Do they have a position on the topic? If so, is it the same as yours?
      _____

   B. How strongly do listeners hold their opinions on the topic?
      _____

3. What level of knowledge about the topic do your listeners have?
   _____

   A. Do they know about more than one side of the issues?
      _____

   B. How much information about the topic have they already gained?
      _____

4. Are your listeners likely to hear counterarguments after your speech?
   _____

EXPERIENCING COMMUNICATION IN OUR LIVES

CASE STUDY: *Persuasive Speech: No Child Left Behind: Addressing the School Dropout Rate among Latinos*

A video of the speech described here is featured in your Chapter 18 Online Resources for *Communication in Our Lives*. Select "Persuasive Speech" to watch the video of Dana Barker's speech entitled "No Child Left Behind: Addressing the School Dropout Rate among Latinos." Improve your own public speaking skills by reading, watching, and evaluating this speech.

 CourseMate

Dana gave this speech in an introductory public speaking class. The assignment was to give a four- to six-minute speech, with a minimum of four sources cited. Students were also asked to create a preparation outline that included a Works Cited section.

I'll begin with a story from *The Santa Fe New Mexican* newspaper about a young woman named Mabel Arellanes. After becoming pregnant and dropping out of school at sixteen, Mabel has re-enrolled in high school and is now the junior class president. Although her dynamic change in attitude toward education has led her to the hope of becoming a lawyer, Mabel's story is not representative of the current trends among other Latinos. I have been conducting extensive research on trends in the socioeconomic status, graduation rates, and the population of Latinos in the United States. Today I will discuss the problem of the Latino dropout rate from high school and college, as well as provide a solution for addressing this intensifying issue. Let me begin by discussing the problem.

The dropout rate among Latinos in secondary schools and colleges must be addressed. Why? Because the dropout rate is simply excessive. Statistics and first-hand accounts attest to this fact. According to *The News and Observer*, one in twelve Latino students dropped out of high school in North Carolina during the 2003–2004 school year, but this statistic does not account for the 47.5 percent of Latino students who have not graduated in the four years since the beginning of the 1999–2000 academic year. Gamaliel Fuentes, who dropped out of school at age 15, said, "We have no money; that's why I dropped out of school. [My father] asked me [to stay in school], but I decided. Now, if I could go back in time, I would stay still in school." The tendency for Latinos to drop out is triggered by their generally low socioeconomic status and a lack of family support. The *Hispanic Outlook in Higher Education* explains that students coming from families of lower socioeconomic status are less likely to succeed in college because high schools do not prepare them well. In addition, Latino families expect their teens and young adults to contribute to the family's economic needs, and work schedules often conflict with studies.

Next, I will discuss the importance of addressing the Latino dropout rate. Addressing the dropout rate will keep Latinos from remaining at a generally low economic status. It is no secret that income is heavily dependent on education level. According to the *Daily Evergreen* newspaper, a person with a bachelor's degree is likely to earn almost one million dollars more over their course of their lifetime than someone with no college education. While a census report in the *San Antonio Express-News* found that Latinos earned merely 6.2 percent of bachelor's degrees awarded in 2001, the U.S. Census Bureau found that Latinos made up 12 percent of the national population in 2000 and 13.3 percent in 2002. In her essay, "Canto, Locura, y Poesia," Olivia Castellano, Latina professor at California State University, writes, "[Latinos] carry a deeply ingrained sense of inferiority, a firm conviction that they are not worthy of success." Ultimately, all who hold the belief that our country is the "land of opportunity" are affected by the Latino dropout rate. Again, referencing the 2001 findings of the U.S. Census Bureau, two out of every ten Hispanics live below the poverty line, while only one out of every four earned a yearly salary of $35,000 or more. Comparatively, around 50 percent of non-Hispanic whites earned $35,000 or more that year. These figures are far from exemplifying opportunity for Latinos.

What will happen if the problem is not solved? Since the percentage of Latinos in our population is still climbing, ignoring this issue will lead to a greater gap between the life of the typical American and the life of the Latino-American. As I proceed to discuss the solutions for this problem, are you beginning to sense the urgency of this situation?

To solve the problem of a high dropout rate, we must fund teacher sensitivity training and programs that help Latinos succeed in education, and Latinos must change their perspective on the importance of education and their ability to succeed. Let me first address teacher sensitivity training. Programs that educate teachers about Latino culture and beliefs and that help Latino students succeed in education will have the most impact on the dropout rate. Properly educated teachers will become aware of how they are able to meet the needs of Latino students. For example, the *Santa Fe New Mexican* reported on the success of a program called AVID, which boasts a 95 percent college entrance rate among its Latino students. This solution, which can be implemented at the national, state, and local levels, is dependent on increased funding and the efforts of educators with experience in Latino culture. Increased funding will help reform educational budgets for Latino communities and fund college success programs like AVID. This solution also requires the collective efforts of highly knowledgeable professionals with experience in education and in Latino culture who can train other educators.

Given proper attention and execution, the plan to address the Latino dropout rate will help the dropout rate begin to fall and will instill pride in the Latino community. Although it will take at least a decade before results are fully apparent, perhaps even a generation, ideally the plan will result in an increase in Latinos earning bachelor's, master's, and doctoral degrees. The sense of accomplishment gained by furthering education will change the typical Latino mindset regarding education and instill an overall sense of pride in the U.S. Latino community.

In summary, today I have discussed the problem of high dropout rate among Latinos, and I have discussed a possible solution for addressing the issue. Hopefully, you can clearly see that the high Latino dropout rate is an issue of great concern, one that requires prompt and thorough attention.

QUESTIONS FOR ANALYSIS AND DISCUSSION

You can answer these questions and see my responses to them online via your Online Resources for Chapter 18.

1. Did Dana provide a strong introduction with an attention device, a clear thesis, and a clear preview?

2. Are the sources of evidence credible? Why or why not? Is there any reason to suspect that the sources are biased?

3. What other kinds of evidence might Dana have used to strengthen the persuasive impact of her message?

4. Did Dana's speech reflect awareness of ethos, pathos, and logos?

5. How did Dana adapt the message to listeners who were 19-to-24-year-old college students? Can you think of additional ways she might have adapted this message to these particular listeners?

SPEECH STUDIO

Access Speech Studio via your Online Resources. You can upload a video of your persuasive speech, share it with your instructor and other students, view other students' persuasive speeches, and read feedback on your speech.

SPEECH BUILDER EXPRESS

Access Speech Builder Express via your Online Resources for *Communication in Our Lives*. Click "Create a New Speech" on the Express Menu. Type in the title of your persuasive speech. If you haven't given it a title, just type in a keyword title such as "Environmental Awareness Speech."

Proceed through the steps in Speech Builder Express to develop your speech and to prepare your list of references (Works Cited). Speech Builder Express is designed so that you can log off and return to it frequently as you move through the process of developing your persuasive speech.

Closing: Pulling Ideas Together

As I reflect on all that we've explored in this book, I find a central theme unifies the many topics we've discussed. The theme is that communication is an intricate tapestry woven from the threads of self, others, perceptions, relationships, contexts, culture, climate, listening, and verbal and nonverbal messages. Each thread has its own distinct character, and yet each thread is also woven into the complex, ever-changing tapestry of human communication. We've taken time to discuss each thread in its own right and then explored how it blends with other threads in particular communication situations.

Sometimes a particular thread stands out boldly, as individual threads sometimes do in woven fabric. For instance, the thread of delivery is quite prominent in public speaking, and the thread of listening is less visible. Yet, as we learned, to be effective, speakers must understand and adapt to their listeners because listeners decide how credible a speaker is and how effective public communication can be. Similarly, in personal relationships the thread of climate stands out as particularly important. Yet, the climate we create through our communication is also important in organizational communication and small group work. Thus, even when threads of communication are restrained in particular interactions, they are present and important.

At other times, an individual thread blends so completely with other threads that we don't perceive it as separate from the overall pattern of the tapestry. Organization, for example, is present in interaction between friends as they decide what to talk about and how to sequence the topics. Yet in friends' conversation, the thread of organization is muted, and other threads, such as sensitive listening, stand out. Similarly, the thread of delivery is subdued in casual conversations, yet our communication with friends is affected by how we articulate our ideas—by vocal force, volume, pace, and other aspects of delivery. The many threads that make up the tapestry of communication vary in intensity and prominence from one point in the tapestry to another, yet all are part of the whole.

To conclude our study of the communication tapestry, let's review what we've discussed and what it means for us. The overall goal of this book is to increase your insight into the ways in which communication is an integral part of our everyday lives.

We launched our journey in Chapter 1, which described the range of human communication and the modern academic field that bears its name. Chapter 2 allowed us to delve into the complicated process of perception so that we could understand how perception, thought, and communication interact. We learned that we seldom, if ever, perceive the full, raw reality around us. Instead, we perceive selectively, noticing only some things and overlooking others. The labels we use to name, classify, and evaluate our perceptions reverberate in our consciousness to shape what we perceive and what it means to us. In fact, most of the time, how we think, feel, and act are based less on objective realities in the external world than on how we label our selective perceptions of it. This is normal, yet it can cause us trouble if we forget that we are responding to our labels, not to the world itself. In Chapter 3 we explored the profound ways in which communication shapes personal identity and, in turn, the ways in which our identities shape how we communicate.

Chapters 4 through 6 focused on primary forms of communication: listening, verbal communication, and nonverbal behavior. As we considered each topic, we examined ways to improve our personal effectiveness as communicators. Particularly important to our understanding of these topics is the realization that people differ in their styles of listening and their verbal and nonverbal communication. Awareness of these differences helps us understand others on their terms. The principles and skills we discussed in these chapters should serve you well throughout your life as you seek to interact effectively and sensitively with others in personal, social, and professional contexts.

The elaborate and fascinating relationships between culture and communication were the focus of Chapter 7. There, we unmasked the subtle ways in which communication creates and sustains the beliefs, values, and practices that define cultures and social communities. Equally important, we saw that cultures shape the forms and content of communication by telling us what is and is not important and what are appropriate and inappropriate ways of interacting with others. Understanding differences between cultures and social communities allows us to appreciate the distinct character of each one and to enlarge our own repertoire of communication skills.

The second part of the book extended the first seven chapters by weaving basic communication concepts and skills into interpersonal, group, organizational, and mass communication. In Chapters 8 and 9, we explored interpersonal communication in general and as it occurs in friendships and romantic relationships. The intimate bonds that grace our lives are communicative achievements because we create and sustain them largely through interaction and the meanings we assign to it. Communication is the lifeblood of intimacy. In dramatic forms, such as declarations of love and disclosure of secrets, and in everyday small talk, it is communication that continually breathes life and meaning into our relationships with others.

We moved to quite a different context in Chapters 10 and 11, which examined communication in small groups. There, we learned what types of communication facilitate and hinder effective group discussion and what communication responsibilities accompany effective membership and leadership. We also studied the standard agenda for problem solving, which gives participants an effective method of organizing group discussion.

Chapter 12 focused on organizational communication, with particular emphasis on how interaction among members of an organization creates an overall culture for the organization. In Chapter 13, we explored mass communication and social media, which permeate our lives. Here we focused on ways to develop critical skills that enhance your media literacy.

Part III of this book concentrated on public speaking. From the early stages of planning presentations, to researching and developing evidence, and finally to

Michael Newman/PhotoEdit

organizing, outlining, and practicing, public speaking involves skills that most of us already have and use in other communication situations. As is true for all interactions, good public speaking centers on others; the values, interests, knowledge, and beliefs of listeners guide what speakers can and cannot wisely say and how they develop and present their ideas. Effective public speaking, like effective everyday conversation, is a genuine interaction between people in which the views and values of all participants should be taken into account.

Whether we are talking to a friend, a co-worker on a task team, or an audience of 500, we rely on common basic ethical principles and communication skills. Among the most important is sensitivity to others and their perspectives. Another principle important in all communication situations is sensitive listening. When we listen mindfully to others, we gain insight into them and their perspectives so that we may communicate effectively with them.

Clarity and responsibility are earmarks of effective verbal and nonverbal communication. To be clear in our messages and to understand those of others, we must recognize the ambiguity and abstractness of communication and must find ways to check with others to make sure we share meanings. Responsibility involves following ethical principles in our communication. In addition to respecting others and their positions, we should be careful to be accurate in making claims, whether in public speech or private conversation. Any evidence we use to support our ideas should be sound, and anything we say should be respectful of others and their differences. Whether we're talking to one person in an intimate setting or to a thousand in a large auditorium, good communication is clear, responsible, and sensitive.

Throughout *Communication in Our Lives*, we've seen that people differ in their communication and in the meanings they attach to words and actions. The cornucopia of cultures and social communities in our world gives rise to a fascinating range of communication styles. No single way of communicating is inherently superior to any other; the differences result from diverse cultural heritages and practices.

Learning not to impose our own communication patterns and our culture's judgments on others and being open to styles of interaction that differ from our own allow us to enlarge and enrich who we are individually and collectively. Curiosity, appreciation, and openness to unfamiliar ways of communicating are the lifeblood of a healthy pluralistic society in which each of us preserves our own distinct identity while remaining part of and engaged with a larger whole.

If you have learned these principles and skills of human communication, then you have the foundation of effectiveness in personal, professional, and social settings. If you are committed to practicing and continually enlarging the principles and skills introduced in this book, then you can look forward to a life of personal growth, meaningful relationships, professional success, and social impact. What is more, you are on the threshold of a life filled with joy. I wish you all of that.

Julia T Wood

Appendix A

Annotated Sample Speeches

BE YOUR OWN STORY: TRANSCRIPT OF 2004 WELLESLEY COMMENCEMENT ADDRESS

Toni Morrison

Abstract: Morrison honors and encourages the graduates of the 2004 class of Wellesley, a prestigious women's college, with her commencement speech. She points out that common themes of commencement speeches make listeners feel good but do not really address the material circumstances of the world and the graduates. Instead, she warns the graduates that the world is hurting and needs change but also encourages them that their individual actions can make that change.

Full Text: Address by Toni Morrison, noted author and recipient of the 1993 Nobel Prize in Literature delivered at Wellesley College in Wellesley, Massachusetts on May 28, 2004.

I have to confess to all of you, Madame President, Board of Trustees, members of the faculty, relatives, friends, students. I have had some conflicted feelings about accepting this invitation to deliver the Commencement Address to Wellesley's Class of 2004. My initial response, of course, was glee, a very strong sense of pleasure at, you know, participating personally and formally in the rites of an institution with this reputation: 125 years of history in women's education, an enviable rostrum of graduates, its commitment sustained over the years in making a difference in the world, and its successful resistance to challenges that women's colleges have

Begins by showing her own challenges and weakness, which creates a connection with the audience.

Honors her audience and the institution.

faced from the beginning and throughout the years. An extraordinary record—and I was delighted to be asked to participate and return to this campus.

But my second response was not so happy. I was very anxious about having to figure out something to say to this particular class at this particular time, because I was really troubled by what could be honestly said in 2004 to over 500 elegantly educated women, or to relatives and friends who are relieved at this moment, but hopeful as well as apprehensive. And to a college faculty and administration dedicated to leadership and knowledgeable about what that entails. Well, of course, I could be sure of the relatives and the friends, just tell them that youth is always insulting because it manages generation after generation not only to survive and replace us, but to triumph over us completely.

And I would remind the faculty and the administration of what each knows: that the work they do takes second place to nothing, nothing at all, and that theirs is a first order profession. Now, of course to the graduates I could make reference to things appropriate to your situations—the future, the past, the present, but most of all happiness. Regarding the future, I would have to rest my case on some bromide, like the future is yours for the taking. Or, that it's whatever you make of it. But the fact is it is *not* yours for the taking. And it is *not* whatever you make of it. The future is also what other people make of it, how other people will participate in it and impinge on your experience of it.

But I'm not going to talk anymore about the future because I'm hesitant to describe or predict because I'm not even certain that it exists. That is to say, I'm not certain that somehow, perhaps, a burgeoning ménage a trois of political interests, corporate interests and military interests will not prevail and literally annihilate an inhabitable, humane future. Because I don't think we can any longer rely on separation of powers, free speech, religious tolerance or unchallengeable civil liberties as a matter of course. That is, not while finite humans in the flux of time make decisions of infinite damage. Not while finite humans make infinite claims of virtue and unassailable power that are beyond their competence, if not their reach. So, no happy talk about the future.

Maybe the past offers a better venue. You already share an old tradition of an uncompromisingly intellectual women's college, and that past and that tradition is important to both understand and preserve. It's worthy of reverence and transmission. You've already learned some strategies for appraising the historical and economical and cultural past that you have inherited. But this is not a speech focusing on the splendor of the national past that you are also inheriting.

You will detect a faint note of apology in the descriptions of this bequest, a kind of sorrow that accompanies it, because it's not good enough for you. Because the past is already in debt to the mismanaged present. And besides, contrary to what you may have heard or learned, the past is not done and it is not over, it's still in process, which is another way of saying that when it's critiqued, analyzed, it yields new information about itself. The past is already changing as it is being reexamined, as it is being listened to for deeper resonances. Actually it can be more liberating than any imagined future if you are willing to identify its evasions, its distortions, its lies, and are willing to unleash its secrets.

Uses humor to identify with another part of the audience (i.e. guests of the graduates)

Acknowledges another part of the audience (i.e. faculty and staff).

Distinguishes her speech from common commencement speeches.

Gets the audience's attention by saying something startling and unexpected in the context (i.e. that the future is not certain or necessarily positive).

Builds anticipation for the thesis as she continues to point out how her speech is different from other commencement speeches.

Uses rich language to make her speech interesting and captivating.

But again, it seemed inappropriate, very inappropriate, for me to delve into a past for people who are in the process of making one, forging their own, so I consider this focusing on your responsibility as graduates—graduates of this institution and citizens of the world—and to tell you once again, repeat to you the admonition, a sort of a wish, that you go out and save the world. That is to suggest to you that with energy and right thinking you can certainly improve, certainly you might even rescue it. Now that's a heavy burden to be placed on one generation by a member of another generation because it's a responsibility we ought to share, not save the world, but simply to love it, meaning don't hurt it, it's already beaten and scoured and gasping for breath. Don't hurt it or enable others who do and will. Know and identify the predators waving flags made of dollar bills. They will say anything, promise anything, do everything to turn the planet into a casino where only the house cards can win—little people with finite lives love to play games with the infinite. But I thought better of that, selecting your responsibilities for you. If I did that, I would assume your education had been in vain and that you were incapable of deciding for yourself what your responsibilities should be.

Again contrasts her speech with other commencement speeches.

Begins to directly address her thesis: Individual action is necessarily and able to make change in the world.

Encourages her audience to indirect action (i.e. to think for themselves).

So, I'm left with the last thing that I sort of ignored as a topic. Happiness. I'm sure you have been told that this is the best time of your life. It may be. But if it's true that this is the best time of your life, if you have already lived or are now living at this age the best years, or if the next few turn out to be the best, then you have my condolences. Because you'll want to remain here, stuck in these so-called best years, never maturing, wanting only to look, to feel and be the adolescent that whole industries are devoted to forcing you to remain.

One more flawless article of clothing, one more elaborate toy, the truly perfect diet, the harmless but necessary drug, the almost final elective surgery, the ultimate cosmetic—all designed to maintain hunger for stasis. While children are being eroticized into adults, adults are being exoticized into eternal juvenilia. I know that happiness has been the real, if covert, target of your labors here, your choices of companions, of the profession that you will enter. You deserve it and I want you to gain it, everybody should. But if that's all you have on your mind, then you do have my sympathy, and if these are indeed the best years of your life, you do have my condolences because there is nothing, believe me, more satisfying, more gratifying than true adulthood. The adulthood that is the span of life before you. The process of becoming one is not inevitable. Its achievement is a difficult beauty, an intensely hard won glory, which commercial forces and cultural vapidity should not be permitted to deprive you of.

Uses specific cultural examples of the need for change.

Encourages her audience towards indirect action (i.e. to continue to learn and critique the world).

Now, if I can't talk inspiringly and hopefully about the future or the past or the present and your responsibility to the present or happiness, you might be wondering why I showed up. If things are that dour, that tentative, you might ask yourself, what's this got to do with me? What about my life? I didn't ask to be born, as they say. I beg to differ with you. Yes, you did! In fact, you insisted upon it. It's too easy, you know, too ordinary, too common to not be born. So your presence here on Earth is a very large part your doing.

Uses a question to suggest that she understands her audience.

Says something unexpected to get her audience's attention.

So it is up to the self, that self that insisted on life that I want to speak to now—candidly—and tell you the truth that I have not really been clearheaded about, the world I have described to you, the one you are inheriting. All my ruminations about the future, the past, responsibility, happiness are really about my generation, not yours. My generation's profligacy, my generation's heedlessness and denial, its frail ego that required endless draughts of power juice and repeated images of weakness in others in order to prop up our own illusion of strength, more and more self congratulation while we sell you more and more games and images of death as entertainment. In short, the palm I was reading wasn't yours, it was the splayed hand of my own generation and I know no generation has a complete grip on the imagination and work of the next one, not mine and not your parents', not if you refuse to let it be so. You don't have to accept those media labels. You need not settle for any defining category. You don't have to be merely a taxpayer or a red state or a blue state or a consumer or a minority or a majority.

Acknowledges her audience's power and ability to accept her challenge.

Of course, you're general, but you're also specific. A citizen and a person, and the person you are is like nobody else on the planet. Nobody has the exact memory that you have. What is now known is not all what you are capable of knowing. You are your own stories and therefore free to imagine and experience what it means to be human without wealth. What it feels like to be human without domination over others, without reckless arrogance, without fear of others unlike you, without rotating, rehearsing and reinventing the hatreds you learned in the sandbox. And although you don't have complete control over the narrative (no author does, I can tell you), you could nevertheless create it.

Uses language that focuses on the individual to encourage her audience.

Uses a metaphor (i.e. a novel).

Although you will never fully know or successfully manipulate the characters who surface or disrupt your plot, you can respect the ones who do by paying them close attention and doing them justice. The theme you choose may change or simply elude you, but being your own story means you can always choose the tone. It also means that you can invent the language to say who you are and what you mean. But then, I am a teller of stories and therefore an optimist, a believer in the ethical bend of the human heart, a believer in the mind's disgust with fraud and its appetite for truth, a believer in the ferocity of beauty. So, from my point of view, which is that of a storyteller, I see your life as already artful, waiting, just waiting and ready for you to make it art.

Concludes with an encouraging and empowering phrase (appropriate for this type of speech).

Thanks her audience.

Thank you.

MARTIN LUTHER KING, JR. REMEMBRANCE SPEECH: TRANSCRIPT OF 2010 SPEECH

Barack Obama

Abstract: President Obama honors Martin Luther King, Jr.'s life and activism while also encouraging Americans that his work is not finished and that individual people must work hard and persevere to end discrimination of all kinds and make our country and world more stable and safe.

Full Text: Address by BARACK OBAMA, 44th President of the United States, during his presidency at the Vermont Avenue Baptist Church in Washington, D.C., delivered on January 17, 2010.

Barack Obama, Martin Luther King, Jr. Remembrance Speech, delivered 17 January 2010, Vermont Avenue Baptist Church, Washington, DC.

Good morning. Praise be to God. Let me begin by thanking the entire Vermont Avenue Baptist Church family for welcoming our family here today. It feels like a family. Thank you for making us feel that way. To Pastor Wheeler, first lady Wheeler, thank you so much for welcoming us here today. Congratulations on Jordan Denice—aka Cornelia.

> Acknowledges and thanks audience and those who invited him.

Michelle and I have been blessed with a new nephew this year as well—Austin Lucas Robinson. So maybe at the appropriate time we can make introductions. Now, if Jordan's father is like me, then that will be in about 30 years. That is a great blessing.

> Uses humor to make a connection.

Michelle and Malia and Sasha and I are thrilled to be here today. And I know that sometimes you have to go through a little fuss to have me as a guest speaker. So let me apologize in advance for all the fuss.

We gather here, on a Sabbath, during a time of profound difficulty for our nation and for our world. In such a time, it soothes the soul to seek out the Divine in a spirit of prayer; to seek solace among a community of believers. But we are not here just to ask the Lord for His blessing. We aren't here just to interpret His Scripture. We're also here to call on the memory of one of His noble servants, the Reverend Dr. Martin Luther King, Jr.

> Identifies the purpose of the speech: to honor Dr. Martin Luther King, Jr.

Now, it's fitting that we do so here, within the four walls of Vermont Avenue Baptist Church—here, in a church that rose like the phoenix from the ashes of the civil war; here in a church formed by freed slaves, whose founding pastor had worn the union blue; here in a church from whose pews congregants set out for marches and from whom choir anthems of freedom were heard; from whose sanctuary King himself would sermonize from time to time.

> Shows respect by honoring the history of the church at which he is speaking.

One of those times was Thursday, December 6, 1956. Pastor, you said you were a little older than me, so were you around at that point? You were three years old—okay. I wasn't born yet.

Provides background information to inform the audience and build credibility.

On Thursday, December 6, 1956. And before Dr. King had pointed us to the mountaintop, before he told us about his dream in front of the Lincoln Memorial, King came here, as a 27-year-old preacher, to speak on what he called "The Challenge of a New Age." "The Challenge of a New Age." It was a period of triumph, but also uncertainty, for Dr. King and his followers—because just weeks earlier, the Supreme Court had ordered the desegregation of Montgomery's buses, a hard-wrought, hard-fought victory that would put an end to the 381-day historic boycott down in Montgomery, Alabama.

Uses detailed imagery to help the audience imagine being at the church at a particular time.

And yet, as Dr. King rose to take that pulpit, the future still seemed daunting. It wasn't clear what would come next for the movement that Dr. King led. It wasn't clear how we were going to reach the Promised Land. Because segregation was still rife; lynchings still a fact. Yes, the Supreme Court had ruled not only on the Montgomery buses, but also on Brown v. Board of Education. And yet that ruling was defied throughout the South—by schools and by states; they ignored it with impunity. And here in the nation's capital, the federal government had yet to fully align itself with the laws on its books and the ideals of its founding.

Continued use of imagery.

So it's not hard for us, then, to imagine that moment. We can imagine folks coming to this church, happy about the boycott being over. We can also imagine them, though, coming here concerned about their future, sometimes second-guessing strategy, maybe fighting off some creeping doubts, perhaps despairing about whether the movement in which they had placed so many of their hopes—a movement in which they believed so deeply—could actually deliver on its promise.

Uses a transition to make a connection between the past and present.

So here we are, more than half a century later, once again facing the challenges of a new age. Here we are, once more marching toward an unknown future, what I call the Joshua generation to their Moses generation—the great inheritors of progress paid for with sweat and blood, and sometimes life itself.

We've inherited the progress of unjust laws that are now overturned. We take for granted the progress of a ballot being available to anybody who wants to take the time to actually vote. We enjoy the fruits of prejudice and bigotry being lifted—slowly, sometimes in fits and starts, but irrevocably—from human hearts. It's that progress that made it possible for me to be here today; for the good people of this country to elect an African American the 44th President of the United States of America.

Addresses a popular counter-argument.

Reverend Wheeler mentioned the inauguration, last year's election. You know, on the heels of that victory over a year ago, there were some who suggested that somehow we had entered into a post-racial America, all those problems would be solved. There were those who argued that because I had spoke of a need for unity in this country that our nation was somehow entering into a period of post-partisanship. That didn't work out so well. There was a hope shared by many that life would be better from the moment that I swore that oath.

Of course, as we meet here today, one year later, we know the promise of that moment has not yet been fully fulfilled. Because of an era of greed and irresponsibility that sowed the seeds of its own demise, because of persistent economic troubles unaddressed through the generations, because of a banking crisis that brought the financial system to the brink of catastrophe, we are being tested—in our own lives and as a nation—as few have been tested before.

Thesis: the work Dr. King began is not finished.

Unemployment is at its highest level in more than a quarter of a century. Nowhere is it higher than the African American community. Poverty is on the rise. Home ownership is slipping. Beyond our shores, our sons and daughters are fighting two wars. Closer to home, our Haitian brothers and sisters are in desperate need. Bruised, battered, many people are legitimately feeling doubt, even despair, about the future. Like those who came to this church on that Thursday in 1956, folks are wondering, where do we go from here?

Uses general statistical information to support the thesis.

I understand those feelings. I understand the frustration and sometimes anger that so many folks feel as they struggle to stay afloat. I get letters from folks around the country every day; I read 10 a night out of the 40,000 that we receive. And there are stories of hardship and desperation, in some cases, pleading for help: I need a job. I'm about to lose my home. I don't have health care—it's about to cause my family to be bankrupt. Sometimes you get letters from children: My mama or my daddy have lost their jobs, is there something you can do to help? Ten letters like that a day we read.

Identifies with audience to create a connection.

Uses and emotional appeal.

So, yes, we're passing through a hard winter. It's the hardest in some time. But let's always remember that, as a people, the American people, we've weathered some hard winters before. This country was founded during some harsh winters. The fishermen, the laborers, the craftsmen who made camp at Valley Forge— they weathered a hard winter. The slaves and the freedmen who rode an underground railroad, seeking the light of justice under the cover of night—they weathered a hard winter. The seamstress whose feet were tired, the pastor whose voice echoes through the ages—they weathered some hard winters. It was for them, as it is for us, difficult, in the dead of winter, to sometimes see spring coming. They, too, sometimes felt their hopes deflate. And yet, each season, the frost melts, the cold recedes, the sun reappears. So it was for earlier generations and so it will be for us.

Uses a metaphor to advance his point.

(metaphor continues)

What we need to do is to just ask what lessons we can learn from those earlier generations about how they sustained themselves during those hard winters, how they persevered and prevailed. Let us in this Joshua generation learn how that Moses generation overcame.

Uses more concrete language to suggest a solution to the problem addressed in the thesis.

Let me offer a few thoughts on this. First and foremost, they did so by remaining firm in their resolve. Despite being threatened by sniper fire or planted bombs, by shoving and punching and spitting and angry stares, they adhered to that

Continues to suggest specific actions for the identified problem.

sweet spirit of resistance, the principles of nonviolence that had accounted for their success.

Continues to suggest specific actions for the identified problem.

Urges people to take action.

Second, they understood that as much as our government and our political parties had betrayed them in the past—as much as our nation itself had betrayed its own ideals—government, if aligned with the interests of its people, can be—and must be—a force for good. So they stayed on the Justice Department. They went into the courts. They pressured Congress, they pressured their President. They didn't give up on this country. They didn't give up on government. They didn't somehow say government was the problem; they said, we're going to change government, we're going to make it better. Imperfect as it was, they continued to believe in the promise of democracy; in America's constant ability to remake itself, to perfect this union.

Uses specific historical examples to encourage the audience towards action in the present.

Third, our predecessors were never so consumed with theoretical debates that they couldn't see progress when it came. Sometimes I get a little frustrated when folks just don't want to see that even if we don't get everything, we're getting something. King understood that the desegregation of the Armed Forces didn't end the civil rights movement, because black and white soldiers still couldn't sit together at the same lunch counter when they came home. But he still insisted on the rightness of desegregating the Armed Forces. That was a good first step—even as he called for more. He didn't suggest that somehow by the signing of the Civil Rights that somehow all discrimination would end. But he also didn't think that we shouldn't sign the Civil Rights Act because it hasn't solved every problem. Let's take a victory, he said, and then keep on marching. Forward steps, large and small, were recognized for what they were—which was progress.

Continues to suggest specific actions for the identified problem.

Fourth, at the core of King's success was an appeal to conscience that touched hearts and opened minds, a commitment to universal ideals—of freedom, of justice, of equality—that spoke to all people, not just some people. For King understood that without broad support, any movement for civil rights could not be sustained. That's why he marched with the white auto worker in Detroit. That's why he linked arm with the Mexican farm worker in California, and united people of all colors in the noble quest for freedom.

Of course, King overcame in other ways as well. He remained strategically focused on gaining ground—his eyes on the prize constantly—understanding that change would not be easy, understand that change wouldn't come overnight, understanding that there would be setbacks and false starts along the way, but understanding, as he said in 1956, that "we can walk and never get weary, because we know there is a great camp meeting in the promised land of freedom and justice."

Effective use of a quotation.

Summarizes the previous main points: to accomplish the task, people must persevere.

And it's because the Moses generation overcame that the trials we face today are very different from the ones that tested us in previous generations. Even after the worst recession in generations, life in America is not even close to being as brutal as it was back then for so many. That's the legacy of Dr. King and his movement. That's our inheritance. Having said that, let there be no doubt the challenges of our new age are serious in their own right, and we must face them as squarely as they faced the challenges they saw.

I know it's been a hard road we've traveled this year to rescue the economy, but the economy is growing again. The job losses have finally slowed, and around the country, there's signs that businesses and families are beginning to rebound. We are making progress.

Uses general examples to encourage and bring a more positive tone.

I know it's been a hard road that we've traveled to reach this point on health reform. I promise you I know. But under the legislation I will sign into law, insurance companies won't be able to drop you when you get sick, and more than 30 million people—our fellow Americans will finally have insurance. More than 30 million men and women and children, mothers and fathers, won't be worried about what might happen to them if they get sick. This will be a victory not for Democrats; this will be a victory for dignity and decency, for our common humanity. This will be a victory for the United States of America.

Uses repetition of a phrase (i.e. "I know it's been a hard road we've traveled …") to emphasize and engage.

Uses repetition again (e.g. "This will be a victory …").

Let's work to change the political system, as imperfect as it is. I know people can feel down about the way things are going sometimes here in Washington. I know it's tempting to give up on the political process. But we've put in place tougher rules on lobbying and ethics and transparency—tougher rules than any administration in history. It's not enough, but it's progress. Progress is possible. Don't give up on voting. Don't give up on advocacy. Don't give up on activism. There are too many needs to be met, too much work to be done. Like Dr. King said, "We must accept finite disappointment but never lose infinite hope."

Uses repetition again ("Don't give up on …")

Uses an effective quotation that supports his point.

Let us broaden our coalition, building a confederation not of liberals or conservatives, not of red states or blue states, but of all Americans who are hurting today, and searching for a better tomorrow. The urgency of the hour demands that we make common cause with all of America's workers—white, black, brown—all of whom are being hammered by this recession, all of whom are yearning for that spring to come. It demands that we reach out to those who've been left out in the cold even when the economy is good, even when we're not in recession—the youth in the inner cities, the youth here in Washington, D.C., people in rural communities who haven't seen prosperity reach them for a very long time. It demands that we fight discrimination, whatever form it may come. That means we fight discrimination against gays and lesbians, and we make common cause to reform our immigration system.

Briefly returns to the metaphor (of winter and spring) used before.

And finally, we have to recognize, as Dr. King did, that progress can't just come from without—it also has to come from within. And over the past year, for example, we've made meaningful improvements in the field of education. I've got a terrific Secretary of Education, Arne Duncan. He's been working hard with states and working hard with the D.C. school district, and we've insisted on reform, and we've insisted on accountability. We we're putting in more money and we've provided more Pell Grants and more tuition tax credits and simpler financial aid forms. We've done all that, but parents still need to parent. Kids still need to own up to their responsibilities. We still have to set high expectations for our young people. Folks can't simply look to government for all the answers without also looking inside themselves, inside their own homes, for some of the answers.

Builds credibility by citing his own work towards the goals that he encourages his audience to work towards.

Progress will only come if we're willing to promote that ethic of hard work, a sense of responsibility, in our own lives. I'm not talking, by the way, just to the African American community. Sometimes when I say these things people assume, well, he's just talking to black people about working hard. No, no, no, no. I'm talking to the American community. Because somewhere along the way, we, as a nation, began to lose touch with some of our core values. You know what I'm talking about. We became enraptured with the false prophets who prophesized an easy path to success, paved with credit cards and home equity loans and get-rich-quick schemes, and the most important thing was to be a celebrity; it doesn't matter what you do, as long as you get on TV. That's everybody.

We forgot what made the bus boycott a success; what made the civil rights movement a success; what made the United States of America a success—that, in this country, there's no substitute for hard work, no substitute for a job well done, no substitute for being responsible stewards of God's blessings.

What we're called to do, then, is rebuild America from its foundation on up. To reinvest in the essentials that we've neglected for too long—like health care, like education, like a better energy policy, like basic infrastructure, like scientific research. Our generation is called to buckle down and get back to basics.

We must do so not only for ourselves, but also for our children, and their children. For Jordan and for Austin. That's a sacrifice that falls on us to make. It's a much smaller sacrifice than the Moses generation had to make, but it's still a sacrifice.

Yes, it's hard to transition to a clean energy economy. Sometimes it may be inconvenient, but it's a sacrifice that we have to make. It's hard to be fiscally responsible when we have all these human needs, and we're inheriting enormous deficits and debt, but that's a sacrifice that we're going to have to make. You know, it's easy, after a hard day's work, to just put your kid in front of the TV set—you're tired, don't want to fuss with them—instead of reading to them, but that's a sacrifice we must joyfully accept.

Sometimes it's hard to be a good father and good mother. Sometimes it's hard to be a good neighbor, or a good citizen, to give up time in service of others, to give something of ourselves to a cause that's greater than ourselves—as Michelle and I are urging folks to do tomorrow to honor and celebrate Dr. King. But these are sacrifices that we are called to make. These are sacrifices that our faith calls us to make. Our faith in the future. Our faith in America. Our faith in God.

And on his sermon all those years ago, Dr. King quoted a poet's verse:

Truth forever on the scaffold
Wrong forever on the throne...
And behind the dim unknown stands God
Within the shadows keeping watch above his own.

Even as Dr. King stood in this church, a victory in the past and uncertainty in the future, he trusted God. He trusted that God would make a way. A way for

Uses vivid, emotional language (i.e. "false prophets," Biblical language for those who pretend to be messengers of God) that will appeal to his audience (i.e. church members).

Personalizes his message by referring to specific individuals (i.e. his nephew and the pastor's daughter, who were mentioned at the start of the speech).

Connects with audience by acknowledging their circumstances.

Continues to connect with the audience by acknowledging their challenges.

Suggests a way (i.e. faith) to meet the difficult challenge he has asked of them

Uses a quotation.

prayers to be answered. A way for our union to be perfected. A way for the arc of the moral universe, no matter how long, to slowly bend towards truth and bend towards freedom, to bend towards justice. He had faith that God would make a way out of no way.

You know, folks ask me sometimes why I look so calm. They say, all this stuff coming at you, how come you just seem calm? And I have a confession to make here. There are times where I'm not so calm. Reggie Love knows. My wife knows. There are times when progress seems too slow. There are times when the words that are spoken about me hurt. There are times when the barbs sting. There are times when it feels like all these efforts are for naught, and change is so painfully slow in coming, and I have to confront my own doubts.

Shares personal information and makes himself vulnerable to relate to the audience.

But let me tell you—during those times it's faith that keeps me calm. It's faith that gives me peace. The same faith that leads a single mother to work two jobs to put a roof over her head when she has doubts. The same faith that keeps an unemployed father to keep on submitting job applications even after he's been rejected a hundred times. The same faith that says to a teacher even if the first nine children she's teaching she can't reach, that that 10th one she's going to be able to reach. The same faith that breaks the silence of an earthquake's wake with the sound of prayers and hymns sung by a Haitian community. A faith in things not seen, in better days ahead, in Him who holds the future in the hollow of His hand. A faith that lets us mount up on wings like eagles; lets us run and not be weary; lets us walk and not faint.

So let us hold fast to that faith, as Joshua held fast to the faith of his fathers, and together, we shall overcome the challenges of a new age. Together, we shall seize the promise of this moment. Together, we shall make a way through winter, and we're going to welcome the spring. Through God all things are possible.

Makes a Biblical reference to further emphasize the point (i.e. faith).

May the memory of Dr. Martin Luther King continue to inspire us and ennoble our world and all who inhabit it. And may God bless the United States of America.

Thank you very much, everybody. God bless you.

Thanks his audience.

"The Dun Dun Drum"

Joshua Valentine

Josh gave this speech in an introductory public speaking class. The assignment was to give a four- to six-minute speech with visual aids. Students were also asked to create a preparation outline that indicated where in the speech the visual aids were to be displayed, that cited the sources of the visual aids, and that included a Works Cited section. As you watch Josh's speech, consider the effectiveness of his use of photographs and audio to illustrate and clarify points.

Josh, a drummer, takes his topic from his interest in music. He catches his audience's attention by asking them to imagine using a musical instrument to communicate language, something people in the United States don't typically do.

In the second main point of his introduction, he introduces his topic. He adapts his topic to his audience by using a familiar source, *Webster's Dictionary*, to define what language is and then explain that although Americans don't use music as language, other cultures do.

He establishes his credibility by indicating that he is a musician and that he learned about his topic in a percussion workshop.

In the last point of his introduction, Josh previews the two main points of his speech.

Because his audience is unfamiliar with his topic, Josh uses his first main point to explain what the *dun dun* drum is, where it originated, and what it is used for.

Imagine that your friend comes up to you and asks you what you did this weekend, and instead of using words, your friend simply beats a drum. You've probably never had this type of encounter. However, there are many cultures in the world where music is used for customs that we're really not accustomed to.

Webster's Dictionary defines language as "any system of symbols, sounds, or gestures used for the purpose of communication." Here in America we don't really have instrumental sounds that represent English words, but there are many cultures around the world where sounds do have meaning.

I've been playing percussion since junior high. I first learned about the *dun dun* drum while attending a percussion workshop two years ago. So, today I'll explain the origins of the *dun dun* drum, its uses as a linguistic tool, and its uses as a musical instrument.

The *dun dun* drum, also known as the Nigerian talking drum, actually does talk in the Yoruba language. *[Display photograph of* dun dun *drum downloaded and used with permission from http://media.dickinson. edu/gallery/Sect5.html.]* The *dun dun* originated in the Oyo Empire of Yoruba-land during the fifteenth century A.D. for the purposes of communication, mainly for spiritual communication. As such, the Yoruba language is easily adaptable to the *dun dun* drum.

Now, the Yoruba language is a tonal language, which basically means it uses three basic tones, or pitches, with glides between them—this is an essential part of how words are pronounced. Listen to this sound clip and see if you can examine the three different glides. *[Play a sound clip downloaded for one-time use from the Internet.]* I'll play that again for you. If you have a sharp ear, you may also be able to pick out three glides that are essential to the pronunciation of the Yoruba language. Melody is the basis for the Yoruba language, since the same word pronounced with a different melody might mean something completely different.

The Yoruba drum, the *dun dun*, functions mainly by using and changing the tension between two different skin heads. *[Point out the straps on the PowerPoint slide.]* By doing such, they can actually have a lot of control about how the *dun dun* operates and its use in communication. And, the *dun dun* was originally created for the purpose of communication.

The Yoruba are people of southwestern Nigeria who have used the *dun dun* drum for communication throughout their history. *[Show photo of carved drum downloaded from www.hamillgallery.com...YorubaDrum01. html.]* It was originally, of course, created first for spiritual communication. Since its inception, the drum has mainly been used to create religious songs and hymns of praise, and these songs are still recited today among the modern Yoruba people.

Here's an example of a very intense spiritual worship song done on talking drums. *[Play example downloaded for one-time use from http://www. world-beats.com/instruments/dundun.htm.]*

The Yoruba talking drum is also used heavily for day-to-day social communication. According to worldbeats.com, a master drummer can maintain a regular monologue while cracking jokes, saying hi to different people, even telling stories on the *dun dun* drum. Additionally, many *dun dun* drummers are known to say the names of friends and family on the *dun dun* drums as a sign of greeting and as a form of respect. So it's used very heavily in those senses, and it's very important—it's a huge part of the Yoruba culture.

And, additionally, the most obvious use of the *dun dun* drum, and its secondary use, really, is as a musical instrument. Now, we've already gone over the fact that the *dun dun* drum originally was used for spiritual communication. But since corporate worship in Yoruba is so prolific, people come together, and making music on the *dun dun* was born. That's essentially an example of how it's evolved. In fact, today, modern Yoruba people still use the *dun dun* for religious songs, although mainly for their musical purposes.

Everyday speech on the Yoruba drum becomes rhythmic when it's used. For example, the word *kabo*, which means "welcome" in the Yoruba language, is only a two-syllable word, so it's really not that exotic—it's not that interesting; it's not that musical. According to Drum Talk Limited, a more common phrase that someone might speak on the Yoruba talking drum is, "Welcome, we are happy that you arrived safely," because it's more musical. It has more of that flair to it. And even when a word spoken, or a phrase spoken, with regular words wouldn't be rhythmic, it is when the Yoruba people use the talking drum, because melody, as I said, is the basis of the talking drum.

By allowing his audience to see and hear a dun dun drum, Josh helps his audience better understand his topic. In particular, the audio clips let the audience hear what is complicated to explain in words alone.

He kept a careful record of where he obtained his visual and audio aids so he could cite his sources accurately in his speech. Note that he downloaded copyrighted material according to the terms of use posted by the websites he accessed—he requested permission or agreed to use the material only for his speech in class.

The visual aid Josh used for subpoint D of his first main point clarifies how the drum works.

In his second main point, Josh explains how the drum is used to communicate. He continues to use his visual and audio aids to enhance and clarify the information in his speech.

In subpoint B, he provides details that his audience can relate to: "saying hi," "cracking jokes," "telling stories." Notice that he cites his sources simply but effectively.

Here Josh uses a specific example to explain how the Yoruba "talk" with the *dun dun* drum.

Here he adapts to his audience by explaining how the *dun dun* drum is used in a way that is familiar to people in the United States, as a musical instrument.

Josh ends the body of his speech with an audio clip that reinforces his final sub-subpoint, that the dun dun drum is now an international instrument.

Josh begins his conclusion by reinforcing that the drum is used for both language and music. He then summarizes his main points.

He ends his speech with an intriguing statement that encourages his audience to remember what he's told them about a particular African drum.

The use of the Nigerian talking drum has spread far beyond Nigeria. In fact, next to the *djembe* drum, the *dun dun* is the most well-known and recognizable African drum used in America today. It's also very versatile. According to Francis Awe, a renowned African American musician, the *dun dun* drum fares well in jazz, blues, R&B, rock and roll, reggae, classical, even choral music. Here's one particular clip from renowned African American musician Francis Awe. [*Play sample clip downloaded from http://www.nitade.com/html/cd1.html.*]

So, in conclusion, whether the *dun dun* drum is used in language or in song, it always has a very unusual and beautiful sound. Today I've talked about the origins of the *dun dun* drum. I've also talked about its linguistic uses, and its uses as a musical instrument. So next time you hear music as simple as someone beating a drum, you might think to yourself that maybe that drummer, maybe that musician, is communicating much more than you first think.

Appendix B

Interviewing

You've probably participated in a number of interviews during your life. Perhaps you were interviewed by committees that appoint students to leadership positions at your school or award scholarships to students. You may have had interviews with members of groups you sought to join. Probably you have interviewed for part-time or full-time jobs.

You've probably been on the other side of the interviewing process, too; you may have interviewed people who were applying to join organizations to which you belong. You may have interviewed experts to gain information about a topic on which you were writing a paper or preparing a speech. Because interviews are common, learning to communicate effectively in interviews is important to your personal and professional success.

An **interview** is a communication transaction that emphasizes questions and answers. In this appendix, we will discuss interviewing and identify ways you can enhance your effectiveness as both interviewer and interviewee. First, we will identify a range of purposes or types of interviews. Second, we will discuss the typical structure and style of interviews. Third, we will describe different kinds of questions interviewers use. Then, we will identify challenges that are part of interviewing. We will focus on hiring interviews because those are particularly important to many college students. Our discussion will provide tips for preparing to interview and for dealing with inappropriate or illegal questions.

UNDERSTANDING COMMUNICATION IN INTERVIEWS

Types and Purposes of Interviews

Communication scholars have identified distinct types of interviews. Each interview is defined by its primary purpose, although many interviews have multiple and sometimes conflicting purposes. For example, an interviewer may want to gain objective information for a speech yet may be biased about the topic that he or she wants to support. We'll discuss 11 types of interviews.

Information-Giving Interviews In the first type of interview, the interviewer provides information to the interviewee. Doctors engage in **information-giving interviews** when they explain to patients how to prepare for procedures, take medicines, follow exercise programs, and observe symptoms. Academic advisers give students information about curricular requirements and administrative processes. Team leaders often inform new members of a work unit about expectations and operating procedures.

Information-Getting Interviews In this type of interview, the interviewer asks questions to learn about the interviewee's opinions, knowledge, attitudes, experience, and so forth. Public opinion polls, census taking, and research surveys are common examples of **information-getting interviews.** Physicians also use these to gain insight into patients' medical histories and current conditions (Farnill, Hayes, & Todisco, 1997). Journalists devote a great deal of time to information-getting interviews to obtain background material for stories they are writing and to learn about experts' opinions on newsworthy topics.

Persuasive Interviews Interviews designed to influence attitudes or actions are **persuasive interviews.** We're all familiar with the sales interview, in which a salesperson attempts to persuade a customer to buy a product or service. Persuasive interviews can sell more than products. They may also promote people (political candidates) and ideas (persuading an administrator to act on your team's report, convincing a company to implement environmental regulations).

Problem-Solving Interviews When people need to address a dilemma, they may engage in **problem-solving interviews.** Perhaps you have met with a professor to discuss difficulties in a course. The two of you may have collaborated to identify ways to improve your note taking, study habits, and writing. Supervisors sometimes hold problem-solving interviews with employees to discover and resolve impediments to maximally effective work.

Counseling Interviews Like problem-solving interviews, **counseling interviews** focus on a problem. In counseling interviews, however, the problem is not mutual. A client has a problem, such as stress, depression, or compulsiveness, that she or he wants to overcome. The counselor attempts to help the client understand the problem more fully and collaborates with the client to develop strategies for coping with or overcoming the difficulty (Evans, Coman, & Goss, 1996). Counseling interviews also occur outside the therapeutic setting: We may seek counseling from attorneys to address (or avoid) legal problems, from accountants to get help with financial matters, and from religious leaders to deal with spiritual issues.

Employment Interviews The purpose of **employment interviews** is to allow employers and job candidates to assess each other and decide whether there is a good fit between them. Typically, employment interviews include periods of information giving and information getting as well as persuasive efforts on the part of both participants. The prospective employer wants to convince the job candidate of the quality of the company, and the candidate wants to convince the prospective employer of the quality of his or her qualifications. Ideally, both participants gain enough information to make a sound judgment of the fit between the candidate and the job.

Complaint Interviews Complaint interviews allow people to register complaints about a product, service, or person. Many firms have departments whose sole purpose is to accept and respond to complaints. Of primary importance is showing the people who complain that they are heard and that they matter. The interviewer (company representative) attempts to gain information about the customer's dissatisfaction: What was defective or disappointing about the product? Was service inadequate? What would it take to satisfy the customer now? The person conducting complaint interviews should call recurring complaints to the attention of those who can diagnose and solve underlying problems.

Performance Reviews Most organizations require **performance reviews,** or performance appraisals, at regular intervals. By building performance appraisals into work life, organizations continually monitor employees' performance and foster their professional growth. The performance review is an occasion on which a supervisor comments on a subordinate's achievements and professional development, identifies any weaknesses or problems, and collaborates to develop goals for future performance. During the interview, subordinates should offer their perceptions of their strengths and weaknesses and participate actively in developing goals for professional development (Kikoski, 1998).

Reprimand Interviews When a person's work is unsatisfactory, a supervisor may conduct a **reprimand interview.** The goals are to identify lapses in professional conduct, determine sources of problems, and establish a plan for improving future performance. Because reprimands tend to evoke defensiveness, developing a constructive, supportive climate for these interviews is especially important. Supervisors may foster a good climate by opening the interview with assurances that the goal is to solve a problem together, not to punish the subordinate. Supervisors should also invite subordinates to express their perceptions and feelings fully.

Stress Interviews Stress interviews are designed to create anxiety in respondents or interviewees. Stress interviews are unique in their deliberate intent to apply pressure. Frequently used communication techniques for inducing stress are rapid-fire questions, intentional misinterpretations and distortions of the interviewee's responses, and hostile or skeptical nonverbal expressions.

Why, you might ask, would anyone deliberately create a high-stress interview situation? Actually, stress interviews may be useful in several contexts. Attorneys may intentionally intimidate reluctant or hostile witnesses or people whose honesty is suspect. Similarly, prison administrators and police officers may communicate aggressively with people they think are withholding important information. This kind of interview also may be used in hiring people for high-stress jobs. By deliberately trying to rattle job candidates, interviewers can assess how well they manage and respond to stress.

Exit Interviews In academic and professional life, **exit interviews** have become increasingly popular. The goal of this type of interview is to gain information, insights, and perceptions about a place of work or education from a person who is leaving. While people are in a job or learning environment, they may be reluctant to mention dissatisfactions or to speak against those who have power over them. When people are leaving an organization or school, however, they can offer honest insights and perceptions with little fear of reprisal. Thus, exit interviews can be especially valuable in providing information about policies, personnel, and organizational culture.

The Structure of Interviews

To be effective, interviews should follow a structure that builds a good communication climate and allows the interviewer and the interviewee to deal with substantive matters. Experienced interviewers, even those without professional training, tend to organize interview communication into a three-stage sequence. Interviewees who understand the purpose of each stage in the sequence increase their ability to participate effectively.

The Opening Stage   The initial stage of an interview tends to be brief and aims to create an effective climate for interaction, clarify the purpose, and preview issues to be discussed (Wilson & Goodall, 1991). Typically, opening small talk encourages a friendly climate:

- "I see you're from Buffalo. Are the winters there still as harsh as they used to be?"

- "It's been 6 months since our last performance review. Any new developments in your life?"

- "I noticed you got your B.A. from State University. I graduated from there, too. Did you ever take any courses with Doctor Barnette in anthropology?"

After opening small talk, effective interviewers state the purpose of the interview and how they plan to accomplish that purpose:

- "As you know, I'm on campus today to talk with liberal arts majors who are interested in joining Hodgeson Marketing. I'd like to ask you some questions about yourself and your background, and then I want to give you an opportunity to ask me anything you want about Hodgeson."

- "Pat, the reason I asked you to meet with me today is that there have been some complaints about your attitude from others on your work team. I know you are good at your job and have a fine history with the firm, so I want us to put our heads together to resolve this matter. Let's begin with me telling you what I've heard, and then I'd like to hear your perceptions of what's happening."

The Substantive Stage   The second stage of an interview, which generally consumes the bulk of time, deals with substance or content relevant to the purpose of the interview. For example, in reprimand interviews the substantive stage would zero in on identifying problem behaviors and devising solutions. In a hiring interview, the substantive stage might concentrate on the job candidate's background, experience, and qualifications.

Because the goal of the substantive stage is to exchange information, it takes careful planning and thought. Most interviewers prepare lists of topics or specific questions and use their notes to make sure they cover all the important topics. During the interview, they may also take notes of responses. Communication during this phase tends to progress from broad topic areas to increasingly specific questions within each topic. After introducing a topic, the interviewer may ask some initial general questions and then follow up with more detailed probes. Because the pattern of communication moves from broad to narrow, it has been called the **funnel sequence** (Cannell & Kahn, 1968; Moffatt, 1979). The interviewer may repeat the funnel sequence for each new topic area in an interview.

During the substantive stage, an interviewer may invite the interviewee to take the lead in communication, either by posing questions or by volunteering perceptions and ideas in response to what has been covered thus far. To be an effective interviewee, you should be prepared with questions and topics that you want to introduce. This portrays you as someone who prepares and takes initiative. It is also important to monitor your nonverbal communication. Interviewers tend to be most impressed with interviewees whose paralanguage and kinesics convey enthusiasm, confidence, and an outgoing personality (Mino, 1996).

The Closing Stage Like the opening stage, the closing stage tends to be brief. Its purposes are to summarize what has been discussed, state what follow-up will occur, if any, and create good will in parting. Summarizing the content of the interview increases the likelihood that an accurate and complete record of the interview will survive. If the interviewer overlooks any topics, the interviewee may appropriately offer a reminder. Interviewees also may ask about follow-up if interviewers fail to mention this.

Most interviews follow the three-step sequence we've discussed, but not all do. Some interviewers are ineffective because they are disorganized, unprepared, and inadequately trained in effective interviewing. They may ramble for 15 minutes or more and fail to provide any closing other than "Gee, our time is up." In other instances, interviewers may deliberately violate the standard pattern to achieve their goals. For example, in stress interviews designed to test how well a person responds to pressure, the interviewer may skip opening comments and jump immediately into tough substantive questions. This allows the interviewer to assess how well the respondent copes with unexpected pressure.

Styles of Interviewing

Like other forms of communication, interviews have climates that may be more or less open, egalitarian, supportive, and cooperative. The climate between participants in interviews is influenced by aspects of communication that we discussed in Part I of this book—for instance, the degree of confirmation provided, cultivation of a defensive or supportive climate, and effective or ineffective listening. Formality and balance of power also affect the climate of an interview.

Interviews may be more or less formal. In highly formal interviews, participants tend to stay within social and professional roles. The content of highly formal interviews tends to follow a standard format, often one that the interviewer has written to structure the interaction. Nonverbal communication provides further clues to formality: clothes, a formal meeting room, stilted postures, and a stiff handshake are all signs of formality.

In contrast, informal interviews are more relaxed, personal, and flexible. The interviewer attempts to engage the interviewee as an individual, not just a person in a general role. Typically, informal interviews aren't as rigidly structured as formal interviews. The interviewer may have a list of standard topics (either memorized or written down), but these provide only guidelines, not a straitjacket for communication. Informal interviews often include nonverbal cues such as smiling, relaxed postures, casual surroundings, and informal dress.

Most interviews fall between the extremes of formality and informality. Also, interviews may become more or less formal as a result of communication between participants. A person who communicates in a stilted manner is likely to encourage formality in the other person. Conversely, a person who communicates casually promotes a relaxed style of response.

Another influence on the communication climate in interviews is the balance of power between interviewer and interviewee. Power may be evenly balanced between participants or skewed toward the interviewer or the interviewee.

Interviewees have the greatest power to direct communication in **mirror interviews,** in which the interviewer consistently reflects the interviewee's comments to the interviewee. This may be done by restating verbatim what an interviewee says, paraphrasing an interviewee's comments, or making limited inferences about an interviewee's thoughts and feelings based on the communication. Skillful listening is essential for effectively using the mirror style (Banville, 1978). Consider this sample excerpt from a mirror interview:

> INTERVIEWER: Tell me about your studies.
>
> INTERVIEWEE: I'm a communication major.
>
> INTERVIEWER: So you've studied communication?
>
> INTERVIEWEE: Yes, especially organizational communication and leadership.
>
> INTERVIEWER: Then you're particularly interested in leadership in organizations?
>
> INTERVIEWEE: Yes. I think communication is the heart of effective leadership, so majoring in communication prepares me to lead.
>
> INTERVIEWER: So you see communication as the heart of effective leadership?
>
> INTERVIEWEE: Well, I see leadership as motivating others and empowering them to achieve their goals. A person who knows how to communicate clearly, listen well, and establish rapport with others is most able to motivate them.

In this exchange, the interviewer lets the interviewee lead. What the interviewee says is the basis for the interviewer's subsequent questions and probes.

Astute interviewees realize that mirror interviews give them significant opportunity to highlight their strengths and introduce topics they wish to discuss.

Distributive Interviews In **distributive interviews**, power is equally divided (or distributed) between participants. Both ask and answer questions, listen and speak, and contribute to shaping the direction and content of communication. The distributive style of interviewing is generally used when participants are equal in professional or social standing. Distributive interviews may also be used between people with unequal power if the interviewer wants to create a relaxed exchange. Recruiters often use distributive styles to put job candidates at ease.

Authoritarian Interviews In **authoritarian interviews**, the interviewer exercises primary control over interaction. The interviewer may avoid or quickly cut off discussion of any topics not on the list and may give the interviewee little or no opportunity to ask questions or initiate topics. Efficiency is the primary strength of the authoritarian style of interviewing: Many topics can be covered quickly. But the authoritarian style of interviewing can be frustrating to interviewees, and the interviewer may miss relevant information by failing to specifically seek it and by not giving the interviewee an opportunity to initiate topics.

In stress interviews, which we discussed previously in this appendix, the interviewer has primary control, as in authoritarian interviews. Unlike authoritarian interviews, however, stress interviews are a deliberate attempt to create anxiety in the interviewee. Thus, the interviewer controls not only the pace and content of interaction but also the psychological agenda.

Interviewees have even less control than in authoritarian interviews because stress interviews often rely on trick questions, surprise turns in topic, and unsettling responses to interviewees. If you find yourself in a stress interview, recognize that it is probably a deliberate attempt to test your ability to cope with pressure. Stay alert and flexible to deal with unpredictable communication from the interviewer.

Forms of Questions in Interviews

Most interviews follow a question–answer pattern in which each person speaks only briefly before the other person speaks. Consequently, skill in asking and responding to questions is central to effectiveness. Skillful interviewers understand that different kinds of questions shape responses, and effective interviewees recognize the opportunities and constraints of distinct forms of questions. We'll consider eight of the most common types of questions and discuss the responses invited by each.

Open Questions Open questions are general queries that invite expansive responses: "What can you tell me about yourself?" "What is your work experience?" Because open questions are broad, they give interviewees opportunities to steer communication toward topics that interest or reflect well on them.

Closed Questions Unlike open questions, closed questions do not invite broad answers. Instead, they ask for a concrete, narrow reply, often in the form of "yes" or "no." Closed questions often are used to follow up on general replies to open questions. "How many business courses have you taken?" "What was your position at the summer camp?" "Do you prefer working individually or on teams?" Closed questions call for short, direct answers, and an interviewer may interpret more broad responses negatively.

Mirror Questions   Mirror questions paraphrase or reflect the previous communication. If an interviewee says, "I have worked in a lot of stressful jobs," the interviewer might respond reflectively by saying, "So you can handle pressure, right?" At the content level of meaning, a mirror question seems pointless because it merely repeats what preceded it. At the relationship level of meaning, however, mirror questions say, "Elaborate; tell me more." Thus, they represent opportunities to expand on ideas.

Hypothetical Questions   Hypothetical questions ask a person to speculate. Recruiters often pose hypothetical questions to see how well job candidates can think on their feet. A student of mine provided the following example of a hypothetical question she was asked in a job interview: "Assume you are supervising an employee who is consistently late to work and sometimes leaves early. What would you do?" My student responded that her first course of action would be to talk with the employee to determine the reason for her tardiness and early departures. Next, she said, she would work with the employee to eliminate the source or, if company policies allowed it, to rearrange the schedule to accommodate the employee's circumstances.

This response showed that the job candidate was collaborative and supportive—precisely the qualities the recruiter wanted to assess. Hypothetical questions are designed to find out how you grasp and approach complex situations (Gladwell, 2000).

Probing Questions   When we probe something, we go beneath its surface to find out more about it. During interviews, probing questions go beneath the surface of a response to gather additional information and insight. Consider this example of several probing questions that follow an open question and a broad response:

> INTERVIEWER: Tell me about your work history.
>
> INTERVIEWEE: I've held 10 jobs while I've been attending college.
>
> INTERVIEWER: Why have you held so many different jobs instead of sticking with one of them?
>
> INTERVIEWEE: I kept switching in the hope of finding one that would be really interesting.
>
> INTERVIEWER: What makes a job interesting to you?
>
> INTERVIEWEE: It would have to be challenging and have enough variety not to bore me.
>
> INTERVIEWER: Are you easily bored?

Note how the interviewer probes to learn more about the interviewee's responses. Each probe seeks more details about the interviewee's attitudes toward work.

Leading Questions   Leading questions predispose a certain response. For example, "You believe in teamwork, don't you?" encourages "Yes" as a response, whereas "You don't drink on a regular basis, do you?" encourages "No" as a response. Leading questions generally are not a good way to get candid responses because they suggest how you want a person to respond (Stewart & Cash, 1991). Leading questions can be useful, however, if an interviewer wants to test an interviewee's commitment to an idea. An acquaintance of mine who recruits employees for sales positions that require a lot of travel often poses this leading question: "After a year or two of travel, the novelty wears off. I assume you expect a permanent location after a year or so with us, right?" Applicants who answer "yes" do not get job offers because travel is an ongoing part of the sales positions.

Loaded Questions   Loaded questions are worded to reflect the emotions or judgments of the person asking the question. The language in the question is laden with emotion and may cause an interviewee to respond emotionally. "How do you feel about slackers who expect to leave work at 5 p.m. every day?" In this question, the word *slackers* suggests the interviewer's negative judgment of employees who expect to quit at 5 p.m. each day. An interviewee is likely to pick up on the bias in the question and reply, "I think an employee should work until the job is done, not until the clock strikes 5 p.m." But this may not reflect the interviewee's actual views, so the question isn't effective in probing the interviewee's attitudes.

Another version of the loaded question involves baiting an interviewee. The classic example of a loaded question is, "When did you stop beating your dog?" The question presumes something (in this case, that the interviewee at some point did beat his or her dog) that hasn't been established. This kind of loaded question is likely to foster defensiveness in an interviewee and to limit what an interviewer learns about the interviewee.

Summary Questions   A final kind of question is the summary question, which covers what has been discussed. Although summary questions often are phrased as statements, they function as questions. For example, "I believe we've covered everything" should be perceived as, "Do we need to discuss anything else?" "It seems we've agreed on expectations for your performance during the next quarter" should be perceived as, "Do you feel we have a common understanding of what's expected of you?" Communication that summarizes topics in an interview provides an opportunity for participants to check whether they agree about what they've discussed and what will follow.

What we've discussed gives us a foundation for discussing two important challenges for communicating in interviews.

CHALLENGES WHEN COMMUNICATING IN INTERVIEWS

Like all other kinds of interaction, interviewing presents challenges that require communication skills. We will discuss two specific challenges: preparing to be interviewed and dealing with illegal questions. We will use the hiring interview to illustrate these challenges, but the ideas we'll discuss pertain to other kinds of interviews as well.

Preparing to Interview Effectively

My students have often told me that they can't prepare for interviews because they don't know what the interviewer will ask. Even without knowing exactly what questions will arise, you can do a great deal to prepare yourself for a successful interview. First, prepare a résumé that is concise, accurate in content and style (proofread carefully!), and professional in appearance. Your résumé is your first chance to "advertise yourself" to potential employers (Krannich & Banis, 1990).

Conduct Research   Every type of interview benefits from advance research, although the appropriate research varies according to the interview's purpose. Before performance appraisals, both the supervisor and the subordinate should review any previous performance appraisals. In addition, both participants should think about what has happened since the last appraisal: Have goals that were set been met? Have there been notable achievements, such as development of new skills or receipt of awards? It's also appropriate to talk with others to learn what is expected of employees at various stages in their careers.

Research is critical for effective employment interviewing. To learn about an organization, you'll want information about its products and services, self-image, history, benefits, organizational culture, and so forth. If you know someone who works for the company, ask that person to share perceptions and information with you. If you aren't personally acquainted with employees at the company, check for materials in your library or placement office or an online service. Standard references such as *Moody's Manuals* and *Standard & Poor's Index* provide information about the size, locations, salary levels, structure, employee benefits, and financial condition of many organizations.

The Internet is an additional source of information. Many companies have web pages that allow you to learn such things as how the company thinks of itself, the image it wants to project, and its size and geographic scope. Because websites are updated regularly, visiting a company's website is a good way to get the current information about a company that interests you.

Research enhances your effectiveness in two ways. First, the information you gather provides a basis for questions that show you've done your homework and understand the company. Second, when you know something about a company's or program's priorities, image, and goals, you can adapt your communication to acknowledge the expectations and norms of the company.

Engage in Person-Centered Communication   In Chapter 2, we discussed person-centered communication, in which one person recognizes and respects the perspective of another person. To prepare for an interview, ask yourself, "What would I want to know if I were interviewing me for this position?" Don't ask what you want to tell the interviewer about yourself or what you think is most important about your record. Instead, take the perspective of the interviewer as you anticipate the interaction.

You are not likely to know the interviewer personally, so you can't realistically expect to understand him or her as a unique individual. What matters is to recognize that in the interview situation the recruiter is a representative of a particular company with distinct goals, history, expectations, and culture. If you have researched the company, you will be able to adapt your communication to the interviewer's frame of reference.

Person-centered communication also requires sensitivity to cultural differences. For instance, people who were raised in some Asian cultures tend to be modest about personal achievements and abilities. Viewed from a Western perspective, such modesty might be misinterpreted as lack of confidence (Kikoski, 1998; U.S. Department of Labor, 1992).

Practice Responding One of the most common complaints of employment recruiters is that candidates are unprepared for interviews (DeVito, 1994). Examples of appearing unprepared include not bringing a résumé to the interview, not knowing about the company, and not recalling specific information, such as names of former supervisors and dates of employment. Ability to recall specific information shows you are prepared and knowledgeable. Yet many people fumble when asked about specifics. Why? Because they assume they know about themselves—after all, it's their life—so they don't bother to review details and practice responses.

You can avoid appearing unprepared by taking time before an interview to review your experiences and accomplishments and to remind yourself of key names, places, and dates. It's also a good idea to practice responding aloud to questions. You want your communication to reflect what employers look for— attentiveness, positive attitude, preparation, clarity, and motivation (Anderson & Killenberg, 1998; Farnill et al., 1997; Peterson, 1997; Ramsay, Gallois, & Callan, 1997). Figure B.1 lists questions commonly asked during employment interviews.

1. Why did you decide to attend this school?
2. Why did you choose _____ as your major?
3. Tell me about yourself.
4. Why are you interested in our company (firm)?
5. How does your academic background pertain to this job?
6. What do you consider your most serious weakness?
7. What are your long-term professional goals?
8. Which of the jobs you've held has been most satisfying to you? Why?
9. What is the most difficult situation you have ever been in? How did you handle it?
10. Who has been the biggest influence in your life?
11. What are your hobbies? How do you spend spare time?
12. How do you define success in sales (marketing, management, training, etc.)?
13. Why should we hire you instead of another person?
14. What kind of people do you prefer to work with? Why?
15. Are you willing to travel?
16. What do you expect your employer to do for you?
17. What do you think of the president's budget proposal (or another current national issue)?
18. Describe your closest friend.
19. How long would you expect to remain with our company?
20. Define *teamwork*. Give me an example of a team on which you worked.

Figure B.1
Common Questions Asked in Employment Interviews

Conducting research, engaging in person-centered communication, and practicing responses will not prepare you for everything that can happen in an interview. However, they will make you better prepared and more impressive than candidates who don't follow the guidelines we've discussed.

Managing Illegal Questions in Interviews

Just a couple of years ago, a student who was completing a professional degree was asked this question by a job recruiter: "What methods of birth control do you use?" Fortunately, this student knew the question was discriminatory, so she refused to answer and reported the interviewer to the campus placement service.

Know the Law The Equal Employment Opportunity Commission (EEOC) is a federally created entity that monitors various kinds of discrimination in hiring decisions. In 1970, the EEOC issued initial guidelines pertinent to employment interviews, and these have been updated periodically. EEOC guidelines also apply to tests, application forms, and other devices used to screen job applicants.

EEOC regulations prohibit discrimination on the basis of criteria that are legally irrelevant to job qualifications. Because the EEOC is an arm of the federal government, it protects interviewees in all states from intrusive questions about race, ethnicity, marital status, age, sex, disability, and arrests. Individual states and institutions may impose additional limits on information about candidates that may be used in hiring decisions. For instance, my school has a policy against discrimination based on military service or sexual orientation.

An illegal question reflects either an interviewer's ignorance of the law or willful disregard of it. People who conduct interviews should review restrictions on questions in a good source such as Arthur Bell's 1989 book *The Complete Manager's Guide to Interviewing*. Whether interviewers intend to ask illegal questions or not, it's important for interviewees to know what questions are not legally permissible in employment interviews. If you don't understand the legal boundaries on questions, you cannot protect your rights.

Respond Deliberately to Illegal Questions Knowing which questions are out of bounds doesn't tell us what to do if we are asked an inappropriate question. You may choose to respond if it doesn't bother you. You also have the right to object and to point out to an interviewer that a question is inappropriate. If you don't care about the job, this is a reasonable way to respond. But realize that even if you exercise your rights diplomatically, doing so may lessen an interviewer's interest in hiring you.

One effective way to respond to unlawful questions is to provide only information that may be sought legally. This strategy preserves a supportive climate in the interview by not directly reprimanding the interviewer. For instance, if an employer asks whether you are a native Chinese speaker, you might respond, "I am fluent in both English and Chinese." If you are asked whether you belong to any political organizations, be wary because this is often an effort to determine

Figure B.2
Legal and Illegal
Questions

It's legal to ask:
1. Are you a law-abiding person?
2. Do you have the physical strength to do this job?
3. Are you fluent in any languages other than English?
4. Could you provide proof that you are old enough to meet the age requirements for this job?
5. Your transcript shows you took a course in socialism. Did you find it valuable?

But illegal to ask:
1. Have you ever been convicted of a felony?
2. Are you physically disabled?
3. Are you a native speaker of English?
4. How old are you?
5. Are you a socialist?
6a. Would you be willing to live in a town without a temple/church/synagogue?
6b. Does your religion allow to work on Saturdays?
7. May I have a picture to put with your file?
8. Do you have (plan to have) children?
9. Are you married?
10. Do you have reliable child care?
11. Do you own a car or a house?
12. What is your political affiliation?

your religion or political affiliation. You might answer, "The only organizations to which I belong that are relevant to this job are the Training and Development Association and the National Communication Association." If a diplomatic response, such as a partial answer, doesn't satisfy the interviewer, it is appropriate for you to be more assertive. You might ask, "How does your question pertain to qualifications for this job?" This more direct response can be effective in protecting your rights without harming the climate. It is possible to be both assertive and cordial, and this is generally advisable. Figure B.2 lists some questions that can and cannot legally be asked by employment interviewers.

CHAPTER SUMMARY

In this appendix, we have gained insight into the structure and processes involved in interviewing. We have learned that most interviews follow a three-part sequence and that different styles and forms of questions are used to achieve different objectives in interview situations.

In the second section of this appendix, we focused on three guidelines for effective communication when interviewing, especially in the context of job seeking. The first guideline is to prepare by researching the company and the interviewer, by reviewing your qualifications and experience, and by practicing dealing with questions, including difficult ones. A second guideline for effectiveness in interviews is to be person-centered in your communication. Adapting the content and style of your communication to the person with whom you are interacting is important. A final suggestion is to become familiar with legal issues relevant to interviewing. Whether you are an interviewer or an interviewee, you should know and abide by laws governing what can and cannot be asked in interviews.

COMMUNICATION IN OUR LIVES ONLINE

The key concepts, For Further Reflection and Discussion questions, and Experiencing Communication in Our Lives case study that follow will help you review, reflect on, and extend the information and ideas presented in this chapter. These resources, and a diverse selection of additional study tools, are also available online at the Premium Website for *Communication in Our Lives*. Your Premium Website includes a student workbook, interactive video activities, a book companion website, Speech Builder Express, and InfoTrac College Edition. For more information or to access this book's online resources, visit **www.cengage.com/login**.

KEY CONCEPTS

authoritarian interview, 473
complaint interview, 469
counseling interview, 468
distributive interview, 473
employment interview, 468
exit interview, 469

funnel sequence, 471
information-getting
  interview, 468
information-giving
  interview, 468
interview, 467

mirror interview, 472
performance review, 469
persuasive interview, 468
problem-solving interview, 468
reprimand interview, 469
stress interview, 469

FOR FURTHER REFLECTION AND DISCUSSION

1. Arrange an information-seeking interview with a person in the field you hope to enter. Ask the person to tell you about the job—its advantages and disadvantages and the skills it requires.

2. Schedule an interview with a peer on a topic of mutual interest. During the interview, experiment with different forms of questions (i.e., open, closed, mirror, stress, hypothetical). How do the different types of questions affect the interviewee's comfort and responses?

3. Think about the ethical issues in choosing how to respond to illegal questions if the questions are not personally offensive or bothersome. For instance, Christians might think they have nothing to lose by responding honestly to the question, "Can you work on Saturdays?" If only members of minority religions refuse to answer questions about religion, how effective are the legal protections provided by EEOC guidelines? If all Protestants answer questions about religion honestly, are members of other religions jeopardized?

    Ethics

4. Identify a company that is of interest to you for future employment. Visit the company's

website and record what is presented there. How does information on the website help you prepare for an effective job interview? Compare what you find on the website with what is available in printed materials (i.e., brochures, annual reports, etc.) about the company.

5. If you would like tips for how to be effective in a virtual interview, use your Premium Website for *Communication in Our Lives* to access **WebLink B.1**.

    CourseMate

6. Watch one television program that features interviews of newsmakers. *Face the Nation*, *Meet the Press*, and *60 Minutes* are programs that feature news interviews. Also watch one television program that features interviews with celebrities or people in the limelight. The talk show of Oprah Winfrey is an example of this genre. Identify the form of each question posed (i.e., open, extended, closed) and the response it generates. Do the different kinds of interviews rely on distinct types of questions? Why? What do you conclude about how the style of question affects responses?

EXPERIENCING COMMUNICATION IN OUR LIVES

CASE STUDY: *Parental Teachings*

A video of the following conversation is featured in your Appendix B Online Resources for *Communication in Our Lives*. Select "Tough Questions" to watch the video. Improve your own interviewing skills by reading, watching, and evaluating this speech.

Elliott Miller is a second-semester senior who has double-majored in business and communication. Today, he is interviewing with Community Savings and Loan, which is recruiting managerial trainees. Elliott has dressed carefully. He is wearing his good suit, a light blue shirt, a conservative necktie, and wingtips. At 10 a.m. sharp, he knocks on the office door of Karen Bourne, the person with whom he will interview. She is in her mid-thirties and is dressed in a conservative navy blue suit. She opens the door and offers her hand to Elliott.

BOURNE: Mr. Miller, I see you're right on time. That's a good start. (*They shake hands.*)

MILLER: Thank you for inviting me to interview today.

BOURNE: Sit down. (*He sits in the chair in front of her desk; she sits behind the desk.*) So, you're about to finish college, are you? I remember that time in my own life—exciting and scary!

MILLER: It's definitely both for me. I'm particularly excited about the job here at Community Savings and Loan.

BOURNE: (*smiles*) Then there's a mutual interest. We had a lot of applications, but we're interviewing only eight of them. What I'd like to do is get a sense of your interests and tell you about our managerial trainee program here, so that we can see if the fit between us is as good as it looks on paper. Sound good to you?

MILLER: Great.

BOURNE: Let me start by telling you about a rather common problem we've had with our past managerial trainees. Many of them run into a problem—something they have trouble learning or doing right. That's normal enough—we expect that. But a lot of the trainees seem to get derailed when that happens. Instead of finding another way to approach the problem, they get discouraged and give up. So I'm very interested in hearing what you've done when you've encountered problems or roadblocks in your life.

MILLER: Well, I can remember one time when I hit a real roadblock. I was taking an advanced chemistry course, and I just couldn't seem to understand the material. I failed the first exam, even though I'd studied hard.

BOURNE: Good example of a problem. What did you do?

MILLER: I started going to all the tutorial sessions that grad assistants offer. That helped a little, but I still wasn't getting the material the way I should. So, I organized a study team and offered to pay for pizzas so that the students who were on top of the class would have a reason to come.

BOURNE: (*nodding with admiration*) That shows a lot of initiative and creativity. Did the study team work?

MILLER: (*smiling*) It sure did. I wound up getting a B in the course, and so did several other members of the study team who had been in the same boat I was in early in the semester.

BOURNE: So you don't mind asking for help if you need it?

MILLER: I'd rather do that than flounder, but I'm usually pretty able to operate independently.

BOURNE: So you prefer working on your own to working with others?

MILLER: That depends on the situation or project. If I have all that I need to do something on my own, I'm comfortable working solo. But there are other cases in which I don't have everything I need to do something well—maybe I don't have experience in some aspect of the job or I don't have a particular skill or I don't understand some perspectives on the issues. In cases like that, I think teams are more effective than individuals.

BOURNE: Good. Banking management requires the ability to be self-initiating and also the ability to work with others. Let me ask another question. As I was looking over your transcript and résumé, I noticed that you changed your major several times. Does that indicate you have difficulty making a commitment and sticking with it?

MILLER: I guess you could think that, but it really shows that I was willing to explore a lot of alternatives before making a firm commitment.

BOURNE: But don't you think that you wasted a lot of time and courses getting to that commitment?

MILLER: I don't think so. I learned something in all of the courses I took. For instance, when I was a philosophy major, I learned about logical thinking and careful reasoning. That's going to be useful to me in management. When I was majoring in English, I learned how to write well and how to read others' writing critically. That's going to serve me well in management too.

BOURNE: So what led you to your final decision to double-major in business and communication? That's kind of an unusual combination.

MILLER: It seems a very natural one to me. I wanted to learn about business because I want to be a manager in an organization. I need to know how organizations work, and I need to understand different management philosophies and styles. At the same time, managers work with people, and that means I have to have strong communication skills.

Glossary

abstract Removed from concrete reality. Symbols are abstract because they are inferences and generalizations derived from a total reality.

acknowledgment The second of three levels of interpersonal confirmation. Acknowledgment communicates that you have heard and understand another's feelings and thoughts.

***ad hominem* argument** Latin for "to the man," an argument that attacks the integrity of the person instead of the person's ideas.

agenda setting Mass media's ability to select and call to the public's attention ideas, events, and people.

ambiguous Subject to more than one interpretation. Symbols are ambiguous because their meanings vary from person to person and context to context.

ambushing Listening carefully in order to attack a speaker.

arbitrary Random; not determined by necessity. Symbols are arbitrary because there is no particular reason for any one symbol to stand for a certain referent.

artifacts Personal objects we use to announce our identities and personalize our environments.

assimilation The giving up of one's own ways for those of another culture.

attachment style Any of several patterns of attachment that result from particular parenting styles that teach children who they are, who others are, and how to approach relationships.

attribution A causal account that explains why a thing happened or why someone acted a certain way.

authoritarian interview An interviewing style in which the interviewer has and exerts greater power than the interviewee.

authoritarian leadership A leadership style in which a leader provides direction, exerts authority, and confers rewards and punishments on group members.

authority rule A group decision-making method in which some person or group with authority tells a group what to do, and the group ratifies the authority's decision.

bandwagon appeal The fallacious argument that because many people believe or act in a certain way, everyone should.

belief An assumption about what is true, accurate, or factual. A belief may be false even though it is accepted as true.

brainstorming A group problem-solving technique in which the free flow of ideas is encouraged without immediate criticism.

chronemics A type of nonverbal communication concerned with how we perceive and use time to define identities and interaction.

claim An assertion. A claim advanced in speaking requires grounds (evidence) and warrants (links between evidence and claims).

climate communication One of three constructive forms of participation in group decision making. Climate communication focuses on creating and sustaining an open, engaged atmosphere for discussion.

closeness in dialogue Interpersonal closeness created through communication.

closeness in the doing Interpersonal closeness created by doing things with and for others.

cognitive complexity The number of constructs used, how abstract they are, and how elaborately they interact to create perceptions.

cognitive restructuring A method of reducing communication apprehension that involves teaching people to revise how they think about speaking situations.

cohesion Closeness among members of a group; esprit de corps.

commitment A decision to remain with a relationship. One of three dimensions of enduring romantic relationships, commitment has more impact on relational continuity than does love alone. It is also an advanced stage in the process of escalation in romantic relationships.

communication A systemic process in which people interact with and through symbols to create and interpret meanings.

communication apprehension Anxiety associated with real or anticipated communication encounters. Communication apprehension is common and can be constructive.

communication network A set of formal and informal links between members of organizations.

communication rules Shared understandings of what communication means and what behaviors are appropriate in various situations.

comparison A form of evidence that uses associations between two things that are similar in some important way.

complaint interview An interview conducted for the purpose of allowing someone to register a complaint about a product, service, person, or company.

compromise A method of group decision making in which members work out a solution that satisfies each person's minimum criteria but does not necessarily fully satisfy all members.

conflict Among people who depend on each other, the expression of different views, interests, and goals and the perception of these differences as incompatible or as opposed by the other.

consensus A decision-making method in which all members of a group support a decision.

constitutive rules Communication rules that define what communication means by specifying how certain communicative acts are to be counted.

constructivism The theory that we organize and interpret experience by applying cognitive structures, called *schemata*.

content level of meaning One of two levels of meaning in communication. The content level of meaning is the literal, or denotative, information in a message.

convergence The integration of mass media, computers, and telecommunications.

counseling interview An interview in which one person with expertise helps another to understand a problem and develop strategies to overcome the difficulty or cope more effectively with it.

covert conflict Conflict that is expressed indirectly. Covert conflict generally is more difficult than overt conflict to manage constructively.

credibility The perception that a person is informed and trustworthy. Listeners confer it, or refuse to confer it, on speakers.

criteria Standards that group members use to evaluate alternative solutions or decisions. Criteria should be established during stage three of the standard agenda.

critical listening Attending to communication to analyze and evaluate the content of communication or the person speaking.

critical thinking Examining ideas reflectively and carefully to decide what you should believe, think, or do.

cultivation The cumulative process by which television fosters beliefs about social reality.

cultivation theory The theory that television promotes an inaccurate worldview that viewers nonetheless assume reflects real life.

cultural calamity Adversity that brings about change in a culture; one of four ways cultures change.

cultural relativism The idea that cultures vary in how they think, act, and behave as well as in what they believe and value; not the same as moral relativism.

culture Beliefs, understandings, practices, and ways of interpreting experience that are shared by a number of people.

deductive reasoning A form of reasoning in which a general premise followed by a specific claim establishes a conclusion.

defensive listening Perceiving personal attacks, criticisms, or hostile undertones in communication where none are intended.

democratic leadership A style of leadership that provides direction without imposing strict authority on a group.

demographic audience analysis A form of audience analysis that seeks information about the general features of a group of listeners.

derived credibility The expertise and trustworthiness that listeners attribute to a speaker as a result of how the speaker communicates during a presentation.

diffusion The incorporation or integration of characteristics of one culture into another as a result of contact between the two. Diffusion is one of four ways cultures change.

digital divide The gap between people and communities with access to media, especially social media, and people and communities with less or no access.

direct definition Communication that explicitly tells us who we are by specifically labeling us and reacting to our behaviors. Direct definition usually occurs first in families and then in interaction with peers and others.

distributive interview A style of interviewing in which roughly equal power is held by interviewer and interviewee.

downer Someone who communicates negatively about a person and reflects negative appraisals of that person's worth as an individual.

dual perspective The ability to understand another person's perspective, beliefs, thoughts, or feelings.

dyadic processes The set of processes in relational deterioration in which established relationship patterns break down and partners discuss problems and alternative futures for the relationship.

dynamic Evolving and changing over time.

ego boundaries A person's internal sense of where he or she stops and the rest of the world begins.

egocentric communication An unconstructive form of group contribution that blocks others or calls attention to oneself.

either–or logic The fallacy of suggesting or assuming that only two options or courses of action exist when in fact there may be more.

emotional intelligence The ability to recognize which feelings are appropriate in which situations and the ability to communicate those feelings effectively.

empathy The ability to feel with another person or to feel what that person feels in a given situation.

employment interview An interview in which employer and job candidate assess each other and decide whether there is a good fit between them.

endorsement The third of three levels of interpersonal confirmation. Endorsement communicates acceptance of another's thoughts and feelings; not the same as agreement.

environmental factors Elements of settings that affect how we feel and act. Environmental factors are a type of nonverbal communication.

ethnocentrism The tendency to regard ourselves and our way of life as superior to other people and other ways of life.

ethos The perceived personal character of the speaker.

evidence Material used to support claims. Types of evidence are statistics, examples, comparisons, and quotations. Visual aids may be used to represent evidence graphically.

example A form of evidence; a single instance that makes a point, dramatizes an idea, or personalizes information. The four types of examples are undetailed, detailed, hypothetical, and anecdotal.

exit interview An interview designed to gain information, insights, and perceptions about a place of work or education from a person who is leaving.

explorational communication The stage in the escalation of romantic relationships in which two people explore various common interests and backgrounds that might provide a basis for further interaction.

extemporaneous speaking A presentational style that includes preparation and practice but not memorization of words and nonverbal behaviors.

fallacy An error in reasoning.

feedback Response to a message; may be verbal, nonverbal, or both. In communication theory, the concept of feedback appeared first in interactive models of communication.

formal outline A complete outline of a speech, including the parts of a speech, main points, supporting material, transitions, and citations for sources.

funnel sequence A pattern of communication in interviews that moves from broad, general questions to progressively narrower, more probing questions.

gatekeeper A person or group that decides which messages pass through the gates of media that control information flow to consumers.

grave-dressing processes The set of processes in the deterioration of romantic relationships in which partners put the relationship to rest.

grounds Evidence that supports claims in a speech.

group Three or more people who interact over time, are interdependent, and follow shared rules of conduct to reach a common goal. The team is one type of group.

groupthink The cessation of critical, independent thought on the part of a group's members about ideas generated by the group.

halo effect The tendency to assume that an expert in one area is also an expert in other unrelated areas.

haptics Nonverbal communication that involves physical touch.

hasty generalization A broad claim based on too few examples or insufficient evidence.

hearing The physiological activity that occurs when sound waves hit our eardrums. Unlike listening, hearing is a passive process.

high-context communication style The indirect and undetailed communication favored in collectivist cultures.

hypothetical thought Cognitive awareness of experiences and ideas that are not part of the concrete, present situation.

identification The recognition and enlargement of common ground between communicators.

identity script A guide to action based on rules for living and identity. Initially communicated in families, identity scripts define our roles, how we are to play them, and basic elements in the plot of our lives.

impromptu speaking Public speaking that involves little preparation. Speakers think on their feet as they talk about ideas and positions with which they are familiar.

indexing A technique of noting that statements reflect specific times and circumstances and may not apply to other times or circumstances.

independence A relationship stage in which a person is characterized by unique needs, goals, experiences, and qualities that affect what he or she looks for in others and relationships.

individualism A strongly held Western value that views each person as unique and important and recognizes individual activities and achievements.

inductive reasoning A form of reasoning that begins with specific instances and forms general conclusions based on them.

informational listening Listening to gain and understand information; tends to focus on the content level of meaning.

information-getting interview An interview in which the interviewer asks questions to learn about the interviewee's qualifications, background, experience, opinions, knowledge, attitudes, or behaviors.

information-giving interview An interview in which the interviewer provides information to the interviewee.

informative speech A presentation that aims to increase listeners' knowledge, understanding, or abilities.

initial credibility The expertise and trustworthiness that listeners attribute to a speaker before a presentation begins. Initial credibility is based on the speaker's titles, positions, experiences, or achievements known to listeners before they hear the speech.

inoculation "Immunization" of listeners to opposing ideas and arguments that they may later encounter.

intensifying communication The stage in the escalation of romantic relationships that increases the depth of a relationship by increasing personal knowledge and allowing a couple to begin creating a private culture. Also called *euphoria*.

interpersonal climate The overall feeling between people, shaped by communication.

interpersonal communication Communication between people, usually in close relationships such as friendship and romance.

interpretation The subjective process of evaluating and explaining perceptions.

interview A communication transaction that emphasizes questions and answers.

intrapersonal communication Communication with ourselves; self-talk.

intrapsychic processes The first set of processes in the disintegration of romantic relationships; involves brooding about problems in the relationship and dissatisfactions with a partner.

invention The creation of tools, ideas, and practices; one of four causes of culture change.

investment Something put into a relationship that cannot be recovered should the relationship end. Investments, more than rewards and love, increase commitment.

invitational communication The second stage in the escalation phase of romantic relationships, in which people signal that they are interested in interacting and respond to invitations from others.

key word outline An abbreviated speaking outline that includes only key words for each point in a speech. The key words trigger the speaker's memory of the full point.

kinesics Body position and body motions, including those of the face.

laissez-faire leadership From the French for "to allow to do," this style of leadership is nondirective and sometimes leads to unproductive group work.

listening A complex process that consists of being mindful, physically receiving messages, selecting and organizing information, interpreting, responding, and remembering.

literal listening Listening only to the content level of meaning and ignoring the relational level of meaning.

loaded language An extreme form of evaluative language that relies on words that strongly slant perceptions and hence meanings.

logos Rational or logical proofs.

low-context communication style The direct, precise, and detailed communication favored in individualistic cultures.

mainstreaming The process by which mass communication stabilizes and homogenizes social perspectives; a concept in cultivation theory.

manuscript speaking A presentational style that involves speaking from the complete manuscript of a speech.

mass media Channels of mass communication, such as television and radio.

meaning The significance we attach to phenomena such as words, actions, people, objects, and events.

media literacy The ability to understand the influence of mass media and to access, analyze, evaluate, and respond to mass media in informed, critical ways.

memorized speaking A presentational style in which a speech is memorized word for word in advance.

metaphor An implicit comparison of two different things that have something in common.

mindfulness From Zen Buddhism, being fully present in the moment; the first step of listening and the foundation of all other steps.

mind map A holistic record of information on a topic. Mind mapping is a method that can be used to narrow speech topics or to keep track of information gathered during research.

mind reading Assuming that we understand what another person thinks or how another person perceives something.

minimal encouragers Communication that, by expressing interest in hearing more, gently invites another person to elaborate.

mirror interview A style of interviewing in which an interviewer's questions reflect previous responses and comments of the interviewee. Mirror interviews allow interviewees substantial power.

monopolizing Continually focusing communication on oneself instead of on the person who is talking.

motivated sequence pattern A pattern for organizing persuasive speeches that consists of five steps: attention, need, satisfaction, visualization, and action.

multilingual Able to speak and think in more than one language.

neutralization One of four responses to relational dialectics; involves balancing or finding a compromise between two dialectical poles.

noise Anything that interferes with intended communication.

nonverbal communication All forms of communication other than words themselves; includes inflection and other vocal qualities as well as several other behaviors.

norm An informal rule that guides how members of a group or culture think, feel, act, and interact. Norms define what is normal or appropriate in various situations.

oral style The visual, vocal, and verbal aspects of the delivery of a public speech.

organizational culture Ways of thinking, acting, and understanding work that are shared by members of an organization and that reflect an organization's distinct identity.

overt conflict Conflict expressed directly and in a straightforward manner.

paralanguage Vocal communication that does not include actual words; for example, sounds, vocal qualities, accents, and inflection.

paraphrasing A method of clarifying others' meaning by restating their communication.

participation A response to cultural diversity in which people incorporate some practices, customs, and traditions of other groups into their own lives.

particular others One source of social perspectives that people use to define themselves and guide how they think, act, and feel. The perspectives of particular others are the viewpoints of people who are significant to the self.

passion Intensely positive feelings and desires for another person. Passion is based on the rewards of involvement and is not equivalent to commitment.

pathos Emotional proofs for claims.

perception The process of actively selecting, organizing, and interpreting people, objects, events, situations, and activities.

performance review An interview in which a supervisor comments on a subordinate's achievements and professional development, identifies any weaknesses or problems, and collaborates with the subordinate to develop goals for future performance. Subordinates should offer perceptions of their strengths and weaknesses and participate actively in developing goals for professional development. Also known as a *performance appraisal.*

personal construct A bipolar mental yardstick that allows us to measure people and situations along specific dimensions of judgment.

personal relationship A relationship defined by uniqueness, rules, relational dialectics, and commitment and affected by contexts. Personal relationships, unlike social ones, are irreplaceable.

person-centered perception The ability to perceive another as a unique and distinct individual apart from social roles and generalizations.

perspective of the generalized other The collection of rules, roles, and attitudes endorsed by the whole social community in which we live.

persuasive interview An interview designed to influence attitudes, beliefs, values, or actions.

persuasive speech A presentation that aims to change listeners by prompting them to think, feel, or act differently.

physical appearance Physical features of people and the values attached to those features; a type of nonverbal communication.

policy A formal statement of an organizational practice. An organization's policies reflect and uphold the overall culture of the organization.

positive visualization A technique of reducing speaking anxiety; a person visualizes herself or himself communicating effectively in progressively challenging speaking situations.

post hoc, ergo propter hoc Latin phrase meaning "After this, therefore because of this." The fallacy of suggesting or assuming that because event B follows event A, event A has therefore caused event B.

power The ability to influence others; a feature of small groups that affects participation.

power over The ability to help or harm others. Power over others usually is communicated in ways that highlight the status and influence of the person using the power.

power to The ability to empower others to reach their goals. People who use power to help others generally do not highlight their own status and influence.

problem-solving interview An interview in which people collaborate to identify sources of a mutual problem and to develop ways to address or resolve it.

procedural communication One of three constructive ways of participating in group decision making. Procedural communication orders ideas and coordinates the contributions of members.

process Something that is ongoing and continuously in motion, the beginnings and endings of which are difficult to identify. Communication is a process.

prototype A knowledge structure that defines the clearest or most representative example of some category.

proxemics A type of nonverbal communication that includes space and how we use it.

pseudolistening Pretending to listen.

psychological responsibility The responsibility for remembering, planning, and coordinating domestic work and child care. In general, women assume the psychological responsibility for child care and housework even if both partners share in the actual tasks.

puffery In advertising, superlative claims for a product that seem factual but are actually meaningless.

punctuation Defining the beginning and ending of interaction or interaction episodes.

qualifier A word or phrase that limits the scope of a claim. Common qualifiers are most, usually, and in general.

quality improvement team A group in which people from different departments or areas in an organization collaborate to solve problems, meet needs, or increase the quality of work life. Also called a *continuous quality improvement team*.

quotation A form of evidence that uses exact citations of statements made by others. Also called *testimony*.

rebuttal A response to listeners' reservations about a claim made by a speaker.

recognition The most basic kind of interpersonal confirmation; communicates awareness that another person exists and is present.

red herring argument An argument that is irrelevant to the topic; an attempt to divert attention from something the arguer can't or doesn't want to address.

reflected appraisal Our perceptions of others' views of us.

reframing One of four responses to relational dialectics. The reframing response transcends the apparent contradiction between two dialectical poles and reinterprets them as not in tension.

regulative rules Communication rules that regulate interaction by specifying when, how, where, and with whom to talk about certain things.

relational culture A private world of rules, understandings, and patterns of acting and interpreting that partners create to give meaning to their relationship; the nucleus of intimacy.

relational dialectics Opposing forces or tensions that are normal parts of all relationships. The three relational dialectics are autonomy/connectedness, novelty/predictability, and openness/closedness.

relational listening Listening to support another person or to understand another person's feelings and perceptions; focuses on the relational level of meaning as much as on the content level of meaning.

relationship level of meaning One of two levels of meaning in communication; expresses the relationship between communicators.

reprimand interview An interview conducted by a supervisor with a subordinate to identify lapses in the subordinate's professional conduct, determine sources of problems, and establish a plan for improving future performance.

resistance A response to cultural diversity in which the cultural practices of others are attacked or the superiority of one's own cultural traditions is proclaimed.

resonance The extent to which media representations are congruent with personal experience.

respect A response to cultural diversity in which one values others' customs, traditions, and values, even if one does not actively incorporate them into one's own life.

resurrection processes The final set of processes in relationship deterioration, in which ex–partners begin to live independent of the former relationship.

rite A dramatic, planned set of activities that brings together aspects of an organization's culture in a single event.

ritual A form of communication that occurs regularly and that members of an organization perceive as a familiar and routine part of organizational life.

revising communication A stage in the escalation of romantic relationships that involves evaluating the relationship and working out any obstacles or problems before committing for the long term. Not all couples experience this stage.

rules Patterned ways of behaving and interpreting behavior; all relationships develop rules.

role The collection of responsibilities and behaviors associated with and expected of a specific position in an organization.

schemata (singular: *schema*) Cognitive structures we use to organize and interpret experiences. Four types of schemata are prototypes, personal constructs, stereotypes, and scripts.

script One of four cognitive schemata. A script defines an expected or appropriate sequence of action in a particular setting.

segmentation One of four responses to relational dialectics. Segmentation responses meet one dialectical need while ignoring or not satisfying the contradictory dialectical need.

selective listening Focusing on only selected parts of communication. We listen selectively when we screen out parts of a message that don't interest us or with which we disagree and also when we rivet attention on parts of communication that do interest us or with which we agree.

self A multidimensional process in which the individual forms and acts from social perspectives that arise and evolve in communication with himself or herself.

self-disclosure The sharing of personal information that others are unlikely to discover in other ways.

self-fulfilling prophecy An expectation or judgment of ourselves brought about by our own actions.

self-sabotage Self-talk that communicates that we're no good, we can't do something, we can't change, and so forth. Undermines belief in ourselves and motivation to change and grow.

self-serving bias The tendency to attribute our positive actions and successes to stable, global, internal influences that we control and to attribute negative actions and failures to unstable, specific, external influences beyond our control.

separation One of four responses to relational dialectics, in which friends or romantic partners assign one pole of a dialectic to certain spheres of activities or topics and the contradictory dialectical pole to distinct spheres of activities or topics.

silence The lack of verbal communication or paralanguage. Silence is a type of nonverbal communication that can express powerful messages.

simile A direct comparison that typically uses the words *like* or *as* to link two things.

situational audience analysis A method of audience analysis that seeks information about specific listeners that relates directly to a topic, speaker, and occasion.

skills training A method of reducing communication apprehension that assumes that anxiety is a result of lack of speaking skills and therefore can be reduced by learning skills.

slippery slope The fallacy of suggesting or assuming that once a certain step is taken, other steps will inevitably follow that will lead to some unacceptable consequence.

social climbing The attempt to increase personal status in a group by winning the approval of high-status members.

social community A group of people who live within a dominant culture yet who also have common distinctive experiences and patterns of communicating.

social comparison Comparing ourselves with others to form judgments of our own talents, abilities, qualities, and so forth.

social media Electronic tools that allow people to connect and to interact actively.

social support processes The set of processes in relational disintegration in which partners figure out how to inform outsiders that the relationship is ending and look to friends and family for support during the trauma of breaking up.

specific purpose A behavioral objective or observable response that a speaker specifies as a gauge of effectiveness; reinforces a speaker's more general speaking goals.

speech to entertain A speech the primary goal of which is to amuse, interest, or engage listeners.

speech to inform A speech the primary goal of which is to increase listeners' understanding, awareness, or knowledge of some topic.

speech to persuade A speech the primary goal of which is to change listeners' attitudes, beliefs, or behaviors or to motivate listeners to action.

standard agenda A logical, seven-step method for making decisions.

standpoint theory The theory that a culture includes a number of social groups that differently shape the knowledge, identities, and opportunities of members of those groups.

static evaluation Assessments that suggest something is unchanging or static. "Bob is impatient" is a static evaluation.

statistics A form of evidence that uses numbers to summarize a great many individual cases or to demonstrate relationships between phenomena.

stonewalling Reliance on the exit response to conflict and refusal to discuss issues. Stonewalling is especially corrosive in relationships because it blocks the possibility of resolving conflicts.

stereotype A predictive generalization about people and situations.

stress interview A style of interviewing in which an interviewer deliberately attempts to create anxiety in the interviewee.

structure In an organization, the set of procedures, relationships, and practices that provides predictability for members so that they understand roles, procedures, and expectations and so that work gets done.

survey research Research that involves asking a number of people about their opinions, preferences, actions, or beliefs relevant to a speaking topic.

symbol An arbitrary, ambiguous, and abstract representation of a phenomenon. Symbols are the basis of language, much nonverbal behavior, and human thought.

synergy A special kind of energy in groups that combines and goes beyond the energies, talents, and strengths of individual members.

system A group of interrelated elements that affect one another. Communication is systemic.

systematic desensitization A method of reducing communication apprehension that teaches people how to relax physiologically and then helps them practice feeling relaxed as they imagine themselves in progressively difficult communication situations.

task communication One of three constructive forms of participation in group decision making; focuses on giving and analyzing information and ideas.

team A special kind of group characterized by different and complementary resources of members and a strong sense of collective identity. All teams are groups, but not all groups are teams.

terminal credibility The cumulative expertise and trustworthiness listeners attribute to a speaker as a result of the speaker's initial and derived credibility; may be greater or less than initial credibility, depending on how effectively a speaker communicates.

thesis statement The main idea of an entire speech. It should capture the key message in a concise sentence that listeners can remember easily.

tolerance A response to diversity in which one accepts differences even though one may not approve of or even understand them.

totalizing Responding to people as if one aspect of them were the sum total of who they are.

Toulmin model of reasoning A representation of effective reasoning that includes five components: claim, grounds (evidence), warrant (link between grounds and claim), qualifier, and rebuttal.

transitions Words and sentences that connect ideas and main points in a speech so that listeners can follow a speaker.

understanding A response to cultural diversity in which it is assumed that differences are rooted in cultural teachings and that no traditions, customs, and behaviors are intrinsically more valuable than others.

upper Someone who communicates positively about a person and confirms with positive appraisals the person's worth as an individual.

uses and gratification theory The theory that people choose to attend to mass communication in order to fulfill personal needs and preferences.

values Views of what is good, right, and important that are shared by members of a particular culture.

visual aids Presentation of evidence by such visual means as charts, graphs, photographs, and physical objects to reinforce ideas presented verbally or to provide information.

voting A method of group decision making that requires the support of a certain number of group members. Some groups have simple majority rule, whereas others require two-thirds or three-fourths support.

vulture The extreme form of a downer. Vultures attack a person's self-concept and sense of self-worth; may be someone else or the person him- or herself.

warrant A justification for grounds (evidence) and claims in persuasive speaking.

working outline A sketch of main ideas and their relationships; used by and intended only for the speaker.

Works Cited A list of sources used in preparing a speech.

References

Abelson, R. (2001, April 29). Online message boards getting nasty. *The Raleigh News & Observer*, p. 8A.

Acitelli, L. (1988). When spouses talk to each other about their relationship. *Journal of Social and Personal Relationships, 5*, 185–199.

Acitelli, L. (1993). You, me, and us: Perspectives on relationship awareness. In S. W. Duck (Ed.), *Understanding relationship processes, 1: Individuals in relationships* (pp. 144–174). Newbury Park, CA: Sage.

Acker, J. (2005). *Class questions: Feminist answers.* Lanham, MD: Rowman & Littlefield.

Adler, J. (2007, March 12). The great sorority purge. *Newsweek*, p. 47.

Adler, R., & Towne, N. (1993). *Looking out/looking in* (7th ed.). Fort Worth: Harcourt Brace Jovanovich.

Afifi, W., & Burgoon, J. (2000). The impact of violations on uncertainty and the consequences for attractiveness. *Human Communication Research, 26*, 203–233.

Agee, W., Ault, P., & Emery, E. (1996). *Introduction to mass communications* (12th ed.). Reading, MA: Addison-Wesley.

Aires, E. (1996). *Men and women in interaction: Reconsidering differences.* New York: Oxford University Press.

Alcoff, L. (1991, Winter). The problem of speaking for others. *Cultural Critique*, 5–32.

Allen, B. J. (2006). Communicating race at WeighCo. In J. T. Wood & S. W. Duck (Eds.), *Composing relationships: Communication in everyday life* (pp. 146–155). Belmont, CA: Thomson Wadsworth.

Allen, M., Hale, J., Mongeau, P., Berkowitz-Stafford, S., Stafford, S., Shanahan, W., Agee, P., Dillon, K., Jackson, R., & Ray, C. (1990). Testing a model of message sidedness: Three replications. *Communication Monographs, 37*, 275–291.

Allen, M., Hunter, J., & Donahue, W. (1989). Meta-analysis of self-report data on the effectiveness of public speaking anxiety treatment techniques. *Communication Education, 38*, 54–76.

Altman, L. K. (2008, August 3). HIV estimates low, CDC study shows. *Raleigh News & Observer*, p. 4A.

Amodio, D., & Showers, C. (2006). 'Similarity breeds liking' revisited: The moderating role of commitment. *Journal of Social and Personal Relationships, 22*, 817–836.

Anders, S. L., & Tucker, J. S. (2000). Adult attachment style, interpersonal communication competence, and social support. *Personal Relationships, 7*, 379–389.

Andersen, M. L., & Collins, P. H. (Eds.). (2006). *Race, class, and gender: An anthology* (6th ed.). Belmont, CA: Wadsworth.

Andersen, P. (1993). Cognitive schemata in personal relationships. In S. W. Duck (Ed.), *Understanding relationship processes, 1: Individuals in relationships* (pp. 1–29). Newbury Park, CA: Sage.

Andersen, P. (1999). *Nonverbal communication: Forms and functions.* Mountain View, CA: Mayfield.

Andersen, P., Hecht, M., Hoobler, G., & Smallwood, M. (2002). Nonverbal communication across cultures. In W. Gudykunst & B. Mody (Eds.), *The handbook of international and intercultural communication* (2nd ed., pp. 89–106). Thousand Oaks, CA: Sage.

Anderson, C., & Martin, M. (1995). The effects of communication motives, interaction, involvement, and loneliness on satisfaction: A model of small groups. *Small Group Research, 16*, 118–137.

Anderson, K., & Leaper, C. (1998). Meta-analyses of gender effects on conversational interruption: Who, when, where, and how? *Sex Roles, 39*, 225–252.

Anderson, R., Baxter, L., & Cissna, K. (Eds.). (2004). *Dialogue: Theorizing difference in communication.* Thousand Oaks, CA: Sage.

Anderson, R., & Killenberg, G. (1998). *Interviewing: Speaking, listening, and learning for professional life.* Mountain View, CA: Mayfield.

Angelou, M. (1990). *I shall not be moved.* New York: Random House.

Anzaldúa, G. (1999). *Borderlands/la frontera: The new mestiza.* San Francisco: Spinsters/Aunt Lute.

Aratani, L. (2007, February 27). Teens aren't studying at 100%. *The Raleigh News & Observer*, p. 4A.

Arenson, K. (2002, January 13). The fine art of listening. *Education Life*, pp. 34–35.

Argyle, M., & Henderson, M. (1984). The rules of friendship. *Journal of Social and Personal Relationships, 1*, 211–237.

Aries, E. (1987). Gender and communication. In P. Shaver (Ed.), *Sex and gender* (pp. 149–176). Newbury Park, CA: Sage.

Armas, G. (2001, June 20). "Multiracial" a youthful category. *The Raleigh News & Observer*, p. 9A.

Arnett, R. (2004). A dialogic ethic "between" Buber and Levinas: A responsive ethical "I." In R. Anderson, L. Baxter, & K. Cissna (Eds.), *Dialogue: Theorizing difference in communication.* (pp. 75–90). Thousand Oaks, CA: Sage.

Ashcraft, K. L. (2006). Back to work: Sights/sites of difference in gender and organizational communication studies. In B. J. Dow & J. T. Wood (Eds.), *The handbook of gender and communication* (pp. 97–122). Thousand Oaks, CA: Sage.

Ashcraft, K. L., & Mumby, D. K. (2004). *Reworking gender: A feminist communicology of organization.* Thousand Oaks, CA: Sage.

Axtell, R. (1990a). *Dos and taboos around the world* (2nd ed.). New York: Wiley.

Axtell, R. (1990b). *Dos and taboos of hosting international visitors.* New York: Wiley.

Axtell, R. (2007). *Essential do's and taboos: The complete guide to international business and leisure travel.* New York: Wiley.

Ayres, J., & Hopf, T. S. (1990). The long-term effect of visualization in the classroom: A brief research report. *Communication Education, 39*, 75–78.

Babbie, E. (2009). *The practice of social research* (11th ed.). Belmont, CA: Wadsworth.

Bachen, C., & Illouz, E. (1996). Imagining romance: Young people's cultural modes of romance and love. *Critical Studies in Mass Communication, 13*, 279–308.

Bailey, A. (1998, February 29). Daily bread. *The Durham Herald-Sun*, p. C5.

Banse, R. (2004). Adult attachment and marital satisfaction: Evidence for dyadic configuration effects. *Journal of Social and Personal Relationships, 21*, 273–282.

Banville, T. (1978). *How to listen: How to be heard.* Chicago: Nelson-Hall.

Baran & Davis 2003 was cited in chapter 13. Please add.

Barash, S. (2006). *Tripping the prom queen.* New York: St. Martin's Griffin.

Barge, K. (2009). Social groups, workgroups, and teams. In W. F. Eadie (Ed.), *21st Century Communication: A Reference Handbook* (pp. 340–348). Thousand Oaks, CA: Sage.

Bargh, J. (1997). *The automaticity of everyday life.* Mahwah, NJ: Erlbaum.

Bargh, J. (1999, January 29). The most powerful manipulative messages are hiding in plain sight. *The Chronicle of Higher Education*, p. B6.

Barlow, J. (1996, October 31). Ethics can boost the bottom line. *Houston Chronicle*, p. C1.

Baron, R. A., & Berne, D. (1994). *Social psychology* (7th ed.). Boston: Allyn & Bacon.

Barry, B. (2001). *Culture and equality: An egalitarian critique of multiculturalism.* New Haven, CT: Harvard University Press.

Bartlett, T. (2003, March 7). Take my chair (please). *The Chronicle of Higher Education*, pp. A36–A38.

Bass, B. M. (1990). *Bass and Stogdill's handbook of leadership: Theory, research, and managerial applications* (3rd ed.). New York: Free Press.

Battaglia, D., Richard, F., Datteri, D., & Lord, C. (1998). Breaking up is (relatively) easy to do: A script for the dissolution of close relationships. *Journal of Social and Personal Relationships, 15*, 829–845.

Baxter, L. A. (1985). Accomplishing relational disengagement. In S. Duck & D. Perlman (Eds.), *Understanding personal relationships: An interdisciplinary approach* (pp. 243–265). Beverly Hills: Sage.

Baxter, L. A. (1987). Symbols of relationship identity in relationship cultures. *Journal of Social and Personal Relationships, 4*, 261–279.

Baxter, L. A. (1990). Dialectical contradictions in relational development. *Journal of Social and Personal Relationships, 7*, 69–88.

Baxter, L. A. (1993). The social side of personal relationships: A dialectical perspective. In S. Duck (Ed.), *Understanding relationship processes, 3: Social context and relationships* (pp. 139–165). Newbury Park, CA: Sage.

Baxter, L. A., & Montgomery, B. (1996). *Relating: Dialogues and dialectics.* New York: Guilford Press.

Bazar, E. (2007, April 24). Stalking "definitely a problem" for women at college. *USA Today*, p. 5A.

Beatty, M. J., & Behnke, R. R. (1991). Effects of public speaking trait anxiety and intensity of speaking task on heart rate during performance. *Human Communication Research, 18,* 147–176.

Beatty, M. J., Plax, T., & Kearney, P. (1985). Reinforcement vs. modeling theory in the development of communication apprehension: A retrospective analysis. *Communication Research Reports, 12,* 80–95.

Beck, A. (1988). *Love is never enough.* New York: Harper & Row.

Beckman, H. (2003). Difficult patients. In M. Feldman & J. Christensen (Eds.), *Behavioral medicine in primary care* (pp. 23–32). New York: McGraw-Hill.

Begley, S. (2009, February 16). Will the BlackBerry sink the presidency? *Newsweek*, pp. 36–39.

Bell, A. (1989). *The complete manager's guide to interviewing.* Homewood, IL: Dow Jones-Irwin.

Bellamy, L. (1996, December 18). Kwanzaa cultivates cultural and culinary connections. *The Raleigh News & Observer*, pp. 1F, 9F.

Belluck, P. (2008, December 5). Strangers may cheer you up, study says. *New York Times*, p. A12.

Benenson, J., Gordon, A., & Roy, R. (2000). Children's evaluative appraisals in competition in tetrads versus dyads. *Small Group Research, 31,* 635–652.

Bergen, K., & Braithwaite, D. O. (2009). Identity as constituted in communication. In W. F. Eadie (Ed.), *21st Century Communication: A Reference Handbook* pp. (pp. 166-173). Thousand Oaks, CA: Sage.

Bergner, R. M., & Bergner, L. L. (1990). Sexual misunderstanding: A descriptive and pragmatic formulation. *Psychotherapy, 27,* 464–467.

Berne, E. (1964). *Games people play.* New York: Grove Press.

Bertman, S. (1998). *Hyperculture: The human cost of speed.* Westport, CT: Praeger.

Birdwhistell, R. (1970). *Kinesics and context.* Philadelphia: University of Pennsylvania Press.

Bites. (1998, September 30). *The Raleigh News & Observer*, p. 1F.

Bixler, S., & Nix-Rice, N. (2005). *The new professional image: Dress your best for every business situation* (2nd ed.). Avon, MA: Adams Media Corporation.

Blanchard, K., Carlos, J., & Randolph, A. (1998). *Empowerment takes more than a minute.* San Francisco: Berrett-Koehler.

Bodey, K., & Wood, J. T. (in press). Grrrlpower: What counts as voice and who does the counting? *Southern Journal of Communication.*

Bohill, C., Owen, C., Jeong, E., Alicea, B., & Bocca, F. (2009). Virtual reality. In W. F. Eadie (Ed.), *21st century communication: A reference handbook* (pp. 534–542). Thousand Oaks, CA: Sage.

Bollier, D. (2002). *Silent theft: The private plunder of common wealth.* New York: Routledge.

Bolman, L., & Deal, T. (1992). What makes a team work? *Organizational Dynamics, 21,* 34–44.

Borchers, T. (2006). *Rhetorical theory: An introduction.* Belmont, CA: Thomson Wadsworth.

Bornstein, M., & Bradley, R. (Eds.). (2003). *Socioeconomic status, parenting, and child development.* Mahwah, NJ: Erlbaum.

Bornstein, R., & Languirand, M. (2003). *Healthy dependency.* New York: Newmarket Press.

Bostrom, R. N. (1988). *Communicating in public: Speaking and listening.* Santa Rosa, CA: Burgess.

Boulding, K. (1990). *Three faces of power.* Newbury Park, CA: Sage.

Bourhis, J., & Allen, M. (1992). Meta-analysis of the relationship between communication apprehension and cognitive performance. *Communication Education, 41,* 68–76.

Bowlby, J. (1973). *Separation: Attachment and loss* (Vol. 2). New York: Basic Books.

Bowlby, J. (1988). *A secure base: Parent–child attachment and healthy human development.* New York: Basic Books.

Bowman, L. (2006, May 19). Teens say dates often are violent. *Raleigh News & Observer*, p. 4A.

Bradbury, T. N., & Fincham, F. D. (1990). Attributions in marriage: Review and critique. *Psychological Bulletin, 107,* 3–33.

Braithwaite, D., & Braithwaite, C. (1997). Viewing persons with disabilities as a culture. In L. Samovar & R. Porter (Eds.), *Intercultural communication: A reader* (8th ed., pp. 154–164). Belmont, CA: Wadsworth.

Braithwaite, D., & Kellas, J. K. (2006). Shopping for and with friends: Everyday communication at the shopping mall. In J. T. Wood & S. W. Duck (Eds.), *Composing relationships: Communication in everyday life* (pp. 86–95). Belmont, CA: Thomson Wadsworth.

Brehm, S., Miller, R., Perlman, D., & Campbell, S. (2001). *Intimate relations* (3rd ed.). New York: McGraw-Hill.

Brooks, D. (2001a). *Bobos in paradise.* New York: Touchstone.

Brooks, D. (2001b, April 30). Time to do everything except think. *Newsweek*, p. 71.

Brooks, R., & Goldstein, S. (2001). *Raising resilient children.* New York: Contemporary Books.

Brown, J., & Cantor, J. (2000). An agenda for research on youth and the media. *Journal of Adolescent Health, 27,* 2–7.

Brown, J., Steele, J., & Walsh-Childers, K. (Eds.). (2002). *Sexual teens, sexual media.* Mahwah, NJ: Erlbaum.

Brown, L. (1997). *Two-spirit people.* Binghamton, NY: Haworth Press.

Brownell, J. (2002). *Listening: Attitudes, principles, and skills* (2nd ed.). Boston: Allyn & Bacon.

Bruess, C., & Hoefs, A. (2006). The cat puzzle recovered: Composing relationships through family ritual. In J. T. Wood & S. W. Duck (Eds.), *Composing relationships: Communication in everyday life* (pp. 65–75). Belmont, CA: Thomson Wadsworth.

Bryant, J., & Oliver, M.B. (Eds.). (2008). *Media effects* (3rd ed.). New York: Routledge.

Buber, M. (1957). Distance and relation. *Psychiatry, 20,* 97–104.

Buber, M. (1970). *I and thou* (Walter Kaufmann, Trans.). New York: Scribner.

Burgoon, J. K., & Le Poire, B. (1999). Nonverbal cues and interpersonal judgments: Participant and observer perceptions of intimacy, dominance, and composure. *Communication Monographs, 66,* 105–124.

Burke, K. (1950). *A rhetoric of motives.* Englewood Cliffs, NJ: Prentice Hall.

Burleson, B. R., & Rack, J. (2008). Constructivism theory. In L. A. Baxter & D. O. Braithwaite (Eds.), *Engaging theories in interpersonal communication: Multiple Perspectives* (pp.51–63). Thousand Oaks, CA: Sage.

Business bulletin. (1996, July 18). *The Wall Street Journal*, p. A1.

Buunk, B., Groothof, H. & Siero, F. (2007). Social comparison and satisfaction with one's social life. *Journal of Social and Personal Relationships, 24,* 197–205.

Buunk, B., & Mutsaers, W. (1999). Equity perceptions and marital satisfaction in former and current marriage: A study among the remarried. *Journal of Social and Personal Relationships, 16,* 123–132.

Buzzanell, P. M., & Lucas, K. (2006). Gendered stories of career: Unfolding discourses of time, space, and identity. In B. J. Dow & J. T. Wood (Eds.), *The handbook of gender and communication* (pp. 161–178). Thousand Oaks, CA: Sage.

Calero, H. (2005). *The power of nonverbal communication: What you do is more important than what you say.* Los Angeles: Silver Lake.

Canary, D., & Dainton, M. (Eds.). (2003). *Maintaining relationships through communication.* Mahwah, NJ: Erlbaum.

Canary, D., & Stafford, L. (Eds.). (1994). *Coimmunication and relational maintenance.* New York: Academic Press.

Cancian, F. (1987). *Love in America.* Cambridge, UK: Cambridge University Press.

Cannell, C., & Kahn, R. (1968). Interviewing. In G. Lindzey & E. Aronson (Eds.), *The handbook of social psychology* (Vol. 2, 2nd ed., pp. 569–584). Reading, MA: Addison-Wesley.

Capella, J. N. (1991). The biological origins of automated patterns of human interaction. *Communication Theory, 1,* 4–35.

Carey, B., & O'Connor, A. (2004, February 15). How to get those at risk to avoid risky sex? *New York Times*, pp. D1, D7.

Carl, W. (1998). A sign of the times. In J. T. Wood, *But I thought you meant . . . Misunderstandings in human communication* (pp. 195–208). Mountain View, CA: Mayfield.

Carl, W. (2006). <where r u? here u?>: Everyday communication with relational technologies. In J. T. Wood & S. W. Duck (Eds.), *Composing relationships: Communication in everyday life* (pp. 96–109). Belmont, CA: Thomson Wadsworth.

Carroll, J., & Russell, J. (1996). Do facial expressions signal specific emotions? Judging emotion from the face in context. *Journal of Personality and Social Psychology, 70,* 205–218.

Cassirer, E. (1944). *An essay on man.* New Haven, CT: Yale University Press.

Caughlin, J., & Vangelisti, A. (2000). An individual difference explanation of why married couples engage in the demand/withdraw pattern of conflict. *Journal of Social and Personal Relationships, 17,* 523–551.

Chan, Y. (1999). Density, crowding, and factors intervening in their relationship: Evidence from a hyper-dense metropolis. *Social Indicators Research, 48,* 103–124.

Chen, H., Luo, S., Yue, G., Xu, D., & Zhaoyang, R. (2009). Do birds of a feather flock together in China? *Personal Relationships, 16,* 167–186.

Christensen, A. (2004). *Patient adherence to medical treatment regiments: Bridging the gap between behavioral science and biomedicine.* New Haven, CT: Yale University Press.

Ciarrochi, J., & Mayer, J. (2007). *Applying emotional intelligence.* Florence, KY: Psychology Press.

Cissna, K. N. L., & Sieburg, E. (1986). Patterns of interactional confirmation and disconfirmation. In J. Stewart (Ed.), *Bridges, not walls* (4th ed., pp. 230–239). New York: Random House.

Clark, R., & Delia, J. (1997). Individuals' preferences for friends' approaches to providing support in distressing situations. *CommunicationReports, 10,* 115-121.

Clemetson, L. (2000, September 18). Love without borders. *Newsweek,* p. 62.

Cloven, D. H., & Roloff, M. E. (1991). Sense-making activities and interpersonal conflict: Communicative cures for the mulling blues. *Western Journal of Speech Communication, 55,* 134–158.

Clydesdale, T. (2009, January 23). Wake up and smell the new epistemology. *Chronicle of Higher Education,* pp. B7–B9.

Cobb, A. T. (2006). *Leading project teams.* Thousand Oaks, CA: Sage.

Cockburn-Wootten, C., & Zorn, T. (2006). Cabbages and headache cures: Work stories within the family. In J. T. Wood & S. W. Duck (Eds.), *Composing relationships: communication in everyday life* (pp. 137–145). Belmont, CA: Thomson Wadsworth.

Cole, T., & Leets, L. (1999). Attachment styles and intimate television viewing: Insecurely forming relationships in a parasocial way. *Journal of Social and Personal Relationships, 16,* 495–511.

Collins, P. (1998). *Fighting words: Black women and the search for justice.* Minneapolis: University of Minnesota Press.

Connerley, M. L., & Pedersen, P. B. (2005). *Leadership in a diverse and multicultural environment.* Thousand Oaks, CA: Sage.

Conrad, C., & Poole, M. (2004). *Strategic organizational communication: Into the twenty-first century* (7th ed.). Fort Worth: Harcourt Brace.

Cooley, C. H. (1912). *Human nature and the social order.* New York: Scribner.

Cooper, L. (1997). Listening competency in the workplace: A model for training. *Business Communication Quarterly, 60,* 75–84.

Cooper, L., Seibold, D., & Suchner, R. (1997). Listening in organizations: An analysis of error structures in models of listening competency. *Communication Research Reports, 14,* 3.

Cox, J. R. (1989). The fulfillment of time: King's "I have a dream" speech (August 28, 1963). In M. C. Leff & F. J. Kaufeld (Eds.), *Texts in context: Critical dialogues on significant episodes in American rhetoric* (pp. 181–204). Davis, CA: Hermagoras Press.

Cox, J. R. (2009). Personal communication.

Cozart, E. (1996, November 1997). *Feng shui. The Raleigh News & Observer,* p. D1.

Cragan, J., Wright, D., & Kasch, C. (2004). *Communication in small groups: Theory, process, skills* (6th ed.). Belmont, CA: Wadsworth.

Crohn, J. (1995). *Mixed matches.* New York: Fawcett Columbine.

Cronen, V., Pearce, W. B., & Snavely, L. (1979). A theory of rule-structure and types of episodes and a study of perceived enmeshment in undesired repetitive patterns ("URPs"). In D. Nimmo (Ed.), *Communication Yearbook, 3.* New Brunswick, NJ: Transaction Books.

Cross, G. (2008). *Men to boys: The making of modern immaturity.* New York: Columbia University Press.

Crossen, C. (1997, July 10). Blah, blah, blah. *The Wall Street Journal,* pp. 1A, 6A.

Crowley, G. (1995, March 6). Dialing the stress-meter down. *Newsweek,* p. 62.

Crowley, G. (1998, March 16). Healer of hearts. *Newsweek,* pp. 50–55.

Cummings, M. (1993). Teaching the African American rhetoric course. In J. Ward (Ed.), *African American communication: An anthology in traditional and contemporary studies* (pp. 239–248). Dubuque, IA: Kendall/Hunt.

Cunningham, J. A., Strassberg, D. S., & Haan, B. (1986). Effects of intimacy and sex-role congruency on self-disclosure. *Journal of Social and Clinical Psychology, 4,* 393–401.

Dailey, R. (2006). Confirmation in parent-adolescent relationships and adolescent openness: Toward extending confirmation theory. *Communication Monographs, 73,* 434–458.

Dainton, M. (2006). Cat walk conversations: Everyday communication in dating relationships. In J. T. Wood & S. W. Duck (Eds.), *Composing relationships: Communication in everyday life* (pp. 36–45). Belmont, CA: Thomson Wadsworth.

Dainton, M., & Zelley, E. (2006). Social exchange theories: Interdependence and equity. In D. O. Braithwaite & L. A. Baxter (Eds.), *Engaging theories in family communication: Multiple perspectives* (pp. 243–259). Thousand Oaks, CA: Sage.

Daly, J., & McCroskey, J. (Eds.). (1984). *Avoiding communication: Shyness, reticence, and communication apprehension.* Beverly Hills, CA: Sage.

Darling, A., & Dannels, D. (2003). Practicing engineers talk about the importance of talk: A report on the role of oral communication in the workplace. *Communication Education, 52,* 1–16.

Davis, S., & Kieffer, J. (1998). Restaurant servers influence tipping behaviors. *Psychological Reports, 83,* 223–236.

Deal, T., & Kennedy, A. (1999). *The new corporate cultures: Revitalizing the workplace after downsizing, mergers, and reengineering.* Reading, MA: Perseus Books.

DeFleur, M. L., & Ball-Rokeach, S. (1989). *Theories of mass communication* (5th ed.). White Plains, NY: Longman.

DeFrancisco, V. (1991). The sounds of silence: How men silence women in marital relations. *Discourse and Society, 2,* 413–423.

Delia, J., Clark, R. A., & Switzer, D. (1974). Cognitive complexity and impression formation in informal social interaction. *Speech Monographs, 41,* 299–308.

DeMaris, A. (2007). The role of relationship inequity in marital disruption. *Journal of Social and Personal Relationships, 24,* 177–195.

Deming, W. E. (1982). *Out of the crisis.* Cambridge, UK: Cambridge University Press.

Demographics. (2009, January 26). *Newsweek,* p. 70.

Dennis, E., & Merrill, J. (2006). *Media debates: Great issues for the digital age* (4th ed.). New York: McGraw-Hill Professional.

Devereux, E. (Ed.). (2007). *Media studies: Key issues and debates.* Thousand Oaks, CA: Sage.

DeVito, J. (1994). *Human communication: The basic course* (6th ed.). New York: HarperCollins.

Dicks, D. (Ed.). (1993). *Breaking convention with intercultural romances.* Weggis, Switzerland: Bergili Books.

Dickson, F. (1995). The best is yet to be: Research on long-lasting marriages. In J. T. Wood & S. W. Duck (Eds.), *Understanding relationship processes, 6: Understudied relationships: Off the beaten track* (pp. 22–50). Thousand Oaks, CA: Sage.

Dieter, P. (1989, March). *Shooting her with video, drugs, bullets, and promises.* Paper presented at the meeting of the Association of Women in Psychology, Newport, RI.

Dindia, K. (1994). A multiphasic view of relationship maintenance strategies. In D. Canary & L. Stafford (Eds.), *Communication and relational maintenance* (pp. 91–112). New York: Academic Press.

Dindia, K. (2000). Sex differences in self-disclosure, reciprocity of self-disclosure, and self-disclosure and liking: Three meta-analyses reviewed. In S. Petronio (Ed.), *Balancing the secrets of private disclosures* (pp. 21–35). Mahwah, NJ: Erlbaum.

Dixon, T. L. (2006). Psychological reactions to crime news portrayals of Black criminals: Understanding the moderating roles of prior news view and stereotype endorsement. *Communication Monographs, 73,* 162–187.

Dixon, T. L., Azocar, C., & Casas, M. (2003). Race and crime on network news. *Journal of Broadcasting and Electronic Media, 47,* 495–520.

Dixon, M., & Duck, S. W. (1993). Understanding relationship processes: Uncovering the human search for meaning. In S. W. Duck (Ed.), *Understanding relationship processes, 1: Individuals in relationships* (pp. 175–206). Newbury Park, CA: Sage.

Donald, D. (1996, February 15). Leadership lessons from Abraham Lincoln. *Fortune,* pp. 13–14.

Donnellon, A. (1996). *Team talk.* Boston: Harvard Business School Press.

Downing, J., & Garmon, C. (2001). Teaching students in the basic course how to use presentation software. *Communication Education, 50,* 218–229.

Doyle, G. (2008). *Understanding media economics* (2nd ed.). Thousand Oaks, CA: Sage.

Drummond, K., & Hopper, R. (1993). Acknowledgment tokens in series. *Communication Reports, 6,* 47–53.

Duck, S. (1982). A topography of relationship disengagement and dissolution. In S. W. Duck (Ed.), *Personal relationships. 4: Dissolving personal relationships* (pp. 1–30). New York: Academic Press.

Duck, S. W. (1990). Relationships as unfinished business: Out of the frying pan and into the 1990s. *Journal of Social and Personal Relationships, 7,* 5–24.

Duck, S. W. (1994). *Meaningful relationships.* Thousand Oaks, CA: Sage.

Duck, S. W. (2006). The play, playfulness, and the players: Everyday interaction as improvised rehearsal of relationships. In J. T. Wood & S. W. Duck (Eds.), *Composing relationships: Communication in everyday life* (pp. 15–23). Belmont, CA: Thomson Wadsworth.

Duck, S. W. (2007). *Human relationships* (4th ed.). Thousand Oaks, CA: Sage.

Duck, S. W., & Wood, J. T. (Eds.). (1995). *Understanding relationship processes, 5: Confronting relationship challenges.* Thousand Oaks, CA: Sage.

Duck, S. W., & Wood, J. T. (2006). What goes up may come down: Gendered patterns in relational dissolution. In M. Fine & J. Harvey (Eds.), *The handbook of divorce and dissolution of romantic relationships* (pp. 169–187). Mahwah, NJ: Erlbaum.

Egan, G. (1973). Listening as empathic support. In J. Stewart (Ed.), *Bridges, not walls.* Reading, MA: Addison-Wesley.

Einhorn, L. (2000). *The Native American or oral tradition: Voices of the spirit and soul.* Westport, CT: Praeger.

Ekins, R., & King, D. (2006). *The transgender phenomenon.* Thousand Oaks, CA: Sage.

Ellis, A. (1988). *How to stubbornly refuse to make yourself miserable about anything—yes, anything.* New York: Lyle Stuart.

Emmons, S. (1998, February 3). The look on his face: Yes, it was culture shock. *The Raleigh News & Observer,* p. 5E.

Erbert, L. (2000). Conflict and dialectics: Perceptions of dialectical contradictions in marital conflict. *Journal of Social and Personal Relationships, 17,* 638–659.

Evans, B., Coman, G., & Goss, B. (1996). Consulting skills training and medical students' interviewing efficiency. *Medical Education, 30,* 121–128.

Fackelmann, K. (2006, March 6). Arguing hurts the heart in more ways than one. *USA Today,* p. 10D.

Faigley, L., & Selzer, J. (2000). *Good reasons.* Needham Heights, MA: Allyn & Bacon.

FAIR. (2000). Pre-convention coverage whitewashes police violence, distorts activists' agenda. Retrieved July 25, 2000, from FAIR-L@listserv. american.edu.

Farnill, D., Hayes, S., & Todisco, J. (1997). Interviewing skills: Self-evaluation by medical students. *Medical Education, 31,* 122–127.

Fehr, B. (1993). How do I love thee: Let me consult my prototype. In S. W. Duck (Ed.), *Understanding relationship processes, 1: Individuals in relationships* (pp. 87–122). Newbury Park, CA: Sage.

Fehr, B., & Russell, J. A. (1991). Concept of love viewed from a prototype perspective. *Journal of Personality and Social Psychology, 60,* 425–438.

Feldman, C., & Ridley, C. (2000). The role of conflict-based responses and outcomes in male domestic violence toward female partners. *Journal of Social and Personal Relationships, 17,* 552-573.

Ferguson, S. D. (2008). *Public speaking: Building competency in stages.* New York: Oxford University Press.

Ferrante, J. (2009). *Sociology: A global perspective* (7th ed.). Belmont, CA: Thomson Wadsworth.

Fincham, F. D., & Beach, S. (2002). Forgiveness in marriage: Implications for psychological aggression and constructive communication. *Personal Relationships, 9,* 239–251.

Fincham, F. D., & Bradbury, T. N. (1987). The impact of attributions in marriage: A longitudinal analysis. *Journal of Personality and Social Psychology, 53,* 510–517.

Fine, A.H. (2006). *Momentum: Igniting social change in the connected age.* San Francisco: Jossey-Bass.

Fisher, A. (1998, June 22). Don't blow your new job. *Fortune, 137,* 159-162.

Fisher, K. (2000). *Leading self-directed work teams: A guide to developing new team leadership skills.* New York: McGraw-Hill.

Fitch, N. (Ed.). (2000). *How sweet the sound: The spirit of African American history.* New York: Harcourt College.

Fitzpatrick, M. A. (1988). *Between husbands and wives: Communication in marriage.* Newbury Park, CA: Sage.

Fitzpatrick, M. A., & Best, P. (1979). Dyadic adjustment in relational types: Consensus, cohesion, affectional expression and satisfaction in enduring relationships. *Communication Monographs, 46,* 167–178.

Fitzpatrick, M. A., & Sollie, D. (1999). Influence of individual and interpersonal factors on satisfaction and stability in romantic relationships. *Personal Relationships, 6,* 337–350.

Flanagin, A., Farinola, W., & Metzger, M. (2000). The technical code of the Internet/World Wide Web. *Critical Studies in Media Communication, 17,* 409–428.

Fletcher, G. J., & Fincham, F. D. (1991). Attribution in close relationships. In G. J. Fletcher & F. D. Fincham (Eds.), *Cognition in close relationships* (pp. 7–35). Hillsdale, NJ: Erlbaum.

Foley, M. (2006). Locating "difficulty": A multi-site model of intimate terrorism. In C. D. Kirpatrick, S. W. Duck, & M. K. Foley (Eds.), *Relating difficulty: The processes of constructing and managing difficult interaction* (pp. 43–59). Mahwah, NJ: Erlbaum.

Ford Foundation (1998, October 6). Americans see many benefits to diversity in higher education, finds first ever national poll on topic. Press release via Business Wire.

Forsyth, D. (2009). *Group dynamics* (5th ed.). Belmont, CA: Wadsworth Cengage.

Foss, K., & Edson, B. (1989). What's in a name: Accounts of married women's name choices. *Western Journal of Communication, 53,* 356–373.

Foster, A. (2007, May 18). Wary of everyware. *The Chronicle of Higher Education,* pp. A26–A29.

Franklin, J. H. (2006). *Mirror to America: The autobiography of John Hope Franklin.* New York: Farrar, Straus & Giroux.

France, D. (2006, January & February). Domestic violence. *AARP Magazine,* pp. 84-85, 112-118.

Fussell, S. (Ed.). (2002). *The verbal communication of emotion.* Mahwah, NJ: Erlbaum.

Gaines, S., Jr. (1995). Relationships between members of cultural minorities. In J. T. Wood & S. W. Duck (Eds.), *Understanding relationship processes, 6: Understudied relationships: Off the beaten track* (pp. 51–88). Thousand Oaks, CA: Sage.

Gabric, D., & McFadden, K. (2001). Student and employer perceptions of desirable entry-level operations management skills. *Mid-American Journal of Business, 16,* 51–59.

Galvin, K. (2006). Gender and family interaction: Dress rehearsal for an improvisation? In B. Dow & J. T. Wood (Eds.), *Handbook of gender and communication research* (pp. 41–55). Thousand Oaks, CA: Sage.

Galvin, K., Dickson, F., & Marrow, S. (2006). Systems theory: Patterns and (w)holes in family communication. In D. O. Braithwaite & L. A. Baxter (Eds.), *Engaging theories in family communication: Multiple perspectives* (pp. 308–324). Thousand Oaks, CA; Sage.

Gammage, K., Carron, A., & Estabrooks, P. (2001). Team cohesion and individual productivity: The influence of the norm for productivity and the identifiability of individual effort. *Small Group Research, 32,* 3–18.

Gangwish, K. (1999). *Living in two worlds: Asian-American women and emotions.* Paper presented at the National Communication Association, Chicago.

Garner, T. (1994). Oral rhetorical practice in African American culture. In M. Houston & V. Chen (Eds.), *Our voices: Essays in culture, ethnicity, and communication* (pp. 81–91). Los Angeles: Roxbury Press.

Gass, R. (1999). Fallacy list: SpCom 335. Advanced argumentation. California State University, Fullerton. Retrieved October 27, 2007, from http://commfaculty.fullerton.edu/rgass/fallacy31.htm.

Gastil, J. (1994). A meta-analytic review of the productivity and satisfaction of democratic and autocratic leadership. *Small Group Research, 25,* 384–410.

Gentner, D., & Boroditsky, L. (2009). Early acquisition of nouns and verbs: Evidence from the Navajo. In V. Gathercole (Ed.), *Routes to language* (pp. 5–86). New York: Taylor & Francis.

George, L. (1995, December 26). Holiday's traditions are being formed. *The Raleigh News & Observer,* pp. C1, C3.

Gerbner, G. (1990). Epilogue: Advancing on the path of righteousness (maybe). In N. Signorielli & M. Morgan (Eds.), *Cultivation analysis: New directions in media effects research* (pp. 250–261). Thousand Oaks, CA: Sage.

Gibb, C. (1969). Leadership. In G. Lindsey & E. Aronson (Eds.), *The handbook of social psychology* (2nd ed., pp. 205–282). Reading, MA: Addison-Wesley.

Gibb, J. R. (1961). Defensive communication. *Journal of Communication, 11,* 141–148.

Gibb, J. R. (1964). Climate for trust formation. In L. Bradford, J. Gibb, & K. Benne (Eds.), *T-group theory and laboratory method* (pp. 279–309). New York: Wiley.

Gibb, J. R. (1970). Sensitivity training as a medium for personal growth and improved interpersonal relationships. *Interpersonal Development, 1,* 6–31.

Gitlin, T. (1995). *The twilight of common dreams.* New York: Metropolitan Books.

Gitlin, T. (2005). Supersaturation, or the media torrent and disposable feeling. In E. Bucy (Ed.), *Living in the information age: A new media reader* (2nd ed., pp 139–146). Belmont, CA: Thomson Wadsworth.

Gladwell, M. (2000, May 29). The new-boy network: What do job interviews really tell us? *The New Yorker,* pp. 68–72, 84–86.

Glascock, N. (1998, February 22). Diversity within Latino arrivals. *The Raleigh News & Observer,* p. 9A.

Glazer, A. (2006, May 20). LAPD cops get personal via blog. *The Raleigh News & Observer,* p. 6A.

Gochenour, T. (1990). *Considering Filipinos.* Yarmouth, ME: Intercultural Press.

Godar, S. H., & Ferris, S. P. (2004). *Virtual and collaborative teams: Process, technologies and practice.* London: Idea Group Publishing.

Golberg, A. E., & Perry-Jenkins, M. (2007). The division of labor and perceptions of parental roles: Lesbian couples across the transion to parenthood. *Journal of Social and Personal Relationships, 24,* 297–318.

Goldsmith, D., & Fulfs, P. (1999). You just don't have the evidence: An analysis of claims and evidence in Deborah Tannen's "You just don't understand."

In M. Roloff (Ed.), *Communication Yearbook, 22* (pp. 1–49). Thousand Oaks, CA: Sage.

Goleman, D. (1995). *Emotional intelligence.* New York: Bantam.

Goleman, D. (1998). *Working with emotional intelligence.* New York: Bantam.

Goleman, D. (2007). *Social intelligence: The new science of human relationships.* New York: Bantam.

Goleman, D., McKee, A., & Boyatzis, R. (2002). *Primal leadership: Realizing the power of emotional intelligence.* Cambridge, MA: Harvard Business School Press.

Gottman, J. (1993). The roles of conflict engagement, escalation, or avoidance in marital interaction: A longitudinal view of five types of couples. *Journal of Consulting and Clinical Psychology, 61,* 6–15.

Gottman, J. (1994a). *What predicts divorce? The relationship between marital processes and marital outcomes.* Hilllsdale, NJ: Erlbaum.

Gottman, J. (1994b). Why marriages fail. *The Family Therapy Newsletter,* pp. 41–48.

Gottman, J. (1999). *Seven principles for making marriages work.* New York: Crown.

Gottman, J., & Carrère (1994). Why can't men and women get along? Developmental roots and marital inequities. In D. Canary & L. Stafford (Eds.), *Communication and relational maintenance* (pp. 203–229). New York: Academic Press.

Greenfield, A. (2006). *Everyware: The dawning age of ubiquitous computing.* Indianapolis, IN: New Riders.

Gregory, G., Healy, R., & Mazierkska, E. (2007). *The essential guide to careers in media and film.* Thousand Oaks, CA: Sage.

Griffin, C. (2008). *An invitation to public speaking* (3rd ed.). Belmont, CA: Wadsworth.

Griffin, C. (2004). *An invitation to public speaking* (2nd ed.). Belmont, CA: Wadsworth.

Gronbeck, B. E., McKerrow, R., Ehninger, D., & Monroe, A. H. (1994). *Principles and types of speech communication* (12th ed.). Glenview, IL: Scott, Foresman.

Groopman, J. (2007). *How doctors think.* Boston, MA: Houghton Mifflin.

Gudykunst, W., & Lee, C. (2002). Cross-cultural communication theories. In W. Gudykunst & B. Mody (Eds.), *The handbook of international and intercultural communication* (2nd ed., pp. 25–50). Thousand Oaks, CA: Sage.

Gueguen, N., & De Gail, M. (2003). The effect of smiling on helping behavior: Smiling and good Samaritan behavior. *Communication Reports, 16,* 133–140.

Guerrero, L. (1996). Attachment style differences in intimacy and involvement: A test of the four-category model. *Communication Monographs, 63,* 269–292.

Guerrero, L., Andersen, P., & Afifi, W. (2008). *Close encounters: Communication in relationships* (2ⁿᵈ ed.). Thousand Oaks, CA: Sage.

Guerrero, L., & Floyd, K. (2006). *Nonverbal communication in close relationships.* Mahwah, NJ: Erlbaum.

Guerrero, L., Jones, S., & Boburka, R. (2006). Sex differences in emotional communication. In K. Dindia & D. Canary (Eds.), *Sex differences and similarities in communication* (pp. 242–261). Mahwah, MJ: Erlbaum.

Guerrero, L., La Valley, A., & Farinelli, L. (2008). The experience and expression of anger, guilt, and sadness in marriage: An equity theory explanation. *Journal of Social and Personal Relationships, 25,* 699–724.

Guldner, G. (2003). *Long-distance relationships: The complete guide.* Corona, CA: JF Milne.

Gunns, R., Johnson, L., & Hudson, S. (2002). Victim selection and kinematics: A point-light investigation of vulnerability to attack. *Journal of Nonverbal Behavior, 26,* 129–158.

Guterl, F. (2003, September 8). Overloaded? *Newsweek,* pp. 422–432.

Hacker, K., Goss, B., & Townley, C. (1998). Employee attitudes regarding electronic mail policies: A case study. *Management Communication Quarterly, 11,* 422–432.

Hager, M., & Springen, K. (1998, March 16). Is love the best drug? *Newsweek,* pp. 54–56.

Hall, E. T. (1966). *The hidden dimension.* New York: Anchor.

Hall, E. T. (1977). *Beyond culture.* New York: Doubleday.

Hall, J. (2006). How big are nonverbal sex differences? The case of smiling and nonverbal sensitivity. In K. Dindia & D. Canary (Eds.), *Sex differences and similarities in communication* (pp. 59–82). Mahwah, NJ: Lawrence Erlbaum.

Hall, J. A. (1987). On explaining gender differences: The case of nonverbal communication. In P.

Shaver & C. Hendricks (Eds.), *Sex and gender* (pp. 177–200). Newbury Park, CA: Sage.

Hall, J. A., & Bernieri, F. J. (Eds.). (2001). *Interpersonal sensitivity: Theory and measurement.* Mahwah, NJ: Erlbaum.

Hall, J. A., Coats, E., & Smith-LeBeau, L. (2004). Nonverbal behavior and the vertical dimension of social relations: A meta-analysis. Cited in M. L. Knapp & J. A. Hall (2006). *Nonverbal communication in human interaction.* Belmont, CA: Thomson Wadsworth.

Hall, S. (1986). The problem of ideology: Marxism without guarantees. *Journal of Communication Inquiry, 10,* 28–44.

Hamachek, D. (1992). *Encounters with the self* (3rd ed.). Fort Worth: Harcourt Brace Jovanovich.

Hamilton, C. (2005). *Essentials of public speaking* (4ᵗʰ ed.). Belmont, CA: Wadsworth.

Hamilton, C. (2008). *Essentials of public speaking.* Belmont, CA: Cengage Wadsworth.

Hamilton, C., & Parker, C. (2001). *Communicating for results* (6th ed.). Belmont, CA: Wadsworth.

Haraway, D. (1988). Situated knowledges: The science question in feminism and the privilege of partial perspective. *Signs, 14,* 575–599.

Harding, S. (1991). *Whose science? Whose knowledge? Thinking from women's lives.* Ithaca, NY: Cornell University Press.

Hargie, O. (Ed.). (2006). *The handbook of communication skills.* Florence, KY: Psychology Press.

Hargraves, O. (2001a). *Culture shock! Morroco.* Portland, OR: Graphic Arts Center.

Hargraves, O. (2001b). *London at your door.* Portland, OR: Graphic Arts Center.

Harlos, K., & Pinder, C. (1999). Patterns of organizational injustice: A taxonomy of what employees regard as unjust. In J. Wagner (Ed.), *Advances in qualitative organizational research* (Vol. 2, pp. 97–125). Stamford, CT: JAI Press.

Harmon, A. (2002). Talk, type, read e-mail: The trials of multitasking. In E. Bucy (Ed.), *Living in the information age* (pp. 79–81). Belmont, CA: Thomson Wadsworth.

Harris, T. (2002). *Applied organizational communication.* Mahwah, NJ: Erlbaum.

Harris, T. J. (1969). *I'm OK, you're OK.* New York: Harper & Row.

Harter, S., Waters, P., Pettitt, L., Whitesell, N., & Kofkin, J. (1997). Autonomy and connectedness as dimensions of relationship styles in men and women. *Journal of Social and Personal Relationships, 14,* 147–164.

Haught, N. (2003, May 30). Beards mean different things to different cultures. *The Raleigh News & Observer,* p. 5E.

Hawkins, K. (1995). Effects of gender and communication content on leadership emergence in small task-oriented groups. *Small Group Research, 26,* 234–249.

Hecht, M., Jackson, R., & Ribeau, S. (2003). *African American communication.* Mahwah, NJ: Erlbaum.

Hegel, G. W. F. (1807). *Phenomenology of mind* (J. B. Baillie, Trans.). Germany: Wurzburg & Bamburg.

Heider, F. (1958). *The psychology of interpersonal relations.* New York: Wiley.

Helgeson, S. (1990). *The female advantage: Women's ways of leadership.* New York: Doubleday/Currency.

Hellweg, S. (1992). Organizational grapevines. In K. L. Hutchinson (Ed.), *Readings in organizational communication* (pp. 159–172). Dubuque, IA: Wm. C. Brown.

Henderson, V., & Henshaw, P. (2007). *Image matters for men.* New York: Hamlyn Press.

Hendrick, C., & Hendrick, S. (1996). Gender and the experience of heterosexual love. In J. T. Wood (Ed.), *Gendered relationships* (pp. 131–148). Mountain View, CA: Mayfield.

Hendrick, C., Hendrick, S., Foote, F. H., & Slapion-Foote, M. J. (1984). Do men and women love differently? *Journal of Social and Personal Relationships, 2,* 177–196.

Hendrick, S., & Hendrick, C. (2006). Measuring respect in close relationships. *Journal of Social and Personal Relationships, 23,* 881–899.

Henley, N. M. (1977). *Body politics: Power, sex and nonverbal communication.* Englewood Cliffs, NJ: Prentice Hall.

Herbert, B. (2009, August 8). Women at risk. *New York Times,* p. A17.

Hernández, D., & Rheman, B. (Eds.). (2002). *Colonize this! Young women of color on today's feminism.* Seattle: Seal Press.

Hesmondhaigh, D. (2007). *The cultural industries* (2nd ed.). Thousand Oaks, CA: Sage.

Hewes, D. (Ed.). (1995). *The cognitive bases of interpersonal perception.* Mahwah, NJ: Erlbaum.

Hickson, M., III, Stacks, D., & Moore, N. (2003). *Nonverbal communication: Studies and applications* (4th ed.). Los Angeles: Roxbury.

Hillis, K. (1999). *Digital sensations: Space, identity, and embodiment in virtual reality.* Minneapolis: University of Minnesota Press.

Hillis, K. (2006). A space for the trace: Memorable eBay and narrative effect. *Space and Culture 9,* 140–156.

Hillis, K. (in press). *Online a lot of the time: Ritual, fetish and display.* Durham, NC: Duke University Press.

Hochschild, A. (1997). *The time bind: When work becomes home and home becomes work.* New York: Metropolitan.

Hochschild, A., with Machung, A. (2003). *The second shift* (Rev. ed.). New York: Viking.

Hodson, R., & Sullivan, T. A. (2002). *The social organization of work* (3rd ed.). Belmont, CA: Wadsworth.

Hofstede, G. (1980). *Cultural consequences: International differences in work-related values.* Beverly Hills, CA: Sage.

Honeycutt, J. M., Woods, B., & Fontenot, K. (1993). The endorsement of communication conflict rules as a function of engagement, marriage and marital ideology. *Journal of Social and Personal Relationships, 10,* 285–304.

Honoré, C. (2005). *In praise of slowness.* San Francisco: Harper.

Houston, M. (2003). When Black women talk with White women: Why dialogues are difficult. In A. González, M. Houston, & V. Chen (Eds.), *Our voices: Essays in culture, ethnicity, and communication* (3rd ed., pp. 98–104). Los Angeles: Roxbury.

Houston, M., & Wood, J. T. (1996). Difficult dialogues, expanded horizons: Communicating across race and class. In J. T. Wood (Ed.), *Gendered relationships* (pp. 39–56). Mountain View, CA: Mayfield.

Huesmann, L. R., Moise-Titus, J., Podolski, C., & Eron, L. D. (2003). Longitudinal relations between children's exposure to TV violence and their aggressive and violent behavior in young adulthood: 1977–1992. *Developmental Psychology, 39,* 201–221.

Huston, M., & Schwartz, P. (1996). Gendered dynamics in the romantic relationships of lesbians and gay men. In J. T. Wood (Ed.), *Gendered relationships* (pp. 163–176). Mountain View, CA: Mayfield.

Hyatt, D. E., & Ruddy, T. M. (1997). An examination of the relationship between work group characteristics and performance: Once more into the breach. *Personnel Psychology, 50,* 533–585.

Inman, C. C. (1996). Friendships among men: Closeness in the doing. In J. T. Wood (Ed.), *Gendered relationships* (pp. 95–110). Mountain View, CA: Mayfield.

International Listening Association. (1995, April). An ILA definition of listening. *ILA Listening Post, 53,* p. 4.

Isaacs, W. (1999). *Dialogue and the art of thinking together.* New York: Doubleday.

Jackson, S., & Allen, J. (1990). Meta-analysis of the effectiveness of one-sided and two-sided argumentation. Paper presented at the International Communication Association, Montreal, Canada.

Jacobson, N., & Gottman, J. (1998). *When men batter women.* New York: Simon & Schuster.

Jaffe, C. (2007). *Public speaking: Concepts and skills for a diverse society* (5th ed.). Belmont, CA: Wadsworth.

Jaffe, E. (2004, October). Peace in the Middle East may be impossible: Lee D. Ross on naïve realism and conflict resolution. *American Psychological Society Observer, 17,* pp. 9–11.

James, N. (2000). When Miss America was always white. In A. González, M. Houston, & V. Chen (Eds.), *Our voices: Essays in culture, ethnicity, and communication* (pp. 42-46). Los Angeles: Roxbury.

James, D., & Clarke, S. (1993). Women, men, and interruptions: A critical review. In D. Tannen (Ed.), *Gender and conversational interaction* (pp. 281–312). New York: Oxford University Press.

Jandt, F. E. (2009). Culture. In W. F. Eadie (Ed.), *21st century communication: A reference handbook* (pp. 396–404). Thousand Oaks, CA: Sage.

Janis, I. L. (1977). *Victims of groupthink.* Boston: Houghton Mifflin.

Janis, I. L. (1989). *Crucial decisions: Leadership in policymaking and crisis management.* New York: Free Press.

Jenkins, H. (2006). *Convergence culture: Where old and new media collide.* New York: NYU Press.

Jenkins, H. (2007, February 16). From YouTube to YouNiversity. *The Chronicle of Higher Education,* pp. B9–10.

Jesdanun, A. (2007, May 6). Video résumés welcomed by some employers. *The Raleigh News & Observer,* p. 4E.

Jhally, S., & Katz, J. (2001, Winter). Big trouble, little pond. *UMass,* pp. 26–31.

Johnson, D., & Johnson, F. (1991). *Joining together: Group theory and group skills.* Englewood Cliffs, NJ: Prentice Hall.

Johnson, F. (2000). *Speaking culturally: Language diversity in the United States.* Thousand Oaks, CA: Sage.

Johnson, F. L. (1989). Women's culture and communication: An analytic perspective. In C. M. Lont & S. A. Friedley (Eds.), *Beyond the boundaries: Sex and gender diversity in communication.* Fairfax, VA: George Mason University Press.

Johnson, F. L. (1996). Friendships among women: Closeness in dialogue. In J. T. Wood (Ed.), *Gendered relationships* (pp. 79–94). Mountain View, CA: Mayfield.

Johnson, M. P. (2006). Gendered communication and intimate partner violence. In B. Dow & J. T. Wood (Eds.), *Handbook of gender and communication research* (pp. 71–87). Thousand Oaks, CA: Sage.

Johnson, M. (2008). *A typology of domestic violence.* Boston: Northeastern University Press.

Jones, D. (2007, March 30). Do foreign executives balk at sports jargon? *USA Today,* pp. 1B–2B.

Jones, E., & Gallois, C. (1989). Spouses' impressions of rules for communication in public and private marital conflicts. *Journal of Marriage and the Family, 51,* 957–967.

Jones, S. (1999, July 24). Some don't get the message. *The Raleigh News & Observer,* pp. 1D, 6D.

Jones, S., & Fox, S. (2009). Generations Online. http://pewinternet.org/pdfs/PIP_Generations_2009.pdf. Accessed February 10, 2009.

Jossi, F. (2001). Teamwork aids HRIS decision process. *HR Magazine, 46,* 165–173.

Kantrowitz, B., & Wingert, P. (2001, May 28). Unmarried, with children. *Newsweek,* pp. 46–55.

Katriel, T. (1990). "Griping" as a verbal ritual in some Israeli discourse. In D. Carbaugh (Ed.), *Cultural communication and intercultural contact* (pp. 99–114). Mahwah, NJ: Erlbaum.

Kelley, H. H. (1967). Attribution theory in social psychology. In D. Levine (Ed.), *Nebraska Symposium on Motivation* (Vol. 15, pp. 192–238). Lincoln: University of Nebraska Press.

Kelley, T., & Littman, J. (2001). *The art of innovation.* New York: Doubleday.

Kennedy, G. (Ed. & trans.). (1991). *Aristotle on rheto- ric.* London: Oxford University Press.

Kiesler, C. A., & Kiesler, S. B. (1971). Role of fore- warning in persuasive communications. *Journal of Abnormal and Social Psychology, 18,* 210–221.

Kikoski, J. (1998). Effective communication in the performance appraisal interview: Face-to-face communication for public managers in the culturally diverse workplace. *Public Personnel Management, 27,* 491–513.

Kilbourne, J. (2004). The more you subtract, the more you add: Cutting girls down to size. In J. Spade & K. Valentine (Eds.), *The kaleidoscope of gender* (pp. 234–244). Belmont, CA: Thomson Wadsworth.

Kimmel, M. (2008). *Guyland: The perilous world where boys become men.* New York: Macmillan.

Kirsh, S. J. (2006). *Children, adolescents, and media violence: A critical look at the research.* Thousand Oaks, CA: Sage.

Klein, R., & Milardo, R. (2000). The social context of couple conflict: Support and criticism from informal third parties. *Journal of Social and Personal Relationships, 17,* 618–637.

Knapp, M., & Hall, J.A. (2006). *Nonverbal com- munication in human interaction.* Belmont, CA: Thomson Wadsworth.

Kohlberg, L. (1958). *The development of modes of thinking and moral choice in the years 10 to 16.* Unpublished doctoral dissertation, University of Chicago.

Kohls, L. R. (2001). *Survival kit for overseas living.* Yarmouth, ME: Nicholas Brealey Intercultural Press.

Köllwitz, K., & Kahlo, F. (2003). Women and the art world: Diary of the feminist masked aveng- ers. In R. Morgan (Ed.), *Sisterhood is forever* (pp. 437–444). New York: Washington Square Press.

Korzybski, A. (1948). *Science and sanity* (4th ed.). Lakeville, CT: International Non-Aristotelian Library.

Kouzes, J., & Posner, B. (1999). *Encouraging the heart: A leader's guide to recognizing and reward- ing others.* New York: Jossey-Bass.

Krannich, R., & Banis, W. (1990). *High-impact résu- més and letters* (4th ed.). Woodridge, VA: Impact Publications.

Kung-Shankleman, L., Towse, R., & Picard, R. G. (Eds.). (2007). *The Internet and the mass media.* Thousand Oaks, CA: Sage.

Kupfer, D., First, M., & Regier, D. (2002). *A research agenda for SSM-V.* Washington, DC: American Psychiatric Press.

LaFasto, F., & Larson, C. (2001). *When teams work best: 6,000 team members and leaders tell what it takes to succeed.* Thosand Oaks, CA: Sage.

La Gaipa, J. J. (1982). Rituals of disengagement. In S. W. Duck (Ed.), *Personal relationships, 4: Dissolving personal relationships* (pp. 189–209). London: Academic Press.

Lamb, S., & Brown, L. (2006). *Packaging girlhood: Rescuing our daughters from marketers' schemes.* New York: St. Martin's Press.

Landrum, R., & Harrold, R. (2003). What employ- ers want from psychology graduates. *Teaching of psychology, 30,* 131–133.

Lane, R. (2000). *The loss of happiness in market democracies.* New Haven, CT: Yale University Press.

Langer, S. (1953). *Feeling and form: A theory of art.* New York: Scribner.

Langer, S. (1979). *Philosophy in a new key: A study in the symbolism of reason, rite, and art* (3rd ed.). Cambridge, MA: Harvard University Press.

Langfred, C. (1998). Is group cohesiveness a dou- ble-edged sword? *Small Group Research, 29,* 124–143.

Langston, D. (2001). Tired of playing monopoly? In M. L. Andersen & P. H. Collins (Eds.), *Race, class, and gender: An anthology* (4th ed., pp. 125–133). Belmont, CA: Wadsworth.

Lareau, A. (2003). *Unequal childhoods: Class, race, and family life.* Berkeley: University of California Press.

Lasch, C. (1990, Spring). Journalism, publicity and the lost art of argument. *Gannett Center Journal,* pp. 1–11.

Laswell, H. D. (1948). The structure and function of communication in society. In L. Bryson (Ed.), *The communication of ideas.* New York: Harper & Row.

Lau, B. (1989). Imagining your path to success. *Management Quarterly, 30,* 30–41.

Le, B., & Agnew, C. (2003). Commitment and its theorized determinants: A meta-analysis of the investment model. *Personal Relationships, 10,* 37–57.

Leaper, N. (1999). How communicators lead at the best global companies. *Communication World, 16,* 33–36.

Lee, J. A. (1973). *The colours of love: An exploration of the ways of loving.* Don Mills, Ontario, Canada: New Press.

Lee, J. A. (1988). Love-styles. In R. J. Sternberg & M. L. Barnes (Eds.), *The psychology of love* (pp. 38–67). New Haven, CT: Yale University Press.

Lee, W. (1994). On not missing the boat: A processual method for intercultural understandings of idioms and lifeworld. *Journal of Applied Communication Research, 22,* 141–161.

Lee, W. (2000). That's Greek to me: Between a rock and a hard place in intercultural encounters. In L. Samovar & R. Porter (Eds.), *Intercultural communication: A reader* (9th ed., pp. 217–224). Belmont, CA: Wadsworth.

Lefebvre, H. (1994). *The production of space.* (Donald Nicholson-Smith, Trans.) Malden, MA: Basil Blackwell.

Lefebvre, H. (2003). *The urban revolution.* (Robert Bononno, Trans.). Minneapolis: University of Minnesota Press.

Lefkowitz, J. (2003). *Ethics and values in industrial-organizational psychology.* Mawah, NJ: Erlbaum.

Lehman, C., & DuFrene, D. (1999). *Business communication* (12th ed.). Cincinnati: South-Western.

Lenhart, A., Madden, M., Macgill, A. R., & Smith, A. (2007, December 19). Teens and social media. Retrieved April 4, 2008 from *Pew Internet and American Life Project.*: http://www.ibiblio.org/fred/inls_490/readings/Week2/Recommended/Lenhart2007Teens-and-Social-Med.pdf.

Le Poire, B. A., Burgoon, J. K., & Parrott, R. (1992). Status and privacy restoring communication in the workplace. *Journal of Applied Communication Research, 4,* 419–436.

Le Poire, B. A., & Yoshimura, S. (1999). The effects of expectancies and actual communication on nonverbal adaptation and communication outcomes: A test of interaction adaptation theory. *Communication Monographs, 66,* 1–30.

Levi, D. (2007). *Group dynamics for teams* (2nd ed.). Thousand Oaks, CA: Sage.

Levin, D., & Kilbourne, J. (2008). *So sexy, so soon.* New York: Ballantine.

Levine, M. (2004, June 1). Tell the doc all your problems, but keep it to less than a minute. *New York Times,* p. D6.

Levine, R., & Norenzayan, A. (1999). The pace of life in 31 countries. *Journal of Cross-Cultural Psychology, 30,* 178–205.

Levy, S. (2004, June 7). A future with nowhere to hide? *Newsweek,* p. 76.

Levy, S. (2006, March 27). (Some) attention must be paid! *Newsweek,* p. 16.

Lewin, K., Lippitt, R., & White, R. K. (1939). Patterns of aggressive behavior in experimentally created "social climates." *Journal of Social Psychology, 10,* 271–299.

Luft, J. (1969). *Of human interaction.* Palo Alto, CA: Natural Press.

Lumsden, G., & Lumsden, D. (2004). *Communicating in groups and teams* (4th ed.). Belmont, CA: Wadsworth.

Lumsden, G., & Lumsden, D. (2009). *Communicating in groups and teams* (6th ed.). Belmont, CA: Wadsworth.

Lund, M. (1985). The development of investment and commitment scales for predicting continuity of personal relationships. *Journal of Social and Personal Relationships, 2,* 3–23.

Lustig, M., & Koester, J. (1999). *Intercultural competence: Interpersonal communication across cultures.* New York: Longman.

Lutz-Zois, C., Bradley, A., Mihalik, J., & Moorman-Eavers, E. (2006). Perceived similarity and relationship success among dating couples: An idiographic approach. *Journal of Social and Personal Relationships, 23,* 865–880.

Major, B., Schmidlin, A. M., & Williams, L. (1990). Gender patterns in social touch: The impact of setting and age. In C. Mayo & N. M. Henley (Eds.), *Gender and nonverbal behavior* (pp. 3–37). New York: Springer-Verlag.

Mangan, K. (2002, July 5). Horse sense or nonsense? Critics decry what they consider the "softening" of medical education. *The Chronicle of Higher Education,* pp. A8–A10.

Manning, M. (2000). *Dispatches from the ebony tower: Intellectuals confront the African American experience.* New York: Columbia University Press.

Manusov, V., & Harvey, J. (2001). *Attribution, communication behavior, and close relationships.* Port Chester, NY: Cambridge University Press.

Manusov, V., & Patterson, M. L. (2006). *The Sage handbook of nonverbal communication.* Thousand Oaks, CA: Sage.

Manusov, V., & Spitzberg, B. (2008). Attribution theory. In L. A. Baxter & D. O. Braithwaite (Eds.), *Engaging theories in interpersonal communication: Multiple Perspectives* (pp. 37–49). Thousand Oaks, CA: Sage.

Mapstone, E. (1998). *War of words: Women and men argue.* London: Random House.

Matsumoto, D., Franklin, B., Choi, J., Rogers, D., & Tatani, H. (2002). Cultural influences on the expression and perception of emotion. In W. Gudykunst & B. Mody (Eds.), *The handbook of international and intercultural communication* (2nd ed., pp. 107–126). Thousand Oaks, CA: Sage.

McCarthy, M. (1991). *Mastering the information age.* Los Angeles: Jeremy P. Tarcher.

McCauley, C., & Van Velsor, E. (Eds.). (2003). *The Center for Creative Leadership handbook of leadership development* (2nd ed.). Indianapolis: Jossey-Bass/Wiley.

McChesney, R. (2004). *The problem of the media: U.S. communication politics in the twenty-first century.* New York: Monthly Review Press.

McChesney, R. (2008). *The political economy of media.* New York: Monthly Review Press.

McCombs, M., Ghanem, S., & Chernov, G. (2009). Agenda setting and framing. In W. F. Eadie (Ed.), *21st century communication: A reference handbook* (pp. 516–524). Thousand Oaks, CA: Sage.

McCroskey, J., & Teven, J. (1999). Goodwill: A reexamination of the construct and its measurement. *Communication Monographs, 66,* 90–103.

McGinn, D. (2004, October 4). Mating behavior 101. *Newsweek,* pp. 44–45.

McGrane, S. (2000, September 4). Absence makes the typing skills grow stronger. *Raleigh Nwes & Observer,* p. 5D.

McGrath, P. (2002, June 10). Public or private? *Newsweek,* p. 32R.

McGuire, W. J. (1989). *Theoretical foundations of campaigns.* In R. E. Rice & C. K. Atkin (Eds.), *Public communication campaigns* (2nd ed., pp. 43–65). Newbury Park, CA: Sage.

McKinney, B., Kelly, L., & Duran, R. (1997). The relationship between conflict message styles and dimensions of communication competence. *Communication Reports, 10,* 185–196.

McKinney, M. (2006, October). Communication among top-10 fields of study. *Spectra,* p. 8.

McQuillen, J. (2003). The influence of technology on the initiation of interpersonal relationships. *Education, 123,* 616–624.

Mead, G. H. (1934). *Mind, self, and society.* Chicago: University of Chicago Press.

Meares, M., Oetzel, J., Torres, A., Derkacs, D., & Ginossar, T. (2004). Employee mistreatment and muted voices in the culturally diverse workplace. *Journal of Applied Communication Research, 32,* 4–27.

Meeks, B., Hendrick, S., & Hendrick, C. (1998). Communication, love, and satisfaction. *Journal of Social and Personal Relationships, 15,* 755–773.

Mehrabian, A. (1981). *Silent messages: Implicit communication of emotion and attitudes* (2nd ed.). Belmont, CA: Wadsworth.

Meloy, R. (2006). *The psychology of stalking: Clinical and forensic perspectives* (2nd ed.). New York: Academic Press.

Men use half a brain to listen, study finds. (2000, November 29). *The Raleigh News & Observer,* p. 8A.

Mernissi, F. (2004). Size 6: The Western woman's harem. In J. Spade & C. Valentine (Eds.), *The kaleidoscope of gener: Prisms, patterns, and possibilities* (pp. 297-301). Belmont, CA: Wadsworth.

Metts, S. (2006a). Hanging out and doing lunch: Enacting friendship closeness. In J. T. Wood & S. W. Duck (Eds.), *Composing relationships: Communication in everyday life* (pp. 76–85). Belmont, CA: Thomson Wadsworth.

Metts, S. (2006b). Gendered communication in dating relationships. In B. Dow & J. T. Wood (Eds.), *Handbook of gender and communication research* (pp. 25–40). Thousand Oaks, CA: Sage.

Metts, S., Cupach, W. R., & Bejlovec, R. A. (1989). "I love you too much to ever start liking you": Redefining romantic relationships. *Journal of Social and Personal Relationships, 6,* 259–274.

Meyers, D. G. (1993). *Social psychology* (4th ed.). New York: McGraw-Hill.

Meyers, M. (1994). News of battering. *Journal of Communication, 44,* 47–62.

Meyers, M. (1997). *News coverage of violence against women: Engendering blame.* Thousand Oaks, CA: Sage.

Milia, T. (2003). *Doctor, you're not listening.* Philadelphia: Xlibris.

Mino, M. (1996). The relative effects of content and vocal delivery during a simulated employment interview. *Communication Research Reports, 13,* 225–238.

Moffatt, T. (1979). *Selection interviewing for managers.* New York: Harper & Row.

Mokros, H. (2006). Composing relationships at work. In J. T. Wood & S. W. Duck (Eds.), *Composing relationships: Communication in everyday life* (pp. 175–185). Belmont, CA: Thomson Wadsworth.

Monastersky, R. (2002, March 29). Speak before you think. *The Chronicle of Higher Education,* pp. A17–A18.

Monmonier, M. (2002). *Spying with maps.* Chicago: University of Chicago Press.

Monroe, A. H. (1935). *Principles and types of speech.* Glenview, IL: Scott, Foresman.

Monsour, M. (2006). Communication and gender among adult friends. In B. Dow & J. T. Wood (Eds.), *Handbook of gender and communication research* (pp. 57–69). Thousand Oaks, CA: Sage.

Moran, R. (2001). *Interracial intimacy: The regulation of race and romance.* Chicago: University of Chicago Press.

Morreale, S. (2001, May). Communication important to employers. *Spectra,* p. 8.

Morreale, S. (2003, September). Importance of communication. *Spectra,* p. 14.

Morreale, S., Osborn, M., & Pearson, J. (2000). Why communication is important: A rationale for the centrality of the study of communication. *Journal of the Association for Communication Administration, 29,* 1–25.

Morreale, S., & Vogl, M. (Eds.). (1998). *Pathways to careers in communication* (5th ed.). Washington, DC: National Communication Association.

Motley, M. (1990). Public speaking anxiety *qua* performance anxiety: A revised model and an alternative therapy. *Journal of Social Behavior and Personality, 5,* 85–104.

Motley, M., & Molloy, J. (1994). An efficacy test of a new therapy ("communication-orientation motivation") for public speaking anxiety. *Journal of Applied Communication Research, 22,* 48–58.

Mudrack, P. & Farrell, G. (1995). An estimation of functional role behavior and its consequences for individuals in group settings. *Small Group Research, 26,* 542–571.

Muehlhoff, T. (2006). "He started it": Everyday communication in parenting. In J. T. Wood & S. W. Duck (Eds.), *Composing relationships: Communication in everyday life* (pp. 46–54). Belmont, CA: Thomson Wadsworth.

Mullen, B. (1994). Group cohesiveness and quality of decision making. *Small Group Research, 25,* 189–204.

Mumby, D. K. (1993). *Narratives and social control: Critical perspectives.* Newbury Park, CA: Sage.

Mumby, D. K. (2006a). Constructing working-class masculinity in the workplace. In J. T. Wood & S. W. Duck (Eds.), *Composing relationships: Communication in everyday life* (pp. 166–174). Belmont, CA: Thomson Wadsworth.

Mumby, D. K. (2006b). Introduction to Part II. In B. J. Dow & J. T. Wood (Eds.), *The handbook of gender and communication* (pp. 89–95). Thousand Oaks, CA: Sage.

Murphy, B. O., & Zorn, T. (1996). Gendered interaction in professional relationships. In J. T. Wood (Ed.), *Gendered relationships* (pp. 213–232). Mountain View, CA: Mayfield.

Mwakalye, N., & DeAngelis, T. (1995, October). The power of touch helps vulnerable babies survive. *APA Monitor,* p. 25.

Nakazawa, D. (2003a, July 6). A new generation is leading the way. *Parade,* pp. 4–5.

Nakazawa, D. (2003b). *Does anybody else look like me? A parent's guide to raising multiracial children.* Oxford, UK: Perseus Press.

Names and faces. (1997, September 11). *The Santa Barbara News-Press,* p. B8.

Namie, G. (2000, September). U.S. hostile workplace survey. Retrieved September 17, 2003, from http://bullyinginstitute.org/home/twd/bb/res/bullyinst.pdf.

Nanda, S. (2004). Multiple genders among North American Indians. In J. Spade & C. Valentine (Eds.), *The kaleidoscope of gender* (pp. 64–70). Belmont, CA: Wadsworth.

Natalle, E. (1996). Gendered issues in the workplace. In J. T. Wood (Ed.), *Gendered relationships* (pp. 253-274). Mountain View, CA: Mayfield.

National Communication Association (NCA). (2000). *Pathways to careers in communication.* Annandale, VA: Author.

National Geographic. (1994, November 5). Public Broadcasting Service, 7:30 P.M. EST.

Nichols, M. (1995). *The lost art of listening: How learning to listen can improve relationships.* New York: Guilford Press.

Nicotera, A., Clinkscales, M., & Walker, F. (2002). *Understanding organization through culture and structure.* Thousand Oaks, CA: Sage.

Nie, N. (2004). *Better off: Flipping the switch on technology.* New York: HarperCollins.

Niedenthal, P. M., Krauth-Gruber, S., & Ric, F. (2006). *Psychology of emotion.* Thousand Oaks, CA: Sage.

Noller, P. (1986). Sex differences in nonverbal communication: Advantage lost or supremacy regained? *Australian Journal of Psychology, 38,* 23–32.

Noller, P. (1987). Nonverbal communication in marriage. In D. Perlman & S. Duck (Eds.), *Intimate relationships: Development, dynamics, and deterioration* (pp. 149–176). Newbury Park, CA: Sage.

Northouse, P. (2006). *Leadership: Theory and practice* (4th ed.). Thousand Oaks, CA: Sage.

Nunes, M. (2006). *Cyberspaces of everyday life.* Minneapolis: University of Minnesota Press.

Oakley, A. (2002). *Gender on planet Earth.* New York: New Press.

Olson, E. (2009, January 4). Killings prompt efforts to spot and reduce abuse of teenagers in dating. *New York Times,* pp. Y1, Y16

Olson, J. M., & Cal, A. V. (1984). Source credibility, attitudes, and the recall of past behaviors. *European Journal of Social Psychology, 14,* 203–210.

One in Four Girls. (2008, March 17). *New York Times,* p. A22.

O'Neill, M. (1997, January 12). Asian folk art of *feng shui* hits home with Americans. *The Raleigh News & Observer,* p. 6E.

Orbe, M., & Harris, T. (2001). *Interracial communication: Theory into practice.* Belmont, CA: Wadsworth.

Orbuch, T., & Veroff, J. (2002). A programmatic review: Building a two-way bridge between social psychology and the study of the early years of marriage. *Journal of Social and Personal Relationships, 19,* 549–568.

Ornish, D. (1998). *Love and survival: The scientific basis for the healing power of intimacy.* New York: HarperCollins.

Ornish, D. (1999). *Love and survival: 8 pathways to intimacy and health.* New York: HarperCollins.

Pacanowsky, M. (1989). Creating and narrating organizational realities. In B. Dervin, L. Grossberg, B. O'Keefe, & E. Wartella (Eds.), *Rethinking communication: Paradigm exemplars* (pp. 250–257). Thousand Oaks, CA: Sage.

Pacanowsky, M., & O'Donnell-Trujillo, N. (1983). Organizational communication as cultural performance. *Communication Monographs, 30,* 126–147.

Palmer, E., & Young, B. (Eds.). (2003). *The faces of televisual media.* Mahwah, NJ: Erlbaum.

Parker-Pope, T. (2009, January 20). Your nest is empty? Enjoy each other. *New York Times,* p. D5.

Parker-Pope, T. (2009, January 13). A problem of the brain, not the hands: Group urges phone ban for drivers. *New York Times,* p. D5.

Paul, E. (2006). Beer goggles, catching feelings and the walk of shame: The myths and realities of the hookup experience. In C. Kirpatrick, S. W. Duck, & M. K. Foley (Eds.), *Relating difficulty: Processes of constructing and managing difficult interaction* (pp. 141–160). Mahwah, NJ: Erlbaum.

Pearce, W. B., Cronen, V. E., & Conklin, F. (1979). On what to look at when analyzing communication: A hierarchical model of actors' meanings. *Communication, 4,* 195–220.

Peter, J., & Valkenburg, P. (2006). Research note: Individual differences in perceptions of Internet communication. *European Journal of Communication, 21,* 213–226.

Peterson, M. (1997). Personnel interviewers' perceptions of the importance and adequacy of applicants' communication skills. *Communication Education, 46,* 287–291.

Petronio, S. (Ed.). (2000). *Balancing the secrets of private disclosures.* Mahwah, NJ: Erlbaum.

Petronio, S., & Caughlin, J. (2006). Communication privacy management theory: Understanding families. In D. O. Braithwaite & L. A. Baxter (Eds.), *Engaging theories in family communication: Multiple perspectives* (pp. 35–49). Thousand Oaks, CA: Sage.

Phillips, G. M. (1991). *Communication incompetencies.* Carbondale: Southern Illinois University Press.

Piaget, J. (1932/1965). *The moral judgment of the child.* New York: Free Press.

Pierson, J. (1995, November 20). If sun shines in, workers work better, buyers buy more. *The Wall Street Journal,* pp. B1, B8.

Potter, J. (2001). *Media literacy* (2nd ed.). Thousand Oaks, CA: Sage.

Potter, J. (2002). *The 11 myths of media violence.* Thousand Oaks, CA: Sage.

Potter, J. (2009). *Media literacy* (4th ed.). Thousand Oaks, CA: Sage.

Previti, D., & Amato, P. R. (2003). Why stay married? Rewards, barriers, and marital stability. *Journal of Marriage and Family, 65,* 561–573.

Purdy, M. (1997). What is listening? In M. Purdy & D. Borisoff (Eds.), *Listening in everyday life: A personal and professional approach* (2nd ed., pp. 1–20). Lanham, MD: University Press of America.

Rae-Dupree, J. (2008, December 7). Teamwork, the true mother of invention. *New York Times,* p. B3.

Ramsay, S., Gallois, C., & Callan, V. (1997). Social rules and attributions in the personnel selection interview. *Journal of Occupational and Organizational Psychology, 70,* 189–203.

Rawlins, W. K. (1981). *Friendship as a communicative achievement: A theory and an interpretive analysis of verbal reports.* Unpublished doctoral dissertation. Philadelphia: Temple University.

Rawlins, W. K. (1994). Being there and growing apart: Sustaining friendships during adulthood. In D. Canary & L. Stafford (Eds.), *Communication and relational maintenance* (pp. 275–294). New York: Academic Press.

Reinhard, C. D., & Dervin, B. J. (2009). Media uses and gratifications. In W. F. Eadie (Ed.), *21st century communication: A reference handbook* (pp. 506–515). Thousand Oaks, CA: Sage.

Reis, H. T., Clark, M. S., & Holmes, J. G. (2004). Perceived partner responsiveness as an organizing construct in the study of intimacy and closeness. In D. J. Mashek & A. P. Aron (Eds.), *Handbook of closeness and intimacy* (pp. 201–225). Mahwah, NJ: Erlbaum.

Remland, M. (2000). *Nonverbal communication in everyday life.* Boston: Houghton Mifflin.

Rhodewalt, F. (Ed.). (2007). *Personality and social behavior.* Florence, KY: Psychology Press.

Ribeau, S. A., Baldwin, J. R., & Hecht, M. L. (1994). An African American communication perspective. In L. Samovar & R. Porter (Eds.), *Intercultural communication: A reader* (7th ed., pp. 140–147). Belmont, CA: Wadsworth.

Richmond, V. P., & McCroskey, J. C. (1992). *Communication: Apprehension, avoidance, and effectiveness* (3rd ed.). Scottsdale, AZ: Gorsuch Scarisbrick.

Richmond, V. P., & McCroskey, J. C. (1995a). *Communication: Apprehension, avoidance, and effectiveness.* Scottsdale, AZ: Gorsuch Scarisbrick.

Richmond, V. P., & McCroskey, J. C. (1995b). *Nonverbal communication in interpersonal relations* (3rd ed.). Boston: Allyn & Bacon.

Riggs, D. (1999, February 28). True love is alive and well, say romance book writers. *The Tallahassee Democrat,* p. 3D.

Risman, B., & Godwin, S. (2001). Twentieth-century changes in economic work and family. In D. Vannoy (Ed.), *Gender mosaics* (pp. 134–144). Los Angeles: Roxbury.

Roberts, S. (2008, August 14). A generation away, minorities may be the majority. *New York Times,* pp. A1, A18.

Robinson, G. (2001, March 4). Sometimes a thank you is enough. *New York Times,* pp. 16, 18.

Robinson, J. D. (2009). Media portrayals and representations. In W. F. Eadie (Ed.), *21st century communication: A reference handbook* (pp. 497–505). Thousand Oaks, CA: Sage.

Rodriguez, R. (2003, September 12). "Blaxicans" and other reinvented Americans. *The Chronicle of Higher Education,* pp. B10–B11.

Rollie, S. S., & Duck, S. W. (2006). Divorce and dissolution of romantic relationships: Stage models and their imitations. In M. Fine & J. Harvey (Eds.), *Handbook of divorce and dissolution of romantic relationships* (pp. 223–240). Mahwah, NJ: Erlbaum.

Rothenberg, P. (2006). *Race, class, and gender in the United States* (7th ed.). New York: Worth.

Rothwell, J. D. (2009). *In mixed company: Small group communication* (7th ed.). Belmont, CA: Wadsworth.

Rowe, A. C., & Carnelley, K. B. (2005). Preliminary support for the use of a hierarchical mapping technique to examine attachment networks. *Personal Relationships, 12,* 499–519.

Ruberman, T. R. (1992, January 22–29). Psychosocial influences on mortality of patients with coronary heart disease. *Journal of the American Medical Association, 267,* 559–560.

Rusbult, C. (1987). Responses to dissatisfaction in close relationships: The exit–voice–loyalty–neglect model. In D. Perlman & S. W. Duck (Eds.), *Intimate relationships: Development, dynamics, and deterioration* (pp. 109–238). London: Sage.

Rusbult, C. E., Johnson, D. J., & Morrow, G. D. (1986). Impact of couple patterns of problem solving on distress and nondistress in dating relationships. *Journal of Personality and Social Psychology, 50,* 744–753.

Rusbult, C. E., & Zembrodt, I. M. (1983). Responses to dissatisfaction in romantic involvement: A multidimensional scaling analysis. *Journal of Experimental Social Psychology, 19,* 274–293.

Rusbult, C. E., Zembrodt, I. M., & Iwaniszek, J. (1986). The impact of gender and sex-role orientation on responses to dissatisfaction in close relationships. *Sex Roles, 15,* 1–20.

Rusk, T., & Rusk, N. (1988). *Mind traps: Change your mind, change your life.* Los Angeles: Price Stern Sloan.

Sahlstein, E. (2006a). Relational life in the 21st century: Managing people, time, and distance. In J. T. Wood & S. W. Duck (Eds.), *Composing relationships: Communication in everyday life* (pp. 110–118). Belmont, CA: Thomson Wadsworth.

Sahlstein, E. (2006b). The trouble with distance. In C. Kirpatrick, S. W. Duck, & M. Foley (Eds.), *Relating difficulty* (pp. 118–140). Mahwah, NJ: Erlbaum.

Salazar, A. (1995). Understanding the synergistic effects of communication in small groups. *Small Group Research, 26,* 169–199.

Sallinen-Kuparinen, A. (1992). Teacher communicator style. *Communication Education, 41,* 153–166.

Samovar, L., & Porter, R. (2001). *Communication between cultures* (4th ed.). Belmont, CA: Wadsworth.

Samovar, L., Porter, R., & McDaniel, E. R. (2009a). *Communication between cultures* (12th ed.). Belmont, CA: Thomson.

Samovar, L., Porter, R., & McDaniel, E. R. (Eds.). (2009b). *Intercultural communication: A reader* (12th ed.). Belmont, CA: Wadsworth.

Samp, J. A., & Palevitz, C. E. (2009). Dating and romantic partners. In W. F. Eadie (Ed.), *21st century communication: A reference handbook* (pp. 322–330). Thousand Oaks, CA: Sage.

Sawyer, K. (2008). *Group genius: The power of creative collaboration.* New York: Basic.

Scarf, M. (2008). *September song: The good news about marriage in the later years.* New York: Riverhead.

Schmidt, J., & Uecker, D. (2007). Increasing understanding of routine/everyday interaction in relationships. *Communication Teacher, 21,* 111–116.

Schmitt, E. (2001, March 13). For 7 million people in census, one race category isn't enough. *The New York Times,* pp. A1, A14.

Schneider, A. (1999, March 26). Taking aim at student incoherence. *The Chronicle of Higher Education,* pp. A16–A18.

Scholz, M. (2005, June). A "simple" way to improve adherence. *RN, 68,* 82.

Schooler, D., Ward, M., Merriwether, A., & Caruthers, A. (2004). Who's that girl: Television's role in the body image of young white and black women. *Psychology of Women Quarterly, 28,* 38–47.

Schott, B. (2008, May 16). Minute waltz. *New York Times,* p. A23.

Schram, P., & Schwartz, H. (2000). *Stories within stories: From the Jewish oral tradition.* Leonia, NJ: Jason Aronson.

Schramm, W. (1955). *The process and effects of mass communication.* Urbana: University of Illinois Press.

Schütz, A. (1999). It was your fault! Self-serving bias in autobiographical accounts of conflicts in married couples. *Journal of Social and Personal Relationships, 16,* 193–208.

Scott, C., & Myers, K. (2005). The socialization of emotion: Learning emotion management at the fire station. *Journal of Applied Communication Research, 33,* 67–92.

Sedikides, C., Campbell, W., Reeder, G., & Elliot, A. (1998). The self-serving bias in relational context. *Journal of Personality and Social Psychology, 74,* 378–386.

Segrin, C. (1998). Interpersonal communication problems associated with depression and loneliness. In P. Andersen & L. Guerrero (Eds.), *Communication and emotion: Theory, research, and applications* (pp. 215–242). San Diego: Academic Press.

Segrin, C., Hanzal, A., & Domschke, T. (2009). Accuracy and bias in newlywed couples' perceptions of conflict styles and the association with marital satisfaction. *Communication Monographs, 76,* 207–233.

Seligman, M. E. P. (1990). *Learned optimism.* New York: Simon & Schuster/Pocket Books.

Seligman, M. E. P. (2002). *Authentic happiness.* New York: Free Press.

Servaty-Seib, H., & Burleson, B. (2007). Bereaved adolescents' evaluations of the helpfulness of support-intended statements: Associations with person centeredness and demographic, personality, and contextual factors. *Journal of Social and Personal Relationships, 24,* 207–223.

Shanahan, J., & Jones, V. (1999). Cultivation and social control. In D. Demers & K. Viswanath (Eds.), *Mass media, social control, and social change* (pp. 89–116). Ames: Iowa State University Press.

Shannon, C., & Weaver, W. (1949). *The mathematical theory of communication.* Urbana: University of Illinois Press.

Shapiro, J., & Kroeger, L. (1991). Is life just a romantic novel? The relationship between attitudes about intimate relationships and the popular media. *American Journal of Family Therapy, 19,* 226–236.

Shattuck, T. R. (1980). *The forbidden experiment: The story of the wild boy of Aveyron.* New York: Farrar, Straus & Giroux.

Sheehan, J. (1996, February). Kiss and well: How to smooch and seduce your way to health. *Longevity,* pp. 50–51, 93.

Shimanoff, S. B. (1980). *Communication rules: Theory and research.* Beverly Hills: Sage.

Shotter, J. (1993). *Conversational realities: The construction of life through language.* Newbury Park, CA: Sage.

Sias, P., Heath, R., Perry, T., Silva, D., & Fix, B. (2004). Narratives of workplace friendship deterioration. *Journal of Social and Personal Relationships, 21,* 321–340.

Signorelli, N. (2009). Cultivation and media exposure. In W. F. Eadie (Ed.), *21st century communication: A reference handbook* (pp. 525–567). Thousand Oaks, CA: Sage.

Simon, S. B. (1977). *Vulture: A modern allegory on the art of putting oneself down.* Niles, IL: Argus Communications.

Smith, R. (1998, December 1). *Civility without censorship: The ethics of the Internet cyberhate.* Speech delivered at the Simon Wiesenthal Center/Museum of Tolerance, Los Angeles.

Snapp, C., & Leary, M. (2001). Hurt feelings among new acquaintances: Moderating effects of interpersonal familiarity. *Journal of Social and Personal Relationships, 18,* 315–326.

Sommerville, D. (1999, May 26). Race, gender attitudes begin early. *The Raleigh News & Observer,* p. 3F.

Sonnentag. S. (2001). High performance and meeting participation: An observational study in software design teams. *Group Dynamics: Theory, Research, and Practice, 5,* 3-18.

Spaeth, M. (1996, July 1). "Prop" up your speaking skills. *The Wall Street Journal,* p. A15.

Spain, D. (1992). *Gendered spaces.* Chapel Hill: University of North Carolina Press.

Spano, S. (2003, June 1). Rude encounters versus cultural differences. *The Raleigh News & Observer,* pp. 1H, 5H.

Sparks, G. (2006). *Media effects research: A basic overview* (2nd ed.). Belmont, CA: Thomson Wadsworth.

Spear, W. (1995). *Feng shui made easy: Designing your life with the ancient art of placement.* New York: HarperCollins.

Spencer, T. (1994). Transforming personal relationships through ordinary talk. In S. W. Duck (Ed.), *Understanding relationship processes, 4: Dynamics of relationships* (pp. 58-85). Thousand Oaks, CA: Sage.

Spenser, L., & Pahl R. (2006). *Rethinking friendship: Hidden solidarities today.* Princeton, NJ: Princeton University Press.

Spitzberg, B., & Cupach, W. (2009). Unwanted communication, aggression and abuse. In W. F. Eadie (Ed.), *21st century communication: A reference handbook* (pp. 444–453). Thousand Oaks, CA: Sage.

Stafford, L. (2005). *Maintaining long-distance and cross-residential relationships.* Mahwah, NJ: Erlbaum.

Stafford, L. (2009). Spouses and other intimate partnershsips. In W. F. Eadie (Ed.), *21st century communication: A reference handbook* (pp. 296–302). Thousand Oaks, CA: Sage.

Stafford, L., Dutton, M., & Haas, S. (2000). Measuring routine maintenance: Scale revision, sex versus gender roles, and the prediction of relational characteristics. *Communication Monographs, 67,* 306–323.

Stafford, L., & Merolla, A. (2007). Idealization, reunions, and stability in long-distance dating relationships. *Journal of Social and Personal Relationships, 24,* 37–54.

Stafford, L., & Merolla, A., & Castle, J. (2006). When long-distance dating partners become geographically close. *Journal of Social and Personal Relationships, 23,* 901–919.

Stanton, E. C., Anthony, S. B., & Gage, M. J. (1881/1969 reprint). *History of woman suffrage, I.* New York: Arno and *The New York Times.*

Stapel, D. A., & Blanton, H. (Eds.). (2006). *Social comparison theories: Key readings.* Florence, KY: Psychology Press.

Steele, R. (2009). Traditional and new media. In W. F. Eadie (Ed.), *21st century communication: A reference handbook* (pp. 489-496). Thousand Oaks, CA: Sage.

Steil, J. (2000). Contemporary marriage: Still an unequal partnership. In C. Hendrick & S. Hendrick (Eds.), *Close relationships: A sourcebook* (pp. 124–136). Thousand Oaks, CA: Sage.

Steil, L. (1997). Listening training: The key to success in today's organizations. In M. Purdy & D. Borisoff (Eds.), *Listening in everyday life: A personal and professional approach* (2nd ed., pp. 213–237). Lanham, MD: University Press of America.

Stewart, C., & Cash, W. (1991). *Interviewing: Principles and practices* (6th ed.). Dubuque, IA: Wm. C. Brown.

Stewart, J., Zediker, K., & Black, L. (2004). Relationships among philosophies of dialogue. In R. Anderson, L. Baxter, & K. Cissna (Eds.), *Dialogue: Theorizing difference in communication.* (pp. 21–38). Thousand Oaks, CA: Sage.

Stiff, J. B. (1994). *Persuasive communication.* New York: Guilford Press.

Stolberg, S. (2009, January 29). From the top, the White House unbuttons formal dress code. *New York Times,* pp. A1, A14.

Strasser, M. (1997). *Legally wed: Same-sex marriage and the Constitution.* Ithaca, New York: Cornell University Press.

Strege, J. (1997). *Tiger: A biography of Tiger Woods.* New York: Bantam/Doubleday.

Stroup, K. (2001, April 30). Business connections: The wired way we work. *Newsweek,* pp. 59–61.

Surfing Web at work is no big deal, judge says. (2006, April 25). *The Raleigh News & Observer,* p. 3A.

Surra, C., Arizzi, P., & Asmussen, L. (1988). The association between reasons for commitment and the development and outcome of marital relationships. *Journal of Social and Personal Relationships, 5,* 47–64.

Swain, S. (1989). Covert intimacy: Closeness in men's friendships. In B. Risman & P. Schwartz (Eds.), *Gender and intimate relationships* (pp. 71–86). Belmont, CA: Wadsworth.

Swidler, A. (2001). *Talk of love: How culture matters.* Chicago: University of Chicago Press.

Swiss, T. (Ed.). (2001). *Unspun key concepts for understanding the World Wide Web.* New York: New York University Press.

Sypher, B., Bostrom, R., & Siebert, J. (1989). Listening, communication abilities, and success at work. *Journal of Business Communication, 26,* 293–303.

Tannen, D. (1990). *You just don't understand: Women and men in conversation.* New York: William Morrow.

Tashiro, T., & Frazier, P. (2003). "I'll never be in a relationship like that again": Personal growth following romantic relationship breakups. *Personal Relationships, 10,* 113–128.

Tavris, C. (1992). *The mismeasure of woman.* New York: Simon & Schuster.

Tavris, C., & Aronson, E. (2007). *Mistakes were made (but not by me): Why we justify foolish beliefs, bad decisions, and hurtful acts.* New York: Harcourt.

Taylor, A., Wiley, A., Kuo, F., & Sullivan, W. (1998). Growing up in the inner city: Green spaces as places to grow. *Environment and Behavior, 30,* 3–27.

Thomas, J. (1999). Do you hear what I hear? *Women in Business, 51,* 1–14.

Thompson, F., & Grundgenett, D. (1999). Helping disadvantaged learners build effective learning skills. *Education, 120,* 130–135.

Timmerman, C., & Scott, C. (2006). Virtually working: Communicative and structural predictors of media use and key outcomes in virtual work teams. *Communication Monographs, 73,* 108–136.

Tolhuizen, J. H. (1989). Communication strategies for intensifying dating relationships: Identification, use, and structure. *Journal of Social and Personal Relationships, 6*, 413–434.

Toulmin, S. (1958). *The uses of argument.* Cambridge, MA: Cambridge University Press.

Toulmin, S., Rieke, R., & Janik, A. (1984). *An introduction to reasoning* (2nd ed.). New York: Macmillan.

Trees, A. (2000). Nonverbal communication and the support process: International sensitivity in interactions between mothers and young adult children. *Communication Monographs, 67*, 239–261.

Trenholm, S. (1991). *Human communication theory* (2nd ed.). Englewood Cliffs, NJ: Prentice Hall.

Triandis, H. C. (1990). Cross-cultural studies of individualism and collectivism. In J. J. Berman (Ed.), *Cross-cultural perspectives* (pp. 41–133). Lincoln: University of Nebraska Press.

Trice, H., & Beyer, J. (1984). Studying organizational cultures through rites and ceremonials. *Academy of Management Review, 9*, 653–669.

Troy, A., & Laurenceau, J. (2006). Interracial and intraracial romantic relationships: The search for differences in satisfaction, conflict, and attachment style. *Journal of Social and Personal Relationships, 23*, 65–80.

Tsai, F., & Reis, H. (2009). Perceptions by and of lonely people in social networks. *Personal Relationships, 16*, 221–238.

Tubbs, S. (1998). *A systems approach to small group communication* (6th ed.). New York: McGraw-Hill.

Tufte, E. (2003). *The cognitive style of PowerPoint.* Cheshire, CT: Graphics Press.

Turow, J. (2008). *Media today* (3rd ed.). New York: Routledge.

Tusing, K., & Dillard, J. (2000). The sounds of dominance: Vocal precursors of perceived dominance during interpersonal influence. *Human Communication Research, 26*, 148–171.

Underwood, A., & Adler, J. (2005, April 25). When cultures clash. *Newsweek,* pp. 68–72.

Urgo, J. (2000). *The age of distraction.* Jackson: Mississippi University Press.

U.S. Bureau of the Census. (2003). *Census 2003.* Washington, DC: Government Printing Office.

U.S. Department of Labor. (1992). *Cultural diversity in the workplace.* Washington, DC: Government Printing Office.

Valentin, E., Rogers, L. E., & Gutierrez, E. (1997). Patterns of relational control and nonverbal affect in clinic and nonclinic couples. *Journal of Social and Personal Relationships, 14*, 5–29.

Valkenburg, P. (2004). *Children's responses to the screen.* Mahwah, NJ: Erlbaum.

van Dijk, J. (2005). *The deepening divide: Inequality in the information society.* Thousand Oaks, CA: Sage.

Van Oostrum, J., & Rabbie, J. (1995). Intergroup competition and cooperation within autocratic and democratic management regimes. *Small Group Research, 26*, 269–295.

Van Styke, E. (1999). *Listening to conflict: Finding constructive solutions to workplace disputes.* New York: AMA Communications.

Vardi, Y., & Weitz, E. (2004). *Misbehavior in organizations.* Thousand Oaks, CA: Sage.

Vito, D. (1999). Affective self-disclosure, conflictresolution, and marital quality. *Dissertation Abstracts International, 60* (3–B), 1319.

Vocate, D. (Ed.). (1994). *Intrapersonal communication: Different voices, different minds.* Hillsdale, NJ: Erlbaum.

Wade, C., & Tavris, C. (1990). *Learning to think critically: The case of close relationships.* New York: HarperCollins.

Walker, K. (2004). Men, women, and friendship: What they say, what they do. In J. Spade & K. Valentine (Eds.), *The kaleidoscope of gender: Prisms, patterns, and possibilities* (pp. 403–413). Belmont, CA: Thomson Wadsworth.

Walker, S. (2007). *Style and status: Selling beauty to African American women.* Lexington: University of Kentucky Press.

Walker, M. B., & Trimboli, A. (1989). Communicating affect: The role of verbal and nonverbal content. *Journal of Language and Social Psychology, 8*, 229–248.

Walther, J. B., & Parks, M. (2002). Cues filtered out, cues filtered in: Computer-mediated communication and relationships. In M. L. Knapp & J. A. Daly (Eds.), *Handbook of interpersonal communication* (pp. 529–563). Thousand Oaks, CA: Sage.

Watzlawick, P., Beavin, J., & Jackson, D. D. (1967). *Pragmatics of human communication.* New York: W. W. Norton.

Wech, B., Mossholder, K., Streel, R., & Bennett, N. (1998). Does work group cohesiveness afflict individuals' performance and organizational commitment? *Small Group Research, 29,* 472–494.

Wegner, H., Jr. (2005). Disconfirming communication and self-verification in marriage: Associations among the demand/withdraw interaction pattern, feeling understood, and marital satisfaction. *Journal of Social and Personal Relationships, 22,* 19–31.

Weimann, G. (2000). *Communicating unreality: Modern media and the reconstruction of reality.* Newbury Park, CA: Sage.

Weinstock, J., & Bond, L. (2000). Conceptions of conflict in close friendships and ways of knowing among young college women: A developmental framework. *Journal of Social and Personal Relationships, 17,* 687–696.

Weisinger, H. (1996). *Anger at work.* New York: William Morrow.

Werner, C., Altman, I., & Oxley, D. (1985). Temporal aspects of homes: A transactional perspective. In I. Altman & C. M. Werner (Eds.), *Home environments, 8. Human behavior and environment: Advances in theory and research* (pp. 1–32). Beverly Hills: Sage.

West, C., & Zimmerman, D. H. (1987). Doing gender. *Gender and Society, 1,* 125–151.

Wheelan, S. A. (2005). *Creating effective teams* (2nd ed.). Thousand Oaks, CA: Sage.

White, R., & Lippitt, R. (1960). *Autocracy and democracy.* New York: Harper & Row.

Whitman, T., White, R., O'Mara, K., & Goeke-Morey, M. (1999). Environmental aspects of infant health and illness. In T. Whitman & T. Merluzzi (Eds.), *Life-span perspectives on health and illness* (pp. 105–124). Mahwah, NJ: Erlbaum.

Whorf, B. (1956). *Language, thought, and reality.* New York: MIT Press/Wiley.

Williams, G. (1995). *Life on the color line: The true story of a White boy who discovered he was Black.* New York: Dutton.

Williams, K. D. (2001). *Ostracism: The power of silence.* New York: Guilford Press.

Williams, R. (1994). *The non-designer's design book: Design and typographic principles for the visual novice.* Berkeley, CA: Peachpit Press.

Wilmot, W., & Hocker, J. (2001). *Interpersonal Conflict.* New York: McGraw-Hill.

Wilson, G., & Goodall, H., Jr. (1991). *Interviewing in context.* New York: McGraw-Hill.

Wilson, J. F., & Arnold, C. C. (1974). *Public speaking as a liberal art* (4th ed.). Boston: Allyn & Bacon.

Winans, J. A. (1938). *Speechmaking.* New York: Appleton-Century-Crofts.

Winbush, G. (2000). African American women. In M. Julia (Ed.,), *Constructing gender: Multicultural perspectives in working with women* (pp. 11-34). Belmont, CA: Wadsworth.

Windsor, J., Curtis, D., & Stephens, R. (1997). National preferences in business and communication education: An update. *Journal of the Association for Communication Administration, 3,* 170–179.

Wolvin, A. (2009). Listening, understanding and misunderstanding. In W. F. Eadie (Ed.), *21st century communication: A reference handbook* (pp. 137–146). Thousand Oaks, CA: Sage.

Wood, A., & Smith, M. (2001). *Online communication: Linking technology, identity, and culture.* Mahwah, NJ: Erlbaum.

Wood, J. T. (1982). Communication and relational culture: Bases for the study of human relationships. *Communication Quarterly, 30,* 75–84.

Wood, J. T. (1992). Telling our stories: Narratives as a basis for theorizing sexual harassment. *Journal of Applied Communication Research, 4,* 349–363.

Wood, J. T. (1993). Engendered relations: Interaction, caring, power, and responsibility in intimacy. In S. W. Duck (Ed.), *Understanding relationship processes, 3: Social context and relationships* (pp. 26–54). Newbury Park, CA: Sage.

Wood, J. T. (1994a). Engendered identities: Shaping voice and mind through gender. In D. Vocate (Ed.), *Intrapersonal communication: Different voices, different minds.* Hillsdale, NJ: Erlbaum.

Wood, J. T. (1994c). Saying it makes it so: The discursive construction of sexual harassment. In S. Bingham (Ed.), *Conceptualizing sexual harassment as discursive practice* (pp. 17–30). Westport, CT: Praeger.

Wood, J. T. (1994d). *Who cares? Women, care, and culture.* Carbondale: Southern Illinois University Press.

Wood, J. T. (1995a). Feminist scholarship and research on personal relationships. *Journal of Social and Personal Relationships, 12,* 103–120.

Wood, J. T. (1995b). The part is not the whole. *Journal of Social and Personal Relationships, 12,* 563–567.

Wood, J. T. (Ed.). (1996). *Gendered relationships.* Mountain View, CA: Mayfield.

Wood, J. T. (1998). *But I thought you meant. . . . Misunderstandings in human communication.* Mountain View, CA: Mayfield.

Wood, J. T. (2000). *Relational communication: Continuity and change in personal relationships* (2nd ed.). Belmont, CA: Wadsworth.

Wood, J. T. (2001). The normalization of violence in heterosexual romantic relationships: Women's narratives of love and violence. *Journal of Social and Personal Relationships, 18,* 239–261.

Wood, J. T. (2002). Gendered speech communities. In L. Samovar & R. Porter (Eds.), *Intercultural Communication: A Reader* (10th ed.). Belmont, CA: Wadsworth. 2002.

Wood, J. T. (2004). *Interpersonal communication: Everyday encounters* (4th ed.). Belmont, CA: Wadsworth.

Wood, J. T. (2005). Feminist standpoint theory and muted group theory: Commonalities and divergences. *Women & Language, 28,* 61–64.

Wood, J. T. (2006a). Chopping the carrots: Creating intimacy moment by moment. In J. T. Wood & S. W. Duck (Eds.), *Composing relationships: Communication in everyday life* (pp. 15–23). Belmont, CA: Thomson Wadsworth.

Wood, J. T. (2006b). Monsters and victims: Male felons' accounts of intimate partner violence. *Journal of Social and Personal Relationships, 21,* 555–576.

Wood, J. T. (2007a). *Gendered lives* (7th ed.). Belmont, CA: Wadsworth

Wood, J. T. (2007b). *Interpersonal communication: Everyday encounters* (5th ed.). Belmont, CA: Wadsworth.

Wood, J. T. (2011). *Gendered lives: Communication, gender and culture* (9th ed.). Belmont, CA: Wadsworth.

Wood, J. T., Dendy, L., Dordek, E., Germany, M., & Varallo, S. (1994). Dialectic of difference: A thematic analysis of intimates' meanings for differences. In K. Carter & M. Presnell (Eds.), *Interpretive approaches to interpersonal communication* (pp. 115–136). New York: State University of New York Press.

Wood, J. T., & Duck, S. (1995a). Off the beaten track: New shores for relationship research. In J. T. Wood & S. Duck (Eds.), *Understanding relationship processes, 6: Understudied relationships: Off the beaten track* (pp. 1–21). Thousand Oaks, CA: Sage.

Wood, J. T., & Duck, S. (Eds.). (1995b). *Understanding relationship processes, 6: Understudied relationships: Off the beaten track.* Newbury Park, CA: Sage.

Wood, J. T., & Duck, S. (2006). Introduction. In J. T. Wood & S. Ducks (Eds.), *Composing relationships: Communication in everyday life* (pp. 1–13). Belmont, CA: Thomson Wadsworth.

Wood, J. T., & Inman, C. C. (1993). In a different mode: Masculine styles of communicating closeness. *Journal of Applied Communication Research, 21,* 279–295.

Wood, J. T., & Phillips, G. M. (1990). The pedagogy of group decision making: Teaching alternative strategies. In G. M. Phillips (Ed.), *Small group communication: Theory and pedagogy.* Norwood, NJ: Ablex.

Woolfolk, A. E. (1987). *Educational psychology.* Englewood Cliffs, NJ: Prentice Hall.

Wu, C., & Shaffer, D. R. (1988). Susceptibility to persuasive appeals as a function of source credibility and prior experience with attitude object. *Journal of Personal and Social Psychology, 52,* 677–688.

Yamato, G. (2001). Something about the subject makes it hard to name. In M. L. Andersen & P. H. Collins (Eds.), *Race, class, and gender: An anthology* (4th ed., pp. 91–94). Belmont, CA: Wadsworth.

Yanes, W. (1990, November 9). Forget consensus: Fight it out, stick with decision. *Investor's Business Daily,* p. 6.

Young, J. (2005, April 22). Knowing when to log off. *The Chronicle of Higher Education,* pp. A27–A29.

Young, S., Wood, J., Phillips, G., & Pedersen, D. (2001). *Group discussion* (3rd ed.). Prospect Heights, IL: Waveland.

Yum, J. (2000). The impact of Confucianism on interpersonal relationships and communication patterns in East Asia. In L. Samovar & R. Porter (Eds.), *Intercultural communication: A reader* (9th ed., pp. 63–73). Belmont, CA: Wadsworth.

Zachary, P. (2002, January 21). The new America. *In These Times*, pp. 22–23.

Zediker, K. (1993, February). *Rediscovering the tradition: Women's history with a relational approach to the basic public speaking course.* Albuquerque: Western States Communication Association.

Zorn, T. (1995). Bosses and buddies: Constructing and performing simultaneously hierarchical and close friendship relationships. In J. T. Wood & S. W. Duck (Eds.), *Understanding relationship processes, 6: Understudied relationships: Off the beaten track* (pp. 122–147). Thousand Oaks, CA: Sage.

Zukerman, L. (1999, April 17). Words go right to the brain, but can they stir the heart? *The New York Times*, p. 9.

Index

abstraction
  in communication, 42–45
  in language, 116
  process, 42–43, 43*f*
  of symbols, 101
Abu Ghraib, 284
abuse
  cycle of, 219*f*
  in romantic relationships,
    218–219, 219*f*
academic degree, 21
Academy Awards ceremonies,
  325
accuracy, 115–117
acknowledgment, 177
action plan, 265
ad hominem arguments,
  441–442, 444*t*
Adler, Ron, 78–79
advertising, 313, 315
advice, 151
advisory groups, 252–253
AFLAC, 279
African Americans
  assertive style of, 152
  bilingualism of, 166
  civil rights movement of, 63,
    161–162, 355
  communal families of, 215
  communication rules of, 103
  connotation of, 108
  language of, 158
  listening style of, 82
  in mainstream culture, 165
  oral traditions of, 328
  paralanguage of, 138
  physical appearance for, 132
agape, 213, 213*f*
age, 153, 157
  at marriage, 160
  perception and, 37
  persuadability from, 332
  of technology users, 296
agenda, in group discussion,
  261–266, 262*f*
agenda setting, 298–299
aggression, 190, 190*t*
Alcoff, Linda, 19
Allstate Insurance, 102
ambiguity, of symbols, 100
ambushing, 85
American Demographics, 346
American Indians, 156, 158
American Sign Language (ASL),
  75
Amos, Dan, 279
analogical organization, 380

Angelou, Maya, 167–168
Anger at Work (Weisinger), 191
anxiety. *see* communication
  apprehension
anxious/ambivalent attachment
  style, 54
arbitrary, symbols as, 98–99
Aristotle, 11, 430
Aronson, Elliot, 34
Arrow Electronics, 279
Arthur Anderson, 284
artifacts, 132–134
Asian culture
  assertiveness in, 237
  collectivism of, 237
  conflict in, 186
  decision-making in, 238
  self-disclosure in, 193
ASL. *see* American Sign
  Language
assertion, 190–191, 190*t*
assertiveness, 152, 237, 238
assimilation, 164
assimilation-preservation
  dialectic, 51
attachment styles, 52–54, 53*f*
attention, 29, 384
attributions, 33–35, 34*t*
audience
  adapting to, 440
  analysis of, 332–333
  attitudes of, 437
  capturing attention of, 384
  connecting with, 405–406
  demographic analysis of,
    332–334
  diverse, 407–408
  expectations of, 437
  for informative speaking,
    405–408, 412–414
  inoculation of, 438
  involving, 412–414, 413*t*
  knowledge of, 438
  motivating, 406–407
  organizing for, 408–409
  orientation of, 334–336
  rhetorical questions for, 413
  situational analysis of,
    334–336
authoritarian leadership, 256
authority rule, decision-making
  by, 260
autoethnography, 51
autonomy, from intimates, 203
autonomy/connection, in
  personal relationships,
  203

Bachen, Christine, 32
Baker, Ron, 135–136
bandwagon appeal, 442, 444*t*
Baran, Stanley, 296
bar graphs, 357, 358*f*
Baxter, Leslie, 18, 203
Beatles, 65
Beck, Aaron, 101
beliefs, 155
Beyer, Janice, 280
bias
  in group discussion, 263
  mass media, 299
  self-serving, 35, 45
Bibliographic Retrieval Service
  (BRS), 345
bilingualism, 165–166
BlackBerry, 297
blaming rites, 291
Blanchard, Ken, 258
"Blaxican," 107
blogging, 276
body, of speech, 373–374
body image, 60
body language, 130–131
Bollier, David, 315
"Bosses and Buddies," 289
bowing, 130, 150
Bowlby, John, 52–53
brainstorming
  electronic, 276
  groups, 251–252, 252*t*, 264
Braithwaite, Dawn, 204
Bratton, Willilam J., 276
Brazil, 129
breast cancer, 5
Brookey, Robert, 304
Brooks, David, 239
Brown, Jane, 306
BRS. *see* Bibliographic Retrieval
  Service
Buber, Martin, 12, 176
Burke, Kenneth, 439
Bush, George W., 132

calendars, 159
"can-do" culture, 13–14
Cannon, Kristopher, 304
Cantor, Joanne, 306
Cappella, Joseph, 438
careers, in communication,
  20–23
Carlos, John, 258
Castle, Janessa, 216
cause–effect pattern, in public
  speaking, 381–382, 434*t*
cell phones, 307

certainty, 180
chi, 135
children
  cognitive complexity of, 40
  media consumption by, 300,
    301, 308, 311, 315
  racism in, 166
China, 125, 157. *see also* Asian
  culture
Cho Seung-Hui, 294
chronemics, 136–137
civil rights movement, 63,
  161–162, 355
claims, 427
classrooms, 135–136
climate communication,
  239, 240*t*, 241. *see
  also* interpersonal
  communication
Clinton, Bill, 353
closedness, 203
closeness. *see also* proxemics
  in dialogue, 192–193
  self-disclosure and, 175–176
clothing
  by culture, 124
  femininity in, 55
  professional, 133
Clydesdale, Tim, 313
CMC. *see* computer-mediated
  communication
code talkers, 99
coercive power, 236
cognitive abilities
  cognitive complexity, 40–41
  person-centered perception,
    41–42
cognitive complexity, 40–41, 333
cognitive restructuring, 389
cognitive schemata, 30–33
  listening through, 77–78
cohesion, of small groups, 232
Cole, Tim, 54
collectivist culture, 150, 237
college students, 219
collegial stories, 280
colloquialisms, 87
colors, 133
colors of love, 213*f*
commencement ceremonies,
  282*f*
commitment, 210
  in groups, 231
  personal relationships,
    200–201
  to self-change, 64
common ground, 439

Student Companion
for
Julia Wood's
Communication in Our Lives
Sixth Edition

Julia T. Wood
University of North Carolina
Chapel Hill

Prepared by

Miri Pardo
St. John Fisher College
Rochester, NY

CONTENTS

Introduction to the Student Companion

Welcome to the Companion to Julia Wood's *Communication in Our Lives*, your exploration into the dynamic world of communication. With the fast-changing pace of today's working world, tomorrow's employees need communication skills that are applicable to a wide range of careers—the job you have in five years may not exist today! Competent communicators will always be prized in the professional world, no matter what the specialization. Building your communication skills as a student will help you to enter the working world confident, prepared, and more valued than those who don't.

This Companion will assist you in applying communication principles to your personal life, helping you assess your newly developed communication competencies, showing you where to develop your skills to equip you to build the life you want to live.

Each chapter in the text has a corresponding chapter in this Companion where skills are developed in depth. Exercises are designed to help you think critically about your life experiences and to learn to apply communication concepts to them in the areas of intrapersonal communication, interpersonal communication, group communication, organizational communication, public communication, mass media and social media, and intercultural communication. You will learn how to communicate with yourself positively, develop healthy social and personal relationships, work effectively in teams and small groups, and learn to enjoy speaking to an audience.

The sixth edition of *Communication in Our Lives* features integrated attention to cultural diversity. Also included is a focus on the intersection of human communication to mass and social media. As you work through the exercises, use your social media interactions for analysis. Why didn't that text message get the response you wanted?

Here's how to use this Companion:

First, each chapter is summarized to outline the essential theories and concepts presented in the textbook.

Second, included are a variety of activities. Some ask you to apply a concept that was introduced in the chapter. Others help you learn about the perceptions of your families and friends. Still others are tied to the Online Resources for *Communication in Our Lives*, allowing you to view videos of students giving speeches and interacting in ways typical of students. To learn how to get started with your Online Resources, see the box on the next page. By figuring out which decisions the participants in the videos made that worked and which did not, you will learn what and what not to do in your own interactions.

Third, a self-test is included for each chapter with answers provided at the end of the book. These test questions will help you prepare you for quizzes and exams.

Online Resources

To access the premium Online Resources for *Communication in Our Lives*, which are referenced throughout your workbook, go to http://academic.cengage.com/sso/to register (if you have not done so already). Instructions for access can also be found on the inside front and back covers of your textbook.

Finally, included are flash cards. Cut out the cards and provide definitions on the back—another great tool for studying for exams and preparing for class.

Using all the tools offered in this guide will help you develop an in depth understanding of yourself and relationships with those in your life.

No matter what you choose to do professionally, effective communication will set you apart from the crowd. The relationships you develop with others can have deeper meaning by understanding how words impact. Life in general can function more smoothly with a finely tuned repertoire of communication skills.

Wouldn't it be great to be the student who aces the speech every time—the one who the other students admire, respect, and perhaps just a little bit, want to be like? Jumping head first into the world of communication will help you to be not only the class speech star, but also the skillful communicator you want to be in all facets of your life.

Have fun! Remember, without communication, we would never laugh. And if we're not laughing, we're not learning!

All the best,

Miri Pardo
"Dr. P"

Chapter 1: The World of Communication

Chapter Summary

I.   Communication is ever present in our world.

II.   The study of Communication is important for several reasons.
- A.   Formal study of the discipline can improve skills.
- B.   Communication theories and principles help us interpret events.
- C.   Studying communication helps you become more competent and confident.

III.   Communication is a systemic process in which people interact with and through symbols to create and interpret meaning.
- A.   When we say that communication is a process, we mean that it is ongoing and always changing.
- B.   The systemic aspect of communication means that it happens in a system of interrelated parts such that a change in one part leads to a change in the other parts.
- C.   Communication uses symbols, which are abstract, arbitrary, and ambiguous representations of things and events.
  - 1.   Language, made up of letters and words, comprises one set of symbols.
  - 2.   Nonverbal communication, such as gestures and facial expressions, comprises a second set of symbols.
- D.   Meaning is the significance we give to certain people, events, behaviors, or things.
  - 1.   The content level of meaning is the literal message.
  - 2.   The relationship level of meaning expresses the relationship between the communicators.

IV.   The values of communication are broad.
- A.   Communication helps us develop our personal values and greatly impacts our physical and emotional well-being.
- B.   Communication is the means through which we establish and maintain personal relationships and learn relationship values.
- C.   Communication skills influence our professional values and success, regardless of career choice.
- D.   Communication is how we learn our cultural values and how to behave in our society, as well as how to understand people of other cultures with whom we live and work.

V.   Over the years, many models of communication have been created.
- A.   The first models of communication were linear models, which viewed communication as an unidirectional linear process from one person to another.
  - 1.   The first linear model, created by Harold Laswell, asked 5 questions.
    - a.   Who?
    - b.   Says what?
    - c.   In what channel?
    - d.   To whom?
    - e.   With what effect?

2.   Shannon and Weaver expanded on Laswell's model by adding the idea that noise interference, can distort a message and lead to misunderstanding.

B.   Models improved upon linear models by including both parties in the communicative process and showing communication flowing both directions.

1.   A communicator is often both sending and receiving messages simultaneously, rather than being only a speaker or only a listener.

2.   Interactive models account for feedback, the response to a message.

3.   Interactive models account for each communicator's field of experience and its influence on her/his interpretation of messages.

C.   Transactional models seek to demonstrate the dynamic process of human communication.

1.   Communicators are often sending and receiving information from one another simultaneously.

2.   Communication is dynamic and changes over time.

3.   Noise, a part of the model, is anything that may interfere with the intended communication.

4.   Communication occurs within systems.

     a.   Shared systems are societal, such as those of a shared campus, a town, or a culture.

     b.   Personal systems are relational, such as family, friends, and religious affiliation.

5.   Communicators actively participate in the communication process of simultaneously sending and receiving messages.

VI.   The field of communication is quite broad in its scope.

A.   The study of communication is more than 2000 years old.

1.   Originally, the field focused on public speaking.

2.   Aristotle thought effective public speaking was essential to participation in civic affairs.

B.   The current study of the communication discipline covers many different communication contexts.

1.   Intrapersonal communication is communication with ourselves, or self-talk.

2.   Interpersonal communication focuses on the communication between two individuals on a continuum from impersonal to highly personal.

3.   Group communication examines different kinds of groups, such as social groups, work groups, and decision-making committees, and it examines the communication processes within these groups. Group communication scholars also study teams.

4.   Organizational communication examines organizational cultures and the types of interaction that occur within a variety of different types of organizations.

5.   The study of mass and social media examines how traditional media and social media influence our thinking, working, and relating.

6.   Public communication is the study and practice of speaking in front of an audience.

7.   Intercultural communication looks at the communication practices of other cultures and how we negotiate communication between cultures.

VII.   Despite its breadth of scope, the field of communication has several unifying themes.

A.   Regardless of the area of interest, all communication is symbolic in nature.

B.   All communication is concerned with meaning and how meaning is communicated and interpreted.

C. Critical thinking, the act of weighing ideas carefully, considering evidence, and looking at alternative courses of action or explanations, is a part of any communicative encounter.

D. Critical thinking, the act of weighing ideas carefully, considering evidence, and looking at alternative courses of action or explanations, is a part of any communicative encounter.

E. Communication in all domains involves issues of ethics, such as freedom of speech, social change, manipulative communication, or corruptive behavior.

VIII. The career opportunities for communication majors are many.

A. Research fields such as media research or marketing are good fields for communication majors.

B. Majors may choose to pursue education in a formal sense such as elementary, junior or senior high, or at the more advanced university level.

C. Majors can choose a career in media production, analysis, and criticism, including news-reporting, script-writing, or television broadcasting.

D. Communication majors can work in a consulting capacity for independent consulting firms or in corporate training and development programs.

E. Human relations and management both require excellent communication skills such as negotiating, customer relations, and persuasion.

IX. Applying Communication in Our Lives

Name_____

1.1   Tuning in to the Relationship Level of Meaning

Purpose
To increase awareness of relationship level meanings in interpersonal communication.

Instructions
Read the dialogue below. Identify relationship levels of meaning that seem to be implied by each line of dialogue.

Jim: Jan, you haven't done the laundry this week.

Jan: Right, and you haven't done the shopping.

Jim: But laundry is more important than shopping. After all, we can't go anywhere without clothes.

Jan: We probably can't do much without food, either.

Jim: You're trying to divert the conversation away from laundry which is the issue I brought up.

Jan: No. I am trying to make you aware that we both agreed to do certain chores around this place and you have been as bad as me about not getting to the chores you agreed to do.

Jim: Okay, fair enough. I see your point and I apologize for not doing the shopping. I'll do it tomorrow.

Jan: Thanks. I can probably find time to do the laundry tonight so you won't have to shop in dirty clothes.

Jim: Good. I knew I could count on you.

Jan: Only if I can count on you, too.

1.2   Learning About Intercultural Communication

Purpose
To increase your awareness of how differently cultures communicate in common exchanges.

Instructions
Interview three fellow students, each from a different country, and all different from your own country. Ask them the following questions and record their answers. Write a short paragraph describing what you now understand about cultural origins of communication that you did not understand before you began this activity.

Questions to ask:

1. How do strangers greet each other in your country?

2. How far apart do strangers stand as they are introduced?

3. How do people choose a place to sit in a café in which 2/3 of the seats are occupied?

4. How do parents typically discipline their children?

5. How would members of a committee in an office workplace work out disagreements?

6. What do people from your country consider polite behavior?

What I understand now about how differently cultures communicate in the same settings that I did not understand before is…

Name_____

1.3   Recognizing Dimensions of Relationship Level Meanings

Purpose
To increase your awareness of relationship level meanings in interpersonal communication.

Instructions
Relationship level meanings have three dimensions: liking, responsiveness, and power. In each of the following examples of communication, identify which dimension of relationship level meaning seems to predominate.

1. When Edwin's parents criticize him for not coming home more often, he responds by saying, "Look, I'm 20 years old and you can't expect me to be at home every weekend."

    Dimension of relationship level of meaning:

2. Frances says to her 5-year-old daughter, "You clean up your room right now."

    Dimension of relationship level of meaning:

3. Adrienne asks her friend, Malcolm, if he wants to come over for dinner and conversation.

    Dimension of relationship level of meaning:

4. Jerry tells his friend, Michael, about a personal problem, and Michael doesn't respond. Jerry then says, "Hey, am I invisible or mute or something?"

    Dimension of relationship level of meaning:

5. Soyanna says to her boyfriend, "I think you are the greatest person in the world."

    Dimension of relationship level of meaning:

6. As Kim talks, Pat nods her head and smiles to show that she is following what Kim says and that she is interested.

   Dimension of relationship level of meaning:

7. Chantelle did not agree with the grade she received on her History essay and says to her professor, "I don't understand why I received such a poor grade on this essay. I really put a lot of effort into this paper."

   Dimension of relationship level of meaning:

8. At a job interview, the interviewer says, "Hi Tom. It's nice to meet you. Thanks for taking the time to visit with me this afternoon."

   Dimension of relationship level of meaning:

Name_____

1.4   Assessing Satisfaction with Communication Skills

Purpose

To allow you to assess how satisfied you are with your ability to communicate in different situations.

Instructions

Listed below are 10 communication situations. Imagine that you are involved in each situation. For each, indicate how confident you are that you could communicate competently. Use the following scale to indicate how satisfied you are that you could communicate well.

1. Very satisfied that I could communicate competently
2. Somewhat satisfied that I could communicate competently
3. Not sure how effectively I could communicate
4. Somewhat dissatisfied with my ability to communicate effectively
5. Very dissatisfied with my ability to communicate effectively

_____1.   Someone asks you personal questions that you feel uncomfortable answering. You'd like to tell the person that you don't want to answer, but you don't want to hurt the person's feelings.

_____2.   You think a friend is starting to drink more alcohol than is healthy. You want to bring up the topic with your friend, but you don't want to create a barrier in the friendship.

_____3.   You really care about the person you've been dating recently, but neither of you has ever put your feelings into words. You'd like to express how you feel, but aren't sure how your partner will respond.

_____4.   During a heated discussion about social issues, the person with whom you are talking says, "Why won't you hear me out fairly??!"

_____5.   A friend shares his creative writing with you and asks if you think he has any talent. You don't think the writing is very good, and you need to respond to his request for an opinion.

_____6.   Your roommate's habits are really getting on your nerves. You want to tell your roommate you're bothered, but you don't want to cause hurt.

_____7.   A classmate asks you for notes for the classes he missed. You agree, but then discover he has missed nearly half of the classes and expects you to bail him out. You feel that's exploitive.

_____8.   You go to a party and discover that you don't know anyone there.

_____9.   The person you have been dating declares "I love you." You care about the person but your feelings are not love, at least not yet. The person expects some response from you.

_____10.   A person you care about comes to you whenever he has problems he wants to discuss, and you give him attention and advice. When you want to talk about your problems, however, he doesn't seem to have time. You want the friendship to continue, but you don't like feeling it's one-way.

Processing

A score of 40 to 50 indicates that you are very satisfied with your ability to communicate in a range of interpersonal situations. A score of 25 to 39 indicates either that you are fairly satisfied with your ability to communicate in various situations, or that you are highly satisfied with your communication skills in some situations and relatively dissatisfied with your skills in other situations. A score of 24 or lower indicates that you are less satisfied with your interpersonal communication skills than you would like to be.

If your score indicates you are moderately satisfied or dissatisfied with your interpersonal communication skills, notice whether your answers are extremes (1s and 5s) or tend to be more average. Extreme ratings indicate that you are very satisfied with your ability to interact in some situations and very dissatisfied with your ability to interact in others. You should focus on improving your skills in the specific situations that make you uneasy. If you have more average scores for most or all of the 10 items, then you might work on further enhancing skills that you already have.

Retake this questionnaire when you complete the course and compare your scores for now and then.

1.5   Understanding Communication Systems

Purpose
To increase your understanding of the interrelatedness of interpersonal communication.

Instructions

1. Describe a major change that occurred in your life. Examples of major changes are coming to college, making a major romantic commitment, and experiencing a serious accident or illness.

2. Describe specific ways in which the change affected you. Explain how it affected your feelings, your ability to do things, the people you interacted with, your priorities, and so forth.

3. Identify 3 people who were close to you at the time the change occurred in your life. Describe how the change in your life affected each of them. Did you interact more or less with them? Did you alter the nature of your communication with them? Did your relationships with them change? Did you ask or expect new things of them?

Person 1:

Person 2:

Person 3:

4. Reflect on the ways in which a change in one aspect of a communication system (in this case, the change you experienced) affects all other elements of a system (in this case, the 3 people who were close to you when the change occurred).

Name_____

1.6   Monitoring in Action

Purpose
To increase your awareness of your monitoring activities in everyday life.

Instructions
On the following pages identify four communication behaviors that you are currently attempting to regulate or change or that you would like to change. For each behavior that you specify, identify three specific behaviors that you associate with the undesirable activity and that you could use to monitor the activity. Then describe three specific statements you do or could say to yourself to call your attention to the behavior and to encourage the desired change.

MONITORING

Behavior to be Monitored	Focus of Attention	Self-Communication
Interrupting others	1. Impatience with others when they are speaking.	1. Be quiet.
	2. Amount of talk by me.	2. You've said enough.
	3. People who are not participating in the conversation.	3. Invite someone else to speak
A.	1.	1.
	2.	2.
	3.	3.
B.	1.	1.
	2.	2.
	3.	3.
C.	1.	1.
	2.	2.
	3.	3.
D.	1.	1.
	2.	2.
	3.	3.

1.7   Social Media: Navigating Your Way

Purpose
To help you become familiar with different types of Social Media.

Instructions
Different types of social media can help you research different communication contexts. Answer each question below, using information and resources you find on the Internet and through interpersonal communication. *Why would having this information be helpful to students in a human communication course?* Report your findings to your class.

1.   How many in your class have a Facebook?

Answer:_____

    A. What are the benefits of having a Facebook?
        1. To your self-image?
        2. To your relationships?
        3. To your profession?
        4. To your culture?
    B. What are the drawbacks of having a Facebook?
        1. To your self-image?
        2. To your relationships?
        3. To your profession?
        4. To your culture?

2.   How many in your class use Twitter?

Answer: _____

    A. How does Twitter change the way people communicate? Find data from interviews, online research, and library databases.
    B. How has Twitter changed the way businesses and customers communicate? Interview business professionals, conduct online research, and consult library databases.

3.   How many in your class use Foursquare?

Answer: _____

    A. What are some of the personal risks involved in using Foursquare?
    B. How can businesses benefit from Foursquare?

1.8   Using Your Online Resources—Applying
      Communication in Our Lives

Chapter 1 Case Study: Speech of Self-Introduction

Purpose
To help you prepare for your own introductory speech assignment by analyzing the Speech of Self-Introduction included under Speech Interactive on your Online Resources for *Communication in Our Lives*. You can complete this activity online or on this worksheet.

Instructions
Evaluate Mona's speech by completing the checklist and answering the questions below.

1. Does Mona's speech give you a sense of who she is?

2. Did Mona's introduction catch your attention and give you a road map of what she would cover in this speech?

3. How did Mona create identification between herself and listeners?

4. How did examples add to the speech?

5. Was the quotation from Sasha effective?

6. Did Mona's conclusion create closure by returning to the theme of her introduction?

Overall, how would you rate the speech?

_____ Excellent   _____ Good   _____ Average   _____ Fair   _____ Poor

1.9   Case Study: Communication Counts

Purpose
To assist you in locating articles about the communication discipline and to demonstrate the practical purpose of communication skills in your life.

Instructions
Locate and read the article listed below, and answer the following questions.

Pearce, W. B. (2008). Toward a new repertoire of communication skills for leaders and managers. The Quality Management Forum, 34 (Fall, #4), 4–7.

1. Explain the mismatch between needs of the organization and the skills of professionals presented in the article?

2. What is the current view of communication?

3. What is the emerging view of communication?

4. According to the article, what should be included in a new repertoire of communication skills?

5. Where do you need to focus or improve your communication skills?

Self-Test for Chapter 1

Multiple Choice

_____ 1. How old is the field of communication?
   A. 1000 years
   B. over 2000 years
   C. 50 years
   D. 100 years

_____ 2. Mr. Davies walks in to find his 6th grade English class having a food fight. He tells them, "EVERYONE SIT DOWN, **RIGHT NOW**!" The content level of Mr. Davies' message is
   A. he is angry with the class
   B. he is an authority figure
   C. he wants the students to sit down
   D. he wants the class to be quiet

_____ 3. The many areas in the field of communication are unified by which central theme(s)?
   A. feedback and symbols
   B. symbols and meaning
   C. noise and feedback
   D. messages and noise

_____ 4. The most sophisticated model of communication is
   A. linear
   B. interactive
   C. pluralistic
   D. transactional

_____ 5. Which of the following is NOT a limitation of the interactive models of communication presented in the textbook?
   A. They don't acknowledge we are simultaneously sending and receiving messages.
   B. They are not dynamic.
   C. They see communication as constant.
   D. They view communicators as active participants.

_____ 6. Ilya is taking notes in his 8:00 a.m. communication class. He is thinking about his brother who is sick at home. While engaged in thought, Ilya doesn't hear what his professor said the assignment is for the next class. Ilya did not get the assignment due to
   A. worry
   B. daydreaming
   C. noise
   D. feedback

_____ 7. In organizations, employees generally have shared understandings of their organization's goals and values, as well as appropriate codes of conduct on the job. These shared understandings are called
A. organizational themes
B. work life codes
C. organizational culture
D. professional etiquette

_____ 8. We would understand Mei-Ling's hesitation to argue for her ideas because to do so would be impolite if we learned which of the following areas of communication?
A. organizational communication
B. intercultural communication
C. public communication
D. interpersonal communication

_____ 9. When Paula goes off to college, her family no longer has long conversations at the dinner table discussing everyone's days. This scenario best exemplifies which definitional component of communication?
A. communication is a process
B. communication is inevitable
C. communication is systemic
D. communication is symbolic

_____ 10. Symbols include all but which of the following?
A. language
B. art and music
C. nonverbal behaviors
D. significance

_____ 11. Darya is sitting in the union having coffee and talking to another professor whom she does not know very well. Darya is engaged in what type of communication?
A. intrapersonal communication
B. interpersonal communication
C. organizational communication
D. public communication

_____ 12. Results of a poll taken in 1999 showed that a majority of Americans perceive which of the following to be the #1 reason marriages fail?
A. sexual difficulties
B. communication difficulties
C. money problems
D. interference from in-laws

_____ 13. Of the values associated with understanding communication, which can be associated with ethical communication?
A. cultural
B. personal
C. professional
D. a, b, and c

_____ 14. Which of the following is not a critical thinking skill?
    A.   interchanging facts and inferences
    B.   applying concepts learned in one context to other contexts
    C.   identifying assumptions behind statements, claims, and arguments
    D.   evaluating evidence to determine relevance, value, and reliability

_____ 15. We engage in self-talk to all but which of the following?
    A.   plan our lives
    B.   rehearse different ways of doing things
    C.   slam on the brakes when an animal jumps in front of our car
    D.   prompt ourselves to do or not to do particular things

True/False

_____ 1. In intimate relationships, the primary values of communication are problem solving and self-disclosure.

_____ 2. Communication with others has no significant impact on recovering from illness.

_____ 3. In the workplace, poor communication can cost time and money.

_____ 4. George Herbert Meade said that humans are "talked into" humanity.

_____ 5. Learning about communication and practicing skills can make you more effective.

_____ 6. We study communication to help us make sense of what happens in our lives.

_____ 7. Most good managers lack effective communication skills.

_____ 8. Communication is a process, meaning it is ongoing and changing continually.

_____ 9. You and your friends are capable of engaging in group communication.

_____ 10. Everyday talk and nonverbal interaction are not nearly so important as significant self-disclosure of feelings in maintaining relationships.

Essay

1. Describe the relationship between communication and personal life. Your essays should discuss both the role of communication in shaping identity and the values of communication to individuals.

2. Define the concept of critical thinking. Explain why critical thinking is a unifying theme in the study of communication.

3. Explore the five "Careers in Communication." Write an essay explaining why each area would or would not be of interest to you.

Chapter 1 Flash Cards

Cut out the cards, write the answers on the back, and you will have a packet of flash cards for each chapter. Paraphrasing definitions will help you remember them.

Communication	Content Level of Meaning	Critical Thinking
Feedback	Interpersonal Communication	Intrapersonal Communication
Noise	Organizational Culture	Process
Relationship Level of Meaning	Symbol	System

Chapter 2: Perception and Communication

Chapter Summary

I.   Perception is the tool to find meaning, and meaning is the heart of communication.

II.   Perception is an active process of selecting, organizing, and interpreting what we encounter in the world, and consists of 3 processes that are interactive, which means that each affects the other two.

    A.   Selection involves choosing which stimuli to attend to.
        1.   We notice stimuli that stand out because they are immediate, relevant, or intense.
        2.   The stimuli to which we attend are influenced by how keen our senses are.
        3.   We tend to notice stimuli when there is a change or variation.
        4.   We attend to stimuli based on our motives and needs.
        5.   We deliberately influence what we notice through self-indication.
        6.   We attend to those stimuli that fulfill our expectations.

    B.   Organization explains how we construct meaning through a variety of cognitive structures called **schemata** using a theory called **constructivism**.
        1.   A prototype is an ideal. It is your notion of the most perfect representation of a category.
        2.   Personal constructs are mental yardsticks that allow us to position people and situations through different dimensions of judgment.
        3.   Stereotypes are generalizations about people and situations. These generalizations can be both truthful and misleading.
        4.   Scripts allow us to define what we expect ourselves and others to do and say in specific situations.

    C.   Interpretation is the subjective process of assigning meaning to our perceptions.
        1.   Attributions are explanations of why things happen and why people act as they do. Attributions have four dimensions.
            a.   Locus is a judgment as to whether the cause is internal or external.
            b.   Stability is a judgment as to whether the cause is stable or unstable.
            c.   Scope is a judgment as to whether the reason is global or specific.
            d.   Responsibility is a judgment as to whether a person has control over the action or not.

    D.   The self-serving bias says that we tend to make attributions that serve our own interests; if something good happens to us, it is because we are always deserving, or we have done something to bring it about. Negative actions and failures are attributed to factors beyond our personal control.

III.   Perceptions are influenced by several different factors.

    A.   Physiology, including our sensory abilities, physiological state, and age impact perception.

    B.   Culture, or the beliefs, values, understandings, practices and ways of interpreting experiences that are shared by a number of people.

     1.   Standpoint theory claims cultures include a number of social communities that have different degrees of social status and privilege. Each social community distinctively shapes the perceptions, identities, and opportunities of its members.

     2.   Gendered locations explain the difference between the amount of effort women and men invest in maintenance communication.

C.   Social roles, how we fill those roles and the demands of those roles shape our perceptions.

D.   Cognitive abilities, or how elaborately we are able to think about something, shapes perception.

     1.   Cognitive complexity refers to the number, level of abstraction, and level of elaboration people use to shape perceptions.

     2.   Person-centered perception allows us to perceive another as a unique individual distinct from his/her social community.

IV.   To enhance our communication competence, we should understand how perception and communication affect each other.

A.   Perceptions, communication, and abstraction clarify and distort how we interact in the world.

B.   Viewing communication as an abstract process offers five guidelines for enhancing competence:

     1.   Recognize that all perceptions are subjective; there is no truth or falsity to people's perceptions.

     2.   Avoid mindreading, assuming we understand what another person thinks.

     3.   Check our perceptions with others to make sure we are interpreting meaning correctly.

     4.   Distinguish between facts and inferences to help us avoid misperceptions.

     5.   Monitor the self-serving bias and critically assess our perceptions and attributions.

2.1   Observing the Impact of Language on Perceptions

Purpose
To increase awareness of the influence of language on human perception.

Instructions

1. Ask 5 people the two questions below and record their answers. ***Did you see the article on tuition increases in today's campus newspaper?***
    Answer 1:

    Answer 2:

    Answer 3:

    Answer 4:

    Answer 5:

    How much do you think this school can inflate the cost of tuition?
    Answer 1:

    Answer 2:

    Answer 3:

    Answer 4:

    Answer 5:

2. Ask 5 different people the two questions below and record their answers. ***Did you see an article on tuition increases in today's campus newspaper?***
    Answer 1:

    Answer 2:

    Answer 3:

    Answer 4:

    Answer 5:

How much do you think this school can nudge the cost of tuition?

Answer 1:

Answer 2:

Answer 3:

Answer 4:

Answer 5:

3. Compare and contrast the answers. How do perceptions differ when the words "inflate" and "nudge" are heard?

2.2   Distinguishing Fact from Inference

Purpose
To increase your skill in distinguishing between facts and inferences.

Instructions
Read the story below. Then decide whether each of the statements that follow the story is a fact or an inference. Correct answers appear with the Chapter 2 Self-Test Answers.

Jane went to the mall to get a new pair of shoes. Even though she didn't have the money to pay for them, Jane felt that she needed the shoes. After looking in several stores, she found a pair she really liked, but they cost $85.00. Jane knew she couldn't afford that. Later when Jane wore her new shoes, she got compliments from all of her friends.

1. Jane bought the $85.00 pair of shoes.

2. Jane stole the $85.00 pair of shoes.

3. After going to the mall, Jane wore the $85.00 pair of shoes.

4. Jane thought she needed a new pair of shoes.

5. Jane is irresponsible with money.

2.3   Remaking the Social World

Purposes

To enhance your awareness of the arbitrariness and the impact of categories societies use to define people.

To allow you to imagine how society would be different if different categories for defining people were used.

Instructions

Join with 5 or 6 other people in your class to form a discussion group. Your group's task is to devise a method of classifying people and to suggest some of the implications of the classifications that you devise. The only restriction on how you complete the task is that you may not use race, class, sex, or sexual orientation to define and classify individuals. After 20 minutes of group discussion, make a report to the class in which you:

A. Describe your system of classifying people.

B. Provide a rationale for the method of classification you chose.

C. Explain some of the political, economic, educational, and social consequences that would be likely if people were classified and thus perceived only with reference to your system.

2.4   Making Attributions

Purposes
To give you practice in making different kinds of attributions.

To heighten your awareness of how different kinds of attributions affect meaning.

Instructions
On the following four pages, you will find seven scenarios that describe what you or others do. For each one, create alternative attributions that explain what happened. Write your attributions in the spaces provided.

After creating alternative attributions, consider how the different explanations affect your interpretation of the scenario. Does it mean different things to you depending on the attributions you make?

Alternate Attributions

Example

While walking down the street, you trip and fall. Explain why you fell.

Internal/stable attribution:	I am a clumsy person.
Internal/unstable attribution:	I am lightheaded today.
External/stable attribution:	This town never fixes sidewalks.
External/unstable attribution:	This sidewalk is temporarily unsafe due to debris from construction.

1. Although you didn't study as much as you thought you should, you make an A on an examination. Explain the grade you received.

    Internal/stable:

    Internal/unstable:

    External/stable:

    External/unstable:

2. You are turned down for admission to the graduate program you wanted to attend. Explain why you were not admitted.

    Internal/stable:

    Internal/unstable:

    External/stable:

    External/unstable:

3. In conversation with a friend, you disagree with your friend's opinion. The friend calls you a jerk. Explain your friend's remark.

    Internal/stable:

    Internal/unstable:

    External/stable:

    External/unstable:

4. You ask a professor if you may come by to talk about your term paper later today. The professor says, "I can't see you today." Explain the professor's comment.

   Internal/stable:

   Internal/unstable:

   External/stable:

   External/unstable:

5. You campaign for a campus office and are defeated in the election. Explain your defeat.

   Internal/stable:

   Internal/unstable:

   External/stable:

   External/unstable:

6. You intend to get up at 6 a.m. to put in a full day studying. You awake at 10 a.m. and realize you turned off your alarm but didn't get up when it went off 4 hours ago. How do you explain sleeping in?

   Internal/stable:

   Internal/unstable:

   External/stable:

   External/unstable:

7. When you return home after classes, your roommate's clothes are strewn all over the place and unwashed dishes are on the table. Explain why your roommate left the room in a mess.

Internal/stable:

Internal/unstable:

External/stable:

External/unstable:

2.5   Perceptions of Groups

Purpose
To help clarify how we perceive different groups of people, the impressions we form, and how easily stereotypes are created.

Instructions
List as many adjectives or descriptive phrases as you can for the following groups of people.

1. Soccer Moms:

    _____
    _____
    _____

2. Football Players:

    _____
    _____
    _____

3. Single Mothers:

    _____
    _____
    _____

4. College Professors/Instructors:

    _____
    _____
    _____

5. Middle-aged Males:

    _____
    _____
    _____

6. Male Cheerleaders:

    _____
    _____
    _____

7. Attorneys:

    _____
    _____
    _____

8. Gay/Lesbian Individuals:

_____
_____
_____

9. Truck Drivers:

_____
_____
_____

10. Sorority/Fraternity Members:

_____
_____
_____

Processing:

1. How easy or difficult was it to come up with adjectives or descriptive phrases?

2. Why might some groups be easier to generate lists for than others?

3. How does your list of terms for each group relate to stereotyping?

4. How might you avoid the negative effects of stereotyping people in these groups or other groups not listed?

2.6 Using Your Online Resources—Experiencing *Communication in Our Lives*

Chapter 2 Case Study: College Success

Purpose
To apply the principles you learned about perception and communication in Chapter 2 to the communication scenario *College Success* included under Communication Scenarios on the Online Resources for *Communication in Our Lives*. You can complete this activity online or on this worksheet.

Instructions
Analyze the *College Success* scenario by answering the questions below.

Scenario Overview
Jim is having a problem with his parents. According to Jim, his father's expectations are too high for Jim's academic work. As you watch and listen to Jim's conversation with his father and Sam, look for examples of mind reading, self-serving bias, and attribution errors.

Conversation Analysis

1. Both Jim and his parents make attributions to explain his grades. Describe the dimensions of Jim's attributions and those of his parents.

2. How might you assess the accuracy of Jim's attributions? What questions could you ask him to help you decide whether his perceptions are well founded or biased?

3. What constructs, prototypes, and scripts seem to operate in how Jim and his parents think about college life and being a student?

4. What could you say to Jim to help him and his parents reach some more shared perspective on his academic work?

Name_____

2.7   What's the Situation?

Purpose
To aid in your understanding of perception.

Instructions
Read the following story and answer the questions below:

After a terrible traffic accident, a father and child are brought into the hospital. The father is unconscious and the child needs emergency surgery. The surgeon comes in to begin the procedure, but stops immediately, exclaiming, "I can't operate on my baby!"

1. Why is the father unconscious?
2. Who is the surgeon?
3. Is the child male or female?
4. How old is the child?

Processing:

Compare your answer with four of your classmates.

Did you all get the same answers? If not, why?

How does perception impact how you interpret the story?

2.8   Analyzing Your Self-Fulfilling Prophecy

Purpose

To increase your awareness of how you perceive yourself and how that perception affects your communication behaviors.

Instructions

List 10 words or phrases that other people said **about** you **to** you as you were growing up. Then describe the self-perception each led you to develop. For example, if your grandfather said, "You are always late," you might perceive yourself as disorganized.

Word or Phrase	Self-Perception
1.	
2.	
3.	
4.	
5.	
6.	
7.	
8.	
9.	
10.	

Look at your list of words. Putting them all together, how would you describe your overall self-perception? For example, if you understand yourself to be disorganized, do you then perceive yourself to be incompetent?

Have you lived up to your label, acting in ways that are consistent with your self-perception? How?

What can you do to develop a more constructive, positive self-perception?

Self-Test for Chapter 2

Multiple Choice

_____ 1.   Which of the following is NOT a dimension of attributions?
  A.   internal/external locus
  B.   stable/unstable
  C.   organized/disorganized
  D.   global/specific scope

_____ 2.   Justin says, "I didn't make the team, but it wasn't because I wasn't good enough. The coach knew everyone but me and he didn't want any unknowns." Justins's explanation for not making the team illustrates
  A.   self-fulfilling prophecy
  B.   self-serving bias
  C.   the influence of social roles
  D.   cultural sense making

_____ 3.   "Dr. Pardo is the best professor I've ever had." In this statement, Dr. Pardo is a
  A.   prototype
  B.   stereotype
  C.   personal construct
  D.   script

_____ 4.   We use schemata to
  A.   determine attributions
  B.   develop empathy
  C.   organize perceptions
  D.   enhance communication competence

_____ 5.   Self-fulfilling prophecy is a phenomenon in which a person
  A.   moves beyond stereotype to person-centered perception
  B.   acts in ways consistent with how they have learned to perceive themselves
  C.   assigns meaning to words, actions, objects, people, and events
  D.   achieves standpoint

_____ 6.   Schemata discussed in the text include all of the following EXCEPT
  A.   themes
  B.   prototypes
  C.   scripts
  D.   personal constructs

_____ 7. A culture is made up of many large groups, such as Caucasian females, students with disabilities, or Native Americans. Each of these groups constitutes a(n)
   A. social community or co-culture
   B. stratum
   C. demographic
   D. attribution

_____ 8. Elvira assumes she knows what her roommate would want for dinner so she fixes what she thinks her roommate would like. Elvira has engaged in
   A. mindreading
   B. static evaluation
   C. polarized thinking
   D. empathy

_____ 9. Michael sees a person stumbling out of a local bar and Michael says to himself, "That dude is drunk." Michael has failed to distinguish between
   A. perception and interpretation
   B. prototypes and scripts
   C. facts and inferences
   D. empathy and person-perception

_____ 10. A word that is especially likely to lead to confusion between facts and inferences is
   A. seems
   B. is
   C. think
   D. true

_____ 11. Explanations of why things happen and why people act as they do best define
   A. attributions
   B. selection
   C. interpretations
   D. schemata

_____ 12. Andrea said to her friend, Tracey, "I'll never find a husband as long as I live in this town. There just aren't any available men here." Andrea is likely communicating
   A. a self-serving bias
   B. poor cognitive complexity
   C. a self-fulfilling prophecy
   D. a person-centered perception

_____ 13. Police officers are friendly, honest, good people who protect society from crime and always enforce the law for the social good. This description of police officers is a(n)
   A. attribution
   B. cognitive construct
   C. schema
   D. stereotype

_____ 14. Carrie came to my office one day to talk about her lack of hope due to anorexia. Typically, I classify everyone I hear about in this situation as dumb and out of control. However, because I knew Carrie as a strong but quiet student, my stereotype did not fit. I was engaging in
A.   cognitive scripting
B.   interpretation
C.   organization
D.   person-centered perception

_____ 15. You decide to switch to another section of your Communication Class because the instructor just isn't as passionate about the subject as your high school Speech teacher was. Your choice is an example of
A.   cognitive construct
B.   attribution
C.   script
D.   perception

True/False

_____ 1. Constructivism is the process of making sense of the world using schemata.

_____ 2. Prototypes are bi-polar mental yardsticks.

_____ 3. People who are cognitively complex tend to be less person-centered than people who are less so.

_____ 4. Understanding that North American culture is highly individualistic can assist your efforts to practice person-centered perception when you are introduced to a North American who lives a communal lifestyle.

_____ 5. Person-centered is synonymous with empathy.

_____ 6. All stereotypes are negative and harmful perceptions.

_____ 7. Because perceptions are objective, we don't need to check them with others.

_____ 8. To move from a social location to a standpoint, a person must develop political awareness.

_____ 9. Standpoint theory states that a culture includes a number of social communities that have different degrees of social status and privilege.

_____ 10. "Professors make a lot of money" is a fact.

Essay

1. Define mindreading and discuss an experience you've had where it caused a disruption in communication.

2. Using a specific example, explain and illustrate the ladder of abstraction. Your essay should demonstrate clearly how the ladder of abstraction pertains to interpersonal communication.

3. Identify and explain 4 of the 5 influences on perception discussed in the text.

Chapter 2 Flash Cards

Cut out the cards, write the answers on the back, and you will have a packet of flash cards for each chapter. Paraphrasing the definitions will help you remember them.

Attribution	Cognitive Complexity	Constructivis
Culture	Empathy	Interpretation
Meaning	Mind Reading	Perception
Personal Construct	Person-centered Perception	Prototype
Schemata	Script	Self-fulfilling Prophecy

Chapter 2 Flash Cards continued

Use the remaining cards for other concepts you would like to remember or study.

Self-serving Bias	Standpoint Theory	Stereotype

Chapter 3: Communication and Personal Identity

Chapter Summary

I.   The self is a process that evolves and changes throughout our lifetime.
   A.   The self involves the internalization of behaviors acquired in the process of communication.

   B.   The self develops through communication with others.
      1.   Family members, especially parents, help shape our self.
         a.   Parents help us define the self through direct definition, telling us what we are, e.g., "boy" or "girl".
         b.   Parents also help us develop our self through identity scripts that teach us who we are and who we should be, such as our social roles and how we are to perform them.
         c.   Parents also shape our self through attachment styles, which determine the value we place on self and others.
            i.   Secure attachment style
            ii.   Fearful attachment style
            iii. Dismissive attachment style
            iv.   Anxious/ambivalent attachment style
      2.   Interaction with peers helps us develop a sense of self.
         a.   We rate ourselves in comparison to others we know to decide who we are like and from whom we are different.
         b.   Through **social comparison**, we compare ourselves with others and judge our own talents, attractiveness, leadership skills, school performance, and other similar characteristics.
      3.   Our interactions with our society shape our self by providing our basic cultural values.
         a.   Our self is shaped by the general interactional patterns that are the norm for our society.
         b.   The media also provides much information about our society which we internalize.
         c.   Other institutions, such as schools and churches, also help to shape our values and our self.
      4.   Our own intrapersonal interactions also may help shape the self through self-fulfilling prophecies.

   C.   The self is multidimensional.
      1.   There is the physical self.
      2.   We have a cognitive self.
      3.   We have an emotional self.
      4.   We have a social self.
      5.   We have a moral self.

   D.   The self is a process that develops and changes over time.
      1.   The self begins when we learn **ego boundaries**, or an understanding of where we stop and the rest of the world begins.
      2.   As we continually encounter new information, we accept some, reject some, and our self changes.

E. The self internalizes and acts from social perspectives.
  1. **Particular others** are people whose opinions and ideas matter to us.
  2. **Reflected appraisal** is seeing ourselves through someone else's eyes.
  3. The **generalized other** is the collection of rules, roles, and attitudes of the social community in which we live—overall society.
   a. We learn about our race.
   b. We learn appropriate gender roles.
   c. We learn sexual orientation.
   d. We learn about our socioeconomic class.
   e. The generalized other helps us see what is "normal" and "right."

F. Social perspectives on the self are constructed and changeable.
  1. Our ideas about the self are socially constructed by society based on what is important to the society at the time.
  2. Social values are constructed and variable.
  3. Social perspectives are fluid and can be changed in response to efforts to weave new meaning into common life. People can collectively work together to create change in terms of social practices or views about certain social groups.

II. The self can be enhanced and improved.

 A. Make a firm commitment to improve yourself.
  1. All change takes persistent effort.
  2. People have a tendency to resist change.

 B. Gain knowledge as a basis for personal change.
  1. First, understand how the self is formed.
  2. Second, develop goals you can achieve.
  3. Look to others as role models or for helpful information and support in making a change.

 C. Set realistic goals.

 D. Accept yourself as being in a process.
  1. Change is not instantaneous.
  2. Accept yourself where you are at present and recognize that you can change.

 E. Create a supportive environment to change.
  1. Surround yourself with people who will encourage you and be supportive.
  2. Avoid self-sabotage by giving yourself negative self-talk; instead, give yourself positive messages.

3.1 Comparing Your Views and Others' Views of Yourself

Purpose
To provide insight into how you and others perceive you and differences in the two views of you.

Instructions
1. Fill out the form below by indicating how true of yourself you think each statement is.
2. Ask someone you think knows you well to fill out the duplicate form that follows. Write your name in the blank space on the second form.
3. Compare the two views of you. Discuss differences with the other person and try to understand why you and the other person might perceive you differently.

Rank each item for how true it is of you. Use the following scale:
1 = very true or always true
2 = mostly true or usually true
3 = somewhat true or true in some situations
4 = mostly untrue or usually untrue
5 = untrue or never true

_____ 1. I am an optimistic person.

_____ 2. I am personally mature.

_____ 3. I am extroverted.

_____ 4. I am thoughtful about others and their feelings.

_____ 5. I am ambitious.

_____ 6. I am generally cheerful, or upbeat.

_____ 7. I am moody.

_____ 8. I am a reliable friend.

_____ 9. I am unconventional in my beliefs.

_____ 10. I am assertive.

Form to be filled out by a person who knows you well

Rank each item for how true it is of _____.

(your name)

Use the following scale:

1 = very true or always true
2 = mostly true or usually true
3 = somewhat true or true in some situations
4 = mostly untrue or usually untrue
5 = untrue or never true

_____   1.   is an optimistic person

_____   2.   is personally mature

_____   3.   is extroverted

_____   4.   is thoughtful about others and their feelings

_____   5.   is ambitious

_____   6.   is cheerful, or upbeat

_____   7.   is moody

_____   8.   is a reliable friend

_____   9.   is unconventional in his/her beliefs

_____ 10. is assertive

3.2   Recognizing the Communication of Uppers, Downers, & Vultures

Purpose
To increase your awareness of the communication styles of people who are uppers, downers, and vultures.

Instructions
Identify three people with whom you interact. One person should be someone who is an upper for you; the second person should be a downer for you; the third person should be a vulture for you. Write the name of the three people in the three blanks at the left of the form below. Beside each name, describe specific verbal and nonverbal communication that the person uses to enact the role of upper, downer, or vulture.

Role/Person	Verbal Communication	Nonverbal Communication
Example Upper/ Louise	Compliments me. Talks about strengths.	Smiles when she sees me. Looks interested when I am talking to her.
Upper/ _____		
Downer/_____		
Vulture/_____		

Name_____

3.3   Recognizing Your Social Comparisons

Purpose
To enhance awareness of the influence of social comparisons on your self-concept.

Instructions
1. List 3 positive qualities or abilities of yours and 3 negative qualities or areas in which you think you are unskillful. Write these in the left column of the chart.
2. Identify two people you consider particularly skilled in each of the 6 areas. Identify how you compare to those two specific people.
3. Substitute two different people as comparison points for each quality. Consider how using the substitutes as comparison points alters your view of your own strengths and weaknesses.
4. Reflect on how the skill of the people you select as points for social comparison affect your views of yourself.
5. With others in your class, discuss the importance of realistic choices of people to be our points of social comparison.

Positive Qualities/Areas of Skill	Person 1	Person 2
1.		
2.		
3.		

Negative Qualities/Areas of Lack of Skill	Person 1	Person 2
1.		
2.		
3.		

Positive Qualities/Areas of Skill	Substitute Person 1	Substitute Person 2
1.		
2.		
3.		

Negative Qualities/Areas of Lack of Skill	Substitute Person 1	Substitute Person 2
1.		
2.		
3.		

3.4   Tracking Changes in Social Perspectives

Purpose
To increase awareness of how social perspectives change over time within a single society.

Instructions
1. Identify a person (a family member, acquaintance, or friend) who is 10 to 15 years older than you. Identify another person who is 25 or more years older than you. Identify a third person who is 10 to 15 years younger than you.
2. Write your views of women and men—what they should be like and do, what is un-feminine and un-masculine.
3. Ask each of the three persons you identified to describe his or her views of women and men. Ask them what women should be like and what men should be like. Encourage them to explain what they consider to be un-feminine and un-masculine behaviors, attitudes, roles, and so forth.
4. Compare the views of people of different ages, including yourself as one of the people.
5. Discuss your findings with others in your class to discover whether there are trends in the views of gender that are common in groups of different ages.

Views of gender of person 10–15 years younger than me.

My views of gender.

Views of gender of person 10–15 years older than me.

Views of gender of person 25+ years older than me.

Name_____

3.5   Improving Self Concept

Purpose
To guide you through the process of initiating changes in yourself.

Instructions
Identify one aspect of your interpersonal communication that you would like to change. Keeping that aspect in mind, apply the guidelines below to help you succeed in bringing about the change that you desire. Since changing the self is a process, don't expect immediate results. Instead, keep the form below with you and refer to it at regular intervals during the academic term. Make notes on progress you make in achieving the change you desire.

1. Identify an aspect of your interpersonal communication that you wish to change (examples: I want to be a better listener; I want to be less judgmental; I want to be more assertive):

2. Identify potential barriers to change (example: many of my friends are judgmental and this reinforces my own tendency to be judgmental):

3. Identify sources of knowledge that might help you achieve the change you desire (examples: I could check the library for books on judgmental attitudes and see what the experts say about changing this; I could observe Shelley closely since I think she is very nonjudgmental):

4. Set realistic goals (example: I am not trying to erase judgment from my attitudes; I only want to lessen its pervasiveness in my thinking).

5. Assess yourself fairly (example: I don't have to be as non-judgmental as Shelley; I could also compare myself to Marilyn who is even more judgmental than I am now):

6. Create a supportive context for change (examples: I will spend more time with Shelley; I will resist engaging in self-sabotage with negative self-talk):

7. Accept yourself as in process, and realize that change is more likely to be gradual and incremental than abrupt and complete.

   Assessment of yourself today:

   Assessment of yourself in 2 weeks:

   Assessment of yourself in 1 month:

   Assessment of yourself in 2 months:

   Assessment of yourself at the end of the term:

3.6   Identifying Your Identity Scripts

Purpose
To help you recognize identity scripts communicated to you by members of your family.

Instructions
Complete each sentence below by filling in what you were told by members of your family when you were a young child. Put a check by each of the scripts that you still act on. Assess how these scripts enhance and/or interfere with your life today and your current goals.

1. Money is

    _____

    _____

2. Nobody in our family has ever

    _____

    _____

3. You can/cannot (circle one) trust others _____

    _____

4. The most important goal in life is

    _____

    _____

5. Good people

    _____

    _____

6. You can't trust people who

    _____

    _____

7. Families should

    _____

    _____

8. If you want others to respect you, you should

_____

_____

3.7   Using Your Online Resources—Experiencing
        Communication in Our Lives

Chapter 3 Case Study: Parental Teachings

Purpose
To apply the principles you learned about personal identity and communication in Chapter 3 to the communication scenario *Parental Teachings* included under Communication Scenarios in your Online Resources for *Communication in Our Lives*. You can complete this activity online or on this worksheet.

Instructions
Analyze the *Parental Teachings* scenario by answering the questions below.

Scenario Overview
Kate McDonald is taking her two children, seven-year-old Emma and five-year-old Jeremy, to the neighborhood park. As the scenario opens, the three of them walk into the park and approach a swing set.

Conversation Analysis

1. Identify examples of direct definition in this scenario. How does Kate define Emma and Jeremy?

2. Identify examples of reflected appraisal in this scenario. What appraisals of her son and daughter does Kate reflect to them?

3. What do Emma and Jeremy's responses to Kate suggest about their acceptance of her views of them?

4. To what extent does Kate's communication with her children reflect gender expectations in Western culture?

3.8   Social Comparison and Reflected Appraisals

Purpose
To more clearly understand how we compare ourselves to others and how others' communication about us to us shapes our sense of self.

Directions
In the first section, list 5 things about yourself that you know because of your social comparisons with others. Give specific examples of the comparisons you have made and how these comparisons have shaped your sense of self. In the second section, ask 5 different people to reflect on the questions provided as they relate to you.

Example
Part 1:   *Whenever I get together with my friends to work on crafts, they always compliment me on how creative and innovative I am. I have learned that I am creative and good with crafts.*

Part 2:   Ask someone about your abilities as a student.
I asked Professor Jones. She said that I am attentive and prepared, and that I bring good insight to class discussion.

Part 1:

1. _____

_____

_____

2. _____

_____

_____

3. _____

_____

_____

4. _____

_____

_____

5. _____

_____

_____

Part 2:

1. Others' perceptions of me as an athlete. Person asked:_____

   Response: _____

   _____

2. Others' perceptions of me as a friend. Person asked: _____

   Response: _____

   _____

3. Others' perceptions of me as a student. Person asked: _____

   Class: _____

   Response: _____

   _____

   _____

4. Others' perception of how I handle conflict. Person: _____

   Response: _____

   _____

5. Others' perception of my best qualities. Person: _____

   Response: _____

   _____

Name_____

3.9   Imagining the Self-Perception of Your Favorite TV Characters

Purpose

To increase your awareness of the role self-perception plays in our choices of behaviors as adults.

Instructions

Imagine the answers of three TV characters—one that is verbose and outgoing, one that is relatively stable, and one that is introverted and shy.

Imagine each character answering the following questions:

1. How did your parents treat you when you were very young? in middle school? in high school?

2. How often did you see a person of your same age, sex, race, and class on TV or in movies? Were these characters portrayed positively or negatively?

3. How well did you feel you "fit in" in high school? Why?

4. Did you ever venture out of your socioeconomic class for an event? What was the event and what happened?

5. Did you graduate from high school? Why or why not?

6. Did you make plans for education or training after high school? Why or why not?

Write a brief paragraph identifying the concepts of identity formation at work in each character's story. Describe the interaction of concepts with the character's self-perception and choices.

Self-Test for Chapter 3

Multiple Choice

_____ 1. Katrina's mom tells her, "You are so creative!" when Katrina shows her mom her school art project. Katrina's mom is using _____ to form Katrina's sense of self.
   A. reflected appraisal
   B. direct definition
   C. attribution
   D. attachment style

_____ 2. Frank is consistently loving and responsive to Chuck when they interact, suggesting that Chuck is experiencing which attachment style?
   A. dismissive
   B. anxious/ambivalent
   C. fearful
   D. secure

_____ 3. Which of the following would NOT be considered a dimension of the self as presented in your text?
   A. emotional self
   B. physical self
   C. social self
   D. hypothetical self

_____ 4. Aaron plays ball with two of his friends who are better catchers than he. After a game in which Aaron plays catcher, Stan says, "You're getting better really fast." Aaron is hearing
   A. social comparison
   B. direct definition
   C. self-sabotage
   D. reflected appraisal

_____ 5. When your professor hands back your exam, you immediately ask your fellow classmates how they did. Your behavior is an example of
   A. the looking glass self
   B. direct definition
   C. social comparison
   D. self-sabotage

_____ 6. The general views and values endorsed by a society or social group are called
   A. the perspective of particular others
   B. self-fulfilling prophecy
   C. the perspective of the generalized other
   D. identity scripts

_____ 7. Jimmie's parents continuously tell him "you can't trust others," "look out for yourself because nobody else will," and "don't believe what people tell you." Jimmie grows up to be very independent and he does not rely on others. The independent, distrustful identity that Jimmie develops is clearly influenced by
   A.   self-fulfilling prophecy
   B.   identity scripts
   C.   direct definition
   D.   the ladder of abstraction

_____ 8. Monique dresses like her mom and wears her hair in a similar way. Monique's mom is shaping Monique's sense of self as
   A.   a reflected appraisal
   B.   a particular other
   C.   a generalized other
   D.   a social comparison

_____ 9. Frank and Edwin were assigned to be roommates. For their first 3 months of living together, Frank liked Edwin and thought he was lucky to have gotten such an interesting and considerate roommate. When Edwin discloses that he is gay, Frank moves out. Frank seems to be motivated by
   A.   reflected appraisal
   B.   perceptual incongruity
   C.   cultural relativism
   D.   homophobia

_____ 10. Whenever Alexander sees Zack, Zack makes a disparaging remark about Alexander's weight problem. For Alexander, Zack is a(n)
   A.   downer
   B.   generalized other
   C.   upper
   D.   attachment style

_____ 11. We come to understand the perspective of the Generalized Other
   A.   by interacting with others
   B.   through the media
   C.   through public institutions
   D.   all of the above
   E.   none of the above

_____ 12. No female in Vered's could drive a stick shift automobile, so she believed she couldn't either. She offered to share the driving on a cross-country trip, thinking the car was an automatic. It wasn't, and rather than miss a cool vacation, Vered practiced every night until she was finally able to drive a stick. You could say she got over her _____.
   A.   direct definition
   B.   identity script
   C.   reflected appraisal
   D.   self-fulfilling prophecy

13. Particular others include
    A. family, friends, teachers, ministers
    B. people we see on TV
    C. characters in stories with whom we identify
    D. historical figures

14. Which of the following is NOT a mechanism for helping change our self?
    A. create a supportive context for change
    B. make a commitment to perfectionism
    C. recognize the role of the generalized other
    D. set realistic goals

15. Your mother tells you, "You'll be great at art school!" She is acting as a(n)
    A. upper
    B. downer
    C. vulture
    D. voice of the Generalized Other

True/False

1. Humans have selves at birth.

2. When we say that social perspectives are constructed, we mean that social views develop in particular cultures at certain times to support dominant ideologies.

3. A child who feels she is unlovable most likely grew up with a dismissive attachment style.

4. Downers are other people who harshly attack our self-concepts.

5. "All Ortegas go to college" is an example of an identity script.

6. The social perspective is made up of a single dimension.

7. Sweden's recognition of same-sex marriages demonstrates that social perspectives are variable.

8. Because the self is a process, we develop our ego boundaries over time.

9. The idea that women were too delicate to do men's work until men went off to war shows us that social perspectives are not changeable.

10. Changing one's self-concept involves overcoming humans' inherent resistance to change.

Essay

1. Describe one change you would like to make in yourself. Relying on the discussion in Chapter 3 of your text, explain how you could create a context that supports the change you wish to make.

2. The chapter identifies four parts of self, cognitive, social, emotional, and moral. Discuss how these four aspects of you help define who you are. Is the picture complete without considering other aspects of yourself? Why or why not?

3. Define the Particular Other. What aspects of yourself are most likely the results of influence from particular others? Who was the particular other who most influenced each of these aspects of yourself that you listed?

Chapter 3 Flash Cards

Cut out the cards, write the answers on the back, and you will have a packet of flash cards for each chapter. Paraphrasing the definitions will help you remember them.

Attachment Styles	Particular Others	Self-sabotage
Direct Definition	Perspective of the Generalized Other	Social Comparison
Downers	Uppers	Ego Boundaries
Reflected Appraisal	Vultures	Identity Scripts
Self		

Chapter 4: Listening Effectively

Chapter Summary

I.   Listening is a fundamental communication process.

    A.   The average person spends 45% to 75% of waking hours listening.

    B.   Listening and hearing are not synonymous.
        1.   Hearing is a passive physiological process that happens when sound hits the eardrums.
        2.   Listening is an active process that requires energy and skill to be mindful, physically receive the message, select and organize information, interpret, respond, and remember.

    C.   Listening is a complex process with many component activities.
        1.   The first step in listening is making a decision to be mindful. Mindfulness is being fully engaged in the moment.
            a.   Mindfulness increases our understanding of others.
            b.   Mindfulness can help enhance others' communication.
        2.   Physically receiving messages means we use our senses to take in another's meaning through hearing, reading lips, or signing.
        3.   Selecting and organizing messages is largely unconscious.
            a.   What we select to attend to depends on many factors, including our sex.
            b.   We are more likely to notice messages that are intense, loud, or unusual.
            c.   We organize what we have selected with cognitive schemata.
            d.   We then choose which script to follow in our interaction.
        4.   We interpret communication by putting together pieces to make sense of the overall situation.
        5.   Responding to the other means that we need to communicate attention and interest and be able to state our own thoughts.
        6.   The final step in the listening process is remembering.
            a.   We tend to remember less than half of what we heard immediately after the message.
            b.   After eight hours, we recall only about one third of the message we heard.

II.   There are several obstacles that impede effective listening.

    A.   External obstacles are those things outside of ourselves that get in the way of listening.
        1.   Message overload occurs when we are bombarded with too much information to effectively listen to all of it.
        2.   Listening is impeded by messages that contain information too complex for us to process.
        3.   Environmental noises and events can also get in the way of effective listening.

B. Internal obstacles are psychological obstacles that interfere with our listening.
   1. Preoccupation with something else keeps us from directing our full attention to the message being presented.
   2. Prejudgments occur when we tune out because we think a message or speaker has nothing to offer us.
      a. We assume others' ideas will contribute nothing of value to the conversation.
      b. We assume we know what another feels, thinks, or is going to say.
   3. A lack of effort due to feeling poorly or being overly tired can keep us from effectively listening to a message.
   4. We also may not listen effectively when we fail to accomodate diverse listening styles.

III. Sometimes we find ourselves engaging in nonlistening behaviors.

A. Pseudolistening is pretending to listen when we are really focused on other things.

B. Monopolizing occurs when we dominate the conversation by focusing on our own stories and circumstances rather than on the person talking.
   1. *Conversational rerouting* is when we switch the topic of talk to ourselves.
   2. *Diversionary interrupting* is the interruption of another while directing the topic to something else.

C. Selective listening is focusing only on certain elements of a message.
   1. We may focus only on information that is directly interesting to us or is in agreement with our values.
   2. Sometimes we tune out information that we feel is boring or that makes us uncomfortable.

D. Defensive listening involves perceiving the message as being a personal attack or criticism of us when there is no such intent behind the message.

E. Ambushing involves listening carefully for the purpose of attacking.

F. Literal listening is paying attention to the content level of meaning in the message and ignoring the relational content of the message.

IV. We adapt our listening to varying communication goals.

A. When we use informational listening, we are listening with the purpose of gaining and understanding information.

B. Critical listening is listening to form opinions, make judgments, or evaluate people or ideas.

C. When we are mindful, we are making a conscious choice to give our full attention to a speaker and the message.

D. To improve our listening, we can strive to control obstacles to listening.

E. Asking questions allows us to clarify another's message to be sure that we understand what the other intends to communicate.

F. Recall aids can assist us in remembering the information we have heard.
   1. Repetition helps move information from short-term memory to long-term memory.
   2. Mnemonic devices are memory aids that create patterns for what you have heard, such as ROY G. BIV to help you remember that the colors of the rainbow are red, orange, yellow, green, blue, indigo, and violet.
   3. Organizing information into clumps of information can help with recall (e.g., academic programs and extracurricular programs).

G. Relational listening helps us support another and maintain important relationships.
   1. Being mindful in relational listening involves listening to understand another's feelings and to "read between the words."
   2. Suspending judgment helps us to truly hear the other's position and take a dual perspective.
   3. Grasp the other's perspective.
      a. Paraphrasing is repeating to the other the general gist of what was said to make sure that you are understanding.
      b. Minimal encouragers are words, sounds, and behaviors that encourage the other to keep on talking and let the other know that you are listening.
      c. Asking questions can help us understand what another is thinking or feeling.
   4. Expressing support lets the other know that you understand and care, even if you don't agree.

V. Besides listening for information, listening critically, and listening to support others, there are other reasons we listen.

A. Listening for pleasure is listening for the sheer enjoyment of what we are listening to (e.g., listening to a movie, a CD, or a concert).

B. Listening to discriminate involves listening in order to decipher the differences between sounds in order to draw a conclusion and act accordingly (e.g., listening to the different sounds an engine makes to determine a particular problem and a potential course of action to resolve the problem).

4.1   Rumor Clinic

Purpose

To demonstrate the ways in which messages are distorted as they are passed along from person to person.

Instructions

Select six people to join you in this experience. They may be other students in your class or friends and acquaintances of yours. Read the story below and then close this book. Tell what you remember of the story to person one and tell that person to relay the story to person two and so forth until the message reaches the sixth person.

Write down the exact words that person six uses to tell the story. Compare the account given by person six with the original one presented below.

Gene thought a lot about what he wanted to do after college, and he finally decided that he would go to law school in order to become a public defender. Last semester Gene sent in applications to eight law schools. So far, he has received rejections from three of them and acceptances from two of them. The other three schools haven't contacted him one way or the other. The problem Gene faces now is that both of the schools that have accepted him require his answer (yes or no) by the end of the month. The three schools he hasn't heard from are higher on his list of preferred schools than the two that have accepted him. He's not sure whether to take one of the sure bets or hold out in the hope that he will be accepted by a better school.

4.2   Noticing Forms of Ineffective Listening

Purpose

To give you experience in recognizing forms of ineffective listening in everyday situations.

Instructions

For the next 3 days pay particular attention to how others listen. Use the form below to record examples of each of the forms of ineffective listening discussed in your textbook.

Listening Form Situation Observed Behaviors
Example:

Selective Listening   Ad about the dangers of smoking   Person who smokes started talking during the ad to divert attention

_____

Pseudolistening

_____

Monopolizing

_____

Selective Listening

_____

Defensive Listening

_____

Ambushing

_____

Literal Listening

_____

4.3   Learning to Paraphrase

Purpose
To give you experience in paraphrasing others' communication.

Instructions
For each of the statements below, write a paraphrase that aims to clarify and check perceptions of what others say. Try to paraphrase in ways that reflect both the thoughts and feelings of the person speaking.

Statement	Paraphrase
Example	
I think we're seeing too much of each other.	So you want us to get together less frequently.
1. I really like communication, but what could I do with a major in this field?	
2. I don't know if Pat and I are getting too serious too fast.	
3. You can borrow my car, if you really need to, but please be careful with it. I can't afford any repairs and if you have an accident, I won't be able to drive to D.C. this weekend.	

Name_____

4.4   **Listening to Support Others**

Purpose
To provide you with experience in listening to support another person and a relationship with that person.

Instructions
Following each statement in the message below, write a response that shows you are listening to support the speaker. Follow the directions for specific kinds of supportive responses.

Example

Speaker: I'm thinking about studying abroad next year.

Minimal encourager: <u>"Oh?"</u>

Speaker: But I've never lived away from my family, and I wonder if I would be okay on my own.

Paraphrase: _____

Speaker: I'm not sure that I'm mature enough to live on my own for a whole year.

Suspending judgment: _____

Speaker: I guess what most interests me about the idea is the chance to really experience another culture.

Minimal encourager: _____

4.5   Identifying Effective Behaviors for Relational Listening

Purpose
To increase your awareness of specific verbal and nonverbal behaviors that accompany effective listening.

Instructions
Identify an individual whom you consider to be especially effective when listening to support others.

Either think back on past situations in which you have observed that individual interacting or observe the person as she or he listens to friends in the next few days. Based on your recollections and/or observations, answer the questions below.

1. What proxemic behaviors contribute to the impression that this person is listening fully? Describe how she or he uses space.

2. What kinesic behaviors does this person use? Describe his or her body posture, facial expressions, and movements when she or he is listening.

3. Does the person use minimal encouragers? If so, identify several that she or he uses.

4. Does the person paraphrase the communication of people to whom she or he listens?

5. How does the person demonstrate support verbally? Be specific in describing phrases and language.

6. How does the person demonstrate support with nonverbal communication? Be specific in describing behaviors.

7. What verbal and/or nonverbal behaviors indicate the person is engaging in dual perspective?

8. Does the person ask questions of the speaker? If so, identify typical questions.

9. Does the person make judgmental comments?

10. Does the person interrupt other than to express minimal encouragers?

Summary
Based on your observations of this individual, write a paragraph that provides a profile of effective relational listening behaviors.

4.6   Using Your Online Resources—Experiencing
Communication in Our Lives

Chapter 4 Case Study: Family Hour

Purpose
To apply the principles you learned about listening effectively in Chapter 4 to the communication scenario *Family Hour* included under Communication Scenarios on your Online Resources for *Communication in Our Lives*. You can complete this activity online or on this worksheet.

Instructions
Analyze the *Family Hour* scenario by answering the questions below.

Scenario Overview
Over spring break, 20-year-old Josh visits his father. He wants to convince his family to support him in joining a fraternity that has given him a bid. On his second day home, after dinner Josh decides to broach the topic. His dad is watching the evening news on television when Josh walks in the living room. Josh sits down and opens the conversation.

Conversation Analysis
1. What forms of ineffective listening are evident in this dialogue?

2. If you could advise Josh's father on listening effectively, what would you tell him to do differently?

3. Would you offer any advice to Josh on how he could listen to his father more effectively?

Name_____

4.7   Listening for Feedback

Purpose
To increase your awareness of the listening skill levels required for supervisory relationships.

Instructions
Imagine your are President Obama visiting troops heading overseas and their families. You have time to meet with two military families. Imagine two different families presented with very serious issues. One family includes a single mother leaving her four children with their grandparents while she is deployed. The other family includes the surviving parents of two soldiers, brothers who both died in battle.

Describe the specific listening skills you would use listening to the first familiy. What effect do you hope to have on them?

Describe the specific listening skills you would use listening to the second family. What effect do you hope to have on them?

Self-Test for Chapter 4

Multiple Choice

_____ 1. Ahmed feels overwhelmed at a meeting he attends. The manager is talking about an upcoming sales conference, his co-workers are engaged in side conversations, and a video is being presented—all at the same time. Ahmed is experiencing
A. message complexity
B. preoccupation
C. message overload
D. prejudgment

_____ 2. Talia goes to a lecture by an author whose works she has read and does not like. Before the author begins, Talia thinks to herself, "Boy, what a waste of time this will be! What could she possibly add to my knowledge if I don't like her work?" Talia's ability to listen effectively is likely to be hampered by
A. message complexity
B. preoccupation
C. message overload
D. prejudgment

_____ 3. Petra tells Carla about the great party she went to this past weekend. Carla immediately begins talking about a different party she went to over the weekend and how great it was. Carla is engaging in which form of nonlistening?
A. pseudolistening
B. selective listening
C. ambushing
D. monopolizing

_____ 4. Dianne is trying to do some last-minute cramming before her economics exam, so while sitting in her psychology class, she reads over her notes. Dianne looks up at the psychology professor often and nods her head to indicate she is attentive. Dianne is engaging in
A. ambushing
B. defensive listening
C. monopolizing
D. pseudolistening

_____ 5. While her friend Orit is speaking, Mojgan interjects these comments: "Go on," "I'm following you," "What happened next?" These are
A. showing dual perspective
B. expressing support
C. minimal encouragers
D. paraphrasings

_____ 6. Eight hours after hearing a message, we are likely to remember _____ of the message.
A. just under half
B. about one third
C. about one half
D. about two thirds

_____ 7. Your ears perk up when your favorite music becomes the focus of conversation at the next table. You eavesdrop until the conversation drifts to another topic and then you return your attention to the conversation at your own table. You are practicing
    A. selective listening
    B. defensive listening
    C. literal listening
    D. relational listening

_____ 8. Which of the following is NOT an internal obstacle to effective listening?
    A. prejudgments
    B. message complexity
    C. lack of effort
    D. preoccupation

_____ 9. To help herself remember a lecture, Tonya makes up a word in which each letter represents a key idea from the lecture. The word Tonya makes up is called a
    A. mnemonic device
    B. memorabilia
    C. retendo
    D. memetic device

_____ 10. You just got tickets to see your favorite musical artist, where you will practice
    A. listening for pleasure
    B. relational listening
    C. critical listening
    D. listening for information

_____ 11. The character in the comedy movie you're watching hears, "Take a hike!" growled at him by an irritated person to whom he has been trying to sell something useless. The salesman looks puzzled, shrugs, turns to the door, and launches into a 3-mile trek. He is practicing
    A. selective listening
    B. defensive listening
    C. literal listening
    D. relational listening

_____ 12. Which of the following is necessary for both informational and relational listening?
    A. asking questions
    B. organizing information
    C. being mindful
    D. using visual aids

_____ 13. When we attend to another with complete attention, we are
    A. listening
    B. being mindful
    C. using empathy
    D. interpreting

_____ 14. The first step in effective listening is to
A. receive a message
B. interpret a message
C. organize a message
D. be mindful

_____ 15. Allen tells Carolyn the baby needs changing. Carolyn snaps, yelling, "Well, I couldn't change the baby AND cook you dinner!" Carolyn is practicing
A. ambushing
B. defensive listening
C. monopolizing
D. pseudolistening

True/False

_____ 1. Someone who has poor hearing cannot be an excellent listener.

_____ 2. Western culture emphasizes judgment.

_____ 3. Your rival approaches in a friendly manner, hears your plan to take a trip this weekend and says, "I knew you weren't really interested in taking Tinisha to the party, so I'll ask her myself!" He is ambushing.

_____ 4. Different cultures teach people different styles of listening.

_____ 5. Men often think women's talk is too detailed and women often think men's talk lacks understanding.

_____ 6. Men listen for what they need to know at the time, while women listen to the whole of a communication event.

_____ 7. Paraphrasing helps us figure out what others feel.

_____ 8. A person spends 45%–75% of waking time listening to others.

_____ 9. Colloquial phrases and slang create listening obstacles for non-native speakers.

_____ 10. To interpret someone's communication with respect for their perspective, whether we agree or not, is one of the greatest gifts we can give.

Essays

1. Describe the attitudes and skills that are particularly useful when the goal of listening is to support others.

2. Describe the attitudes and skills that are particularly useful when the goal of listening is to gain information or to form an opinion.

3. Do people who use ASL to communicate need good listening skills? Discuss how people who are deaf or hard of hearing can listen and not hear.

Chapter 4 Flash Cards

Cut out the cards, write the answers on the back, and you will have a packet of flash cards for each chapter. Paraphrasing the definitions will help you remember them.

Ambushing	Listening	Paraphrasing
Critical Listening	Literal Listening	Pseudolistening
Defensive Listening	Mindfulness	Relational Listening
Informational Listening	Hearing	Minimal Encouragers
Selective Listening	Monopolizing	

Chapter 5: The Verbal Dimension of Communication

Chapter Summary

I.   Communication is the result of using shared symbols to create meaning.
   A.   Our perceptions are shaped by symbols that represent phenomena.

   B.   Language and much nonverbal behavior is symbolic.

   C.   Symbols are arbitrary.
      1.   Symbols are not intrinsically connected to what they represent.
      2.   Because language is arbitrary, we can create private communication codes.
      3.   Symbols, and thus language and meanings, change over time.

   D.   Symbols are ambiguous.
      1.   Symbols don't mean the same thing to everyone; most have an agreed-on range of meanings within a culture.
      2.   Symbol ambiguity helps to explain why miscommunication is so common.

   E.   Symbols are abstract, intangible.
      1.   Abstraction leads to overgeneralization that causes confusion.
      2.   Overly abstract language can also complicate personal relationships.

II. Verbal communication has several basic principles.
   A.   How we interpret symbols creates the meaning we assign them.

   B.   Communication is rule-guided.
      1.   **Regulative rules** specify when, how, where, and with whom to talk about certain things.
      2.   **Constitutive rules** define what an interaction means by telling us how to interpret certain kinds of communication.
   C.   Punctuation, the mental mark of the beginnings and endings of particular interactions, affects meaning.

III. Symbolic abilities affect our lives in several ways.
   A.   Symbols define experiences, people, relationships, feelings, and thoughts.
      1.   **Totalizing** is using a single label to represent the totality of a person.
      2.   Labeling can lead to self-fulfilling prophecies.

   B.   Symbols evaluate—they are not neutral; they assign value and worth to what they represent.
      1.   There are degrees of evaluation in language.
      2.   **Loaded language** consists of words that strongly slant perceptions and meanings.

   C.   Symbols organize perceptions.
      1.   Symbols help us to organize abstract thought.
      2.   Abstract thought can easily lead to stereotyping as a form of generalizing.

D. Symbols allow hypothetical thought.
  1. Hypothetical thought allows us to think about the past and the future.
  2. Hypothetical thought allows us to reflect on and improve ourselves.

E. Symbols allow for self-reflection.
  1. The *I* is the spontaneous, creative self that acts impulsively in response to inner needs and desires, regardless of social norms.
  2. The *me* is the reflective part of the self that monitors the *I* and helps us behave appropriately.
  3. Self-reflection also allows us to manage our identity and the image we present to others.

IV. We are able to enhance our own verbal communication competence.
  A. We can engage in **dual perspective**, or recognizing another's point of view, critical for improving our verbal communication.

  B. We can own our own feelings and thoughts.
    1. Others cannot make us feel a particular way.
    2. *I*-language helps us take ownership of our own thoughts and feelings.

  C. We can respect what others say about their feelings and ideas.
    1. Speaking for others is arrogant and disempowering toward them.
    2. Speaking for others is often associated with mindreading.

  D. We can strive for accuracy and clarity in communication.
    1. Be aware of levels of abstraction.
    2. Qualify language to limit times, places, circumstances, or conditions, especially when judging people.
      a. Limit generalizations so that we don't mislead.
      b. Qualify language (e.g., "seems") to avoid static evaluation.
      c. Index (avoid using "is") only specific times and circumstances.

5.1   Recognizing Ambiguity in Verbal Language

Purpose
To provide you with concrete examples of ambiguous verbal symbols.

Instructions
For each of the statements below, write 2 distinct ways it might be interpreted.

	Interpretation 1	**Interpretation 2**
A. That party was sick.		
B. I found grass in your room.		
C. Are you straight?		
D. My professor is psycho.		
E. That skateboard is hot.		
F. I'm going to holler at you later.		
G. His shirt is sweet.		
H. The house was wasted.		

5.2   Good Enough to Eat

Purpose

To increase awareness of how language is used to shape perceptions.

Instructions

Get together with 5 or 6 other students in your class. Assign each member of your group 3 local restaurants that he or she will study. Make sure that your group includes restaurants of different types (fast food, expensive, etc.). Each member of the group should go the 3 assigned restaurants and ask for a menu. Many restaurants have take-out menus. If a restaurant doesn't have a takeout menu, you might ask to borrow a menu to photocopy and then return it. When all members of your group have collected their menus, meet and discuss the language used to describe foods. As guidelines for your discussion, use the questions that follow.

1. Can you identify language used in describing entrees that refers to taste, texture, and other features that contribute to dining pleasure?

2. Can you identify language used in describing entrees that emphasizes the health values of the entrees? For example, are entrees described as "low fat," "nutritional," "healthy," "low calorie," and so forth?

3. Can you identify language used in describing entrees that emphasizes value? For example, are menu items described as "bargains," "specials," "super buys," and so forth?

4. What differences can you identify in the menu language of expensive restaurants and fast food eateries? Which of the above 3 emphases is most pronounced for different kinds of restaurants?

5.3   Understanding Communication Rules

Purpose

To increase your awareness of communication rules.

Instructions

For each of the statements listed below, indicate whether it expresses a constitutive or a regulative communication rule. In the blanks on the left, place an R if the statement expresses a regulative rule and a C if it expresses a constitutive rule of communication. Answers appear with the Chapter 5 Self-Test answers.

_____   1.   Don't talk when you have food in your mouth.

_____   2.   Never engage in conflict in front of others.

_____   3.   True friends listen to what each other says.

_____   4.   It's impolite to interrupt others when they are speaking.

_____   5.   Good buddies don't reveal confidences.

_____   6.   Look at your elders when they speak to you so that you show you respect them.

_____   7.   Children should not speak back to parents.

_____   8.   It's thoughtful to ask others what is going on in their lives.

5.4   Punctuation in Practice

Purpose
To increase your sensitivity to different ways that communication might be punctuated.

Instructions
Read the dialogue between Ann and Max that appears below. Then write a description of how Ann seems to punctuate the interaction and a second description of how Max appears to punctuate the interaction.

Max: You seem awfully quiet tonight. Are you okay?

Ann: Hardly (said in a sarcastic voice).

Max: You sound angry.

Ann: Brilliant deduction on your part.

Max: Are you angry with me?

Ann: A second brilliant deduction.

Max: But I just got home—literally just walked in the door. How could I have done anything to make you angry?

Ann: My, you have a short memory.

Max: Cut the sarcasm, will you? My memory is fine. What's the matter with you?

Ann: The "matter with me," as you call it, is our discussion this morning when we were getting ready to go to work.

Max: Yeah. What about it?

Ann: I can't believe you've forgotten how nasty you were. I said I wanted to go back to school next year and you said we couldn't afford it, like that ended the issue.

Max: That's what you're mad about now? We resolved that issue nearly 10 hours ago.

Ann: I didn't. It's not resolved for me.

Ann's punctuation of the interaction:

Max's punctuation of the interaction:

How does their punctuation of the incident impact their communication with one another?

5.5   Learning to Use I-Language

Purpose
To give you experience in using I-language.

Instructions
Read each of the 10 statements below. Each one relies on you-language. Rephrase each statement so that it is expressed using I-language.

Example
Your stubbornness makes me angry.
Rephrasing: I get angry when you are stubborn.

1. You are so arrogant.
   Rephrasing:

2. You embarrassed me in front of my friends.
   Rephrasing:

3. You make me feel guilty.
   Rephrasing:

4. You get me so upset that I forget things.
   Rephrasing:

5. You're so inconsiderate of me.
   Rephrasing:

6. You're very loving.
   Rephrasing:

7. You're insensitive.
   Rephrasing:

8. You're so understanding about my situation.
   Rephrasing:

9. You really are self-centered.
   Rephrasing:

10. You're very helpful when I talk to you about problems.
    Rephrasing:

Name_____

5.6   Reducing the Abstractness of Language

Purposes
To increase your ability to recognize highly abstract language.
To increase your skill in reducing the abstractness of language.

Instructions
Each of the statements below is expressed in highly abstract language, which increases the chances of misunderstanding between communicators. Rephrase each statement so that it is less abstract and more clear.

Example
This course is conceptually difficult.
Rephrasing: This course requires students to learn a great many new concepts and to understand how they relate to one another.

1. Edward always finds something critical to say.
   Rephrasing:

2. The American concept of freedom is diminishing.
   Rephrasing:

3. Most people have lost any sense of personal responsibility.
   Rephrasing:

4. Let's try to keep our trip from getting too expensive.
   Rephrasing:

5. I wish you would be more responsible.
   Rephrasing:

6. I'd like for us to be better friends.
   Rephrasing:

7. Politicians are dishonest.
   Rephrasing:

5.7   Practicing Using Qualified Language

Purpose
To give you experience in using qualified language.

Instructions
Below are 8 statements that are unqualified. Each statement is very broad generalization. In the space below each statement, write a rephrased statement that is more qualified.

Example
Politicians are crooks.
Rephrasing: Some politicians sometimes engage in illegal acts.

1. You always interrupt me.
    Rephrasing:

2. Bureaucrats just follow rules; they never think for themselves.
    Rephrasing:

3. Democrats want to tax everyone with money.
    Rephrasing:

4. Professors think students have nothing else going on but classes.
    Rephrasing:

5. Women are much more emotional than men.
    Rephrasing:

6. Required courses are boring.
    Rephrasing:

7. Children should not watch television.
    Rephrasing:

8. Men's nature will never let them nurture a child.
    Rephrasing:

9. College students are always looking for the next party.
    Rephrasing:

10. He never goes out with his friends.

Name_____

5.8   Guarding Against Static Language

Purpose

To give you practice in recognizing and correcting static language.

Instructions

Listed below are 10 statements that include static language. Rephrase each statement to qualify it in terms of specific times, events, and/or situations.

Example

Marion is irresponsible.

Rephrasing: Marion was irresponsible about returning the sweater he borrowed from me.

1. Aaron is selfish.
    Rephrasing:

2. Emily is very supportive.
    Rephrasing:

3. Dr. Dowler is not interested in talking with students.
    Rephrasing:

4. Andy cares more about how a woman looks than what kind of personality and values she has.
    Rephrasing:

5. Aimee is immature.
    Rephrasing:

6. Pat can't be relied on to complete assignments.
    Rephrasing:

7. I am stupid.
    Rephrasing:

8. Kim is a real gossip.
    Rephrasing:

9. American cars are poorly made.
    Rephrasing:

10. You are disrespectful of your parents.
    Rephrasing:

5.9   The Personal Nature of Meanings

Purpose
To provide you with concrete examples of the variations in meanings for words among people.

Instructions
Select 7 people who are diverse. They should represent a range of ages, sexes, political leanings, races, and so forth. Ask each person to tell you what each of the 4 terms listed below means to her or him. Record the answers. With others in your class, discuss the variations in meanings for the "same words."

	Feminism	Affirmative Action	Alcoholic	Conflict
Person 1				
Person 2				
Person 3				
Person 4				
Person 5				
Person 6				
Person 7				

Name_____

5.10   Breaking the Rules of Gendered Communication

Purposes
To increase your awareness of how gender socialization shapes your verbal communication.

To increase your insight into others' perceptions of verbal communication that is and is not appropriate for each sex.

Instructions
1. Read about gender cultures on pages 176–177 in your textbook.
2. Select a social prescription for how your sex is supposed to communicate verbally and deliberately violate that prescription in your interactions with others for one day.
3. Record how others respond to your violation of a gender prescription for verbal behavior.
4. Record how you feel when you violate the prescription and when others respond to your violation.

Example

Description of Verbal Violation
I chose to break the prescription that women should be empathic by giving only minimal responses and not emotional responses when people talked to me. I kept it up even when my best friend told me about a problem she was having.

Responses of Others
Several people asked me if I was sick or angry. When I said I wasn't, they said that I surely was acting cold. My best friend said that I was acting like I didn't care about her.

My Reactions
I felt really weird not responding emotionally to other people. Also, I felt bad when others criticized me, because I felt like I was letting them down by not being my usual empathic self. But when I reflected further, a part of me felt like it isn't fair that women are expected to always be caring and empathic.

REPORT OF VERBAL VIOLATION

1. Description of verbal violation:

2. Description of others' responses to the violation:

3. Report on personal feelings and responses:

Name_____

5.11   Using Loaded Language

Purpose
To give you practice in selecting words to shape perceptions of listeners to match your own.

Instructions
Imagine that your friend, a travel agent, has offered you a free cruise if you can find 3 more people to join a group who want to vacation in the Caribbean Islands. You have invited to lunch ten co-workers who you know usually plan their vacations a year in advance. Write a few things you might say to get yourself on that cruise.

5.12 Using Your Online Resources—Experiencing *Communication in Our Lives*

Chapter 5 Case Study: The Roommates

Purpose

To apply the principles you learned about the verbal dimension of communication in Chapter 5 to the communication scenario *The Roommates* included under Communication Scenarios on your Online Resources for *Communication in Our Lives*. You can complete this activity online or on this worksheet.

Instructions

Analyze *The Roommates* scenario by answering the questions below.

Video Preview

Bernadette and Celia were assigned to be roommates a month ago when the school year began. Both were initially pleased with the match because they discovered commonalities in their interests and backgrounds. They are both sophomores from small towns, they have similar tastes in music and television programs, and they both like to stay up late and sleep in on mornings. Lately, however, Bernadette has been irritated by Celia's housekeeping—or lack of it! Celia leaves her clothes lying all over the room.

Conversation Analysis

1. Identify examples of you-language in this conversation. How would you change it to I-language?

2. Identify examples of loaded language and ambiguous language.

3. Do you agree with Celia that the problem is Bernadette's, not hers?

4. Do Celia and Bernadette seem to engage in dual perspective to understand each other?

Self-Test for Chapter 5

Multiple Choice

_____ 1. When we say words are arbitrary we mean
   A. their meaning may change over time
   B. its meaning has no natural connection to it
   C. meaning may be shared only by certain people
   D. all of the above

_____ 2. Which of the following terms is the LEAST abstract?
   A. William Zachary
   B. resident of Brighton
   C. male
   D. person

_____ 3. "Do not chew with your mouth open." This is an example of a(n)
   A. constitutive rule
   B. regulative rule
   C. punctuation
   D. abstraction

_____ 4. "Paying attention when others speak is a sign of respect." This is an example of a(n)
   A. constitutive rule
   B. regulative rule
   C. punctuation
   D. abstraction

_____ 5. When we overlook many aspects of a person and define the person only by a single aspect of her or his identity, we are
   A. organizing
   B. engaging in dual perspective
   C. totalizing
   D. stereotyping

_____ 6. "Too much abstraction" means language has
   A. resulted in broad claims that no one will accept
   B. become too general to understand exactly what you mean
   C. become inaccurate
   D. all of the above

_____ 7. "When I was a teenager, I never would have dreamed I'd be able to fly a plane."
   A. using symbols to define
   B. using symbols to organize
   C. engaging in hypothetical thought
   D. engaging in punctuation

_____ 8. "Unwed mothers are irresponsible and a drain on our public assistance programs." This statement is an example of
A. stereotyping
B. hypothesizing
C. using I-language
D. self-reflecting

_____ 9. "People who support gay marriage are all liberal." This is an example of
A. indexing
B. loaded language
C. impulse control
D. hypothetical thought

_____ 10. The ability to consciously manage how we appear to others by monitoring and regulating our self presentation is called
A. facework
B. reflected-appraisal
C. damage control
D. owing self

_____ 11. In the middle of your chemistry class, you think that you want to stand up and scream out of frustration because you do not understand the material. You know that to do so would be socially inappropriate. The part of yourself that wants to stand up and scream is
A. the *I* aspect of yourself
B. the *me* aspect of yourself
C. a nonregulative rule
D. none of the above

_____ 12. We construct meaning of symbols
A. in the process of interacting with others
B. through dialogues we carry on in our own heads
C. using symbols
D. all of the above

_____ 13. Which of the following is NOT a way in which symbols affect our lives?
A. they define
B. they evaluate
C. they organize perceptions
D. all of the above are functions of symbols

_____ 14. Even though Elizabeth does not believe in taking a life for a life, she understands her friend Marissa's desire to have her brother's convicted murderer put to death by lethal injection. Elizabeth is engaging in
A. cultural sensitivity
B. dual perspective
C. meaning enhancement
D. social awareness

_____ 15. Which of the following are means for enhancing verbal effectiveness?
     A.   know your own perspective
     B.   own your own feelings
     C.   respect what others say and feel
     D.   B and C

True/False

_____ 1. The most effective language is neutral—it doesn't contain biased words.

_____ 2. Static evaluations focus only on what is negative about a person.

_____ 3. There is no objectively accurate (correct) way to punctuate interaction.

_____ 4. Interpretation is not an objective process.

_____ 5. Indexing fixes perceptions by using the word "is".

_____ 6. Words may change in meaning depending upon how we classify who says them.

_____ 7. Perceptions are shaped by symbols.

_____ 8. "You look really hot" is an example of ambiguous language.

_____ 9. All words are symbols but not all symbols are words.

_____ 10. Agreeing with another person's point of view is the basis of adopting a dual perspective.

Essays

1. Did you know the 'magic' word **abracadabra** means, "I create as I speak" in Hebrew? Does speech create? Using your knowledge about language, defend your answer.

2. Define I-language and You-language, and provide concrete examples of each. Explain the values of using I-language.

3. You have been asked to give a presentation on how to enhance verbal communication. Give an example of a poor verbal communication exchange and then use the four suggestions for enhancing verbal communication to make it a better exchange.

Chapter 5 Flash Cards

Cut out the cards, write the answers on the back, and you will have a packet of flash cards for each chapter. Paraphrasing the definitions will help you remember them.

Totalizing	Ambiguous	Arbitrary
Communication Rules	Constitutive Rules	Dual Perspective
Hypothetical Thought	Indexing	Loaded Language
Punctuation	Regulative Rules	Static Evaluation

Chapter 6: The Nonverbal Dimension of Communication

Chapter Summary

I.   Nonverbal communication is a major dimension of human communication.
    A.   Nonverbal communication accounts for 65% – 93% of all communication.
    B.   Nonverbal communication is everything from dress to vocal inflections.

II.   Nonverbal communication is all aspects of communication other than words themselves.
    A.   There are similarities and differences between verbal and nonverbal communication.
        1.   There are many similarities between the two.
            a.   Both verbal and nonverbal communication are symbolic, meaning they are ambiguous, abstract, and arbitrary.
            b.   Both are guided by constitutive and regulative rules.
            c.   Both are culture bound.
            d.   Both can be either intentional or unintentional.
        2.   There are differences between both systems.
            a.   Nonverbal communication is perceived as more honest.
            b.   Nonverbal communication is multi-channeled rather than single-channeled.
            c.   Nonverbal communication is more continuous, while verbal communication is more discrete.
    B.   Nonverbal communication supplements or replaces verbal communication.
        1.   Nonverbal behaviors can repeat verbal messages.
        2.   Nonverbal behaviors may highlight verbal communication.
        3.   Nonverbal behaviors complement or add to words.
        4.   Nonverbal behaviors may contradict verbal messages.
        5.   Nonverbal behaviors may substitute for verbal messages.

    C.   Nonverbal communication regulates our communicative interactions.

    D.   Nonverbal communication establishes relationship-level meanings.
        1.   Nonverbal behavior communicates responsiveness.
        2.   Nonverbal behavior communicates liking.
        3.   Nonverbal behavior communicates power or control.

    E.   Nonverbal communication reflects cultural values.

III. There are nine different types of nonverbal communication.
    A.   Kinesics is body position and movements, including facial expressions.
        1.   Posture and gestures indicate interest in interacting with others.
        2.   The face, especially the eyes, conveyances emotions.
        3.   Our body positioning communicates our feelings toward others.

    B.   Haptics is physical touch.
        1.   Touch is the first sense to develop.
        2.   Touch has been found to be necessary for human development and survival.
        3.   Touch communicates power and status.

C. Physical appearance forms most of our initial evaluations.
   1. Physical qualities, such as age, race, sex, features, skin color, and size are some of the aspects of others that we notice first.
   2. We make assessments about another's attractiveness based on physical characteristics.
   3. Culture greatly influences our interpretations of physical appearance and attractiveness.

D. Artifacts are the personal objects with which we announce our ideas and personalize our environments.
   1. We craft our image by how we dress, the jewelry we wear, and the objects we carry and use.
   2. We define settings and personalize our territories using artifacts.
   3. We use artifacts to express personal and ethnic identities.
   4. We communicate important relational meanings using artifacts.

E. Proxemics is space and how we use it.
   1. Space communicates intimacy or relational closeness.
   2. Space also communicates status and power.
   3. Space indicates our desire for relational interaction.

F. Environmental factors are elements of settings, like colors, music, smells, lighting, and furniture arrangement.
   1. Included are all other physical elements of the environment that impact how we feel and act.
   2. Feng shui is a cultural use of environmental factors to create balance with chi, the earth's energy.

G. Chronemics is how we use and perceive time to define identities and interaction.
   1. Chronemics communicate status.
   2. Chronemics express cultural attitudes toward time.
   3. The amount of time we spend with people or on certain activities reflects our interpersonal priorities.

H. Paralanguage is vocal communication that does not include words.
   1. Vocal characteristics such as pitch, rate, articulation, inflection, sighs, giggles, gasps, and rhythms are considered paralanguage.
   2. Paralanguage helps communicate feelings and our relationships with others.
   3. We use our voices to communicate how we see ourselves and how we wish to be seen by others.
   4. Paralanguage reflects our cultural heritage.

I. Silence is a nonverbal form of communication that can serve to disconfirm others or can show how comfortable we are in the presence of another.

IV. Like all aspects of communication, there are things a person can do to improve his or her nonverbal communication skills.
   A. The first step in improving your nonverbal skills is to monitor and become aware of your nonverbal behaviors.

B.   Others' nonverbal behaviors need to be interpreted tentatively and with caution.
1.   Not all people use nonverbal communication in the same way, so what means one thing with one friend may mean something different when done by someone else.
2.   There are contextual factors that may affect how a nonverbal behavior is interpreted.
3.   Cultural rules may affect the way we interpret a particular nonverbal behavior.
4.   Even within a single culture, social communities have distinct rules for nonverbal behavior.

Name_____

6.1 Gendered Communication

Purpose
To demonstrate gender differences in nonverbal communication.

Instructions
Divide your class (or, alternatively, a group of your friends) into two groups based on gender. Being certain neither group can hear the other, come up with as many gender-based names, words, or titles for the other as possible in 10 minutes. At the end, have each a representative from each group read aloud the other's list.

How were the gender-based names, words or titles different for each group?

Which gender had more sex-based occupations?

Did either gender use terms they reserved for members of that group ('for the guys only,' for example)?

What do these terms communicate nonverbally?

6.2   Nonverbal Exclusions

Purpose
To increase awareness of how environmental features of settings include and exclude social groups.

Instructions
Choose 5 places to visit: (1) a business office, such as a realty company, (2) an administrator's office on your campus, (3) a commercial building, such as a bank, (4) a waiting lounge in a hospital or doctor's office, and (5) a conference room in one of the campus buildings.

Visit each of the five locations and record answers to the questions below.

1. How many pictures or paintings of non-white people are present?

    Business office

    Administrative office

    Commercial building

    Waiting lounge

    Conference room

2. Which parts (rooms, floors) are accessible to persons who have disabilities that restrict their movement?

    Business office

    Administrative office

    Commercial building

    Waiting lounge

    Conference room

3. Are rooms identified with Braille and are there reading materials in Braille?

    Business office

    Administrative office

    Commercial building

    Waiting lounge

    Conference room

---

4. How many photographs or paintings of women are present?

    Business office

    Administrative office

    Commercial building

    Waiting lounge

    Conference room

Processing

Discuss your observations with other students in your class. Are there consistent trends in your observations? What can you conclude about nonverbal communication of inclusion and exclusion?

6.3   Portrait of Myself

Purpose
To increase your awareness of the ways in which you use artifacts to personalize your environment.

Instructions
Go to your dormitory room or your room in your apartment. Using the form below, list the personal artifacts that you have put there. Do not list any that you didn't choose. Beside each item that you list, explain its significance to you and what it communicates about your identity.

Artifact	Significance/What It Communicates
Example	
Photo of me in Nepal	This photo reminds me of a very special trek I made in Nepal. It also communicates to others that I am adventurous.
1.	
2.	
3.	
4.	
5.	
6.	
7.	

Name_____

6.4   Nonverbal Designs

Purpose
To increase your awareness of the ways in which settings influence interaction.

Instructions
Select three restaurants to visit. One should be a very elegant restaurant; one should be an inexpensive fast-food restaurant; and one should be a specialty or novelty restaurant. Describe the setting of each restaurant by answering the questions on Form A, which appears on the two pages that follow this page. Describe interaction patterns among diners by answering the questions on Form B, which follows on the pages after Form A.

FORM A: DESCRIPTION OF THE SETTING

1. What is the average distance between tables or booths in each restaurant?

   Elegant restaurant

   Fast-food restaurant

   Novelty restaurant

2. How are the restaurants lit (candles, soft side lighting, overhead bulbs, fluorescent lighting) and how brightly lit is each restaurant?

   Elegant restaurant

   Fast-food restaurant

   Novelty restaurant

3. What kind of music, if any, is playing in each restaurant? Describe the style and tempo of music and the mood it invites in diners.

   Elegant restaurant

   Fast-food restaurant

   Novelty restaurant

4. How are members of the staff dressed? Notice the receptionist as well as waitpersons. Are they dressed formally or informally, in uniforms or not?

   Elegant restaurant

   Fast-food restaurant

   Novelty restaurant

5. Describe the decor of each restaurant? Identify artwork, if any; quality of carpeting; presence of plants and other items.

   Elegant restaurant

   Fast-food restaurant

   Novelty restaurant

FORM B: DESCRIPTION OF INTERACTION PATTERNS

1. What is the average time that diners spend in each restaurant?

   Elegant restaurant

   Fast-food restaurant

   Novelty restaurant

2. How much do diners, in general, look at one another while eating?

   Elegant restaurant

   Fast-food restaurant

   Novelty restaurant

3. How loudly do diners talk in each restaurant?

   Elegant restaurant

   Fast-food restaurant

   Novelty restaurant

4. What is the average number of people in dining groups at each restaurant?

   Elegant restaurant

   Fast-food restaurant

   Novelty restaurant

5. How intimate do diners' conversations appear to be, judging from touching, eye behavior, and other nonverbals?

   Elegant restaurant

   Fast-food restaurant

   Novelty restaurant

6.5   Identifying Nonverbal Cues

Purpose
To make you more aware of nonverbal cues that lead you to particular interpretations of others.

Instructions
Using the form below, identify 2 or more nonverbal behaviors that you associate with the states described on the left. When you have competed the form, consider whether the nonverbal behaviors you listed might have meanings other than those you assign to them.

Example

State	Associated Nonverbal Cues
Happiness	Smiling, laughing

1. Anger

2. Lack of interest

3. Arrogance

4. Boredom

5. Romantic interest

6. Fear

7. Embarrassment

8. Type A personality

9. Nervous

10. Disapproval

Name_____

6.6   Monitoring Your Nonverbal Communication

Purposes
To heighten your awareness of nonverbal behaviors that others may misinterpret.

To assist you in identifying alternative nonverbal behaviors that are consistent with the messages you intend to send to others.

Instructions
First, on the form provided, write 6 statements about you that others have made but that you do not think are accurate descriptions of you.   Second, identify nonverbal behaviors of yours that others may interpret as the basis of their descriptions of you. You may find it useful to ask others for feedback on your nonverbal communication so that you can understand the cues on which they are relying. Third, identify alternative nonverbal behaviors you might use to decrease the likelihood that others will misinterpret you.

Description of You	Nonverbal Cues	Alternative Nonverbal Cues
Example My husband says I often seem critical when I'm listening to him.		
1.		
2.		
3.		
4.		
5.		

6.7   Sculpting Personal Image with Nonverbal Communication

Purpose
To highlight the ways in which you use nonverbal communication to project different images of yourself.

Instructions
Using the form below, describe how you would use nonverbal communication, including artifacts, kinesics, and proxemics to project an identity for yourself that is congruent with the goal and situation that are described.

Example

Desired Image & Situation	Appropriate Nonverbal Communication
You are going to interview for a job with a bank.	Wear a suit and dress shoes; offer a firm handshake; keep good eye contact; avoid funky jewelry.
1. Your friend just broke up with his or her significant other, and you want to appear caring and concerned.	
2. You are very angry because the product you just bought does not work as promised. You are at the customer service desk to return it.	
3. You are at a campus social activity and want to appear attractive and available to be asked on a date.	
4. You just did poorly on an exam and are now working with the same professor to help organize a public speaker on campus. You are trying to appear responsible and reliable.	
5. You just got stopped for speeding and you want to appear like a responsible citizen.	
6. Your friend just told your secret to several other people. You are talking to your friend and you are angry and disappointed.	

Name_____

6.8   Using Your Online Resources—Experiencing
Communication in Our Lives

Chapter 6 Case Study: Teamwork

Purpose
To apply the principles you learned about the nonverbal dimension of communication in Chapter 6 to the communication scenario *Nonverbal Cues* included under Communication Scenarios on your Online Resources for Communication in Our Lives. You can complete this activity online or on this worksheet.

Instructions
Analyze *Nonverbal Cues* scenario by answering the questions below.

Scenario Overview
A project team is meeting to discuss the most effective way to present its recommendations for implementing a flextime policy on a trial basis. Members of the team are: Jason Brown (team leader), Erika Filene, Victoria Lawrence, Bill Williams, and Jensen Chen. They are sitting around a rectangular table with Jason at the head.

Conversation Analysis
1. Identify nonverbal behaviors that regulate turn-taking within the team.

2. Identify nonverbal behaviors that express relational level meanings of communication. What aspects of team members' nonverbal communication expresses liking or disliking, responsiveness or lack of responsiveness, and power?

3. How do artifacts affect interaction among members of the team?

4. If you were the sixth member of this team, what kinds of communication might you enact to help relieve tension in the group?

6.9   Understanding Cultural Values Through Proxemics

Purpose
To increase your awareness of how culture is reflected in people's use of space.

Instructions
Walk around campus, especially dining halls, cafeterias, and spaces for socializing. Observe the following use of space.

1. How far apart does a pair or group of people from the same culture sit or stand as they talk? What value do you think each culture places on personal territory?

2. How much space do students from various cultures leave between themselves and others as they walk between buildings to change classes? What value do you think each person places on speed? Time? How does the space tell you this?

3. How much space do students from various cultures leave between themselves and others as they walk through hallways to change classes? What value do you think each culture places on politeness?

4. Note couples from same cultures walking. Does one partner walk ahead of the other? Do partners walk side-by-side? What value do you think each culture places on equality of sexes?

5. Do you think the persons you observed typified their cultures? Do you think any expressed individual variation? What would you need to do to be sure?

Self-Test for Chapter 6

Multiple Choice

_____ 1. The three dimensions of relational-level meanings that may be expressed nonverbally are
   A. power, control, and liking
   B. power, liking, and disliking
   C. power, liking, and responsiveness
   D. liking, responsiveness, and disliking

_____ 2. Which of the following statements is/are true of nonverbal communication?
   A. Most nonverbal communication is instinctual.
   B. Most nonverbal communication is learned in socialization.
   C. Nonverbal patterns vary from culture to culture and social community to social community.
   D. B and C are both true.

_____ 3. In the United States, close friends and romantic partners are generally comfortable interacting at what distance?
   A. about 4 feet
   B. about 3 feet
   C. about 18 inches
   D. about 6 inches

_____ 4. We communicate nonverbally to perform or "do"
   A. race and class
   B. kinesics and haptics
   C. sexual orientation and gender
   D. A and C

_____ 5. Views of what is an attractive weight in women are influenced by
   A. socio-economic class
   B. race and ethnicity
   C. age
   D. A and B

_____ 6. The first sense to develop in humans is
   A. sight
   B. smell
   C. touch
   D. hearing

_____ 7. The professor always arrives 6 minutes late to class. He has the power to be late, whereas others don't. The professor's late arrival to remind the others that he is in charge illustrates
   A. chronemics
   B. proxemics
   C. paralanguage
   D. kinesics

_____ 8. Which of the following is true regarding the responsiveness facet of nonverbal communication?
  A. Women demonstrate more sensitivity to others than do men.
  B. Men are more adept at interpreting nonverbal communication than are women.
  C. People in subordinate standpoints fail to be as responsive and skilled in nonverbal communication as members of the dominant standpoint.
  D. None of the above is true.

_____ 9. In showing the trainee how to conduct the analysis, the manager says, "The MOST important thing to know is..." and uses greater volume when saying "most." His volume illustrates using which nonverbal behavior to reinforce the verbal message?
  A. haptics
  B. paralanguage
  C. chronemics
  D. kinesics

_____ 10. Professor Rigor lists 4 concepts on the board and points at one he regards as especially important. His gesture illustrates using which kind of nonverbal behavior to reinforce his verbal message?
  A. haptics
  B. paralanguage
  C. chronemics
  D. kinesics

_____ 11. When meeting in groups, we signal that we have finished speaking using
  A. hand gestures
  B. eye contact
  C. posture
  D. both B and C are correct

_____ 12. Peter walks into Yaakov's apartment. He notices a small tube on the doorpost (a *mezuzah*) and a copy of the *The Torah* on the end table. Peter is reacting to which type of nonverbal communication?
  A. kinesics
  B. physical appearance
  C. artifacts
  D. haptics

_____ 13. Which of the following types of nonverbal communication are you most likely to use to convey intimacy with your partner?
  A. haptics
  B. paralanguage
  C. physical appearance
  D. A and B

_____ 14. Which of the following helps improve nonverbal communication?
  A. contextual qualifications
  B. personal qualifications
  C. self reflection
  D. A, B, and C

_____ 15. Which of the following is a type of interaction between verbal and nonverbal communication?
A. Nonverbal communication regulates interpersonal interaction.
B. Nonverbal symbols are discrete.
C. Verbal communication needs to occur before nonverbal communication.
D. B and C

True/False

_____ 1. Verbal communication is almost always intentional, while nonverbal is almost always unintentional.

_____ 2. The face is capable of roughly 1,000 distinct emotional expressions.

_____ 3. Silence can convey both liking and power.

_____ 4. In the United States we often talk about, and orient ourselves toward, time as a commodity.

_____ 5. Nonverbal communication accounts for 65% to 93% of the total meaning of a message.

_____ 6. A clock is a wonderful gift for a Chinese person.

_____ 7. We create and sustain our identity by performing it day in and day out.

_____ 8. Verbal communication is perceived as more dishonest.

_____ 9. Verbal communication is culture bound and nonverbal communication is not.

_____ 10. Environmental racism is an example of using nonverbal communication to further harm those from the lower classes of society.

Essay

1. Design an environment that encourages relaxed, friendly interaction among people. Explain decisions you make about nonverbal features of the environment that you intend to contribute to the relaxed atmosphere.

2. A friend tells you that he just bought a book titled "Read Anyone's Nonverbal Communication with 100% Accuracy" and that he intends to break the "hidden code" of communication. Based on your study of nonverbal communication, what advice would you give to your friend?

3. Explain at least three cultural differences in nonverbal communication.

Chapter 6 Flash Cards

Cut out the cards, write the answers on the back, and you will have a packet of flash cards for each chapter. Paraphrasing the definition will help reinforce the definition and ideas.

Artifacts	Kinesics	Proxemics
Chronemics	Nonverbal Communication	Silence
Environmental Factors	Paralanguage	Haptics
Physical Appearance		

Chapter 7: Communication and Culture

Chapter Summary

I. Culture is a way of life that includes a system of ideas, values, beliefs, structures, and practices that are handed down from one generation to the next.
   A. Cultures are systems.
      1. The various parts of a culture are not merely a collection of ideas; the parts are related.
      2. Parts of a culture system are interdependent; change in one part will result in change in others.

   B. Multiple social communities in a single culture.
      1. Mainstream values may be in tension with social communities.
         a. High-context communication style is indirect and undetailed.
         b. Low-context communication style is explicit, detailed, and precise.
      2. Gender is one social community that exists concurrently with a larger mainstream culture.
         a. Men's talk tends to be instrumental and competitive.
         b. Women's talk expresses feelings and creates relationships.
      3. Other social communities exist.
         a. Social classes are a plagued by misunderstanding.
         b. Race and ethnicity shape social communities.

II. Communication and culture cannot be separated, because each influences the other.
   A. Communication expresses and sustains cultures.
      1. Patterns of communication reflect cultural values and perspectives.
      2. We express cultural values as we perpetuate them.

   B. Culture consists of material and nonmaterial components.
      1. Material components are those things we can see, such as housing styles, types of automobiles, clothing, and other artifacts.
      2. Nonmaterial components include beliefs, values, norms, and language.
         a. Beliefs are ideas about what is true, factual, or valid.
         b. Values are generally shared ideas about what is good, right, worthwhile, and important with regard to behavior and existence.
         c. Norms are informal rules that guide the behaviors of a given culture or social group.
         d. Language is a tool that shapes how we think about ourselves and the world.

   C. Historical and geographic forces shape culture.

   D. Culture is learned through the process of communicating.

   E. Cultures are dynamic and must evolve in order to survive.
      1. One way culture changes is through the invention of new tools, ideas, and practices.
      2. Culture can also change as a result of diffusion, or the borrowing from other cultures.
      3. Cultural changes may result from cultural calamity.
      4. Communication changes cultures by challenging the status quo.

III. We can improve communication among cultures and social communities.
  A. We can resist the ethnocentric bias.
    1. Ethnocentrism is seeing our culture of origin as right and other cultures as wrong.
    2. We can strive for cultural relativism that recognizes the unique qualities of other cultures.

  B. Recognize that responding to diversity is a process.
    1. Resistance occurs when we attack the cultural practices of others or hold ethnocentric views.
    2. Assimilation occurs when minority group members reject their own culture to adopt the ways of the dominant culture.
    3. Tolerance is accepting differences, respecting others' rights to their own ways without necessarily respecting the values of other cultures.
    4. Understanding occurs when we realize that no customs, traditions, or behaviors are superior.
    5. Respecting differences can come from understanding.
    6. We engage in participation when we borrow practices and values, becoming multilingual.

7.1   Identifying Sexist and Racist Language

Purpose
To increase awareness of language that may be perceived as sexist or racist by some people.

Instructions
Read over the ten sentences below. For each one indicate whether you think it includes language that is sexist or racist by writing an S for sexist or a R for racist in the blank at the left. If you think a sentence is neither sexist nor racist, write nothing in the blank. For any sentence that you think contains sexist or racist language, write out a revised sentence that avoids sexism and racism. Compare your answers with those of others in your class.

Example

_____   I now pronounce you man and wife.
Revision: I now pronounce you husband and wife.
_____

_____ 1.   The waitress took our order.
Revision:

_____ 2.   He's the black sheep in the family.
Revision:

_____ 3.   Anne is a woman doctor.
Revision:

_____ 4.   It's okay to tell white lies.
Revision:

_____ 5.   Edward babysat his son while his wife was away on business.
Revision:

_____ 6.   Good guys wear white hats.
Revision:

_____ 7.   A lot of Asians are really just like regular people.
Revision:

_____ 8.   She's in a black mood—stay away from her until she gets over it.
Revision:

_____ 9.   The partners in the law firm are Mr. Thompson, Mr. Flagler, Mr. Winstead, and Emily.
Revision:

_____ 10.   Asians are so indirect and deferential.
Revision:

Name_____

7.2   Cultural Variations in Social Perspectives

Purpose
To conduct cultural self-reflection and develop interpersonal skills with individuals from a variety of cultures.

Instructions
Find an artifact that is representative of a culture of which you identify. It could be a family heirloom, photographs of a significant cultural experience, or something that signifies group membership, like a pin or certificate. Share your artifact with someone that is NOT a part of your culture, then answer the following questions:

What is your artifact? Does it have a history?

What is the significance of the artifact to your culture?

Does that significance transfer to people not part of your culture? Why or why not?

How could you make the artifact meaningful to someone that doesn't share your culture?

7.3   Self-Description

Purpose
To develop awareness of facets of your identity that affect how you communicate and how you interpret the communication of others.

Instructions
On the blank lines below, fill in answers to the questions posed.

1. What is your race/ethnicity?_____

2. What is your sex?
    _____

3. What is your sexual orientation?
    _____

4. What is your socioeconomic class?
    _____

5. What is (are) your ethnic identification(s)?
    _____

6. Describe any disabilities that you have.
    _____

7. What are your spiritual beliefs (these may or may not be part of a formal religion)?
    _____

8. What is your age? _____

9. Are you currently involved in a serious romantic relationship? _____ yes _____ no

10. What are your basic political views?
    _____

11. What is your education level? _____

12. Identify other facets of your identity that you consider important influences on who you are.

Processing
Look over your answers to the above questions. What do they tell you about who you are? Compare your communication style and goals with the communication styles and goals of others in your class who answered the questions in different ways. Can you identify connections between aspects of personal identity and communication behaviors?

Name_____

7.4   Appreciating Differences Among People

Purpose
To encourage appreciation of cultural differences.

Instructions
Attend a meeting of a group of people who differ from you in some definable way. For example, if you are white, you might attend services at a black church; if you are heterosexual, you might attend a meeting of gay and lesbian students; if you are European American, you might attend a meeting of Native Americans, Asian Americans or another cultural group. Pay attention to interaction patterns and styles while you are at the meeting. Afterwards, answer the following questions.

1. Did you notice any patterns of interacting that differ from ones to which you are accustomed? Describe them:

2. Did you notice any words, phrases, or nonverbal behaviors that differ from those you normally use? Describe them:

3. Describe how it felt to be a minority in the group that you visited.

4. Discuss your responses with other students in your class.

7.5   The Nestle Case: The Impact of Social Media Communities

Purpose
To think critically about the impact of social media communities.

Instructions
Read the article listed below and use this worksheet to record your thoughts.

McKay, L. (2010). Crashing the Community. *CRM Magazine*, 14(6), 14–15. Retrieved from Academic Search Complete database.

1. According to your text, what is a social community?

2. According to McKay, are Facebook fans a community?

3. How did the Facebook community impact the way Nestle communicates online? How has social media impacted the way companies interact with their customers?

Name_____

7.6 Using Your Online Resources—Experiencing *Communication in Our Lives*

Chapter 7 Case Study: The Job Interview

Purpose

To apply the principles you learned about culture and communication in Chapter 7 to the communication scenario *The Job Interview* included under Communication Scenarios on your Online Resources for *Communication in Our Lives*. You can complete this activity online or on this worksheet.

Instructions

Analyze the *Job Interview* scenario by answering the questions below.

Scenario Overview

Mei-ying Yung is a senior who has majored in computer programming. Mei-ying's aptitude for computer programming has earned her much attention at her college. She has developed and installed complex new programs to make advising more efficient and to reduce the frustration and errors in registration for courses. Although she has been in the United States for six years, in many ways Mei-ying reflects the Chinese culture where she was born and where she spent the first 15 years of her life. Today Mei-Ying is interviewing for a position at New Thinking, a fast-growing tech company that specializes in developing programs tailored to the needs of individual companies. The interviewer, Barton Hingham, is 32 years old and a native of California, where New Thinking is based. As the scenario opens, Ms. Yung walks into the small room where Mr. Hingham is seated behind a desk. He rises to greet her and walks over with his hand stretched out to shake hers.

Conversation Analysis

1. How does Mei-ying Yung's communication reflect her socialization in Chinese culture?

2. How could Mei-ying be more effective without abandoning the values of her native culture?

3. What could enhance Barton Hingham's ability to communicate effectively with people who were raised in non-Western cultures?

7.7   Recognizing Low/High Context

Purpose
To give you practice interacting in the context not typical of your culture of origin.

Instructions
Select a few friends and acquaintances from a culture that uses high context if your culture of origin uses low or vice versa. Or attend a meeting of a campus group or an event that will be attended by members of a culture that uses the context not employed by yours. Listen for details, explanations, and descriptions, and respond to the following questions.

1. How did you know which people or event to choose for this activity?

2. How did you physically arrange or fit yourself into the arrangement of people as they conversed in the space provided?

3. How much eye contact did you note during exchanges?

4. How much time was spent explaining "how" or "why" something happened, compared to time spent describing "what" happened?

5. Did the members of the other culture get right to the point, lead up to the point gradually, or move toward the point, then away, closer toward, then away?

6. How did you feel as you participated in this exercise? What can you use from this experience to aid your communication with people of other cultures in the future?

Self-Test for Chapter 7

Multiple Choice

_____ 1. Collectivistic cultures tend to rely on a style of communication that is indirect and undetailed called
  A. low context
  B. high context
  C. no context
  D. universal context

_____ 2. Which of the following is (are) rule(s) of feminine communication?
  A. assert yourself
  B. use talk to solve problems and give advice
  C. use talk expressively
  D. B and C

_____ 3. A common misunderstanding between genders occurs when a male interprets which of the following as agreement?
  A. deferential communication
  B. symmetrical communication
  C. listening noises
  D. maximal encouragers

_____ 4. In general, individuals who have been socialized into masculine social communities tend to regard talking about relationships
  A. as useful only if there is a problem that needs to be resolved
  B. as pointless
  C. as diminishing intimacy
  D. A and C

_____ 5. Members of feminine social communities tend to form relationships centered primarily around
  A. activities
  B. common backgrounds
  C. similar values
  D. communication

_____ 6. The 'McMansions' of many suburban neighborhoods communicates the American value of "bigger is better." This would best be an example of which principle of the communication-culture relationship?
  A. cultures consist of material and non-material components
  B. communication expresses and sustains culture
  C. cultures are shaped by historical and geographic forces
  D. cultures are dynamic

_____ 7. Views of what is good, right, and worthwhile that are shared among members of a culture are called
A. values
B. beliefs
C. norms
D. properties

_____ 8. Americans' language includes terms such as "bungalow," "robot," and "fog," which originated in other cultures. Importing words from other cultures is an example of
A. invention
B. diffusion
C. reappropriation
D. consciousness

_____ 9. The tendency to think one's own culture is superior to other cultures is called
A. egocentrism
B. cultural relativism
C. moral relativism
D. ethnocentrism

_____ 10. In the 19th and 20th centuries, whites placed Native American children in "Indian Schools" where they learned to speak English and were forbidden to speak their native languages. Whites were forcing the issue of
A. ethnocentrism
B. assimilation
C. resistance
D. cultural relativism

_____ 11. "Penicillin cures infections" is an example of a
A. belief
B. language
C. norm
D. value

_____ 12. Calling a carbonated soft drink 'pop' in Detroit and 'soda' in Los Angeles is an example of
A. beliefs
B. language
C. diffusion
D. values

_____ 13. Having so many words that start with "self-" in American English demonstrates our culture's
A. beliefs
B. language
C. norms
D. values

_____ 14. Increased technological tools such as pagers, cell phones, and the Internet have changed cultures across the world. These technologies represent which source of cultural change?
A. assimilation
B. diffusion
C. invention
D. cultural calamity

_____ 15. When communicatively competent individuals recognize that different cultures think, act, and communicate in different ways, they are adopting the perspective of
A. egocentrism
B. cultural relativism
C. moral relativism
D. ethnocentrism

True/False

_____ 1. Geographic boundaries define cultures.

_____ 2. Cultural relativism is the same as moral relativism.

_____ 3. Members of a culture may give up their native ways and adopt those of a different culture.

_____ 4. Multiple social communities may co-exist within a single society or culture.

_____ 5. A culture is simply a collection of ideas, beliefs, values, and customs.

_____ 6. Communication patterns are the same between social classes and between ethnicities.

_____ 7. A culture is a system of inter-related parts.

_____ 8. Individualistic cultures value harmony, group welfare, and interdependence.

_____ 9. All social communities identify equally and exclusively with the dominant culture.

_____ 10. To participate in diversity, we must be multilingual.

Essays

1. Explain how communication functions as an agent of cultural change. Provide specific examples to support your answer.

2. Do you belong to any cybercommunities? Is it a culture? What are the shared values, beliefs, practices, and languages?

3. Name and give an example of a norm, value, belief, and language choice that exists within our society. Using the principles of culture, explain from where these nonmaterial components came.

Chapter 7 Flash Cards

Cut out the cards, write the answers on the back, and you will have a packet of flash cards for each chapter. Paraphrasing the definitions will help you remember them.

Assimilation	Dynamic	Resistance
Belief	Culture	Cultural Calamity
Cultural Relativism	Diffusion	Ethnocentrism
Invention	Multilingual	Norm
Participation	Respect	Social Community

Chapter 7 Flash Cards continued

Use the remaining cards for other concepts you would like to remember or study.

Tolerance	Understanding	Values
	High Context Communication Style	Low Context Communication Style

Chapter 8: Foundations of Interpersonal Communication

Chapter Summary

I. All interpersonal relationships have a climate that characterizes the relationship.
   A. Interpersonal climate is the overall feeling between people that comes about primarily from how they interact with one another.

   B. Interpersonal climate is an important foundation of communication in all contexts.

II. Self-disclosure is the revelation of personal information about ourselves that is not readily known to others.
   A. Self-disclosure is an important part of creating and maintaining interpersonal relationships with numerous benefits.
      1. Sharing personal feelings, etc., enhances closeness between people.
      2. Self-disclosing invites self-disclosure.
      3. Self-disclosure affects how we feel about ourselves.

   B. Self-disclosure is related to our own personal growth and the formation of relationships with others.
      1. The Johari Window is a model that helps describe self-disclosure in a relationship.
         a. The open area is information that we know and that the other knows.
         b. The blind area is information that we do not know, but that the other does know.
         c. The hidden area is information that we know but have not shared with the other.
         d. The unknown area is information that is not yet known to ourselves or to the other.
      2. The Johari Window is not static, but changes over time and changes with different individuals.

   C. Self-disclosure is related to closeness, especially among Westerners.
      1. Self-disclosure should take place gradually and with appropriate caution.
      2. In the early stages of relationships, self-disclosures are more frequent, and reciprocity is important.
      3. Reciprocation of self-disclosure is not as important once trust becomes established.
      4. The longer relationships endure over time, the less self-disclosure plays a role in the communication between the two partners.

III. Communication is an integral part of building communication climates.
   A. Supportive or confirming communication behaviors have a great influence on interpersonal climate.

   B. There are several levels of confirmation and disconfirmation.
      1. **Recognition**, reflecting another's existence, is the most basic form of confirmation.
      2. **Acknowledgment**, reflecting another's feelings, is the second level of confirmation.
      3. **Endorsement**, validating another's feelings, is the highest level of confirmation.

IV. Communication can create either supportive or defensive communication climates.
   A. Evaluative (judgmental) communication is defensive, while descriptive language is supportive.

B.   Certainty (declaration) is defensive; provisionalism (tentativeness) is supportive.

C.   Strategy (manipulation) is defensive; spontaneity (saying what we want up front) is supportive.

D.   Control (looking to blame) is defensive; problem orientation (looking for a solution) is supportive.

E.   Neutrality (not caring) is defensive; empathy (having compassion) is supportive.

F.   Superiority (believing that one partner is more important than the other) is defensive; Equality (understanding that both partners are equally important) is supportive.

V.   Conflict is a normal part of interpersonal relationships.

    A.   Conflict occurs when two interdependent people have different views, interests, and goals, and perceive those differences as incompatible.

    B.   Conflict may be over or covert.
        1.   Overt conflict occurs when people express their differences in a straightforward manner.
        2.   Covert conflict exists when partners deny or camouflage disagreements or anger and express it indirectly.

    C.   Conflict may be managed well or poorly.
        1.   Conflicts of interest occur when there are seemingly incompatible opinions, goals, or interests.
        2.   Conflict orientations relate to the attitudes people hold toward conflict.
        3.   Conflict responses are the actual behaviors people enact when in conflict.
            a.   Responses can be active or passive.
            b.   Responses can be constructive or destructive.
            c.   The exit response involves leaving the relationship physically or emotionally.
            d.   The neglect response occurs when the person minimizes or denies the problem.
            e.   The loyalty response is staying committed to the relationship despite conflict.
            f.   Voice is an active, constructive strategy that deals with conflict by talking about problems, offering sincere apologies, or trying to resolve differences so that a relationship remains healthy.
        4.   Conflict outcomes are the results of the conflict once it has been addressed, including the impact upon the relationship.

    D.   Different cultures express and deal with conflict differently.

    E.   Conflict can be beneficial for both individuals and the relationship.

VI.   Several steps can be taken to create and sustain healthy relational climates.
    A.   Communication can be used to shape the climate.
        1.   We must first recognize and acknowledge other people.
        2.   We should use confirming, supportive communication.
        3.   We should be mindful, use perception checking, and use I-language when faced with conflict.
        4.   We need to accept and be willing to grow from the conflicts in a relationship.

B.   We need to accept and confirm others.

C.   We need to accept and confirm ourselves and our own needs.

D.   We should use self-disclosure appropriately to help build relationships.

E.   We need to acknowledge and respect diversity in relationships.
     1.   Men value closeness in the doing.
     2.   Women value closeness in dialogue.

8.1   Your Many Windows

Purposes
To allow you to apply the Johari Window to your life to discover content in the different windows of yourself.

To increase awareness of differences in what is communicated about the self in different relationships.

Instructions
On the following pages you will find three copies of blank Johari Windows—one each for your parent, your best friend, and a past or current romantic partner or another person not a member of your family who knows you well. Fill in each Johari Window by writing information about you that fits each pane in the window for that particular relationship.

Processing
When you have filled in all three Johari Windows, compare the kinds of information that fits in each pane among the different relationships.

Relationship 1: With a parent (either parent)

	Known to Self	Unknown to Self
known to others	Open Area	Blind Area
unknown to others	Hidden Area	Unknown Area

Relationship 2: With your best friend

	Known to Self	Unknown to Self
k n o w n t o o t h e r s	Open Area	Blind Area
u n k n o w n t o o t h e r s	Hidden Area	Unknown Area

Relationship 3: With a current or former romantic partner

	Known to Self	Unknown to Self
k n o w n t o o t h e r s	Open Area	Blind Area
u n k n o w n t o o t h e r s	Hidden Area	Unknown Area

8.2   Changing Windows of Yourself

Purpose

To increase your awareness of how knowledge about yourself that others have changes over the course of a relationship.

Instructions

Identify a friend or romantic partner with whom you have had a long relationship. For this activity, it's important that you think about a relationship that has endured for quite a while. First, recall the early stages of this relationship. You might think about the first two or three dates with a romantic partner or the first long talks with someone who became a close friend. Fill in Johari Window #1 with content for each pane at the early stage of your relationship. Second, think back to a mid-point in the relationship's development. It might be when you and a romantic partner first expressed love for each other or when you and a friend took a vacation together.   Fill in Johari Window #2 with content for each pane at the mid-point in the relationship. Third, think about the relationship as it is today. Fill in Johari Window #3 with content for each pane at the current stage in the relationship.

Johari Window #1
Time 1: Early Stage of Relationship

	Known to Self	Unknown to Self
k n o w n t o o t h e r s	Open Area	Blind Area
u n k n o w n t o o t h e r s	Hidden Area	Unknown Area

Johari Window #2
Time 2: Mid-point in the Relationship

	Known to Self	Unknown to Self
k n o w n t o o t h e r s	Open Area	Blind Area
u n k n o w n t o o t h e r s	Hidden Area	Unknown Area

Johari Window #3
Time 3: Current Stage of the Relationship

	Known to Self	Unknown to Self
known to others	Open Area	Blind Area
unknown to others	Hidden Area	Unknown Area

8.3   Using Supportive Communication

Purpose
To provide you with concrete experience in creating supportive communication.

Instructions
Following each statement below, write out responses that foster a supportive interpersonal climate.

Example
Statement: I should have studied harder for the test.

Response: (descriptive)   You don't think you studied enough.
               (empathic)   I know how you feel.

Statement 1: I think Pat is cheating on me.

Response: (provisionalism) _____

               (problem-orientation) _____

Statement 2: I think I need to go on a diet.

Response: (empathy) _____

               (provisionalism) _____

               (equality) _____

Statement 3: Do you think it's ever right to tell a lie?

Response: (spontaneity) _____

               (provisionalism) _____

Statement 4: My counselor suggested that I go on medication to control my depression.

Response: (problem-orientation) _____

               (description) _____

               (equality) _____

8.4 **Transforming Defensive Communication Into Supportive Communication**

Purposes

To provide you with concrete examples of communication that cultivates defensiveness.

To give you experience in transforming communication that fosters defensive climates into communication that fosters supportive climates.

Instructions

Listed below are six statements that use language that cultivates defensive communication climates. Following each statement listed below, write out an alternative statement that is more likely to build a supportive communication climate. Follow directions for the type of supportive language to use.

Example

Defense-producing Language	Supportive Language
Change evaluation to description.	
You are such a whiner.	You seem to be making a lot of complaints lately.

---

1. Change certainty to provisionalism.

   The right thing to do is crystal clear.

   ---

2. Change strategy to spontaneity.

   Don't you owe me a favor from when I typed that paper for you last term?

   ---

3. Change evaluation to description.

   You're acting very immaturely.

4. Change control orientation to problem orientation.

   I think we should move where I have the good job offer since I'll make a bigger salary than you anyway.

5. Change superiority to equality.

   I can't believe you got yourself into such a dumb predicament.

6. Change neutrality to empathy.

   I don't want to get involved in your disagreement with your parents.

8.5   Distinguishing Aggressive, Assertive, and Deferential Forms of Communication

Purpose

To increase your awareness of distinctions among aggressive, assertive, and deferential styles of communicating.

Instructions

Listed below are five scenarios that describe a situation and your goal in the situation. For each scenario, write an aggressive, assertive, and deferential statement expressing your goal.

Example

Scenario: You need to study for an examination, but your boyfriend/girlfriend really wants to go out for dinner and a movie.

Aggressive response: I don't care about your preferences. I'm not going out tonight.

Assertive response: I'd like to go out tomorrow or this weekend, but I have to study tonight.

Deferential response: I guess studying isn't really that important. We can go out if you want to.

Scenario 1:   You think your roommate is angry with you, but you have no idea why and s/he denied being angry when you stated your perception. But s/he is acting very distant and unfriendly.

Aggressive response:

Assertive response:

Deferential response:

Scenario 2:   One of your close friends asks to borrow your car. Normally, you wouldn't mind lending your car to a friend, but this person has a record of speeding and being careless behind the wheel. You can't afford to have your car wrecked.

Aggressive response:

Assertive response:

Deferential response:

Scenario 3: A close friend asks you about something very personal. You want to show that you trust the friend, but you don't want to discuss this topic—even with a close friend.

Aggressive response:

Assertive response:

Deferential response:

Scenario 4: Ten days ago you lent $20 to one of your co-workers with the understanding that he would repay you within a week. He has not repaid the money, nor has he offered any explanation. You need the loan repaid.

Aggressive response:

Assertive response:

Deferential response:

Scenario 5: One of the people in a group to which you belong tells racist and sexist jokes. You find the jokes very offensive, but you don't want to create tension in the group or make the person who tells the jokes feel bad. You just want the jokes to stop.

Aggressive response:

Assertive response:

Deferential response:

Name_____

8.6   Rating the Supportiveness of Communication Climates

Purposes
To provide you with experience in identifying communication that tends to foster defensive and supportive climates between people.

To demonstrate the practical value of knowledge about supportive and defense-producing styles of communicating.

Instructions
Identify two personal relationships that you can observe. One relationship should have a supportive climate in which partners seem to feel safe, at ease, and supported by each other. The second relationship should be one in which a defensive climate prevails. Partners should seem to feel on guard and unsure of each other's motives and support. You may wish to select relationships between characters in television programs or films so that your observations do not interfere with the relationships.

Use form A below to identify examples of communication that are linked to defensive and supportive climates in the relationship that has a supportive climate. Try to record each example of supportive and defense-producing communication.

Use form B below to identify examples of communication that are linked to defensive and supportive climates in the relationship that has a defensive climate. Try to record each example of supportive and defense-producing communication.

Processing
What are the similarities and differences for the two relationships?

FORM A: USE TO CODE COMMUNICATION IN A RELATIONSHIP THAT HAS A SUPPORTIVE CLIMATE

Communication Type	Number of Instances Observed
Evaluation	
Description	
Certainty	
Provisionalism	
Strategy	
Spontaneity	
Control-orientation	
Problem-orientation	
Neutrality	
Empathy	
Superiority	
Equality	

FORM B: USE TO CODE COMMUNICATION IN A RELATIONSHIP THAT HAS A DEFENSIVE CLIMATE

Communication Type	Number of Instances Observed
Evaluation	
Description	
Certainty	
Provisionalism	
Strategy	
Spontaneity	
Control-orientation	
Problem-orientation	
Neutrality	
Empathy	
Superiority	
Equality	

8.7 Using Your Online Resources—Experiencing *Communication in Our Lives*

Chapter 8 Case Study: Cloudy Climate

Purpose

To apply the principles you learned about interpersonal communication in Chapter 8 to the communication scenario *Cloudy Climate* included under Communication Scenarios on your Online Resources for *Communication in Our Lives*. You can complete this activity online or on this worksheet.

Instructions

Analyze the *Cloudy Climate* scenario by answering the questions below.

Video Preview

Andy and Martha married five years ago when both completed graduate school. Last week Andy got the job offer of his dreams, with one problem—he would have to move 1,500 miles away. Martha loves her current job and has no interest in moving or in living apart. Andy sees this job as one that could really advance his career. For the past week they have talked and argued continuously about the job offer. Tonight, while they are preparing dinner in their kitchen, they have returned to the topic once again. We join them mid-way in their discussion, just as it is heating up.

Conversation Analysis

1. Identify examples of mind reading and describe their impact on Martha and Andy's discussion.

2. Identify communication that fosters a defensive interpersonal climate.

3. To what extent do you think Andy and Martha feel listened to by the other?

4. Do you perceive any relational level meanings that aren't being addressed in this conversation?

8.8   Communicating Levels of Confirmation

Purpose

To give you practice in creating communication that expresses different levels of confirmation of another person.

Instructions

Listed below are four situations. For each one, write a statement that expresses each of the three levels of confirmation: recognition, acknowledgment, and endorsement. Use parentheses to indicate nonverbal communication of each level of confirmation.

Example

A two-year-old child runs up to you and says, "Look, look, I found a four leaf clover."

    A. Recognition: Hello. (Smile)

    B. Acknowledgment: So you're pretty excited, aren't you?

    C. Endorsement: Wow! You're right. You did find a four leaf clover.

---

1. Your best friend comes to your place without having mentioned she/he was coming by. Your friend walks in and says, "I'm really worried about what's happening between my parents. They seem angry with each other all the time lately, and I think they may be thinking about a separation or divorce."

    A. Recognition:

    B. Acknowledgment:

    C. Endorsement:

---

2. At a meeting of a political group, someone whom you know only casually says to you, "All we ever do in this group is talk. We never really DO anything. I am very frustrated by the lack of action."

    A. Recognition:

    B. Acknowledgment:

    C. Endorsement:

---

3. While you are home over break, one of your parents says to you, "I'm worried about your uncle. His health is failing, and I think maybe we need to move him into a nursing home."

    A. Recognition:

    B. Acknowledgment:

    C. Endorsement:

---

4. The person whom you have been dating steadily for 4 months tells you, "I don't like the way we handle conflict. Whenever we disagree about something, it seems that each of us digs our heels in and refuses to listen to the other or to even try to understand the other's point of view."

    A. Recognition:

    B. Acknowledgment:

    C. Endorsement:

Name_____

8.9   Identifying Your Style(s) of Responding to Conflict

Purpose
To provide you with feedback on your preferred responses to interpersonal conflict.

Instructions
Read the 5 scenarios below. For each one, indicate which of the four possible responses you think is most likely you would follow. To score your conflict response inventory, turn to the key on the page following the inventory.

1. The person you have been dating for 6 months tells you she/he is upset by your lack of interest in spending time with her/his friends. You don't want to spend time with your partner's friends, but she/he sees this as an issue that the two of you need to resolve. In this situation, you would be most likely to

    A. walk out on the conversation.
    B. tell her/him that the issue isn't important.
    C. say nothing and hope the issue will go away.
    D. actively work to find a resolution that satisfies both of you.

2. Last week a friend let you use his/her computer when yours crashed. Accidentally, you erased a couple of files on your friend's computer. Later, the friend confronts you about the erased files and the friend seems really angry. In this situation, you would be most likely to

    A. tune out your friend's criticism and anger.
    B. agree that you had made an error and ask how you could make it up to your friend.
    C. say nothing and hope your friend's anger blows over and the friendship continues.
    D. tell your friend that it's not a big deal since he/she always backs up the hard disk on diskettes.

3. Your roommate tells you that you are a slob and that she/he wants the two of you to agree to some ground rules about cleaning and putting things away. In this situation, you would be most likely to

    A. agree to be more neat, even though you don't think it's fair that you should have to operate by your roommate's standards.
    B. tell your roommate that cleaning is not a big deal in the big picture of living together.
    C. agree that the two of you differ in how you like the place to look and offer to work out some mutually acceptable rules.
    D. leave the situation and hope that your roommate will let the matter drop.

4. The person you have been dating for a while says that you are too critical and too negative, and she/he says she/he wants you to work on changing that aspect of your behavior. Although you realize this may be a fair criticism of you, you find it uncomfortable to hear. Further, you have no idea how you could eliminate or improve your tendency to be judgmental. In this situation, you would be most likely to

   A. agree with your dating partner's perceptions and ask if she/he has any suggestions for how you might reduce your critical, negative tendencies.
   B. shrug and ignore the criticism.
   C. say nothing and hope things get better.
   D. point out that being critical is not really a major issue in whether two people are compatible.

5. Your parents call you to criticize you for not staying in touch. They say they want you to come home more often and call a couple of times each week. You are very involved in the campus scene and don't want to be running home all the time. In this situation, you would be most likely to

   A. tell your parents they are creating a problem when none really exists
   B. agree that you haven't stayed in touch and promise to be better in the future; then follow through on your promise even though it isn't your preference.
   C. tell your parents that you want to work with them to come up with ways you can stay in better touch without separating you from the campus too much.
   D. tell your parents that you don't wish to discuss this and hang up the phone.

Scoring the Conflict Response Inventory

The four choices for your action in each scenario represent the responses of exit, voice, loyalty, and neglect.

Scoring:

	Exit	_Voice_	_Loyalty_	_Neglect_
1.	A	D	C	B
2.	A	B	C	D
3.	D	C	A	B
4.	B	A	C	D
5.	D	C	B	A

Processing

Questions to consider in interpreting your scores:

1. Did you rely on a single response in 3 or more of the situations?

2. Did you rely more on exit and neglect (combined) than on voice and loyalty (combined)?

3. What are the advantages and disadvantages of your response style(s)?

Name_____

8.10   Generating Different Responses to Conflict

Purposes

To give you practice in generating communication that reflects each of the four responses to interpersonal conflict.

To increase your repertoire of methods for responding to interpersonal conflict.

Instructions

Listed below are 5 conflict scenarios. For each one, write 4 responses, one each that reflects exit, voice, loyalty, and neglect responses.

Scenario 1

The person you have been dating suggests that it's time the two of you talked about commitment. You feel unready to discuss a serious relationship, but your partner insists that she/he thinks the two of you need to talk about it.

A. Exit response:

B. Voice response:

C. Loyalty response:

D. Neglect response:

Scenario 2

One of your friends brings up a political race, and you make a comment about the strengths of the candidate you support. Your friend says, "I can't believe you support that jerk. What has he done for the environment?"

A. Exit response:

B. Voice response:

C. Loyalty response:

D. Neglect response:

Scenario 3

One of your co-workers continuously misses deadlines in turning in reports to you. Since your reports require information from the co-worker's reports, your reports are also late. You don't want your late reports to interfere with your raises and advancement. You'd like for the co-worker to be more prompt.

A. Exit response:

B. Voice response:

C. Loyalty response:

D. Neglect response:

Scenario 4

You tell your parents you'd like to take a term off from school. They are strongly opposed to the idea and they tell you to stay in school.

A. Exit response:

B. Voice response:

C. Loyalty response:

D. Neglect response

Scenario 5

You and your friend generally get together to watch the play-offs at his apartment. This year, your friend suggests that the two of you go downtown to one of the bars that has a giant screen. Where you watch doesn't really matter to you.

A. Exit response:

B. Voice response:

C. Loyalty response:

D. Neglect response

8.11   Understanding Your Conflict Script

Purpose
To help you recognize ways in which your family shaped your views of conflict.

To invite you to reconsider any unproductive conflict scripts that you learned.

Instructions
First, respond to the questions below. Second, to summarize your responses to the questions, create a written description of the conflict script you learned in your family. Third, identify any aspects of your conflict script that you would like to change. Finally, indicate strategies you will follow for revising aspects of your conflict script that you do not want to retain.

1. Did you ever witness your parents engaging in conflict?

2. If so, how often did they adopt win-win, win-lose, and lose-lose orientations toward conflict?

3. How often did each of your (step)parents rely on exit, voice, loyalty, and neglect responses to conflict?

   A. Father
   B. Mother
   C. Stepfather
   D. Stepmother

4. Do you recall any explicit statements about conflict that your parents made? For example, some parents tell children "conflict is bad" or "conflict is healthy." What do you recall hearing from your (step)parents?

5. What happened when conflict occurred in your family?

   A. Did individuals demonstrate respect for one another and one another's views?

   B. Was there any residual anger or negative feeling following conflicts?

    C. Did your parents try to get others to take sides?

6. Write the conflict script that you were taught in your family:

Identify any aspects of the conflict script that you learned in your family that you would like to revise or eliminate from your own views of conflict. For each aspect of your conflict script that you would like to revise, indicate two specific strategies you might follow to create the desired change.

Example

Desired Change in Script	Strategies for Changing
I want to change what I learned about trying to win in every case.	a. I will monitor my inclination to try to win just for the sake of winning. b. I will paraphrase other people's views to encourage myself to consider what they think and feel.
1.	a. b.
2.	a. b.
3.	a. b.

Name_____

8.12   The Smith Family

Purpose
To give you practice recognizing defensive and supportive climates.

Instructions
Watch an episode of "American Dad." As you watch the episode, list as many comments made by members of the Smith family that shape a defensive climate. What happened after the character(s) on the receiving end heard the comment? Identify the comment using Gibb's 6 pairs of Communication Behaviors. Rewrite the script for the cartoon so that members of the Smith family create a positive climate.

Self-Test for Chapter 8

Multiple Choice

_____ 1.   The Johari Window is a model of self-disclosure that
  A.   describes our self-disclosure in certain relationships
  B.   presents a constant, steady view of shared information in a relationship
  C.   helps create awareness of ourselves in relationships with others
  D.   both A and C

_____ 2.   Bia has noticed that Manijah drums her fingers while studying. Manijah doesn't realize she's doing it. Bia's observations would fall into which pane of Manijah's Johari Window with Bia?
  A.   open area
  B.   blind area
  C.   unknown area
  D.   hidden area

_____ 3.   Guy wants to be a pilot because his uncle, an Air Force pilot, was shot down in battle and never recovered. Guy has never shared the reason for his career choice with anyone. His reason is in his
  A.   open area
  B.   blind area
  C.   unknown area
  D.   hidden area

_____ 4.   Using the loyalty response to conflict may be helpful if
  A.   partners know there's no hope of resolving the conflict
  B.   the conflict is one of orientation
  C.   partners need a cooling off period
  D.   the loyalty response is never helpful

_____ 5.   You happen to run into your family doctor in the supermarket. Your doctor says, "hello," calls you by name, and asks about your family. Your doctor has just engaged in
  A.   distinction
  B.   recognition
  C.   endorsement
  D.   acknowledgment

_____ 6.   Which of the following statements about self disclosure is TRUE?
  A.   Self-disclosure is much greater in later stages of a relationship than in early stages.
  B.   When one person self-discloses, the other usually feels obligated to reciprocate, especially in later stages of the relationship.
  C.   Self-disclosure is closely related to relational satisfaction in romantic relationships.
  D.   Both A and C are true statements.

7. When interacting with a person who has a severe visual impairment, which of the following is (are) good guidelines?
    A. Avoid phrases such as "see you later."
    B. In groups, preface comments to the visually impaired person with her or his name.
    C. Speak to the person's companion or interpreter rather than directly to the person with the visual impairment.
    D. A, B, and C

8. Rob and Laura discover they have a strong difference of opinion when they discuss a job offer Rob got that would require them to move. When Rob says he wants to take the offer, Laura walks out. This exemplifies which response to conflict?
    A. exit
    B. voice
    C. loyalty
    D. neglect

9. Rob decides not to push things but to just remain quietly committed to Laura and to hope their relationship recovers.
    A. exit
    B. voice
    C. loyalty
    D. neglect

10. Assertive communication
    A. clearly expresses one's own needs or preferences
    B. recognizes and respects others' needs or preferences
    C. adopts a neutral perspective
    D. A and B

11. Farley comes to a meeting and says, "The best way to build the department is with a Health Communication minor." He is engaging in
    A. certainty
    B. evaluation
    C. problem orientation
    D. provisionalism

12. Manipulation is most like
    A. control
    B. evaluation
    C. neutrality
    D. strategy

13. While discussing sustainable resources, Wayne makes a comment about wind power. Marshall strongly disagrees with Wayne's statement. Marshall replies, "Well, I suppose that could be possible." Marshall's response is an example of
    A. evaluation
    B. provisionalism
    C. strategy
    D. neutrality

14. Assertive statements begin with the word "I" and follow with language that is
    A. loaded
    B. neutral
    C. evaluative
    D. descriptive

15. Which of the following is/are guidelines for creating and sustaining healthy climates?
    A. assert yourself
    B. confirm others
    C. self disclose continuously
    D. A and B

True/False

1. Conflict is the sign of a problem and should be avoided.

2. The highest level of confirmation is acknowledgment.

3. Voice is considered a constructive and active approach to conflict.

4. Both positive and negative evaluations can foster defensive communication climates.

5. Covert conflict is more difficult to resolve than overt conflict.

6. The most corrosive communication behavior of all to use when managing conflict is stonewalling.

7. Conflict is something that should be avoided to preserve interpersonal relationships.

8. Beth Le Poire and Stephen Yoshimura's research showed that pleasant behaviors were consistently reciprocated.

9. Problem orientation creates a more defensive climate than control.

10. Neutrality is communication that shows lack of regard and caring for another.

Essays

1. Identify and describe the specific kinds of communication that tend to foster defensive and supportive communication climates. Provide specific examples of each.

2. How would you help a friend transform a relationship plagued with toxic communication? What advice can you offer about building a supportive climate?

3. Describe Gottman's "4 Horsemen of the Apocalypse" metaphor for corrosive communication patterns and explain what effect each "horseman" has on the relationship.

Chapter 8 Flash Cards

Cut out the cards, write the answers on the back, and you will have a packet of flash cards for each chapter. Paraphrasing the definition will help reinforce the definition and ideas.

Acknowledgment	Covert Conflict	Recognition
Closeness in Dialogue	Endorsement	Self-disclosure
Closeness in the Doing	Interpersonal Climate	Stonewalling
Conflict	Overt Conflict	

Chapter 9: Communication in Personal Relationships

Chapter Summary

I. Personal relationships are unique commitments between irreplaceable individuals who are influenced by rules, relational dialectics, and surrounding contexts.

    A. Parties interact as unique individuals who could not be replaced by anyone else.

    B. Personal relationships are characterized by a commitment to the other person and to the continuation of the relationship.

        1. Passion is the intense positive feelings and desires for another person.

        2. Commitment is a decision to remain in a relationship with the intention of sharing the future together.

        3. Investments, or those things we put into the relationship that we cannot retrieve if the relationship were to end, are the basis of commitment.

    C. Personal relationships have rules that guide how partners interact.

        1. *Constitutive rules* define the meaning of various types of communication in personal relationships.

        2. *Regulative rules* influence interactions by specifying when and with whom to engage in various kinds of communication.

    D. Personal relationships are affected by the contexts in which they form, such as neighborhood, families, social units, distance, etc.

    E. Personal relationships have relational dialectics, or the opposing and continual tensions normal in relationships.

        1. Autonomy vs. connection is a dialectic that balances wanting to be connected to another individual and still maintaining one's own independence.

        2. Novelty vs. predictability is a tension between wanting familiarity and consistency and wanting surprises and spontaneity different from the daily routine.

        3. Openness vs. closedness is a tension between wanting to share things openly with a relational partner and maintaining a degree of privacy and not sharing everything.

        4. There are several techniques people use to help manage dialectic tensions.

            a. Neutralization is the negotiation of a balance between the dialectical needs.

            b. Separation, the least successful strategy, gives priority to one aspect of the dialectic while ignoring the other.

            c. Segmentation occurs when partners assign each need to certain areas, activities, or issues within the relationship.

            d. Reframing is redefining the two opposing tensions in such a way that they are not really oppositional.

II. Personal relationships evolve as they develop.

    A. Rawlins defined a six-stage model of how friendships form and develop over time.

        1. Role-limited interaction occurs in the initial stages of interaction where we follow social rules and roles.

        2. Friendly relations stage involves each person checking out the other to discover similar interests and common ground.

        3. Moving toward friendship involves stepping beyond social roles and norms and spending more time together.

4.   In nascent friendship, people think of themselves as friends or as becoming friends and begin to work out their own private way of relating.

5.   Stabilized friendship occurs when both members are established in each other lives. Stabilized friends share intimate information and reveal vulnerabilities and may continue indefinitely.

6.   Waning friendship occurs when either one or both parties decide they are no longer committed to the relationship.

B.   Romantic relationships also follow a unique pattern of development, including the stages of escalation navigation, and deterioration.

   1.   *Escalation* progressively moves two people to the point of commitment.

      a.   **Independence** is the awareness of the kind of individual we are seeking for a romantic relationship.

      b.   **Invitational communication** is the stage where people express interest in interacting with one another.

      c.   In the **explorational communication** stage, we begin considering the possibility of a relationship and begin to increase the breadth and depth of the communication.

      d.   **Intensifying communication** is the point where we begin to increase the amount and intimacy of interaction with another, and is nicknamed *euphoria*.

      e.   **Revising communication** is not always a part of escalation, but often partners back up and begin talking about the relationship itself, examining the strengths, weaknesses, and potential future.

      f.   **Commitment** is a decision to stay with the relationship permanently.

   2.   Not all couples follow this standard pattern.

      a.   Some may skip steps.

      b.   As long as intimacy exists, the constant is commitment to a future and investment in the relationships.

C.   Navigation characterizes the ongoing process of communication necessary to maintain intimacy when other parts of the relationship (oneself, one's partner, the relationship, the context) are changing.

   1.   Couples work through new problems and revisit old ones in their individual and joint lives.

   2.   Couples continuously define and redefine the **relational culture** of the relationship, or how a couple manages relational dialectics.

D.   Steve Duck and colleagues have identified a complex and dynamic series of processes that represent relationship deterioration.

   1.   **Intrapsychic processes** occur when one or both partners reflect on dissatisfaction.

   2.   **Dyadic processes** usually follow—this involves the breakdown of established patterns, understandings, and relational rules.

   3.   **Social support processes** involve telling others about problems within the relationship to receive support.

   4.   **Grave-dressing processes** occur as individuals decide they will definitely part ways and decide how to explain the deterioration in relationship with others.

   5.   **Resurrection processes** see each former partner moving into futures of their own.

III.   Personal relationships involve many challenges.
   A.   When people are unable to adapt to different communication styles, relationships may become strained.
   B.   Geographical separation may be a significant struggle for a relationship.
      1.   The greatest difficulty with geographical distance is the couples' lack of daily communication about small events and issues.
      2.   Couples often have unrealistic expectations for the time that they do share together, often expecting that time to be perfect while they are together.
      3.   Idealization of the long-distance partner can cause strain when the relationship becomes geographically close.

   C.   Equity between partners affects relationship satisfaction.
      1.   The happiest couples are those where both partners have equal investment in the relationship.
      2.   There are multiple dimensions of equity, including fairness surrounding finances, emotional contributions, physical contributions, and other elements partners deem important.
      3.   Often, inequitable distribution of domestic responsibilities creates dissatisfaction.
      4.   Women often assume psychological responsibility, even if the actual domestic workload is equal.

   D.   Violence and abuse between intimates are widespread.
      1.   Most reported partner violence is committed by men against women.
      2.   Stalking is on the rise, especially on college campuses.
      3.   Relational violence tends to follow a predictable pattern of mounting tension in the abuser, followed by a violent explosion where the abuser lashes out, and then a period of remorsefulness and caring until the tension begins to increase again.
      4.   Partner violence has been promoted by the normalization of violence in our society.
      5.   Violent relationships are not the fault of the victim.

   E.   Negotiating safer sex is difficult for some relationships, but must be engaged.
      1.   Many people find it more embarrassing to talk about sex than to engage in it.
      2.   Many people hold erroneous and dangerous misperceptions about practicing safer sex.
      3.   Sometimes people do not discuss safer sex because drugs or alcohol has impaired their rational thought.

9.1   Distinguishing Between Love and Commitment

Purposes
To increase your understanding of the difference between love and commitment.

To provide concrete experience in identifying language that reflects love and commitment.

Instructions
Listed below are 10 statements that friends and romantic partners might make to each other. In the blank to the left of each statement indicate whether the statement expresses commitment (C) or love (L). Answers appear with the Chapter 9 Self-Test Answers.

_____   1.   I have a really great time with you.

_____   2.   Talking with you is so helpful in sorting out my feelings.

_____   3.   I like to think about how we'll be 10 or 15 years from now.

_____   4.   I feel great when I'm with you.

_____   5.   I intend to be faithful to you all of my life.

_____   6.   I've never felt this way about anyone else before.

_____   7.   I'm crazy about you, but if you don't learn to control your temper, our relationship is over.

_____   8.   Our relationship would be so much more enjoyable if you didn't have these outbursts of temper.

_____   9.   I feel so close to you right now.

_____   10.   Nothing will ever come between us.

Name_____

9.2   Features of Relationships

Purposes
To allow you to apply research on close relationships to two important relationships in your life.

To help you understand the bases of satisfaction in two important relationships in your life.

Instructions
Identify a close friend and a current or past romantic partner. Each person should be one with whom you did or do have a satisfying close relationship. Use forms A and B on the following two pages to describe the central features of satisfying relationships as they operate in your personal relationships.

FORM A: FEATURES IN FRIENDSHIP

Feature	Presence in Your Relationship
1. Investments	
• What have you invested?	
• What has your friend invested?	
2. Commitment	
• How certain are you that the two of you will remain close friends?	
• To what extent do the two of you talk about a shared future or future plans?	
3. Trust	
• How much do you feel you can rely on your friend to do what she/he says she/he will do?	
• How much do you count on your friend to look out for you and your welfare?	
4. Relational Dialectics	
• How do you manage needs for autonomy and connection?	
• How do you manage needs for novelty and predictability?	
• How do you manage needs for openness and closedness?	

FORM B: FEATURES IN A ROMANTIC RELATIONSHIP

Feature	Presence in Your Relationship
1. Investments	
• What have you invested?	
• What has your partner invested?	
2. Commitment	
• How certain are you that the two of you will remain together in a romantic relationship?	
• To what extent do the two of you talk about a shared future or future plans?	
3. Trust	
• How much do you feel you can rely on your partner to do what she/he says she/he will do?	
• How much do you count on your partner to look out for you and your welfare?	
4. Relational Dialectics	
• How do you manage needs for autonomy and connection?	
• How do you manage needs for novelty and predictability?	
• How do you manage needs for openness and closedness?	

9.3   Recognizing Relational Dialectics

Purpose
To give you experience in identifying relational dialectics in everyday situations.

Instructions
Listed below are 6 descriptions of common dynamics in personal relationships. Identify which relational dialectic is most prominent in each. Record your answers in the blanks to the left of the descriptions. Answers appear with the Chapter 9 Self-Test Answers.

Example

_____*novelty/predictability*_____
Erin and Mike want to take a vacation and are undecided whether to return to a place they know and like or to go somewhere new and different.

1. _____
Emiko just got off the phone with her best friend. Emiko's husband walked in and overheard the end of the conversation. He starts asking Emiko to tell him about what she and her friend were discussing. Emiko shares almost everything with her husband, but isn't sure she wants to reveal the details of their conversation.

2. _____
Tyrone and David have gotten together to watch football games every weekend for two years. They really enjoy their time together, but they are starting to get bored with the ritual.

3. _____
Marilyn likes the fact that her boyfriend, Jim, respects her right to not tell him about certain aspects of her life. At the same time, she sometimes feels that what they don't know about each other creates a barrier between them.

4. _____
Jay isn't sure what to do. He really loves spending time with Anna and really wants to go out with her tonight. But his friends just asked him to come over, watch the game, and have pizza— just the guys.

5. _____
Kelly loves the security and predictability in her relationship with Scott, but sometimes she wishes their relationship was just a little more exciting.

6. _____
Eva and Sylvia went to Chicago for the weekend to visit a mutual friend and go shopping. When they get home, they don't call or see each other for several days.

Name_____

9.4   Features of Friendships

Purpose
To allow you to identify common features of friendship that operate in an important friendship in your life.

Instructions
The form that begins on the next page identifies 5 features that researchers have found are important in satisfying friendships in Western culture. Identify your closest friend. The friend may be your sex or the other sex as long as this is the person you regard as your closest friend. For each feature described on the form, indicate ways in which it is expressed and experienced in your friendship.

FEATURES OF FRIENDSHIP

Feature	How expressed and experienced
1. Willingness to invest in the friendship. • How do you invest? • How does your friend invest?	
2. Intimacy • How do you express emotional closeness? • How important is closeness through dialogue? • How important is closeness through doing?	
3. Acceptance • How do you let your friend know that you accept her/him, faults and all? • How does your friend demonstrate that she/he accepts you, faults and all?	

4. Trust

- Can you count on your friend to do what she/he says she/he will do?

- Can your friend count on you to do what you say you will?

- How does your friend show that she/he cares about you and your welfare?

- How do you show your friend that you care about him/her and his/her welfare?

---

5. Support

- How does your friend communicate that she/he supports you? Identify verbal and nonverbal forms of communication.

- How do you communicate to your friend that you support her/him? Identify verbal and nonverbal forms of communication.

9.5   Relational Dialectics in Your Friendships

Purposes
To heighten your awareness of the presence of relational dialectics in an important friendship in your life.

To give you insight into the normalcy and health of opposing needs in a friendship of yours.

Instructions
Identify an important friendship in your life. Use that friendship as the referent for responding to the form on the following pages. Using the form that appears on the following page, first provide an example from your friendship of each pole of the three relational dialectics. Second, identify what would be lost if the example you identified were not in your friendship.

Relational Dialectics in Your Friendship

Dialectic	Specific example in your friendship	What would be lost if this were not present
Example		
Openness	I disclose to Jenetta about my worries about getting into graduate school.	Jenetta would not know me as well; I would not get her support.
A. Autonomy/ Connectedness		
A-1: Autonomy		
A-2: Connectedness		

B. Novelty/ Predictability

B-1: Novelty

B-2: Predictability

C. Openness/ Closedness

C-1: Openness

C-2: Closedness

Can you think of other dialectics that operate in your personal relationships?

Name_____

9.6 Gendered Styles of Friendship

Purposes

To recognize masculine and feminine styles of experiencing and expressing closeness in friendships.

To identify multiple styles of closeness in your friendships.

Instructions

Identify a close friend of your sex and a second close friend of the other sex. Answer the questions on the form that follows this page. When you have completed your form, discuss features of friendship with others in your class. Are there common features that distinguish interaction in male-male, male-female, and female-female friendships?

Use the following scale to respond to questions about interaction in your friendships:
  1 = occurs very often in the friendship
  2 = occurs fairly often in the friendship
  3 = occurs, but is not a regular feature of the friendship
  4 = seldom occurs in the friendship
  5 = never or virtually never occurs in the friendship

Same Sex Friend	Opposite Sex Friend		
_____	_____	1.	We talk about family issues and problems.
_____	_____	2.	We help each other out with repairs, loans, etc.
_____	_____	3.	We play sports together.
_____	_____	4.	We listen to each other's personal problems.
_____	_____	5.	We talk directly about our feelings for one another.
_____	_____	6.	We do things together like watching games, back packing, and going out to bars.
_____	_____	7.	We go get a cup of coffee and sit and talk about what is going on in our lives.
_____	_____	8.	We give each other hugs.
_____	_____	9.	We offer advice for whatever problem the other is experiencing.
_____	_____	10.	We talk on the phone regularly just to talk to one another.

9.7 Why Friendships Wane

Purposes
To allow you to apply research discussed in the textbook to understand better friendships that have faded.

To enhance your understanding of internal and external factors that can erode friendships in our lives.

Instructions
Identify a past friendship that was very important to you at one time, but that has waned or ended entirely. Check each of the statements on the form on the following page that accurately describes that friendship when it was becoming less intimate.

Signs of Waning Friendship

Check if applies to your friendship

Sign of Waning Friendship

_____ 1. My friend was less interested in getting together or talking with me.

_____ 2. I was less interested in getting together or talking with my friend.

_____ 3. Career demands took too much of my time.

_____ 4. Career demands took too much of my friend's time.

_____ 5. My family situation changed (I married, had or adopted a child, etc.).

_____ 6. My friend's family situation changed.

_____ 7. My friend violated my trust.

_____ 8. I violated my friend's trust.

_____ 9. My friend moved.

_____ 10. I moved.

_____ 11. There was sexual tension in the friendship.

_____ 12. My friend's and my interests changed so that we no longer had strong common interests.

_____ 13. I developed a new, strong friendship with another person.

_____ 14. My friend developed a new, strong friendship with another person.

_____ 15. The friendship became too routine and boring.

9.8   Long Distance Friendship

Purposes
To allow you to apply research discussed in the textbook to a long-distance friendship of yours.

To increase your awareness of ways in which communication can ease the difficulty of sustaining a long-distance friendship.

Instructions
Listed below are 5 strategies for maintaining good communication in long-distance friendships. Identify a friend of yours who lives more than 60 miles away. Check each of the communication strategies listed below that you use to maintain the friendship. For communication strategies that you are not now using, consider the value of including them in your friendship.

Use	Do Not Use	Communication Strategy
_____	_____	1. Call at least once a week.
_____	_____	2. Send electronic mail at least once a week.
_____	_____	3. Visit at least three times a year.
_____	_____	4. Write letters at least once a month.
_____	_____	5. Talk to the friend in your head.

9.9   Let's Get Personal

Purposes

To increase your awareness of the bases of romantic attraction in our era.

To increase your sensitivity to differences in criteria for romantic partners that are used by heterosexual women, heterosexual men, lesbians, and gay men.

Instructions

Obtain one or more state-wide newspapers or other publications that include a large section of personal ads. Or, use a personal service on the Internet such as Yahoo.Com. You should have a large enough sample of ads to have at least ten ads each for: men seeking men, men seeking women, women seeking men, and women seeking women. Use the four forms that follow this page to record the criteria specified by ad-writers when they describe desirable romantic partners. Compare trends in the criteria used by the four groups of individuals.

Form for Analyzing Personal Ads by Men for Men

Ad #	Physical Qualities	Personal Qualities	Career Success	Interest in Talk	Activities	Financial Resources
1.						
2.						
3.						
4.						
5.						
6.						
7.						
8.						
9.						
10.						

Form for Analyzing Personal Ads by Men for Women

Ad #	Physical Qualities	Personal Qualities	Career Success	Interest in Talk	Activities	Financial Resources
1.						
2.						
3.						
4.						
5.						
6.						
7.						
8.						
9.						
10.						

Form for Analyzing Personal Ads by Women for Men

Ad #	Physical Qualities	Personal Qualities	Career Success	Interest in Talk	Activities	Financial Resources
1.						
2.						
3.						
4.						
5.						
6.						
7.						
8.						
9.						
10.						

Form for Analyzing Personal Ads by Women for Women

Ad #	Physical Qualities	Personal Qualities	Career Success	Interest in Talk	Activities	Financial Resources
1.						
2.						
3.						
4.						
5.						
6.						
7.						
8.						
9.						
10.						

9.10   A Fine 'Bromance'

Purposes

To identify stages of male non-sexual relationships in popular film.

To understand better how stages of relationships are experienced and expressed in popular communication.

Instructions

What is a 'bromance'? This activity invites you to identify stages of relationships that are emphasized in currently popular 'buddy' or 'bromantic' films. Using the form that begins on the next page, identify a current or recent popular buddy movie. How is each stage played out in the movie? Note specific examples in the space provided.

When you have completed the form, notice which stages of relationships were highlighted in the movie. What does this tell you about the phases of relationships celebrated in popular culture? Is a romantic model of relationship analysis appropriate for a 'bromantic' relationship?

(Examples of this genre of film include *I Love You, Man*, *Star Trek: The Search for Spock*, and the originator, *The Odd Couple*.)

A Fine Bromance

Stage	Movie	Specific Example
Intensifying Together		
Invitational Communication		
Explorational Communication		
Intensifying Communication (Euphoria)		
Revising Communication		
Intimate Bonding		
Navigating	*Wedding Crashers*	Jeremy and John develop 'Wedding Crasher Rules'
Dyadic Breakdown		
Intrapsychic Phase		
Dyadic Negotiation		
Social Phase of Deterioration		
Social Support		
Grave Dressing		

9.11 Recognizing Styles of Love

Purpose
To give you experience in identifying communication that reflects particular styles of loving.

Instructions
Listed below are 15 statements that might be made by a person about romance or a romantic partner. Identify the style of love reflected in each of the statements. Answers appear with the Chapter 9 Self-Test Answers.

Style of Love	Statement
Example	
Agape	Your happiness is my happiness.

_____ 1. I want to tell my partner everything about me as soon as I fall in love.

_____ 2. My partner is my best friend.

_____ 3. I could only fall in love with someone of my race and class.

_____ 4. I am looking for a partner who will be a good parent.

_____ 5. Love's a game—I never take it too seriously.

_____ 6. I wish I could be sure Pat loves me. I worry all the time.

_____ 7. I put Kim's welfare and desires ahead of my own, and that's the way I want it to be.

_____ 8. I fall in love hard and fast.

_____ 9. I am not looking for a committed relationship—just some fun.

_____ 10. All I can think about is this relationship. Nothing and nobody else matters to me.

_____ 11. I am happiest when my partner is happy.

_____ 12. What I like best about my relationship is that it is so steady and peaceful—none of those dramatic ups and downs that some couples have.

_____ 13. I need to make sure my partner loves me, so I come up with tests a lot of the time.

_____ 14. I intend to marry someone who is professionally ambitious.

_____ 15. Our love just grew very gradually. We started off as friends, and eventually romantic interest developed an extra layer on the basic foundation of friendship.

Name_____

9.12   Identifying Stages in Romantic Relationships

Purpose
To give you experience in identifying communication that reflects different stages in the evolution of romantic relationships.

Instructions
Listed on this page and the next are 12 interactions between partners A and B that would be most likely to occur at specific stages in a romantic relationship. Identify the stage of romance most clearly reflected in each of the interactions. Answers appear with Chapter 9 Self-Test answers.

Revising
A: Before I could consider a permanent relationship, you need to stop smoking.
B: I understand that condition.

1. _____
   A: Where are you from?
   B: Ohio. Where is your home?

2. _____
   A: I plan to spend the rest of my life with you.
   B: I feel the same way.

3. _____
   A: (thought, not stated) I'm just not happy in this relationship. We don't communicate any more.
   B: (thought, not stated) I really miss doing things together.

4. _____
   A: Do you enjoy bands like this one?
   B: Sure, but I like jazz even more. Do you like jazz?

5. _____
   A: I think I finally understand what went wrong in our relationship and why we couldn't make it work.
   B: Me too, so now we can let it go.

6. _____
   A: It's so comfortable to have established our routines and understandings in our relationships.
   B: Yeah, there's a nice basic rhythm in our lives together.

7. _____

A: I just called to say good night. Even though we spent 4 hours just talking tonight, I wanted to talk to you once more before going to sleep.

B: I'm glad you called. I can't get enough of you.

8. _____

A: We have some problems that I think we should talk about.

B: You're right—things aren't very smooth right now.

9. _____

A: (unstated realization) We don't ask about each other's day anymore like we used to do all the time.

B: (unstated realization) We used to go out for brunch every Sunday, but we don't anymore.

10. _____

A: (to parent) It's over between Pat and me, and I'm really sad.

B: (to friend) Kim and I just broke up, and I'm kind of down.

11. _____

A: I know that I love you, but I'm not sure we can make a permanent life together.

B: Why not? Let's talk about your questions and see if we can find answers to them. I want to make this work.

12. _____

A: How are we going to tell our parents we're separating? There's never been a divorce in either of our families.

B: I know. I think it's really important that neither of us blame the other when we talk to our families. Will you agree to that?

Name_____

9.13   Identifying Your Love Style

Purpose
To help you recognize your own love style and predict how it will fit with each of the others in a potential romantic relationship, or does fit with the style of your current partner.

Instructions
Look at the statements in exercise 9.11. Which of those describe you? Write your style name below and copy the descriptive statements. If you are currently in a romantic relationship, repeat the previous instruction for your partner. If you are not currently in a relationship, follow instruction 1, then select the style that most appeals to you.

My Style Description _____ **My Partner's Style Description** _____

Compare the styles. Are they congruent (the same)? Adjacent (nearly the same)? Opposite?

What communication behaviors will you and your partner (real or hypothetical) have to engage in to accommodate differences or balance the potential negative effects of sameness?

9.14   Using Your Online Resources—Experiencing
Communication in Our Lives

Chapter 9 Case Study: Wedding Bells

Purpose
To apply the principles you learned about communication in personal relationships in Chapter 9 to the communication scenario *Wedding Bells* on your Online Resources for *Communication in Our Lives*. You can complete this activity online or on this worksheet.

Instructions
Analyze the *Wedding Bells* scenario by answering the questions below.

Scenario Overview
After meeting at a New Year's party in the spring of their senior year at Agora College, Trevor and Meg quickly developed an exclusive dating relationship. Now, 4 months later, they are trying to figure out what to do about their relationship. Listen to and analyze the following conversation which occurred after lunch on a Sunday afternoon. Based on their conversation, answer the following questions:

Conversation Analysis
1. Based on the scenario, which styles of loving do you think Meg and Trevor have? What communication by each of them leads you to perceive particular styles of loving?

2. Based on their conversation, what do you perceive to be Meg's and Trevor's levels of commitment to the relationship?

3. What aspects of context seem to influence Meg's and Trevor's preferences for how the relationship should proceed?

Name_____

9.15   Case Study —Experiencing Communication in Our Lives

Purpose
To assist you in locating research about communication and help you analyze and apply the concepts from Chapter 9.

Instructions
Locate and read the article listed below, and answer the following questions.

Karbo, K. (November, 2006). Friendship: The Laws of Attraction. *Psychology Today*.

1. What does the author refer to as, 'the dark matter of friendship'?

2. When does a pair leave 'buddyhood' for real friendship?

3. Why do only some friendships stick?

4. What are the four basic behaviors necessary to maintain friendship bonds?

5. Why is being positive so important to a lasting friendship, according to this author?

Self-Test for Chapter 9

Multiple Choice

_____ 1. Pat and Lynn feel torn between going square dancing every Tuesday night and wanting to try ballroom dance. They are experiencing tension from which relational dialectic?
A. autonomy/connection
B. novelty/predictability
C. openness/closedness
D. structure/flexibility

_____ 2. Pat and Lynn then discover they are uncomfortable not knowing what's going on Saturday night. Instead of trying something new, they decide maybe they should just continue what they've been doing. This illustrates which response to relational dialectics?
A. neutralization
B. separation
C. segmentation
D. reframing

_____ 3. Ella and Ben have been dating for six months. Ben wants to take Ella to a party at his sister's house Friday night. Ella had a hard week. She wants to go to the party with Ben, but she'd rather just stay at home and chill. Ella is struggling with which relational dialectic?
A. autonomy/connection
B. novelty/predictability
C. openness/closedness
D. independence/interdependence

_____ 4. Ella suggests to Ben that they get together on Saturday night instead. She explains this way she can relax Friday night but also spend time with Ben. Her method of managing dialectics is
A. segmentation
B. reframing
C. separation
D. neutralization

_____ 5. The part of relationship that is the primary building block of enduring relationships is
A. passion
B. commitment
C. investments
D. relationship rules

_____ 6. The unique feature of personal relationships is
A. the persons involved are not replaceable
B. the value of the persons involved is determined by the roles they play
C. personal relationships constitute the greater proportion of all our relationships
D. the relationship does not end when one person leaves it

_____ 7. Ada and Louis call to say 'good morning' to each other before they leave for work each day, and have done so for the past five years. Their phone calls are an example of
A. constitutive rules
B. regulative rules
C. passion
D. dialectics

_____ 8. The greatest problem(s) reported by partners in long-distance relationships is (are)
A. not being able to share small talk and daily routines
B. unrealistic expectations for time together
C. inability to share major events with each other
D. A and B

_____ 9. In heterosexual dual-worker families, approximately what percentage of men assume domestic responsibilities equal to their partners?
A. 10%
B. 20%
C. 25%
D. 50%

_____ 10. The most egalitarian relationships in terms of shared homemaking and child care are in
A. Heterosexual marriages
B. heterosexual cohabitation
C. gay commitments
D. lesbian commitments

_____ 11. According to research cited in the textbook, what percentage of teenage dating relationships includes violence?
A. 0%
B. 5%
C. 10%
D. 25%

_____ 12. At what point do social norms and roles become less important in a friendship?
A. friendly relations
B. nascent friendship
C. stabilized friendship
D. waning friendship

_____ 13. Which of the following is the nucleus of intimacy?
A. commitment
B. relational culture
C. relational dialectics
D. satisfaction

_____ 14. Why do people choose NOT to engage in safer sex?
A. use of alcohol and/or other drugs
B. they find it embarrassing to talk about sex
C. they ignore the risks
D. A and B

15. Investments, what we put into a relationship that we don't get back out of it when the relationship ends, include
    A. thoughts
    B. feelings
    C. time
    D. A, B, and C are all investments

True/False

_____ 1. Social relationships are commitments between individuals who are irreplaceable.

_____ 2. A passion for the other person is the primary building block of relationships.

_____ 3. Regulative rules in relationships define what various kinds of communication means.

_____ 4. Relationships that are driven by external events and circumstances tend to result in less long-term satisfaction than relationships that develop in response to feelings and fit between individuals.

_____ 5. Violence and abuse in intimate relationships seldom stops without intervention.

_____ 6. Psychological responsibility, remembering, planning, and coordinating activities is typically assigned to men.

_____ 7. The three greatest influences on initial attraction are self-concept, proximity, and similarity.

_____ 8. People of different races and cultural heritages are building relationships in greater numbers today than 20 years ago.

_____ 9. Idealization and the consequent euphoria we feel as passion is greater in on-line relationships because they develop faster.

_____ 10. Media include many narratives that normalize violence between intimate partners.

Essay

1. Describe the cycle of abuse that occurs in some intimate relationships. Explain how intrapersonal communication of abusers contributes to abuse.

2. How are relationships characterized on TV commercials? Watch a few commercials that feature relationships. How do the relational dialectics of the relationship play out in the ads?

3. Friendships and romantic relationships have different stages of development. List and define each of the stages of romantic relationship development.

Chapter 9 Flash Cards

Cut out the cards, write the answers on the back, and you will have a packet of flash cards for each chapter. Paraphrasing the definitions will help you remember them.

Commitment	Investments	Relational Dialectics
Dyadic Processes	Invitational Communication	Resurrection Processes
Explorational Communication	Neutralization	Revising Communication
Grave Dressing Processes	Personal Relationship	Segmentation
Independence	Reframing	Social Support Processes

Chapter 9 Flash Cards continued

Use the remaining cards for other concepts you would like to remember or study.

Intensifying Communication	Relational Culture	Psychological Responsibility
Intrapsychic Processes	Passion	Rules
Separation		

Chapter 10: Foundations of Group and Team Communication

Chapter Summary

I.   Groups and teams are an important context of our regular communication activities.
    A.   Business increasingly relies on groups and teams because they often do better work than individuals.

    B.   Groups and teams are related, but are not the same.
        1.   Groups are comprised of three or more people who interact over time, depend on each other, and follow shared rules of conduct to achieve a common goal.
        2.   Teams are a special kind of group that are characterized by people with diverse skills and by a greater interdependence and sense of collective identity than most groups.
        3.   All groups are not teams, but all teams are groups.

    C.   If the shared goal of a group or team goes away, the group will dissolve unless another goal or shared activity is found.

II.   Groups have potential limitations and strengths.
    A.   There are two potential limitations to group work.
        1.   The first is the amount of time groups demand.
        2.   A second is the emphasis on conformity and the possible suppression of individual creativity.

    B.   Groups have many strengths that often outweigh the limitations.
        1.   Groups contain greater resources than any one individual can bring to bear on a problem, decision, or project.
        2.   Groups tend to be more thorough in their tasks than do individuals because the group members act as a check-and-balance system for one another and often develop synergy.
        3.   Groups tend to generate greater creativity.
        4.   Groups tend to generate greater commitment to a decision.
            a.   Participation in the decision-making process enhances the group members' commitment to the decision made.
            b.   Group decisions generally take into account a greater number of perspectives and thus are likely to yield to greater cooperation by those impacted by the group's decision.

III. There are several features that characterize small groups.
    A.   Cohesion is the degree of closeness, esprit de corps, and group identity that members feel.
        1.   Greater cohesion often leads to greater member satisfaction.
        2.   Cohesion can be built by emphasizing communication that focuses on shared goals and on the team as a whole.
        3.   Cohesion can be built by fostering communication that highlights similarities among group members.
        4.   Cohesion can be enhanced by expressing affection, inclusion, and respect so group members feel valued.
        5.   Cohesion and participation influence each other reciprocally.
        6.   When groups are too cohesive, Groupthink can occur.

B. Group size impacts group interaction.
    1. Large groups may encourage the formation of cliques or subgroups.
    2. The ideal group size is between 5 and 7 members.
    3. Groups that are too small have disadvantages as well.

C. Power, or the ability to influence others, impacts group functioning.
    1. *Power over* is one type of power where an individual is clearly highlighted as the leader who has the ability to make decisions and control others.
    2. *Power to* is using power to empower others to reach their goals, often behind the scenes, in order to support a win-win group climate.
    3. A *distributive power structure* occurs when all members in a group have equal power.
    4. A *hierarchical power structure* occurs when one or more members have greater power than others.
    5. **Social climbing** is the attempt to gain approval of high status individuals in the hope of achieving higher status through association.
    6. *Earned power* is gained when a member provides skills valued by the group.

D. A group's interaction patterns can impact how a group functions.
    1. A centralized group has one or two key individuals through whom most communication flows.
    2. In a decentralized group, communication is more balanced among all members, usually leading to greater member satisfaction.

E. Group norms are guidelines that regulate how members behave and interact with one another.
    1. Norms define what is allowed, what is not allowed, and what is rewarded within the group.
    2. Group norms regulate all aspects of group interaction from the trivial to the critical.
    3. Norms are the direct result of interaction among group members.

IV. Culture influences group decision making.
    A. **Individualism** is one of the most strongly held values of Western society.

    B. We value **assertiveness**, and we expect that people will speak up and assert their ideas and stand up for their rights.

    C. Western cultures strongly value **equality** and equal participation of all members.

    D. **Progress, change, and speed** are also valued, leading many Westerners to want a quick pace of interaction and quick results or answers.

    E. Westerners tolerate more **risk and uncertainty** as a normal part of progress.

    F. Westerners also value **informality** leading them to interact with others in a direct and relaxed way.

V.   There are a variety of communicative processes that take place in small groups.
   A.   There are four kinds of communication in small group interaction.
      1.   Task communication focuses on the problems, issues, or information before the group.
      2.   Procedural communication focuses on how the group will accomplish its task and carry out its interactions.
      3.   Climate communication focuses on maintaining a supportive and effective climate that is comfortable for the members and is positive for the completion of the task.
      4.   Egocentric communication is dysfunctional communication that focuses on one or more particular individuals at the expense of the group and task.

   B.   Effective group communication focuses on task, procedural, and climate communication while avoiding egocentric communication.

10.1   Identifying Kinds of Communication in Groups

Purpose
To sharpen your awareness of different kinds of communication that affect group process and outcomes.

Instructions
Below is an excerpt from a group discussion. In the blank, write whether each contribution is task, procedural, climate, or egocentric. Correct answers appear with Chapter 10 Self-Test Answers.

Coding Group Discussion

1. _____ I think we should talk first about the background each of us has relevant to our task. Then we can move into discussion of the task itself.

2. _____ I think it would be better to get right into the task. If we didn't have relevant backgrounds we wouldn't have been put in this group.

3. _____ I think the two of you agree. Both of you think our backgrounds are important and that talking about the task is also important. Perhaps we could indicate what relevant experience we have in the process of discussing the task.

4. _____ Okay, then I'll start by saying that I think our priority should be developing a strong marketing campaign. That is the foundation of succeeding with this new product.

5. _____ Do we have any information on effective marketing strategies for similar products?

6. _____ Whoa! Aren't we putting the cart before the horse? Let's focus first on the product, and then consider the best way to market it.

7. _____ Who gives a darn about the product? We know our job is to push it whether it has any value.

8. _____ That kind of thinking isn't going to help us. Let's try to stay positive.

9. _____ I agree. I see the product as a very creative addition to our line of office supplies. It promises to increase efficiency for workers.

10. _____ Right. And my background in developing other products in our office supply line indicates that a lot of workers are going to love our new note-a-pad system.

11. _____ Great! So what we're doing is something that will be appreciated by the customers and do well for our company. It's a win-win situation.

10.2   Distinguishing Power Over and Power To

Purposes
To give you practice in recognizing power over and power to forms of power in groups.

To heighten your ability to distinguish between communication that expresses *power over* and *power to* styles of exerting influence.

Instructions
Below are statements that might be made by a group leader. In the blanks to the left of each statement indicate whether it expresses *power over* or *power to*. Correct answers appear with Chapter 10 Self-Test Answers.

Distinguishing Power Over and Power To

_____   1.   If you get this project in on time, I will guarantee you a bonus.

_____   2.   If you don't get the project in on time, your job is gone.

_____   3.   I notice and appreciate all that you're doing to keep our team on target.

_____   4.   Since you indicated you want to get field experience, I decided to put you on a special assignment.

_____   5.   Each of you is making the others' work easier—you're a fabulous team.

_____   6.   My position as CEO entitles me to decide which of you is laid off and which of you stays.

_____   7.   I'm going to put a good word in for you with the head guy. I might as well use the power I have.

_____   8.   If you do your work right, I can help you advance in this company.

_____   9.   If we all work together, I think each of us will succeed.

_____   10.   Not everyone going to win points on this project, so the competition is on.

Name_____

10.3   Assessing Group Discussion

Purposes
To heighten your awareness of aspects of groups that influence effectiveness.

To assist you in applying conceptual information about groups to your own experiences working in groups.

Instructions
Think about your experiences in groups and teams. Identify the single best and the single worst group or team experience you have had. Use Form A: Rating the Best Group Experience on the following page to assess the best group experience you have had. Use Form B: Rating the Worst Group Experience to assess the worst group experience you have had.

Processing
Compare your assessments for the two group experiences. To what extent do your judgments of best and worst groups reflect the textbook's discussion of group features?

FORM A: RATING THE BEST GROUP EXPERIENCE

Check whether you agree or disagree with each statement.

Aspect of Group	Agree	Disagree
1. Members were committed to the group.	_____	_____
2. Members were enthusiastic when discussing issues in the group.	_____	_____
3. Members listened to one another.	_____	_____
4. Differences of opinion were respected and considered fairly.	_____	_____
5. There was a strong sense of group identity (cohesion).	_____	_____
6. Everyone participated.	_____	_____
7. Meetings were organized.	_____	_____
8. There were not strong disparities of power among members.	_____	_____
9. Discussion was productive—we got things done.	_____	_____
10. Members provided procedural communication to keep the group organized and on schedule.	_____	_____
11. Members provided good climate communication to maintain a healthy working relationship.	_____	_____
12. Members exercised critical thinking and analysis when working on the task.	_____	_____
13. Members supported and helped one another.	_____	_____

FORM B: RATING THE WORST GROUP EXPERIENCE

Check whether you agree or disagree with each statement.

Aspect of Group	Agree	Disagree
1. Members were committed to the group.	_____	_____
2. Members were enthusiastic when discussing issues in the group.	_____	_____
3. Members listened to one another.	_____	_____
4. Differences of opinion were respected and considered fairly.	_____	_____
5. There was a strong sense of group identity (cohesion).	_____	_____
6. Everyone participated.	_____	_____
7. Meetings were organized.	_____	_____
8. There were not strong disparities of power among members.	_____	_____
9. Discussion was productive—we got things done.	_____	_____
10. Members provided procedural communication to keep the group organized and on schedule.	_____	_____
11. Members provided good climate communication to maintain a healthy working relationship.	_____	_____
12. Members exercised critical thinking and analysis when working on the task.	_____	_____
13. Members supported and helped one another.	_____	_____

10.4 Using Your Online Resources—Experiencing *Communication in Our Lives*

Chapter 10 Case Study: Group Communication

Purpose
To apply the principles you learned about group communication in Chapter 10 to the scenario *Group Communication* included under Communication Scenarios on your Online Resources for *Communication in Our Lives*. You can complete this activity online or on this worksheet.

Instructions
Analyze the *Group Communication* scenario by answering the questions below.

Video Preview
As members of the Student Government Financial Committee, Davinia, Joyce, Thomas, and Pat make decisions on how much funding, if any, to give to various student groups that request support from the funds collected from student fees. They are meeting for the first time, in a campus cafeteria.

Conversation Analysis
1. Classify each of the following statements as forms of group communication (task, procedural, climate, egocentric). For some statements, you might be able to appropriately select more than one communication form (for instance, as both procedural and climate).

Thomas: Well, we've got 23 applications for funding and a total of $19,000.00 that we can distribute.

_____ **Task** _____ **Procedural**_____ **Climate** _____ **Egocentric**

Davinia: Maybe we should start by listing how much each of the 23 groups wants.

_____ **Task** _____ **Procedural**_____ **Climate** _____ **Egocentric**

Joyce: It might be better to start by determining the criteria that we will use to decide if groups get any funding from student fees.

_____ **Task** _____ **Procedural**_____ **Climate** _____ **Egocentric**

Pat: Yeah, right. We should set up our criteria before we look at applications.

_____ **Task** _____ **Procedural**_____ **Climate** _____ **Egocentric**

Davinia: Sounds good to me. Pat, what do you think?

_____ **Task** _____ **Procedural**_____ **Climate** _____ **Egocentric**

Pat: I'm on board. Let's set up criteria first and then review the applications against those.

_____ **Task** _____ **Procedural**_____ **Climate** _____ **Egocentric**

Joyce: Okay, we might start by looking at the criteria used last year by the Financial Committee. Does anyone have a copy of those?

_____ **Task** _____ **Procedural**_____ **Climate** _____ **Egocentric**

Thomas: I do. They had three criteria: service to a significant number of students, compliance with the college's non-discrimination policies, and educational benefit.

_____ **Task** _____ **Procedural**_____ **Climate** _____ **Egocentric**

Davinia: What counts as 'educational benefit?' Did last year's committee specify that?

_____ **Task** _____ **Procedural**_____ **Climate** _____ **Egocentric**

Joyce: Good question. Thomas, you were on the committee last year. Do you remember what they counted as educational benefit?

_____ **Task** _____ **Procedural**_____ **Climate** _____ **Egocentric**

Thomas: The main thing I remember is that it was distinguished from artistic benefit—like a concert or art exhibit or something like that.

_____ **Task** _____ **Procedural**_____ **Climate** _____ **Egocentric**

Pat: But can't art be educational?

_____ **Task** _____ **Procedural**_____ **Climate** _____ **Egocentric**

Davinia: Yeah, I think so. Thomas, Joyce, do you?

_____ **Task** _____ **Procedural**_____ **Climate** _____ **Egocentric**

Thomas: I guess, but it's like art's primary purpose isn't to educate.

_____ **Task** _____ **Procedural**_____ **Climate** _____ **Egocentric**

Joyce: I agree. It's kind of hard to put into words, but I think educational benefit has more to do with information and the mind, while art has more to do with the soul. Does that sound too hokey?

_____ **Task** _____ **Procedural**_____ **Climate** _____ **Egocentric**

Pat: Okay, so we want to say that we don't distribute funds to any hokey groups, right?

_____ **Task** _____ **Procedural**_____ **Climate** _____ **Egocentric**

Davinia: It's not like we're against art or anything. It's just that the funding we can distribute is for educational benefit, right?

_____ **Task** _____ **Procedural**_____ **Climate** _____ **Egocentric**

Joyce: Okay, let's move onto another criterion. What is a significant number of students?

_____ **Task** _____ **Procedural**_____ **Climate** _____ **Egocentric**

Thomas: Last year we said that the proposals for using money had to be of potential interest to at least 20% of students to get funding. How does that sound to you?

_____ **Task** _____ **Procedural**_____ **Climate** _____ **Egocentric**

Pat: Sounds okay as long as we remember that something can be of potential interest to students who aren't members of specific groups. Like, for instance, I might want to attend a program on Native American customs even though I'm not a Native American. See what I mean?

_____ **Task** _____ **Procedural**_____ **Climate** _____ **Egocentric**

Davinia: Good point—we don't want to define student interest as student identity or anything like that.

_____ **Task** _____ **Procedural**_____ **Climate** _____ **Egocentric**

Thomas: Okay, so are we agreed that 20% is about right, with the understanding that the 20% can include students who aren't in a group applying for funding? Okay, then do we need to discuss the criterion of compliance with the college's policies on nondiscrimination?

_____ **Task** _____ **Procedural**_____ **Climate** _____ **Egocentric**

2. Based on the above discussion, does this group seem to have a single leader or do different members provide leadership to the group?

3. How do you perceive the interaction pattern among members? Does everyone seem to be involved and participating?

4. Are any of the potential values of group vs. individual decision making evident in this discussion?

10.5   Case Study: Creating High-Performing Teams

Purpose
To develop your research skills in communication and to develop cognitive links between the research and material presented in the chapter.

Instructions
Locate and read the article listed below, and answer the following questions.

Nelson, B. (2010). Creating High-Performing Teams. Health Care Registration: The Newsletter for Health Care Registration Professionals, 19(9), 10–12. Retrieved from Business Source Complete database.

1. According to this article, how are employees motivated?

2. What are the characteristics of a high-performing team?

3. What should a manager do to recognize team success?

4. What are some of the dilemmas team recognition presents?

5. What conclusions does the author draw about recognizing teams as a whole?

Name_____

10.6   Group Doctor Part I

Purpose
To help you assess your group's need at any particular point in your interaction.

Instructions
Think about the stage in which your group was just forming and think about it as it is functioning now. Rank the group's success in each question on a scale of 1–5, with 5 highest.

If you have a particular memory of something being said or done that relates to the question, write it in the comment column.

	1	2	3	4	5	Comment
1. Did your group arrange seats so every member could see every other member?						
2. Did your members sit the same distance from the center of the gathering?						
3. Did members introduce themselves with confidence?						
4. Did quiet members receive invitations to talk?						
5. Did one person start the talk and then continue to direct other members?						
6. Did members chat about topics not related to the group?						
7. Did members exhibit positive attitudes toward working together?						
8. Did members talk about how they would like this group to be different from previous groups?						
9. Did members exchange contact information?						
10. Did members willingly coordinate schedules to arrange the next group meeting?						

Looking at the start, would you say the group got off well or poorly?

How did the forming stage affect your attitude toward the group?

If one thing could make the group work more smoothly and productively, what would that be?

Commit to one action you can take to make the change you identified above come true. What is that action?

Self-Test for Chapter 10

Multiple Choice

_____ 1. Which of the following is necessary for a group to exist?
    A. there must be a clear leader
    B. members must be interdependent
    C. the group must follow shared rules of behavior
    D. both B and C are necessary

_____ 2. Potential limitations of small groups in comparison to individuals include
    A. time required
    B. cohesion
    C. conformity pressures
    D. A and C

_____ 3. The special energy in groups that is more than the additive energy of members is called
    A. synergy
    B. cohesion
    C. commitment
    D. groupthink

_____ 4. "The Dominators" is a work team that has been together for a while. They have a high level of cohesion and harmonious group spirit. One day, the team members begin deliberating. Individuals offer very little critical analysis and agree with everything presented by the leader. The Dominators seem to be experiencing
    A. synergy
    B. power over
    C. groupthink
    D. decentralization

_____ 5. Pharrell knows how to use Twitter, but no one in his group does. He brings his group to the computer lab and demonstrates all the different things Twitter can do. He is exhibiting
    A. conformity
    B. groupthink
    C. power over
    D. power to

_____ 6. Pronounced Western values include
    A. assertiveness
    B. progress and change
    C. risk and uncertainty
    D. A, B, and C

_____ 7. Joyce is going through a bad breakup, and repeatedly uses group time to burden the group with her problems. Communication of this nature is
    A. procedural
    B. task
    C. climate
    D. egocentric

8. Wayne shares, "Before we choose the best MC for the event, I think we should first decide what qualities make a good MC." He is contributing which form of leadership communication?
   A. procedural
   B. task
   C. climate
   D. conflictual

9. Communication that initiates ideas, seeks information, and evaluates ideas is called
   A. procedural
   B. task
   C. climate
   D. egocentric

10. A form of communication that is undesirable in group discussion is
    A. procedural
    B. task
    C. climate
    D. egocentric

11. Missy arrives to the meeting first. She moves the chairs into a circle, as usual. She is exhibiting which group feature?
    A. cohesion
    B. norm
    C. commitment
    D. social climbing

12. Miranda is the captain of her ROTC military unit on campus. When Miranda tells her unit to do something, they all immediately do what she says. Miranda is utilizing which kind of power?
    A. distributive power
    B. power over
    C. power to
    D. domination

13. Most researchers agree that the ideal small group has _____ members.
    A. 3 to 5
    B. 5 to 7
    C. 7 to 9
    D. 11 or fewer

14. Andre notices that Gina looks a little down as she joins the group and says, "Are you okay?" He is contributing which form of leadership communication?
    A. procedural
    B. task
    C. climate
    D. egocentric

_____ 15. Group Epic members look forward to working together. Spending time together energizes them individually. They are experiencing
A. cohesion
B. individualism
C. groupthink
D. climate communication

True/False

_____ 1. All groups are teams.

_____ 2. All teams are groups.

_____ 3. Gali's habit of bringing Dexter, her boss, a donut every morning demonstrates social climbing.

_____ 4. Centralized interaction patterns tend to lead to higher member satisfaction than decentralized interaction patterns.

_____ 5. Cohesion increases commitment, which increases satisfaction, which in turn increases cohesion.

_____ 6. If a group's primary goal ceases to exist, the group will likely cease to exist.

_____ 7. Satisfaction is not related to commitment, participation, or cohesion.

_____ 8. Power over can be both positive and negative.

_____ 9. Each power structure has an inherent interaction pattern.

_____ 10. Most group members are not particularly skilled in group communication.

Essays

1. Have you experienced challenges with group communication because of a difference in cultural values?   Discuss how cultural values influence our group communication behaviors.

2. Identify, discuss, and provide examples of important potential strengths of groups in comparison to individuals.

3. Identify, define, and provide an example of each of the four types of group communication.

Chapter 10 Flash Cards

Cut out the cards, write the answers on the back, and you will have a packet of flash cards for each chapter. Paraphrasing the definitions will help you remember them.

Climate Communication	Individualism	Procedural Communication
Cohesion	Norms	Social Climbing
Egocentric Communication	Power	Synergy
Group	Power Over	Task Communication
Power To	Groupthink	Team

Chapter 11: Effective Communication in Task Groups and Teams

Chapter Summary

I. Task groups and teams exist for the purpose of accomplishing a particular objective.
- A. Project teams consist of people who have special expertise and work together over an extended time to achieve a common goal.
- B. Focus groups are used to find out what people think about a specific idea, product, or person.
  1. Focus groups are guided by a leader or facilitator who guides the communication and interaction.
  2. The facilitator encourages group members to discuss their ideas, beliefs, feelings, and perceptions about the relevant topic of discussion, but offers no opinion.
- C. Brainstorming groups generate ideas and stimulate thinking "outside the box."
  1. No evaluation is done during the brainstorming session.
  2. The leader should set the tone for creative communication.
- D. Advisory groups are set up to provide advice and guidance to those who will make the actual policy or decision.
  1. Advisory groups may consist of both experts and peers.
  2. Advisory groups allow leaders to develop effective policy and make informed decisions.
- E. A quality improvement team is three or more people from different areas of an organization who work together to improve quality in the organization's hierarchy.
  1. It is usually comprised of people from different levels of the organization.
  2. In order to be effective, quality improvement teams must be given the power to solve problems.
- F. Decision-making groups are formed to render a specific decision or policy.

II. Leadership communication is an important aspect of small group interaction.
- A. Leadership may be provided by one individual or by several members who contribute to guiding the process and ensuring effective communication within the group.
- B. There are several functions of effective leadership.
  1. Leadership establishes good working climate.
  2. Leadership organizes group processes.
  3. Leadership focuses discussion productively to the task at hand.
  4. Leadership controls disruptive members.
- C. There are three primary styles of leadership.
  1. **Laissez-faire leadership** is a laid-back, non-directive style that does not provide the group with guidance or suggestions regarding behaviors or decisions.
  2. **Authoritarian leadership** is highly directive and tends to be used by a lone leader.
     a. Authoritarian leadership fosters a centralized pattern of leader-to-member, member-to-leader communication.
     b. Dependence, apathy, low cohesion, and resentment are common responses to authoritarian leadership.
     c. This style of leadership can be appropriate in emergency situations.

3. **Democratic leadership** provides guidance and direction but does not impose rigid authority.
   a. Democratic leadership usually results in high group participation and increased satisfaction.
   b. Democratic leadership style is linked to high-quality results that are more creative and original than the other two leadership styles.

D. Effective leadership often changes over time in relation to the different points in the group's life cycle and the changes in member maturity.

III. There are four common methods groups use to make decisions.
A. **Consensus**, the most popular method of decision making, occurs when all members of a group express their ideas and the group agrees on a decision.
   1. Consensus involves wide participation, but can be time consuming.
   2. Since everyone has been involved and agrees on the decision, there is usually very strong support of the decision.

B. **Voting** is when a decision is made based on the support of a certain number of group members.
   1. Number of group members ranges from just over half to up to a 75% majority.
   2. Voting may lead to dissatisfaction since not everyone agrees with the decision.
   3. Voting may sometimes lead to less thoroughly considered decision.
   4. Voting is often used because of its efficiency and resolution.

C. **Compromise** is a third decision-making technique.
   1. Members work out a solution that is at least partially satisfactory to everyone, but does not always fully satisfy all members.
   2. Decisions are not always coherent.
   3. Compromise doesn't always yield a lot of support from members.

D. **Authority rule** doesn't actually involve decision made by a group.
   1. Authority rule occurs when an individual or a group with power tells the group what it will do, and the group merely ratifies the authority's decision.
   2. Authority rule often generates resentment and group dissatisfaction.
   3. The major advantage of authority rule is that it is highly efficient.

E. The best decision-making method is dependent upon such factors as the nature of the decision, preferences of group members, time available for reaching decisions, and cultural values and norms.

IV. The **standard agenda**, a seven-stage method of decision making, is a highly effective way to organize group discussion.
A. Defining the problem is the first stage of the standard agenda.
   1. At this stage, members often determine whether they are dealing with a question of fact, value, or policy.
      a. Questions of fact deal with finding out what is true or untrue, and what exists.
      b. Questions of value have to do with the worth, ethicality, or importance of a policy, procedure, concept, or action.
      c. Questions of policy deal with actions or positions that should be taken and who will be responsible for taking them.

2. The group then defines all terms related to the issue at hand.
3. Group members should attempt to minimize bias.

B. The second stage is to analyze the issue(s).
1. Members must decide what information they need.
2. Communication between members focuses on presenting and evaluating information.

C. The third stage is to establish the criteria for making the decision.
1. Criteria are standards members use to evaluate alternative solutions or decisions.
2. Establishing clear criteria before solutions helps a group avoid decision making pitfalls.

D. In the fourth stage, generating solutions, members consider ways to solve the problem.
1. Research conducted during stage two often uncovers a number of possible solutions.
2. Brainstorming, the free flow of ideas without immediate criticism, is a second source of alternative solutions.

E. In stage five members evaluate solutions based on research and the criteria established in stage three.
1. Solutions that do not meet all criteria are discarded.
2. Ideally, members arrive at a consensus on the best decision.

F. Step six, choosing and implementing the best decision, involves the implementation of whatever plan the group has decided upon.

G. Stage seven is the development of an action plan to monitor the solution after implementation.
1. The group needs to check on the effectiveness of the solution after implementation.
2. Members should specify how they will measure success.
3. Monitoring allows the plan to be adjusted if it is not working as the group envisioned.

V. Conflict exists when people who are independent have different views, interests, or goals that seem incompatible.
A. Conflict in groups can be desirable and beneficial.
1. Conflict stimulates thinking among members.
2. Conflict helps to enlarge the members' grasp of the issues involved.

B. Disruptive conflict exists when disagreements interfere with the effective work and healthy communication climate of a group.
1. Disruptive conflict is conflict that interferes with the effective work and healthy communication climate of a group.
2. Disruptive conflict is often domineering, rigid, and competitive communication.
3. Disruptive conflict lowers group satisfaction.
4. Disruptive conflict is often the result of communication that produces defensiveness and draws people away from the collective goals of the group.

C. Constructive conflict is conflict that is accepted as a natural part of the group process and that helps the group achieve its goals.
1. Constructive conflict focuses on the issues rather than on personalities.
2. Constructive conflict encourages a win-win orientation to problems.

11.1   The Many Types of Task Groups

Purpose
To reinforce your understanding of different kinds of task groups.

Instructions
Below are ten statements, each of which defines a group's charge, or task. In the blank to the left of each statement, indicate which kind of task group is illustrated in the statement. Answers appear with the Chapter 11 Self-Test Answers.

IDENTIFYING TASK GROUPS

_____   1.   We'd like to get your reactions to a new perfume we've developed.

_____   2.   I want the five of you to work together on this problem since each of you is integral to solving it and you need to coordinate with one another.

_____   3.   I simply don't have the personal expertise to make a decision, so I'm asking you 6 to deliberate among yourselves and then give me your best advice.

_____   4.   Today our goal is to come up with as many ideas as we possibly can.

_____   5.   I'd like to know what you think about the 3 candidates running for mayor.

_____   6.   Our task is to develop a policy for student appeals of grades.

_____   7.   The five of you come from different departments in the company. I want you to work together to develop suggestions for reducing on-the-job accidents.

_____   8.   It is our responsibility to come up with a method of determining raises.

_____   9.   We need to generate some creative, new ideas for organizing work, so let your creative juices flow and don't offer any criticisms.

_____   10.   Each of you brings a special resource to this group. By working together you can keep the project coherent and keep each other informed of things that affect all of you.

11.2   Organizing Group Discussion

Purpose
To give you experience in organizing group work using the standard agenda.

Instructions
On the following page are statements that could occur during a group problem-solving discussion. The statements, however, are not ordered most effectively. Your task is to reorder the statements so that they follow the sequence represented in standard agenda. The proper sequence of statements appears with the Chapter 11 Self-Test Answers.

Scrambled Discussion

Reorder the following statements so that they follow the sequence for problem solving that standard agenda prescribes.

Do we have all the information we need now?

How are we going to define "beneficial"?

Do you think this poll is reliable?

I can think of four standards that any solution would have to meet in order to be effective.

If there is a negative reaction when the solution is implemented, we could modify it in this way. . .

Okay, we seem to be ready to start identifying possible solutions for our problem. Any ideas?

Of the two solutions left, one seems to satisfy all criteria most fully.

Let's make sure our implementation plan really spells things out in the most clear language possible.

Are we dealing with a factual or value question?

How can we tell if our solution solves the problem?

What might go wrong with the solution we're recommending?

Solutions 3 and 4 don't meet all of our criteria so we should throw them out.

11.3   Orientations to Conflict

Purpose
To give you practice in recognizing orientations to conflict in group situations.

Instructions
For each of the statements listed below, indicate which orientation to conflict it most clearly reflects. Use the letters below to indicate the corresponding orientations to conflict. Correct answers appear with Chapter 11 Self-Test Answers.

A. win-lose
B. lose-lose
C. win-win

_____   1.   We can't all be satisfied with a resolution to this problem.

_____   2.   Since we disagree on how to recognize excellence, let's not bother.

_____   3.   We are never going to see eye to eye on this. I think my preference should prevail.

_____   4.   I think if we keep talking, we will figure out something that all of us can live with.

_____   5.   I can't stand fighting. Everyone loses.

_____   6.   No matter what you say, I'm not giving any ground on this issue. I feel very strongly and I expect you to go along with me this time.

_____   7.   There's no point in arguing about the policy. All we ever do is disagree and create hard feelings without solving anything.

_____   8.   I'm willing to go along with your preference on the schedule if you'll go along with my preference for labor arrangements.

_____   9.   Look: There are only two possibilities in this situation, so both factions in our group can't be satisfied.

_____   10.   Maybe there are solutions other than the two we have come up with so far. I think if we keep talking, we might be able to come up with something workable for everyone.

11.4   Fitting Leadership to Group Situations

Purposes
To reinforce understanding of styles of leadership.

To demonstrate that each style of leadership can be appropriate in specific situations.

Instructions
Below you will find six descriptions of group situations. Decide which style or styles of leadership is (are) most appropriate in each situation and explain the reasons for your choices. Answers and explanations for them appear with the Chapter 11 Self-Test Answers.

WHICH STYLE(S) OF LEADERSHIP IS(ARE) RIGHT?

---

1. This group is having its first meeting. Members have good expertise and knowledge relevant to the task, but they have limited experience working in groups. It is essential that all members participate in the group process and develop strong commitment to the decision they develop.

    Recommended leadership style:
    Reasons:

---

2. This group consists of 5 people who are very experienced in working in groups to achieve goals. The members are mature and all have initiative and self-direction. Each of the members has served as leader of other groups.

    Recommended leadership style:
    Reasons:

---

3. This group must produce a high-quality decision that is creative and well thought through. Members have some experience in group process, but have not held leadership positions.

    Recommended leadership style:
    Reasons:

---

4. This group is floundering. Members don't seem able to organize themselves productively. After two months of meetings, they have virtually nothing to show. Time is running out—the group must complete its work. Members' morale and satisfaction is less important than getting the job done.

    Recommended leadership style:
    Reasons:

5. This group is made up of six people who are highly enthusiastic about their task and who are eager to get going. All members have the necessary expertise relevant to the task and they have some experience in group process.

    Recommended leadership style:
    Reasons:

6. Members of this group have lost a lot of time bickering about minor details. They have trouble staying on track and keeping the big picture in mind. The leader has provided guidance and suggested direction for the group, but members have not responded well to these efforts. The group's deadline for a decision is near.

    Recommended leadership style:
    Reasons:

Name_____

11.5   Using Your Online Resources—Experiencing
Communication in Our Lives

Chapter 11 Case Study: Team Work

Purpose
To apply the principles you learned about task group communication in Chapter 11 to the communication scenario *Team Work* included under Communication Scenarios on your Online Resources for *Communication in Our Lives*. You can complete this activity online or on this worksheet.

Instructions
Analyze the *Team Work* scenario by answering the questions below.

Video Preview
You'll recognize the scenario if you have already watched the "Non-Verbal Cues" scenario. Here in "Team Work," the focus is on group dynamics and communication. A project team is meeting to discuss the most effective way to present its recommendations for implementing a flextime policy on a trial basis. Members of the team are: Jason Brown, team leader; Erika Filene, Victoria Lawrence, Bill Williams, and Jensen Chen. They are sitting around a rectangular table with Jason at the head.

Conversation Analysis
1. Identify leadership behaviors on the team. Is Jason the single leader or do other team members contribute leadership to the group?

2. Is the conflict on this team constructive or disruptive or both? If you were a member of the team, how might you communicate to enhance the constructiveness of disagreements?

3. Judging from Jason's comments, which leadership style does he seem to use?

11.6   Chapter 11 Case Study

Purpose

To learn how to do communication research and to understand how the concepts of this chapter are used in an applied communication setting.

Instructions

Locate and read the article listed below, and answer the following questions.

Galanes, G. (2009). Dialectical Tensions of Small Group Leadership. Communication Studies, 60(5), 409–425. doi:10.1080/10510970903260228.

1. According to the article, what is dialectical theory?

2. Why should group leaders be aware of dialectical tensions in a group?

3. What are the six factors distinguishing excellent leadership?

4. What did Galenes find are the four factors effective leaders consciously attend to?

5. What did the researcher seek to find out in this study?

6. Briefly summarize the method the researcher used.

7. What were the basic results of this study?

8. What were the researcher's three main conclusions?

Name_____

11.7   Group Doctor Part II

Purpose
To help you identify your group's need at any particular point in your process.

Instructions
Think about your class group at a certain point in your history of working together. Examine the interaction from the viewpoint of each of the four forms of group communication. On a scale of 1–5, with 5 highest, rank how well you feel your group did contributing leadership in that area.

1. Climate: How skillfully do you feel your group built the climate to be a positive one that encourages participation?

    1   2   3   4   5

2. Procedure: How skillfully do you feel your group defined the goal or mission and proceeded through the steps of the standard agenda that are applicable at this time?

    1   2   3   4   5

3. Climate: How skillfully do you feel your group defined your goal, defined language within the goal statement, decided what information was needed, analyzed issues, and assigned tasks to members?

    1   2   3   4   5

4. Egocentric: How skillfully do you feel your group encouraged constructive conflict and handled disruptive conflict?

    1   2   3   4   5

5. Examine each rating as if it were a vital sign of a patient coming to you, a doctor, for a routine checkup. Put them all together and describe your group's prognosis. How successful do you predict your group will be?

6. What does your group most need right now to steer it to optimal function?

7. What can you do to provide that need?

Self-Test for Chapter 11

Multiple Choice

_____ 1. Nidun works for a local radio station. He has gathered five listeners and is getting their opinions on the morning show personalities. Nidun is most likely facilitating which type of task group?
- A. project team
- B. focus group
- C. brainstorming
- D. advisory group

_____ 2. The CEO of a national distribution company is looking to expand his operations. He assembles a group of experts with more knowledge of the local area to get their opinions. The group of experts are most likely members of a(n)
- A. quality improvement team
- B. focus group
- C. advisory group
- D. project team

_____ 3. Leadership that provides guidance, but does not impose rigid authority is referred to as
- A. laissez-faire
- B. democratic
- C. dialectical
- D. ratification

_____ 4. The word "laissez-faire" comes from a French phrase that means
- A. the bottom line
- B. do nothing
- C. guide gently
- D. combine carrot and stick

_____ 5. When all members of a group express their opinions and then agree on a decision, they are using which method of decision making?
- A. voting
- B. compromise
- C. authority rule
- D. consensus

_____ 6. The decision-making method that is most time consuming is
- A. consensus
- B. voting
- C. compromise/group ratification
- D. authority rule

_____ 7. Moshe agreed to interview students to get their opinions. Pearl is gathering information from the library. Jon checked government databases. The group is involved in which stage of the standard agenda method of decision making?

    A. defining the problem

    B. analyzing the problem

    C. establishing criteria

    D. evaluating the possible solutions

_____ 8. A group faced with deciding how to increase student enrollment at the university is dealing with a question of

    A. fact

    B. value

    C. policy

    D. advising

_____ 9. Sources for solutions to problems on which groups work include

    A. the group's research and the group's study of how similar problems have been solved by others

    B. the group's research and criteria

    C. the group's research and brainstorming

    D. brainstorming and monitoring

_____ 10. Disruptive conflict typically includes which of the following communication behaviors?

    A. personal attacks

    B. self-interested comments

    C. competitive remarks

    D. A, B, and C are all typical of disruptive conflict

_____ 11. Which of the following would be considered brainstorming rule(s)?

    A. go for quality

    B. record ideas on a board or newsprint

    C. verbal and nonverbal criticism are appropriate

    D. A and B

_____ 12. Which type of group typically spends the first few meetings complaining about problems?

    A. advisory

    B. decision-making

    C. focus

    D. quality circle

_____ 13. Majority rule is another name for

    A. compromise

    B. consensus

    C. group ratification

    D. voting

_____ 14. Constructive conflict occurs when members understand
A. disagreements are natural and can help them achieve their goals
B. that's just the way the members are when they are together and adjust to the conflict
C. some groups actually enjoy quarreling
D. none of the above statements accurately describes necessary conditions for constructive conflict

_____ 15. Compromise works when no other method of deciding does, but it has which disadvantage?
A. members are not fully satisfied
B. decisions do not emerge fully integrated
C. support may be unenthusiastic
D. A, B, and C

True/False

_____ 1. Emotionally intelligent people have difficulty with leadership.

_____ 2. The most effective leadership generally is provided by a single individual.

_____ 3. An important strength of compromise method of making decisions is that it works when nothing else does.

_____ 4. No criticism is allowed when a group is brainstorming.

_____ 5. Conflict does not improve group work.

_____ 6. Groups that function under laissez-faire leadership usually have the greatest member satisfaction.

_____ 7. Leadership is a set of functions, not a person.

_____ 8. Leadership should shape a positive climate, organize process, clarify the goal and generate solutions, and manage conflict.

_____ 9. In order to achieve maximum effectiveness, a group needs both task and climate leadership.

_____ 10. Leadership may be a blend of styles and the blend may change over time.

Essay

1. Think about three different groups in which you are a member. What are the leadership styles of each? What are the benefits and drawbacks of each?

2. Define and contrast disruptive and constructive conflict in groups. Your answer should discuss ways that each form of conflict is represented in communication, as well as how each form influences communication in groups.

3. Name the five types of task groups and give an example of a question each would attempt to answer.

Chapter 11 Flash Cards

Cut out the cards, write the answers on the back, and you will have a packet of flash cards for each chapter. Paraphrasing the definitions will help you remember them.

Authoritarian Leadership	Consensus	Laissez-faire
Authority Rule	Criteria	Quality Improvement Team
Brainstorming	Democratic Leadership	Standard Agenda
Compromise	Emotional Intelligence	Voting

Chapter 12: Communication in Organizations

Chapter Summary

I. Organizational communication has three distinct features: structure, communication networks, and links to external environments.

    A. The word organization means **structure**.

        1. Structure provides predictability for members so that they understand roles, procedures, and expectations.

        2. Most modern organizations rely on a hierarchical structure.

            a. Different levels of power and status are assigned to members.

            b. A chain of command specifies who is to communicate with whom about what.

    B. **Communication networks** are formal and informal links between people.

        1. In most organizations, people belong to multiple networks.

        2. An increasing number of workers are part of virtual networks.

        3. Electronic brainstorming groups are increasingly effective.

    C. Links to external environments are the means by which organizations interact with the society in which they operate.

        1. We must look outside the organization to understand how it is affected by its contexts.

        2. Sometimes external threats cause businesses to suffer.

II. Organizational culture consists of ways of thinking, acting, and understanding that are shared by members of an organization that reflect an organization's distinct identity.

    A. Organizational cultures consist of meanings shared by members of organizations.

    B. The relationship between communication and organizational culture is reciprocal: communication creates, sustains, and sometimes alters the culture while organizational culture influences patterns of communication between members.

    C. Four kinds of communication are particularly important in developing and conveying organizational culture, vocabularies, stories, rites and rituals, and structures.

        1. Vocabularies reflect and express the history, norms, values, and identity of an organization.

            a. Many organizations use hierarchical language that distinguishes levels of status among members.

            b. Because organizations have historically been run by men, language developed that is more related to men's traditional interests and experiences than women's.

        2. Stories are narratives of experiences that establish and sustain organizational culture.

            a. Corporate stories convey the values, style, and history of an organization.

            b. Personal stories are accounts that announce how people see themselves and how they want to be seen by others.

            c. Collegial stories are accounts of other members of the organization that teach new members how to get along.

3.   Rites and rituals are planned events that provide standardized ways of expressing organizational values and identities.
    a.   Rites are dramatic, planned sets of activities that bring together aspects of an organization's culture in a single event.
    b.   Rituals are forms of communication that occur regularly and that members of an organization perceive as familiar and routine parts of organizational life.
4.   Structures organize relationships and interaction between members of an organization.
    a.   Roles are responsibilities and behaviors expected of people because of their specific positions.
    b.   Rules are patterned ways of interacting.
    c.   Policies are formal statements of practices that reflect and uphold the overall culture, such as how sexual harassment will be defined and dealt with.
    d.   Communication networks link members through formal and informal forms of interaction and relationships.

III.   Knowing three guidelines for communicating in organizations can make your experiences with them more positive.

    A.   Adapt to diverse needs, situations, and people; the most effective professionals will be those who are comfortable with a stream of changes in people and ways of working.

    B.   Expect to move in and out of teams.
        1.   Effective communication in today's and tomorrow's organizations requires interacting intensely with members of teams that may form and dissolve quickly.
        2.   The team player is most highly sought today.
        3.   The greater your repertoire of communication skills, the more effectively you will be able to move in and out of teams on the job.

    C.   Manage personal relationships on the job.

Name_____

12.1   Understanding Culture within an Organization

Purpose
To help you become aware of how you are affected by an organization's culture.

Instructions
Visit an organization such as a place of work, a congregation, a student activity meeting, etc. Observe the members.

How do they dress?

How do they greet one another?

How do they talk?

What is the "climate" like? Positive? Negative? Neutral? How formal or informal would you say this group is? Why do you think this is so or how do you know?

Can you determine whether there is a leader of the organization? How do you know who it is?

Can you determine a "pecking order" among members? How do you know who fits where in it?

What sort of manners do you see being observed?

Do you see evidence of structure in the proceedings? What happens how?

Do you see subgroups? How many and how tightly do their members stick together? Or do you see people interacting freely with anyone they wish?

Do the members of this organization like each other? Do they like being where they are? Do they like having you among them?

12.2   Seeing Structures

Purpose

To help you become aware of the structure of the organizations to which you belong.

Instructions

Think about the school where you are currently a student. What is the chain of command, from your instructor to the president (or chancellor)? Now, consider a student organization to which you belong. How is the chain of command for the organization different from your school? Is it hierarchical? Decentralized? How does the structure of an organization affect the way you communicate? Think of an example for each.

Name_____

12.3   Counting Networks

Purpose
To help you become aware of the number of networks in which you participate on a daily basis.

Instructions
In addition to being a member of your community, you are a student and therefore a member of the organization that is your college or university. Count the number of networks in which you participate on a daily basis.

Picture yourself as you wake in the morning. Do you live in student housing? An apartment complex? Do you talk with other people who live in the same housing?

Each class you attend is an organization within the organization. How many classes do you attend?

Do you belong to any student organizations, such as Student Government or the Chemistry Club?

Do you have a job either on campus or off?

Are you a member of a church, or attend one enough to interact with other congregants?

Do you belong to any civic clubs, such as the Big Brothers/Big Sisters of America?

12.4   Recognizing Rites

Purpose
To help you become aware of the role that rites play in your identity.

Instructions
Think back over your life. How many events have you participated in that marked your progression from childhood to adulthood? List a few. For each, answer the following questions: Which organization planned the event? How widely was it recognized in your community? What was each event designed to accomplish? How did you feel as you participated in each?

Event #1

Event #2

Event # 3

Event #4

Event #5

Name_____

12.5   Recalling Rituals

Purpose
To help you recognize the importance of the role ritual plays in your life.

Instructions
Think of a typical year in your life. List the occasions for which you observe certain rituals, such as the Seder Meal at Passover.

How many of these occasions are national holidays?

How many are particular to your community?

Your family?

What small group rituals do you participate in, as in gathering with a group of friends regularly? What is your "usual" behavior?

How important do you feel these rituals are to your sense of belonging in each of the groups practicing the occasions you named?

Self-Test for Chapter 12

Multiple Choice

_____ 1. Organizational communication has three distinct features. Which of the following is NOT one of them?
  A. communication networks
  B. guidelines for communicating in our era
  C. structures
  D. links to external environments

_____ 2. Hierarchical structure is characterized by
  A. a specific chain of command
  B. many levels of power between the CEO and the lowest-status worker
  C. power and status that are assigned to different members
  D. A and C are both correct

_____ 3. Communication networks are
  A. systems in which the organization operates
  B. ways of thinking, acting, and understanding work that are shared by members of an organization
  C. the language of an organization
  D. formal and informal links between members of an organization

_____ 4. When we say that an organization is embedded in multiple contexts, we mean that
  A. its operation can only be understood by looking outside it
  B. organizations must change and adapt to emerging social, political, and economic conditions
  C. communication within organizations is influenced by the systems in which they operate
  D. A, B, and C

_____ 5. Organizational culture consists of all but which of the following elements that are shared by its members?
  A. ways of thinking
  B. ways of acting
  C. ways of philosophizing
  D. ways of understanding

_____ 6. Four kinds of communication are particularly important in conveying organizational culture. Which of the following is not?
  A. fairytales
  B. vocabularies and stories
  C. rites and rituals
  D. structures

_____ 7. Vocabulary refers to the nature of the language used within an organization. For many, the language is
   A. decentralized and masculine
   B. decentralized and feminine
   C. hierarchical and masculine
   D. hierarchical and feminine

_____ 8. Stories do all but which for the organization?
   A. convey values and style
   B. convey history and socialize new members into the culture
   C. reflect the economic growth of the company
   D. reflect the collective vision of itself

_____ 9. Stories are one of the following types except
   A. personal
   B. corporate
   C. collegial
   D. private

_____ 10. Rites serve all but which of the following functions?
   A. mark a member's passage into a new level of the organization
   B. explain the chain of command to interviewees
   C. revitalize the organization
   D. manage conflict

_____ 11. Rituals differ from rites in that they
   A. always involve the same people
   B. consist of repeated behaviors that communicate a particular role
   C. are planned by the CEO
   D. are spontaneous

_____ 12. Structures do what for the organization?
   A. allow members to choose status
   B. provide predictability
   C. limit the number of interactions between members
   D. A and B

_____ 13. Roles are responsibilities and behaviors expected because of
   A. members' special abilities
   B. the boss's ambitions
   C. members' specific positions in the organization
   D. the boss's preferences

_____ 14. Formal rules are patterned ways of interacting that are
   A. found in the contract or organizational chart
   B. norms for interacting
   C. only constitutive
   D. only regulative

787

15. The Communication Department has formulated a way to give transfer students credits for internships done over the summer. This is called a
    A. policy
    B. rite
    C. ritual
    D. structure

True/False

1. 75% – 90% of details pass through the grapevine accurately.

2. Being a team player is a desirable quality in an organization.

3. Employees must be comfortable with change in people and job responsibilities in most organizations today.

4. The employee of today and tomorrow will be expected to stay with his/her team for years.

5. Conrad and Poole (2002) found that the power structures, norms, and cultures in many organizations encourage unethical activities.

6. Masculine language dominates most organizations and many women may feel uncomfortable in the community of men it bonds together.

7. Blogging is not a recommended way for an organization to get feedback because the credibility of the blogger cannot be verified.

8. Electronic brainstorming groups work because anonymity encourages creativity.

9. In most organizations, people belong to multiple networks.

10. US sports jargon is universal and widely received by foreign business people.

Essay

1. Discuss the role of stories in creating and sustaining organizational culture.

2. Discuss the role of networks in creating and sustaining organizational culture.

3. Watch and compare 'Mad Men' and 'The Office'. What is the organizational structure of each company? How do the offices function? What organizational stories create and sustain each organizational structure?

Chapter 12 Flash Cards

Cut out the cards, write the answers on the back, and you will have a packet of flash cards for each chapter. Paraphrasing the definitions will help you remember them.

Communication Network	Organizational Culture	Policy
Rite	Ritual	Role
Structure		

Chapter 13: Media and Media Literacy

Chapter Summary

I. Media is a broad term that includes both mass and social media.
   A. **Mass media** are electronic or mechanical channels of delivering one-to-many communication.
      1. Mass media broadcast messages to a large group of people.
      2. Mass media include radio, television, books, newspapers, compact discs, and billboards.

   B. **Social media** are means of connecting and interacting actively.
      1. Social media include cell phone, e-mail, PDA, iPods, MP3s, the web and other tools.
      2. The primary difference between mass media and social media is digitalization, which has three key implications:
         a. Ease of manipulation blurs the line between production and consumption.
         b. Digital convergence creates communication ease.
         c. Nearly instant speed jeopardizes accuracy.

II. Mass media and social media both work in and affect our lives.
   A. There are several theories that help to explain the functions and effects of mass media.
      1. **Uses and gratification theory** assumes that people are active agents who make deliberate choices among media to gratify themselves.
         a. We use media to gain information, alleviate loneliness, divert from problems, or fulfill any other number of possible needs.
         b. People exercise control over their interactions with mediated mass communication.
      2. **Agenda setting** is selecting and calling to the public's attention ideas, people, or events while ignoring or diverting public attention from others.
         a. Mass media controls the events, people, and issues that reach public consciousness.
         b. A **gatekeeper** is a person or group that decides which messages pass through the gates of the media to reach consumers.
            i.   With the excessive amount of information and with the sheer volume of events, people, and situations in the world, gatekeepers are a necessity in making choices about what the media will present to the public.
            ii. There are many different gatekeepers, including reporters, editors, owners, producers, government agencies, advertisers, and political groups.

791

        iii.   The choices that gatekeepers make affect our knowledge and perspectives.

        iv.   Gatekeepers screen both information content and sources of information.

    c.   Agenda setting theory states that the what and how stories impact the way in which we view the world, including values, beliefs, and attitudes of a culture.

    3.   **Cultivation theory claims** that television promotes a worldview that is inaccurate but that viewers nonetheless assume reflects real life.

        a.   Cultivation is defined as the cumulative process by which television creates and influences beliefs about social reality.

        b.   Cultivation theory holds that television fosters beliefs about the world being more violent and dangerous than the facts demonstrate.

        c.   *Mainstreaming*, one means by which cultivation occurs, says that television teaches viewers that what they see is normal and creates a situation where people tend to be more alike than different in how they view groups of people, events, and other social realities in the world.

        d.   *Resonance*, the second way that cultivation occurs, says that when media representations of events are congruent with one's personal experiences, then the images presented in the media are reinforced as being representative of reality.

        e.   While the high incidence in violence in news programming does not reflect reality, it does reflect the fact that the abnormal is usually more newsworthy than the normal, and thus is often more reported.

    4.   **Ideological control**, a fourth media theory, asserts that media function as tools that represent the dominant ideology in a culture as normal and right.

        a.   Mass media are powerful in representing the ideology of privileged groups as natural and good.

        b.   Minorities continue to be portrayed as criminals, victims, subordinates, or less respectable people.

B.   Theories of mass media do not easily apply to social media. Five characteristics of social media help us understand how they fit into and change our lives.

    1.   Social media blur production and consumption.

    2.   Social media alter conceptions of space.

    3.   Social media invite supersaturation.

    4.   Social media encourage multitasking.

    5.   Social media promote visual thinking.

III.   Media literacy is an important perspective to have to truly be an informed consumer of mass media.

A.   Understanding the influence of media helps us develop media literacy.

B.   Access to media includes the capacity to own and use televisions, radios, computers, cell phones, etc.

    1.   Democratic access is not universal, and is creating a digital divide between people and communities that convergence will increase.

    2.   Exposing yourself to a range of media sources to be an informed consumer of media.

    3.   Attend to more than just entertainment for media literacy.

C.   Analyzing media allows us to understand how it works.

    1.   Learning to recognize patterns in media empowers you to engage media in critical and sophisticated ways.

    2.   There are a few standard patterns that media use repeatedly.

        a.   Stories open with a conflict or problem that escalates until it climaxes in final dramatic scenes.

        b.   Romance stories work through a pattern that resolves in characters living happily ever after.

        c.   Media construct the news by selecting what gets covered, choosing the hook, and choosing how to tell the story.

    3.   Critically evaluate media messages.

        a.   Interaction with mass communication should be thoughtful and skeptical.

        b.   Media literate individuals continually question sources, motives, viewpoints, bias, and other similar issues.

    4.   Responding actively to mass communication helps in recognizing that worldviews presented are partial and subjective.

        a.   Use mass communication consciously.

        b.   Participate in decision making about media.

13.1   Your Personal Media Use Questionnaire

Purpose
To understand how you personally use and interact with media and to help you think critically about the impact of media in your life.

Instructions
As consumers of the media, your life is impacted by what is presented and what you consume. Address the following questions based on your experience with the media.

1. What types of media do you consume? What media do you *not* consume? For the media you use, about how much time each day do you spend with that media?

2. In general, how does the media make you feel? Do you feel positive, represented, and respected? Or do you feel negative (angry, misrepresented, misunderstood) when you interact with the media?

3. What kinds of stereotypes exist in the media? Consider sex, race, jobs, places, children, values, relationships, etc.

4. Do you feel like the media represent and are representative of you? In what ways? Are you personally represented in terms of age, sex, race, talents, socioeconomic status, education, values, morals, etc.?

5. Who and/or what does the media make visible? Invisible?

6. Are certain sectors of your society over- or under-represented in the media? Which ones?

7. What might be some implications for yourself as you interact with the media and the views you noted above?

8. Do you think you need or want to change some of your media habits? Which ones? Why?

13.2   Critical Media Literacy

Purpose
To help you use critical thinking skills and practice media literacy when interacting with media.

Instructions
Choose a sitcom or drama program that you especially enjoy watching. Watch the program from a critical perspective. Address the following questions.

Show: _____   Date:_____   Time:_____

1. Who are the major characters? What is their sex, race, age, profession, and socioeconomic class?

A. Name: _____

Race: _____   Sex: _____   Age: _____

Occupation: _____

B. Name: _____

Race: _____   Sex: _____   Age: _____

Occupation: _____

C. Name: _____

Race: _____   Sex: _____   Age: _____

Occupation: _____

D. Name: _____

Race: _____   Sex: _____   Age: _____

Occupation: _____

2. What does this program communicate about sex/gender, race, age, and class in a general sense?

3. What do these messages about sex/gender, race, age, and class mean for society?

4. Who is visible and who is invisible in this program? Is this program similar to other programs on television? How do(es) the message(s) of this program make you feel? Why?

5. Do you feel differently about this program now that you have watched it from a more media literate perspective? Why or why not?

13.3   Case Study: Media Literacy

Purpose
To help you learn how to conduct research about the communication discipline and to see how concepts from this chapter are used in an applied setting.

Instructions
Locate and read the article listed below, and answer the following questions.

Rogow, Faith. "Voices from the Field: Teaching Media Literacy in Less Than an Hour." Journal of Media Literacy Education 1.1 (2009): 72–73. Education Research Complete. EBSCO. Web. 2 Aug. 2010.

1.   How long does the author usually have to address an audience?

2.   What serves as a foundation for her presentation?

3.   What does the author say is the purpose of teaching media literacy?

4.   What is meant by a 'habit of inquiry'?

5.   What do you think is the author's opinion of teachers? Why?

13.4   Case Study: Media Effects and New Media

Purpose

To help you learn how to locate communication research about the topics discussed in this chapter and to assist you in reading research and understanding how theories are supported or refuted by data.

Instructions

Locate and read the article listed below, and answer the related questions.

Metzger, M. (2009). The Study of Media Effects in the Era of Internet Communication. Conference Papers—International Communication Association, 1–31. Retrieved from Communication & Mass Media Complete database.

1. What is purpose of this paper?

2. What has the Internet changed, according to the author? Use specific examples from the paper to support your position.

3. How do new media challenge core theories of media effects in the mass communication literature?

4. What is the role of agenda setting and cultivation theory in new media?

5. What conclusions does the author draw about theories of media effects and new media?

6. Are you surprised at the results of this study based on your experiences and knowledge of the media? Why or why not?

Name_____

13.5   Case Study: Violence in Video Games

Purpose
To aid you in researching communication subjects and to provide greater insight to the ideas discussed in this chapter.

Instructions
Locate and read the article listed below, and answer the following questions.

Hartmann, T., & Vorderer, P. (2010). It's Okay to Shoot a Character: Moral Disengagement in Violent Video Games. Journal of Communication, 60(1), 94–119. doi:10.1111/j.1460-2466.2009.01459.x.

1.   What are the critics' concerns about violent video games? How do the authors define virtual violence?

2.   Why is virtual violence enjoyable for many players? What do the authors feel are the costs of this enjoyment? What is moral disengagement?

3.   What did the experiments test?

4.   What was the method?

5.   What were the results? What were the limitations and flaws of the study?

6.   How do you personally feel about shooting a character in a video game? Do you support the authors' findings?

13.6   Using Your Online Resources—Power Zapper

Purpose
To assist you in analyzing and applying the concepts from Chapter 13 to The Power Zapper scenario.

Instructions
Locate The Power Zapper under the Communication Scenarios section of your Online Resources for *Communication in Our Lives*. Watch the video clip and address the following questions. You may use this worksheet or answer the questions online.

Scenario
Charles and Tina Washington are in their kitchen area of their great room working on dinner. At the other end of the room their six-year-old son, Derek, is watching television. Tina is tearing lettuce for a salad, while Charles stirs a pot on the stove.

Analysis
1. Identify an example of puffery in the advertisement for a Power Zapper.

2. Are Charles and Tina Washington teaching Derek to be a critical viewer of mass communication?

3. How does this scenario illustrate the process of mainstreaming?

4. Are you more in agreement with Charles or Tina about whether toys teach important lessons?

Self-Test for Chapter 13

Multiple Choice

____ 1. Newspapers, books, CDs, Television, and radio are all examples of
   A. mass communication
   B. mass media
   C. electronic communication
   D. both A and B

____ 2. Miriam can't sleep soundly at night unless she has watched the 11 o'clock news. Which theory best explains the interaction between Miriam and the media?
   A. uses and gratification theory
   B. cultivation theory
   C. agenda setting
   D. ideological control

____ 3. Jenny is taking her first trip to New York City, but says she wont, take the subway because she's seen on TV how dangerous it can be. Jenny is operating under which theory?
   A. uses and gratification theory
   B. cultivation theory
   C. agenda setting
   D. ideological control

____ 4. Media literacy can best be defined as
   A. an understanding of the different kinds of media
   B. knowing how to operate all types of media, including television, computers, and DVD players
   C. the ability to understand the influence of mass media and respond in informed, critical ways
   D. knowledge and skill about the production of mediated messages

____ 5. Bryan is the head of a non-profit organization dedicated to improving road safety. He sends out Twitter and Facebook messages he designs to 'go viral' in order to get the word out about an upcoming fund raising campaign. A viral message reflects which response to mass media?
   A. responding actively by being mindful
   B. responding actively by using mass communication consciously
   C. critically evaluating messages
   D. exposing herself to a variety of media sources

____ 6. Technological means of connecting and interacting is called
   A. mass media
   B. social media
   C. electronic media
   D. print media

_____ 7. The nearly instant contact social media affords us also allows others constant access to us. That phenomenon is called
   A. multitasking
   B. perpetual linkage
   C. visual thinking
   D. altered space conception

_____ 8. The effects of social media consumption include all but which of the following?
   A. altered conception
   B. supersaturation
   C. multitasking
   D. gatekeeping

_____ 9. The only theory of the use and effects of mass media that also applies to social media is
   A. agenda setting
   B. ideological control
   C. cultivation theory
   D. uses and gratification

_____ 10. Social media blurs the lines between
   A. production and consumption
   B. assembly and consumption
   C. consumption and theory
   D. ideology and production

_____ 11. Kombu drove past an accident returning to campus after a weekend at home. He was certain the local paper would have a story the next day about such a large accident, but when he read the paper, there was no story. Which theory best explains the lack of coverage?
   A. agenda setting
   B. uses and gratification
   C. cultivation
   D. ideological control

_____ 12. Society's acceptance of the media portrayal of a group of people regardless of its accuracy is known as
   A. mainstreaming
   B. resonance
   C. gatekeeping
   D. cultivation

_____ 13. Regarding television violence and aggression, which statement is accurate?
   A. Children who watch a lot of television violence score higher on measures of personal aggression than children who watch less television violence.
   B. Realistic aggression is less likely to be modeled by viewers.
   C. The less one identifies with a character, the more likely the viewer is to model the aggression.
   D. Young females are more likely to model unrealistic aggression than are young male viewers.

_____ 14. The degree to which a media portrayal is congruent with personal experience is called
    A. mainstreaming
    B. resonance
    C. gatekeeping
    D. cultivation

_____ 15. Asking, "Why is this story getting so much attention?" would be engaging in which component of media literacy?
    A. understanding media influence
    B. analyzing mass communication
    C. critical evaluation of messages
    D. being involved in media issues

True/False

_____ 1. Media portrayals of interpersonal romantic relationship represents a fairly accurate portrayal of most romantic relationship.

_____ 2. One reason there is so much violence in the media is because the media tends to emphasize the abnormal over the normal.

_____ 3. There is always a clear and distinct difference between interpersonal and mass-mediated communication.

_____ 4. Children spend nearly as much time each week interacting with media as they spend at school.

_____ 5. A reporter writing a story for the local paper could be considered a gatekeeper.

_____ 6. An editor choosing which story to put in the front page is easily explained by cultivation theory.

_____ 7. Newspapers present minorities as violent criminals more than they present minorities in positive stories.

_____ 8. The media promote a fairly accurate worldview reflective of real life.

_____ 9. People who watch a lot of television have a more realistic understanding of the nature of crime than those who watch very little TV.

_____ 10. While the high incidence in violence in news programming does not reflect reality, it does reflect the fact that the abnormal is usually more newsworthy than the normal, and thus is often more reported.

Essay

1. Compare and contrast cultivation theory with the theory of ideological control.

2. What is meant by the statement, "social media blur the line between production and consumption"? Give examples from your own life to support your answer.

3. Define media literacy, and identify and describe the components.

Chapter 13 Flash Cards

Cut out the cards, write the answers on the back, and you will have a packet of flash cards for each chapter. Paraphrasing the definitions will help you remember them.

Agenda Setting	Mainstreaming	Puffery
Convergence	Mass Communication	Resonance
Cultivation	Mass Media	Uses and Gratifications Theory
Gatekeeper	Cultivation Theory	Mean World Syndrome
Media Literacy	Cultivation Theory	Digital Divide
Social Media		

Chapter 14: Planning Public Speaking

Chapter Summary

I. Public speaking can be compared to enlarged conversation.
   A. Public speaking and conversation both require us to consider the listeners' perspectives.

   B. Both public speaking and conversation necessitate that we create a good climate for communication.

   C. Both require that we express our ideas clearly.

   D. Both require that we organize what we say so that others can follow our thinking.

   E. Both require that we support our ideas.

   F. Both require that we present information in an engaging manner.

   G. While public speaking may be slightly more formal, a relaxed conversational delivery style helps listeners feel talked to rather than lectured to.

II. The first step in planning an effective public speech is to choose a topic.
   A. You need to choose a topic that matters to you.

   B. You should also select a topic that is appropriate for the speaking occasion.
      1. Know the expectations, demands, and constraints of a speaking situation.
      2. Take into consideration the physical setting for the presentation.

   C. Effective speakers will also select topics that will appeal to the needs, interests, and situations of listeners.

   D. Effective speakers limit their speeches to a manageable focus.
      1. A mind map, a holistic record of information on a topic, may help you think about the focus you want your speech to take.
      2. You need to consider the purpose of the speech, the audience, and the time constraints as just some of the variables that will impact the focus of your speech.

III. Next, define the general and specific purposes in speaking.
   A. Three general (but overlapping) speaking purposes have been recognized:
      1. Speeches to entertain, with the primary objective to engage, interest, amuse, or please listeners.
      2. Speeches to inform, with the primary objective to increase listeners' understanding, awareness, or knowledge about some topic.
      3. Speeches to persuade aim to change people's attitudes, beliefs, or behaviors or to motivate people to act.

B.   Identify the specific purpose of your speech, a behavioral object or observable response that indicates that you have been effective in achieving your goal.
        a.   Your specific purpose will help you understand your goals.
        b.   Your specific purpose will help you narrow your focus with your topic.
C.   Next, you will need to develop a thesis statement for your speech.
    1.   A thesis statement is the main idea of an entire speech.
    2.   The thesis statement concisely states the heart of your speech.
    3.   The thesis statement should be a sentence that your audience can easily remember.

III.   Analyzing your audience is an important aspect of planning a speech.
    A.   Demographic audience analysis identifies general features common to your audience.
        1.   Examples of demographics include race, age, education, sex, occupation, political affiliation, cultural heritage, marital status, etc.
        2.   Demographic information can help you adapt your speech to your listeners, for example by adapting to education level or age.
        3.   It provides general insights into what and whom listeners may find credible.
        4.   Demographic analysis provides an overview of your audience, but cannot provide precise information about each and every audience member.
        5.   When using demographic information, take precautions against stereotyping your audience.

    B.   Situational audience analysis seeks information that relates directly to the speaker's topic and purpose.
        1.   Understanding listeners' orientation toward your topic may help you know what information needs more or less emphasis.
            a.   You can find out your audience's knowledge of your topic.
            b.   You can also find out your audience's attitudes about your topic.
        2.   Insight about the listeners' orientation toward the speaker and the speaker's credibility can shape how they respond to the message.
        3.   Understanding listeners' orientation toward the speaking occasion impacts the message.
            a.   You may be able to find out what expectations your audience holds for the occasion.
            b.   You can also gather information about how long the audience expects the speech to be, as well as their expectations regarding content, tone, etc.
            c.   Adapting to the length of speech is also required.
        4.   Situational audience analysis can be conducted by simply making observations of your audience or through conversations, interviews, or surveys.

14.1 Developing Effective Thesis Statements

Purpose
To give you practice in composing strong thesis statements for speeches.

Instructions
Below are five weak thesis statements. Revise each one so that it provides a short and precise statement of the main idea for a speech.

DEVELOPING EFFECTIVE THESIS STATEMENTS

Weak thesis statement	Revised thesis statement
Example	
I want to talk about gun control.	Effective gun control is needed to save innocent lives.
1. Everyone should vote in elections.	
2. Health care in America needs help.	
3. Terrorism is a problem in the world.	
4. The affirmative action policy is not fair.	
5. Children shouldn't be allowed to watch commercial television.	

14.2   Analyzing Your Audience

Purpose
To give you practice in assessing the characteristics of your audience.

Instructions
Below are five possible speech topics. Next to each topic, make a list of the demographic and goal-focused analysis you would need to do before preparing your speech.

Speech Topics	**Audience Analysis**
1. Importance of voting in local elections	
2. Value of taking communication classes	
3. Extracurricular activities on campus	
4. Role of student government on campus	
5. Most exotic vacation spot	

14.3   Generating Topics

Purpose
To give you practice in developing topics for your presentations.

Instructions
Answer each of the ten questions below and consider it a possible topic for a classroom speech. After you generate the topics, narrow them to something that is reasonable for a five to six minute speech. Finally, using the guidelines presented in Chapter 14, rank them from one (most likely to meet the situational and audience criteria) to ten (least likely to meet the situational and audience criteria).

1. What are three hobbies or interests you possess outside of school and work?

2. What three fictional characters would you most like to meet?

3. Which three people, living or dead, would you most like to meet?

4. Read a current newspaper or magazine and list three topics that interest you.

5. What jobs have you held?

6. Where would you like to visit or travel?

7. Where have you traveled?

8. Who is your hero?

9. If you could live in any era of history except this one, which era would you choose?

10. What is the last book you read for pleasure? If you don't, why not?

Narrow your topics to something manageable within the situational and audience constraints you have been given for your class assignment. Now rank the topics from one (most likely to be successful given the assignment) to ten (least likely to be successful).

Rank	**Narrowed Topic**
_____1.	
_____2.	
_____3.	
_____4.	
_____5.	
_____6.	
_____7.	
_____8.	
_____9.	
_____10.	

What makes your top three choices most likely to be successful?

14.4   Developing Effective Specific Purpose Statements

Purpose
To give you practice in composing strong specific purpose statements for speeches.

Instructions
Below are five weak specific statements. Revise each one so that it provides a short and precise statement of what you should attempt to accomplish in a speech.

DEVELOPING EFFECTIVE SPECIFIC PURPOSE STATEMENTS

Weak specific purpose statement	Revised specific purpose statement
Example	
I want to talk about donating organs.	To persuade 25 percent of my class to sign organ donation cards.
1. Voting is a privilege.	
2. I've been thinking about the two-party system in American politics.	
3. We should buy cars made in America.	
4. There are some problems with the idea of having quotas in hiring.	
5. Parents shouldn't let their children watch commercial television.	

14.5   Listening for the Specific Purpose

Purpose

To give you practice in discerning the specific purpose of a speech.

Instructions

Find three short speeches on campus, on the radio, on TV, or online. Listen with the express purpose of "catching" the specific purpose of each and list the purposes here.

Specific Purpose #1

Specific Purpose #2

Specific Purpose #3

Compare the three purposes.

Which do you feel was most easily discernable? What qualities did the purpose possess that made it discernable?

Which was the least discernable? What did it lack?

14.6   Using Your Online Resources—Experiencing
Communication in Our Lives

Chapter 14 Case Study: Speech of Introduction

Purpose
To help you prepare for your own introductory speech assignment by analyzing the Speech of Introduction included under Student Resources on the *Communication in Our Lives* web site. You can complete this activity online or on this worksheet.

Instructions
Evaluate Dan's speech by completing the checklist and answering the questions below. The assignment was to present a 2–3-minute speech introducing a professional who uses communication skills in his or her career. In this speech, Dan introduces Dr. Evelyn Horton and explains the importance of communication skills in her work with patients.

Evaluation
1.   Does the speaker use appropriate rate and volume?

2.   Does he sound conversational?

3.   Does he use vocal variety to convey emotion?

4.   Does he appear poised and confident?

5.   Does the speaker's attire bolster credibility?

6.   Does he use effective eye contact?

7.   Does he use gestures to emphasize points and clarify structure?

8.   Does the introduction capture listeners' attention?

9.   Does the introduction provide a clear thesis and preview?

10. Does the speaker provide smooth transitions between main points?

11. Does the speaker provide evidence to develop main points?

12. Does the speaker summarize main points in the conclusion?

13. Does the speaker end with a strong idea?

_____ Excellent   _____ Good   _____ Average   _____ Fair   _____ Poor

Name_____

14.7   Checklist for Planning a Public Speech

My speech topic is:

My general purpose is to:

My specific purpose is to:

My thesis statement is:

List demographic characteristics of your listeners:

Age range _____   Average age _____
Educational level _____
Political positions _____
Number of women _____ Number of men _____
Ethnic-race composition of listeners _____
Other demographic information

Describe what you know about listeners that is directly relevant to your speech topic and purpose:

1. How much do listeners already know about your topic?

2. How much experience, if any, do listeners have with the topic of your speech?

3. Do listeners have strong opinions about the topic?

4. How strong an interest in the topic do listeners have?

14.8   Case Study: Target Your Audience

Purpose
To assist you in locating research about communication and help you analyze and apply the concepts from Chapter 14.

Instructions
Using the InfoTrac College Edition online library, locate and read the article listed below, and answer the following questions.

Newman, A.A. (2010). Half Baked: With boys more interested in cooking than ever, why do toy brands still market almost exclusively to girls? Adweek, 51, 11.

1. What is the basic story line or idea presented in this article?

2. According to the article, why should toy companies be interested in advertising cooking toys to boys?

3. How can toy companies use demographic information to develop products? Use specific examples from this article.

4. Explain how this article is related to audience analysis and your speaking assignment in this class.

Self-Test for Chapter 14

Multiple Choice

_____ 1. Freedom of speech is guaranteed by which amendment to the U. S. Constitution?
   A. first
   B. fifth
   C. sixth
   D. tenth

_____ 2. Creating a mind map is part of which stage of planning for public speaking?
   A. analyzing your audience
   B. choosing a topic
   C. defining your general and specific purpose
   D. developing a thesis statement

_____ 3. Which purpose uses a story to share experiences, build community, pass on history, or teach a lesson?
   A. entertainment
   B. informative
   C. narrative
   D. persuasive

_____ 4. Gabriel wants to give a speech on the history of Thomas the Tank Engine. His primary general purpose will be to
   A. entertain
   B. inform
   C. persuade
   D. none of the above

_____ 5. When we say that good public speaking is conversational, we mean that
   A. ethical consideration is as important in speaking as in conversation
   B. minor mistakes don't impair credibility or effectiveness
   C. both A and B
   D. Neither A nor B

_____ 6. Guidelines for selecting a good topic for a speech include
   A. choose a topic that you are unfamiliar with
   B. avoid narrowing the topic
   C. select a topic appropriate to listeners
   D. B and C

_____ 7. Giving a eulogy at a wedding dinner would offend the listeners' orientation toward the
   A. speaking occasion
   B. you, the speaker
   C. topic
   D. general purpose

_____ 8. "I want my listeners to agree to give up meat for one meal." This is an example of a
    A. thesis statement
    B. general purpose
    C. demographic purpose
    D. specific purpose

_____ 9. Which of the following would NOT be a general purpose
    A. to motivate
    B. to entertain
    C. to defend
    D. both A and C are not general purposes

_____ 10. Lou finds out the ages, educational levels, races, sexes, and political positions of his audience before his speech on owning your first home. This kind of analysis is called
    A. situational analysis
    B. satisfactory analysis
    C. demographic analysis
    D. democratic analysis

_____ 11. If Joanne were giving a speech about the differences between aerobic, anaerobic, and strength training exercise, her general purpose would be to
    A. entertain
    B. inform
    C. persuade
    D. none of the above

_____ 12. Lisa wants to give a speech on why her audience should practice yoga. Her general purpose is to
    A. entertain
    B. inform
    C. persuade
    D. none of the above

_____ 13. Demographic analysis allows you to
    A. make inferences about listeners' attitudes, beliefs, and values
    B. gain information that is useful in developing a speech
    C. survey your listeners' experiences and attitudes relevant to your speaking goal
    D. A and B

_____ 14. Which of the following is considered an element of situational audience analysis?
    A. education level
    B. knowledge about the topic
    C. age
    D. housing arrangements

_____ 15. Which of the following is an ineffective thesis statement?
    A. People should think about safe sex.
    B. Preserving rainforests is critical to global ecology.
    C. You should always have a designated driver when you go out.
    D. You should vote for Eleanor Johnston.

True/False

_____ 1. Demographic analysis provides in-depth insight into listeners' attitudes toward a topic.

_____ 2. Public speaking that is conversational is too informal for most American audiences.

_____ 3. Humor is part of all speeches that have the goal of entertaining.

_____ 4. It is important to avoid stereotyping groups about whom we collect demographic information.

_____ 5. Creating a mind map is the same as brainstorming.

_____ 6. Being a critical listener is essential for being an effective speaker.

_____ 7. Critically analyzing a speech is not necessary to respond effectively.

_____ 8. Your listeners' gender is a demographic.

Essays

1. State the content of the first amendment to the United States Constitution. You may paraphrase it.

2. Cite and define three parts of demographic audience analysis. What impact does each part have on your speech?

3. You have been asked to give a speech at your high school about why the current juniors would choose to attend the same college or university you do. What are your general purpose, specific purpose, and thesis statements?

Chapter 14 Flash Cards

Cut out the cards, write the answers on the back, and you will have a packet of flash cards for each chapter. Paraphrasing the definitions will help you remember them.

Demographic Audience Analysis	Specific Purpose	Speech to Persuade
Mind Map	Speech to Entertain	Thesis Statement
Situational Audience Analysis	Speech to Inform	

Chapter 15: Researching and Developing Support
for Public Speeches

Chapter Summary

I.   Conducting good research is a critical part of being an effective public speaker.
- A.   Library and online research are rich resources for gathering materials for your speech.
    1. Begin your research with a visit to your reference librarian.
    2. The Internet provides a great deal of information that isn't necessarily credible or reliable.
    3. Indexes summarize various publications and backgrounds of individuals.
    4. Databases and search engines allow you to search a library's or service's holdings from a computer terminal.
        a. DIRS is a database of over 1 million records from popular and academic publications.
        b. InfoTrac College Edition is a special edition of the InfoTrac database specifically for college students.
        c. There are also specialized databases for fields such as medicine and law.
    5. Specialized reference works can provide a wealth of information.
        a. *The Reader's Guide to Periodical Literature* summarizes articles from 125 popular magazines.
        b. *American Demographics* provides information about American's lives, including behavioral patterns, work habits, possessions, etc.

- B.   Personal knowledge is another source of information.
    1. You will feel more comfortable and be more engaging if you have personal involvement with a topic.
    2. Personal content enhances your credibility.

- C.   Interviews allow you to gather information, check the accuracy of ideas, and understand expert perspectives.
    1. Ask permission to take notes during the interview.
    2. Never record an interview without the consent of the interviewee.
    3. Conducting interviews often increases a speaker's credibility.

- D.   Survey research involves asking a number of people about their opinions, views, values, actions, or beliefs.
    1. Surveys are useful when there is no published research on a topic.
    2. Surveys can help you learn about your audience's knowledge and attitudes toward your topic.

II.   Evidence is material used to support claims a speaker makes.
- A.   Evidence tends to make ideas clearer, more compelling, and more dramatic for the listener.

- B.   Evidence fortifies a speaker's opinions, which is almost always necessary to be persuasive.

- C.   Evidence heightens a speaker's credibility.

D. There are several kinds of evidence that can be used in speeches.
    1. **Statistics** are numbers that summarize many individual cases that demonstrate relationships between phenomena.
        a. Statistics allow us to state quickly large amounts of information.
        b. Statistics can enhance a speaker's credibility.
    2. **Examples** are single instances used to make a point, dramatize an idea, or personalize information.
        a. *Undetailed examples* are quick and undetailed.
        b. *Detailed examples* provide more elaborate information and are valuable when listeners are not familiar with an idea.
        c. *Hypothetical examples* are realistic illustrations used to make a point.
        d. *Stories* are longer examples that humanize the topic, connecting it with what the listeners understand or know.
    3. **Comparisons** are associations between two things that are similar in some important way or ways.
        a. **Similies** are explicit comparisons using the words "like" or "as." (Communication is like an all-purpose tool for human interaction.)
        b. **Metaphors** are implicit comparisons that suggest the likeness of two things. (Education is opening the door to your future.)
    4. **Quotations**, or testimony, are exact citations of statements made by others.
        a. Quotations are used to clarify ideas or make them more credible.
        b. Quotations are used to substantiate ideas.
        c. Whenever you quote someone else, you are ethically obligated to give that person credit for the statement.
        d. Effective quotations must meet four criteria in order to be effective.
            i. Sources should be people whom listeners know and respect or whom they will respect once you identify credentials.
            ii. Testimony should come from someone qualified to speak on the issue.
            iii. Ethical quotations must be accurate and used in an appropriate context.
            iv. Quotations should come from unbiased sources.
    5. **Visual Aids** can provide support to a speech through charts, graphs, photographs, transparencies, computer graphics, and physical objects.
        a. Visual aids increase listeners' understanding and retention.
        b. Visual aids increase listeners' interest by providing variety.
        c. Visual aids provide content clues to speakers, freeing you from reliance on notes.
        d. Diagrams or models are best for explaining complex concepts and unfamiliar topics.
        e. Photographs can be used to reinforce verbal messages or as messages in their own right, but they must be large enough to be seen by the audience.
        f. Handouts are an effective way to give information that the listener can take with them, but handouts are best given at the end of a speech to avoid interrupting your presentation.

E. There are several guidelines for using visual aids effectively.
    1. A visual aid needs to be large enough and clear enough for the whole audience to see it.
    2. Visual aids should be kept simple and uncluttered.
    3. Visual aids should be safe and nondistracting.

4. When using a visual text, there should be no more than six lines of text written in simple phrases and using a plain typeface.
5. The maximum number of visual aids for a speech should be the length of speech/2 + 1.
   a. Visual aids should only be put up or shown when you are referring to them, and then should be covered or removed when you are done speaking about them.
   b. When using visual aids, be sure to maintain eye contact with your audience rather than speaking to the visual aid.
6. Keeping track of evidence while preparing a speech is important.
   a. The traditional method is to put each piece of evidence on a separate note card.
   b. Mind maps also keep track of evidence.

Name_____

15.1 Identifying Evidence

Purpose
To increase your familiarity with types of evidence.

Instructions
Below are 10 statements containing evidence. In the blank to the left of each statement, identify the specific type of evidence presented. Answers appear with the Chapter 15 Self-Test Answers.

IDENTIFYING EVIDENCE

Example

statistic   Nearly 25% of children in America do not get adequate nutrition.

1. _____   Only 1 in 4 Americans votes in local elections.

2. _____   According to Jacob Robinson, President of ABC Chemicals, "no toxic chemicals are released from plant operations."

3. _____   Walking home last night, I picked up three soft drink cans in one block.

4. _____   The Outward Bound Course is a journey of self discovery.

5. _____   This bar graph shows the relative proportions of money spent on welfare and support of businesses.

6. _____   My grandmother used to say, "Life is what happens when you're busy doing other things."

7. _____   To understand what it's like to be homeless, imagine that your room is suddenly gone. You have no place to keep your stuff or to sleep.

8. _____   College is like a key to success.

9. _____   Over 400,000 individuals have been diagnosed with HIV.

10. _____   This enlarged photograph shows what happens when land is clear-cut.

15.2   Translating Statistics

Purpose
To give you experience in making statistics interesting and clear.

Instructions
Below are statistics that are dry, cluttered, or otherwise ineffective for use in a speech. Translate each statistic into one that is interesting and understandable. When you have completed the exercise, compare your translations with those of other students in your class. There are multiple ways to translate each statistic in the exercise.

BRINGING STATISTICS TO LIFE

Statistic	Translated Statistic
Of the 20,000 students at this university, 5,000 will not have jobs waiting when they graduate.	1 in 4 of the students at our school will not have a job on graduation day.
1. 3,678,921 cars were recalled last year.	
2. We spend $100,000 million annually on offensive weapons and less than 1 million on job training.	
3. During this century the average life span has grown from 40.1 years to 65.4 years.	
4. Women make only 72% of what men make.	
5. Each year in this country, 2,742 children accidentally consume poisons.	

6. The average person spends 8 hours sleeping and 16 hours communicating every day.

_____

7. Less than half of the citizens in the U.S. today are Caucasian.

_____

8. Each year over 5,689 small businesses are forced to close in the United States.

_____

9. There are only 3 women in the U. S. Senate.

_____

10. More than 60% of elderly people below the poverty line are women.

_____

15.3   Recognizing Ineffective Speaking

Purpose
To give you experience in identifying ineffective and/or unethical features in a speech.

Instructions
The following is an excerpt from a speech. There are a number of aspects of the speech that are ineffective and/or unethical. Circle any parts of the speech you think should be revised. With the Chapter 15 Self-Test answers is a second copy of the speech with errors noted in parenthetical comments that appear in boldface type. Compare your analysis with the one provided.

Merck: A Socially Conscious Business

According to <u>American Attitudes</u>, 75% of people in 1976 said big business contributes nothing to the common good. Merck is an exception.

Merck is the second largest pharmaceutical company in the world. This bar graph shows how much Merck spends each year on R and D, contributions to social programs, and donations to indigenous populations in third world countries. As you can see, Merck is sharing its wealth. In this second graph, you see how Merck's contributions to social issues compare to those of the three other largest pharmaceutical companies in the world.

One of Merck's projects is a two-year research and sampling budget of $1,142,857.00 to fund drug research in Costa Rica. In the chart I'm now showing, you can see that this is 500% more than Costa Rica previously had for its drug research.

According to Merck's CEO, "we are a company that cares about the world. Contributing to global health is our first and most important priority." Others agree. Basketball superstar James Jordan says, "Merck is a company with a heart." In this photo, you can see Jordan attending a meeting of Merck's shareholders.

Name_____

15.4   Finding Sources

Purpose
To give you experience identifying potential sources for a speech.

Instructions
For each of the three topics you listed at the end of activity 13.7, identify 3 specific sources for each. If you list a book, be sure to give the call number. If you list an Internet source, be sure to include the URL (web address).

Topic 1:_____

    1.

    2.

    3.

Topic 2:_____

    1.

    2.

    3.

Topic 3:_____

    1.

    2.

    3.

15.5   Survey Construction Guidelines

Purpose
To give you experience in identifying properly and improperly constructed survey questions.

Instructions
For each question or behavior below, list what, if anything, is wrong according to the Survey Construction Guidelines presented in Chapter 15. Answers appear with the Chapter 15 Self-Test answers.

MARTHA'S SURVEY PLANS

1.   Martha is planning to give a speech on why the campus should become vehicle free.

2.   She decides that she has approximately 30 sisters in her sorority and knows approximately 40 students in other organizations that she can have fill out the survey so her plan is to get at least 50 surveys completed.

3.   On her survey, there are eight questions that deal with various aspects of driving, pedestrian walkways, and grass/trees and flowers on campus.

4.   Question one asks students, "Do you agree or disagree that there is not enough parking on campus?"

5.   Question two asks students, "Do you think we should have less traffic and more walkways on campus?"

6.   Question three asks students, "Should we increase the greenway on campus?"

7.   Question four asks students, "You would rather be able to walk safely on campus, wouldn't you?"

8.   Question five asks students, "Would you be willing to take a trolley/shuttle bus from an outlying parking lot?"

9.   Question six asks, "Do you favor less pollution or parking closer to campus?"

10.   Question seven asks, "Do you think more grassy areas (e.g., to sit and study, play frisbee, etc.) are an important part of campus life?"

11.   Question eight asks, "Do you think both students and faculty should have to park in shuttlebus lots?"

15.6   Choosing Speech Evidence

Purpose
To give you experience in identifying different types of evidence to include in your speech.

Instructions
For each of the types of evidence listed below, name three pieces of information you found in your research that could be included in your speech. Be sure to indicate which source contained the information so you can cite it properly in your speech.

Statistics
    1.

    2.

    3.

Examples
    1.

    2.

    3.

Comparisons
    1.

    2.

    3.

Quotations

1.

2.

3.

Visual Aids

1.

2.

3.

Now go back and circle the number of the one item listed under each type of evidence that is most likely to be useful in your speech. Why are these more likely to be effective than the other items you listed?

15.7 Slide Construction Guidelines

Purpose
To give you experience in identifying effective or ineffective use of slides in a presentation.

Instructions
Alexa is planning to use slides as her visual aid for a presentation on the importance of interpersonal communication in organizational settings. Below is a list of plans she has made for her PowerPoint slides. Below each plan, list what slide guideline she has used properly or improperly. Answers appear with the Chapter 14 Self-Test answers.

Alexa's Planned PowerPoint Slides

EXAMPLE
Alexa is having a difficult time deciding if she should use the seashell or waves background design for her slides so she decides to do the introduction and conclusion with seashells and the main points with waves.

ANSWER Should use one design consistently.

1. In her introduction, Alexa decides to use a model of communication she found in her organizational communication textbook. The model takes up the entire slide.

   ANSWER:

2. Her next decision is to use a 12-point italicized font. She really likes the Funky font and decides to go with it because she can get more information on each slide.

   ANSWER:

3. Because the main points are such an important part of the speech, she decides to preview them on a single slide with all capital letters.

   ANSWER:

4. In the body of her speech, there is a slide about manager-employee relationships and so she splits the slide in half with text on the left and a piece of clipart on the right.

ANSWER:

5. During the next main point, she decides that she wants to make sure the audience is paying attention so she has all of the sub-point slides flash back and forth between red and green.

ANSWER:

6. Alexa is less sure about her third main point, so she decides to write out her examples and statistics in full sentences on the slides.

ANSWER:

7. In the conclusion, Alexa wants to highlight her closing quotation, so she places it in a bright color with boldface to make it memorable.

ANSWER:

8. When she gets to the room to practice her speech with the slides, Alexa finds that the color schemes she has chosen are lighter/paler on the screen in the room than on her computer screen so it will work best if she turns off the lights.

ANSWER:

15.8 Using Your Online Resources—Experiencing *Communication in Our Lives*

Chapter 15 Case Study: Effective Evidence

Purpose
To help you prepare for your own speech assignment by analyzing the speech excerpt from Effective Evidence included under Speech Interactive on your Online Resources for *Communication in Our Lives*. You can complete this activity online or on this worksheet.

Instructions
Evaluate Shannon's speech by completing the checklist and answering the questions below.

Assignment
The assignment was to present a 7–9 minute persuasive speech. In her speech, Shannon Navarro delivers a persuasive speech against the dumping of toxins in low-income and minority neighborhoods. The second point in Shannon's speech is presented online to illustrate the use of effective evidence in persuasive speaking. This second point presents and develops the claim that environmental racism has health effects on communities.

Evaluation
1. Does Shannon use a variety of types of evidence?

2. Does Shannon use sufficient evidence to support her point?

3. Does Shannon cite her sources properly?

4. Does Shannon's evidence meet the five tests for effective and ethical evidence?

   _____   Excellent
   _____   Good
   _____   Average
   _____   Fair
   _____   Poor

Name_____

15.9   Case Study: Planning Your Presentation

Purpose

To assist you in learning how to locate materials about communication and public speaking, and to provide you with additional tips to help you plan and organize your speech.

Instructions

Locate and read the article listed below, and answer the following questions.

Reiffenstein, K. (2010, May). Speaking Up: 10 Tips for Making a C-Level Presentation. T + D, 64(5), 33–35. Retrieved August 4, 2010, from ABI/INFORM Global. (Document ID: 2034038391).

1. What is the purpose of this article?

2. Why don't most presentations succeed, according to the article?

3. Why does the author suggest to start with the conclusions?

4. How many slides should you use in your presentation?

5. In applying the ideas of this article, what specific steps should you take to plan presentation?

15.10   Practicing Oral Footnotes

Purpose
To give you practice constructing oral footnotes, which are essential to speaker credibility.

Instructions
Construct written footnotes for three sources you intend to use in your speech. For each source write a sentence that you will incorporate into your speech to tell your audience where you found your information.

An oral footnote has three parts: signal phrase, source identification, qualification.

A signal phrase is one that alerts the listener to the fact that information to follow is not of the speaker's invention. Typical signal phrases include "according to", "in the words of…", and [name of author, interviewee, etc.] says…".

Source identification is the name of the person, organization, or agency offering the information. The source is not the web address. Rather, it is the author of the information you read at that address.

Qualification is an explanation of the connection between the author's experience and the information. For example, if we use statistics on spying made available by the CIA, we would explain to an audience unfamiliar with the CIA that it is the Central Intelligence Agency, the federal government agency responsible for espionage.

Construct the footnotes, then in each, underscore the 3 parts.

Oral footnote #1

Oral footnote #2

Oral footnote #3

Name_____

15.11   Case Study: Developing Professional Presence

Purpose
To learn how to locate materials about the discipline of communication and to provide you with additional reasons for public speaking proficiency.

Instructions
Locate and read the article listed below, and answer the questions.

Bass, A. (2010). From Business Dining To Public Speaking: Tips For Acquiring Professional Presence And Its Role In The Business Curricula. American Journal of Business Education, 3(2), 57–63. Retrieved August 4, 2010, from ABI/INFORM Global. (Document ID: 1981614011).

1. What is 'professional presence'?

2. According to this article, why is business etiquette important to a competitive global environment?

3. List three ways the author suggests to express confidence through nonverbal communication.

4. Why are introductions important to business communication?

5. What is the role of dining etiquette to business presence?

6. How can you improve your business presence?

Self-Test for Chapter 15

Multiple Choice

_____ 1. What is the first step in the research process?
    A.   construct a survey
    B.   look for personal examples
    C.   surf the web
    D.   visit the reference librarian

_____ 2. Indexes can help you research your speech by
    A.   summarizing publications
    B.   summarizing backgrounds of individuals
    C.   allowing you to search government documents
    D.   A, B, C

_____ 3. Numbers that summarize a great many individual cases are called
    A.   statistics
    B.   analogies
    C.   similes
    D.   direct comparisons

_____ 4. "Starting a business is like giving birth" is an example of a(n)
    A.   analogy
    B.   simile
    C.   reference
    D.   hypothetical example

_____ 5. According to Edward Klinzer, chair of the AMA, "If everyone had an annual physical, we would save more than a half million lives each year." This is an example of which kind of evidence?
    A.   statistics
    B.   analogy
    C.   detailed example
    D.   quotation

_____ 6. "Starting college is the first step in the rest of your life." This is an example of which kind of evidence?
    A.   statistics
    B.   metaphor
    C.   simile
    D.   comparison

_____ 7. In a speech on face cream, the speaker states, "Joan Rivers says WrinkleBGone is the best for relieving deep wrinkles on the face." This evidence is an example of
    A.   quotation
    B.   halo effect
    C.   analogy
    D.   A and B

8. A print reference work that describes such things as the behaviors exhibited by, or possessions owned by, members of our society is
   A. The Reader's Guide to Periodical Literature
   B. The Public Affairs Information Service Bulletin
   C. American Demographics
   D. Facts on File

9. To determine the maximum number of visual aids that can be used effectively in a speech, which formula is advised?
   A. Length of speech/3 + 1
   B. Length of speech/4 + 2
   C. Length of speech/2 + 1
   D. Length of speech/2

10. Which of the following should be avoided in interviews?
    A. notetaking
    B. having a prepared list of questions
    C. undisclosed tape recording
    D. both A and C

11. DIRS and InfoTrac are examples of
    A. databases
    B. indexes
    C. search engines
    D. web sites

12. Horace wants to find out more background information on Hillary Clinton, the US Secretary of State. An excellent reference would be
    A. Encyclopedia Britannica
    B. Who's Who in American Women
    C. Reader's Guide to Periodical Literature
    D. American Demographics

13. Jayden says in his speech on fire safety, "for example, if you awaken to a smoke alarm and need to get out of the house quickly…" Jayden is using a(n)
    A. undetailed example
    B. detailed example
    C. story
    D. hypothetical example

14. Which of the following constitute criteria for quotations?
    A. accurate
    B. biased
    C. respected sources
    D. A and C

15. Which form of visual aid would be most effective for clarifying proportions?
    A. bar graph
    B. line graph
    C. pie chart
    D. diagram

True/False

_____ 1. It's generally advisable to pass handouts to listeners after a speaker has completed his or her speech.

_____ 2. Visual aids help reduce speaker dependence on notes.

_____ 3. Hypothetical examples are inappropriate in speeches to entertain.

_____ 4. A source who acknowledges other sources and opposing viewpoints is more credible than one who does not.

_____ 5. Sensational visual aids are most effective.

_____ 6. The Internet has many sources that are neither credible nor reliable.

_____ 7. Information from the Internet is usually accurate.

_____ 8. One way to test the credibility of information found on the Internet is to find it in another source or by consulting an expert.

_____ 9. Evidence's effectiveness depends upon whether listeners can understand it.

_____ 10. Scientific evidence favorable to industry that results from research funded by that industry is not considered biased.

Essay

1. Give three examples of similes and three examples of metaphors. How will you use each in your speech?

2. Name five guidelines for using slides in a presentation and explain why it is important to follow them.

3. You are giving a speech on why the United States should promote democracy in Third World countries. Name three of the four types of research and give an example of how you would go about researching this topic using each.

Chapter 15 Flash Cards

Cut out the cards, write the answers on the back, and you will have a packet of flash cards for each chapter. Paraphrasing the definitions will help you remember them.

Comparisons	Metaphors	Survey Research
Evidence	Quotations	Visual Aids
Examples	Similes	Halo Effect
Statistics		

Chapter 16: Organizing and Presenting Public Speeches

Chapter Summary

I.   Organization is a crucial to delivering an effective speech.
   A.   Organization increases your speaking effectiveness because audiences like and expect structure.

   B.   Organization influences comprehension of ideas by your listeners.

   C.   Listeners are better persuaded by organized speech than by a disorganized one.

   D.   Organization enhances your credibility as a speaker with your audience.

   E.   Organizing an effective speech is not the same as organizing a good paper, even though they share some structural principles.
      1.   Oral communication requires more explicit organization.
      2.   Oral communication benefits from greater redundancy within the message.
      3.   Oral communication should rely on less complex sentence structures.

   F.   Effective organization of your speech begins with a good outline that helps you organize your ideas and makes sure you have enough evidence to support your claims.
      1.   A **working outline** is a brief sketch of your speech with main ideas and phrases for the purpose of seeing how your ideas fit together.
      2.   A **formal outline** includes all main points and subpoints, supporting materials, and transitions, as well as a bibliography.
      3.   A **key word** uses only key words for each point in order to trigger the speaker's memory of each point.

   G.   Organizing the body of the speech is the first priority in creating the actual speech.
      1.   The body of the speech develops and supports the central idea by organizing it into several related, but distinct points.
         a.   In short speeches of 5 to 10 minutes, no more than three points can be developed.
         b.   In longer speeches of 11 to 20 minutes, more points can be developed.
      2.   There are eight organizational patterns for organizing the speech.
         a.   The time pattern (also called temporal or chronological pattern) organizes ideas on the basis of temporal relationships.
         b.   The spatial pattern organizes ideas according to physical relationships.
         c.   The topical pattern orders a presentation into several different categories, classes, or areas of distinction.
         d.   The star pattern is a type of topical pattern that ties each point to an overriding theme.
         e.   The wave pattern consists of repetition of a key idea.
            i.   The speaker presents evidence and then crests at a main point.
            ii.   Each crest repeats the main theme using the same words, or a variation on the theme.
         f.   The comparative pattern (also called comparison/contrast and analogical organization) encourages listeners to be aware of similarities or differences between two or more things.

g. The problem-solution pattern divides a topic into a basic problem and the solution to it.
   i. Usually the problem is presented before the solution, but can be reversed.
   ii. This organizational pattern is especially useful in persuasive speeches advocating policies and practices.
h. The cause-effect and effect-cause patterns are used to argue a direct relationship between two things.
   i. This pattern is appropriate for both informative and persuasive speeches.
   ii. It is extremely difficult to *prove* a cause and effect relationship, but thorough evidence of the relationship is often sufficient to persuade.

H. The introduction to a speech is the first thing listeners hear, and has four goals.
   1. The introduction gains listeners' attention and give them a reason to listen.
      a. Dramatic evidence, such as a stirring quotation, a striking visual aid, a strong example, or a startling statistic may be used.
      b. Rhetorical questions get listeners thinking about a topic.
      c. Action questions require listeners to respond.
      d. Referring to current events helps capture audience attention.
      e. Provide direct experience to listeners by having them directly do or try something related to the speech.
      f. Humor can also be an appropriate way to open a speech.
   2. The introduction functions to present the main message of your speech, the thesis statement discussed in Chapter 14.
   3. The audience functions to establish a speaker's credibility.
      a. A speaker is deemed credible if she or he seems qualified to speak on the topic, shows good will toward the audience, and demonstrates dynamism in the presentation.
      b. Speakers should be especially focused on establishing good will if they are speaking on an unpopular topic.
   4. The final purpose of an introduction is to tell listeners the main points of the speech to assist your audience in listening for your main ideas.

I. The final part of constructing a public speech is creating the conclusion.
   1. An effective conclusion is the last chance to drive home the main points of a presentation.
      a. Restate the thesis and major points.
      b. Leave your audience with a memorable and lasting thought, returning to the main idea to provide closure.
   2. Your conclusion should take less than 5% of your total speaking time.

J. The final organizational issue is **transitions**.
   1. Transitions are words and sentences that connect ideas and main points in a speech so that listeners can follow a speaker.
      a. Transitions may be words, phrases, or entire sentences.
      b. Transitions may also be nonverbal, such as moving to a new location as you present a new point.
      c. Silence may serve as a transition.
      d. Visual aids may be used to signal a move to a new thought.
   2. Effective transitions tell audiences where you have been and where you are going next.

II. Communication apprehension is a natural fear of communicating, especially in public speaking settings.
   A. Some communication apprehension is normal and can be beneficial; extreme anxiety can be debilitating.

   B. There are two types of communication apprehension.
      1. Situational communication apprehension occurs when an individual has a fear of communicating in specific communication settings, such as giving a speech, or one-on-one settings.
      2. Chronic communication apprehension is when an individual is apprehensive in almost all communication settings.

   C. There are four ways to help alleviate communication apprehension.
      1. Systematic desensitization teaches people to relax, alleviating the physiological effects of the anxiety.
      2. Cognitive restructuring is a method designed to help people change how they think about the speaking situations.
      3. Positive visualization aims to reduce anxiety, guiding speakers through imagined positive speaking experiences.
      4. Skills training assumes that lack of speaking skills causes us to be apprehensive about speaking, and teaches people effective skills such as starting a conversation, organizing ideas, and creating strong introductions.

III. Once the speech has been crafted, speakers need to decide how to best deliver the speech.
   A. **Oral style** refers to visual, vocal, and verbal communication with listeners.
      1. *Vocal delivery* includes volume, pitch, pronunciation, articulation, inflections, pauses, and speaking rate.
      2. *Verbal delivery* consists of word choice and sentence structure.

   B. There are three qualities of effective oral communication.
      1. It is more informal than written communication.
      2. It tends to be more personal than written style.
      3. It tends to be more immediate and more active than written style.

   C. Oral style may follow one of 4 patterns called presentational styles.
      1. Impromptu speaking involves little preparation.
      2. Extemporaneous speaking is the most common style and relies on preparation and practice, but is not memorized.
      3. Manuscript speaking involves speaking from the complete manuscript of a speech.
      4. Memorized speaking sees the speaker committing the manuscript to memory.

   D. Effective public speeches always involve significant practice and rehearsal by the speaker.
      1. Begin practicing several days before you plan to deliver it.
      2. There are many ways to practice, including alone or with a mirror.
      3. Record yourself to refine your delivery.
      4. Practice in front of others.
      5. Don't overrehearse.

16.1   Identifying Clues to Organization

Purposes

To demonstrate how a thesis statement can provide clues to the organization of a speech.

To give you practice in recognizing signals of diverse organizational patterns for speeches.

Instructions

Below are 10 thesis statements. Each one suggests a specific organizational pattern. In the blank to the left of each statement, write the organizational pattern that it signals. Answers appear with the Chapter 16 Self-Test answers.

IDENTIFYING ORGANIZATIONAL CLUES

Example	
<u>comparative</u>	Rape is unlike any other violent crime.

_____ 1. The population of America has become increasingly diverse over time.

_____ 2. There are three reasons to vote.

_____ 3. The epidemic of domestic violence could be reduced by more vigorous enforcement of existing laws.

_____ 4. Excessive reliance on computers undermines literacy.

_____ 5. Pollution spreads from its original source to surrounding areas.

_____ 6. Graduate education is more intense and self-directed than undergraduate education.

_____ 7. Motivation to learn in school rises when students begin the day with a nutritious breakfast.

_____ 8. Universal health care should provide both preventive services and treatment for specific problems.

_____ 9. Children develop language in a series of stages during the first 3 years.

_____10. Disneyworld is designed to move people through the entire theme park.

Name_____

16.2   Evaluating Public Speeches

Purposes
To give you experience identifying aspects of public speeches in applied situations.

To demonstrate how features of speeches affect effectiveness.

Instructions
Select a public speech being given on your campus or in your community. Plan to attend the speech. The next page is an assessment form for evaluating public speeches. Use this form to evaluate the speech that you attend. Reflect on the impact of features of speeches listed on the form, on the effectiveness of the speech you observe.

EVALUATION FORM FOR A PUBLIC SPEECH

Feature of Speech	Excellent	Satisfactory	Poor
I. **Organization**			
A. Attention device	_____	_____	_____
B. Clear thesis statement	_____	_____	_____
C. Relevance stated	_____	_____	_____
D. Preview of body	_____	_____	_____
E. Appropriate pattern for organizing body	_____	_____	_____
F. Conclusion restated main ideas	_____	_____	_____
G. Speech ended with a strong, memorable idea	_____	_____	_____
H. Strong transitions	_____	_____	_____
I. Organization enhanced speaker's credibility	_____	_____	_____
II. **Evidence**			
A. Statistics were interesting & clear	_____	_____	_____
B. Cited sources were explained, qualified, & identified properly	_____	_____	_____
C. Comparisons were logical & useful	_____	_____	_____
D. Examples were strong & vivid	_____	_____	_____
E. Visual aids were clear & helpful	_____	_____	_____
F. Evidence strengthened speaker's credibility	_____	_____	_____

III. Delivery

A. Language was clear & immediate   _____   _____   _____

B. Speaker seemed spontaneous   _____   _____   _____

C. Speaker kept good eye-contact with listeners   _____   _____   _____

D. Delivery strengthened speaker's credibility   _____   _____   _____

Name_____

16.3   Positive Visualization

Purposes
To give you experience in using positive visualization to reduce speaking anxiety.

To assist you in creating a positive expectation for your public speech.

Instructions

1. Find a place that is quiet and where others will not disturb you. Make yourself comfortable.

2. Breathe deeply until you feel relaxed.

3. Imagine yourself talking with your closest friend about the topic of a speech you want to present. Visualize your friend looking interested, nodding, and responding positively to your ideas.

4. Visualize a second friend joining the two of you. See yourself continuing to talk about your ideas and notice that the second friend is showing clear interest and attention.

5. Visualize two other people in the open doorway. Notice that they are there because you were expressing your ideas effectively and they want to hear more. See yourself continuing to talk as several more people stop in the doorway to listen.

6. Imagine one of the people listening in the doorway asks you to talk about your ideas to a student group. Visualize 25 students who care about your topic.

7. Visualize yourself walking into a room with the 25 students who have come to hear your ideas. As you walk in, several students you know greet you and say they're excited about what you have to say. Feel yourself relaxing and feeling at ease with this group.

8. Imagine yourself standing before the group and beginning to speak. See the listeners responding with interest and admiration for you.

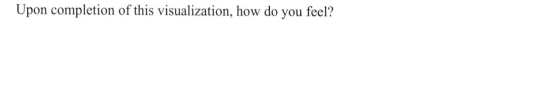

Upon completion of this visualization, how do you feel?

Has your confidence about giving your speech changed? If so, how? Be honest in your answer.

What other steps can you take to help alleviate nervousness associated with public speaking?

16.4   Outlining Speeches

Purpose

To give you experience in understanding the importance of a good outline.

Instructions

Below is a full sentence speech outline template. Use the template on the following page to prepare your key word outline.

I.   Introduction
    A. Gain Attention/Motivate to Listen

    B. Thesis Statement

    C. Establish Credibility

    D. Preview of Main Points

Transition
II. Body
    A. Main Point One

        1. Evidence/Source

        2. Evidence/Source

        3. Evidence/Source

Transition
    B. Main Point Two

        1. Evidence/Source

        2. Evidence/Source

        3. Evidence/Source

Transition
    C. Main Point Three

        1. Evidence/Source

        2. Evidence/Source

        3. Evidence/Source

Transition
III. Conclusion
    A. Summary of Main Points
    B. Memorable Closing Statement

Key Word Outline

I.   Introduction

    A.   Attention Getting Device
    B.   Thesis Statement
    C.   Establish Credibility
    D.   Preview of Main Points

Transition
II.   Body
    A.   Main Point One

        1.   Evidence/Source
        2.   Evidence/Source
        3.   Evidence/Source

Transition
    B.   Main Point Two

        1.   Evidence/Source
        2.   Evidence/Source
        3.   Evidence/Source

Transition
    C.   Main Point Three

        1.   Evidence/Source
        2.   Evidence/Source
        3.   Evidence/Source

Transition
III. Conclusion
    A.   Summary of Main Points
    B.   Memorable Closing Statement

16.5   Introductions and Conclusions

Purpose
To give you experience in creating introductions and conclusions.

Instructions
Below is a list of thesis statements for classroom presentations. For each one, find a quotation, a statistic, and an example that you can use in the introduction or conclusion of your speech. Be sure to include a reference for each so that you can cite it in a speech.

Thesis Statement: The mission of public school K-12 education is job preparation.

Quotation:

Example:

Statistic:

Thesis Statement: Socialist medical practices are inferior to medical practices in a private market, like in the US.

Quotation:

Example:

Statistic:

Thesis Statement: Reforming immigration law would be bad for our economy.

Quotation:

Example:

Statistic:

16.6   Checklist for Organizing and Presenting a Speech

Purpose
To help you learn how the same topic can be presented using a variety of organizational patterns.

Instructions
Structure your speech using each of the organizational patterns we discussed. To learn which pattern best fits your topic, write out a thesis statement for each pattern.

My topic: _____

Time:

Space:

Topical:

Star:

Wave:

Comparative:

Problem-Solution:

Cause-Effect/Effect-Cause:

Which pattern have you decided to use for your speech? _____

List the two or three main points into which you have divided your topic.

Point 1:

Point 2:

Point 3:

Describe the four parts of your introduction.

Attention:

Thesis:

Credibility:

Preview of Main Points:

Describe the transitions you have developed.

Describe the two parts of your conclusion

Summary of Main Points

Memorable Concluding Thought

The delivery style I will use is _____ because _____

I've practiced my speech (circle all that apply)

On my own   In front of others

In front of a mirror   In the room where I will deliver it

Recorded

16.7   Using Your Online Resources—Experiencing
Communication in Our Lives

Chapter 16 Case Study: Effective Delivery

Purpose
To help you prepare for your own delivery by analyzing the speech excerpt from Effective Delivery included under Speech Interactive on your Online Resources for *Communication in Our Lives*. You can complete this activity online or on this worksheet.

Instruction
Evaluate Adam's speech by completing the checklist and answering the questions below.

Assignment
The assignment was to present a 2–3 minute speech introducing yourself to the class. In his speech, Adam Currier introduces himself by talking about the quotes he has on the wall in his room—quotes that reflect who he is and what he values. In the excerpt included online, Adam explains how his grandfather taught him to enjoy every minute of life.

Criteria
1. Is Adam's speaking style conversational?

2. Is his articulation clear?

3. Is his volume appropriate—loud enough, but not too loud?

4. Does he choose an appropriate speaking style?

5. Does he engage in good eye contact with listeners?

6. Does his delivery convey that he cares about the topic?

7. Does he rely on oral (not written) style?

8. Is his appearance appropriate?

9. Does he use effective gestures?

10. Does he use pauses effectively?

11. Does he use effective vocal inflection and variety?

12. Does he use effective facial expressions?

13. Does he use body movement effectively?

Evaluate the Speech:

_____Excellent   _____Good   _____Average   _____Fair   _____Poor

16.8   Getting Attention

Purpose
To give you practice in focusing your audience's attention on you and directing it into your topic.

Instructions
Imagine that you are to deliver a 5-minute speech on forming study groups. Write an attention-getter employing each of the following strategies. You may use hypothetical evidence.

1. Dramatic evidence

2. Rhetorical question

3. Action question

4. Reference to current events

5. Direct experience

6. Humor

Self-Test for Chapter 16

Multiple Choice

_____ 1. Speeches differ from papers in that they need all but which of the following?
   A. more than one pattern
   B. more repetition
   C. simpler sentences
   D. more organization

_____ 2. A speech designed to inform the audience how to apply for graduate school would most likely use which organizational structure?
   A. spatial
   B. time pattern
   C. topical
   D. wave

_____ 3. Erryn is giving a speech on the White House after having gone on a tour which she was in Washington, D.C. Which organizational pattern would you recommend?
   A. spatial
   B. time pattern
   C. topical
   D. wave

_____ 4. A speaker who has several different topics of equal concerns changes the order and emphasis of the topic depending upon the audience would likely use which pattern?
   A. spatial
   B. chronological
   C. problem-solution
   D. star

_____ 5. Organization increases the effectiveness of a speech for which of the following reasons?
   A. people like order and so order enhances credibility
   B. an organized speech is easier to remember
   C. people are more persuaded by an organized speech
   D. A, B, and C

_____ 6. The statement "I have a dream" is repeated in Martin Luther King's speech to indicate which organizational pattern?
   A. cause-effect
   B. star
   C. time
   D. wave

_____ 7. Research indicates that roughly _____ people suffer from some sort of communication apprehension.
   A. 85%
   B. 90%
   C. 95%
   D. 100%

_____ 8. Words and sentences like, "first of all…" or "
   A. tie-lines
   B. transitions
   C. previews
   D. visualizations

_____ 9. Credibility includes all but which of the following?
   A. audience involvement
   B. trustworthiness
   C. goodwill
   D. preparedness

_____ 10. Answering a question in class is equivalent to which style of speech delivery?
   A. extemporaneous
   B. manuscript
   C. impromptu
   D. memorized

_____ 11. A thesis statement
   A. fully explains the content of the speech
   B. hints at the main theme
   C. announces the key idea
   D. is repeated in the body

_____ 12. Situational causes of communication apprehension include
   A. communicating with unfamiliar people
   B. being in the spotlight
   C. novel situations
   D. A, B, and C

_____ 13. The introduction of a speech should accomplish all but which of the following?
   A. get the audience's attention
   B. expand upon main points
   C. present a clear thesis
   D. preview the points that will be addressed

_____ 14. Which of the following is NOT an attention device?
   A. dramatic example
   B. personal involvement
   C. question to create suspense
   D. A, B, and C are all effective devices

_____ 15. One way to reduce our nervousness is to imagine ourselves in a speaking situation performing well. This method of reducing communication apprehension is called
   A. cognitive restructuring
   B. skills training
   C. positive visualization
   D. systematic desensitization

True/False

_____ 1. Transitions in speeches may be nonverbal, as well as verbal.

_____ 2. Effective conclusions are extended reviews of main ideas and supporting evidence presented in a speech.

_____ 3. The comparative pattern is also known as the analogical pattern.

_____ 4. Speaking from a manuscript is advisable when a speech must be precise and with no errors.

_____ 5. Written communication is informal, personal, and immediate.

_____ 6. Introductions and conclusions should each constitute 5% of the total speaking time.

_____ 7. The three kinds of outlines are working, formal, and delivery.

_____ 8. A degree of communication anxiety can enhance speaking effectiveness.

_____ 9. A rhetorical question is one that requires a response from the audience.

_____ 10. Probably the most common presentational style is extemporaneous.

Essay

1. Develop an introduction for an informative speech on the history of Rock and Roll. Identify and explain each of the four components necessary to an effective introduction. How do the components work together to give your listeners a reason to pay attention?

2. You have been invited back to your high school to convince current juniors that they should attend the same college or university you do. Name five pieces of evidence you would use. What specifically would you include in the introduction and conclusion?

3. Define effective oral style and identify at least eight features of effective oral style that distinguish it from effective written style in communication.

Chapter 16 Flash Cards

Cut out the cards, write the answers on the back, and you will have a packet of flash cards for each chapter. Paraphrasing the definitions will help you remember them.

Cognitive Restructuring	Key Word Outline	Systematic Desensitization
Communication Apprehension	Manuscript Speaking	Transitions
Extemporaneous Speaking	Oral Style	Working Outline
Formal Outline	Positive Visualization	Impromptu Speaking
Skills Training	Memorized Speaking	Positive Visualization
Works Cited		

Chapter 17: Informative Speaking

Chapter Summary

I. An informative speech is a presentation that aims to increase listeners' knowledge, understanding, or abilities.
   A. The majority of speeches you give in your life will be informative.
      1. Some will be formal.
      2. Some will be informal.

   B. Informative speeches differ from persuasive speeches in four ways.
      1. Informative speeches are generally less controversial in nature than persuasive speeches.
      2. The response sought is different; informative speeches want listeners to understand information, while persuasive speeches seek to change the audience's mind or behavior.
      3. Persuasive speeches require more evidence and stronger supporting materials than do informative to convince listeners to change in some way.
      4. Persuasive speeches seeking to change people generally require more credibility than informative.

II. Eight guidelines are particularly important for informative speeches.
   A. Provide listeners with a clear thesis statement.

   B. Connect with listeners' values and experiences.
      1. Focus on connecting with listeners' values and experience.
      2. Use "we" language to establish a connection with listeners.

   C. Motivate listeners to want information.
      1. Sometimes listeners are motivated for their own reason.
      2. The speaker may need to motivate people to want information.

   D. Build credibility with listeners.
      1. Demonstrate that you have some knowledge of the topic.
      2. Show that you care about your listener or that your information will aid them in some way.
      3. Appear friendly and honest.

   E. Adapt to the diversity of listeners.

   F. Organize so listeners can follow easily.
      1. Structure your speech clearly.
      2. Weave transitions throughout the speech to assist listeners with the flow of ideas.
      3. Organize the body of your speech using a pattern adapted to informative speeches.

   G. Design your speech to enhance learning and retention.
      1. Limit the information you present to avoid overload.
      2. Move from familiar to unfamiliar.

3.   Repeat important ideas.
4.   Highlight key material.
5.   Rely on multiple communication channels.
6.   Involve listeners.
     a.   Call for participation.
     b.   Ask rhetorical questions.
     c.   Poll listeners.
     d.   Refer to specific listeners.

H.   Use effective and ethical supporting materials to add interest and clarity to a speech.

17.1 Informative Speaking in our Everyday Lives

Purpose

To give you a sense of how much public speaking you experience over the course of a week.

Instructions

For the next week, make a list of all of the times that you hear a presentation (if you are unsure what to include, check your textbook for a list). Be sure to include the date, place, speaker, topic, and your evaluation of the presentation.

Date	Place	Speaker	Topic	Evaluation (Excellent, Good, Fair, Poor)

What do your experiences tell you about how much informative speaking occurs every day?

Name_____

17.2   Involving Listeners

Purpose
To give you experience in identifying ways to involve listeners in your public speeches.

Instructions
Below is a list of topics. For each topic, choose two of the mechanisms for involving listeners and give an example of how you would incorporate them into the speech.

Topic	Mechanism	Example
Student fees fund artistic, extracurricular, and intellectual activities on campus.	1	
	2	
Advising on campus should include career planning as well as class planning.	1	
	2	
Additional students from different countries and ethnic or racial backgrounds would enhance learning at our school.	1	
	2	
People without homes need to be treated with respect and dignity.	1	
	2	
Speaking in public causes more stress for most people than death, divorce, or exams.	1	
	2	

17.3   Outlining Informative Speeches

Purpose
To give you experience in providing a full outline of your informative speech.

Instructions
In each of the blanks below, complete your full-sentence outline for the informative speech you are going to give in class.

I. **Introduction**
   A. Attention device

   B. Thesis statement

   C. Establish credibility

   D. Preview of speech

II. **Body**
   A. First main point

       1. Supporting material/source

       2. Supporting material/source

       3. Supporting material/source

       4. Transition

   B. Second main point

       1. Supporting material/source

       2. Supporting material/source

       3. Supporting material/source

       4. Transition

  C. Third main point (if there is one)

    1. Supporting material/source

    2. Supporting material/source

    3. Supporting material/source

    4. Transition

III. Conclusion

  A. Summary of main points

  B. Strong closing statement

References

17.4   Informative Speech Evaluation Form

Speaker's Name: _____

Speech Topic: _____

Date: _____

	Strongly Disagree	Disagree	Neither Agree nor Disagree	Agree	Strongly Agree
The speaker captured the audience's initial attention.					
The speaker stated a clear thesis.					
The speaker established credibility.					
The speaker previewed the body of the speech.					
The speech was structured clearly and appropriately.					
Strong transitions were used between parts of the speech and main points in the body of the speech.					
The speaker provided effective supporting material.					
The speaker used ethical supporting material.					
The speaker involved the listeners.					
The speaker used strategies to enhance listeners' learning and retention.					
The conclusion summarized the main points of the speech.					
The speech ended on a strong note.					

The most effective aspect of this speech was: _____.

If I were making recommendations for a structure goal for the next speech, it would be

to: _____.

Name_____

17.5   Using the Web Site for *Communication in Our Lives*

Chapter 17 Case Study: The Black Box

Purpose

To help you prepare for your own informative speech by analyzing the speech excerpt from *The Black Box* Speech Interactive section of the web site for *Communication in Our Lives*. You can complete this activity online or on this worksheet.

Instructions

Evaluate Michael's speech by completing the checklist and answering the questions below.

Assignment

The assignment was to prepare and deliver an informative speech no longer than 10 minutes using few or no notes and multiple sources. Michael Daniels chose to present a speech titled "The Black Box."

Criteria

1.   Does the speaker use appropriate rate and volume?

2.   Does he sound conversational?

3.   Does the speaker use an effective presentational style?

4.   Does he use vocal variety to convey emotion?

5.   Does he appear poised and confident?

6.   Does the speaker's attire bolster credibility?

7.   Does he use effective eye contact?

8.   Does he use gestures to emphasize points and clarify structure?

9.   Does the introduction capture listeners' attention?

10. Does the introduction provide a clear thesis and preview?

11. Does the speaker provide smooth transitions between main points?

12. Does the speaker provide evidence to develop main points?

13. Does the evidence meet the five tests for effective and ethical evidence?

14. Does the speaker summarize main points in the conclusion?

15. Does the speaker end with a strong idea?

<u>Evaluate the Speech</u>

——— Excellent
——— Good
——— Average
——— Fair
——— Poor

17.6   Case Study: Toward Better Presentations

Purpose
To aid you in locating research materials in communication and to provide you with additional resources regarding effective speech delivery.

Instructions
Locate and read the article listed below, and answer the following questions.

Boettcher, D. (2010, February). Toward Better Presentations. United States Naval Institute. Proceedings, 136(2), 81–82. Retrieved August 5, 2010, from Research Library. (Document ID: 1961419711).

1. According to the author, what did Lincoln's, Kennedy's, and King's speeches have in common?

2. What does the author say is the purpose of communication?

3. What are the ramifications of lack of effective communication?

4. Does the author suggest writing an outline? Show information from the article to support your point.

5. What are some specific risks involved with graphics?

6. What are five specific delivery tips to improve ineffective communication given by this author?

Name_____

17.7　Understanding Diversity Among Listeners

Purpose
To give you practice in anticipating the range of values an audience may bring to the speaking occasion.

Instructions
Imagine that you are giving a 10-minute speech outlining the benefits to society of having a national health insurance program. Your audience will be composed of a cross-section of your community's socio-economic classes. Predict the perceptions each of the following groups will have of each claim by putting a +, −, or 0 in
each box to indicate positive, neutral, or negative perception.

Income Level	High	Middle	Low
American business would become more competitive.			
We would see an increase in our Gross Domestic Product if we had a healthier work force.			
Absenteeism in public schools would go down, so we would know our graduates were better prepared to enter the work force.			
Universal access would ensure equitable health care among all groups within our society, reducing friction among segments of the population.			

Did you encounter any surprises as you thought about each claim? What?

Did you discover an important principle to follow while constructing your speech? What?

Self-Test for Chapter 17

Multiple Choice

_____ 1. Which of the following thesis statements would be most appropriate for a speech whose general purpose is "to inform"?
- A. There are three ways you can change the world.
- B. Arizona's immigration policy will not solve the problem of illegal immigration.
- C. It should be illegal to text and drive.
- D. People need to know how to change a tire.

_____ 2. Which of the following is a difference between informative and persuasive speaking?
- A. Informative speeches are equally as controversial as persuasive speeches.
- B. The desired audience responses to informative and persuasive speeches are the same.
- C. Credibility is more important for informative speeches than persuasive speeches.
- D. Informative speeches usually require less evidence than persuasive speeches.

_____ 3. Suri tells her audience, "Like you, I'm a student at Brighton College who can't find a place to park." Which guideline for effective informative speaking best describes Siri's comment?
- A. provide listeners with a clear thesis statement
- B. connect to listeners' values and experiences
- C. adapt to diverse listeners
- D. clearly organize your speech so listeners can easily follow the speech

_____ 4. When we employ multiple communication channels we are
- A. engaging as many of the listeners' senses as possible
- B. asking listeners to stay tuned
- C. focusing attention when the audience drifts
- D. showing artifacts

_____ 5. You decide to do your speech on "The Importance of Good Study Habits" and in the introduction tell your classmates that you have information that can increase their GPAs with less study time. You are employing which informative speaking technique?
- A. build credibility
- B. motivate listeners to want the information
- C. assist recall
- D. adapt to diverse listeners

_____ 6. Which is not a quality that supporting material must possess to be ethical?
- A. timeliness
- B. authenticity
- C. accuracy
- D. impartiality

7. Which of the following is NOT a technique to help the audience learn and retain the information presented?
   A. limit the number of main points presented
   B. move from the unfamiliar to the familiar
   C. highlight key materials
   D. call for audience participation

8. Which of the following is effective in both informative and persuasive presentations?
   A. delivery
   B. evidence
   C. research
   D. A, B, and C

9. If we want to add interest and clarity to a speech, we must
   A. include effective and ethical evidence
   B. use only simple sentences
   C. repeat, repeat, repeat
   D. refer to specific listeners

10. Telling your audience, "My next point highlights the seriousness of the problem," is
    A. limiting the information you present
    B. relying on multiple communication channels
    C. highlighting key material
    D. repeating important ideas

True/False

1. Informative speeches are the most common type we encounter in everyday life.

2. The thesis statement in an introduction is critical to effective informative speaking.

3. Problem-solution is a popular informative organizational pattern.

4. Polling listeners and then referring to their vote later in a speech keeps listeners involved.

5. The difference between an informative response sought and that of a persuasive is that it is more ethical.

6. Directly involving your audience during your speech is not recommended for effective public speaking.

7. Rhetorical questions are questions the speaker wants listeners to answer in their heads.

8. Using multiple channels of communication tend to confuse audiences and limit the effectiveness of your presentation.

Essay

1. Louise grew up in London and is planning to give a speech to her American classmates about the similarities and differences between the education systems in England and the United States. She has come to you for advice on how to motivate her audience to listen. What advice will you give her?

2. Describe the similarities and differences between informative and persuasive speaking.

3. List five of the guidelines for effective informative speaking. How would you incorporate them into a speech?

Chapter 17 Flash Cards

Cut out the cards, write the answers on the back, and you will have a packet of flash cards for each chapter. Paraphrasing definitions will help you remember them.

Informative Speech	Persuasive Speech	

Chapter 18: Persuasive Speaking

Chapter Summary

I. Persuasive speeches seek to change others by prompting them to think, feel, believe, or act differently.
    A. Effective persuasion keeps listeners in mind.
    B. Persuasion is not coercion or force—it relies on artistic proofs.
    C. Persuasion is usually gradual and incremental.

II. There are three pillars of persuasion that hail from the time of the Greek philosopher, Aristotle.
    A. **Ethos** refers to the perceived personal character of the speaker.
        1. We are more likely to believe people we trust.
        2. Ethos involves the speaker's integrity, trustworthiness, goodwill, knowledge, and dynamism.
    B. **Pathos** refers to emotional reasons for attitudes, beliefs, and actions.
        1. Emotional proofs help your listeners feel a certain way about your ideas.
        2. Appeals to emotions can easily alienate listeners instead of involving them.
        3. Generally, it is better to get audience members to do something about which they will feel good than to berate them for something they either are or are not doing.
    C. **Logos** is using rational or logical proofs, such as arguments, reasoning, and evidence to support claims.
        1. Inductive reasoning begins with specific examples and uses them to draw a general conclusion.
        2. Deductive begins with a general claim that is widely accepted, then offers a very specific claim.
        3. The Toulmin Model is a third way to think about logic.
            a. The claim is an assertion.
            b. Grounds are the evidence or data that support the claim.
            c. The warrant is the justification of the grounds—the relevance or connection for the grounds of the claim.
            d. A qualifier is a word or phrase that limits the scope of the claim.
            e. Rebuttal anticipates and addresses reservations or counterarguments that listeners are likely to have about claims.

III. Another word for ethos is **credibility**, which a speaker earns by convincing listeners that s/he has integrity, goodwill, and trustworthiness.
    A. Credibility is something the audience confers on the speaker.
    B. Credibility arises from the three pillars of persuasion.
        a. Listeners find speakers who demonstrate personal integrity as credible.
        b. Speakers who establish emotional meaning for their messages are more persuasive.
        c. Speakers who present tight, rational, and logical evidence are viewed as more credible.

C.   There are several different types of credibility.
    1.   **Initial credibility** is the speaker's expertise and trustworthiness before a presentation begins.
    2.   **Derived credibility** is a result of how speakers communicate during presentations.
    3.   **Terminal credibility** is a combination of initial and derived granted at the end of the presentation.

D.   A speaker can do several things to enhance credibility with an audience.

IV.   The organization of a persuasive speech impacts its effectiveness.
    A.   The motivated sequence model has been shown to be quite effective in diverse communication situations.
        1.   The first step is to draw attention to the subject.
        2.   The second establishes a need by showing a real and serious problem exists.
        3.   Next is the satisfaction step, in which a speaker presents a reasonable solution.
        4.   Visualization helps listeners to visualize the outcomes or results.
        5.   The action step then involves a direct appeal for concrete action on the part of the audience.

    B.   Persuasive speeches can be organized to present only one side of an issue or both sides.
        1.   Listeners' expectations of the speaker will impact whether you choose to present one or both viewpoints of an issue.
        2.   Listeners' attitude will also impact your choice of a one-sided or two-sided approach.
            a.   Audiences that are already somewhat in favor of your position are more likely to accept your argument with only one point of view.
            b.   Audiences that are hostile to your views are more likely to need to hear both sides of an argument before they will consider change.
        3.   Listeners' knowledge of a topic influences decisions on whether to present one or more sides of an issue.
        4.   Generally, the most persuasive strategy is to present both sides and refute arguments from the other side.

V.   There are several guidelines that will increase your effectiveness when giving persuasive speeches.
    A.   Create common ground with listeners to increase your goodwill and increase the likelihood that they will pay close attention to you.

    B.   Adapt to listeners by considering their knowledge, attitudes, motives, experiences, values, and expectations. This helps ensure that you reach the greatest portion of your audience in a way that is most effective for them.

    C.   Avoid fallacious reasoning to increase your credibility and effectiveness.
        1.   *Ad hominem* arguments attack individuals rather than ideas.
        2.   *Post hoc, ergo propter hoc* arguments present two things as being related such that the first thing causes the second, even though causality may not be true.
        3.   *Bandwagon appeals* seek to change people by suggesting that everyone else is already thinking, feeling, or behaving in a particular way, so the listener should do so, too.
        4.   The *slippery slope* fallacy claims that once we take the first step, more and more steps inevitably will follow until some unacceptable consequence results.

5. A *hasty generalization* is a broad, general claim with insufficient evidence.
6. *Red Herring* arguments try to deflect listeners from relevant issues to some irrelevant topic.
7. *Either-or logic* implies there are only two possible outcomes or viewpoints, when in fact there are many options.
8. The halo effect occurs when the speaker generalizes a person's authority or expertise to areas in which the person's authority or expertise is irrelevant.

18.1   Cornerstones of Persuasion

Purpose
To give you experience in understanding how ethos, pathos, and logos operate in persuasive situations.

Instructions
For one week, collect the editorials written by the editorial staff from a local or national paper. After collecting these, make a list of the ethos, pathos, and logos appeals used in these opinion editorials.

Ethos Appeals

Pathos Appeals

Logos Appeals

Processing
Discuss the appeals that you found most persuasive. Were they ethos, pathos, logos, or some combination of the three? What made these appeals more persuasive than the other ones?

18.2   Motivated Sequence

Purpose
To give you experience in working with the Motivated Sequence for persuasive speaking.

Instructions
Find five print, television, or radio advertisements. For each one, indicate how the advertisement accomplishes the five steps in the Motivated Sequence. If the advertisement does not accomplish this, indicate how it might have done that step.

Advertisement 1

Attention:

Need:

Satisfaction:

Visualization:

Action:

Advertisement 2

Attention:

Need:

Satisfaction:

Visualization:

Action:

Advertisement 3

Attention:

Need:

Satisfaction:

Visualization:

Action:

Advertisement 4

Attention:

Need:

Satisfaction:

Visualization:

Action:

Advertisement 5

Attention:

Need:

Satisfaction:

Visualization:

Action:

Processing

Which of these advertisements was most persuasive? Why was it more persuasive than the others?

18.3 Recognizing Fallacies

Purpose
To give you experience in picking fallacies out of a main point's evidence.

Instructions
Below is a list of statements made in a speech. Next to each one, indicate the logical reasoning fallacy that has occurred. Correct answers appear with the Chapter 18 Self-Test answers.

Statement	Fallacy
Example: Dr. Izzie Stevens, from *Grey's Anatomy*, promotes the use of Zyrtec for allergy sufferers and encourages you to ask your doctor about trying this drug to relieve your allergy symptoms.	Halo Effect
Accounting standards should be kept as they are.	
Most first-year students live on campus and you should too.	
All people should have security systems installed because there have been so many break-ins and child abductions in the area lately.	
The standardized test scores for first graders declined in 1998, one year after Lindsey was named superintendent of schools.	
Avoid following Donna's advice about children because she has never had any.	
We need to raise taxes or decrease services.	
People who believe in the death penalty should volunteer their time in prisons. Let me tell you why volunteering is such a worthwhile endeavor.	
Lindsey Lohan is quoted on the virtues of being an organ donor.	

Because melamine was found in milk in China, we should avoid drinking milk in the United States.

If we give 18-year-olds the right to drink alcohol, they will come to class drunk and give alcohol to minors.

Heeding David's comments about stock investing is like asking a liberal whether social programs are beneficial.

Support candidate Saporta with a lawn sign, just like your neighbors did.

Name_____

18.4   Persuasive Speech Evaluation Form

Speaker's Name: _____

Speech Topic: _____

Date: _____

	Strongly Disagree	Disagree	Neither Agree nor Disagree	Agree	Strongly Agree
The speaker captured the audience's initial attention.					
The speaker motivated the listeners to want information.					
The speaker stated a clear thesis.					
The speaker previewed the body of the speech.					
The speech was structured clearly and appropriately.					
Strong transitions were used between parts of the speech and main points in the body of the speech.					
The speaker provided effective evidence to support main points.					
The speaker gained ethos during the speech.					
The speaker engaged listeners directly.					
The speaker built pathos.					
The speaker attended to logos.					

The conclusion summarized the main points of the speech.					
The speech ended on a strong note.					
The speaker used appropriate volume and pace.					
The speaker used a conversational presentation style.					
The speaker used vocal variety to convey emotion.					
The speaker used effective facial expressions and body movement.					
The speaker made direct eye contact.					
The speaker's attire bolstered credibility.					
The speaker appeared poised and confident.					

The most effective aspect of this speech was:

_____

If I were making recommendations for a structure goal for the next speech, it would be

to:

_____

_____

Name_____

18.5   Using Your Online Resources—Experiencing
Communication in Our Lives

Chapter 18 Case Study: The Case for Graduated Licensing

Purpose
To help you prepare for your own persuasive speech by analyzing the speech excerpt from The Case for Graduate Licensing under Speech Interactive on your Online Resources for *Communication in Our Lives*. You can complete this activity online or on this worksheet.

Instruction
Evaluate Rebecca's speech by completing the checklist and answering the questions below.

Assignment
The assignment was to prepare and deliver a persuasive speech 7 to 9 minutes in length. Rebecca Ewing chose to present a speech titled, "The Case for Graduated Licensing."

Criteria
1.   Does the speaker use appropriate volume?

2.   Is the speaker articulate?

3.   Is the rate of speaking effective?

4.   Does she sound conversational?

5.   Does she use an effective presentational style?

6.   Does she use vocal variety to convey emotion?

7.   Does she appear poised and confident?

8.   Does the speaker's attire bolster credibility?

Delivery

1. Does she use effective eye contact?

2. Does she use gestures to emphasize points and clarify structure?

3. Does she use effective facial expressions?

4. Does the speaker use effective body movements?

5. Does the introduction capture listeners' attention?

6. Does the introduction provide clear thesis and preview?

7. Does the speaker engage listeners directly?

8. Does the speaker provide smooth transitions between main points?

9. Does the speaker provide effective evidence to develop main points?

10. Does the speaker gain ethos during the speech?

11. Does the speaker build pathos?

12. Does the speaker attend to logos?

13. Does the speaker summarize main points in the conclusion?

14. Does the speaker end with a strong idea?

Evaluate the Speech

_____ Excellent   _____ Good   _____ Average   _____ Fair   _____ Poor

Name_____

18.6   Case Study: Critical Thinking and Logic

Purpose
To aid you in locating research articles about communication, and to aid you in critical thinking and logic regarding persuasive messages.

Instructions
Locate and read the article listed below, and answer the following questions.

Rex, L., Thomas, E., & Engel, S. (2010). Applying Toulmin: Teaching Logical Reasoning and Argumentative Writing. English Journal, 99(6), 56–62. Retrieved August 9, 2010, from Research Library. (Document ID: 2070589451).

1. What did the authors feel has been given "short shrift"?

2. What did the students teach the authors?

3. How was Toulmin's framework modified?

4. What were the three components of the framework?

5. How did the framework help improve Adrian's essay?

6. How could Toulmin's framework help your communication skills?

18.7   Advertising Audience Diversity

Purpose
To deepen your understanding of the scope of perceptions listeners.

Instructions
Watch commercials on five different cable channels. Note the differences in advertising –for example, what is being sold on Nick Jr? On BET? Telemundo? How are the same products sold differently on each of the five channels?

Create a chart listing each of the channels you view. Include a column for the product sold and a column for specific words, behaviors or images you find to be persuasive in nature. Now look at each of the channels. How are advertisements modified to be persuasive to each specific audience?

Self-Test for Chapter 18

Multiple Choice

_____ 1. Which of the following is true of persuasive speaking?
A. It is coercive.
B. It usually seeks immediate changes.
C. It is interactive.
D. B and C

_____ 2. The error in "either/or" logic is that it assumes
A. the audience needs simplicity
B. the time is too short to include other options
C. there are no other options
D. the issue is suited to this form of logic

_____ 3. If a speaker wanted to enhance pathos by bringing material alive, he or she should
A. include quotations from respected sources
B. incorporate familiar examples
C. rely on vivid language to paint a picture
D. translate statistics to make them interesting

_____ 4. Toulmin's model is an example of
A. deductive reasoning
B. ethos
C. inductive reasoning
D. none of the above

_____ 5. Which of the following is a common and highly effective persuasive organization pattern?
A. comparative
B. motivated sequence
C. star
D. topical

_____ 6. Four acting students left school to try their luck in Hollywood. Acting students must not be serious about their studies. This is an example of
A. either-or logic
B. hasty generalization
C. red herring
D. reduction to absurdity

_____ 7. President Obama's credibility based upon his rank and title is called
A. initial
B. derived
C. terminal
D. expert

_____ 8. Your credibility based upon you giving an excellent speech to your classmates is called
   A.   initial
   B.   derived
   C.   terminal
   D.   expert

_____ 9. The step in the motivated sequence that prepares the audience to take action is
   A.   attention
   B.   need
   C.   transition
   D.   visualization

_____ 10. When a speaker tells listeners about ideas that oppose those she or he is presenting, the speaker is engaging in
   A.   immunity
   B.   visualization
   C.   inoculation
   D.   enhancement

_____ 11. Josh tells his audience that he is qualified to speak about this history of the Boy Scouts because he has been involved with the organization since he was six years old. He also relays that he earned the rank of Eagle Scout at 17 and now works for his local Scout Council as a professional employee. Josh's comments are best described as
   A.   logos
   B.   pathos
   C.   ethos
   D.   fallacy

_____ 12. When Miriam tells her audience that as soon as the college decides to add a technology fee, there will be no end to the future addition of more and more fees. Which fallacy has Miriam presented?
   A.   ad hominem attack
   B.   red herring
   C.   slippery slope
   D.   bandwagon appeal

_____ 13. Evan strongly says, "The college got a new president last year. This year enrollment is down significantly. What does that tell you about our new president's effectiveness at our school?!" Evan is using what type of fallacious appeal?
   A.   bandwagon
   B.   post hoc, ergo propter hoc
   C.   halo effect
   D.   red herring

_____ 14. Julian tells his audience, "You may be thinking to yourself that my proposal sounds like a great idea but wondering if we can really afford this program. We can. Let me show you how". Julian's statement is an example of which part of Toulmin's Model of Reasoning?
A. claim
B. warrant
C. rebuttal
D. qualifier

_____ 15. "Our social security system desperately needs to be revamped." This statement is an example of which part of Toulmin's Model of Reasoning?
A. qualifier
B. data
C. warrant
D. claim

True/False

_____ 1. Visual aids are an excellent way to increase persuasive appeal.

_____ 2. Looking at ten different case studies and drawing a general conclusion is a deductive appeal.

_____ 3. The amount of perceived goodwill affects credibility.

_____ 4. Recognizing and enlarging commonalities between speaker and audience is an effective persuasive strategy known as identification.

_____ 5. Fallacies may be intentional or unintentional.

_____ 6. Red herring errors attack individuals.

_____ 7. Ethical and effective persuasive speakers avoid reasoning fallacies.

_____ 8. Fear and guilt are usually less effective pathos appeals.

_____ 9. Credibility is a trait the speaker possesses.

_____ 10. Effective evidence increases a speaker's credibility.

Essay

1. Identify the six audience characteristics a speaker must learn in order to tailor a persuasive speech to that particular audience. Explain why it is important to know each, using hypothetical examples to illustrate your points.

2. Describe the factors that influence whether a speaker should present a one-sided or two-sided speech.

3. Watch your favorite TV advertisement. Identify how the steps in the motivated sequence organizational pattern are or are not followed. Is the motivated sequence an effective method for organizing persuasive appeals? Why or why not?

Chapter 18 Flash Cards

Cut out the cards, write the answers on the back, and you will have a packet of flash cards for each chapter. Paraphrasing the definition will help you remember them.

Ad hominem Argument	Halo Effect	*Post Hoc, Ergo Propter Hoc*
Bandwagon Appeal	Hasty Generalization	Qualifier
Claim	Identification	Rebuttal
Credibility	Inductive Reasoning	Red Herring Argument
Deductive Reasoning	Initial Credibility	Slippery Slope

Chapter 18 Flash Cards continued

Use the remaining cards for other concepts you would like to remember or study.

Derived Credibility	Inoculation	Terminal Credibility
Ethos	Motivated Sequence Pattern	Fallacy
Pathos	Warrant	Grounds
Persuasive Speech	Logos	Toulmin Model of Reasoning
Either-Or Logic		

Chapter 1

Multiple Choice
1. B
2. C
3. B
4. D
5. D
6. C
7. C
8. B
9. B
10. D
11. B
12. B
13. D
14. A
15. C

True/False
1. False
2. False
3. True
4. True
5. True
6. True
7. False
8. True
9. True
10. False

Essay
1. Answers may vary.
2. Answers may vary.
3. Answers may vary.

Chapter 2

2.2 Distinguishing Fact from Inference:

Only statement 4 is factual. The others are inferences that go beyond the facts presented in the story. We only know that Jane went to the mall to get shoes and that later she wore new shoes. We do not know WHICH pair of new shoes she was wearing and we do not know whether she charged them on credit, paid in cash, or shoplifted the shoes. We also don't have facts that would allow us to determine whether Jane is irresponsible with money.

Multiple Choice
1. C
2. B
3. A
4. C
5. B
6. A
7. A
8. A
9. C
10. B
11. A
12. C
13. D
14. D
15. C

True/False
1. True
2. False
3. False
4. True
5. False
6. False
7. False
8. True
9. True
10. False

Essay
1. Answers may vary.
2. Answers may vary.
3. Answers may vary.

Chapter 3

Multiple Choice

1. B
2. D
3. D
4. D
5. C
6. C
7. B
8. B
9. D
10. A
11. D
12. D
13. A
14. B
15. A

True/False

1. False
2. True
3. False
4. False
5. True
6. False
7. True
8. True
9. True
10. True

Essay

1. Answers may vary.
2. Answers may vary.
3. Answers may vary.

Chapter 4

Multiple Choice

1. C
2. D
3. D
4. D
5. C
6. B
7. A
8. B
9. A
10. A
11. C
12. A
13. B
14. D
15. B

True/False

1. False
2. True
3. True
4. True
5. True
6. True
7. True
8. True
9. True
10. True

Essay

1. Answers may vary.
2. Answers may vary.
3. Answers may vary.

Chapter 5

Answers to Understanding Communication Rules

Items 1, 2, 4 and 7 express regulative rules.

Items 3, 5, and 8 express constitutive rules.

Item 6 includes both a regulative rule (Look at elders) and a constitutive rule (looking at elders counts as respect).

Self-Test

Multiple Choice
1. D
2. A
3. B
4. A
5. C
6. D
7. C
8. A
9. B
10. A
11. A
12. D
13. D
14. B
15. D

True/False
1. False
2. False
3. True
4. True
5. False
6. True
7. True
8. True
9. True
10. False

Essay
1. Answers may vary.
2. Answers may vary.
3. Answers may vary.

Chapter 6

Multiple Choice
1. C
2. D
3. C
4. D
5. B
6. C
7. A
8. A
9. B
10. D
11. A
12. D
13. D
14. D
15. A

True/False
1. True
2. True
3. True
4. True
5. True
6. False
7. True
8. True
9. False
10. True

Essay
1. Answers may vary.
2. Answers may vary.
3. Answers may vary.

Chapter 7

Multiple Choice
1. B
2. C
3. C
4. A
5. D
6. A
7. A
8. B
9. D
10. B
11. A
12. B
13. C
14. C
15. B

True/False
1. False
2. True
3. True
4. True
5. False
6. False
7. True
8. False
9. False
10. True

Essay
1. Answers may vary.
2. Answers may vary.
3. Answers may vary.

Chapter 8

Multiple Choice
1. D
2. B
3. D
4. C
5. B
6. C
7. B
8. A
9. C
10. D
11. A
12. D
13. B
14. D
15. D

True/False
1. False
2. False
3. True
4. True
5. True
6. True
7. False
8. True
9. True
10. True

Essay
1. Answers may vary.
2. Answers may vary.
3. Answers may vary.

Chapter 9

Answers to Distinguishing Between Love and Commitment:

1, 2, 4, 6, 7, and 9 are statements of love. Each expresses a feeling and/or refers to the present time.

3, 5, and 8 are statements of commitment. Each expresses an intention or assumption that the relationship will continue.

10 is both a statement of love and a statement of commitment.

Note especially the difference between statements 7 and 8. In statement 7, the continuity of the relationship is contingent on the partner's learning to control her or his temper. In statement 8, the continuity of the relationship is assumed and only the level of enjoyment it affords is uncertain.

Answers to Recognizing Relational Dialectics

1. openness/closedness
2. novelty/predictability
3. openness/closedness
4. autonomy/connection
5. novelty/predictability
6. autonomy/connection

Answers to Recognizing Styles of Love

Answers to Identifying Stages in Romantic Relationships

Invitational communication
Intimate bonding
Intrapsychic phase (of deterioration)
Explorational communication
Grave dressing
Navigating
Intensifying communication (euphoria)
Dyadic negotiation, (could also be the revising stage)
Dyadic breakdown
Social support
Revising communication
Social phase (of deterioration)

Ch. 9 Self-Test

Multiple Choice

1. B
2. A
3. B
4. B
5. A
6. B
7. D
8. B
9. D
10. A
11. C
12. B
13. B
14. D
15. D

True/False

1. False
2. False
3. False
4. True
5. True
6. False
7. True
8. True
9. False
10. True

Essay

1. Answers may vary.

1. Eros	9. Ludus
2. Storge	10. Mania
3. Pragma	11. Agape
4. Pragma	12. Storge
5. Ludus	13. Mania
6. Mania	14. Pragma
7. Agape	15. Storge
8. Eros	

2. Answers may vary.
3. Answers may vary.

913

Chapter 10

Correct Codings for Group Discussion
1. Procedural
2. Procedural
3. Climate and Procedural
4. Task
5. Task
6. Procedural
7. Egocentric
8. Climate
9. Task
10. Task
11. Climate

Answers for Power Over/ Power To Distinctions
1. Power over
2. Power over
3. Power to
4. Power to
5. Power to
6. Power over
7. Power over
8. Power over
9. Power to
10. Power over

Ch. 10 Self-Test

Multiple Choice
1. D
2. D
3. A
4. C
5. D
6. D
7. D
8. A
9. B
10. D
11. B
12. B
13. B
14. C
15. A

True/False
1. False
2. True
3. True
4. False
5. True
6. True
7. False
8. True
9. True
10. True

Essay
1. Answers may vary.
2. Answers may vary.
3. Answers may vary.

Chapter 11

Answers to Identifying Task Groups Exercise

1. Focus group
2. Project team
3. Advisory group
4. Brainstorming group
5. Focus group
6. Decision-making group
7. Quality circle
8. Decision-making group
9. Brainstorming group
10. Project team

Unscrambled Discussion

1. Are we dealing with a factual or value question?

2. How are we going to define "beneficial"?

3 or 4. Do we have all the information we need now?

3 or 4. Do you think this poll is reliable?

5. I can think of four standards that any solution would have to meet in order to be effective.

6. Okay, we seem to be ready to start identifying possible solutions for our problem. Any ideas?

7. Solutions 3 and 4 don't meet all of our criteria so we should throw them out.

8. Of the two solutions left, one seems to satisfy all criteria most fully.

9. Let's make sure our implementation plan really spells things out in the most clear language possible.

10. How can we tell if our solution solves the problem?

11. What might go wrong with the solution we're recommending?

12. If there is a negative reaction when the solution is implemented, we could modify it in this way. . .

Answers to the Conflict Orientations Instrument

1. A	6. A
2. B	7. B
3. A	8. C
4. C	9. A
5. B	10. C

Answers to Leadership Exercise

1. Democratic style is recommended since this group needs some guidance and since participation and commitment are important.

2. Laissez-faire leadership is appropriate since this group doesn't need a lot of guidance. Members have the maturity and experience with group process to be effective without any specific guidance from a leader.

3. Democratic leadership is the most appropriate style because it generally results in the most creative and high-quality outcomes. Another reason to select democratic leadership is that members' lack of experience leading groups suggests they could benefit from guidance and direction provided by a leader.

4. This situation is made to order for authoritarian leadership. The group clearly needs strong direction from a leader. Since morale and member satisfaction are not high priorities in this situation, the negative effects of authoritarian leadership on these are not salient.

5. Laissez-faire leadership seems appropriate since members are highly motivated and have expertise. These qualities suggest the group might be able to operate effectively without direction from a leader. However, if the group does not proceed smoothly, the guidance of democratic leadership is in order.

6. Authoritarian leadership is recommended. The group has not responded well to the more gentle guidance of democratic leadership and the deadline for completion of the task is closing in.

Ch.11 Self-Test

Multiple Choice

1. B
2. C
3. B
4. B
5. D
6. A
7. B
8. C
9. C
10. D
11. B
12. D
13. D
14. A
15. D

True/False

1. False
2. False
3. False
4. True
5. False
6. False
7. True
8. True
9. True
10. True

Essay

1. Answers may vary.
2. Answers may vary.
3. Answers may vary.

Chapter 12

Multiple Choice

1. B
2. D
3. D
4. D
5. C
6. A
7. C
8. C
9. D
10. B
11. B
12. B
13. C
14. A
15. A

True/False

1. True
2. True
3. True
4. True
5. True
6. True
7. False
8. True
9. True
10. False

Essay

1. Answers may vary.
2. Answers may vary.
3. Answers may vary.

Chapter 13

Multiple Choice

1. B
2. A
3. B
4. C
5. B
6. B
7. B
8. D
9. D
10. A
11. A
12. A
13. A
14. B
15. C

True/False

1. False
2. True
3. False
4. True
5. True
6. False
7. True
8. False
9. False
10. True

Essay

1. Answers may vary.
2. Answers may vary.
3. Answers may vary.

Chapter 14

Multiple Choice
1. A
2. B
3. C
4. B
5. C
6. C
7. A
8. D
9. D
10. C
11. B
12. C
13. D
14. B
15. A

True/False
1. False
2. False
3. False
4. True
5. True
6. True
7. False
8. True

Essay
1. Answers may vary.
2. Answers may vary.
3. Answers may vary.

Chapter 15

Answers to Evidence Exercise
1. statistic
2. quotation
3. example (undetailed)
4. comparison (analogy)
5. visual aid
6. quotation
7. example (hypothetical)
8. comparison (simile)
9. statistic
10. visual aid

Answers to Merck Evidence Exercise

Merck: A Socially Conscious Business
According to <u>American Attitudes</u>, 75% of people in 1976 [*statistics are out of date*] said big businesses contribute nothing to the common good. Merck is an exception.

Merck is the second largest pharmaceutical company in the world. This bar graph shows how much Merck spends each year on R and D, contributions to social programs, and donations to indigenous populations in third world countries. As you can see, Merck is sharing its wealth. In this second graph, you see how Merck's contributions to social issues compare to those of the three other largest pharmaceutical companies in the world [*a second graph so close to the first one might overload listeners*].

One of Merck's projects is a two-year research and sampling budget of $1,142,857.00 [*listeners are more likely to remember a rounded figure such as $1.14 million*] to fund drug research in Costa Rica. In the chart I'm now showing, you can see that this is 500% more than Costa Rica previously had for its drug research [*too many visuals*].

According to Merck's CEO, "we are a company that cares about the world. Contributing to global health is our first and most important priority." [*Merck's CEO has a vested interest in praising the company*] Others agree. Basketball superstar James Jordan says "Merck is a company with a heart." [*the halo effect*] In this photo, you can see Jordan attending a meeting of Merck's shareholders. [*Too many visuals; what purpose is served by this photograph?*]

Answers to Survey Construction Guidelines Exercise
Nothing wrong with topic
Respondents should reflect the population
Need eight respondents for each question
Avoid negative language
Focus on one issue
Rely on clear language
Avoid biased wording
Correct as is
Allow for all possible responses
Correct as is
Focus on one issue

Answers to Guidelines for Using Slides in a Speech Exercise
No credit was given for the model.

The font was not large enough and the typeface was not clear.

Used all capital letters instead of capital and lowercase.

Incorporated clipart appropriately to provide visual relief.

Should have used special effects more sparingly and not sacrificed content for flashy visuals.

Slide should have focused on key information not full examples.

Used visual highlighting effectively.

Slides were not bright enough and the color scheme should have been visually stronger.

Ch. 15 Self-Test

Multiple Choice

1. D
2. D
3. A
4. B
5. D
6. B
7. D
8. C
9. C
10. C
11. A
12. B
13. D
14. D
15. C

True/False

1. True
2. True
3. False
4. True
5. False
6. True
7. False
8. True
9. True
10. False

Essay

1. Answers may vary.
2. Answers may vary.
3. Answers may vary.

Chapter 16

Answers to Organizational Clues Exercise
1. Time pattern
2. Topical pattern
3. Problem-solution pattern
4. Cause-effect pattern
5. Space pattern
6. Comparative pattern
7. Effect-cause pattern
8. Topical pattern
9. Time pattern
10. Space pattern

Multiple Choice
1. A
2. B
3. A
4. D
5. D
6. D
7. C
8. B
9. A
10. C
11. C
12. D
13. B
14. D
15. C

True/False
1. True
2. False
3. True
4. True
5. False
6. True
7. False
8. True
9. False
10. True

Essay
1. Answers may vary.
2. Answers may vary.
3. Answers may vary.

Chapter 17

Multiple Choice
1. D
2. D
3. B
4. A
5. B
6. B
7. D
8. D
9. A
10. C

True/False
1. True
2. True
3. False
4. True
5. False
6. False
7. True
8. False

Essay
1. Answers may vary.
2. Answers may vary.
3. Answers may vary.

Chapter 18

Answers to Recognizing Fallacies
Either-or
Bandwagon Appeal
Hasty Generalization
After this, therefore because of this
Ad Hominem Attack
Either-or
Red Herring Argument
Reliance on the Halo Effect
Hasty Generalization
Reduction to Absurdity
Ad Hominem Attack
Bandwagon Appeal

Multiple Choice
1. C
2. C
3. C
4. D
5. B
6. B
7. A
8. B
9. D
10. C
11. C
12. C
13. B
14. C
15. D

True/False
1. True
2. False
3. True
4. True
5. True
6. False
7. True
8. True
9. False
10. True

Essay
1. Answers may vary.
2. Answers may vary.
3. Answers may vary.